THE SCOUTING
REPORT: 1985

THE SCOUTING REPORT: 1985

An in-depth analysis of the strengths
and weaknesses of every
active major league baseball player

by
Dave Campbell
Denny Matthews
Brooks Robinson
and
Duke Snider

Edited by
Marybeth Sullivan

1817

HARPER & ROW, PUBLISHERS, New York
Cambridge, Philadelphia, San Francisco, London,
Mexico City, São Paulo, Singapore, Sydney

The player photographs which appear in THE SCOUTING REPORT were furnished individually by the twenty-six teams that comprise Major League Baseball. Their cooperation is gratefully acknowledged: Baltimore Orioles, Boston Red Sox, California Angels, Chicago White Sox, Cleveland Indians, Detroit Tigers, Kansas City Royals, Milwaukee Brewers, Minnesota Twins, New York Yankees, Oakland A's, Seattle Mariners, Texas Rangers, Toronto Blue Jays, Atlanta Braves, Chicago Cubs, Cincinnati Reds, Houston Astros, Los Angeles Dodgers, Montreal Expos, New York Mets, Philadelphia Phillies, Pittsburgh Pirates, St. Louis Cardinals, San Diego Padres and San Francisco Giants.

EDITORIAL STAFF

Dan Donovan	Larry LaRue	Mark Ruda
Bruce Jenkins	Bob Markus	Harry Shattuck
Paul Hagan	Al Mari	Tim Tucker
Greg Hoard	Nick Peters	Gordon Verrell
Paul Hoynes	Rusty Pray	Andrea Schneider,
Rick Hummell	Tracy Ringolsby	Production Assistant

THE SCOUTING REPORT: 1985

Copyright © 1985 by TeamWork Enterprises, Inc.

Designer: Marybeth Sullivan

ISSN: 0743-1309
ISBN: 0-06-091245-6

85 86 87 88 89 10 9 8 7 6 5 4 3 2 1

CONTENTS

INTRODUCTION

This is it! This is THE BOOK! Baseball people are always talking about THE BOOK--and you have it right in your hands!

Six hundred and seventy-four scouting reports--fully detailed, comprehensive, easy-to-read reports on the 674 players in both the American and National Leagues. THE SCOUTING REPORT: 1985 is a baseball fan's treasure!

The reports were written by four of the most knowledgeable men in baseball: Brooks Robinson, former Baltimore Oriole third baseman and a member of the Hall of Fame, who has been broadcasting Orioles' games since 1978; Denny Matthews, who has been the Kansas City Royals' play-by-play man since the team was added to the American League in 1969; Dave Campbell, former second baseman, minor league manager and now a broadcaster for the San Diego Padres; and Duke Snider, all-time great Dodger center fielder and another Hall of Famer, who has been broadcasting for the Montreal Expos since 1973.

The book begins with the scouting reports of the players on the fourteen teams of the American League. The American League East reports were provided by Brooks Robinson; Denny Matthews contributed the evaluations of the players in the American League West. The second portion of THE SCOUTING REPORT: 1985 is made up of the reports of the players of the National League. Dave Campbell offered his insights on the players of the National League West, while Duke Snider contributed his perspectives on the National League East.

The reports include detailed and easy-to-follow information on each player's strengths and weaknesses in all phases of major league play: hitting, baserunning, fielding, pitching, etc. While player statistics are an integral part of baseball, a line of numbers does not tell the whole story. THE SCOUTING REPORT: 1985 lets baseball fans in on the kind of information that no major league team would release. Hitters are evaluated on the basis of their aggressiveness at the plate, the way they select pitches, how they swing, how they hit, how fast they get down to first and around the bases and how well they perform at their positions. Pitchers are described as to how well they mix up their pitches, which is their best pitch, worst pitch, what they will throw when behind in the count, how well they field and respond to pressure.

This is it, this is THE BOOK. There has never been another book like it available to the general public. For that matter, THE SCOUTING REPORT: 1985 may contain more information than many teams have in their own files! Major league scouts, management and even players have been spotted traveling with THE SCOUTING REPORT. And most of them agree--THE SCOUTING REPORT is right on target.

The format:

THE SCOUTING REPORT: 1985 is divided into two sections--first, the fourteen teams of the American League, then the twelve teams of the National League. Player reports are located alphabetically with their team, with the exception of some players who are used on a limited basis; these players appear at the end of their team's section.

Free agency and trades make it impossible to keep up with all of the players' movements, use the index located on page 657 to find players who have been traded to or signed by other teams since this book went to press.

On each page, the player's name appears in the upper right corner, followed by his position and his uniform number. The third line displays a two-letter code indicating (1) which side of the plate he bats from, right (R), left (L), or switch-hitter (S), and (2) whether the player throws with his right (R) or left (L) arm. The player's height and weight are also provided. The fourth line gives you a quick indication as to how long the player has been in the major leagues. These numbers have been rounded off to the closest number of seasons and do not reflect the player's time, if any, in the minors. The last two lines are the player's date and place of birth.

One of the most interesting features of THE SCOUTING REPORT: 1985 is the batter's diagram. Each batter's page includes a "strike zone chart." It provides an on-the-spot report of the player's "power zone"; this is the player's strongest area, and pitchers should keep their pitches away from here! Also included is a diagram indicating the location on the field where each batter is most likely to hit the ball.

Bring THE SCOUTING REPORT: 1985 to the ballpark or keep it handy while watching games on television. You'll see how the defense will shift to play each individual hitter and you can become your own scout, following the reports on each player to analyze when the manager should put on the hit-and-run, which baserunners will be trying to run on a weak-armed catcher, what are the signs that indicate when the pitcher is starting to "lose it," and on and on. It's all here--THE SCOUTING REPORT: 1985--and you have it right in your own hands!

Acknowledgments

Nothing ever stays the same--especially major league ballplayers. With few exceptions, ballplayers' abilities and skills change with each passing season. Some, like the abundance of rookies who appeared on the scene in 1984, are on a high-speed chase to the top of their profession. You can be certain that their 1986 reports will reflect the changes they go through in their sophomore year of 1985. The veterans evolve as well. In recent seasons, we have seen more "older" players (35 years old plus) than in the past, and they change, too. In most cases, they adjust to new roles; former power pitchers begin to finesse the hitters a bit more, while power hitters find new ways to get on base. The scouting reports that appear in this book reflect these new dimensions, and are completely re-written and are fresh each year.

THE SCOUTING REPORT: 1985 is made possible by a group of hard-working and dedicated people who believe in bringing this book's unique information to baseball fans everywhere. For their efforts, we would like to thank the entire editorial staff whose names appear on page 4. These writers are the baseball "beat writers" who travel with the teams, and their contribution to the flavor of this book is invaluable. The nuts-and-bolts work of putting this together is a fast-paced team task; Jim Armstrong, Bob Eisner, Mary Kay Fama, Terry Karten, Peter Lillienfield, Rose Petersons, Walter Schatz, Sue Schwer and Andrea Schneider are All Star members of the team. Brooks Robinson, Denny Matthews, Dave Campbell and Duke Snider are the beginning of this book; without their willingness to share their experience and knowledge, none of this would even begin to be possible. Special appreciation goes to Buz Wyeth of Harper & Row for his encouragement and support for three seasons.

THE AUTHORS

DAVE CAMPBELL

Dave Campbell began his eight-year playing career with the Detroit Tigers in 1967. After his first season with them, he was traded to the San Diego Padres and played there at both second base and third base until 1973. Continuing on to St. Louis, Mr. Campbell played briefly for the Cardinals before he was traded to the Houston Astros. He finished his playing career, but not his ties to major league baseball, in Houston in 1974. Immediately thereafter, he began broadcasting at KCST-TV and KSDO Radio while also managing in the San Diego farm system. In 1985, he enters his eighth year as a San Diego Padre broadcaster.

Dave Campbell was born in Manistee, Michigan, and while attending the University of Michigan, played on the 1962 NCAA Championship team, and captained the 1964 squad. Mr. Campbell, his wife, Diane, and their two daughters, Courtney, 14, and Shelby, 11, reside in San Diego.

DENNY MATTHEWS

Offering his insights from the broadcast booth on the players of the American League West is Denny Matthews. He is the play-by-play man for the Kansas City Royals; his voice has been on the airwaves surrounding Kansas City since the Royals played their first game in 1969.

Raised in Bloomington-Normal, Illinois, Mr. Matthews graduated from Illinois Wesleyan University where he played both football and baseball. In 1965, he was rated in the Top Ten in the nation among small college pass receivers.

Alongside Hall of Fame broadcaster, Mr. Ernie Harwell of Detroit, Mr. Matthews called the action of the 1982 American League Championship Series on the CBS world-wide radio network.

During baseball's off-season, he picks up his own stick and is an aggressive amateur hockey player. Mr. Matthews makes his home in Overland Park, Kansas.

BROOKS ROBINSON

Known as "Mr. Third Base," Brooks Robinson continues to be the standard by which all other third basemen are measured. None have played the game as well as he did during his 23-year major league career. He was inducted into baseball's Hall of Fame in Cooperstown, New York, in 1983, one of the few players to be so honored in his first year of eligibility. Mr. Robinson has filled his shelves with just about every award that baseball has to offer. He played in 18 consecutive All Star games from 1960 through 1974, and was the All Star game's Most Valuable Player in 1966. Beyond that, he was voted MVP of the American League in 1964, and in 1970 he was the MVP of the World Series. For his spectacular play at third base, he won 16 straight Gold Gloves from 1960 to 1975.

Mr. Robinson begins his eighth year as color broadcaster for the Baltimore Orioles in 1985. He is also Executive Vice-President and Director of Personal Management Associates, a Baltimore firm which provides athletes with advice and assistance in areas of professional, personal and financial management. He also serves as Special Assistant for the Crown Petroleum Company.

DUKE SNIDER

Duke Snider, "The Silver Fox," is considered by many to be the greatest Dodger center fielder of all time. He played in the major leagues for eighteen seasons, most of that time as a Dodger in both Brooklyn and Los Angeles. He began his pro career in Montreal in 1944 at the age of 17, and during his long career also played for the San Francisco Giants and the New York Mets.

Mr. Snider appeared in seven All Star games and received baseball's highest honor when he was elected to the Hall of Fame in 1980. He is the Dodgers' all-time home run leader, finishing his career with 407 round-trippers. He has more home runs (11) and RBIs (26) in World Series competition than any other National Leaguer in history.

Entering his twelfth season as a member of the Montreal Expos' broadcasting team, Mr. Snider is frequently sought out by many of today's top stars for his advice and coaching skills.

THE
AMERICAN LEAGUE

BALTIMORE ORIOLES

HITTING:

When a World Championship team slips from first place to fifth place in one year with virtually the entire roster the same, you know that something is wrong. When many of the players are over 30, you have your first clue. All of the Orioles seemed to get old all at once last season, Benny Ayala included.

While Ayala had slumped badly during the championship season (.221), he fell into an even worse one last year. He was always a good high fastball hitter; pitchers who think they can throw the heater past him are mistaken. They finally realized that they could show Ayala the fastball away because he likes to pull everything, then come back with curves, sliders and junk. Ayala looks fastball all the time, so some pitchers will try to get ahead in the count with the breaking ball. When they do, they can throw the fastball away and curves and sliders low and away.

He has a square, straight-up stance with a level swing, but can be made to look bad on off-speed pitches. He saw such limited playing time last season that he started missing pitches that he once hammered. He is a poor bunter but in the past was always tough coming off the bench, particularly with men on base and against a lefthander.

BASERUNNING:

He does not steal, will not steal and is a slow runner. He is a powerfully built player, yet he does not use his bulk to frighten infielders when breaking up the double play. He will rarely take the extra base and may not even go from first to third on a hit to right field.

FIELDING:

He used to be an outfielder but now

BENNY AYALA
DH/OF, No. 27
RR, 6'1", 195 lbs.
ML Svc: 7 years
Born: 2-7-51 in
Yauco, PR

1984 STATISTICS
AVG	G	AB	R	H	2B	3B	HR	RBI	BB	SO	SB
.212	60	118	9	25	6	0	4	24	8	24	1

CAREER STATISTICS
AVG	G	AB	R	H	2B	3B	HR	RBI	BB	SO	SB
.251	379	789	104	198	35	1	36	130	67	119	2

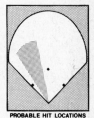

VS. RHP   VS. LHP   PROBABLE HIT LOCATIONS

is a designated hitter or pinch-hitter. If he does catch on with another major league team, he won't play the field.

OVERALL:

Ayala is the all-time Oriole leader in pinch-hit home runs with seven and gave Baltimore several fine years--not the last two, however.

Robinson: "Benny will be in the big leagues somewhere in 1985. You don't find many people who can come off the bench and swing the bat so aggressively. The only way he can help you, however, is to get more at-bats. He is confident and a definite threat with a bat in his hands."

PITCHING:

Mike Boddicker must now be considered the best starter in the American League. He led the league in ERA and wins and was second in the league in complete games and shutouts. He was the top rookie pitcher in the majors in 1983, proved himself in the playoffs and World Series by throwing shutouts against the White Sox and Phillies, respectively, and came back to be an even better pitcher with a worse team. Here's why . . .

Boddicker will not give a hitter the fastball over the plate. His fastball is really a slow ball, about 85 MPH, but he moves it from the black to the black. He throws from three-quarters, can drop down against righthanded hitters occasionally and has superb control. He has supreme confidence in his curve and forkball (he calls it a "fosh").

Boddicker can throw curveballs for strikes in any situation and can put a little extra on it or take something off. He also fools around with a knuckler, but his basic plan is to let the batter know that he will throw breaking pitches 90% of the time. The so-called fosh has the effect of Bruce Sutter's split-fingered fastball: it breaks down sharply. The curve is usually thrown at righthanded hitters and will break over the plate or at the heart of the plate and will break outside. A batter simply does not know what the pitch will do and how fast it will be thrown.

Boddicker has the ability to shake off a bad inning or a bad outing because he knows that he will get the ball over the plate soon enough. He finishes what he starts more often than 99% of the other pitchers in the league.

FIELDING:

Good fielding is another of his fine

MIKE BODDICKER
RHP, No. 52
RR, 5'11", 172 lbs.
ML Svc: 2 years
Born: 8-23-57 in
    Cedar Rapids, IA

1984 STATISTICS

W	L	ERA	G	GS	CG	IP	H	R	ER	BB	SO	SV
20	11	2.79	34	34	16	261	218	95	81	81	128	0

CAREER STATISTICS

W	L	ERA	G	GS	CG	IP	H	R	ER	BB	SO	SV
37	20	2.89	71	61	26	479	396	180	154	152	274	0

qualities. He is outstanding at fielding comebackers, protecting both lines against bunts and covering first base. He keeps runners close, is alert and quick off the mound and always throws to the right base at the right time.

OVERALL:

Boddicker won 20 games last year after starting off the season at 0-3. It took him a while (five and a half years) to get to the majors. He made sure that his time in the minors was time well-spent.

Robinson: "I think I'll call him the ultimate pitcher. He proved it last season. Before that, despite his 1983 performance, there were doubts in the minds of some players. They said that he wouldn't do it again, but he did. Mike is tough and will ask for the ball even when he is hurting. Get used to him, folks!"

HITTING:

Al Bumbry's 1984 season was almost a mirror image of his previous one; he was platooned in center field with John Shelby, who happens to be a switch-hitter. Bumbry played against righthanded pitchers and Shelby against lefties. He out-hit Shelby by 70 points but is finished as a Bird. Seventy points will not change the 38-year-old Bumbry into a 27-year-old Shelby.

Bumbry is a notorious bad ball hitter who likes low fastballs and chases high ones. He has a square stance but is a straightaway hitter with surprising power to left and left-center. He made one change in his stance in the middle of 1984 that helped him pick up 30 points in his average. Instead of standing almost straight up, he began to crouch and hold his bat lower so he could lay off the high fastball.

Pitchers will give Bumbry the high fastball every chance they get because he will always swing at it--or at least he did until he changed his stance. Once ahead in the count, the pitcher should come back with sliders and curves and almost invariably try to slip the big hard one past him. The mistake that some pitchers make with Bumbry is that they try the fastball up and away, but he can go the other way against them with that pitch. A smart pitcher will get him up and in.

Bumbry was always a good bunter and a fair clutch hitter but has not bunted much in the past two years. He remains an impatient hitter who will swing at the first pitch, or swing even when he is ahead in the count 2-0 or 3-1.

BASERUNNING:

Bumbry is fast but not as quick as he once was. He recovered from a broken leg in 1978 and assorted leg injuries in 1982, but he is not considered too much of a threat to steal. He may try to take some bases with his new team. He takes

AL BUMBRY
CF, No. 1
LR, 5'8", 175 lbs.
ML Svc: 12 years
Born: 4-21-47 in
    Fredricksburg, VA

1984 STATISTICS

AVG	G	AB	R	H	2B	3B	HR	RBI	BB	SO	SB
.270	119	344	47	93	12	1	3	24	25	35	9

CAREER STATISTICS

AVG	G	AB	R	H	2B	3B	HR	RBI	BB	SO	SB
.283	1428	4958	772	1403	217	52	53	392	464	701	252

VS. RHP   VS. LHP   PROBABLE HIT LOCATIONS

care when he slides (he broke his ankle while sliding) but is aggressive and daring on the bases.

FIELDING:

He still has good range and still comes in on a ball better than he goes back. He plays a deep center and does not move around to position himself as much as other center fielders who play everyplace from behind second to behind short. His arm is weak and runners will go on him.

OVERALL:

Robinson: "The Orioles made up their minds that they were going to give center field to Shelby--lock, stock and barrel. Bumbry can still help some major league team, not as an everyday player, but as a platoon player. He has played on winning teams and has a good attitude."

HITTING:

Todd Cruz bounced around from team to team and finally seemed to find a place in the sun with the Seattle Mariners in 1982. He played a full year and pounded out 16 homers, but they may have made him a worse hitter than he was before. He does not have long ball power except in parks like the Kingdome, where balls fly out quite easily.

Cruz swings hard at everything and tries to pull too much. He has a slightly closed stance and bats straight up. He looks for and likes fastballs belt-high and toward the inside. He will not see those pitches with men on base. Pitchers can get him out by throwing fastballs up and away and curves any-place. He can hit the inside curve from lefties--he only plays against lefthand-ers because he has so much trouble with breaking balls and off-speed pitches from righthanded pitchers.

He has success against lefties who try to jam him or who try to throw hard stuff past him on the inside. Lefties who get him out will use hard stuff away and an occasional high fastball out of the strike zone. Cruz is an impatient hitter, but he has started to be more selective and stay away from the "suck-er" high fastball. He is a good bunter who does not bunt enough.

BASERUNNING:

Cruz does not pay that much attention to running the bases despite the fact that he has natural speed and gets a good jump from the batter's box. He is prone to baserunning mistakes. In one game he may try to take the extra base for no earthly reason and in another game he may be too tentative. He is not a threat to steal.

FIELDING:

Cruz came up as a shortstop and played there with California, Kansas City, the White Sox and the Mariners. The Orioles switched him to third in the

TODD CRUZ
3B, No. 10
RR, 6'1", 185 lbs.
ML Svc: 5 years
Born: 11-23-55 in
  Highland Park, MI

1984 STATISTICS

AVG	G	AB	R	H	2B	3B	HR	RBI	BB	SO	SB
.218	96	142	15	31	4	0	3	9	8	33	1

CAREER STATISTICS

AVG	G	AB	R	H	2B	3B	HR	RBI	BB	SO	SB
.221	544	1526	133	338	58	6	34	154	59	317	9

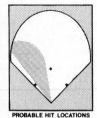

VS. RHP   VS. LHP   PROBABLE HIT LOCATIONS

middle of 1983, where he had a difficult time adjusting. He has improved defen-sively but still does not play the hit-ters well. He has trouble because he lets the ball play him. His arm, howev-er, is one of the strongest in the AL and turns the around-the-horn double play very well. He has a quick release and an accurate arm.

OVERALL:

The Orioles' forte has always been defense. In 1984 they used both Cruz and Wayne Gross at third, neither of whom played like the Oriole third baseman of the past. To make that comparison, how-ever, is unfair.

Robinson: "He played less in 1984 than he did the year before. He is a platoon player and he may play even less in 1985. He can help a team because he plays all the infield positions, but he is just not going to hit for average. I do not think his attitude is quite what it should be."

HITTING:

Rich Dauer is another Oriole who gets paid for his defense, not his offense. He hit better than .280 in past years, which was an Oriole bonus, but his average has dropped noticeably in the past two seasons. He hit 20 points higher in 1984 than he did in 1983, but for a team that lost its punch it was not good enough.

Dauer has a slightly closed stance, with his weight evenly distributed. He has a tendency to hit off his front foot and pull the ball too much. He is one of the best hit-and-run men in baseball and will almost always hit behind the runner when asked to, but he does not go with the pitch in other situations.

He is one of the most difficult men in the league to strike out and always gets a piece of the ball. He will not hit for power or hit the long ball, but he is annually among the club leaders in doubles because he can pull the ball past the third baseman or hit to the gap in right-center.

He has become a bit more impatient at home plate, swinging at too many first pitches. He will make contact with two strikes, but he has to become a defensive hitter on those occasions. He would have more success if he went the other way, but pitchers who have him in the hole will use the curve on the corner or hard stuff low and in. He likes fastballs up and in. He is a fair bunter.

BASERUNNING:

Dauer has no speed, either out of the batter's box or on the bases, but is a knowledgeable runner who does not hurt his team. He knows when and how to take the extra base. He can break up a double play but will not steal a base.

FIELDING:

He had an off year in 1984 but is

RICH DAUER
2B, No. 25
RR, 6'0", 180 lbs.
ML Svc: 8 years
Born: 7-27-52 in
San Bernardino, CA

```
1984 STATISTICS
AVG   G   AB    R    H   2B  3B  HR  RBI  BB   SO  SB
.254 127  397   29  101  26   0   2   24   24   23   1
CAREER STATISTICS
AVG   G    AB    R    H   2B  3B  HR  RBI  BB   SO  SB
.260 1055 3621  423  942 186  3  41  358  277  212  6
```

  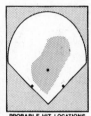

STRONG   STRONG

VS. RHP   VS. LHP   PROBABLE HIT LOCATIONS

still one of the most solid second basemen in the league. His range is limited, but he knows where to play to hitters and always seems to be in the right place. He will dive either way and go down on one knee to stop hard smashes. Very few balls that he can reach get past him. He can turn the double play with the best of them and is not afraid of contact.

OVERALL:

Dauer has the all-time highest fielding average of any American League second baseman who has played more than 10 years, but his hitting is a puzzlement. In the past two years he was flirting with .220 before late-season drives.

Robinson: "The Orioles were worried about him in the first half in both fielding and hitting. He bounced back and got the job done . . . he is steady and a good team player in every way."

PITCHING:

After an outstanding year in 1983, Storm Davis was hailed as the second coming of Jim Palmer. After a fairly decent year in 1984, Storm Davis is hailed as being Storm Davis . . . just what he is. That's plenty.

He is a big starting pitcher who can overpower batters with a 93 MPH fastball, sharp curve, change and forkball. He does bear a striking resemblance to Palmer, particularly in his delivery. He comes almost straight over-the-top and can come from three-quarters. He has excellent control for a power pitcher. Basically, he starts hitters off with the fastball, and if he gets ahead, may throw the forkball or change. He will, however, come back with the fastball for the strikeout.

Davis's pitching patterns are the same to both left and righthanded hitters. He is one of the toughest pitchers in the league to hit a home run off. He throws what is called a "heavy" ball. He can be hurt at times when he hangs his breaking ball. In addition, his forkball does not move enough to be effective, though he throws it quite hard and it looks like a fastball to the hitter. If it doesn't break down or away, it can be hit.

If he had had a good September, Davis would have been among the league leaders in wins and winning percentage, but he lost his last two starts and saw his ERA jump to over 3.00. His finishing ERA of 3.12 was still good enough to tie him for fifth-best in the league.

FIELDING:

Davis has the Palmer move to first.

STORM DAVIS
RHP, No. 34
RR, 6'4", 207 lbs.
ML Svc: 3 years
Born: 12-26-61 in Dallas, TX

1984 STATISTICS

W	L	ERA	G	GS	CG	IP	H	R	ER	BB	SO	SV
14	9	3.12	35	31	10	225	205	86	78	71	105	1

CAREER STATISTICS

W	L	ERA	G	GS	CG	IP	H	R	ER	BB	SO	SV
35	20	3.37	98	68	17	526	481	216	197	163	297	1

He holds his hands very high when coming to the stop and runners have a difficult time telling when he comes to a full stop. Davis's fielding has improved and he is rated better than average in fielding bunts and grounders to the mound.

OVERALL:

He has had three straight winning seasons and is only 23 years old. Davis has outstanding ability, but despite doing well in post-season play in 1983, he must acquire more mental toughness, as teammate Mike Boddicker has. In 1984 Davis was inconsistent and had a series of winning and losing streaks.

Robinson: "He is still an outstanding young pitcher with a world of poise. Maturity and more innings pitched will help him because he has so much stuff. He's getting better every year, and that trend should continue."

HITTING:

It took Rick Dempsey three years to knock in 100 runs, but the Orioles do not pay their 1983 World Series MVP to hit homers or drive in runs. They pay him to catch, throw out runners and handle a basically young pitching staff.

He decided to hit the long ball in 1984 and wound up with a career-high 10 homers. Most of them came late in the year when the weather turned cool. He did, however, have nine home runs in 1980 so it should not be much of a surprise.

What is surprising is that Dempsey continues to try to pull everything. Because of that, his average suffers. He could hit for a higher average if he went the other way. He likes the fastball from the middle of the plate on in. He can golf a low fastball and hammer a high fastball. He will see those pitches only on rare occasions, usually with nobody on base.

Pitchers will try to get him out with hard sliders low and in or low and away and fastballs or curves on the outside part of the plate. Most of Dempsey's arguments with umpires come when the ump calls a strike on the outside corner and Dempsey thinks it is a ball. A pitcher with control will have success against Dempsey if he keeps the ball low and away at all times.

Dempsey is a good bunter and a better hitter with a runner on third, because he can squeeze, get the ball up in the air or hit it up the middle.

BASERUNNING:

Not fast, but like his friend, the late Thurman Munson, Dempsey runs as hard as he can in every at-bat and will always try to knock over anything or anyone in his path. He will not steal but will take a bigger lead now than he did in the past.

FIELDING:

Dempsey's probably one-two with Lance

RICK DEMPSEY
C, No. 24
RR, 6'0", 184 lbs.
ML Svc: 12 years
Born: 9-13-49 in
Fayetteville, TN

1984 STATISTICS

AVG	G	AB	R	H	2B	3B	HR	RBI	BB	SO	SB
.230	109	330	37	76	11	0	11	34	40	58	1

CAREER STATISTICS

AVG	G	AB	R	H	2B	3B	HR	RBI	BB	SO	SB
.239	1165	3260	342	779	149	11	53	299	371	410	16

VS. RHP

VS. LHP

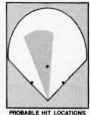

PROBABLE HIT LOCATIONS

Parrish as the best defensive catcher in the league. His arm is strong and accurate, he has a quick release and is usually near the top in throwing runners out. He blocks pitches in the dirt, is quick on bunts and slow rollers and knows what base to throw the ball to. He is not afraid to throw to any base, in any situation, in an attempt to pick a runner off or keep him close. He calls an excellent game behind the plate and the pitchers respect him.

OVERALL:

He is as close to Munson as you will find.

Robinson: "He was hurt in 1984 but he's still one of the best around. No one tries harder than Dempsey. He won't hit for average but can catch and throw with the best. His attitude and drive help him."

HITTING:

1984 was The Lost Year for most of the Oriole oufielders and Jim Dwyer was no exception. The Great Plan of 1983, when manager Joe Altobelli platooned all three outfield positions, fell into the Chesapeake Bay last year because half the outfielders decided to stop hitting and the other half were injured.

Dwyer underwent knee surgery and saw limited playing time in right field. He missed from the middle of July to the end of August with his knee problems and never got untracked either before or after the injury.

He has a square stance, weight evenly distributed and bat held high. He plays only against righthanded pitching and always looks for the fastball from the belt on up and toward the middle portion of the plate. Righties will not let him beat them with that pitch, but if they get it too close to his power zone, Dwyer has the ability to hit it out of parks with short right field porches.

He tries to pull everything so pitchers will keep the fastball away and use curves, sliders and off-speed pitches against him. Dwyer swings at many first pitches, hoping the pitcher will try to get ahead in the count with the fastball. He normally does not hit to the opposite field, but he is a good bunter who can move runners along, although he will not bunt for a base hit.

BASERUNNING:

Never fast, Dwyer was slowed by the ailing kneee and is not a threat to steal or take the extra base. He does, however, know how to run the bases, and when he is healthy he is aggressive and will slide hard to break up the double play.

FIELDING:

He is a smooth fielder who gets a

JIM DWYER
RF, No. 28
LL, 5'10", 175 lbs.
ML Svc: 10 years
Born: 1-3-50 in
    Evergreen, IL

1984 STATISTICS
AVG	G	AB	R	H	2B	3B	HR	RBI	BB	SO	SB
.255	76	161	22	41	9	1	2	21	23	24	0

CAREER STATISTICS
AVG	G	AB	R	H	2B	3B	HR	RBI	BB	SO	SB
.257	848	1735	251	446	74	12	41	201	239	233	20

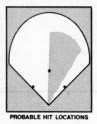

VS. RHP   VS. LHP   PROBABLE HIT LOCATIONS

decent jump on the ball but who has an average arm. Runners will challenge him. Dwyer does not get to the ball quickly down the line or in the gap in right-center. He can go back on a ball very well. His arm is accurate though not strong and he hits the cutoff man.

OVERALL:

He and Dan Ford had excellent years in right field as the O's won it all in 1983, but both of them found themselves in hospital beds in 1984.

Robinson: "In his capacity he can help you because he is a role player and he knows it. If the knee is better this season he will be the player that he was in 1983 (.286/8 HRs/38 RBIs). There are not too many stops left in the major leagues for Jim."

PITCHING:

Mike Flanagan is a pitcher in the purest sense of the word.

He throws overhand, drops to three-quarters and sometimes to sidearm when facing lefthanded hitters. He throws the basic four pitches: fastball (87-89 MPH), curveball, slider and change. He is a power pitcher who becomes more of a control pitcher as the seasons pass. He is helped by the fact that he has good command of all of his pitches and is not afraid to throw any of them with two strikes on a batter.

He is tough on lefthanded hitters because of his three-quarters to sidearm curveball. He is tough on anybody because his fastball sinks. His curve is rated among the top three in the league.

A hitter cannot expect to follow a pattern with Flanagan. He will start off one batter with a fastball and another with a curve.

His 1984 record is deceiving because of the poor-hitting 1984 Orioles. The book on the man they call "Iron Mike" is to get him early in the game. That is possible because if he starts to overthrow in the early innings, his fastball will not sink but stay in the hitter's spot.

He is tough with men on base and gets the grounders when he needs them.

FIELDING:

He and teammate Scott McGregor are two crafty southpaws when it comes to holding runners on first and picking them off. Flanagan is always among the league leaders in pickoffs. Despite a knee injury in 1983, Flanagan can still

MIKE FLANAGAN
LHP, No. 46
LL, 6'0", 195 lbs.
ML Svc: 9 years
Born: 12-16-51 in
Manchester, NH

1984 STATISTICS

W	L	ERA	G	GS	CG	IP	H	R	ER	BB	SO	SV
13	13	3.53	34	34	10	226	213	103	89	81	115	0

CAREER STATISTICS

W	L	ERA	G	GS	CG	IP	H	R	ER	BB	SO	SV
125	87	3.75	284	268	91	1831	1810	822	762	562	1037	1

move around on the mound and is outstanding at getting to slow choppers to his right or left and at throwing runners out. He is an excellent fielder who uses his fielding ability to help him win games.

OVERALL:

He has logged a lot of innings in his nine years. He may soon realize that he cannot blow the fastball by as many hitters as he did in the past. Hitters may start to see him spotting the fastball and using the curveball and slider for strikeouts and grounders.

Robinson: "He might be the best 13-13 pitcher in baseball. He pitched his heart out but got no offensive support; it was pathetic. He will be here next season and will keep giving his best. For seven innings, he will keep them in the game. Mentally, he is probably the toughest pitcher on the staff."

HITTING:

Dan Ford was jeered by Oriole fans in 1982 and cheered by Oriole fans in the championship year of 1983. In 1984, Dan Ford heard neither knocks nor kudos. He did not play for six months of the season.

It wasn't his fault because his ailing knee and ankle kept him on the disabled list for virtually the entire season. He has an extremely closed stance and almost faces the first baseman when batting. His platooning in right field was stopped when he went down with the injury, so the line on Ford is based on what he did when he did hit, run, field, and play.

Ford's stance indicates that he looks for fastballs to hit the opposite way. If teams play him away and pitch him away, he can hit, and with power, to center, right-center and right. He can also pull a fastball because his bat is quick. A pitcher makes a mistake if he hangs a belt-high curve to Ford.

Pitchers will use hard stuff up and in or down and in and hard stuff down and away. He is a better than average off-speed hitter who has patience at the plate. He faces only lefthanded pitching and realizes he will see hard sliders away and fastballs up, but when healthy, Ford is a good mistake hitter who can hit with gap power. He is, however, a poor bunter.

BASERUNNING:

Ford has good speed and stole nine bases in 1983, but late-year knee problems in 1983 and all of 1984 made it certain he would not steal, run hard or take the extra base. When healthy, Ford will make rookie mistakes on the basepaths. He is either too tentative or too foolhardy. Outfielders must always throw to the base ahead of Ford because they can never be sure if he will try to run or simply stay put.

DAN FORD
RF, No. 15
RR, 6'1", 185 lbs.
ML Svc: 10 years
Born: 5-19-52 in
    Los Angeles, CA

1984 STATISTICS											
AVG	G	AB	R	H	2B	3B	HR	RBI	BB	SO	SB
.231	25	91	7	21	4	0	1	5	7	13	1

CAREER STATISTICS											
AVG	G	AB	R	H	2B	3B	HR	RBI	BB	SO	SB
.271	1125	4088	594	1109	212	38	120	565	296	705	61

  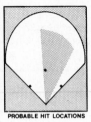

STRONG   STRONG

VS. RHP   VS. LHP   PROBABLE HIT LOCATIONS

FIELDING:

He is not a good outfielder in any aspect of fielding. He can make an outstanding catch on one play and let a grounder roll through his legs the next. He is better at going to his right than to his left and has a good but erratic arm; runners will run on him.

OVERALL:

He had a good year with the O's in 1983 and opted for free agency. The O's rewarded him by keeping him and giving him a three-year contract. One of those years is already gone and Ford's knees are worse.

Robinson: "I think it will be tough for him to come back and have a good year in Baltimore. Where is he going to play? I look for him to be somewhere else this year."

HITTING:

Wayne Gross knew exactly why he was acquired by the Orioles after the 1983 season. The World Champions needed some power at third base. That seemed to be all that was lacking on the team that was labeled "The Dynasty."

The Dynasty turned out to be a dinosaur in 1984, but Gross gave them power, knocking in more runs than he had ever driven in before and matching his home run total for a single year.

Gross has a classic slugger's stance and resembles Jim Rice. Gross uses a square stance, stands straight up and holds the bat high. He has trouble with breaking balls from lefthanded pitchers who will always keep the ball away and use fastballs away. Baltimore, however, used him as either a first baseman or third baseman against righthanded pitchers.

You cannot make a mistake to Gross and try to throw a fastball past him--anyplace. Although he tries to pull and jerk anything out, Gross can hit a fastball out of any park, to any field.

Righthanders will let him see the fastball out of the strike zone and then come back with curves and change-ups. Gross can hit a hard slider or curve but has trouble with off-speed pitches. He will either be off stride or try to pull them rather than go the other way.

BASERUNNING:

He is big and is what is usually called "lumbering" on the bases. He does not have good speed. In 1984 he managed his first triple in three years. He runs hard, however, is aggressive on the paths and is not afraid to knock infielders over. He will not steal or take chances on the bases and knows his limitations.

FIELDING:

Big third basemen always look awkward

WAYNE GROSS
1B, No. 14
LR, 6'2", 205 lbs.
ML Svc: 9 years
Born: 1-14-52 in
   Riverside, CA

1984 STATISTICS											
AVG	G	AB	R	H	2B	3B	HR	RBI	BB	SO	SB
.216	127	342	54	74	9	1	22	64	68	69	1

CAREER STATISTICS											
AVG	G	AB	R	H	2B	3B	HR	RBI	BB	SO	SB
.233	1000	2906	343	676	118	9	110	378	435	447	23

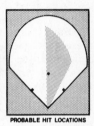

VS. RHP   VS. LHP   PROBABLE HIT LOCATIONS

and Gross is no exception. He is, however, a decent fielder with limited range. He does not get a good jump on balls hit to his left but can knock down hard smashes hit to his right. His arm is strong and accurate. He is no gazelle around third but does manage to get a good jump on pop flies and can handle anything hit near him.

OVERALL:

He knew he would be platooned, knew he would only see righties and made up his mind to go deep as often as he could. Gross obviously accomplished what he set out to do and finished in the top five in the league in homers-per-at-bat ratio.

Robinson: "The O's got what they wanted. This year, he may play third against righties and DH on other occasions."

HITTING:

A newspaper reporter asked manager Joe Altobelli last September how it was that the World Champions could sink to fifth place in 1984, and he replied, "I have no idea. All I do know is that when I look at our lineup, I see seven guys hitting .230." John Lowenstein was one of those seven. He simply stopped hitting last year.

Just when it looked as if he was about to make his usual late-season run at the plate, Lowenstein went on the disabled list with a pulled rib muscle and was later hampered by a bruised heel.

He stands straight up, square to plate, and looks for fastballs from the middle of the plate in. He faces only righthanded pitchers and they do not like to give him that pitch, considering his past success against it. Pitchers will throw him the fastball but spot it down and away. Then they will use curves and low sliders mixed with occasional change-ups to get him out.

Lowenstein looks to go deep on many occasions but is a smart hitter with men on base. The one thing he won't do is go the other way. He will look to pull any pitch he can reach. When he is healthy, he is a better than average hitter of breaking balls, particularly high ones.

He is a decent bunter who occasionally surprises infielders by beating out bunts. He did not bunt much in 1984.

BASERUNNING:

Lowenstein had excellent speed early in his career and was a smart runner. At this stage of his career he does not have excellent speed but is still smart. He does not make mental mistakes and will take the extra base if the opportunity is there. Ankle injuries have slowed him down and the added rib and heel problems in 1983 slowed him even further.

JOHN LOWENSTEIN
LF, No. 38
LR, 6'1", 180 lbs.
ML Svc: 14 years
Born: 1-27-47 in
Wolf Point, MT

1984 STATISTICS

AVG	G	AB	R	H	2B	3B	HR	RBI	BB	SO	SB
.237	105	270	34	64	13	0	8	28	33	54	1

CAREER STATISTICS

AVG	G	AB	R	H	2B	3B	HR	RBI	BB	SO	SB
.255	1356	3450	510	879	137	18	116	439	444	593	128

  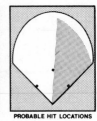

VS. RHP   VS. LHP   PROBABLE HIT LOCATIONS

FIELDING:

He is not a graceful fielder but gets a good jump on fly balls and catches everything he gets his glove on. John has a better than average arm and surprises runners who think they can take an extra base against him. His is an alert outfielder who can think along with a runner and make accurate throws to the right base. He hits his cutoff man.

OVERALL:

Very quietly, Lowenstein has joined the ranks of Oriole players who have grown a little bit older, a little slower and a little less effective.

Robinson: "I expect him to bounce back. He will hit if he is healthy, but I wonder about the age factor with him. True, injuries have taken their toll, but I think he has one good year left in him."

PITCHING:

It would appear that a pitcher with a losing record might feel that his year was a total loss, but such is not the case with Dennis Martinez. 1983 was a different story of course, when he had a record of 7-16. Prior to that, this starter/reliever was used exclusively as a starter for six years and posted more than 14 wins in five of those years.

He began 1984 in the bullpen but joined the starting rotation in June and stayed there. He is the type of pitcher who can totally confuse fans, writers, scouts, managers and maybe even himself. He has an explosive fastball (90-92 MPH) and a sharp curve, a hard slider and a change-up. He throws from three-quarters with a quick windup and release. His control is excellent.

He is confusing because if he has command of all his pitches, he is tough to beat. He will throw all of his pitches to many batters and they will not be able to hit them. But in so doing, he may actually hurt himself more than help himself. If he stayed with the fastball and slider, throwing in an occasional change-up, he might be better off. When he is on track, he will use all of his pitches but throw the fastball or curve for a third strike.

Control does hurt him despite the fact that he does not walk more than 2.5 batters a game. If he gets his pitches in the wrong place he can be taken deep. Martinez led the staff in home runs allowed. Although his windup is rapid, he is still a slow, deliberate worker on the mound.

FIELDING:

Martinez has a good move to first and

DENNIS MARTINEZ
RHP, No. 30
RR, 6'1", 185 lbs.
ML Svc: 8 years
Born: 5-14-55 in
Granada, NIC

1984 STATISTICS

W	L	ERA	G	GS	CG	IP	H	R	ER	BB	SO	SV
6	9	5.02	34	20	2	141	145	81	79	37	77	0

CAREER STATISTICS

W	L	ERA	G	GS	CG	IP	H	R	ER	BB	SO	SV
95	82	4.04	282	212	66	1588	1608	784	712	518	788	5

is quick off the mound. He can get to balls that others pitchers cannot. He is good at covering bunts but does have trouble in certain situations with runners on. He tends to throw too much to first, losing some of his concentration on the batter.

OVERALL:

His personal problems have been well documented. He has admitted publicly to an alcohol problem and has worked his butt off to come back for his own self-esteem and to be the pitcher he was and is expected to be. He is still, however, an inconsistent pitcher who is liable to pitch a no-hitter in one start and a 50-hitter the next.

Robinson: "Dennis is working harder now than ever before. He has a great arm, maybe the best on the team, and that is in his favor. I look for him to get back on track and win at least 15 games this year."

PITCHING:

In 1984, Tippy Martinez had his first losing season in eight years with the Orioles, and it came as a surprise. He has one of the best curveballs in baseball, but lost control of it too many times, had a variety of arm problems and slumped in almost every pitching category.

He has a short, compact delivery and quick release. He does not look as if he is throwing hard or can throw hard, but he does . . . really. His fastball has been clocked at 88-89 MPH and gets on top of a hitter before he knows it.

Martinez always had ultimate faith in his ability to throw the curve in any situation, to any hitter, and to throw it for a strike. After missing with it so often last season, that faith may be wavering.

He is a better pitcher against left-handed hitters because even though they know the curve is coming, it has a tremendous break and drops down sharply. He can also flatten out the curve to keep it in a wide, sweeping plane, making it almost impossible for lefthanders to hit if he can keep it on the outside corner.

Martinez moves his fastball around very well, usually up and away and low and in. He will use it for a strikeout in a key situation. He is used in short relief and knows what must be done.

He has had outstanding success with basically two pitches and could always get both of them over. Last season, he began to lose his control and led the team in wild pitches. He averaged a walk every two innings. He was not able to pitch himself out of jams as well as he had in the past.

FIELDING:

Tippy is an average fielder who will

TIPPY MARTINEZ
LHP, No. 23
LL, 5'10", 175 lbs.
ML Svc: 9 years
Born: 5-31-50 in
     LaJunta, CO

1984 STATISTICS

W	L	ERA	G	GS	CG	IP	H	R	ER	BB	SO	SV
4	9	3.91	55	0	0	89	88	42	39	51	71	17

CAREER STATISTICS

W	L	ERA	G	GS	CG	IP	H	R	ER	BB	SO	SV
52	37	3.15	480	2	0	744	636	290	260	372	570	110

let his middle infielders handle hard grounders just past the mound. He does cover first base well but has only an average move there. He will throw to first just to see if the runner is leaning rather than to try to pick him off.

OVERALL:

He is a no-nonsense pitcher who comes at the hitters with his curve and fastball. He is proof that a live arm and good control (mostly), coupled with the ability to shake off a bad outing, can lead to a career as an excellent short man.

Robinson: "Tippy might have to prove to everyone this year that he can still be effective. He has got to get the curve over. This year, it is a cinch that he will get competition from Sammy Stewart for the role of number one man out of the bullpen."

PITCHING:

It was only instinct--anyone would try to protect themselves--but Scott McGregor stuck out his pitching hand in front of a grounder and wound up breaking his pinkie. He was lost to the team for the last six weeks of the 1984 season.

But long before that, it seems that the Orioles' lack of hitting was affecting their pitchers---except McGregor. He was humming along somewhat ignorant of what the rest of his team was not doing, had 15 wins and looked sure to notch 20. Before the pinkie.

He throws from an extremely deceptive three-quarters motion and can occasionally drop down further against certain lefthanded hitters. He has a slight hesitation in his motion that makes it difficult for hitters to time his pitches. No matter, though, McGregor will not throw a pitch over the middle of the plate unless he makes a mistake.

He will throw fastball, curve and change, over and over, keeping the ball low and away. He hits the corners very well and is one of the best control pitchers in the game. He will throw the fastball when he has to and can strike out many hitters with it because he will feed them off-speed curves, and get them leaning, then bust the fastball in on their hands.

He never seems to throw the pitch the batter is expecting. Even if the batter guesses curve, he will have trouble hitting it because it always moves. In 1984, however, McGregor's ERA and hits-per-innings climbed because he had a tendency to get too many pitches up in the strike zone.

SCOTT McGREGOR
LHP, No. 16
SL, 6'1", 190 lbs.
ML Svc: 8 years
Born: 1-18-54 in
    Inglewood, CA

1984 STATISTICS

W	L	ERA	G	GS	CG	IP	H	R	ER	BB	SO	SV
15	12	3.94	30	30	10	196	216	93	86	54	67	0

CAREER STATISTICS

W	L	ERA	G	GS	CG	IP	H	R	ER	BB	SO	SV
111	69	3.63	257	223	70	1631	1664	716	658	354	674	5

FIELDING:

With the exception of Mike Flanagan, no pitcher on the staff has a better move to first than McGregor. The only way a runner can steal off him is to guess right and take off. Otherwise, he is a dead man.

McGregor is an excellent fielder who covers his ground, covers first and always throws to the right base and backs up other infielders.

OVERALL:

He seems to have some arm problems every year but is always near the top in all pitching categories. He is simply tough to beat and does not moan and groan if he does lose a tough game or gets blasted.

Robinson: "He stays with the pitches that are working, does not beat himself and always makes you beat him. I see no reason why he can't win 20 this year."

HITTING:

As a rule, pitchers are a clever lot. They proved it again in 1984 with Eddie Murray. They realized that there were only two Oriole hitters who could beat them--Murray and Ripken. Since no Baltimore player was hitting even .250 behind Murray in the cleanup spot, the solution was simple--walk him. He wound up leading the league in walks with 107, and the Orioles finished in fifth place.

Nonetheless, Murray stood tall and led the league in game-winning hits with 19 and in on-base percentage with .410, keeping up his usual totals of RBIs and home runs.

This power-hitting first baseman hits for a higher average and gets more home runs from the left side. He bats basically the same either way, a slightly open and slightly crouched stance. He is a devastating fastball hitter from the left side and likes the fastball from the belt to the knees. Pitchers may try to throw the high fastball past him when he bats either way, but if they get it in the wrong spot it will become a souvenir in the stands.

Lefthanders will throw him hard sliders low and fastballs away. Both left and righthanded pitchers now throw him many more trick pitches such as the forkball, palmball, split-fingered fastball or knuckler (if they have them). A pitcher who can throw him nothing but off-speed breaking balls will have success against him--but how many pitchers can do that?

BASERUNNING:

Murray is faster than people think, and in 1984 he stole ten bases just to prove it. He could steal even more if he wanted to or had to. He runs hard, slides hard and is aggresseive on the basepaths. He may make one or two more mental errors than he should, however.

FIELDING:

Not very long ago, Eddie Murray stood

EDDIE MURRAY
1B, No. 33
SR, 6'2", 200 lbs.
ML Svc: 8 years
Born: 2-24-56 in
    Los Angeles, CA

1984 STATISTICS

AVG	G	AB	R	H	2B	3B	HR	RBI	BB	SO	SB
.306	162	588	97	180	26	3	29	110	107	87	10

CAREER STATISTICS

AVG	G	AB	R	H	2B	3B	HR	RBI	BB	SO	SB
.298	1206	4546	712	1355	234	18	227	807	546	651	47

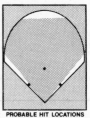

VS. RHP   VS. LHP   PROBABLE HIT LOCATIONS

alone at the top of the heap of American League first baseman. Now, players like Don Mattingly of the Yankees and Kent Hrbek of the Twins are giving him a run for the money.

Murray handles all throws and has excellent jumping ability and a sweep tag if a throw pulls him off first. He can go either way on hard smashes, has excellent range, is accurate on his throws to pitchers covering first in his stead and has no peer when it comes to charging bunts and throwing runners out.

OVERALL:

Like Ripken, Murray played every game of the season. He is a team player and one of the most durable players in the league.

Robinson: "An outstanding year. He was the Orioles' MVP and the leader of the team. One of these years, he will be MVP of the league. Outstanding past, present and future."

HITTING:

At the rate that Floyd Rayford is going, he will wind up in the broadcasting booth. He signed a major league contract with the Angels, who converted him from an outfielder to an infielder. The O's had him later, traded him to St. Louis, got him back in 1984 and converted him to a catcher. He is moving closer and closer to the booth but he did catch some earlier in his career.

He had several good years in the high minors but could not hit big league pitching. He perked up when he was back with Baltimore in 1984.

He has a slightly closed stance and is a straightaway line drive hitter with occasional pop. He loves low pitches, particularly fastballs, but has trouble with breaking balls away and fastballs up. He is an impatient hitter, swings at many first pitches and does not like to take a walk. He is a better than average bunter.

BASERUNNING:

Rayford takes a long lead off first but is no threat to steal. He has average speed. He will not take chances on the bases and will not take the extra base.

FIELDING:

Rayford has played everywhere but the mound in his tenure in the minors and majors, but Baltimore has been grooming him as a catcher. He did play a little in the infield and outfield but is considered average in both spots. He had better success as a catcher and displayed a quick release and accurate arm. His arm is not strong--runners will run on him. He exhibited an ability to get along well with the pitching staff and can call the game they expected him to with no frills attached. He caught 68 games last season.

FLOYD RAYFORD
C/INF, No. 12
RR, 5'10", 205 lbs.
ML Svc: 3 years
Born: 7-27-57 in
Memphis, TN

1984 STATISTICS

AVG	G	AB	R	H	2B	3B	HR	RBI	BB	SO	SB
.256	86	250	24	64	14	0	4	27	12	51	0

CAREER STATISTICS

AVG	G	AB	R	H	2B	3B	HR	RBI	BB	SO	SB
.256	86	250	24	64	14	0	4	27	12	51	0

VS. RHP   VS. LHP   PROBABLE HIT LOCATIONS

OVERALL:

By a quirk of fate, the Orioles sent him to St. Louis and got Tito Landrum in return. Landrum homered in the championship series and helped the Orioles beat the White Sox. The following April, both teams changed their minds and, thank you very much, sent both back to the other.

Robinson: "He can help you in several positions and is by no means an automatic out. He is a better player than anyone gives him credit for. Look for him to be in an Orioles' uniform playing at a couple of different positions. He has a great attitude, the players love him and he just goes about his business. He really deserves a lot more playing time than most might expect."

HITTING:

To show you how good this shortstop is, Cal Ripken dropped off in batting average, hits, doubles, RBIs, at-bats, slugging percentage and total bases in 1984--and was still among the league leaders in almost every offensive category!

He was third in the league in hits, tied for fourth in doubles, third in total bases (327) and third in extra-base hits (71). The figures were all slightly less than his incredible MVP year of 1983 but it hardly mattered.

He has a closed stance, bat held away from his body, and sees the ball better than 99% of the players in baseball. He is on top of every pitch, murders high fastballs and high curves and has the ability to hit the ball hard and far in any direction. He goes with the pitch, but will pull the inside fastball or slider to left for a homer.

He is patient but aggressive at home plate and with men on base will make contact. He does not cut down his swing with two strikes and always looks to drive the ball. The only book on him has been for pitchers to throw him up and away with fastballs and low and away with sliders and curves. He is a better than average off-speed hitter who can double-clutch at the plate and slash the ball to right-center.

He is not a streak hitter and manages to keep his average at or near .300 all year. In 1984 he did struggle a bit early (if you call .287 on June 27th a struggle) but rallied and hit over .300 for a team that hit .252 as a whole.

BASERUNNING:

Ripken has great instincts, rarely makes a mistake and has good speed. He is very aggressive, breaks up double plays and will always take the extra base on a bobble or an outfielder's laziness. He doesn't steal but could if he had to. Ripken bats in front of Eddie Murray so he never gets the steal sign.

CAL RIPKEN
SS, No. 8
RR, 6'4", 200 lbs.
ML Svc: 3 years
Born: 8-24-60 in
    Havre de Grace, MD

1984 STATISTICS

AVG	G	AB	R	H	2B	3B	HR	RBI	BB	SO	SB
.304	162	641	103	195	37	7	27	86	71	89	2

CAREER STATISTICS

AVG	G	AB	R	H	2B	3B	HR	RBI	BB	SO	SB
.293	507	1941	315	569	116	14	82	281	176	289	5

  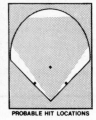

VS. RHP — VS. LHP — PROBABLE HIT LOCATIONS

FIELDING:

Ripken is not one of the best, but he is certainly the best all-around shortstop day in and day out. He has not missed a game at short since July 1, 1982. He is a steady, smart player who knows how to play the hitters. He has good range and a strong arm.

Cal can turn the double play and go to his right or left with equal ease; he makes all the necessary plays. He might have been better at short if the Orioles had a better third baseman.

OVERALL:

After Rookie of the Year in 1982 and MVP in 1983, the Orioles pay him a million dollars a year. He is worth it.

Robinson: "One of the best players in the game. You put his name in the lineup every day, forget about him and watch the results. And I'll tell you something--he can play better!"

HITTING:

Roenicke & Lowenstein. Lewis & Clark. Hope & Crosby. Johnson & Johnson. You get the idea: think of one, think of the other.

Roenicke and Lowenstein platoon in left field; they do a good job of it and have enjoyed a lot of publicity as well. In 1982, the first year of The Big Platoon, they combined for 41 homers and 123 RBIs. In 1983, they had 35 homers and 131 RBIs. In 1984, they were nowhere.

Roenicke has a closed stance, stands deep in the box and holds the bat at shoulder level and further back than most hitters. He is a pull hitter and a long ball hitter who loves belt-high fastballs from the middle of the plate in. He is a dead fastball hitter who prefers the ball high in the strike zone. He plays only against lefthanded pitchers. Those who have good control and keep the ball away and down will enjoy good success against him. Roenicke is a good clutch hitter.

Pressure does not bother him, but in 1984 he did not hit in any situation. It appeared as though he did not have a definite plan of attack when he came to the plate and was unsure of himself; furthermore, he didn't have one of his usual hot streaks. He slumped badly in September. He can bunt if he has to either with men on base or for a hit.

BASERUNNING:

He has good baseball instincts but does not have enough speed to stretch hits or take foolish chances on the bases. He will not steal but will take the extra base in obvious situations and is very aggressive on the bases. He gets out of the batter's box fairly well.

FIELDING:

When all is well and everyone's head is on straight, Roenicke is a very good

GARY ROENICKE
LF, No. 35
RR, 6'3", 200 lbs.
ML Svc: 6 years
Born: 12-5-54 in
Covina, CA

1984 STATISTICS

AVG	G	AB	R	H	2B	3B	HR	RBI	BB	SO	SB
.224	121	326	36	73	19	1	10	44	58	43	1

CAREER STATISTICS

AVG	G	AB	R	H	2B	3B	HR	RBI	BB	SO	SB
.253	765	2082	284	526	108	4	93	314	295	324	13

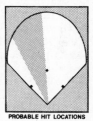

VS. RHP   VS. LHP   PROBABLE HIT LOCATIONS

major league outfielder who rates above average in all categories. He gets a good jump on balls hit either way, can come in or go back and has a good arm. He keeps his throw low as an outfielder should.

Roenicke makes tough plays look easy.

OVERALL:

Roenicke's year was worse than John Lowenstein's because Gary was healthy, while Lowenstein had an excuse.

Robinson: "The Orioles think that he can come back and have a good year, but I wonder. Too many things seemed to happen to him during the year. The team would like him to play every day, but that is almost impossible. His big swing makes him quite susceptible to dry spells. I think that it would be best to continue the platoon system with him. It is that combination that seems to hold the secret to the success of the Orioles."

HITTING:

As Dave Winfield and Don Mattingly were battling it out last season for the batting title, Bob Boone, Dick Schofield and John Shelby were in a race of their own: the one for the lowest batting average in the American League. At the finish line, it was Schofield in last place at .193, Boone at .202 and John Shelby at .209.

Shelby was platooned last season and hit .202 as a lefthanded hitter and .219 as a righty. His stance is slightly closed, with his feet fairly wide apart. He is not a power hitter and tries to hit straightaway but has the tendency to swing too hard. He can hit a fastball down the middle of the plate but not much else. Pitchers will show him the fastball down or away because although he is able at times to handle a high fastball, he chases too many out of the strike zone.

Many pitchers throw Shelby nothing but breaking balls, and he has trouble with them in any location. He is an impatient hitter who swings at many first pitches and does not draw many walks, something he should try to do because he bats high in the order.

BASERUNNING:

In 1983, Shelby led the Orioles with 15 steals. A year later, he took 12. He has outstanding speed from the batter's box and on the bases, but he must learn the pitchers' moves better in order to be able to steal at will. He is an aggressive runner who will always take chances.

FIELDING:

A young center fielder with blazing speed and an above average arm should progress from year to year, but Shelby slipped in 1984. He does not make errors but lets too many fly balls play him rather than the otherway around.

He plays deeper than most center fielders and relies on his speed to

JOHN SHELBY
OF, No. 37
SR, 6'1", 175 lbs.
ML Svc: 2 years
Born: 2-23-58 in
Lexington, KY

1984 STATISTICS											
AVG	G	AB	R	H	2B	3B	HR	RBI	BB	SO	SB
.209	128	383	44	80	12	5	6	30	20	71	12

CAREER STATISTICS											
AVG	G	AB	R	H	2B	3B	HR	RBI	BB	SO	SB
.235	287	745	106	175	30	7	12	59	38	141	29

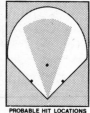

VS. RHP   VS. LHP   PROBABLE HIT LOCATIONS

catch bloops or balls hit in the gaps. He can out run anything that is hit but lets too many balls drop in front of him. Runners have learned that he has a good arm and do not take chances against him.

OVERALL:

Shelby must learn the strike zone and must be able to regain his confidence. He is the best bunter on the team and did a lot of excellent bunting in the second half of the season. He has to start hitting and not let what may be lack of production at the plate carry over into the field.

Robinson: "With Al Bumbry not coming back to the Orioles, Shelby has the center field job. It might prove to be the best thing for him—just what he needs. He has the tools, and is a coachable player but he must make use of what he has. There has to be some improvement this year."

HITTING:

Hitting? Try "walking." Last season, Ken Singleton's highlight was chasing Boog Powell's all-time Oriole record for bases-on-balls. He didn't reach it, falling short of Powell's record of 889 walks by four short trips.

The switch-hitting Singleton lost the pop in his bat last season from both sides of the plate (.224 right vs. 213 left). He still uses basically the same stance, slightly open and straight up. He is a high fastball hitter batting left and a low fastball hitter the other way.

His lifetime batting average is excellent because he has always had the best eye in baseball. He is very selective and patient at the plate. He usually gets the pitch he wants to hit when pitchers fall behind on him 2-0 or 3-1.

He does not always look fastball when he is behind and can hit belt-high curveballs batting either way. When he did hit well last season, righthanded pitchers would try to keep the ball away and down and then throw sliders low and in, then turn the fastball over or throw him an off-speed pitch. He does not bunt but has always had the reputation for being a dangerous clutch hitter with a high on-base percentage.

BASERUNNING:

He was never a fast runner, is steadily getting slower, does not steal but certainly knows how to run the bases. He gives it everything he can on the bases and is a good slider who can avoid a tag with a hook slide.

KEN SINGLETON
DH, No. 29
SR, 6'4", 212 lbs.
ML Svc: 14 years
Born: 6-10-47 in
Mt. Vernon, NY

1984 STATISTICS

AVG	G	AB	R	H	2B	3B	HR	RBI	BB	SO	SB
.215	111	363	28	78	7	1	6	36	37	60	0

CAREER STATISTICS

AVG	G	AB	R	H	2B	3B	HR	RBI	BB	SO	SB
.282	2082	7189	985	2029	317	25	246	1066	1262	1246	21

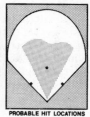

VS. RHP   VS. LHP   PROBABLE HIT LOCATIONS

OVERALL:

He has played with the Baltimore Orioles for ten years and has given them nine excellent ones. He is an intelligent player of vast experience. The presence of this respected veteran could be the punch that another club needs.

Robinson: "Kenny really slipped last year. As the DH, he must hit--it is all he does--but he lost some snap. He believes that a certain set of exercises will help there, but no exercise can make you younger. He'll get a look-see in the spring, and then we'll all see."

PITCHING:

Sammy Stewart--power pitcher--93 MPH fastball--reliever--doesn't fool around.

Additionally, Stewart has a curveball, slider and straight change, but above all else, he is a power pitcher. Whether he comes into a game for short or long relief, Stewart challenges every hitter with the hard stuff. His slider is also hard, and he is similar to Dave Stieb in that they are both able to send their two big pitches in at the same speed.

Stewart has worked on perfecting a curve, and he throws it to righties from an over-the-top motion that makes it a tough pitch to hit.

His fastball moves in and out but usually rises. If he has control of the slider and fastball he is equally effective against either left or right-handed hitters. He has supreme confidence in his ability to overpower a hitter.

Last season, he had trouble with his location and control.

FIELDING:

Stewart has a quick move to first and tries to keep runners close. At times, he throws over too much and loses some of his effectiveness. He is in good position to field grounders hit back at him but in general is rated below average in all aspects of fielding. He does

SAMMY STEWART
RHP, No. 53
RR, 6'3", 208 lbs.
ML Svc: 6 years
Born: 10-28-54 in
Asheville, NC

1984 STATISTICS												
W	L	ERA	G	GS	CG	IP	H	R	ER	BB	SO	SV
7	4	3.29	60	0	0	93	81	42	34	47	56	13

CAREER STATISTICS												
W	L	ERA	G	GS	CG	IP	H	R	ER	BB	SO	SV
46	38	3.45	251	24	4	736	657	306	282	367	437	33

not take his fielding as seriously as he should.

OVERALL:

Stewart was a combination starter/reliever for the better part of four years with the Orioles. In 1984, he made only one start in 58 games so it looks as if Stewart will be their stopper.

Robinson: "He did a good job in long relief and then did a good job in short as the year progressed. This year, he will get his chance to become top dog in the bullpen and he will just eat it up. Last season, he did not always like the way he was being used and said so."

PITCHING:

Nobody seems to know what to do with Bill Swaggerty. In the minors he was used as both a starter and a reliever. When he came up to Baltimore in 1984 he was used the same way. When Scott McGregor broke his finger in late August Swaggerty replaced him in the starting rotation.

He has a quick windup and throws from over-the-top. The ball seems to get to home plate before the batter realizes it, but Swaggerty does not really have a good fastball. He usually cuts the fastball and tries to run it in to righties and away from lefties. He is more effective against righthanded hitters because he can make the fastball move and mix it with a hard slider. One problem he has is that his slider and fastball, regardless of how fast or slow they come to home plate, come at the same speed. He uses an occasional change to right-handed hitters, but will have to come up with another pitch to effectively handle the lefthanders. He will also have to learn to vary speeds.

His success comes when he moves the ball around and keeps the hard stuff low and away. Like the majority of pitchers, when he falls behind in the count or starts getting his pitches up he gets in trouble.

FIELDING:

Swaggerty has a good move to first and keeps runners close. He is rated average as a fielder but moves around well and works hard to improve his fielding.

BILL SWAGGERTY
RHP, No. 32
RR, 6'2", 186 lbs.
ML Svc: 1 year plus
Born: 12-5-56 in
    Sanford, FL

1984 STATISTICS

W	L	ERA	G	GS	CG	IP	H	R	ER	BB	SO	SV
3	2	5.21	23	6	0	57	68	41	33	21	18	0

CAREER STATISTICS

W	L	ERA	G	GS	CG	IP	H	R	ER	BB	SO	SV
4	3	4.62	30	8	0	78	91	49	40	27	25	0

OVERALL:

Because Swaggerty does not have a good fastball, he may not be the reliever Baltimore thinks he might be. He can be used in long relief, but he would have trouble coming in late in the game in tough situations. He has the stuff to be a starter but must develop another pitch to become more effective.

Robinson: "He was the best pitcher the O's had in spring training, when he was unhittable. There was just no place for him on the staff so he was up-and-down between Rochester and Baltimore all year. That didn't help. He can pitch but he needs to do it every fourth or fifth day. He will be a major league pitcher this year either with Baltimore or somebody else. He has the ability, is ready and is a fast learner."

PITCHING:

Tom Underwood has always been a pitcher a team could use just about anywhere. Long, short, start--with reliable get-the-job-done type of performances against a lefty batter. But because of some control problems last season, Underwood became the last man on the pitching staff.

He went through a vicious cycle: he was not pitching well and couldn't find the spots because he wasn't pitching often--he wasn't pitching often because he couldn't find a cow on the highway.

He throws a fastball, curve and short slider and he has a change-up he rarely uses. He can pitch well to lefthanded hitters if he keeps the curve away and the fastball up and in. He is not afraid to come inside with his 86 MPH fastball but missed getting it in the right spots too often in 1984 and was hit hard.

Dugout chatter about Underwood is that he will always find a way to lose a game and that he can be caught up to in the late innings. Many of his problems stem from inactivity and the lack of a true "killer instinct" coupled with the fact that he never knows what is expected of him. If his sharp curve is not working, he will get hit pretty badly because the hitters are just waiting for him.

TOM UNDERWOOD
LHP, No. 42
RL, 5'11", 177 lbs.
ML Svc: 10 years
Born: 12-22-53 in
　　　Kokomo, IN

1984 STATISTICS
W	L	ERA	G	GS	CG	IP	H	R	ER	BB	SO	SV
1	0	3.52	37	1	0	71	78	33	28	31	39	1

CAREER STATISTICS
W	L	ERA	G	GS	CG	IP	H	R	ER	BB	SO	SV
86	87	3.89	379	203	35	1585	1554	772	685	662	948	18

FIELDING:

His move to first is fair, but Tom is quick off the mound, fields bunts well and does a good job covering first. He sees his fielding as a part of his job, not just an adventure.

OVERALL:

Robinson: "He has a rubber arm and can pitch anytime. He might need a better off-speed pitch to go with the hard curve and fastball. He should help someone this season; teams are always in the market for lefthanders with a live arm."

HITTING:

About the only power Baltimore generated from their outfield last season was from Mike Young. The switch-hitting Young, who led the International League in strikeouts in 1982, is slowly learning to cut down on the Ks and to improve as a hitter.

He bats from a slightly closed stance either way and strides into pitches. He was hit by pitches six times last year, a club high. Young is a power hitter but hits basically straightaway and looks for fastballs belt-high. He has trouble with breaking balls, and pitchers will invariably feed him curves and sliders low and away. They will do so even more in 1985 because Young has shown that he has power from both sides of the plate and was one of the top rookie home run hitters in the league in 1984.

Despite his successes at the plate, Young still struck out too many times. He is a guy who looks at the first pitch and in that way, he is a patient hitter. He is slowly gaining the reputation for being a better than average clutch hitter who can hit for power with men on base. He is much better left-handed than righthanded (.276 vs. .195).

BASERUNNING:

Young has excellent speed and can steal bases but does not know how to. When he does learn, he will probably take 10-15 bases a year, an excellent number for an individual on a team that does not run much. He takes a long lead at first and is very aggressive on the bases. He will take the extra base every chance he gets.

FIELDING:

Mike played various positions in 1984 but seems best suited to right field.

MIKE YOUNG
OF, No. 43
SR, 6'2", 194 lbs.
ML Svc: 1 year plus
Born: 3-20-60 in
    Oakland, CA

1984 STATISTICS

AVG	G	AB	R	H	2B	3B	HR	RBI	BB	SO	SB
.252	123	401	59	101	17	2	17	52	58	110	6

CAREER STATISTICS

AVG	G	AB	R	H	2B	3B	HR	RBI	BB	SO	SB
.244	153	439	66	107	19	3	17	54	60	119	7

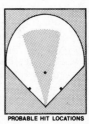

VS. RHP   VS. LHP   PROBABLE HIT LOCATIONS

His arm is rated fair but accurate. He has trouble playing "position" outfield and must learn to move around more. Balls hit in front of him give him trouble. He can go back on a ball with his speed but generally does not get a good jump on the ball.

OVERALL:

He was the only bright spot in an outfield that fell apart last season.

Robinson: "Mike came on with a rush in August and September and I can smell a bright future in the wind for him. With a full year under his belt now, he should only get better. While he has some things to work on and has a lot to learn about playing in the big leagues, Young has all the tools to become an outstanding player. He'll come along fast."

RON JACKSON
INF/OF, No. 15
RR, 6'0", 217 lbs.
ML Svc: 10 years
Born: 5-9-53 in
Birmingham, AL

HITTING, BASERUNNING, FIELDING:

Ron Jackson played in the minors for most of the 1984 season and was called up to the parent club in September. He is a solidly built righthander with a slightly closed stance who will try to hit the ball where it is pitched. He likes the ball out over the plate so he can extend his arms, and he is a good low ball, fastball hitter.

Pitchers will throw him curves away and hard stuff up and in. He tries to think with the pitchers and looks for a pitch that has struck him out the prior at-bat. He is a better than average off-speed hitter. At one time a notorious free-swinger, Jackson has been trying to meet the ball and hit it in the alleys, but he has lost some aggressiveness at the plate. He seems to fight the ball off more than just driving it hard.

He is not fast but is intelligent and rarely makes foolish mistakes on the bases. He will not steal but can be used in hit-and-run situations because he will take the extra base.

He can play first and third and fill in in the outfield. He does not have good range but stays in front of hard smashes and is not afraid of the ball. He will dive either way to stop a ball from getting by him at first or third.

OVERALL:

Robinson: "He plays a lot of positions, but I don't know if that helps him or hurts him. I really don't know where he would fit in best with the Orioles, so I think he'll be with another team. He has a super attitude."

JOE NOLAN
C, No. 17
LR, 6'0", 190 lbs.
ML Svc: 8 years
Born: 5-21-51 in
St. Louis, MO

HITTING, BASERUNNING, FIELDING:

Joe Nolan was just getting used to American League pitching when his knee gave him trouble after the 1983 season. It was operated on but did not come around, and Nolan was lost for virtually the entire 1984 season.

The lefthanded-hitting catcher enjoyed a good season in 1983, platooning with Rick Dempsey. In the National League he enjoyed hitting against primarily fastball, power pitchers; he had trouble adjusting to breaking balls in the American League. He can hit fast-balls from the knees to the shoulders but likes the fastball up and from the middle of the plate on in. He will try to pull anything he can get his bat on.

A control pitcher will have good success against Nolan because he will spot the fastball away then come back with sinkers, sliders and curves. Nolan was learning to adjust to junk and off-speed pitches but the bad knee ruined him in 1984.

He is not fast, will not take the extra base and will not steal. He is rated a good defensive catcher who calls a good game and has a fair and accurate arm, but not a quick release nor a particularly strong arm. Runners will run on him.

OVERALL:

Robinson: "I have my doubts that he will make it in 1985. That knee operation slowed him down considerably. He has to catch to help, and right now, I don't think his knees will let him."

LENN SAKATA
2B, No. 12
RR, 5'9", 160 lbs.
ML Svc: 6 years
Born: 6-8-53 in
   Honolulu, HI

HITTING, BASERUNNING, FIELDING:

Lenn Sakata can play any infield position and can catch in an emergency, but in 1984 he sat on the bench. When someone got hurt, he played, or when someone was pinch-hit for, he played. In short, he never knew when he was going to play so he simply stopped hitting.

In 1982 and 1983, he hit fairly well, with surprising power, and performed some late-inning, clutch-hitting heroics. He has a slightly open stance and likes the fastball up and in. He can handle that pitch from either righties or lefties. He has the ability to get his bat on the ball with a runner on third, and can either squeeze him in or manage a fly ball. Basically, however, he is an impatient hitter who swings at the first pitch and tries to pull. Pitchers will try to keep the ball away from him, usually low and away.

He has speed and can steal when asked to. He is a good baserunner who always watches his coach's signs.

At second base, he has good range and is excellent at turning the double play. He gets rid of the ball quickly because he doesn't want opposing runners bearing down on him. He was a bit too flashy at short, but has steadied down at second. His arm is average, but his release is good.

OVERALL:

Robinson: "It was a lost year for him. He did not play enough to help and his overall play suffered. He is a good utility man, but with the Orioles he has to play to help. His future seems very much up in the air."

BOSTON RED SOX

HITTING:

Tony Armas hits and hits for power, as was evident by his major league leading home run and RBI totals. A free swinger, Armas is a dead fastball hitter who can also hammer curves if they get up in his eyes. He raised his average almost 50 points in 1984 because he did not try to pull everything he saw. He made much better contact, despite his career high in strikeouts. He had a 19-game hitting streak from June 17th to July 6th.

Armas has a square stance, stands upright and holds the bat high near his shoulder. If he is looking for the fastball, he can hit it, but there are times when a pitcher can sneak the pitch by him with two strikes if Armas is thinking curve. Righties usually try to feed him the fastball in, then throw curves and sliders low and away. In 1984, he was able to hit those outside pitches to the opposite field, giving him more of a chance to see fastballs in clutch situations.

Armas has always been a notorious streak hitter, and when he is hot, he hits for power, day in and day out.

BASERUNNING:

While Armas does not steal a lot of bases, he always tries to take an extra base. Leg injuries have slowed him down, but he has enough competitive juices flowing to try his best to break up the double play.

FIELDING:

A converted right fielder, Armas handles center field as well as anybody in the league. Rick Manning and Fred Lynn cover more ground, but Armas has a better than average arm. Runners will rarely try to test him by going from first to third.

TONY ARMAS
CF, No. 20
RR, 6'1", 200 lbs.
ML Svc: 8 years
Born: 7-12-53 in
       Anzoategui, VEN

1984 STATISTICS

AVG	G	AB	R	H	2B	3B	HR	RBI	BB	SO	SB
.268	157	639	107	171	29	5	43	123	32	156	1

CAREER STATISTICS

AVG	G	AB	R	H	2B	3B	HR	RBI	BB	SO	SB
.248	1000	3703	452	920	136	26	190	605	188	888	16

  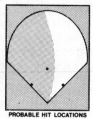

VS. RHP   VS. LHP   PROBABLE HIT LOCATIONS

He gets an excellent jump on the ball and is perfect for the Red Sox, with classy Dwight Evans in right and the ever-improving Jim Rice in left. Armas seems to make outstanding catches when the game is on the line.

OVERALL:

In his two years in Boston, Armas has 79 homers and 230 RBIs. He does not walk much, hits into an extraordinary number of double plays and strikes out a lot. Not much matter, though; an average of 40 homers and 115 RBIs per season simply cannot be overlooked.

Robinson: "He worked hard at hitting the ball the other way. He even changed his stroke with two strikes on him. It all added up to a great year. Nothing seems to bother him anymore."

HITTING:

Howard Cosell likes to use the word "plethora," as in "There are a plethora of good-hitting second basemen in the American League." He is right, of course--there is Lou Whitaker, Damaso Garcia, Frank White and the rookie Tim Teufel. But Boston's Marty Barrett out-hit them all.

Barrett has closed his stance severely and virtually faces the first baseman. That stance has enabled him to hit to all fields. Not for power, but he cannot be taken lightly. He has a quick bat and makes contact. Barrett is one of the toughest players in the league to strike out (25 times for the season and only 5 in September).

Basically, he likes the low fastball, and righthanded pitchers will accordingly try hard stuff up and in as well as a variety of curves. Lefties move the ball around on him, but Barrett has an excellent eye and can pull the curve or slash the fastball to right or right-center.

Barrett's concentration level has improved 100%. He led the Sox in hitting for most of the year, until Wade Boggs remembered that he was Wade Boggs. Barrett hit close to .300 both on the road and at Fenway.

His only slump came in September when his average dropped 15 points. Barrett was given the second baseman's job on an everyday basis after Jerry Remy was injured. The regular play, something that Barrett was not used to, probably accounted for the slump.

He is an excellent bunter and will bunt at any time to any place in the infield. He is also a good hit-and-run man who goes with the pitch.

BASERUNNING:

Barrett is becoming as aggressive on the basepaths as he is in the batter's box. He has good speed from the plate and around the bases; he will definitely

MARTY BARRETT
2B, No. 17
RR, 5'10", 175 lbs.
ML Svc: 2 years
Born: 6-23-58 in
    Arcadia, CA

1984 STATISTICS

AVG	G	AB	R	H	2B	3B	HR	RBI	BB	SO	SB
.303	139	475	56	144	23	3	3	45	42	25	5

CAREER STATISTICS

AVG	G	AB	R	H	2B	3B	HR	RBI	BB	SO	SB
.289	180	537	63	155	24	4	3	47	45	27	5

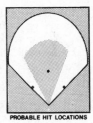

VS. RHP   VS. LHP   PROBABLE HIT LOCATIONS

take the extra base if an outfielder loafs on a hit. Despite his slender frame, Barrett is not afraid to take out the second baseman.

FIELDING:

Much improved as a fielder, Barrett is learning the pivot almost inning by inning. He has a strong arm and good range both ways.

Barrett is working at learning to play each hitter. He was among the best-fielding second basemen in the league.

OVERALL:

He has a "plethora" of assets.

Robinson: "He started out as insurance for Boston and Remy. Remy got hurt and a star war began. He was one of the most pleasant surprises in the league in 1984."

HITTING:

Wade Boggs had his worst offensive year in 1984, his third year with the Red Sox--he hit only .325 and finished third in the batting race!

Despite a slow start, Wade Boggs lifted his average more than 30 points from mid-August through the end of the year. He had 25 hits in the last two weeks of the season and hit close to .500 in September, one of the strongest major league finishes ever.

Boggs has an extremely wide stance, slightly closed and in the middle of the box. It is obvious that he has learned a lot from Hall of Famer Ted Williams because he refuses to swing at pitches out of the strike zone. He would sooner take a walk than swing at a pitch an inch off the corner, even with men on base. That accounts for his extremely low RBI production.

If Boggs has another hitting flaw, it is that he has trouble getting the ball in the air.

His bat is quick and he is able to hit to all fields against both left and righthanded pitchers. Lefthanders will try fastballs up and in, and off-speed curves and sliders low and away. Right-handers will also throw him hard stuff up and in, then try to turn the ball over, keeping it low and on the outside.

He is a better than .300 hitter with men on base, but most of his hits are singles. He had 203 hits and drove in fewer than 60 runs--but as a leadoff hitter, that figure might not be as low as it looks.

BASERUNNING:

He is quick out of the box, and has good speed running to first. Boggs is not, however, a threat to steal or take chances on the basepaths. He is not overly aggressive when breaking up double plays or sliding hard into fielders.

WADE BOGGS
3B, No. 26
LR, 6'2", 190 lbs.
ML Svc: 3 years
Born: 6-15-58 in
Omaha, NE

1984 STATISTICS

AVG	G	AB	R	H	2B	3B	HR	RBI	BB	SO	SB
.325	158	625	109	203	31	4	6	55	89	44	3

CAREER STATISTICS

AVG	G	AB	R	H	2B	3B	HR	RBI	BB	SO	SB
.344	415	1545	260	531	89	12	16	173	216	101	7

VS. RHP   VS. LHP   PROBABLE HIT LOCATIONS

FIELDING:

He managed to cut down on his errors at third base, but still has trouble going to his right. Hard hit balls go right by Boggs, but he has improved coming in on high chops and going to his left. He does not have a strong arm, but has improved his accuracy.

OVERALL:

The Red Sox must keep him in the lineup because of his superb hitting, but they may have to move him out of the leadoff spot. He sets the table perfectly for Dwight Evans, Jim Rice and Tony Armas, but it would seem he could be more valuable in the second or third spot in the batting order.

Robinson: "An outstanding year with the bat, and he was actually disappointed that he hadn't hit better than .325. I see no reason why his average won't be even better this year."

PITCHING:

Dennis Boyd is a member of Boston's crew of hard throwing righthanded starters. Unlike teammate Roger Clemens, it took Boyd a while to learn that he could not throw the fastball past every major league hitter. When Boyd gets too cocky, the Sox send him back to Pawtucket.

It appears that Boyd has learned his lesson and has learned how to pitch. He was one of a trio of Sox starters who went 12-12 in 1984. Boyd now mixes in his slider and curve when he is setting up a hitter. He will use his 90 MPH fastball for the strikeout pitch, and try to get it up and in to some batters and low and away to others.

He is a very fast worker on the mound and throws the ball with a snakelike delivery, tough for batters to hit. He can pitch overhand and three-quarters and may even drop lower than that against some righthanded hitters. His control has improved and he is rapidly learning to throw the curve and the slider for strikes, regardless of the count.

When he is in trouble, he will throw the fastball. He will do well against both left and righthanded hitters if he keeps the ball down and on the corners. He can be hurt when he gets any of his pitches too high in the strike zone. His attitude has improved because he has earned a spot in the rotation, knows he will pitch every fifth day and knows he must shake off a bad inning or a bad outing, which he has the ability to do.

FIELDING:

Boyd is an excellent all-around athlete who loves fielding and would play short or third if given the chance. When

DENNIS BOYD
RHP, No. 23
RR, 6'1", 155 lbs.
ML Svc: 2 years
Born: 10-6-59 in
Meridian, MS

1984 STATISTICS
W	L	ERA	B	GS	CG	IP	H	R	ER	BB	SO	SV
12	12	4.37	29	26	10	197	207	109	96	53	134	0

CAREER STATISTICS
W	L	ERA	G	GS	CG	IP	H	R	ER	BB	SO	SV
16	21	4.06	47	40	15	304	321	160	137	78	179	0

Bill Buckner joined the team, he made sure that Boyd covered first on everything and anything hit to the right side, and Boyd did. "Oil Can" is very quick off the mound and handles bunts much better than he did in the past. He must still work a bit harder when it comes to keeping runners on base.

OVERALL:

He is fun to watch when pitching important ball games. He is emotional and will often pump his fist, raise his arms or gesticulate at an infielder or outfielder who makes a good defensive play behind him. He is becoming Boston's answer to Mark (The Bird) Fidrych.

Robinson: "When he returned from the minors, he was a much better pitcher. I think that he needed a kick in the butt because he did not seem to concentrate enough early in the year. He has definitely got the tools now to be a much better pitcher this year. Now he knows that he has to do more than just throw the ball."

PITCHING:

Mike Brown has an excellent fastball and great control. He was counted on to be the big righthanded winner among 1984 starters for the Red Sox, but wound up with the worst record and the highest ERA of any pitcher on the staff.

He was the 11th man on a ten-man staff and may have been a bit anxious when he did start. He throws overhand to three-quarters and uses his fastball (88 MPH) to set up his slider, curve and change.

Brown's fastball sinks, but he got into a lot of trouble last season because he got the ball up in the strike zone; he gave up a staggering amount of hits in proportion to his number of innings-pitched. Through it all, he kept excellent control, but it might have been too good because batters hit everything he threw to home plate.

Subsequent lack of confidence may have caused Brown to suffer even more through the horrendous year. He had a lot of difficulty trying to pitch out of jams.

At his best, he will keep the slider down and in against lefties and righties, and put the sinker in the same spot. The sinker/fastball is his out pitch, but if he does not get it in there and just misses the corner, he invariably comes in with fat pitches.

Brown has a fluid motion, is not deceptive and generally is a fast worker when he is on the mound.

FIELDING:

Brown is a good fielder when his mind is in the game. He has a good move to first base. He fields his position well, covers first base and knows what to do

MIKE BROWN
RHP, No. 27
RR, 6'2", 195 lbs.
ML Svc: 2 years
Born: 3-4-59 in
   Haddon Township, NJ

1984 STATISTICS

W	L	ERA	B	GS	CG	IP	H	R	ER	BB	SO	SV
1	8	6.85	15	11	0	67	104	63	51	19	32	0

CAREER STATISTICS

W	L	ERA	G	GS	CG	IP	H	R	ER	BB	SO	SV
8	14	5.34	37	29	3	177	221	125	105	63	71	0

with the ball when he picks it up. He works hard at his fielding.

OVERALL:

No one can climb inside the mind of another, but it looks as if Brown is doubting himself. The emergence of Roger Clemens as a star of the future, and a righthanded one at that, might have helped to sow the seeds of doubt in Brown's mind. The Sox have their three lefthanded starters, and two righthanders in Boyd and Clemens, so where does that leave Mike Brown?

Robinson: "I think that he has to be a little more aggressive in his approach to the game. Up and down all year and a 1-8 record with a 6.85 ERA is a bit too much. I do not think that he will be effective if the Red Sox try to make him a reliever; no, he has to be a starter. He has both the fastball and the control, but he must overcome his arm problems and come back. Boston is still very high on him, and that tells you something."

HITTING:

The great columnist Jim Murray once did a feature on Bill Buckner (when Buckner was hitting .300 every year with the Dodgers and Cubs) and wrote: "Bill Buckner is the only major leaguer who can foul off machine gun bullets." It was quite a compliment, and Bill deserves it.

Year in and year out, this former NL batting champ does not draw walks, does not strike out and hits everything he sees, if not the first time then the next time.

He uses a square stance, slight crouch, stands in the middle of the box, deep, and holds the bat slightly off his shoulder. He has an excellent eye and looks for location and speed. Buckner can inside-out his swing or time an off-speed pitch and dump it to any field. He is basically a fastball hitter who likes the ball up and over the plate. Lefties and righties will try to jam him with sliders or fastballs and throw the change to him. A straight change from a pitcher with a good fastball can give Buckner trouble. He hits to all fields, but has shown more power in the past few years. When he is swinging for the long ball, Buckner's average suffers. He hit .306 with a (then) career-high 15 homers for the Cubs in 1982, came back with 16 homers but a .280 average in 1983. He continued to hit the long ball and drive in runs for both the Cubs and Sox in 1984. He did, however, lead the Sox in batting with men on base (.352) and averaged an RBI every game and a half in September.

BASERUNNING:

Buckner is a smart runner who knows he cannot run because of injury-plagued ankles. His ankles are so bad that he actually falls off balance at the plate. He cannot run, but does everything he can to be aggressive on the basepaths. He is a superb slider who often eludes tags when the ball is waiting for him. He is no threat to steal, but if the

BILL BUCKNER
1B, No. 22
LL, 6'1", 185 lbs.
ML Svc: 14 years
Born: 12-14-49 in
Vallejo, CA

1984 STATISTICS

AVG	G	AB	R	H	2B	3B	HR	RBI	BB	SO	SB
.278	114	439	51	122	21	2	11	67	24	38	2

CAREER STATISTICS

AVG	G	AB	R	H	2B	3B	HR	RBI	BB	SO	SB
.295	1840	7079	843	2086	377	41	130	858	331	333	151

VS. RHP

VS. LHP

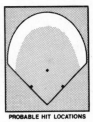

PROBABLE HIT LOCATIONS

pennant were on the line, and you least expected it, Buckner would take second.

FIELDING:

A former outfielder, Buckner has developed into a very good defensive first baseman. His range is limited, but he can dive either way. He is excellent at handling throws off the line.

He fields bunts very well, and works well with pitchers when someone must cover first base on grounders to the right side.

OVERALL:

Robinson: "Bill steadied an infield that was awful defensively. He is a leader who swung a respected bat in the No. 6 spot. His attitude improved a great deal after the trade from the Cubs and he fit in perfectly with Boston. Look for him to have a good year this year."

PITCHING:

On a Clear day, you will never know what to expect. Mark Clear, the second man in Boston's bullpen, can easily come into a game and strike out five batters in a row. Just as easily, he can come into a game and walk five batters in a row. The only thing he did differently in 1984 from 1983 was improve his record from 4-5 to 8-3 and double his saves from four to eight.

Those figures might seem admirable, but Clear clearly has one of the best curves in baseball. In addition, his fastball hums and has been clocked at 92 MPH. He does not have that good a slider, but with two power pitches he should be unhittable.

The trouble is Clear is a long and a short relief pitcher who walks more than one batter an inning. If he comes in with men on base, he is liable to walk another batter. If he comes in to start an inning, he is liable to put two men on with walks, just not the thing to do.

Clear has driven managers and coaches to distraction because he is so fast and has such an excellent curve. At 6'4", he has long arms, and throws from three-quarters to sidearm. It makes him a terror to most righthanded hiters. His curve is not as effective against lefties unless he spots it or keeps it low and in or low and away.

His fastball is his out pitch. When he runs it in to righties and away to lefties, Clear is one of the best short men in the game. But he walks too many batters; the hitters all know it, and they wait for something in the strike zone.

FIELDING:

He is not a good fielder. He resem-

MARK CLEAR
RHP, No. 25
RR, 6'4", 215 lbs.
ML Svc: 6 years
Born: 5-27-56 in
    Los Angeles, CA

1984 STATISTICS

W	L	ERA	B	GS	CG	IP	H	R	ER	BB	SO	SV
8	3	4.03	47	0	0	67	47	38	30	70	76	8

CAREER STATISTICS

W	L	ERA	G	GS	CG	IP	H	R	ER	BB	SO	SV
56	36	4.02	294	0	0	560	478	283	250	383	551	58

bles a robot when he's pitching--very mechanical. He does not get a good jump on balls hit back through the box. He is also not quick off the mound when fielding bunts, and his deliberate style and slow delivery leaves him very susceptible to the stolen base.

OVERALL:

He has to be pleased with an improved 1984 season, but deep down Clear knows that the Sox rely on Stanley, not him, for crucial situations.

Robinson: "He knows that he could be one of the best if he could get the ball over consistently. He will strike out one, then walk another, all in the same inning. That is not good. I believe that the Sox lost confidence in him and then were afraid to use him in tight spots."

PITCHING:

Roger Clemens arrived at Fenway last season without fanfare, looked around and said, "I can beat these guys." And beat them he did. That is, until he strained a muscle in his forearm on the last day of August.

Once he got his baby shoes wet, Clemens ripped off six straight wins; fanned 15 batters in one start, 10 in the next start and he had seven strike-outs in four innings before he strained the muscle and was through for the year. The turning point for Clemens came on July 26th, when he fanned 11 batters to even his record at 4-4. After that, he was untouchable.

He has been clocked at 96 MPH, the highest reading of any pitcher in the league. He is a pure power pitcher with an excellent curve and a straight change who throws from three-quarters. Unlike many young pitchers, Clemens is a fast worker who likes challenges and will come at the hitters with hard stuff with men on base. They may know that it is coming, but they won't be able to hit it.

Ironically, Clemens seemed to get himself into trouble when he was ahead in the count, rather than when he was behind. With two strikes on many bat-ters, he aimed the ball too much. His only other flaw seems to be getting the curve too high in the strike zone. His mechanics, delivery and basics are ex-cellent.

FIELDING:

He is a good fielder who takes it seriously and is working on perfecting

ROGER CLEMENS
RHP, No. 21
RR, 6'4", 205 lbs.
ML Svc: 1 year
Born: 7-18-59 in Dayton, OH

1984 STATISTICS												
W	L	ERA	B	GS	CG	IP	H	R	ER	BB	SO	SV
9	4	4.32	21	20	5	133	146	67	64	29	126	0

CAREER STATISTICS												
W	L	ERA	G	GS	CG	IP	H	R	ER	BB	SO	SV
9	4	4.32	21	20	5	133	146	67	64	29	126	0

his move to first. He is quick off the mound and makes a strong throw to which-ever base he is throwing to.

OVERALL:

There is always fear in the heart of a manager when a young flamethrower without too much minor league experience comes up, strikes out a batter with a blazing fastball and then winds up with a strained forearm. Yet, should Clemens follow the path of a Nolan Ryan, he may injure himself frequently and then wind up with 5 no-hitters and every strike-out record in the book.

Robinson: "He is probably the hard-est thrower in the American League and will lead the league in strikeouts this season. He is an extremely confident young man with a fastball that makes it tough for batters to lay off. It looks good, but the batters are not able to hit it. Look for 1985 to be outstand-ing."

PITCHING:

When Don Larsen pitched his perfect game in the World Series in 1956, one newspaper reported that, "The Imperfect Man Pitched the Perfect Game." In 1984, Steve Crawford was the perfect man. He had the lowest ERA on a staff that gave up too many runs. He was not used in too many games or too many innings, but he did fill his role of long reliever and spot pitcher in certain situations.

Crawford is a big man and a former star football player, but he lost his fastball career after a 1981 arm operation. He throws from three-quarters and relies on getting his pitches in certain locations. He cannot overpower hitters as he once did, but can still throw his fastball in the 85 MPH range. He uses his curve, slider and change-up and will try to get a batter out on a fastball by keeping it low and in or low and away.

Crawford has a deceptive delivery which helps to keeps the batters unsettled in the box, particularly batters who think that his size means that they will see hard stuff up and in. He can fool batters with a big motion and come in with something off-speed or a breaking ball. His off-speed pitch could be better than it is, and a straight change would help, as well. Most of his off-speed pitches are sliders and curves.

FIELDING:

He has an average move to first but is always aware of runners who are a threat to steal. He works hard at his fielding but is basically a bit too slow on comebackers and balls hit around him.

STEVE CRAWFORD
RHP, No. 28
RR, 6'5", 225 lbs.
ML Svc: 1 year plus
Born: 4-29-58 in
    Pryor, OK

1984 STATISTICS

W	L	ERA	G	GS	CG	IP	H	R	ER	BB	SO	SV
5	0	3.34	35	0	0	62	69	31	23	21	21	1

CAREER STATISTICS

W	L	ERA	G	GS	CG	IP	H	R	ER	BB	SO	SV
8	5	3.91	60	15	2	161	193	86	70	47	62	1

OVERALL:

Crawford's job is crystal clear. He is the righthanded reliever on a team that has Mark Clear, Bob Stanley and the young Charlie Mitchell, and they are all righthanded, too. Crawford won't be the short man because he does not have the trick pitch or the overpowering fastball, so he must be ready, willing and able to hold his job.

Robinson: "He is still trying to get back to where he was before the arm operation, but even though he was the eighth or ninth pitcher on the staff, he was able to get righthanded hitters out. He responded with a 5-0 record, but in all honesty, he was not used in too many pressure situations. I do think, however, that he will be able to regain his spot on the staff because he can help you in a lot of ways. If he gets all of his confidence back, he will definitely help the Red Sox."

HITTING:

They called him the "Hit Man" when he played with the Pirates. The Pirates needed a long ball hitting outfielder like Mike Easler, so, for the oddest reasons, they traded him to the Red Sox. Without him, the Pirates finished in last place . . . the Red Sox, using him as the everyday DH, finished close to third.

He bats from a severe, exaggerated crouch with a closed stance. He looks as though he is sitting in a chair.

He is an excellent low ball, fastball hitter who keeps his bat cocked and coiled and his head high. His bat is as quick as anyone's in the league, and he makes sure to swing at everything he sees. That accounts for so few walks and a high percentage of strikeouts.

He had a good start in the American League and closed strong, too, to finish eighth in the league in hitting. He adjusted to the extraordinary amount of breaking balls thrown at him, and hit both left and righthanders.

Easler is an excellent "mistake" hitter. He uses the alleys in both left and right to power the long ball. Lefthanders will curve him and try to keep the fastball away, but he can go the other way with them.

Pitchers should show him the fastball off the plate and then come in with nothing but junk and off-speed pitches. Easler improved against certain off-speed pitches late in the year accounting for his excellent offensive year. He had a 20-game hitting streak from May 23rd through June 15th.

BASERUNNING:

Easler does not have good speed, but hustles on grounders hit to the infield. He is not a particularly smart baserunner, taking one base at a time, and will never steal a base. He will, however, be aggressive in trying to break up double plays and knocking over fielders who

MIKE EASLER
OF/DH, No. 7
LR, 6'1", 196 lbs.
ML Svc: 7 years
Born: 11-29-50 in
Cleveland, OH

1984 STATISTICS

AVG	G	AB	R	H	2B	3B	HR	RBI	BB	SO	SB
.313	156	601	87	188	31	5	27	91	58	134	1

CAREER STATISTICS

AVG	G	AB	R	H	2B	3B	HR	RBI	BB	SO	SB
.300	752	2342	310	703	124	19	83	339	199	428	16

VS. RHP

VS. LHP

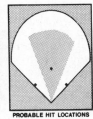

PROBABLE HIT LOCATIONS

have the ball waiting for him at any base.

FIELDING:

Easler was a defensive liability in the outfield for the Pirates, and played only sparingly with Boston in 1984. He tries his best, but does not have a strong arm or any special defensive instincts.

OVERALL:

Robinson: "He fit right in with a hitting Sox team. He learned a bit more patience and discipline at the plate and is at his best right now. He got his chance to play every day with the Sox and made the most of it. Look for more of the same this year. The DH is perfect for him because it allows him to concentrate on hitting, something he does very well and very naturally."

HITTING:

In 1984, Dwight Evans went over the 1,000 mark in career strikeouts--but that was the only blot on his best year ever. He was part of an outfield that hit close to 30 home runs apiece and drove in more than 100 runs each. Evans led the league in runs scored, tied for the league lead in extra-base hits (77) finished third in the league in walks, fifth in game winning RBIs (15), third in slugging percentage (.532) and fourth in doubles.

Evans did nothing different in 1984 from the previous two years, except stay healthy. He maintained his closed stance with a slight crouch, weight back, and his front foot barely touching the dirt.

He is an excellent high ball hitter who can hit with power to all fields. He can hit a low pitch up the middle. He looks for fastballs out and over the plate, but can murder high curves from righties or lefties. Righthanders will try to keep the curve low and away, and sneak the fastball in on his hands to tie him up. Lefthanders will throw him low, inside sliders and fastballs away.

Despite his strikeouts, Evans has an excellent batting eye and is a patient hitter. He is a good clutch hitter, but for some reason the media in Boston have never believed he hits often enough in the clutch. He bunts well and can hit behind the runner.

BASERUNNING:

Evans takes a short lead, will not steal, but is a smart baserunner who knows when to take the extra base. He will go from first to third if an outfielder does not hustle on a hit, and he breaks up double plays with hard slides.

FIELDING:

Next to Dave Winfield, Evans is the best right fielder in the league. He

DWIGHT EVANS
RF, No. 24
RR, 6'3", 205 lbs.
ML Svc: 12 years
Born: 11-3-51 in
    Santa Monica, CA

1984 STATISTICS
AVG	G	AB	R	H	2B	3B	HR	RBI	BB	SO	SB
.295	162	630	121	186	37	8	32	104	96	115	3

CAREER STATISTICS
AVG	G	AB	R	H	2B	3B	HR	RBI	BB	SO	SB
.269	1622	5515	886	1486	299	54	236	774	778	1067	51

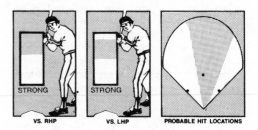

VS. RHP   VS. LHP   PROBABLE HIT LOCATIONS

has a shotgun for an arm and can go to his right or left. He gets a good jump on the ball and is always aware of where the fences are.

Evans can and will knock down a fence in order to catch a ball. He charges hits like an infielder and runners will rarely challenge him.

OVERALL:

Critics claim he throws too hard, showing off his arm, when he knows nobody is going anywhere, and that he doesn't hit enough in the clutch, but his record speaks for itself--in every phase of the game.

Robinson: "The best year of his career. A power hitter with an excellent on-base percentage (.388, sixth in the league.) That is a rare combination. No reason 1985 won't be the same."

HITTING:

Since February 21, 1981 the Red Sox have been looking for a catcher. That was the day Carlton Fisk was granted free agency (he later signed with the White Sox). The Red Sox have finally found a catcher--Rich Gedman.

A year of winter ball after the 1983 season helped Gedman to earn the catching job. An extremely hard and dedicated worker, Gedman had many flaws in both his hitting and fielding. He ironed out the wrinkles in his hitting by playing the extra season.

He bats from various stances, but settled on one that is slightly open with a slight crouch, his weight back and his front foot barely touching the ground.

He has huge shoulders and arms. Rich seems unable to handle high inside fastballs, but he has learned bat control and a bit more patience and he began to get around on those pitches in 1984. He also has excellent power to left-center and was helped by the Green Monster in Fenway.

Lefthanders will try the hard fastball up and in, and then come back with curves and sliders, generally low and away. Righties will try to spot the fastball and try to get him out with off-speed breaking balls. Gedman strides quickly into the ball, and is vulnerable to off-speed pitches.

He has learned to look for location and can easily pull a high fastball with his quick bat. Against lefties, Gedman learned to go the other way with breaking balls. He wound up hitting more home runs than any catcher in the league except Detroit's Lance Parrish.

BASERUNNING:

An average baserunner with no speed. Gedman is no threat to steal or take an extra base. He will slide hard when breaking up double plays, but rarely gets close enough to the middle infielders to knock them down with his bulk and strength.

RICH GEDMAN
C, No. 10
LR, 6'0", 215 lbs.
ML Svc: 4 years
Born: 9-26-59 in
    Worcester, MA

1984 STATISTICS
AVG	G	AB	R	H	2B	3B	HR	RBI	BB	SO	SB
.269	133	449	54	121	26	4	24	72	29	72	0

CAREER STATISTICS
AVG	G	AB	R	H	2B	3B	HR	RBI	BB	SO	SB
.271	377	1171	129	317	74	7	35	143	63	182	0

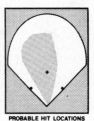

VS. RHP   VS. LHP   PROBABLE HIT LOCATIONS

FIELDING:

Rich improved greatly as a catcher, despite his error total. He has learned to release the ball more quickly and has a strong arm. He still has to be more accurate with his throws and keep a closer eye on the baserunners.

To be more effective behind the plate, he must be decisive in fielding bunts and slow chops near home plate. He is improving on cutting down his passed-ball total.

OVERALL:

Unless Gary Allenson does something dramatic, or the Red Sox make a big trade, Gedman is their everyday catcher.

Robinson: "Former manager Ralph Houk said that Gedman improved more than any player he has ever managed. That is quite a compliment. You could see him getting better day by day because he worked hard and took extra batting. It has been a long haul for him, but Gedman is finally an everyday player."

HITTING:

Jackie Gutierrez performed at shortstop last season as few others could. The fact that he showed he could hit as well and was able to maintain a batting average over .300 for the last month of the season was icing on the cake.

He has a square stance, bat held high, and likes to jump on the high fastball. He is a very impatient hitter who will swing at the first pitch more often than not. He will also swing at anything near the plate when there are two strikes on him. Despite his anxiety, he does not strike out a lot, but drew fewer walks per at-bat than any infielder in the league.

One of Jackie's flaws is that he tries to pull the ball too much and does not go to the opposite field enough. For that reason, a pitcher who gets ahead in the count can feed him a steady diet of pitches on the outside corner, be they breaking balls or hard stuff.

Gutierrez can be struck out by that pattern, particularly if the pitcher can keep the ball low. If Gutierrez starts leaning, a pitcher will come high, hard, and up and in with the fastball.

He is an outstanding bunter who easily led the Sox in sacrifice bunts, and will bunt for a base hit if an infielder is napping. His RBI total was low, but he did bat ninth and rarely hit with men in scoring position.

BASERUNNING:

Gutierrez led the Sox in steals in 1984 and will undoubtedly lead them this year. He is the only player with enough speed to get the steal sign when he is on base (unless Jerry Remy returns to good health).

He is fast and gets a good jump, but does not have the sound fundamentals of a good baserunner at this point in his career. Like most rookies, he likes to steal, but makes mental mistakes on the basepaths.

FIELDING:

Gutierrez is an outstanding fielder

JACKIE GUTIERREZ
SS, No. 41
RR, 5'11", 175 lbs.
ML Svc: 1 year
Born: 6-27-60 in
  Cartagena, COL

1984 STATISTICS

AVG	G	AB	R	H	2B	3B	HR	RBI	BB	SO	SB
.263	151	449	55	118	12	3	2	29	15	49	12

CAREER STATISTICS

AVG	G	AB	R	H	2B	3B	HR	RBI	BB	SO	SB
.264	156	459	57	121	12	3	2	29	16	50	12

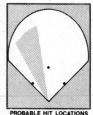

VS. RHP   VS. LHP   PROBABLE HIT LOCATIONS

with excellent range, particularly to his right--into the hole. He can also go to his left, but must release the ball more quickly when fielding grounders over second base.

Gutierrez reaches balls no other shortstop (with the exception of Julio Franco) can reach, but is charged with many errors. His arm (reputed to be the best in the league) saves him some errors, but also gives him some because he often rushes his throws.

OVERALL:

It is doubtful any Sox infielder will move this young man off short this year.

Robinson: "This kid has great range and will get better when he is more consistent. I don't know if he'll hit any higher than he did in 1984, but he sure was a big surprise and gave the Sox a tremendous boost when Hoffman couldn't play. He should have a long career."

PITCHING:

Like waiting for water to boil, the Red Sox have been patiently keeping their eye on Bruce Hurst. They have been watching his pot for three years. He has yet to steam, never mind boil.

Hurst has four pitches: the fastball, curve, slider and change-up. He used them all pretty effectively until the middle of August, when he seemed to lose confidence. From an 11-6 record, he tumbled to finish 12-12; he lost four in a row and in one stretch allowed 35 earned runs in 41 innings.

With good cause, the Red Sox starters were pitching with concern for their lack of a quality bullpen. Starting pitchers throw a lot differently when there is a Quisenberry or Sutter blowing bubbles in the pen. Boston had neither.

Hurst has a big windup and a high leg kick, an advantage when pitching to lefthanders because of his big sweeping curve. He throws from over the top to three-quarters and is effective against lefthanded hitters. Against righthanded power hitters, Hurst is not afraid to start off with his curve, spot the fastball low and in, then use a lot of off-speed pitches. He loves to send the off-speed pitches as a finale to power hitters. Against most righthanded hitters, however, Hurst starts them off with hard stuff away and down and in, then gives them off-speed stuff while setting them up. He will use his curve as his strikeout pitch when ahead in the count.

Hurst loses something off his fastball in the late innings, and he gives up far too many home runs for a starter. He led the Boston staff with 25 home runs allowed, despite the fact that he is actually pretty good at challenging righties in Fenway.

BRUCE HURST
LHP, No. 47
LL, 6'3", 215 lbs.
ML Svc: 3 years
Born: 3-24-58 in
St. George, UT

1984 STATISTICS

W	L	ERA	B	GS	CG	IP	H	R	ER	BB	SO	SV
12	12	3.92	33	33	9	218	232	106	95	88	136	0

CAREER STATISTICS

W	L	ERA	G	GS	CG	IP	H	R	ER	BB	SO	SV
31	33	4.62	111	96	15	600	696	339	308	218	331	0

FIELDING:

His excellent follow-through usually leaves him in good position to field balls hit back to him. He should move around the mound a bit more and be a bit quicker on handling choppers and bunts. His pickoff move is the best on the staff and is one of the best in the league. He led the Sox with 15 pickoffs.

OVERALL:

Elbow problems seem to follow him and have bothered him since 1983. But because he knows HOW to pitch, Boston will probably continue to wait for his water to boil.

Robinson: "It seems that he should be a better than .500 pitcher. This year will determine if he can be a winning pitcher. He has got to produce soon; the rest of the team should help him to do just that in 1983.

PITCHING:

The Boston Red Sox had 32 saves from their bullpen in 1984. You-know-who (Bob Stanley, of course) saved 22 of them. Mark Clear had eight. John Henry Johnson had one and Steve Crawford the other. Despite that horrible ratio, Johnson was the only Sox lefty out of the bullpen, and for that reason must be considered a valuable piece of property.

He does not have the fastball he once had, but he can still throw an 87 MPH fastball past many hitters. In his arsenal he has the fastball, slider, curve and change, but his situation in the pen calls for him to throw strikes and get the fastball and slider over the plate quickly. He is very effective against lefty hitters because he can use his sweeping curve, one which he throws from three-quarters to sidearm. If he gets ahead of a lefthanded hitter with men on base, he will use the curve or throw a low, hard slider. He likes to show his fastball up and away to righties, then come back with low sliders and an occasional change.

When his fastball moves in on a righty, he is very effective; but when his fastball comes in straight, he can be hit. He did allow a hit an inning. His control is good, and he is continually working on trying to get all of his pitches in the strike zone.

His basic job is to come in and get a lefthanded hitter out, and he does that extremely well, unless the other team sends up a pinch-hitter. He is not afraid to challenge the best lefthanded hitters in the league because he has seen adversity and has become mentally tough. He can pitch in long relief, but has not done so in the past two years.

JOHN HENRY JOHNSON
LHP, No. 48
LL, 6'2", 210 lbs.
ML Svc: 6 years
Born: 8-21-56 in
Houston, TX

1984 STATISTICS

W	L	ERA	B	GS	CG	IP	H	R	ER	BB	SO	SV
1	2	3.53	30	3	0	63	64	26	25	27	57	1

CAREER STATISTICS

W	L	ERA	G	GS	CG	IP	H	R	ER	BB	SO	SV
24	31	3.72	185	59	9	532	500	249	220	222	347	8

FIELDING:

Johnson is only an average fielder. His move to first is nothing spectacular. He is adequate at covering the bag and fielding bunts. He does take his fielding seriously but stays aware of the baserunners.

OVERALL:

It is surprising that Boston has not been able to acquire a strong lefthanded stopper. Johnson does his job, but the Red Sox have fallen in love with Bob Stanley, who can pitch to both left and righthanded hitters. Still, it makes you wonder about how they trade . . . especially when you see what Hernandez has done for the Tigers.

Robinson: "He is still battling and struggling as the low man on the totem pole and is trying to overcome slight arm problems. He does the job, he can get the tough lefthanded hitter."

HITTING:

In 1983, Rick Miller was the best pinch-hitter in the world (.457). He did not have that good a year in 1984, but it was ironic that he had exactly half the pinch-hits the Red Sox managed (14), exactly one-half the at-bats the pinch-hitters managed (53) and obviously hit exactly what Sox pinch-hitters managed (.264).

Miller maintains a severely closed, very wide stance and faces the third baseman. Teams will play him to hit to the opposite field and pitch him that way. That is exactly what Miller thrives on because he can slap grounders between third and short and dump short hits into left and left-center.

He does have trouble with hard stuff up and in. Pitchers who can get their pitches there will have good success against him because he has no power.

On occasion, Miller will pull the ball, but it will usually come off a low inside pitch from a righthander. Lefties curve him and keep the ball down and away, and can throw the fastball by him, again, up and in.

When Miller is pinch-hitting, he is not called upon to bunt, though he can do it very well. The Red Sox need him to hit and swing the bat. His additional at-bats come when he is sent into the game as a late-inning defensive replacement. By that time, the Sox have either won or lost the game. They rarely replace their outfield of Jim Rice, Tony Armas and Dwight Evans.

BASERUNNING:

Miller can run--he always has had good speed and he always will, although he will not steal bases. He takes a long lead from first in an attempt to trick the pitcher and is always faking a break toward second base. He gets a

RICK MILLER
OF, No. 3
LL, 6'0", 180 lbs.
ML Svc: 13 years
Born: 4-19-48 in
Grand Rapids, MI

1984 STATISTICS

AVG	G	AB	R	H	2B	3B	HR	RBI	BB	SO	SB
.260	95	123	17	32	5	1	0	12	17	22	1

CAREER STATISTICS

AVG	G	AB	R	H	2B	3B	HR	RBI	BB	SO	SB
.268	1441	3842	547	1031	159	35	28	360	449	577	77

VS. RHP

VS. LHP

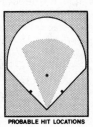
PROBABLE HIT LOCATIONS

good jump from the box and off a base and is always willing to take an extra base. He will definitely take out a middle infielder on potential double play grounders.

OVERALL:

The Sox are stockpiling young players, but Miller has proven that he can pinch-hit with the game on the line. Next season, he may be asked to continue to pinch-hit for a younger player.

Robinson: "He won't play much in 1985, but he is a valuable man to have around because he does so many things. He hasn't lost his speed, can play defense, knows the game, knows he won't play much but is always ready."

HITTING:

Reid Nichols, who just might be the best defensive outfielder in the league, is far from the best hitter. Nichols carried a .280 lifetime batting average into the 1984 season, but dropped 50 points in 1984. He simply does not get much playing time with Boston's awesome outfield. He has a closed stance with his weight perfectly distributed and keeps his bat belt high.

He is not a power hitter, but rather a contact hitter who can drill liners to either left or right-center. He has enough speed to stretch what would be ordinary singles into doubles.

Pitchers who are unaware of his bat speed will be burned by Nichols because he can get around (when he plays regualrly) on hard stuff inside. He is a good clutch hitter and bears down after the sixth inning.

He has an extremely level swing and will hit the ball where it is pitched, especially with men on base. Control pitchers can get him out with breaking balls, sliders and sinkers low and away. He can hit a belt-high pitch to any field, depending upon its location.

BASERUNNING:

Nichols takes a long lead at first and can be counted on to go from first to third on hits to center or right. At times he will gamble on the arms of some outfielders and take the extra base if they think he will automatically stop at second. He will always try to score from second on a hit and is very aggressive and not afraid to break up double plays.

FIELDING:

He has incredible range in center field. Nichols gets a tremendous jump on balls, and if he doesn't, has the speed to outrun them. He is not afraid

REID NICHOLS
OF, No. 51
RR, 5'11", 172 lbs.
ML Svc: 4 years
Born: 8-5-58 in
    Ocala, FL

1984 STATISTICS

AVG	G	AB	R	H	2B	3B	HR	RBI	BB	SO	SB
.226	73	124	14	28	5	1	1	14	12	18	2

CAREER STATISTICS

AVG	G	AB	R	H	2B	3B	HR	RBI	BB	SO	SB
.271	316	727	102	197	43	5	14	75	57	96	14

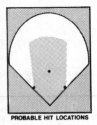

VS. RHP   VS. LHP   PROBABLE HIT LOCATIONS

to dive head-long, whether to his left or right, on line drives in the gaps. He rarely lets a ball get past him.

He has an arm that can equal that of Dwight Evans, but might even be better because he keeps his throws low. They can always be cut off by infielders--unlike the throws of certain outfielders who like to throw the ball 300 feet in the air so the fans can "ooh and aah."

OVERALL:

Somebody would do well to acquire this player, put him in either center or left and leave him there for 162 games.

Robinson: "The jury might still be out on whether or not he can play every day, but he has a great attitude for a backup outfielder. I think the Sox might send him to winter ball and convert him into an infielder. Unless they do, he has no future with Boston except as an insurance policy."

PITCHING:

He pitches in diametric opposition to his name: Al Nipper comes right at the hitters--no "nipping" here. One of the top young pitchers in the league, in 1984 he finished with a winning percentage of .647, seventh in the league.

Nipper uses all of his pitches, the fastball, curve, slider and change. He has the ability to sink the fastball. The amazing part about Nipper is that he can and will throw the curve in any spot to any batter, regardless of the count or the number of men on base. He has supreme confidence in his curveball, which he releases from a three-quarters delivery.

He gets the majority of his strikeouts with the curve, which stunned the American League hitters--they just froze and took it. He also will catch the hitters for a fan on his sinking fastball, a pitch they swing at.

Near-perfect control is another factor that the young Nipper has in his favor. With a runner on second or third, he becomes more deliberate in his pitching patterns, takes his time and works to spots. He will throw the fastball/sinker low and away to lefties with men on base, so that the batter cannot pull it and he keeps his slider and curve down and away to righties.

His fastball has not been clocked at more than 88 MPH, but because he throws the sinker/slider/curve pattern, the fastball looks much faster than it actually is. Nipper will, of course, get hurt if he gets his pitches up in the strike zone. Particularly when there are no men on base, Nipper follows through with his whole body and seems to be charging off the mound at the hitter. In that way, he resembles Ron Guidry.

AL NIPPER
RHP, No. 49
RR, 6'0", 188 lbs.
ML Svc: 1 year plus
Born: 4-22-59 in
  San Diego, CA

1984 STATISTICS
W	L	ERA	B	GS	CG	IP	H	R	ER	BB	SO	SV
11	6	3.89	29	24	6	182	183	86	79	52	84	0

CAREER STATISTICS
W	L	ERA	G	GS	CG	IP	H	R	ER	BB	SO	SV
12	7	3.77	32	26	7	198	200	90	83	59	89	0

FIELDING:

He is a good athlete who fields his position very well, has an excellent move to first, especially for a righty, moves around on the mound well and can be considered a fifth infielder. He takes pride in his fielding and works hard at it.

OVERALL:

He was given his chance as a starter and made the most of it. Nipper ripped off six wins in a row at the end of last season, and in one stretch had a record of 9-3 as a starter in 15 consecutive games. The Red Sox won 12 of those 15 games. Clearly, Nipper keeps his team in the game.

Robinson: "This guy is a pitcher. The only thing that hurt him was his inexperience, but it is just a matter of time. Nipper has now had his first go-around and is only going to get better. The Sox are going to be a better overall team in 1985, and Al Nipper will be a part of that, better himself."

PITCHING:

No one on this planet, except maybe Bob Ojeda, knows what to expect when he takes the mound for one of his 30-35 starts. He can shut down a powerful offensive team, be the game at Fenway or Yankee Stadium, and then get clubbed half to death the next time out. In 11 of his starts last season, he allowed only four earned runs and was 9-1 in those games. What does this say for his 12-12 overall record?

He throws from three-quarters with a deceptive herky-jerky motion that keeps most batters off stride. He uses his 85-87 MPH fastball, curve and change-up. He has more confidence in his fastball than in any other pitch, but when he overthrows he misses home plate and his control suffers. When he throws too hard and too straight, he can be hit. He is at his best when he gets all of his pitches over the plate so the batter has no idea of what to look for.

Ojeda is not afraid to challenge hitters in any situation and gets tougher in the late innings. He would not have been able to throw five shutouts if he didn't buckle down, but at other times he seems to lose his concentraion. He knows how to pitch, is tough against lefties, but when he walks a batter he thinks he should have struck out, Ojeda loses even more of his concentration.

FIELDING:

His pickoff move is very good and particularly effective because he has

BOB OJEDA
LHP, No. 19
LL, 6'1", 190 lbs.
ML Svc: 3 years
Born: 12-17-57 in
Los Angeles, CA

1984 STATISTICS

W	L	ERA	B	GS	CG	IP	H	R	ER	BB	SO	SV
12	12	3.99	33	32	8	216	211	106	96	96	137	0

CAREER STATISTICS

W	L	ERA	G	GS	CG	IP	H	R	ER	BB	SO	SV
35	28	4.28	101	91	15	560	568	289	266	237	323	0

the same herky-jerky motion when pitching from the stretch as he does from the windup. Runners find it difficult to get a jump on him, but will steal if he deliberates too long on the mound. His overall fielding is good, but not as good as it should be, particularly his throws to second on double play grounders. He is, however, working hard at his fielding prowess.

OVERALL:

Robinson: "He has got to be better than 12-12. I definitely look for him to be better than that this year because he pitches a lot of innings and gives you a good effort."

HITTING:

Jerry Remy has hit close to .300 in six full years of playing in Fenway Park, but those seem to be days gone by. In 1984, Remy again injured his left knee, played in only 30 games, hit only .250 and was on the disabled list for virtually the entire year. He will have the knee operated on again, but it remains to be seen if he can bounce back.

He is the best bunter in the league, and gets away with beating out bunts and advancing runners despite the fact that infielders play him on the grass at first and third. He has excellent bat control, standing with a closed stance and a slight crouch.

Like other intelligent lefthanded batters (Wade Boggs, George Brett, Don Mattingly), Remy will hit to left field against lefthanded pitchers who think they can get him out by pitching him on the outside corner. Remy actually has hit better against lefties in the past few years.

He will pull the ball if he gets his pitch, one about belt-high and out over the plate. Remy has no power, but hits to all fields and is a situation hitter. With men on base, Remy would rather swing the bat than take a walk, and he draws very few walks. Pitchers try to keep the fastball up and away and throw him hard sliders low and in. A pitcher who can change speeds can get Remy out, by showing him hard stuff inside and coming back with off-speed pitches. Although he bats leadoff, Remy will swing on a 2-0 or 3-1 count.

BASERUNNING:

Whatever speed the Red Sox had in the recent past, it was Remy. The Sox do not steal bases, but a healthy Remy averages 15 to 20 stolen bases a year. He is quick in all aspects of running, from the batter's box to the basepaths, and is aggressive. He always hustles and can be counted on to take the extra base.

JERRY REMY
2B, No. 2
LR, 5'9", 165 lbs.
ML Svc: 10 years
Born: 11-8-52 in
   Fall River, MA

1984 STATISTICS

AVG	G	AB	R	H	2B	3B	HR	RBI	BB	SO	SB
.250	30	104	8	26	1	1	0	8	7	11	4

CAREER STATISTICS

AVG	G	AB	R	H	2B	3B	HR	RBI	BB	SO	SB
.275	1154	4455	605	1226	140	38	7	329	356	404	208

  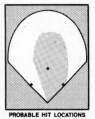

VS. RHP   VS. LHP   PROBABLE HIT LOCATIONS

FIELDING:

Remy is a solid fielder in every department. He may take a back seat to Willie Randolph when it comes to turning the double play, a back seat to Frank White in term of range and a back seat to Damaso Garcia when it comes to arm strength, but Remy puts it all together.

He is better at going to his left than to his right, but goes back well in any direction on short pops. He makes all the plays needed at second.

OVERALL:

He was a tough clutch hitter and a good team player. It may be harsh to use the word "was," but his left knee makes him a liability.

Robinson: "He probably won't regain his starting job in 1985. When he got hurt, Marty Barrett got a chance to play and had a great year. Injuries have caused Jerry to slip, so I believe he may be a backup this year."

HITTING:

Jim Rice, the Boston Strong Man, put together an excellent year in 1984. Excellent, that is, for anyone but Rice. A career .300 hitter, Rice did not approach that mark and hit lower than he has in seven years. He was bogged down with 27 home runs for most of September, and teammates Dwight Evans and Tony Armas both passed him in homers down the stretch. Evans and Armas both hit more than 30 homers, but Rice could not quite make it. From September 15th through the end of the season, Rice drove in only five runs, leaving him one behind Armas for the RBI lead in the league.

He has the classic slugger's stance, square to the plate, straight up, deep in the box. He is basically a low ball hitter, but can hit the high pitch if it is not the pitcher's best. He looks for the fastball out over the plate because he has so much power he can clear any fence, in any park, in either left, center or right. He is a straightaway hitter and is usually jammed by hard stuff up and in, from either righties or lefties.

Rice usually knows what is coming, but tends to be impatient at times if he sees nothing but low sliders from lefties and sliders and changes from righties. He will chase a bad pitch if he is not going well at the plate, and he set a record for grounding into the most double plays in a season (36). That record stems from a combination of not being too fast when leaving the batter's box, hitting the ball hard and right at somebody and trying to pull the outside pitch.

BASERUNNING·

He is hard, tough and aggressive. Jim Rice reminds one of a linebacker on a blitz when he heads into second. He is no threat to steal and rarely takes too many chances on the basepaths. On a close play however, he is odds on to knock over the fielder (or catcher).

JIM RICE
LF, No. 14
RR, 6'2", 205 lbs.
ML Svc: 11 years
Born: 3-8-53 in
Anderson, SC

1984 STATISTICS

AVG	G	AB	R	H	2B	3B	HR	RBI	BB	SO	SB
.280	159	657	98	184	25	7	28	122	44	102	4

CAREER STATISTICS

AVG	G	AB	R	H	2B	3B	HR	RBI	BB	SO	SB
.303	1493	5963	921	1804	272	69	304	1076	451	1065	53

  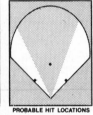

VS. RHP   VS. LHP   PROBABLE HIT LOCATIONS

FIELDING:

Rice continues to improve in the field. Runners do not run on him as they used to, and his throws, particularly on potential sacrifice flies, have become very accurate. He gets a good jump on the ball, but is better at going to his right than to his left. He plays The Wall perfectly at Fenway, and holds many hits to singles.

OVERALL:

His September slump was inexplicable. He was among the league leaders in hits, homers, RBIs and total bases, but simply stopped hitting for power and with men on base. He frankly admitted he was disappointed in his RBI production, because he hit behind Wade Boggs and Evans, who had almost 400 hits between them.

Robinson: "He is a very good player with a good attitude. The year was solid, power-wise, but I believe he knows he should have driven in more runs. I'm not worried--he will have a big year this year."

PITCHING:

Bob Stanley has the perfect disposi-
tion for a short relief man. Pressure
does not bother him, righties do not
bother him, lefties do not bother him,
managers do not bother him--but for the
first time in three years, Stanley heard
the boo-birds at Fenway.

It may or may not have had an effect
on this 6'4" hard throwing specialist.
His saves dropped from 33 to 22, but he
again had an abnormal number of decisions (19) for someone who is basically
a short relief man.

He has a fastball, but seemed to lose
some velocity on it in 1984. In addition, he has a fastball with a slight
wrinkle and several off-speed pitches
and hard pitches that all sink. It is
the sinker that makes him valuable out
of the pen. He uses a palmball, forkball and slider (the fastball with the
wrinkle) which all sink. He tries to
jam righties low and in and keep his
pitches down against lefties.

He is one of the best control pitchers in the league, and rarely gets into
trouble with walks. He would sooner let
a batter hit the ball than walk and relies on good outfield and infield defense to help him in many games. He is
another Guidry-type of pitcher who seems
to be on top of you after he releases
the ball. He is always coming forward
after his release, and is extremely intimidating. In addition, his motion is
not smooth, and you rarely know where
his release point will be. Batters know
he will not give in, regardless of the
count, and they can look for something
hard and low when he comes in to pitch
with men on base. If he has his control, he is tough to hit.

BOB STANLEY
RHP, No. 46
RR, 6'4", 220 lbs.
ML Svc: 8 years
Born: 11-10-54 in
Portland, ME

1984 STATISTICS

W	L	ERA	B	GS	CG	IP	H	R	ER	BB	SO	SV
9	10	3.54	57	0	0	106	113	57	42	23	52	22

CAREER STATISTICS

W	L	ERA	G	GS	CG	IP	H	R	ER	BB	SO	SV
88	64	3.43	389	64	17	1203	1283	528	458	322	437	97

FIELDING:

Stanley is not especially quick, but
he is very knowledgeable around the
mound. He anticipates bunt situations
and handles them very well. He does not
have a good move to first, but compensates for it by throwing over an inordinate number of times.

OVERALL:

He cannot go on forever. If Boston
had one more stopper they could count
on, they would have potentially one of
the best overall pitching staffs in the
league.

Robinson: "He is always tough, but I
wonder if the fans getting on him bothered him. A 9-10 record is pretty high
for a reliever. I think that he had
trouble in 1984 because his ball stayed
up a bit too much. This man needs some
help in the pen if he is to regain the
touch that made him one of the best
relievers in the league."

GARY ALLENSON
C, No. 39
RR, 5'11", 193 lbs.
ML Svc: 6 years
Born: 2-4-55 in
Culver City, CA

HITTING, BASERUNNING, FIELDING:

Gary Allenson was handed the catching job in 1983, but then lost it. It appears that he will never get it back. He cannot hit major league pitching and is not strong enough defensively behind the plate to earn the starting job again.

He stands straight up with a square stance and is a good fastball hitter if the ball is belt-high. Pitchers will rarely give him that type of pitch; instead, they will throw him nothing but fastballs low and away and every breaking ball they can devise. Because of a lack of playing time, Allenson had trouble with almost every pitch and was particularly vulnerable to breaking balls and change-ups.

He has not stolen a base in the last four years and doesn't figure to ever steal one. He tries his best on the basepaths and at everything he does, but he does not have good speed. He has a strong arm and can surprise runners with his throws, but still has trouble handling pitches in the dirt.

OVERALL:

Two years ago, they wrote that Gary would make Red Sox fans forget Carlton Fisk. At the rate Allenson is going, he may make Boston fans forget him first.

Robinson: "He is going to be a back-up catcher forever because he has not hit major league pitching. It is too bad in a way, because he has a good attitude and has better than average defensive skills. Whether he stays in Boston or goes elsewhere, he will be a backup catcher."

RICH GALE
RHP, No. 32
RR, 6'7", 225 lbs.
ML Svc: 7 years
Born: 1-19-54 in
Littleton, NH

PITCHING, FIELDING:

The Boston Red Sox wait for no man, especially a righthanded reliever who may be better off as a starter. Rich Gale falls into that category. He agreed to a Triple A contract, pitched well in the minors and was called up the the Sox in June but was sent back in August.

Once the Rookie Pitcher of the Year with the Royals (1978), the 6'7" Gale has never been able to follow up that season with success. His fastball comes in too straight, although it is fast (88 MPH). He has a slider, a change and a curve, but must rely on control and perfect location in order to be effective. He is a very deliberate worker who some observers claim thinks too much on every pitch to every batter.

He was ineffective in his short stint with Boston last year, but he does have 53 major league career wins. He is not a particularly agile fielder and must improve his leg kick in order to keep the runners close.

OVERALL:

Robinson: "I think that he would probably be better off as a starter than as a reliever, but I know that arm problems have slowed him down. I also know that he has lost some of the zip from his fastball and must rely on better control and location. Rich needs to re-regain his lost confidence."

GLENN HOFFMAN
SS, No. 18
RR, 6'2", 190 lbs.
ML Svc: 5 years
Born: 7-7-58 in
Orange, CA

HITTING, BASERUNNING, FIELDING:

Glenn Hoffman was pencilled in as the everyday shortstop in 1984, but his left knee, which was operated on in the off-season, gave him problems and his hitting and fielding suffered. He hit less than .200 and saw very little playing time.

He has a square stance and bats straight-up. He can handle high fastballs and is usually more of a contact and line drive hitter than one with power. He is one of the best bunters in the league.

Pitchers will give him a high fastball, but will try to keep it up and in. Hoffman can be struck out by righthanders who feed him a steady diet of sweeping curves and low sliders. Any control pitcher with a breaking ball, righty or lefty, can have success with Hoffman, particularly if they can spot the fastball.

Hoffman is not fleet afoot, will not steal or scare a pitcher, will not take extraordinary chances on the basepaths and may take even less in the future unless his knee heals completely. He does have good baserunning instincts.

At short, Hoffman has one of the best arms in the league and good range to his right. He can make spectacular plays and throws, but will follow them with simple errors on easy grounders. He reaches balls other shortstops cannot, and is therefore charged with an unusually high number of errors.

OVERALL:

Robinson: "I doubt if he'll crack the starting lineup in 1985. The fact that he can play several positions will keep him in the big leagues."

DAVE STAPLETON
INF, No. 11
RR, 6'1", 185 lbs.
ML Svc: 4 years
Born: 1-16-54 in
Fairhope, AL

HITTING, BASERUNNING, FIELDING:

Last season, Dave Stapleton had no chance to play first base and no chance to overcome a poor percentage year in 1983. He injured his knee in his very first game at Fenway, played hurt for several weeks and finally packed his bags and went home after 13 games.

He stands deep in the box with a square stance, which he often closes against certain pitchers. When he did hit, Stapleton liked to stride into every pitch and could handle high fastballs and curves. He has trouble with low pitches, particularly fastballs in and sliders away. He can hit to all fields, but is better with men on base when called upon to hit behind the runner. He might be the best hit-and-run man in the league and can hit any pitch to right field. When he does not play regularly, however, he appears overanxious and impatient at the plate and tries to pull, and his average suffers.

He is a solid, fundamental baserunner and fielder, no threat to steal, but no embarrassment when fielding or running. He has (or had) excellent leaping ability and handled high throws very well at first base.

OVERALL:

Robinson: "I can't see Dave playing much in 1985. He can play several positions, a definite plus, but his performances have gone downhill every year since he became a regular."

ED JURAK
INF, No. 22
RR, 6'2", 185 lbs.
ML Svc: 2 years
Born: 10-24-57 in
Los Angeles, CA

HITTING, BASERUNNING, FIELDING:

Ed Jurak seems to be the prototypical infielder for Beantown--good high ball hitter, good contact hitter, no-power hitter who can play any infield position.

He has a square stance and strides into every pitch, giving him a chance to pull a curve or off-speed pitch to left-center or hit a fastball out over the plate to right-center. Righties and lefties can get him out by throwing fastballs up and in and curves and sliders low and away. Late in 1983, he had outstanding success with a runner on third, but did not get the chance in 1984 when youngsters Marty Barrett and Jackie Gutierrez were inserted into the starting lineup and played every day.

He does not have good speed but does get out of the batter's box well. He does not take chances on the basepaths and will not steal a base. The Sox thought he was a good shortstop, but his play proved erratic. He fired the ball on several occasions with straight and true throws, but seemed to simply lob it on other occasions. He was starting to learn to play the hitters, and improving on his pivot at second, but the bench beckoned and the bell tolled for him.

OVERALL:

It's tough to find a spot for Jurak because his defense is not overly outstanding and he has no power.

Robinson: "The best he can do is be a utility man. He does have a good attitude and knows his limitations. His problem is that he plays on a team that uses the same guys and the same lineup more than any other team."

JEFF NEWMAN
C, No. 5
RR, 6'2", 215 lbs.
ML Svc: 9 years
Born: 9-11-48 in
Fort Worth, TX

HITTING, BASERUNNING, FIELDING:

In 1983 Jeff Newman hit .189. In 1984 he hit 33 points higher.

Perhaps it is not fair to condemn this catcher/first baseman, because he just does not get enough at-bats and does not come to the plate in pressure situations. With Boston, he is a third-string catcher who plays once a month.

He has a closed stance and likes high fastballs. Hard stuff up and in, however, can get him out, as well as sliders away. Newman has a tendency to try to pull, whether at Fenway or elsewhere, but again, when you bat only once a week what else can you do? He has never tried going the opposite way at Boston, so pitchers will throw everything away and on the outside corner to him.

He is fundamentally sound behind the plate and calls a good, smart game. He has a good throwing arm and is accurate. He is better than most at catching foul pops. On the bases he will not run, will not take chances, but does not make foolish mistakes.

OVERALL:

He knows he cannot play too much, and he does take the time to talk to Gedman and Allenson, imparting the knowledge of his eight years in the majors. Now, Boston has a young catcher named Marc Sullivan, the son of part-owner Haywood Sullivan, primed and ready to make the team. Where does that leave Newman?

Robinson: "It leaves Newman as a third-string catcher who may be able to pinch-hit for you on occasion, but I'd be surprised if he is back with Boston this year."

CALIFORNIA ANGELS

PITCHING:

Don Aase returned to the majors last season after a nearly two-year absence. He came back with a reconstructed right arm and the same 95 MPH fastball that had made him a quality short relief pitcher before his 1982 injury.

Brought along slowly at mid-year, Aase never worked two consecutive games and rarely worked more than three times a week--a concession to continued rehabilitation programs. Yet when he did pitch, it was the Aase the Angels had hoped would return.

Delivering that fastball from over the top or, occasionally, three-quarters, Aase challenged both lefthanded and righthanded batters, mixing in a hard slider, depending upon the situation. Though he hadn't pitched in the majors since July of 1982, Aase's control was on a par with his pre-injury years: in 39 innings he walked 19 men, and struck out 28.

While the fastball was testament to Aase's arm strength, the question about his resiliency remains unanswered. In 1984, the Angels used him sparingly, rarely for more than an inning, though he did pitch well in his longer outings, too.

Aase's on-the-mound philosophy hasn't changed. His strength is the fastball and he'll throw it letter-high to high ball hitters or knee-high to low ball hitters. When he's got his best one working, Aase's strength-on-strength approach works.

Always a fast worker, Aase was moved to the bullpen in 1980 partly because of his inability to pace himself. Relief pitching allows him to do what he does best--go all out, every pitch, as long as he can. His concentration is solid and maturity has left him nearly unshakable in the toughest situations.

He's largely shelved his secondary pitches, a change-up and slow curve, and refuses to lose a game on anything less than his best pitch. Perhaps one of the

DON AASE
RHP, No. 46
RR, 6'3", 215 lbs.
ML Svc: 7 years
Born: 9-8-54 in
 Orange, CA

1984 STATISTICS
W	L	ERA	G	GS	CG	IP	H	R	ER	BB	SO	SV
4	1	1.62	23	0	0	39	30	7	7	19	28	8

CAREER STATISTICS
W	L	ERA	G	GS	CG	IP	H	R	ER	BB	SO	SV
45	41	3.82	205	91	22	787	794	355	334	308	418	27

more amazing statistics of his comeback was that in 23 games he gave up only one home run.

FIELDING:

Aase's fielding is average, although his mechanics are sound. He gets himself in position to field after delivering a pitch, has a quick move to first base and because of his delivery and primary pitch--the fastball--is tough to run against.

In the situations Aase usually finds himself in, baserunners aren't trying to steal and hitters aren't trying to bunt.

OVERALL:

Aase's intensity and competitiveness are exemplified by his comeback. After undergoing surgery in which a ligament in his right forearm had to be reconstructed, Aase worked non-stop for 23 months to earn his return to the majors. He is a power pitcher who still hasn't reached his potential since the injury.

Matthews: "Aase showed that he has a chance to continue his comeback and possibly become the late-inning relief pitcher the Angels need so desperately. He was quite effective in some of his late-season appearances."

HITTING:

Always a streak hitter, Juan Beniquez put together a year-long streak in 1984, batting a career high .336 in 110 games by disciplining both his approach and his free-spirit attitude toward the game.

Over the past two seasons, Beniquez has matured immensely, and what was once a pull-or-nothing approach at the plate has now changed drastically. Borrowing an inside swing from teammate Rod Carew, Beniquez had as many hits to right field as left field last season.

Beniquez remains a first pitch hitter, though when he batted leadoff last season he did show far more patience at the plate, even though he walked just 18 times in 354 at-bats.

And while the fastball is still the pitch he hits best, Beniquez has discovered new confidence in taking breaking pitches the other way, a confidence that translated into base hits.

At times, he will crowd the plate against a pitcher he thinks he can handle, trying to force an inside pitch he can turn on.

Though most of his power is to left field, he can drive a ball up either alley, and a third of his 17 doubles last season were shots down the right field line.

Pitchers generally try to keep him off stride, though he's less likely to chase breaking pitches off the plate than in the past. When he goes into a slump, some of the old undisciplined swings are usually on display again.

BASERUNNING:

A good, instinctive baserunner, Juan was 0 for 3 in stealing bases last season, but that's never been his forte. His basestealing attempts are actually hit-and-run plays gone awry. However, when going from first to third, or from second to home, he's rarely thrown out, and he will take the extra base if he senses the opportunity.

FIELDING:

When he's at his best, Beniquez is

JUAN BENIQUEZ
OF, No. 12
RR, 5'11", 175 lbs.
ML Svc: 12 years
Born: 5-13-50 in
    San Sebastian, PR

1984 STATISTICS

AVG	G	AB	R	H	2B	3B	HR	RBI	BB	SO	SB
.336	110	354	60	119	17	0	8	39	18	43	0

CAREER STATISTICS

AVG	G	AB	R	H	2B	3B	HR	RBI	BB	SO	SB
.269	1132	3584	479	965	148	24	56	343	251	411	98

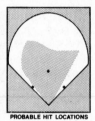

VS. RHP   VS. LHP   PROBABLE HIT LOCATIONS

among the best defensive outfielders in the game. He gets an excellent jump on the ball, has a strong, accurate arm and will at times throw behind baserunners.

Beniquez's weakness in the outfield is his tendency to be flashier than is necessary. He will nonchalantly play outs into errors several times a season, then make a stunning defensive play an inning or two later.

OVERALL:

The rap on Beniquez has long been that the more you play him, the less his value is, that he was a platoon player and should remain one. Since 1983, however, Beniquez has hit well over .300 against all comers. If he remains a fourth outfielder, he may be the best in the game for all he can do once in the game.

Matthews: "Beniquez finally matured to the point where he is a very good all-around player . . . especially at the plate. He is now a pretty tough out and pretty effective in the clutch."

HITTING:

No ifs, ands or buts about it, Bob Boone had the worst season of his career in 1984, batting in the .190s from mid-June until late September, when he rallied to finish at .202.

An intelligent, analytical player--at the plate and when behind it--Boone tried new stances, new approaches and new bats last season. None worked.

Some teammates said Boone's hitting suffered immeasurably because Dick Schofield, hitting ahead of him in the lineup in 1984, batted .193 and was rarely on base. That prevented Boone from hitting his way through a slump by playing "little ball"--sacrifice bunts, hit-and-run plays, moving the runner along.

Boone does all those things as well as anyone, with excellent bat control, and though he didn't hit at all last season, he still struck out only once every ten at-bats.

Most pitchers try to jam Boone--stop him from going the other way or up the middle and force him to pull. Good righthanders have given him trouble the past few years.

Boone is still at his best with men on base, good at moving them over or scoring them from third with less than one out.

What power he has is all to left field, and that's limited. Boone, however, knows his limitations and remains a contact hitter who'll rarely try to do more than he's capable of.

BASERUNNING:

The tendency when Boone is on base is for everyone to forget him, figuring it will take at least two hits to score him from first, and maybe more. Though he is a slow runner now, Boone's instincts are good and he'll get two or three surprise steals a year when pitchers ignore him. Instincts and bad legs, however, don't add up to a threat on the bases. Boone isn't one.

BOB BOONE
C, No. 8
RR, 6'2", 202 lbs.
ML Svc: 12 years
Born: 11-19-47 in
San Diego, CA

1984 STATISTICS											
AVG	G	AB	R	H	2B	3B	HR	RBI	BB	SO	SB
.202	139	450	33	91	16	1	3	32	25	45	3

CAREER STATISTICS											
AVG	G	AB	R	H	2B	3B	HR	RBI	BB	SO	SB
.254	1549	5080	470	1289	223	22	84	598	453	432	30

  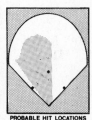

VS. RHP   VS. LHP   PROBABLE HIT LOCATIONS

FIELDING:

His knowledge of opposing hitters is great, and in close games, he simply doesn't make mistakes on his selection of pitches.

OVERALL:

He still has a strong, accurate arm and, given the chance by his pitcher, will throw out a potential basestealer more than 45% of the time. If he has a weakness, it's that he won't block the plate too aggressively against a hard-charging baserunner.

Boone's the kind of player who's in the lineup every day, giving 100 percent and expecting his teammates to do the same.

Matthews: "I wonder if Bob has managerial aspirations after he finishes what has been a wonderful career. Being an intelligent catcher and baseball-smart, he would be an excellent choice."

HITTING:

One of the few good young hitters to come out of the Angels organization—and remain with the team—Mike Brown had the reputation in the minors as being a man who hit for average, power and run production. In limited duty last season, Brown showed no inclination to change that reputation.

In fewer than half as many at-bats, Brown had more extra-base hits than either Rod Carew or Dick Schofield, batted .284 and showed potential that will make it hard for the Angels to keep him out of the lineup this season.

A fine fastball hitter, Brown is an aggressive student of the game and is rarely fooled more than a few times by the same pitch.

One of the stronger men on the team, Brown hits mistakes a long way but isn't just a pull hitter by any means. He's disciplined and will try to make hard contact when behind. In key pinch-hit situations last season, Brown three times showed the patience to take the base on balls rather than chase pitches out of the strike zone.

Like most young hitters, Brown finds himself worked hard inside and then away with off-speed pitches. The problem with that is he learns fast.

He has a good knowledge of the strike zone, but hasn't yet gained the confidence in the majors that made him such a tremendous minor league hitter. If he gets that, he'll get similar results.

BASERUNNING:

Brown isn't fast but he's aggressive, and he'll take anyone out at second base to break up a double play. He shows good instincts but still lacks confidence on the bases in the majors, partly because he doesn't know pitchers, partly because he didn't want to make mistakes. He is not really a basestealing threat.

FIELDING:

Brown is a strong defensive player

MIKE BROWN
OF, No. 3
RR, 6'2", 195 lbs.
ML Svc: 1 year plus
Born: 12-29-59 in
    San Francisco, CA

1984 STATISTICS

AVG	G	AB	R	H	2B	3B	HR	RBI	BB	SO	SB
.284	62	148	19	42	8	3	7	22	13	23	0

CAREER STATISTICS

AVG	G	AB	R	H	2B	3B	HR	RBI	BB	SO	SB
.262	93	252	31	66	13	4	10	31	20	43	1

STRONG   STRONG
VS. RHP   VS. LHP   PROBABLE HIT LOCATIONS

whose outfield play is marked by the same aggression that appears at the plate and on the basepaths. Brown's greatest strength may be that aggression, coupled with his enthusiasm and God-given ability.

The owner of a strong arm, Brown will charge base hits and dare runners to test him. He goes back on balls well.

OVERALL:

Brown has the potential to be a .280s hitter with 25 home run power but needs the opportunity to prove it to himself as well as others. Whenever the Angels talked trade with other teams, Brown's name came up first. He is the best-hitting prospect the Angels have produced since Tom Brunansky.

Matthews: "It appears that Mike has a chance to be a good everyday player— but that's what he needs—a chance to play every day. He does a number of things well."

NOTE: Burleson sat out most of last season, recuperating from surgery to correct a torn rotator cuff in 1982. When he was activated, his role was as a pinch-runner and pinch-hitter. He didn't play an inning in the field.

HITTING:

A battler at the plate, Rick Burleson is a hard line drive hitter who'll spray the ball anywhere from left field over to the right field corner. He is a better hitter to the opposite field.

Hitting from a slightly crouched stance, Burleson is a contact hitter with superb bat control who seems to view every at-bat as a minor war. A good fastball hitter, Burleson is patient at the plate and an excellent hit-and-run prospect.

With very little power, Burleson slumps when he begins hitting fly balls. Since he goes the other way so well, pitchers often try to jam him, daring him to try to pull the ball.

He is a smart hitter and will drop a bunt if he thinks the third baseman is too deep. Whatever it takes to win, Rick is willing to do it.

BASERUNNING:

While not especially fast, Burleson is very quick. His aggression on the basepaths does not include basestealing. He is a fiery competitor, as his nickname, "The Rooster," indicates and infielders don't take force plays for granted when he is the runner. He comes in hard. Burleson will take the extra base and often forces throws to be made from the outfield.

FIELDING:

Once among the best shortstops in baseball with one of the strongest arms, Burleson faces an uncertain future and his career remains in jeopardy because of his shoulder injury. He has talked of making the transition from short to second or even to first.

Burleson's injury requires that his

RICK BURLESON
SS, No. 7
RR, 5'10", 160 lbs.
ML Svc: 11 years
Born: 4-29-51 in
 Lynwood, CA

1984 STATISTICS

AVG	G	AB	R	H	2B	3B	HR	RBI	BB	SO	SB
.000	7	4	2	0	0	0	0	0	0	2	0

CAREER STATISTICS

AVG	G	AB	R	H	2B	3B	HR	RBI	BB	SO	SB
.275	1191	4662	595	1281	228	22	43	406	370	415	71

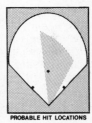

STRONG   STRONG

VS. RHP   VS. LHP   PROBABLE HIT LOCATIONS

throws be over-the-top most of the time, and he's altered his mechanics accordingly. His advantage is that despite the circumstances, he is an all-out player. If Burleson plays, he's giving all he has.

He has good range for an infielder, and improves it by knowing the hitters and his pitchers. He is fearless in the pivot.

OVERALL:

The kind of player teams make team captains, Burleson is a spark plug and has been all his career. His attitude on the field is that he can be beaten but refuses to lose, and there are few more competitive men in sports. No one seeing the pain he's gone through the past two years in his comeback effort could doubt his desire to reach the top again.

Matthews: "He is still battling back from the shoulder injury, but battling has been the Burleson style since he started playing professionally. If the will and desire count for quite a bit, then Burleson will be back."

HITTING:

Although Rod Carew remains one of the more phenomenal hitters in the game, his best years are behind him--perhaps far behind him--and his value to a team is limited to the role of a singles hitter.

An inside-out swinger, Carew is played as if he were a righthanded power hitter; most of his hits are soft line drives to left field. He will rarely turn on a pitch and pull the ball; instead, he takes the hard inside fastball the other way. Few have ever done that-- but then few have career averages of .330.

That said, it must be noted that Carew, long dubbed the best bunter in the league, is rarely a major factor in a game these days. Batting second behind a basestealing threat last season, Carew complained that he was distracted by having to take pitches. Never a patient man at the plate, Carew rarely pulls the ball, so he is not a sure bet to move runners along in any situation since, oddly enough, he is not a good sacrifice bunter.

His declining speed has also limited his bunting, especially when third basemen play him in close. Carew has not dragged a bunt in more than three years.

Still, what he does in laying wood on the ball, consistently and in any situation, is amazing. Last season, in a game-on-the-line at-bat against Kansas City's Dan Quisenberry, Carew fell behind 0-2. He lost his helmet chasing an off-speed pitch, then calmly lined a game-tying single up the middle on the third pitch. Amazing.

BASERUNNING:

Carew has terrible instincts for a man who has been on base as many times as he has. He may get thrown out going from first to third more often than anyone in the league, and certainly leads his team every year in that regard.

He is no longer a threat to steal, and he is aggressive on the bases only when something provokes him.

ROD CAREW
1B, No. 29
LR, 6'0", 182 lbs.
ML Svc: 18 years
Born: 10-1-45 in
Gatun, PAN

1984 STATISTICS

AVG	G	AB	R	H	2B	3B	HR	RBI	BB	SO	SB
.295	93	329	42	97	8	1	3	31	40	39	4

CAREER STATISTICS

AVG	G	AB	R	H	2B	3B	HR	RBI	BB	SO	SB
.330	2342	8872	1355	2929	428	109	90	976	954	981	348

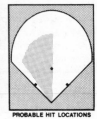

VS. RHP   VS. LHP   PROBABLE HIT LOCATIONS

FIELDING:

Carew has never been a great defensive player, and last year he led the team in errors--a rarity for a first baseman. While his range is limited, he has an accurate, but not strong, arm. He can be fooled on trick plays but usually makes a safe play on a fielder's choice rather than throw for the force at second.

OVERALL:

Carew is approaching the 3,000-hit plateau but is doing it slowly. He is being held back by injuries and the fact that he is not as great an asset to his club as he was in the past. Even when he is healthy, he is platooned. The result was his first below-.300 season in 16 years.

Matthews: "Rod is winding down a career that has been dominated by awe-inspiring hitting. I don't think that he will ever be too old to step up to the plate and hit the ball."

PITCHING:

Though Aase's return to form last season was more dramatic, teammate Doug Corbett's was no less unexpected. He is a sinkerball pitcher with 20-save seasons in Minnesota, but he began last year in the minor leagues, with both his pitches and his mental toughness questioned by teammates and managers.

Recalled early in the year, Corbett erased the mental question marks by winning his first career start and then by pitching superbly in middle and short relief roles. Corbett's style is still not favored by everyone. His propensity for yelling "Look out!" to batters when a pitch gets away inside leads some to question his on-the-field personality, but Corbett is competitive.

Never a power pitcher, his strength is a sinker. When he's on his game, his infielders are making a lot of plays. His delivery drops anywhere from three-quarters to sidearm, and though he may be a bit more effective against right-handers than lefthanders, his sinker seems equally difficult for either.

Corbett's biggest weakness is lack of control. When he has his control, he'll only get beat by ground balls that get through the infield—a hazard for any sinkerball specialist—and when he does not, he gets himself in trouble.

An emotional player, Corbett has a number of on-the-field trademarks; among them is his habit of sprinting to the mound from the bullpen when called upon to relieve. Another is cheering on teammates who make plays behind him.

A chain-smoker off the field, Doug's demeanor on the mound can appear frantic to the uninitiated, but last year he proved at last that he can pitch well in clutch situations when his team is in a pennant race.

FIELDING:

He is an average fielder who often

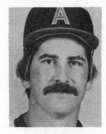

DOUG CORBETT
RHP, No. 23
RR, 6'1", 185 lbs.
ML Svc: 4 years
Born: 11-4-52 in Sarasota, FL

1984 STATISTICS
W	L	ERA	G	GS	CG	IP	H	R	ER	BB	SO	SV
5	1	2.12	45	1	0	85	76	22	20	30	48	4

CAREER STATISTICS
W	L	ERA	G	GS	CG	IP	H	R	ER	BB	SO	SV
17	23	2.82	226	1	0	405	357	137	127	145	266	55

makes plays on adrenaline alone. Like most sinkerballers, Corbett has learned to prepare for comebackers. He has quick hands. With only an average move to first base, Corbett will nonetheless work at keeping men close to give his catcher an edge.

OVERALL:

Since coming to the Angels from the Twins in 1982, the questions about him centered around his ability to cope with pressure and his reliance on one pitch, the sinker.

For the first time since that trade, Corbett pitched consistently for an entire season, and his ERA was as good as any righthanded reliever in the AL with over 50 innings pitched. A one-time short reliever turned now to more long relief situations, Corbett is expected to challenge for more and more save situations this season.

Matthews: "A sinkerball pitcher, Doug must have razor-sharp control for him to be effective. He showed signs in 1984 of the consistency needed by a late inning reliever."

HITTING:

A clean-up hitter last season on reputation alone, Doug DeCinces suffered through an off-year in which he never really put together the kind of streak the California Angels had grown to expect from him.

A line drive hitter with good power, DeCinces can be awesome when he gets into a groove. In one 1983 game, he hit three home runs--one each on a fastball, slider and change-up.

Many pitchers pitch DeCinces inside, since he tends to dive after the outside-corner fastball, and DeCinces frequently goes down, though rarely because he's in any physical danger. He does not hang in on inside balls.

He has an excellent grasp of the strike zone and rarely passes the opportunity to complain on a called strike. He can be a very patient hitter, especially when he's hot. When he's slumping, he'll lunge at bad balls, usually high or just off the plate.

DeCinces's power goes from left field to the right-center field power alley, and he can drive the ball anywhere.

A great low ball hitter, DeCinces can lose a sinker fast. High fastballs are far less combustible.

BASERUNNING:

A very intelligent--but slow--runner, DeCinces isn't likely to steal or, for that matter, get thrown out often on the bases. An aggressive runner, he'll challenge outfielders for the extra base. He is not overly aggressive at breaking up the double play.

FIELDING:

DeCinces takes great pride in his defense and can often make the big play. Good hands, good instincts; DeCinces rarely makes a bad throw--he has a strong, accurate arm and can throw from nearly any position.

DOUG DeCINCES
3B, No. 11
RR, 6'2", 194 lbs.
ML Svc: 10 years
Born: 8-29-50 in
  Burbank, CA

1984 STATISTICS

AVG	G	AB	R	H	2B	3B	HR	RBI	BB	SO	SB
.269	146	547	77	147	23	3	20	82	53	79	4

CAREER STATISTICS

AVG	G	AB	R	H	2B	3B	HR	RBI	BB	SO	SB
.264	1252	4408	593	1162	245	25	175	641	449	671	53

  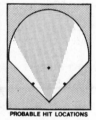

STRONG — VS. RHP   STRONG — VS. LHP   PROBABLE HIT LOCATIONS

He willingly leaves his feet for balls hit to either side, and DeCinces is at his absolute best in a big game. When his team is out of it, DeCinces can be, too.

OVERALL:

DeCinces has fallen victim to injuries and slumps since putting together his career-best season in 1982, troubled by a succession of back problems and good fastballs that were a little too good. He remains a big game player, however, though he may not be the clean-up man he was much of that 1982 season. He is a good clutch player, on offense or defense.

Matthews: "Doug is one of the many California players who has had a long and brilliant career. As a whole, the team is getting very old; Doug is injury-prone and it takes longer to recover as the years add up."

HITTING:

Brian Downing never met a book on hitting he wouldn't buy and probably find a use for. Downing is constantly searching for the perfect stance, the perfect swing, the perfect at-bat. Along the way, he's become a dangerous hitter and a man who may be underrated in the press but never by opposing pitchers.

Downing may be a better hitter now simply because he can do more things. Still able to go the other way, Downing has shown in the last three seasons that he has 20-25 home run power.

He'll also play games with pitching staffs, setting up situations by taking the first pitch at-bat after at-bat, then laying on that first pitch in a critical, late game at-bat. He feels confident against certain pitchers and is a very disciplined hitter. He's also a guess hitter, which makes him vulnerable at times, but the former catcher in him guesses right the majority of the time.

A great fastball hitter and a very strong hitter, Downing has determination. His refusal to give in makes him a consistent threat, and he's become even more dangerous with men on base.

Most pitchers try to work him away with off-speed pitches or fastballs around the letters. He can be induced to chase such pitches. The problem is, he can also hit them great distances if he gets them.

BASERUNNING:

Downing will never be a great baserunner simply because he hasn't the confidence; he runs like a man terrified that he's just made a mistake in judgment. What he lacks in instinct he makes up for in aggression. Lots of players run better, few run harder. But he still can't break himself of the headfirst slide.

FIELDING:

Downing's made one outfield error-- total--in the past three seasons, and in 1984 he may have finally shed some of

BRIAN DOWNING
OF, No. 5
RR, 5'10", 200 lbs.
ML Svc: 11 years
Born: 10-9-50 in
   Los Angeles, CA

1984 STATISTICS

AVG	G	AB	R	H	2B	3B	HR	RBI	BB	SO	SB
.275	156	539	66	148	28	2	23	91	70	66	0

CAREER STATISTICS

AVG	G	AB	R	H	2B	3B	HR	RBI	BB	SO	SB
.266	1284	4168	594	1108	185	12	126	554	616	574	31

  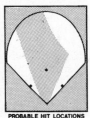

VS. RHP   VS. LHP   PROBABLE HIT LOCATIONS

his own inhibitions about his defense. A converted catcher, Downing doesn't have the strongest arm, best reflexes or sharpest skills, but has worked hard to become an an above average fielder. Balls hit directly over his head still give him trouble.

Downing, however, refuses to let a ball drop in his area and will take on fences, tarp rollers or carpet burns to get an out. He's become more aggressive on ground balls, more confident on fly balls and showed last season he's beginning to know American League hitters. He is a better outfielder than he's given credit for.

OVERALL:

Downing's devotion to the game made him a major leaguer even after he could not make his high school team, and that same dedication has made him a good major league player.

Matthews: "Brian is a tough, aggressive, battling player. Originally a catcher, he worked hard to become an excellent outfielder. He changed his stance in 1984. He used to have the most wide-open stance in baseball."

HITTING:

Always a steady, get-the-job done hitter with better than average power, Bobby Grich slumped badly in the first half of last season before larceny put his offense back together--he stole Juan Beniquez's stance.

Discarded was the straight up and down stance of the past in which Grich kept his hands down and bat perfectly straight. When he went to a flatter approach that included a crouch and a bat held back behind his head, he got results.

Despite fighting minor injuries and a platoon system that saw him play three positions a week the last half of the year, Grich's numbers at the end were compatible with his career stats--and those have always been solid if unspectacular. Still a strong hitter, especially when pitchers make mistakes or he guesses dead right, Grich's new approach made him more of a contact hitter without sacrificing opposite field power.

Few second baseman have reached the 200 home run mark in their careers, and though Grich has, he remains a team player at the plate, a well-schooled fundamentalist who'll move his man over with the ground ball and who can bunt well in sacrifice situations.

Grich has good bat control with a weakness for high fastballs that, thrown fast enough, elude him. He has a good eye at the plate and will take the base on balls, as he has 967 times in his career.

BASERUNNING:

A product of the Orioles' organization, Grich remains one of the more aggressive, intelligent baserunners in the game. Not a basestealing threat, he will, however, challenge defenses to stop him from stretching singles and is fearless at going from first to third on hits to any field. There are, though, times that his mind is faster than his body. In one game last season, he was thrown out at three different bases, and complained after being removed that he

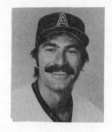

BOBBY GRICH
2B, No. 4
RR, 6'2", 190 lbs.
ML Svc: 14 years
Born: 1-15-49 in
Muskegon, MI

1984 STATISTICS

AVG	G	AB	R	H	2B	3B	HR	RBI	BB	SO	SB
.256	116	363	60	93	15	1	18	58	57	70	2

CAREER STATISTICS

AVG	G	AB	R	H	2B	3B	HR	RBI	BB	SO	SB
.268	1766	6098	917	1633	285	44	202	781	967	1147	100

VS. RHP   VS. LHP   PROBABLE HIT LOCATIONS

was deprived of a chance to run for the cycle.

FIELDING:

For the first time in his career, Bob found himself not the everyday second baseman and opened up a "Dial-A-Glove" franchise that saw him play first, second and third base, each well. Now at the stage of a career when utility play begins to become a strength, not a drawback, Grich still has soft hands, a great knowledge of the hitters and a strong, accurate arm. He may turn the double play from second as well as anyone ever has.

OVERALL:

Unselfish at the plate, he remains a rarity, a middle infielder capable of making the plays, hitting .260 and getting his 15-20 home runs per season.

Matthews: "Bob is the type of player who is always trying to figure out a way to beat you. Still a most effective offensive player who can do a lot of things."

HITTING:

Reggie Jackson's toughest job last season may have been proving to Reggie Jackson that he could still hit. While the results weren't an MVP-level season, given the disaster of 1983, he had a fine 1984.

Good, high fastballs still went by last season, but mistakes disappeared as Jackson moved past the 500 home run mark in his career and showed a willingness to cut down on his swing in situations that called for base hits. How serious was Jackson's transition from his well-known style of all-or-nothing at-bats? Well, he dropped his first sacrifice bunt in 12 years in September and it helped win a game.

Still a long ball threat, Jackson remains one of those rare players who rises to occasions, if not as often as in his best years, often enough still to remain a force. He goes to left and left-center more than in the past, and because he has such upper-body strength he has the ability to hit home runs to the opposite field.

Bat control, however, will never be a Jackson strength. He has struck out more times than anyone in baseball history and doesn't figure to be caught in the next millennium. But one, even two bad swings does not an at-bat make, and Jackson's A-1 swing is still among the most awesome in baseball.

For all his strength, Jackson remains a smart hitter at the plate and has shown he can adjust to the pitching book on him. Except for a month-long drought that began in August, Jackson had a consistent season, and his 25 home runs nearly doubled his 1983 production.

BASERUNNING:

Among the many Jackson trademarks that have made him a crowd favorite to cheer or boo is his baserunning, an ears back, head down charge usually capped with a hard slide that, if not artistic, is exuberant. Jackson's speed to first base is surprising, and he beat out more than a half dozen infield hits last season.

REGGIE JACKSON
DH/RF, No. 44
LL, 6'0", 204 lbs.
ML Svc: 17 years
Born: 5-18-46 in
    Wyncote, PA

1984 STATISTICS

AVG	G	AB	R	H	2B	3B	HR	RBI	BB	SO	SB
.223	143	525	67	117	17	2	25	81	55	141	8

CAREER STATISTICS

AVG	G	AB	R	H	2B	3B	HR	RBI	BB	SO	SB
.265	2430	8649	1380	2293	410	46	503	1516	1173	2247	224

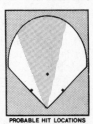

VS. RHP   VS. LHP   PROBABLE HIT LOCATIONS

He's also a threat to steal, especially in situations where one run might make a difference. He'll steal on the count, when a pitcher is ahead and more likely to throw off-speed pitches, and last year he guessed right eight of the twelve times he went.

FIELDING:

Jackson's first defensive play of 1984 came in the All Star game and, yep, he played a ball off his leg. Still, for a man who played only a half dozen times in the field, Jackson was hardly an embarrassment and still showed both the hustle and the arm that made him an average fielder at his absolute worst.

OVERALL:

Simply by his presence in a lineup, Reggie Jackson can make hitters around him better, and he's proven he is a winner. And he is still capable of 25-30 home runs.

Matthews: "Reggie made a few offensive adjustments in 1984 and had a fine comeback year. Few players have ever had his flair for the dramatic. People still love to watch him hit."

PITCHING:

Anyone--whether he's 21 or, as in Tommy John's case, 41--can have a bad year. For Tommy John, however, the sad truth is that since opening day 1982, his record is 32-38 and his ERA is over 4.00.

A finesse pitcher who has relied for more than a decade on a sinker for outs, John has tinkered in the past few seasons with a slider but junked that pitch at mid-season last year. It wasn't working, but then nothing has been working for him consistently. It has changed John's game entirely.

When he's on, he forces batters to hit pitches on the corners or chase bad balls at their shins. Since his best fastball is in the low-to-mid-80 MPH range, he has to spot that pitch and mesmerize a hitter with off-speed offerings. John has to rely on a batter putting the ball in play for outs.

Without the velocity to work a hitter inside, John has had to cope in recent seasons with the fact that batters are beginning to show more patience against him. If John isn't hitting the outer corner and falls behind, he has no advantage and becomes eminently hittable.

A fast worker, John has a delivery that varies from three-quarters to a bit lower, usually dropping down against lefthanders. Because his breaking pitches are slow, not quick breaking and sharp, he has no particular advantage against lefthanders.

A starter for most of his career, John found himself in the Angels' bullpen last August, asked to pitch in long relief. Though he was effective in that capacity, John may find that his effectiveness is limited to three- or four-inning assignments. He shows no inclination to accept that assignment.

John's biggest strength at this point in his career may lie in his experience, and in his desire to reach the 300-win mark. Effective when he works regularly and has both offensive support and a bullpen ready to relief after six or

TOMMY JOHN
LHP, No. 25
RL, 6'3", 200 lbs.
ML Svc: 22 years
Born: 5-22-43 in
   Terre Haute, IN

1984 STATISTICS

W	L	ERA	G	GS	CG	IP	H	R	ER	BB	SO	SV
7	13	4.52	32	29	4	181	223	97	91	56	47	0

CAREER STATISTICS

W	L	ERA	G	GS	CG	IP	H	R	ER	BB	SO	SV
255	197	3.19	646	598	158	4122	4073	1695	1460	1101	2030	4

seven innings, John has reached the stage where he must accept a role as the fourth or fifth starter in a rotation--if he can find that situation available.

FIELDING:

John's range on the field is limited to the mound and whatever he can reach from a crouched position. Not quick, not aggressive, John seems to believe that once he throws the pitch he's done his job.

A slow delivery makes him easier to run on than he would be if he altered his motion, but John will throw to first base. He'll also fake throws to second, though he hasn't actually thrown a ball there in more than two years.

OVERALL:

A very knowledgeable pitcher, John might be better suited as a pitching coach than as a starter, but can still be effective. The question is for how long. John pitched well early in 1984 and had no offensive support. When the offense did come later in the year, John rarely survived long enough to prosper with it.

Matthews: "Tommy had some tough outings in 1984. One of the best sinker-ball pitchers, he'll have to battle hard for a job in 1985."

PITCHING:

A short reliever in the minors, Curt Kaufman was cast into the role of long reliever last season and responded with a good attitude, if not always good results.

Used sporadically, Kaufman showed that his main strength was control. He walked only 20 men in 69 innings while striking out 41 batters. But being around the plate had its drawbacks: 13 home runs given up.

Kaufman's most effective performances in the minor leagues came when he was used frequently. A resilient arm seems to be getting better with more use, and when Kaufman was used two or three times in a week, his second and third assignments were always his most effective.

Along with a good fastball (88-92 MPH), Kaufman has a slider and off-speed breaking pitch, but he relies mostly on control. He's not going to overpower a batter, but he will catch more than his share looking at called third strikes.

Extremely competitive, Kaufman is an intelligent, teachable pitcher willing to pitch in any capacity. And in any situation, he'll give his absolute best that day. He maintains his poise.

With a very smooth motion, Kaufman will deliver his pitches from over the top to three-quarters. He is a good student of the game, and Kaufman figures to improve with experience and more consistent work.

FIELDING:

Good mechanics on the mound leave him

CURT KAUFMAN
RHP, No. 48
RR, 6'2", 175 lbs.
ML Svc: 1 year plus
Born: 7-19-57 in
Omaha, NE

1984 STATISTICS												
W	L	ERA	G	GS	CG	IP	H	R	ER	BB	SO	SV
2	3	4.57	29	1	0	69	68	37	35	20	41	1
CAREER STATISTICS												
W	L	ERA	G	GS	CG	IP	H	R	ER	BB	SO	SV
3	3	4.50	40	1	0	86	87	45	43	30	50	1

in solid fielding position, and the little things like hustling to first base to cover probably make him a better than average fielding pitcher.

He has an average move to first base, but will hasten his delivery out of the stretch. Kaufman is alert on the mound.

OVERALL:

Trying to adjust to a new role and the worst of pitching situations--sporadic work and long periods between assignments--Kaufman probably pitched better than his season numbers indicate.

Kaufman has solid ability and a great attitude. What he lacks at this point is experience and a well-defined role on a pitching staff.

Matthews: "A control type of pitcher, Kaufman should improve as he continues to adjust to the major leagues."

PITCHING:

The way Bruce Kison pitches is often more impressive than the results he gets, simply because courage and tenacity seem to be as big a key to his game as a fastball and his ability to change speeds.

Injured often in his major league career, Kison was back on a mound last June just eight months after undergoing spinal surgery. He shouldn't have been, but pain has never been enough to stop Kison from pitching.

On the mound he is the consummate competitor, known to be totally unafraid to pitch inside to anyone in any situation. Kison demands the inside of the plate, especially against righthanded batters. Because the natural break of his pitches runs in on a righthander, he is less effective against lefties.

Once a power pitcher, Kison's back, elbow and wrist injuries have reduced the velocity of his fastball, though his continued rehab work to strengthen his right arm and shoulder may again bring his fastball into the 90 MPH range.

In lieu of the overpowering fastball, Kison has mastered off-speed, change-of-speed pitches that come at a batter from any number of release points. Since he's 6'4" and thin, Kison has a delivery that can seem to be a jumble of elbows and knees. He conceals the ball well to heighten the perception.

A starter throughout his career, Kison has had injuries the past few seasons that have forced him to work in a number of roles. Last year, he was used in long and short relief, and his endurance, because of the surgery, was limited--and so was his effectiveness when starting. Pitching with a back brace that limited his flexibility, he was nonetheless the only pitcher on the staff with more strikeouts (66) than innings pitched (65), and he walked only 28 men.

In big game situations, Kison is the kind of man managers love to have on the mound. As his pitching coach, Marcel

BRUCE KISON
RHP, No. 24
RR, 6'4", 180 lbs.
ML Svc: 13 years
Born: 2-18-50 in
Pasco, WA

1984 STATISTICS
W	L	ERA	G	GS	CG	IP	H	R	ER	BB	SO	SV
4	5	5.37	20	7	0	65	72	42	39	28	66	2

CAREER STATISTICS
W	L	ERA	G	GS	CG	IP	H	R	ER	BB	SO	SV
110	85	3.64	358	237	36	1717	1595	796	694	630	1017	11

Lachemann, said last season, "Kison is the kind of pitcher who refuses to lose. Even if you're beating him, he won't acknowledge it. He'll come at you every pitch."

FIELDING:

Given the fact that he was coming off surgery and wearing a back brace, it was somewhat of a surprise that opponents didn't challenge Kison with bunts last season. But, again, since pain is no drawback for Kison, fielding in pain is not a disadvantage.

A smart pitcher on the mound, Kison fields well and knows hitters. His move to first is average, but he has ruined more than a few hit-and-run situations by buzzing a fastball up and in--a good pitch for the catcher to throw and impossible for the hitter to hit.

OVERALL:

A team player out of the old school of pitching, Kison will do anything to win. A student of the game and especially of major league hitters, he thrives on challenges--the bigger the better.

Matthews: "There aren't many pitchers as mentally tough as Kison. Always takes that highly competitive, 'never back down' attitude to the mound with him. He has overcome several physical setbacks."

PITCHING:

A man who lives for competition, Frank LaCorte endured the most frustrating year of his career last season when injuries and ineffectiveness limited him to 29 innings of work.

When healthy, LaCorte has survived on pure power, a fastball in the mid-90s that some hitters have compared to a heat-seeking missile. Intimidation is part of the game when LaCorte's right.

While his fastball is his show pitch, LaCorte's strikeouts often come on a sharp slider delivered with the same three-quarters motion. In situations where he can waste a pitch or try to lure a hitter into chasing something, he will also throw a curve as an off-speed pitch.

LaCorte's weakness is control. When he has it, he's a very tough relief pitcher. When he doesn't, he falls behind, tries to be too fine and gets into trouble.

Extremely competitive, LaCorte is the type of pitcher who can march into someone else's jam, escape trouble--but then get into his own the next inning. He is at his best with someone else's runners on base.

LaCorte also thrives on work; when he's not getting it, his tendency is to push sanity to the outer limits. He is an emotional, hard-working pitcher, and loves the game and lives and dies with each outing.

FIELDING:

On the mound, LaCorte has the look of a man in fifth gear. He will field most

FRANK LaCORTE
RHP, No. 31
RR, 6'1", 180 lbs.
ML Svc: 7 years
Born: 10-13-51 in
San Jose, CA

1984 STATISTICS

W	L	ERA	G	GS	CG	IP	H	R	ER	BB	SO	SV
1	2	7.06	13	1	0	29	33	26	23	13	13	0

CAREER STATISTICS

W	L	ERA	G	GS	CG	IP	H	R	ER	BB	SO	SV
23	44	5.02	253	32	1	489	457	297	273	258	372	26

anything hit at him, though not necessarily with grace. LaCorte will throw himself in front of anything. Base hits up the middle sometimes have to go right through him--literally.

He has an average move to first, but his live fastball makes him tough to run against.

OVERALL:

At one time, he was a starting pitcher, but now LaCorte's great love is game-on-the-line situations and short relief. When every pitch might mean a win or loss, LaCorte's concentration is at its peak. He is a streak pitcher and is capable of being the best he can be--or the worst--for considerable periods of time.

Matthews: "Frank can be overpowering. He had a frustrating 1984 season, but could come back and be a most effective pitcher for the Angels in 1985."

HITTING:

One of the great mysteries of sports is why Fred Lynn, since his move from Boston in 1981, has rarely, and only briefly, recaptured the form that at one time made him a regular MVP candidate. As an Angel the past four years, his numbers were (gasp!) average, far below his Red Sox form and unsatisfying both to Lynn and to his team.

When he is hot, he is as good as anyone in the game in every offensive category. He can hit, hit with power and produce runs at a pace few can match. But Lynn has yet to put a full season of that potential on the field since leaving Fenway Park. Instead, he has become a streak hitter whose good streaks last about as long as his bad ones. One reason may be that when Lynn struggles he seems lost, as if unable to believe that the natural swing that made him both Rookie of the Year and American League MVP in 1975 isn't working.

Lynn may adjust less than anyone in his class as a hitter. Though he can use the whole field, most of his hits fall from left-center on over to the right field line, and his power is from right-center to the line. When he's hot, he hits anything, though he still hits the fastball best. And when he's cold, he can look bad on mediocre off-speed pitches.

He continues to be at his best in game situations, a clutch hitter who prides himself on RBI production. He is a very good low ball hitter, and pitchers tend to work him away and in the top half of the strike zone. When he is slumping, his tendency is to pull the ball too much since he hits with power from right-center to the line.

BASERUNNING:

Though he rarely makes a mistake on the bases, he's relatively unaggressive at taking the extra base. He is a smart baserunner. When he does gamble, it's usually on an outfielder he wants to test.

FRED LYNN
OF, No. 19
LL, 6'1", 190 lbs.
ML Svc: 10 years
Born: 2-3-52 in
  Chicago, IL

1984 STATISTICS

AVG	G	AB	R	H	2B	3B	HR	RBI	BB	SO	SB
.271	142	517	84	140	28	4	23	79	77	98	2

CAREER STATISTICS

AVG	G	AB	R	H	2B	3B	HR	RBI	BB	SO	SB
.295	1301	4744	780	1400	311	38	195	791	610	689	55

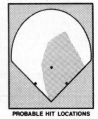

VS. RHP   VS. LHP   PROBABLE HIT LOCATIONS

FIELDING:

Once considered without peer in center field, Lynn has been proven mortal the last few seasons, although a gifted mortal. He still gets a great jump on balls and plays hitters well. Lynn's arm is above average, but recently he hasn't really gone after runners as aggressively as he once did.

Lynn's greatest strength may be his complete disregard of fences, and he's particularly fearless in big play situations. Many of his errors come at times when the game is gone, one way or the other, and his concentration may lag. He's probably not the best anymore, but he's still close to the top of the line.

OVERALL:

Matthews: "Lynn shows his outstanding ability from time to time, especially in clutch situations. He is very smooth and graceful in all facets of the game."

HITTING:

In his rookie season last year, Gary Pettis set team records in stolen bases and in driving teammates and his manager crazy with his failure to adjust his swing at the plate.

Among the fastest players in the league, Pettis entered 1984 with a power hitter's stroke--hands high, big swing--and didn't change it a bit even when he began striking out every other at-bat. Though nearly everyone tried, no one seemed able to change Pettis's approach.

A better hitter righthanded than lefthanded, Pettis proved he could hit most any kind of pitching, unless it was really good pitching--and that kind gave him fits.

The team project this off-season was sending Pettis to the Instructional League to teach him another swing, that of a contact hitter, and to work on his bunting. If Pettis shortens the stroke, he'll hit .260 in a bad year and rank among the league leaders in stolen bases. Pettis is a better bunter than he's shown, and his problem at this point is more confidence than execution.

If he makes the adjustment, he'll be a major league leadoff hitter. If he doesn't, he may find himself a pinch-runner and defensive specialist.

BASERUNNING:

The strength of Pettis' game is his running, and there aren't many American Leaguers capable of staying with him. His speed to first is exceptional, and, until his confidence dropped off late in the season, he was almost perfect in stealing.

He takes a good lead and has a great first few steps toward second and, even without a good jump, can outrun many throws. Once he learns pitchers, Pettis will be even more dangerous--providing, of course, that he's on base.

FIELDING:

One of the brightest outfield finds

GARY PETTIS
CF, No. 20
SR, 6'1", 166 lbs.
ML Svc: 2 years
Born: 4-3-58 in
  Oakland, CA

1984 STATISTICS

AVG	G	AB	R	H	2B	3B	HR	RBI	BB	SO	SB
.227	140	397	63	90	11	6	2	29	60	115	48

CAREER STATISTICS

AVG	G	AB	R	H	2B	3B	HR	RBI	BB	SO	SB
.238	172	487	87	116	13	9	6	36	67	132	56

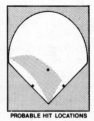

VS. RHP   VS. LHP   PROBABLE HIT LOCATIONS

of the season was Pettis, who showed Willie Wilson-like defensive speed in center and surprised most people with a strong, accurate arm that he was more than willing to display.

Pettis can reach balls few outfielders get to because of his speed and is at his most aggressive on defense. He will charge grounders and come up firing. Last season, he caught five men at home plate.

OVERALL:

No one doubts Pettis's potential. On base, he's a disruptive force to any defense, and in the outfield he's already among the best. The future of Pettis's value to a team, however, still lies in his ability to make contact with major league pitching. He hasn't shown that he can do that yet.

Matthews: "Pettis could become a very good leadoff man, but he has work to do offensively. Some players adjust to the big leagues, some never do. The jury remains out on Gary."

PITCHING:

A strong rookie showing on Ron Romanick's part would have been possible had he been given either offensive support or a better bullpen. If he had received both, he would have won 18 games, minimum, in his first season.

The 24-year-old righthander made the jump to the majors from Double A ball without any single overpowering pitch. What impressed the Angels, instead, was his poise and command of four pitches, the fastball, change, curve and slider, coupled with his ability to use them all. It is not unusual to get a 3-2 change from Romanick.

A sneaky quick fastball in the high 80 MPH range is made all the more effective because Romanick can and does deliver all his pitches from the same release point, an almost over-the-top motion. The smoothness of his delivery can deceive hitters.

Very much in control on the mound, Romanick maintains a professional cool in any situation.

Because he's not a power pitcher, Romanick must rely on control to win, and when he begins to tire, it is his control that he loses first. When that happened last season, he was wild in the strike zone, which led to his giving up a staff high of 23 home runs.

Still, Romanick is most effective when he is given a lead to protect. A tough competitor, Romanick is among a handful of good young finesse pitchers beginning to make their presence felt in the American League.

FIELDING:

Sound mechanics make up for the fact that Romanick is not especially quick,

RON ROMANICK
RHP, No. 37
RR, 6'4", 195 lbs.
ML Svc: 1 year
Born: 11-6-60 in
  Burley, ID

1984 STATISTICS

W	L	ERA	G	GS	CG	IP	H	R	ER	BB	SO	SV
12	12	3.76	33	33	8	229	240	107	96	61	87	0

CAREER STATISTICS

W	L	ERA	G	GS	CG	IP	H	R	ER	BB	SO	SV
12	12	3.76	33	33	8	229	240	107	96	61	87	0

and his cool on the field is an asset, too. He has a pair of moves to first base: one for show and one that's deceptively quick.

OVERALL:

Ron is a mature young pitcher who knows he must rely on ability, not raw power. He proved in 1984 that he is a determined competitor. He displayed winning form consistently all season, and had a fine rookie year and figures to improve with experience.

Because he relies exclusively upon command and a variety of pitches, he may never be the ace of a staff. But a pitcher with stuff who is capable of 15 wins or more is always at a premium in the majors. Romanick has it.

Matthews: "Ron is an impressive young pitcher. He pitched with more poise than you would expect from a rookie who skipped Triple A ball. He must continue to work hard and improve. Most think he will."

PITCHING:

If Luis Sanchez's right arm got him to the majors, his lack of concentration --or of a killer instinct--continually threatens to send him packing.

Sanchez throws as hard as all but a handful of short relievers, and he has a slider and a forkball to complement that heat. The problem? Sanchez seems incapable, or unconcerned, about remembering what works against which batters. When he's successful, and even more so when he's not, Sanchez remains more of a thrower than a pitcher.

Anyone requiring proof need only note that, when used exclusively in short relief, Sanchez has more wins than saves in his career. His propensity for giving up the tying run has driven three different Angels managers crazy, and if Sanchez is back this season, he may well drive a fourth Angels manager nutty.

His strength is that fastball, delivered with a smooth motion that seems to make the ball explode on the batter, and a resilient arm that reminds some of Pedro Borbon and his ability to pitch game after game, month after month.

On the mound, however, Sanchez is easily distracted by base hits, baserunners or noise from the stands. Several times a season, he will upset a teammate with a hands-on-the-hip look of disgust following an error behind him.

Sanchez's control improved in 1984, with a nearly 2-to-1 ration of strikeouts to walks, but his career ERA as a short man out of the bullpen says most of what needs to be said. Sanchez is hardly a lock when he comes in to stop a rally.

FIELDING:

Sanchez is a fine enough athlete, but

LUIS SANCHEZ
RHP, No. 40
RR, 6'2", 210 lbs.
ML Svc: 3 years
Born: 8-24-53 in
    Cariaco, VEN

1984 STATISTICS
W	L	ERA	G	GS	CG	IP	H	R	ER	BB	SO	SV
9	7	3.33	49	0	0	83	84	34	31	33	62	11

CAREER STATISTICS
W	L	ERA	G	GS	CG	IP	H	R	ER	BB	SO	SV
26	21	3.36	168	1	0	308	304	128	115	118	182	25

his fielding suffers from the same flaw as his pitching--no concentration. At one time or another, he has forgotten the number of outs, thrown to the wrong base and failed to cover bases simply by forgetting the situation.

Once he gets the ball in his glove, he's no certainty, either. Twice last year (in back-to-back games), his throwing error set up extra-inning losses.

OVERALL:

Sanchez remains a pitcher of immense potential and raw ability, but until someone can harness his mental focus, he will probably remain an inconsistent force on the mound.

He is capable of overpowering a team simply blowing pitch after pitch by the hitters. Sanchez has never put together a season that reflected his ability.

Matthews: "His inconsistency has frustrated many managers and pitching coaches. No one questions his 'stuff'; many have questioned his mode of operation."

HITTING:

A major disappointment in 1984, Dick Schofield remains long on potential and short on results at the plate, a man with a great-looking swing, but a man who all too rarely hits a baseball.

Schofield struggled all season, dropping into the .190s early and leveling off there against all comers. From June through late August, nearly two months, he didn't have an RBI.

Contact wasn't Schofield's main problem, though he struck out 79 times in 400 at-bats. The problem was he didn't adjust his swing, and instead of going for contact swung hard every time. The result was a lot of routine fly balls. Major league pitchers know how to handle kids who swing one way at everything.

Schofield's numbers throughout his minor league days, however, would seem to indicate that last year may have been a case of overanxiousness and an inability to change tactics in mid-season.

Schofield still possesses the raw athletic ability that attracted scouts to him in high school, it's just a question of whether he'll adjust.

Schofield showed an inclination to use only the left half of the field, with most of his hits coming to the left field side of second base, though he showed good bat control when asked to hit-and-run. Not an exceptional bunter, Schofield mostly seemed overmatched last season.

BASERUNNING:

At this point, Schofield is a basic run-by-number baserunner, a man who'll go from first to second and then think about whether or not to go on to third. He's not aggressive, though he's got above average speed. It was tough to assess Schofield's baserunning in 1984. He simply wasn't on the bases often enough.

FIELDING:

Schofield surprised many with his

DICK SCHOFIELD
SS, No. 22
RR, 5'10", 175 lbs.
ML Svc: 2 years
Born: 11-21-62 in
  Springfield, IL

1984 STATISTICS

AVG	G	AB	R	H	2B	3B	HR	RBI	BB	SO	SB
.193	140	400	39	77	10	3	4	21	33	79	4

CAREER STATISTICS

AVG	G	AB	R	H	2B	3B	HR	RBI	BB	SO	SB
.194	161	454	43	88	12	3	7	25	39	87	4

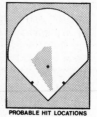

VS. RHP   VS. LHP   PROBABLE HIT LOCATIONS

ability at shortstop, showing better range and a slightly better arm than anyone had expected.

Possessing good range, Schofield can make the play in the hole and behind second base, too. If he has a weakness, it's his lack of fundamental knowledge. Several times last year Dick was not in the proper position on relay plays. The majority of his errors were throwing errors, rookie mistakes on hurried throws that shouldn't have been made.

OVERALL:

Schofield's attitude, a "Who cares," approach that irritated many teammates, may have been a coverup for his own intimidation at his jump into the majors. Whatever the reason, it has to change.

Matthews: "He is another rookie with potential who must show more than that if he's going to avoid the utility man role down the line."

HITTING:

For years Daryl Sconiers, a minor league hitter with few flaws, occasional power and the ability to hit to all fields, was hailed by the Angels as the someday-replacement for Rod Carew. All of the potential that big league teams saw in Sconiers is still there--and it is still potential.

Sconiers is a fine raw hitter, a man who can hit just about any pitch. Tough to strike out, he's also tough to walk, and therein lies Sconiers's weakness. He is totally undisciplined at the plate, a man who seems to treat every at-bat as a new adventure. If he has a book on opposing pitchers, what they throw, how they pitch him, he hasn't read it yet.

Nonetheless, he remains a threat every time he comes up. He is a strong fastball hitter; the fact that he can be made to swing at nearly anything isn't always to the pitcher's advantage. When he's hot, this guy can hit almost anything.

Sconiers does have a long, looping kind of swing and can be jammed. If he guesses with you, though, he can pull. Mostly, however, he tries to lay wood on the ball and let it go wherever it chooses to.

Many scouts still feel that if Daryl fills out and adds a little strength and a lot of discipline he could be a .300 hitter with 15-20 home run potential.

BASERUNNING:

On the bases, Sconiers is a threat only to himself and perhaps his team's rally. He has poor judgment, modest speed and no real idea of how to slide. The best you can say about his baserunning is that it's often as enthusiastic as it is eccentric. A long, lean lanky runner, Sconiers takes a while to get things unfolded. He also has a history of knee problems that don't help the situation.

DARYL SCONIERS
1B, No. 6
LL, 6'2", 195 lbs.
ML Svc: 2 years
Born: 10-3-58 in
San Bernardino, CA

1984 STATISTICS											
AVG	G	AB	R	H	2B	3B	HR	RBI	BB	SO	SB
.244	57	160	14	39	4	0	4	17	13	16	1
CAREER STATISTICS											
AVG	G	AB	R	H	2B	3B	HR	RBI	BB	SO	SB
.262	190	539	69	141	24	4	13	72	33	68	5

  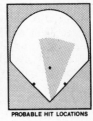

VS. RHP   VS. LHP   PROBABLE HIT LOCATIONS

FIELDING:

Sconiers may have among the worst hands in the majors, though he will stick himself in front of anything and, most of the time, make the play.

Balls hit to first--hard or soft-- have a tendency to bounce off Sconiers's glove, a situation that reminds pitchers to cover first on the most routine of ground balls. Sometimes it is tough to tell whether Sconiers lacks fundamentals or motor skills.

He also lacks confidence in his arm and opposing runners have tried on occasion to take advantage of that. Usually, they're glad they did.

OVERALL:

Matthews: "I am not really sure just where Sconiers's career is heading. He has trouble in the field and at the plate. The Angels see a lot of potential in him and are apparently willing to wait him out."

PITCHING:

After pitching exclusively in long relief for most of the past two seasons, Jim Slaton moved back into a starting role last June and proved, if nothing else, that he's still capable of some fine, complete game showings.

A tenacious competitor, Slaton has as his best pitch a fastball that is in the high 80 MPH range, but he sets it up with a good breaking ball, a slider and an occasional change-up. An experienced pitcher, he knows the hitters well.

Slaton's pattern is generally to get ahead with the curve and spot the fastball, mixing in other pitches to keep the hitter off stride. When the breaking pitch isn't working or if his control is off, his pitching suffers. When he is wild, it's usually around the plate. In later innings when he tires, his pitches come up and he's vulnerable to the long ball.

His main strength, tenacity, may also be his greatest flaw. Slaton is the kind of pitcher who won't come out of a game on his own--he has to be pulled. He will often pitch even when tiring, and thus, can be hit late in a game.

Slaton is a quick worker, and has a smooth, economical delivery that puts little wear on a shoulder that once suffered a small tear in the rotator cuff.

FIELDING:

Slaton may be one of the best at spearing shots back up the middle or simply fielding his position in general. He has very good hands, and is always in good defensive position on the mound, perhaps because he knows he must

JIM SLATON
RHP, No. 47
RR, 6'0", 185 lbs.
ML Svc: 13 years
Born: 6-20-50 in
    Long Beach, CA

1984 STATISTICS

W	L	ERA	G	GS	CG	IP	H	R	ER	BB	SO	SV
7	10	4.97	32	22	5	163	192	95	90	56	67	0

CAREER STATISTICS

W	L	ERA	G	GS	CG	IP	H	R	ER	BB	SO	SV
141	142	3.96	431	324	85	2422	2480	1183	1066	901	1088	11

rely on having the batter put the ball in play.

He has a quick move to first base, and will shorten his delivery with runners aboard. Slaton is smart with men on base.

OVERALL:

A "game situation" journeyman, Slaton has survived and even flourished on some bad teams in his career. His bulldog attitude on the mound has won more than 140 major league games.

Jim is an old-school team player; he willingly pitches in any role, though starting allows him to use all of his pitches and may be what he's still best suited for.

Matthews: "Jim had some fine outings in 1984. He gets the most out of his ability--he pitches 'smart'. He is versatile and can fill any pitching role."

HITTING:

If you rank the elements of his game on the basis of his strengths, Derrel Thomas's hitting would come last. Nevertheless, he can still do some damage with the bat.

He is a switch-hitter who likes to spray the ball around and use the entire field. He will hit an occasional home run; he has more power from the right side than from the left.

The one key to pitching to him is to keep the ball down. Thomas likes to hit mistakes up in the strike zone.

BASERUNNING:

Growing up in Los Angeles, Thomas had Maury Wills as his idol. He even insisted on wearing Wills's number when he broke into the big leagues with the Dodgers.

Thomas has great speed, but he has never stolen bases in Wills-like quantities. Two reasons: one is that he doesn't hit enough to get himself stealing opportunities, and also, he does not have Wills's quickness. Remember: quickness and speed are not synonymous.

But because of his pure speed, Thomas is a better than average baserunner, certainly capable of stealing a base at a pivotal time. He has a tendency to be careless at times, however.

FIELDING:

Derrel broke in as a second baseman and has played every position on the field except pitcher. His strongest position, however, is center field.

In fact, if he had the bat to match, he could be one of the more distinguished center fielders in baseball. He has a great throwing arm, is an exceptional judge of fly balls and appears to have gotten away from his troublesome basket catches.

Thomas can also do an adequate job in left and right, in addition to third

DERREL THOMAS
INF, No. 13
SR, 6'0", 160 lbs.
ML Svc: 14 years
Born: 1-14-51 in
Los Angeles, CA

1984 STATISTICS

AVG	G	AB	R	H	2B	3B	HR	RBI	BB	SO	SB
.243	122	272	29	66	12	3	0	22	23	37	0

CAREER STATISTICS

AVG	G	AB	R	H	2B	3B	HR	RBI	BB	SO	SB
.250	1534	4585	569	1144	152	54	39	358	445	579	138

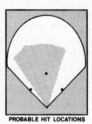

VS. RHP   VS. LHP   PROBABLE HIT LOCATIONS

base, shortstop and second base. He is a better defensive outfielder.

OVERALL:

Thomas is a very good person to have on a team, if only for his versatility. It gives a manager invaluable maneuverability to be able to use one player at eight defensive positions, plus as a high quality pinch-runner and occasional pinch-hitter from either side of the plate.

Campbell: "If Thomas were a strong hitter, he'd be one of the best players in the history of baseball. His versatility is just incredible. If he has one problem defensively, it is that he's a better outfielder than infielder, and he isn't going to hit enough to play the outfield regularly. But he has played 14 years in the big leagues, and I fully expect he will play 20 years."

HITTING:

For years in Minnesota under Gene Mauch, Rob Wilfong was the consummate throwback second baseman—a man who made contact, bunted superbly, moved his men along and did all the right things. That made him a good, solid player if rarely a spectacular one.

Wilfong languished on the bench most of 1983, got a chance to play in 1984 and surprised a lot of people, reminding the American League once again that in the right situation, Wilfong helps win games.

A lefthanded spray hitter, Wilfong will go to left, though the majority of his hits are up the middle or to right field. Virtually all his occasional power is to right.

He remains one of the premier bunters in baseball and has excellent bat control. He is much stronger against right-handed pitchers; lefties with big breaking balls wear Wilfong out.

At the plate, he's a much better hitter in situation-baseball, in at-bats where men are on base, moving or needing to be moved. He is a very, very unselfish player.

BASERUNNING:

Wilfong's speed is about average, but his ability on the bases is above average. He'll take the extra base, force throws and slide hard in double play situations and rarely makes mistakes. An aggressive runner, Wilfong is also an exceptional, creative slider. Block a base on him and he'll invent a way to get around you.

FIELDING:

Again, Wilfong is a solid if unspectacular player, with good hands and an average arm and great instincts. His range doesn't rank with the best in

ROB WILFONG
INF, No. 9
LR, 6'1", 185 lbs.
ML Svc: 8 years
Born: 9-1-53 in
Pasadena, CA

1984 STATISTICS

AVG	G	AB	R	H	2B	3B	HR	RBI	BB	SO	SB
.248	108	307	30	76	13	2	6	33	20	53	3

CAREER STATISTICS

AVG	G	AB	R	H	2B	3B	HR	RBI	BB	SO	SB
.259	782	2177	274	563	82	20	31	213	172	319	48

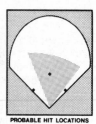

VS. RHP   VS. LHP   PROBABLE HIT LOCATIONS

baseball, but he rarely loses anything he should reach and turns the double play very well.

His arm blew out with too many Little League curveballs, and Wilfong can't play anywhere but second—unless, in an emergency, it's the outfield.

OVERALL:

Wilfong is a much better player than he's given credit for—his only problem is that he doesn't do any one thing exceptionally well—except bunt. He's not strong, has little power and probably won't hit .300 again, although he did one year.

Matthews: "Just wind him up and let him go, and he'll 'little ball' you to death, give you good defense and end up among the more popular men on the team."

PITCHING:

Mike Witt grew into the role of quality starting pitcher in 1984, leading the Angels in victories, strikeouts and highlights. He capped the season with a closing day perfect game, the first in team history.

That was an appropriate end to Witt's finest season, an indication perhaps that he may at last have harnessed control not only of his pitches but of his concentration as well. Early in the year he consulted a hypnotist and worked on focusing his attention for nine innings, not just five or six. The result was the blossoming of his big league potential.

Catcher Bob Boone, a veteran who has caught or hit the best of them, says Witt's fastball/curveball combination is the best in the league. Few pitchers would seem to have two out pitches of similar quality.

Witt's fastball has hit the mid-90 MPH mark on radar guns, and when he has control of his breaking pitch he can dominate both lefthanded and righthanded batters. He was in the league's top four in strikeouts last season.

The question mark on Witt has always been his lack of concentration--his inability to focus on what he's doing on the mound for a full game. His tendency in the past had always been to pitch marvelously, only to lose close games on a bad pitch.

Last season, he avoided those problems to a large extent, though he lost a 1-0 game in Baltimore by taking his eyes off a comeback roller and booting it.

Overall, he's on the threshold of becoming the pitcher the Angels believed they saw three years ago.

MIKE WITT
RHP, No. 39
RR, 6'7", 185 lbs.
ML Svc: 4 years
Born: 7-20-60 in
  Fullerton, CA

1984 STATISTICS

W	L	ERA	G	GS	CG	IP	H	R	ER	BB	SO	SV
15	11	3.47	34	34	9	246	227	103	95	84	196	0

CAREER STATISTICS

W	L	ERA	G	GS	CG	IP	H	R	ER	BB	SO	SV
38	40	3.76	132	100	23	708	699	330	296	253	433	5

FIELDING:

Angels coaches labored long and hard with Witt in spring training on fielding balls hit back at him. At 6'7", he understandably has problems fielding low ground balls.

However, Witt does have good athletic ability and quick hands. His move to first is average, but he has worked on keeping runners on base and shortening his high leg kick with men on.

OVERALL:

Witt may have one of the finest curves in the big leagues, and once he has batters looking for it, his fastball becomes all the more effective. He has 20-win potential right now and could be ready for that kind of season if he continues to make consistency an actuality, not just a goal.

Matthews: "Mike has a devastating breaking ball, one that can buckle the knees of a righthanded hitter. He could become one of the American League's premier pitchers."

PITCHING:

Few pitchers in the American League have been more consistent over the past three seasons--and had less to show for it--than Geoff Zahn.

Three years ago, he won 18 games utilizing change of speed and remarkable control. Though his ERA for the last two seasons has been lower than in that 18-win year, he's only been a .500 pitcher.

Simply put, Zahn is a quiet competitor whose stuff tries the patience of even the most disciplined hitters. He may have the best change-up in the game, and even when hitters look for it, they don't often handle it. His location is excellent.

Zahn's poise on the mound is unwavering, as is his faith in his off-speed pitches, his junk, to leave major league hitters spellbound. Because he seems to work inside and outside corners equally well and equally low, Zahn frequently survives three-hit innings without giving up a run.

Zahn's competitive instincts were illustrated best in 1984 by his rebound from injuries. A shoulder problem sidelined him early, yet he still nearly made the All Star team. Then he bounced back from arthroscopic knee surgery in August to pitch down the stretch in mid-September. Zahn will pitch with pain.

When he tires, his pitches tend to come up in the strike zone, a dangerous place for off-speed offerings. Rarely will he get burned with a fastball, the mid-80 MPH pitch he spots carefully. He will mix in sliders and sinkers and the most successful hitters against him seem content to take his pitches to the opposite field. Zahn forces batters to adjust to him.

FIELDING:

A product of the Dodger organization,

GEOFF ZAHN
LHP, No. 38
LL, 6'1", 175 lbs.
ML Svc: 10 years
Born: 12-19-46 in
  Baltimore, MD

1984 STATISTICS

W	L	ERA	G	GS	CG	IP	H	R	ER	BB	SO	SV
13	10	3.12	28	27	9	199	200	78	69	48	61	0

CAREER STATISTICS

W	L	ERA	G	GS	CG	IP	H	R	ER	BB	SO	SV
109	107	3.73	297	263	78	1811	1934	870	751	512	691	1

Zahn is well schooled in the fundamentals. He isn't quick and certainly isn't fast, but he gets the job done. No baserunner stole a base against Zahn all last season, credit both to a fine move and a slimmed-down delivery with men on base.

OVERALL:

Zahn is the portrait of a successful finesse pitcher, a man who will get beat only on HIS pitches and is resolute in his refusal to pitch beyond himself. A patient, crafty pitcher, Zahn has proved he can win big games without power pitches.

He's also the kind of pitcher teams feel they've beaten, even after they've lost. Zahn gives up lots of hits over the course of a season, but his ERA for the last two years is just 3.20.

Matthews: "Geoff is a very interesting pitcher to watch--very good at setting up the hitters, pitching to spots, changing speeds and utilizing all his pitches. He is really a pitcher, a craftsman."

JERRY NARRON
C, No. 34
LR, 6'3", 195 lbs.
ML Svc: 4 years
Born: 1-15-56 in
Goldsboro, NC

HITTING, BASERUNNING, FIELDING:

Used infrequently as a pinch-hitter and backup catcher, Narron proved last season that he could hit anybody's fastball and that he could hold his own with off-speed pitching, too.

Narron isn't likely to go the other way often, instead lining most of his hits to center and right field. He has a very quick bat, and he'll sit fastball first and try to adjust to anything else. He is a good hitter coming off the bench.

On the bases, Narron is a heads-up runner without much speed, but he's ag-gressive breaking up the double play. If he's running from first, it's a hit-and-run play.

Defensively, Narron won the confidence of the pitching staff with the games he called, and his arm was stronger than some scouts thought. A quiet player off the field, Narron loves to mix it up and be in the middle of things on the field. He can also play first base.

OVERALL:

He may be the best second-string catcher the Angels have had in years. A good reserve hitter and defensive player, Narron accepts his role and comes off the bench as an aggressive hitter. He is the type of player who would play anywhere to help a team.

Matthews: "Narron proved to be a capable pinch-hitter. Being a lefthanded batter was an added asset. He will hurt the opposition if the pitcher makes a mistake."

ROB PICCIOLO
INF, No. 10
Rr, 6'2", 180 lbs.
ML Svc: 8 years
Born: 2-4-53 in
Santa Monica, CA

HITTING, BASERUNNING, FIELDING:

Rob Picciolo's major league career has been based on his ability to fill holes on a utility role basis and his willingness to be the 24th or 25th man on a roster.

He may be the hardest man in the major leagues to walk: Picciolo's strategy at the plate is see the ball and swing. He didn't walk once last season. He has good bat control but too little discipline and can be made to pursue most any pitch within reach.

Still, he's adept at "little ball," can hit-and-run, bunt and move runners over. He's at his worst with no one on base.

Once on base, Picciolo is quick if not fast, and probably more cautious than uncertain. He's never been a base-stealer, nor particularly aggressive.

He does play hard. Defensively, Rob's best position is shortstop, though he can play any of the infield spots and, if asked, the outfield. He makes up for an average arm with a quick release and with his knowledge of the hitters.

OVERALL:

A quiet man who accepts his role, Picciolo is a journeyman utility player who can do a little of everything relatively well while not excelling at any single phase of the game. Forced into a starting role over a two-week period last year, Picciolo showed apprehension. He found himself with a bad case of the jitters before every game he started.

Matthews: "Rob has been a utility man throughout his career. His length of service in the big leagues suggests how well he has filled that role."

CHICAGO WHITE SOX

HITTING:

Quietly, oh so very quietly, Harold Baines has become one of the best hitters in baseball. This lithe lefty who speaks softly, if at all, now carries one of the biggest sticks in the American League. He cracked the .300 barrier for the first time in his career with his .304 average in 1984 and led the AL in slugging percentage with .541.

He also had a career high 29 homers and 94 RBIs, which was down a bit from his previous two seasons but understandable when considering the White Sox were last in the league in batting average. Perhaps Willie Keeler could "hit 'em where they ain't," but not even Harold Baines can drive 'em in when they ain't out there.

Impatience has always been Baines's chief flaw. A first ball swinger, he hits from a closed, upright stance. He likes the fastball anywhere he can get it but has become better at hitting the breaking ball.

When he first came up, lefthanders could paralyze him with breaking stuff. He has learned to handle breaking stuff much better. He has a tendency to chase breaking balls in the dirt from right-handers. Although it's coming along slowly, Baines is getting more disciplined at the plate. His 54 walks in 1984 were a career high, and his 75 Ks were the fewest since he became a full-time player.

What sets Baines apart as a hitter is his clutch ability. A phlegmatic sort who never gets too high or too low, he does not cave in to pressure. He is a streaky hitter who always seems to start slowly. If the season began in June, he'd be all-world.

BASERUNNING:

Baines has never utilized his good speed on the bases, particularly as a basestealer. He does not get a good jump and stole only one base in 1984.

HAROLD BAINES
RF, No. 3
LL, 6'2", 175 lbs.
ML Svc: 5 years
Born: 3-15-59 in
  Easton, MD

1984 STATISTICS

AVG	G	AB	R	H	2B	3B	HR	RBI	BB	SO	SB
.304	147	569	72	173	28	10	29	94	54	75	1

CAREER STATISTICS

AVG	G	AB	R	H	2B	3B	HR	RBI	BB	SO	SB
.279	687	2544	334	710	123	34	97	388	183	361	26

VS. RHP

VS. LHP

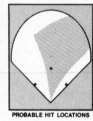
PROBABLE HIT LOCATIONS

FIELDING:

He is becoming one of the better right fielders in the game. If he has a problem, it is going back on a ball, but he has good range and a superior arm. He is fundamentally sound, hits the cutoff man and throws instinctively to the right base.

OVERALL:

Because he won't blow his own horn, Baines is often overlooked when it comes to post-season honors. But there are few better all-around players in baseball today.

Matthews: "Baines is not a player who sticks out every time you see the club, but he is always there doing his job. He is a quiet sort of player who just goes about his business. His strategy seems to be working because every time we see him, he is a better player than he was before."

PITCHING:

Floyd Bannister defies the mathematical theory that the whole is equal to the sum of its parts. Here is a pitcher who seems to have everything: four outstanding pitches, excellent control, and a delivery so smooth it looks as if it came from a Cuisinart. But so far it has not added up to the greatness that has been predicted time and again for him.

Can it be there is a missing ingredient? If there is one, it could be that Bannister lacks a mean streak. He is reluctant to move batters off the plate. As a consequence, he surrendered 30 home runs last year.

It is difficult to assess Bannister's performance in 1984. On one hand, he had a winning record (14-11) for a losing team. On the other, he had a career-worst 4.83 ERA.

Bannister comes over-the-top to three-quarters and is definitely a power pitcher who, because he has such a good curve, sometimes throws it too often.

He busts the fastball in on right-handers and tries to get them to chase his slider. He has a tendency to try to use all of his pitches rather than to rely on the ones that are going best for him on a given night.

For one so talented, Bannister sometimes seems to lack confidence in himself. At least he no longer seems burdened by the huge free agent contract he signed two years ago. A more aggressive approach overall might do wonders for him.

FIELDING:

The smoothness of his delivery is echoed in the manner in which Bannister fields his position. He is cat-quick

FLOYD BANNISTER
LHP, No. 24
LL, 6'2", 189 lbs.
ML Svc: 8 years
Born: 6-10-55 in
  Pierre, SD

```
1984 STATISTICS
W  L  ERA  G   GS  CG IP   H    R   ER  BB  SO  SV
14 11 4.83 34  33  4  218  211  127 117 80  152 0
CAREER STATISTICS
W  L  ERA  G   GS  CG IP   H    R   ER  BB  SO   SV
81 89 3.96 238 223 39 1456 1398 706 641 532 1115 0
```

on bunts and meticulous in mopping up balls hit up the middle. His move to first is above average, and he also will try for the pickoff at second base without hesitation.

OVERALL:

Although he still has not had the 20-game season everyone has predicted for him, Bannister has had two winning years in a row and seems to be on the right track. He will turn 30 during the 1985 season, and if he ever is going to make that leap from good to great, this should be the year.

Matthews: "It is time for Bannister to get up on the mound and throw--really throw the ball! He has to grip the ball, grit his teeth and growl at the hitters. There are some pitchers who are never expected to reach great heights: no one complains, because they do the job expected of them. But this guy, well, he could be so much better if he would act more like tough Mr. T instead of nice-guy Mr. B."

PITCHING:

Too bad Britt Burns didn't spend some time in the army: then he would have learned never to volunteer. With a pitching staff loaded with quality starters, Burns volunteered to open last season in the White Sox bullpen. It turned out to be the worst decision since Jesse James turned his back on Robert Ford.

Burns was semi-successful but little used as a reliever early in the year, was finally shoved back into the rotation and eventually ended up in limbo. Once one of the most promising lefthanders in baseball, Burns, still only 25, ended the season with a 4-12 record and a gross 5.00 ERA.

The gangly lefty has been pitching in tough luck since sustaining a shoulder injury in August of 1982, which apparently has taken a few inches off his fastball. Although he has a slow curve and a straight change to go with his fastball and hard slider, Burns is definitely a power pitcher who seems in need of a tuneup.

He generally has excellent control, but when he nibbles and gets behind in the count he gets in trouble. That seems to happen most often when he falls into a slow tempo, for which he is notorious. On the occasions when Burns has been persuaded to pitch faster, he has usually had success. Probably more than anything else, Burns needs to get his confidence back. A little luck wouldn't hurt, either. He has missed portions of each of the last three seasons because of illness or injury.

FIELDING:

Burns is awkward in the field and

BRITT BURNS
LHP, No. 40
RL, 6'5", 218 lbs.
ML Svc: 5 years
Born: 6-8-59 in
Houston, TX

1984 STATISTICS

W	L	ERA	G	GS	CG	IP	H	R	ER	BB	SO	SV
4	12	5.00	34	16	2	117	130	74	65	45	85	3

CAREER STATISTICS

W	L	ERA	G	GS	CG	IP	H	R	ER	BB	SO	SV
52	49	3.58	157	127	31	868	839	394	345	283	562	3

probably will never be better than adequate, no matter how hard he works. A congenital hip problem is largely responsible for that. He is not good at fielding bunts and is slow to react to balls hit through the middle. His teammates fear for his safety when they see hard liners go through the box. His move to first base is just average.

OVERALL:

Burns is a nice kid, maybe too nice sometimes, and a willing worker. He is too young and talented to be written off, but a change of scenery might help.

Matthews: "Burns needs to find a place for himself. He should get some expert advice and blend it with his own feeling about his best use as a pitcher. Then, he should set a course of action."

HITTING:

Julio Cruz got a lot of the credit for turning the White Sox into runaway winners when he came in a June 15 trade in 1983. So perhaps it wasn't altogether unfair that he received so much of the blame for the team's 1984 collapse.

Cruz did have an abysmal year any way you want to look at it. You want to look at batting average? Only once in his career had he ever hit lower than his .222 final average, and much of the year he hovered at the .200 mark. You want to look at stolen bases? His lowest previous total for a full season was 43. Cruz had 14 last year. How about errors? His 18 were a career high.

A sensitive player, Cruz probably tried too hard to justify the $4 million contract he had signed. The fact that the rest of the club stopped hitting, magnifying his own batting problems, also played on his mind and carried over into the field.

The fact is, Cruz was never a great hitter. A switch-hitter, he has much more power and hits for a higher average righthanded (.203 lefthanded vs .253 righthanded in 1984). Yet because most pitchers are righthanded, he hits from his weaker side two-thirds of the time.

He bats from a closed stance which is much more pronounced righthanded. When he bats lefthanded, teams play him over to the left and shallow. He likes the fastball up, so pitchers change speeds and keep the fastball down.

He could help himself immensely if he could bunt, especially from the left side, but he has never learned how.

BASERUNNING:

Despite his off-year, Cruz is regarded as a superior baserunner. When he was with Seattle, he was always near the top of the league in stolen bases. He seems to have tightened up since coming to the White Sox and is not getting as good a jump. He still has outstanding speed and needs to relax and use it.

FIELDING:

Cruz makes the spectacular play rou-

JULIO CRUZ
2B, No. 16
SR, 5'9", 180 lbs.
ML Svc: 7 years
Born: 12-2-54 in
Brooklyn, NY

1984 STATISTICS

AVG	G	AB	R	H	2B	3B	HR	RBI	BB	SO	SB
.222	143	415	42	92	14	4	5	43	45	58	14

CAREER STATISTICS

AVG	G	AB	R	H	2B	3B	HR	RBI	BB	SO	SB
.242	984	3416	491	825	109	24	23	245	404	440	328

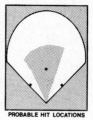

VS. RHP   VS. LHP   PROBABLE HIT LOCATIONS

tinely but sometimes makes the routine play with great difficulty. He has outstanding range and good hands, and his arm is far above average. He has a unique and exciting style in turning the double play, leaping over the runner, with both feet tucked under him, while still getting plenty of mustard on the throw. It sometimes enables him to complete a play that would be impossible for the more conventional second baseman.

OVERALL:

If White Sox fans, and Cruz himself, allow him to just be himself, he can be a tremendous asset.

Matthews: "He is such a good defensive second baseman and has such good baserunning skills that he really does not have to hit much to be valuable. He got down on himself for not hitting almost as quickly as the customers did, and the result was he didn't do the other things he can do to help a club."

PITCHING:

The White Sox might have been more concerned about Richard Dotson's puzzling slide in the second half of the 1984 season if they hadn't known there was a reason for it. He pitched well enough to make the All Star team in the first half, but ended the season a sub-.500 pitcher (14-15).

Explanation? Dotson suffered a slight groin pull in his last start before the All Star game; although the injury was not serious, it caused Dotson to make adjustments in his motion that messed up his mechanics.

Dotson has often been compared to Tom Seaver, but more for the compact, over-the-top delivery than for his repertoire, which is still limited. Dotson is very sound mechanically, but when he goes awry it sometimes takes weeks for him to get put back together. It happened the first half of the 1982 season, too.

Dotson's meat-and-potatoes pitches are his fastball and change-up. The fastball is good, but nothing like the buzz-bomb he used to throw in the minors before he learned that control was more important than MPH. It's the change that sets him apart.

For years Dotson has been struggling to perfect a breaking pitch for dessert, but for the most part his efforts have been a flat souffle. He gave up on the slider after one lamentable experiment and now has a big-breaking curve that he sometimes has difficulty controlling.

Control has always been a problem, and in 1984 he walked more than 100 batters for the second year in a row.

Dotson is extremely competitive and is not afraid to throw inside. His confidence has increased immeasurably, and he is a better pitcher for it. Last

RICH DOTSON
RHP, No. 34
RR, 6'0", 196 lbs.
ML Svc: 5 years
Born: 1-10-59 in
Cincinnati, OH

1984 STATISTICS

W	L	ERA	G	GS	CG	IP	H	R	ER	BB	SO	SV
14	15	3.59	32	32	14	245	216	110	98	103	120	0

CAREER STATISTICS

W	L	ERA	G	GS	CG	IP	H	R	ER	BB	SO	SV
70	55	3.71	163	155	39	1045	1002	484	431	424	561	0

year, he experimented with a split-fingered fastball (which he had never even thrown on the sidelines) in the late stages of a close game, and was pleased with the results.

But that was early in the year when everything was going his way.

FIELDING:

Dotson is slow delivering the ball to the plate, but compensates somewhat with a move to first that is above average for a righthander. He is a good athlete, quick off the mound, and above average at fielding his position.

OVERALL:

Dotson is already an accomplished pitcher, and he is young enough (26 years old) and willing enough to learn that he should get even better.

Matthews: "Although he is still a young man, it seems that Rich has been around a long time. He has developed a great change-up that really fools a lot of good hitters."

HITTING:

In all respects but one, 1984 was Carlton Fisk's worst year, and at age 37, the veteran catcher stands at a crossroads in his career. His .231 average was by far lower than he'd ever hit before, but he did hit 21 homers while missing 60 ball games.

There's no question that part of his problems were physical. An abdominal muscle pull kept Fisk out for long stretches at a time, and when he did play, he often played hurt. He was still able to rise to the occasion, however, as he did on the night he returned to action and he hit two big homers.

Fisk uses a straight-up stance and likes the fastball up, but he will go down and get one if he has to. He is a disciplined hitter who will wait for his pitch. When he gets it, he is a line drive type who will use all fields. When he's in a groove, he'll pull the ball more frequently, and pitchers will try to jam him and lefthanders will try to set him up first with breaking balls down and away. He is patient enough to sit back on a pitch, which helps him handle the breaking pitch.

He is a good bunter and hit-and-run man.

BASERUNNING:

Fisk is one of the best baserunners in the game, despite average speed. He seldom makes a mistake when going for the extra base, and he can steal on occasion. He was 6 for 6 in 1984. Fisk plays the game hard and is good at breaking up the double play.

FIELDING:

A take-charge type behind the plate, Fisk believes in working to the pitcher's strength rather than the batter's weakness. Most pitchers thrive under

CARLTON FISK
C, No. 72
RR, 6'2", 215 lbs.
ML Svc: 13 years
Born: 12-26-47 in
  Bellows Falls, VT

1984 STATISTICS

AVG	G	AB	R	H	2B	3B	HR	RBI	BB	SO	SB
.231	102	359	54	83	20	1	21	43	26	60	6

CAREER STATISTICS

AVG	G	AB	R	H	2B	3B	HR	RBI	BB	SO	SB
.278	1549	5521	876	1537	282	41	230	807	545	833	106

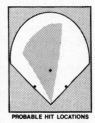

VS. RHP   VS. LHP   PROBABLE HIT LOCATIONS

his tutelage. He still has a strong arm, but the stomach injury cut his effectiveness. He is one of the best at keeping the ball in front of him. The big rap is still his deliberate style behind the plate, which some feel is detrimental to young pitchers like Britt Burns.

OVERALL:

When he's healthy, he is still one of the better catchers in the game. Fisk is fiercely proud and can be expected to work hard to regain his eminence in the game.

Matthews: "A good catcher, one who really knows what he is doing, can make all the difference to a team. Fisk is that kind of player. He missed 60 games last season, and you can't help but wonder if that could account for the White Sox's 1984 slide."

HITTING:

In his first two seasons in the major leagues, Scott Fletcher has not done anything to cause the White Sox to feel they have a shortstop problem. On the other hand, he has not done anything to convince them they don't.

In a word, he has been ordinary. He raised his average to .250 in his second year and displayed some occasional, very occasional, pop in his bat. He is patient at the plate and makes contact, so there is still chance for improvement.

Fletcher is a spray hitter who employs a straightaway stance. He likes the ball up but can be jammed with inside fastballs. Breaking balls outside have proved effective against him. He is a good hit-and-run man and an above average bunter who led the club in sacrifice hits.

He became the regular shortstop after sharing the position the year before with Jerry Dybzinski. The White Sox have not indicated any great rush to trade for another shortstop. If he continues to improve, they probably won't.

BASERUNNING:

Fletcher has above average speed and is becoming a little more willing to use it. He stole 10 bases in 1984, double the total in his rookie year. He goes from first to third well, and is an intelligent, scrappy player.

FIELDING:

Fletcher has a good arm and his range is a little above average. He now appears to be making the routine play a

SCOTT FLETCHER
SS, No. 1
RR, 5'11", 168 lbs.
ML Svc: 2 years
Born: 7-30-58 in
   Fort Walton, FL

1984 STATISTICS
AVG	G	AB	R	H	2B	3B	HR	RBI	BB	SO	SB
.250	149	456	46	114	13	3	3	35	46	46	10

CAREER STATISTICS
AVG	G	AB	R	H	2B	3B	HR	RBI	BB	SO	SB
.241	293	788	98	190	33	8	6	68	81	77	15

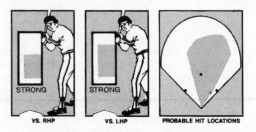

little more routinely than he did in his rookie season.

OVERALL:

Fletcher is a good player, but he has limited ability both at the plate and in the field. If he works hard, he can be an adequate shortstop and hold down a starting job at the major league level.

Matthews: "Scott is holding his own at short. The Sox must think that he has lots of potential, but so far, I haven't seen much. He had some defensive difficulties in 1983, though he seemed to smooth things out a bit last season."

HITTING:

Jerry Hairston is the Cadillac of pinch-hitters. For the second year in a row he led the American League with pinch-hits (18), and with 50 in his career with the White Sox, he is tied with Smoky Burgess for the club's all-time lead.

Although most hitters do better when playing regularly, Hairston seems to thrive on the do-or-die diet. His .304 average as a pinch-hitter was far better than his overall .260.

Although he now is pretty rough on the diamond, Hairston once was a diamond in the rough. Originally a White Sox, he had drifted into oblivion (sometimes known as the Mexican League), where White Sox manager Tony LaRussa stumbled on him during the 1981 players' strike.

Always a capable hitter, Hairston had failed because of defensive shortcomings but had improved enough that when LaRussa saw him, he was playing center field. He still plays the outfield occasionally and sometimes is used as a designated hitter, but it is his pinch-hitting ability that has finally given him some security.

Although he switch-hits, he has more power and is a better hitter from the left side. Of his ten homers over the last two years, nine have come as a lefthanded hitter.

Righthanded, he uses a straightaway stance and prefers the fastball up. From the left side, he opens up a little, which enables him to pull more. He will jump on any fastball in the strike zone. Pitchers try to change speeds on him and feed him breaking stuff down. If they make a mistake and hang one upstairs, he'll kill it.

BASERUNNING:

He has good speed but doesn't use it much (only two steals the last two seasons). He seems to lack confidence in his ability to steal and does not get a

JERRY HAIRSTON
PH/OF, No. 17
SR, 5'10", 180 lbs.
ML Svc: 7 years
Born: 2-16-52 in
   Birmingham, AL

1984 STATISTICS

AVG	G	AB	R	H	2B	3B	HR	RBI	BB	SO	SB
.260	115	227	41	59	13	2	5	19	41	29	2

CAREER STATISTICS

AVG	G	AB	R	H	2B	3B	HR	RBI	BB	SO	SB
.260	592	1203	161	313	60	6	18	139	202	171	4

VS. RHP   VS. LHP   PROBABLE HIT LOCATIONS

good jump. Conversely, Hairston tends to be a little overaggressive when running the bases.

FIELDING:

No matter what they thought in Mexico, Hairston is not a great outfielder —just a capable one. He has fair range and a fair arm. Runners don't go wild on him. He will catch anything in reach and can play all three positions.

OVERALL:

Hairston gets the most out of his limited ability.

Matthews: "He seems to concentrate more as a pinch-hitter, perhaps because that usually means the game is on the line. He's the type of player who won't hurt you and can help you in a lot of little ways."

HITTING:

What you see is not what you get when you look at Marc Hill. What you see is a strapping giant who should hit the ball to the moon. In batting practice, he does. But once the game starts, Hill becomes a spray hitter.

Earlier in his career, when he was with the Giants, Hill was expected to hit home runs. When he didn't, they gave up on him. Now he is determined to play within himself, to make contact, to advance the runner, to occasionally go for the long ball.

His five homers in 1984 were his most since 1977 and his at-bats (193) and hits (45) were his most since 1978. He is by no means an outstanding hitter, but he is no longer an automatic out, either.

Hill swings from a straight-up stance and is known as a strictly fastball hitter. So, of course, he sees almost nothing but breaking balls and off-speed pitches. He is a first ball hitter, but has become tenacious when he gets behind in the count.

BASERUNNING:

Notorious for his lack of speed, Hill represents no basestealing threat. In his entire professional career, going all the way back to 1970, he has attempted just a dozen steals and has been successful only twice. Yet, like many slow men, he has good baserunning judgment, and two years ago scored from second base on a sacrifice fly.

FIELDING:

He has just average hands, but a strong arm, and baserunners advance at their peril. His greatest asset as a catcher is his knowledge of the hitters

MARC HILL
C, No. 7
RR, 6'3", 240 lbs.
ML Svc: 10 years
Born: 2-18-52 in
   Elsberry, MO

1984 STATISTICS

AVG	G	AB	R	H	2B	3B	HR	RBI	BB	SO	SB
.233	77	193	15	45	10	1	5	20	9	26	0

CAREER STATISTICS

AVG	G	AB	R	H	2B	3B	HR	RBI	BB	SO	SB
.228	654	1715	139	391	60	3	34	194	172	231	2

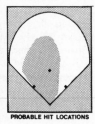

VS. RHP   VS. LHP   PROBABLE HIT LOCATIONS

and his rapport with his pitchers. He has the knack of making his pitchers feel comfortable.

OVERALL:

Hill is the ideal backup catcher because he accepts his role, and, defensively, there is little if any drop-off when he plays. If he played more often, he might hit better, too. He is an outstanding team player, and the White Sox realized that when they gave him a new two-year contract.

Matthews: "Chicago is very lucky to have someone as good as Marc Hill waiting in the wings to back up Carlton Fisk. He does a good job behind the plate and is willing to play the second-man role."

PITCHING:

Although he is a menacing presence when viewed from a pitching mound, LaMarr Hoyt is basically a pleasant person. But if you call him Fat Man, well, you'd better smile when you say that, pardner. When Hoyt was winning the Cy Young Award in 1983, he was looked on as pleasingly plump. After he suffered through the first losing season of his big league career, however, Hoyt was viewed in some quarters as being overweight. Hogwash, he says. "I am not any heavier now than when I was winning."

Something IS different, however. Hoyt gave up 31 homers in 1984, and except for one nearly perfect game against the New York Yankees he rarely resembled the pitcher who won 14 in a row to end the 1983 season.

Hoyt never did have blinding stuff. His fastball (he throws two kinds) is not overpowering but has good movement, particularly the sinker. He also has two kinds of sliders: one is more like a slurve, and the other is a straight change. If you can come up with another kind of pitch, Hoyt will oblige you and throw it, too.

His main assets have always been his pinpoint control and bulldog determination. It would be wrong to say his control deserted him last year, since he still walked only 43 batters in 235.2 innings. But he was getting behind in the count much more frequently than in the past, and his natural aggressiveness would be more a liability than an asset in those circumstances. Too often, when he challenged hitters, they accepted the challenge.

Hoyt has always been a great finisher but was having trouble getting started last year. Most of his problems come in

LaMARR HOYT
RHP, No. 31
RR, 6'3", 244 lbs.
ML Svc: 5 years
Born: 1-1-55 in
Columbia, SC

1984 STATISTICS

W	L	ERA	G	GS	CG	IP	H	R	ER	BB	SO	SV
13	18	4.47	34	34	11	235	244	127	117	43	126	0

CAREER STATISTICS

W	L	ERA	G	GS	CG	IP	H	R	ER	BB	SO	SV
74	49	3.92	178	116	39	941	1033	452	410	191	513	10

the first inning. Despite that, there has been talk that he will return to the bullpen as a short man in 1985.

FIELDING:

His delivery to home is slow, but he has an above average move to first base and is not reluctant to throw to second, either. He's slow to react on bunts and not a good fielder in general.

OVERALL:

Despite his off year (13-18), Hoyt has averaged nearly 19 wins a season in the three years he's been a starter. He is a streaky pitcher who can get in a groove and stay in it over long periods. Look for him to bounce back.

Matthews: "Cy Young Award winners seem to have difficulty repeating their success in the next year. The White Sox, as a whole, sort of fell apart last season, and while Hoyt did not really pitch badly, he did not get a lot of help."

HITTING:

When Ron Kittle hit .254 with 35 homers and 100 RBIs as a rookie, he was a little disappointed in himself. Imagine how he felt in 1984, when he hit only .215 (although he had 32 home runs and banged in 74 RBIs). If you said "devastated," then you don't know Ron Kittle.

Like his teammate Harold Baines, Kittle does not get down on himself when things are going badly. Unlike Baines, he seems to enjoy the good times. And either way, he is adept at articulating his feelings.

While most power hitters look to their home run and RBI totals for solace, Kittle feels he's too good a hitter to be batting .215. He has history to back him up. He batted .345 in Triple A the year he hit 50 homers.

Many of those home runs went to the opposite field, whereas in the majors Kittle has become more of a pull hitter. That is because the pitchers have been literally forcing him to pull, jamming him with fastballs up and in, and breaking bats, if not his heart.

When they're not jamming him, pitchers tease him with breaking stuff in the dirt. He hasn't developed the discipline yet to lay off. He struck out 137 times in 1984 and walked only 49 times.

He hits best when he has a chance to extend his arms and take advantage of his tremendous power to all fields.

BASERUNNING:

Kittle is faster than he looks and has good baserunning instincts. He had some success stealing as a rookie but in 1984 was thrown out on six of nine attempts.

FIELDING:

As his hitting suffered, so did his

RON KITTLE
LF, No. 42
RR, 6'4", 200 lbs.
ML Svc: 2 years
Born: 1-5-58 in
   Gary, IN

1984 STATISTICS

AVG	G	AB	R	H	2B	3B	HR	RBI	BB	SO	SB
.215	139	466	67	100	15	0	32	74	49	137	3

CAREER STATISTICS

AVG	G	AB	R	H	2B	3B	HR	RBI	BB	SO	SB
.235	304	1015	146	239	36	3	68	181	91	299	11

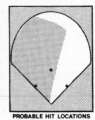

VS. RHP   VS. LHP   PROBABLE HIT LOCATIONS

defense. He has a strong arm, but does not judge fly balls well and does not get a good jump on the ball. He makes the routine play, but does not often make the difficult one.

OVERALL:

Kittle needs to assert mastery over the pitcher by being patient enough to wait for his pitch. He needs to improve considerably on defense, but could end up being a full-time DH.

Matthews: "Ron Kittle is a fellow who is going to be around a long time. Not only does he have tremendous power, he has the right kind of attitude."

HITTING:

After a big start, Rudy Law had an off year, hitting only .251. That's not enough for an outfielder with no power and a rag arm. So Law, an avid boxing fan, will have to pick himself off the canvas.

It won't be that easy. Law could be caught in a squeeze for playing time in 1985. Manager Tony LaRussa would rather move him from center field to left because of his arm, but he has to contend with both Ron Kittle and Tom Paciorek.

The biggest thing in his favor is that he is the best leadoff hitter on the club. Even there, however, he is not ideal, because he is a first ball hitter who does not walk much. He drew only 39 free passes in 1984. So in order to use his great speed once he gets on base, Law virtually has to hit .300 to be effective.

Law bats from an open stance and likes the fastball up and away. Righthanders can jam him with a slider on the fists, and he will chase pitches out of the strike zone. In general, pitchers try to change speeds and keep the ball down.

Although he uses the whole field, most teams play him to pull. He is a good bunter and, with his great speed, is a threat to beat it out when he does lay one down. He no longer is intimidated by lefthanders and usually is allowed to face them when he's going well.

BASERUNNING:

Hampered by nagging leg injuries, Law was as bad on the bases as he was at trying to get on them. He stole only 29 bases and was thrown out 17 times, which was five more times than in 1983, when he stole 77 bases. He still does not get a particularly good jump, but relies on his speed. He is not an aggressive slider. When he's right, he can be a disruptive force.

FIELDING:

He has improved as a flychaser to the

RUDY LAW
CF, No. 11
LL, 6'2", 176 lbs.
ML Svc: 5 years
Born: 10-7-56 in
Waco, TX

1984 STATISTICS

AVG	G	AB	R	H	2B	3B	HR	RBI	BB	SO	SB
.251	136	487	68	122	14	7	6	37	39	42	29

CAREER STATISTICS

AVG	G	AB	R	H	2B	3B	HR	RBI	BB	SO	SB
.276	537	1724	365	475	54	26	13	127	128	148	185

VS. RHP   VS. LHP   PROBABLE HIT LOCATIONS

extent that the only defensive rap on him now is that weak arm. Because he can chase down most balls hit over his head, he is able to play shallow and minimize his greatest deficiency. Runners still take advantage of him.

OVERALL:

Law should be playing left field, where his weak arm could be better hidden. With his great speed, he can create havoc in a defense once he gets on base. But because of his limited power, he must hit for a high average and utilize his speed to be effective.

Matthews: "He's got to have been disappointed with his 1984 season. Leg injuries to a player like Rudy are as worrisome as a rotator cuff to a pitcher. There are only a handful of players in the majors who can steal the way Law can: watching the way that some defenses go nuts when he is on base can be a treat."

HITTING:

Vance Law is an astute young man who knows that there are not too many .250 hitters with no power who survive long at third base. So, he made a conscious decision that transformed him into a .250 hitter with adequate power.

All of which makes Law living testimony to the power of positive thinking. Law banged out 17 homers in 1984 while actually raising his average nine points to .252. In his previous major league career, Law had totaled just nine home runs.

He did it by merely deciding that he was going to pull the ball and try for home runs instead of spraying it to all fields the way Charlie Lau had taught him. That might have been all right for a shortstop, which Law was when he came to the White Sox, but because third base has traditionally been a power position, it was not good enough.

He uses a straight-up stance and likes the fastball up and in. Most pitchers throw him breaking stuff down and in or show him the fastball up and away. He sometimes will chase it out of the strike zone. He will still take the fastball down and away to right field with good effect.

BASERUNNING:

Vance has just average speed and is an average baserunner with a tendency toward conservatism. He attempted only five steals last year and was caught once. He has never really applied himself to this phase of the game.

FIELDING:

The son of Vern Law, Vance has inherited his father's strong arm. In the past he was erratic at shortstop, but he

VANCE LAW
3B, No. 5
RR, 6'2", 185 lbs.
ML Svc: 4 years
Born: 10-1-56 in
Boise, ID

1984 STATISTICS
AVG	G	AB	R	H	2B	3B	HR	RBI	BB	SO	SB
.252	151	481	60	121	18	2	17	59	41	75	4

CAREER STATISTICS
AVG	G	AB	R	H	2B	3B	HR	RBI	BB	SO	SB
.250	465	1389	167	347	61	11	26	161	123	199	14

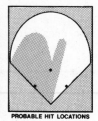

STRONG VS. RHP   STRONG VS. LHP   PROBABLE HIT LOCATIONS

has become solid and sometimes even spectacular at third base. He plays well off the line, but makes the backhanded dive play very well and can afford to give hitters the line.

OVERALL:

If he can continue to demonstrate the kind of power he showed in 1984, Law is a good enough fielder to be a quite adequate third baseman for years to come. It is doubtful he'll ever go beyond that level, however.

Matthews: "I have seen him make some really great plays in the field--he can dive and make the backhanded catch with the best of them. His defensive prowess, however, seems to come and go. At this stage, Chicago is getting the best of him."

HITTING:

It has often been said that with Greg Luzinski's compact swing, he could hit a home run in a phone booth. Alas, in 1984 it seemed that a phone booth was the only place The Bull could hit a home run.

Luzinski can still hit the ball a long way. He proved that when he won the major league longball contest and its $50,000 first prize. But that was against a batting practice pitcher. Luzinski has always been spectacular in batting practice. Until 1984, he was often spectacular in the game, too.

But he hit only 13 home runs, and most of those came in bunches. His awesome power was shackled by fastballs that jammed him and shattered both his bat and his confidence. Luzinski, who in the past had been able to ride out his slumps comfortable in the knowledge that this, too, would pass, for once admitted he was shaken and pressing.

Luzinski has always been a patient hitter who will sit on a pitch. But there were times when White Sox fans thought he was too patient. It seemed to them that their sitting Bull was going to wait forever before pulling the trigger.

Whereas in the past he could fight off inside pitches and hit them to the opposite field, in 1984 he more often than not was popping them up. He has always had some trouble hitting breaking balls, but he has also been one of the game's best mistake hitters. Last season, either pitchers were making no mistakes, or Luzinski simply was not getting around on the ball when they did.

Despite his power, Luzinski is not a dead pull hitter and still takes the outside pitch to right.

BASERUNNING:

He has an uncanny knowledge of when to take the extra base, which he does more frequently than one would expect in a man so ponderous. Although knee surgery has wrecked his speed, it did not take away his baserunning instincts: and if he catches a pitcher napping, he will

GREG LUZINSKI
DH, No. 19
RR, 6'1", 256 lbs.
ML Svc: 13 years
Born: 11-22-50 in
Chicago, IL

1984 STATISTICS											
AVG	G	AB	R	H	2B	3B	HR	RBI	BB	SO	SB
.238	125	412	47	98	13	0	13	58	56	80	5
CAREER STATISTICS											
AVG	G	AB	R	H	2B	3B	HR	RBI	BB	SO	SB
.276	1821	6505	880	1795	344	24	307	1128	845	1495	37

STRONG

VS. RHP

STRONG

VS. LHP

PROBABLE HIT LOCATIONS

steal, something he did five times in 1984.

FIELDING:

He no longer plays in the field. His knees will not permit him to roam the outfield. He could play first base in a pinch (his original position in the minors) and not disgrace himself.

OVERALL:

Luzinski at 34 years of age is not old, but his batting average has slipped drastically over the last two years and last year his power production fell off with it. He needs to get off to a good start in 1985, but he generally does not perform well in cold weather. The odds seem to be stacked against him, but this is one time the Bull needs to grab the situation by the horns.

Matthews: "It is hard to imagine Greg not hitting; he looks as if he could just stand at the plate and smash a home run. But even the best players get older, and it just doesn't get any easier."

PITCHING:

He's only 24 years old, but already Gene Nelson is pitching for his third major league team. Nelson has been living in the fast lane since he was 19, when his 20-3 season in A ball earned him the big leap right to the New York Yankees.

He wasn't ready then, and there are those who wonder if he ever will be. Time and a live arm are on his side, however. His fastball has such great movement on it that White Sox bullpen catcher Art Kusnyer says Nelson is the only pitcher on the staff he refuses to warm up without a mask.

Nelson also throws a good forkball, a straight change and a slider. Although he generally has above average control of the fastball, he sometimes has a tendency to let the hummer ride up belt-high. He was tagged for 9 homers in 74 innings with the White Sox.

He sometimes hangs the forkball, too, another invitation for the big boppers to do their thing. He generally throws the forkball when he is ahead of the hitter, but if he knows the batter is a good fastball hitter, he may start him out with the forkball.

He went on a weight-training program over the winter in hopes of adding even more pop to his fastball, and the White Sox were considering trying him as their late-inning stopper. In that role, he would probably go exclusively with the fastball and forkball, which, when he gets it down, can be a strikeout pitch for him.

GENE NELSON
RHP, No. 30
RR, 6'0", 172 lbs.
ML Svc: 3 years
Born: 12-3-60 in
  Tampa, FL

1984 STATISTICS

W	L	ERA	G	GS	CG	IP	H	R	ER	BB	SO	SV
3	5	4.46	20	9	2	74	72	38	37	17	36	1

CAREER STATISTICS

W	L	ERA	G	GS	CG	IP	H	R	ER	BB	SO	SV
12	18	5.02	60	40	5	267	283	161	149	121	134	1

FIELDING:

Nelson is a good fielder who has two distinct moves to first base that make him dangerous to take off on. One is a sort of snap move that will catch runners off guard and the other is just your basic move to first.

OVERALL:

Matthews: "Nelson has been used as a starter and a reliever, and because he's so young that might be disconcerting for him. He would benefit from knowing his role at the outset. If he goes to his fastball more and throws strikes consistently on the inside with it, he can be a very tough pitcher."

HITTING:

Tom Paciorek would do well to pay heed to Satchel Paige's advice: Never look back, something may be gaining on you. In Paciorek's case, that something could be age, although a case could be made that it was the broken hand that limited the 38-year-old veteran to 111 ball games in 1984.

Paciorek, who in six previous American League campaigns had averaged .301, batted only .256 and without much pop. It was a long struggle for Paciorek to prove he was a major league hitter, but he did it. Now he's going to have to prove he can be effective in the limited role he'll probably be assigned by the White Sox.

Paciorek is a streaky hitter, hence he does much better when he plays every day. He bats from a slightly open, crouched stance that resembles a right-handed Rod Carew. Like most hitters, he thrives on fastballs, particularly down in the strike zone. Righthanders try to ride the fastball up and in on his fists and keep the breaking ball down.

Lefthanders hope he'll chase fastballs away. They try to change speeds and they, too, want the breaking ball down. Smart pitchers know better than to feed him a first pitch in his comfort zone. Although he is not a home run hitter per se, it would be foolish to ignore him as a longball threat. He uses the whole ballpark and has decent power to the opposite field.

While he's never hit more than 15 homers in a year, he hits lots of doubles and is well suited to Comiskey Park with its deep power alleys. He's enough of a contact hitter to be effective on the hit-and-run and is a good bunter.

BASERUNNING:

Once, he was fast enough to be an All-America defensive back (Houston), but now his speed is average at best. He has a knack for picking his spots, however, and in the last two years he has been successful in 12 out of 13

TOM PACIOREK
OF/INF, No. 44
RR, 6'4", 210 lbs.
ML Svc: 13 years
Born: 11-2-46 in
Detroit, MI

1984 STATISTICS
AVG	G	AB	R	H	2B	3B	HR	RBI	BB	SO	SB
.256	111	363	35	93	21	2	4	29	25	69	6

CAREER STATISTICS
AVG	G	AB	R	H	2B	3B	HR	RBI	BB	SO	SB
.283	1185	3610	443	1021	217	29	78	449	230	605	51

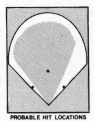

STRONG — VS. RHP   STRONG — VS. LHP   PROBABLE HIT LOCATIONS

stolen base attempts.

FIELDING:

With deteriorating speed and a below average arm, Paciorek is not a good outfielder, although he will catch balls that are within his range. He is now better suited to first base because of his good hands. He is becoming much more adept at digging throws out of the dirt, and is more an asset than a liability at first.

OVERALL:

Paciorek is at an age where it is difficult to determine if his slippage in 1984 was just a slump or the beginning of a trend.

Matthews: "He is a hardworking player who will get the most out of the talent that remains. He has had some difficulty making a mental adjustment to his more limited role, but if he can do that, he will be a handy guy to have on the team."

PITCHING:

Like many other White Sox pitchers, Ron Reed was miscast last year in the role of principal closer. Although he had been a short reliever for most of his eight years in Philadelphia, he had been principally the setup man and certainly was never called on to save a game two nights in a row. He had never had more than 17 saves in a season for the Phils and, since 1978, when he recorded his career high, only once had more than nine.

So the staff-leading 12 saves he recorded in 1984 would seem respectable, were it not for the fact that, for some reason, the club had greater needs and expectations for this 42-year-old pitcher.

Reed is still a power pitcher. He has always kept himself in excellent physical condition, minimizing the age factor. His sinking fastball is so "heavy" that some hitters liken it to hitting a shotput. His second pitch is a slider. Never one to rest on his laurels, he has been developing a forkball as well.

For a reliever, Reed does not have exceptional control, but he exploits his 6'6" frame with a lot of motion, and that makes him tough on righthanders. Reed tries to keep the fastball in on the hands and hit the corners with his breaking stuff. He comes at the hitters from three-quarters and has a high leg kick, making it difficult for them to pick up his pitches.

FIELDING:

The high leg kick and slow delivery

RON REED
RHP, No. 36
RR, 6'6", 225 lbs.
ML Svc: 17 years
Born: 11-2-42 in
LaPorte, IN

1984 STATISTICS												
W	L	ERA	G	GS	CG	IP	H	R	ER	BB	SO	SV
0	6	3.10	51	0	0	72	67	29	25	14	57	12
CAREER STATISTICS												
W	L	ERA	G	GS	CG	IP	H	R	ER	BB	SO	SV
146	140	3.46	751	236	55	2476	2374	1084	953	633	1481	10

allow runners to take advantage, especially since his move to first is just average. Despite his athletic ability, Reed is not a particularly good fielder. He does not cover first well and has trouble with bunts to his right.

OVERALL:

Given his age, you have to wonder how much longer he can continue to be effective. If he is used right, pitching the seventh and eighth innings to set up the short man, Reed can probably be an asset again.

Matthews: "Now, here is a guy who can pitch. He has been around so long and seen so many changes, I wonder what goes through his mind as he faces each season's phenoms. Many of them have come and gone and are long gone now, but Reed just keeps on tossing the ball."

PITCHING:

If Tom Seaver left his heart in New York, it would come as a surprise to anyone who saw him pitch for the Chicago White Sox in 1984. Reluctant as he might have been to leave the Mets, Seaver proved to be the consummate professional in his first season in the American League.

His fastball may be but a whisper of what it once was, but it was good enough to win 15 games for the disappointing White Sox. Check that! It was good enough to win 20, but repeated bullpen failures hurt Seaver more than opposition bats did.

Seaver is a bit of an enigma. While he still is basically a power pitcher, he tries to keep the fastball out of the strike zone—or at least out of the hitting zone. That he is successful at this is attested by those 15 wins and the fact that his 131 strikeouts were second high on the team. That he is sometimes not successful would account for the 27 homers he surrendered, a career high.

The rest of Seaver's repertoire includes a slider, curve, and straight change. His control is outstanding and his mechanics impeccable. He's been told that he could pitch until he's 45 years old because his delivery does not exact a toll on his arm. His legs, which provide his tremendous thrust, do take a beating, and he has had occasional problems there.

He is the classic overhand pitcher, but now occasionally comes down against righthanders.

FIELDING:

Seaver has a high leg kick and thus

TOM SEAVER
RHP, No. 41
RR, 6'1", 210 lbs.
ML Svc: 18 years
Born: 11-17-44 in
       Fresno, CA

1984 STATISTICS
W	L	ERA	G	GS	CG	IP	H	R	ER	BB	SO	SV
15	11	3.95	34	33	10	236	216	108	104	61	131	0

CAREER STATISTICS
W	L	ERA	G	GS	CG	IP	H	R	ER	BB	SO	SV
288	181	2.80	593	586	223	4366	3568	1488	1358	1265	3403	0

is slow in delivering to home and, moreover, does not have an exceptional move to first. But, as in all things, he is meticulous in holding the runner and knows when to be particularly wary. He is a better than average fielder.

OVERALL:

Even when he had blinding stuff, Seaver was a thinking man's pitcher. Every pitch he throws has a purpose and he is outstanding at setting up a hitter. With a year in the American League under his belt, and provided he brings the same physical skills to the mound, he could have an even better year in 1985.

Matthews: "He is a total professional and a worthy role model both personally and professionally. He has one of the most intelligent approaches in the game and largely because of it, Seaver will be around for still a few more years."

HITTING:

Roy Smalley was too young to remember how Chicago fans booed his father when he played shortstop for the North Side Cubs in the early 1950s. But he got a taste of how it must have been when he was traded to the White Sox in the middle of the 1984 season.

Smalley was singled out as a target for the fans' dissatisfaction with the poor showing of the 1983 AL West champs; and the more they booed him, the worse he performed.

A dependable hitter for his entire career, Smalley ended up hitting only .170 for the White Sox in his 47 games.

A chronic back problem which surfaced in the 1981 season has blighted but not extinguished Smalley's once bright career. Since then, although he is a switch-hitter, he has been used primarily as a lefthanded hitter. He still swings from the right side when he faces lefthanders, but he doesn't face them often anymore.

Smalley has decent power and before the injury once hit 24 home runs for the Twins. When he was with the Yankees and batting almost exclusively lefthanded, he was able to aim at the short porch in right field and produce some good power totals, but in spacious Comiskey Park the home runs don't come as readily for him.

He is a smart hitter who will sit on a pitch, and he makes enough contact to be a hit-and-run man. Pitchers try to crowd him with fastballs in on the fists.

BASERUNNING:

Smalley is an intelligent baserunner, but because of his back problems has below average speed. He is not a threat to steal.

FIELDING:

Roy has inherited his father's strong arm, but has a better idea of where he's throwing the ball. When they weren't

ROY SMALLEY
SS/3B, No. 12
SR, 6'1", 182 lbs.
ML Svc: 10 years
Born: 10-25-52 in
Los Angeles, CA

1984 STATISTICS

AVG	G	AB	R	H	2B	3B	HR	RBI	BB	SO	SB
.212	114	344	32	73	12	1	11	39	37	65	3

CAREER STATISTICS

AVG	G	AB	R	H	2B	3B	HR	RBI	BB	SO	SB
.257	1301	4501	597	1156	188	20	123	558	607	711	24

booing the elder Smalley because of his frequent throwing errors, Cubs' fans used to joke about their double play combo of Miksis-to-Smalley-to-Addison Street (which lies behind first base at Wrigley Field). Roy Jr. still has the arm to play shortstop, but not the range. He's better at third, but again his range is limited so first base may now be his best position.

OVERALL:

Matthews: "With thanks to George Steinbrenner, Smalley is working on a long-term contract that is said to pay him $800,000 a year. Not many teams are willing to pay that much for a player who is not going to play every day. The White Sox gambled that Smalley could add enough punch to their offense to pull them out of their tailspin, but it was a gamble that failed. There does not ap-appear to be a regular spot for Smalley on the White Sox, so he will remain a very high-priced utility player."

PITCHING:

When a French detective has a puzzle to solve, the maxim used is "Cherchez la femme"; that is, "Look for the woman." But when baseball people scratch their heads over a pitcher who has had two bad years in a row after being one of the most dependable relievers in his league, it's usually "Look to the fastball."

Dan Spillner had two outstanding seasons under his belt when he inexplicably started to unravel in 1983. He started 1984 just as poorly, and although he did a little better after joining the White Sox he still was not the Dan Spillner who had posted a 12-10 record with 24 saves and a 2.49 ERA for Cleveland in 1982.

Cherchez le fastball? To be sure, Dan Spillner's fastball is probably not quite what it used to be. But it still is his primary pitch and an effective weapon, as long as he can keep it down. When he does, the pitch has good movement, running in on righthanders and dipping away from lefties.

But Spillner has been plagued with mechanical problems which sometimes cause his fastball to ride up into the strike zone. That accounts for the seven home run balls he served up in just 48 innings after coming to the White Sox in mid-season.

Spillner has a slider, but it is just average, and he has been working on a curveball. So far he has had trouble controlling it. He is also working on a straight change. Spillner knows how to pitch and has good control. He uses the corners very effectively and is not afraid to go after hitters with his good fastball.

DAN SPILLNER
RHP, No. 37
RR, 6'1", 190 lbs.
ML Svc: 11 years
Born: 11-27-51 in
Casper, WY

1984 STATISTICS

W	L	ERA	G	GS	CG	IP	H	R	ER	BB	SO	SV
1	5	4.89	36	8	0	99	121	61	54	36	49	2

CAREER STATISTICS

W	L	ERA	G	GS	CG	IP	H	R	ER	BB	SO	SV
71	86	4.27	504	120	19	1401	1502	747	664	572	837	49

He needs to get more consistent control of his breaking pitches.

FIELDING:

Spillner has just an average move to first base. He is a thorough professional who understands the importance of fielding his position well and does a good job of it.

OVERALL:

Matthews: "Spillner is one of those versatile types who has been used as a starter, long reliever, and short man. In the latter capacity he was outstanding for two years with Cleveland, but is now more suited to being the setup man. If he can keep the fastball down and master the curveball, Spillner, a gutsy type and a good competitor, can be a valuable contributor to the White Sox staff."

HITTING:

When a hitter bats .294 and clouts 24 homers in only his second season in the major leagues, that is usually considered a pretty good year's work. But more is expected of Greg Walker. Much more. Walker made strides as a hitter in 1984, but there are those who expect him to one day challenge for a batting championship. And he is already giving evidence that, as he matures, his power figures will blossom, too.

What has everyone so excited is his picture-book swing. A disciple of the late Charlie Lau, Walker is close to mechanical perfection. He is also a student of the art of hitting.

He has a slightly closed stance and is a first-ball hitter. A little more selectivity would make him an even better hitter. He is a tremendous fastball hitter and disciplined enough that he will take the outside fastball to the opposite field, where he has good power.

Righthanded pitchers try to jam him, change speeds, and keep the ball down. Lefthanders feed him breaking stuff. But Walker is the type who learns from his mistakes, as a result, most pitchers try to change their pattern when facing him.

He still has some trouble against lefthanders, and when he first started playing every day because of an injury to Tom Paciorek, he went into a slump against all kinds of pitching. But he finished with a rush, hitting .315 in August and .381 in September. His 24 homers were most for a White Sox first baseman since Richie Allen hit 32 in 1974.

BASERUNNING:

He has average speed, but knows when to take the extra base. Though he is not a great threat to steal, he had eight in 13 attempts last season.

FIELDING:

Walker made great improvements in

GREG WALKER
1B, No. 29
LR, 6'3", 205 lbs.
ML Svc: 2 years
Born: 10-6-59 in
Douglas, GA

1984 STATISTICS

AVG	G	AB	R	H	2B	3B	HR	RBI	BB	SO	SB
.294	136	442	62	130	29	2	24	75	35	66	8

CAREER STATISTICS

AVG	G	AB	R	H	2B	3B	HR	RBI	BB	SO	SB
.287	265	766	97	220	47	6	36	137	65	126	10

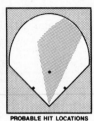

VS. RHP   VS. LHP   PROBABLE HIT LOCATIONS

1984 after attending an off-season aerobic dance class to improve his agility. He committed only four errors all season, just one more than he had made on opening day alone as a rookie. He handles the routine play well, but still has just average range. Walker's arm is only average, too.

OVERALL:

His ability plus his attitude make Walker a candidate for future stardom. He still needs to hit lefthanders better, but he won't do it until he is given the opportunity to play every day. That should come this season.

Matthews: "Greg appears to have the makings of a real major league power hitter. His swing is so mechanically sound that it could be used as an example to all young hitters. He should have an exciting career."

JUAN AGOSTO
LHP, No. 50
LL, 6'2", 187 lbs.
ML Svc: 2 years
Born: 2-23-58 in
      Rio Piedras, PR

PITCHING, FIELDING:

A cursory glance at Juan Agosto's numbers for 1984 would indicate a fairly successful season. He had a 2-1 record with 7 saves, and his 3.09 ERA was a full run better than in his rookie year of 1983.

But one telling number tells a different story: Agosto walked 34 batters in 55 innings, a figure that is anathema to a relief specialist. In addition to too many walks, Agosto got behind in the count too often. That is particularly bothersome to a pitcher whose fastball is just ordinary.

Although he once threw a pretty fair curve, Agosto abandoned it when he went to the bullpen and now throws just the fastball and a pretty good slider that is particularly effective against left-handed hitters.

Agosto's regular move to first is ordinary, but he also has a snap throw from the hip that can be dangerous. He is an average fielder.

OVERALL:

Matthews: "Agosto is not afraid to challenge hitters. He tries to throw strikes, but he just can't always do it and that is his downfall. Because of the control problems he is not suited to short relief, but when he's on target he's tough on lefties."

JERRY DYBZINSKI
SS, No. 20
RR, 6'2", 180 lbs.
ML Svc: 5 years
Born: 7-7-55 in
      Cleveland, OH

HITTING, BASERUNNING, FIELDING:

Jerry Dybzinski looks like a croquet wicket at shortstop but has been treated more like a croquet ball during his major league career. In other words, he's been knocked around a bit and never has had a chance to play on a regular basis.

Still, he is a decent player who works hard. He has a little better than average range in the field, but his arm is only average for a shortstop, which is his primary position. He has good speed, though, and is a good baserunner.

As a batter, Dybzinski is strictly a spray hitter. He's had only three home runs in over 900 at-bats in the major leagues. He bats from a straight-up stance and hits much better against lefthanders. Dybzinski can be jammed with fastballs or fooled by breaking pitches low and away.

OVERALL:

Matthews: "Dybzinski is the kind of player who appreciates what he has and does not make waves. He's good for the chemistry of a team that can afford to carry a light-hitting utility player."

BERT ROBERGE
RHP, No. 53
RR, 6'4", 190 lbs.
ML Svc: 3 years
Born: 10-3-54 in
    Lewiston, ME

PITCHING, FIELDING:

Bert Roberge was ready to call it a career when White Sox general manager Roland Hemond talked him into giving it another try. The likable righthander was glad he did when he got an early call up to the big club.

He did not dazzle anyone but didn't disgrace himself, either. Consistency was lacking, however. Roberge's big pitch is the forkball, which he has developed in recent years. His fastball sinks and when he is right his infielders get a lot of ground balls.

Roberge tries to get ahead of the hitter and establish superiority in the count. And he has to keep his pitches down, down, down, or they might go up, up, and out.

He fields his position well, which is an asset for a pitcher who lives on a ground ball diet. His move to first is just fair.

OVERALL:

Matthews: "Roberge is the type of player who has knocked around the fringes for quite a while. He is better suited to short relief, but he is not consistent enough to be a closer."

MIKE SQUIRES
1B, No. 25
LL, 5'10", 190 lbs.
ML Svc: 7 years
Born: 3-5-52 in
    Kalamazoo, MI

HITTING, BASERUNNING, FIELDING:

Mike Squires can just about do everything. He can play first base, he can catch and he can play third base. But the one thing he cannot do keeps him from being an everyday ballplayer.

Squires cannot hit for power, and the position he plays best--first base--demands a power hitter. Squires is a very disciplined hitter who will make the pitcher throw strikes. If the pitcher has to come in the strike zone with a fastball, Squires can punish him.

He makes good contact and uses the whole field, but in 1984 he had his worst year with the bat, probably because he saw such limited duty. As a first baseman, Squires has few equals. As a baserunner, he has better than average speed, but doesn't use it aggressively. He will, however, go hard into second to break up the double play.

OVERALL:

Matthews: "He can save an infield a lot of errors with his deft glovework at first base, but few clubs can afford the luxury of a first baseman who hits almost no home runs. A pity, because he is not a bad hitter and is a good man to have around."

CLEVELAND INDIANS

PITCHING:

No one made much of a fuss when the Indians obtained righthanded reliever Luis Aponte from Boston before the end of spring training last year, and that's the way it stayed.

Aponte has a tricky herky-jerky side-arm delivery that produces good results against righthanded hitters. He throws a fastball, curve, slider, forkball and an alleged spitter. Aponte never admitted throwing an illegal pitch, and the Indians' coaching staff swore he didn't. There are some hitters, however, who will tell a different tale.

Manager Pat Corrales didn't show much faith in Aponte from the start of the season. Aponte was used strictly in long relief, a role he disliked a great deal. Aponte wanted to pitch more often, but he couldn't even buy time in the team's crowded bullpen.

The Indians farmed Aponte to Triple A in July 1984 when Joe Carter was activated. Aponte was angry over the demotion and said he never wanted to pitch for Corrales again. At Triple A, Aponte came down with a sore elbow and pitched only 14.2 innings the rest of the season.

Aponte relies more on guile and control than overpowering stuff. He throws in the 85-86 MPH range and uses a sinking fastball as his out pitch. His forkball--which is the pitch that some interpret as a spitter--is another lethal pitch.

While he was with the Boston Red Sox, Aponte at least got a shot at saving a game now and then. That was not the case in Cleveland, and it frustrated him. He does have a professional attitude about his work and can shake some things off.

He is best when he keeps the ball down and can do so consistently with all

LUIS APONTE
RHP, No. 45
RR, 6'0", 165 lbs.
ML Svc: 3 years
Born: 7-14-54 in
   Lel Tigre, VEN

1984 STATISTICS
W	L	ERA	G	GS	CG	IP	H	R	ER	BB	SO	SV
1	0	4.11	25	0	0	50	53	25	23	15	25	0

CAREER STATISTICS
W	L	ERA	G	GS	CG	IP	H	R	ER	BB	SO	SV
9	6	3.27	110	0	0	220	222	86	80	68	113	7

his pitches. He has trouble when he gets behind in the count, but his outlook on relief pitching goes like this: either the ball goes over the fence or somebody catches it.

FIELDING:

Aponte's unorthodox delivery would lead one to believe that he would be far from nimble in fielding his position. Nothing could be further from the truth. He hops off the mound well after bunts. He keeps runners close at first with a quick throw. At times, however, Aponte throws to first too often.

OVERALL:

He can pitch short or long relief, but first must make peace with Corrales. It will be interesting to see how his elbow responds and where he fits in with the Tribe's other relievers.

Robinson: "I see him being part of the Indians' staff, but I don't see him pitching that much. There are too many other guys who do the same job he does."

HITTING:

Chris Bando proved a lot of things to a lot of people last year. Most of all, he proved he could not only survive in the big leagues as a switch-hitting catcher but prosper while he's at it.

Promoted from the minors in June 1984, Bando hit .291 with 12 home runs and 41 RBIs in only 220 at-bats. In the process, he showed the power the team thought he had in the minors. Before last season, Bando had hit only seven home runs in two big league seasons--all of them from the right side of the plate. Last year, Bando learned about distribution, hitting eight homers left-handed and four righthanded.

Bando uses a closed to slightly open stance. Hitting righthanded, he likes the ball up and in. Hitting lefthanded, he prefers the ball down and in. Breaking ball pitchers bother Bando the most, but he is a patient hitter and uses the whole field.

Before last season, Bando appeared to have no pop at all, but in 1984 he became much more aggressive at the plate. No longer tentative, Bando swung with authority from both sides of the plate. He still struck out a lot (35 times in 220 at-bats), but he also started to look for off-speed pitches. Pitchers know they'll have to try something different against him in 1985.

Bando is a better hitter from the right side of the plate. Batting righty, he hit .315 last year, with 14 RBIs.

BASERUNNING:

Bando will never be mistaken for a speedster. When he runs, he runs hard, he just doesn't go very fast. Bando likes to run the bases, but sometimes that aggressiveness gets him in trouble. He doesn't mind breaking up a double play.

FIELDING:

When Bando returned from Triple A

CHRIS BANDO
C, No. 23
SR, 6'0", 195 lbs.
ML Svc: 3 years
Born: 2-4-56 in
Cleveland, OH

1984 STATISTICS

AVG	G	AB	R	H	2B	3B	HR	RBI	BB	SO	SB
.291	75	220	38	64	11	0	12	41	33	35	1

CAREER STATISTICS

AVG	G	AB	R	H	2B	3B	HR	RBI	BB	SO	SB
.252	210	572	69	144	23	1	19	78	74	86	1

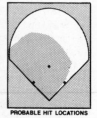

VS. RHP VS. LHP PROBABLE HIT LOCATIONS

last year, he simply took charge on the field and moved into the starting job. He has a good working relationship with the pitching staff and blocks balls in the dirt well. Bando has a strong arm and good accuracy, but he was bothered by a strained rotator cuff late in the season--he did not catch the last two weeks of the season because of it. Although he is definitely not a toothpick, Bando went into last season 15 to 20 pounds lighter, and his range behind the plate increased.

OVERALL:

Perhaps figuring that it was now or never, Bando became the take-charge catcher the Indians were looking for last year. His power figures were a plus, and now he figures to be the full-time catcher.

Robinson: "He played more often and better than ever in 1984. He is still prone to injury, but he swung the bat well. He should get even better."

HITTING:

Tony Bernazard has always been known as an average defensive second baseman who made a living with his bat. Last year the bottom fell out on all phases of this switch-hitter's game. It eventually drove him to the bench for the last month and a half of the season.

Bernazard is a natural righthanded hitter and uses a squared stance from both sides of the plate. From the left side, he likes the ball up and in; and from the right side, he likes the ball down and in. He is a singles hitter with gap power.

After a hot start, Bernazard went into an 0 for 44 slump and never got back on track. He became impatient at the plate, often swinging at the first pitch. Breaking ball pitchers who kept the ball away from him gave him the most trouble.

Bernazard became an easy out last season, striking out 70 times, a career high. A decent bunter with good speed, Bernazard rarely used it to help break out of his slump. He has to become a more selective hitter.

He hit two home runs last year, both from the right side. However, 24 of his 38 RBIs came when Bernazard was batting lefthanded.

BASERUNNING:

Bernazard has good speed out of the box and down the line. For all of his problems last year, he almost never loafed to first base. Bernazard stole 20 bases, three shy of a career high, but did not show good judgment. He was caught stealing 13 times and was vulnerable to the pickoff. He has enough speed to take the extra base on hits to right field.

FIELDING:

Bernazard's problems at the plate

TONY BERNAZARD
2B, No. 4
SR, 5'9", 160 lbs.
ML Svc: 5 years
Born: 8-24-56 in
Caguas, PR

1984 STATISTICS											
AVG	G	AB	R	H	2B	3B	HR	RBI	BB	SO	SB
.221	140	439	44	97	15	4	2	38	43	70	20
CAREER STATISTICS											
AVG	G	AB	R	H	2B	3B	HR	RBI	BB	SO	SB
.252	626	2119	289	535	97	21	33	210	233	374	68

VS. RHP   VS. LHP   PROBABLE HIT LOCATIONS

followed him into the field, where he committed a career high 20 errors in 1984. He often seemed tentative on balls hit right at him. His range was not the best either, especially going behind second base. Tony has an average arm and is mechanical when turning the double play. He cannot depend solely on his defense to keep him in the big leagues.

OVERALL:

At first, Bernazard was glad to be in Cleveland following his trade from Seattle. By the end of the season, however, he expressed his displeasure with the manager and talked about demanding a trade (an option he did not exercise).

Robinson: "It was a poor year for him. Cleveland even started rotating second basemen in the second half of the season. It will be his job until he loses it in 1985."

PITCHING:

After two years of injuries, Bert Blyleven was transformed into The Dutchman of old in 1984. His curveball made hitter's knees bend from one end of the league to the other, and he added a 90 MPH sinking fastball to his repertoire.

Blyleven is a medical miracle. In 1982, his right elbow went snap, crackkle, pop. The doctors put it back together and said it would take two years to rehabilitate. As Blyleven's 19-7 record of 1984 indicates, the doctors were right on schedule.

Consistency and control are his lifelines. He had them both at maximum last season, leading the Indians with 170 strikeouts and lasting at least seven innings in 26 of his 32 starts.

After two years of doubt, Blyleven proved his right arm could stand the strain of his cracking curve, which is rated as one of the best in the AL. He pitched 245 innings and probably would have had 20 or more wins if he hadn't missed six starts because of a broken bone in his foot.

He is an excellent competitor. He seems to pitch better when he's behind in the count or with runners on base. His curveball is his strikeout pitch but at 33 years old Blyleven knows not to rely on it totally. He has no qualms about going with his fastball in tough situations and was actually throwing harder at the end of the season than at the start.

He is a joy to watch. "Captain Bly" even seemed to shed his hard-luck loser image. True, the Tribe scored only six runs in Blyleven's seven losses when he was on the mound, but they also scored more than 100 runs in his 19 wins.

FIELDING:

Blyleven is the best fielding pitcher

BERT BLYLEVEN
RHP, No. 28
RR, 6'3", 208 lbs.
ML Svc: 15 years
Born: 4-6-51 in
    Zeist, Holland

1984 STATISTICS

W	L	ERA	G	GS	CG	IP	H	R	ER	BB	SO	SV
19	7	2.87	33	32	12	245	204	86	78	74	170	0

CAREER STATISTICS

W	L	ERA	G	GS	CG	IP	H	R	ER	BB	SO	SV
195	167	3.00	468	462	176	3422	3079	1277	1141	939	2669	0

on the Indians. He works hard for that honor. He routinely helps himself during games by fielding hot shots back at the mound. He always knows what base to throw to and gets off the mound quickly on bunts.

OVERALL:

Going into the 1984 season, all Bert wanted was a season of good health. He said that if he stayed in one piece, he would win some games. No one is arguing with him now.

His desire to win is always there. The Indians become a contender each time Blyleven's on the mound. He works quickly and keeps the ball in the strike zone and his fielders in the game.

Robinson: "I think injuries have taken their toll, but I saw the Blyleven of old in 1984. He has acquired a sinking fastball, which has helped him. He was extremely consistent all year and was one of the best pitchers in the AL in 1984. This season should be even better for him."

HITTING:

In 1984, Brett Butler gave the Indians something they've needed for a long time, a dependable leadoff hitter. Although he didn't hit for a high average (.269), Butler drew 86 walks, scored 108 runs and stole 52 bases.

Butler uses a squared and slightly open stance. He's basically a singles hitter with some gap power aided by good speed. Butler likes fastballs, but has trouble with high inside heat and breaking balls in the same location.

Butler is a patient hitter who rarely swings at the first pitch. He doesn't strike out often and stays away from deep slumps because of his bunting ability and speed. Last year he led American League hitters with 29 bunt-singles.

His style hasn't changed from 1983, when he played with Atlanta, but adjusting to AL pitching may have resulted in the drop in his batting average from .281 to .269. Butler sometimes has a tendency to hit the ball in the air instead of putting it on the ground and using his speed to reach base.

BASERUNNING:

The rap on Butler when the Indians obtained him from Atlanta was that he was a "dumb" baserunner. The rap was that he took unnecessary chances, got thrown out a lot and was easy to pick off. At first he lived up to that reputation in Cleveland. Slowly, though, he became more disciplined on the bases and didn't take foolish leads. He stole 52 bases and was caught 22 times. He was still vulnerable to pickoffs, but that may have been because he was unfamiliar with American League pitchers. By the end of the year, Butler was keeping a notebook on pitchers' moves to first.

FIELDING:

Butler fooled some people with his

BRETT BUTLER
LF, No. 2
LL, 5'10", 160 lbs.
ML Svc: 3 years
Born: 6-15-57 in
Los Angeles, CA

1984 STATISTICS

AVG	G	AB	R	H	2B	3B	HR	RBI	BB	SO	SB
.269	159	602	108	162	25	9	3	49	86	62	52

CAREER STATISTICS

AVG	G	AB	R	H	2B	3B	HR	RBI	BB	SO	SB
.264	439	1517	244	400	50	25	8	97	184	170	121

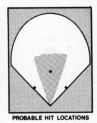

VS. RHP   VS. LHP   PROBABLE HIT LOCATIONS

arm from center field. Said to be below average, Butler showed good strength and accuracy. Baserunners didn't take too many chances with him. He covers a lot of ground in center and excelled in coming in on short flies. Butler was not as graceful going back to the fence--he plays shallow--and had trouble with the ball hit directly over his head.

OVERALL:

Pound for pound, it's hard not to appreciate Butler. He is a consistent, all-around performer.

Robinson: "Brett played well for the Indians. I think you are seeing him at his best. He might add a few more points to his batting average in 1985."

PITCHING:

Ernie "No Tricks" Camacho shocked everyone in the Cleveland organization in 1984. As long as Pat Corrales's vocal chords hold together, he has a good chance of shocking them again this season.

Watching Camacho pitch is a study in conversation--loud conversation. When Camacho is pitching, manager Corrales stands on the top step of the dugout and screams his lungs out. Ernie will take a peek at his manager, tip his cap and throw a sinking fastball anywhere from 92 to 96 MPH across the plate. That act earned Camacho a team record 23 saves in 1984.

The nickname "No Tricks" is no accident. Camacho used to have five, maybe six pitches. All it did was get him bounced out of five organizations AND the Mexican League. Two years ago, he reached the end of the line in Charleston, West Virginia, the Tribe's former Triple A farmclub.

That's where Corrales saw him. He remembered the righthanded Camacho the next time he saw him, in spring training 1984. Corrales's message was direct: "Throw the fastball and nothing else, Ernie. Remember, no tricks, just the fastball."

Tentative at the start of the season, Camacho's confidence grew as the summer progressed. He became the team's No. 1 stopper, with an easy three-quarters delivery that belies the velocity of his pitch.

Labeled a "head case" for most of his career, Camacho showed he could pitch out of jams and under pressure last year. In fact, he had never saved a game in the big leagues until last year. He was 23 of 34 in save situations, with 11 saves coming in the last two months of the season.

Despite his overpowering speed, he is not a big strikeout pitcher. Control is

ERNIE CAMACHO
RHP, No. 40
RR, 6'1", 180 lbs.
ML Svc: 1 year plus
Born: 2-1-56 in
       Salinas, CA

1984 STATISTICS												
W	L	ERA	G	GS	CG	IP	H	R	ER	BB	SO	SV
5	9	2.43	69	0	0	100	83	31	27	37	48	23
CAREER STATISTICS												
W	L	ERA	G	GS	CG	IP	H	R	ER	BB	SO	SV
5	11	3.30	85	3	0	139	131	56	51	59	70	23

his major problem and when he loses it, Corrales jogs out to the mound, pounds him on the chest and tells him to throw it over the plate or else. Camacho listens.

FIELDING:

He has one move to first base but doesn't worry much about runners. He gets off the mound quickly, but fielding is sometimes an adventure for him. He covers first base well.

OVERALL:

Camacho is strictly a one-pitch pitcher, but that's not too bad when the pitch travels in the low-to-mid 90s. It is doubtful that Camacho could have performed as he did in 1984 for any other manager than Corrales. It bears watching as to whether or not Corrales's macho approach will work with Camacho in 1985.

Robinson: "Camacho seemed to get more confident as the year went on. As long as his control holds up, he will be a good pitcher. He is just hard to hit. You know what's coming and he says, 'Here it is, hit it if you can.'"

HITTING:

The Indians gave away a lot when they traded Rick Sutcliffe to the Cubs, but some say they received a lot in return in the form of Joe Carter, a righthanded-hitting rookie.

Carter batted only 244 times for the Indians, but managed to finish second on the team with 13 home runs. Projected over a 500 at-bat season, Carter would have had 27 home runs and 83 RBIs.

Tall and lean, Carter uses a slightly closed stance and loves to pull fastballs to left field. However, he has good bat control and was often used in hit-and-run situations because of his ability to go to right field.

Aggressive at the plate, Carter has the most problem with breaking ball pitchers. He is an impatient hitter and often swings at the first pitch no matter where it is. He strikes out frequently, but it doesn't curtail his aggressiveness.

He aggravated an old knee injury when he ran into an outfield fence in his second game with the Tribe last season. When Carter got off the disabled list, he hit his way into the everyday lineup in center field and left field and at first base. He may be best in the No. 3 spot in the batting order, but last year he was also used as the leadoff and in the No. 5 spot behind DH Andre Thornton.

BASERUNNING:

Carter is a good baserunner for his size, but the knee injury took that part of his game away last season. He underwent knee surgery in the off-season and is expected to become more of a base-stealing threat this year. He stole 40 bases at Triple A with the Cubs in 1983.

Carter gets down the first base line quickly. He has the speed to beat out infield hits, and slides hard into second base, even with his tender knee.

FIELDING:

Carter's natural position is center

JOE CARTER
OF, No. 30
RR, 6'3", 215 lbs.
ML Svc: 1 year
Born: 3-7-60 in
 Oklahoma City, OK

1984 STATISTICS
AVG	G	AB	R	H	2B	3B	HR	RBI	BB	SO	SB
.275	66	244	32	67	6	1	13	41	11	48	2

CAREER STATISTICS
AVG	G	AB	R	H	2B	3B	HR	RBI	BB	SO	SB
.275	66	244	32	67	6	1	13	41	11	48	2

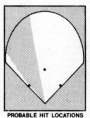

STRONG — VS. RHP   STRONG — VS. LHP   PROBABLE HIT LOCATIONS

field, but he spent most of his time in left field. He has good athletic ability and enough speed to make a mistake in judgment and still make the catch. He seems to have more trouble coming in on the ball than going back. Carter isn't afraid of the fence and has good leaping ability against it. For the first time in his career, he played first base in 1984 and didn't make an error in six games. He has a good arm with fair accuracy.

OVERALL:

He will be an everyday player for the Indians this year. They must decide whether to play him at first base or in the outfield.

Robinson: "The reports have been mixed on Carter. They range from terrific to questioning whether he'll hit in the big leagues. From what I saw, he is going to have a spot on the Cleveland club somewhere. He has a lot of holes in his swing--but don't make a mistake or he'll hit it. If he plays 150 games, he will hit 25-30 home runs."

HITTING

Carmelo Castillo picked the wrong time to have his best season in the big leagues. George Vukovich, his platoon partner in right field, followed his lead, and Castillo was virtually lost in Vukovich's statistics.

Powerfully built through the upper body, the righthanded hitting Castillo produced 10 home runs and 36 RBIs in only 211 at-bats. Facing an almost exclusive diet of lefthanded pitchers, he disappeared after the All Star break. In the second half, he came to the plate only 85 times.

He uses a slightly closed stance and shows good power to left and straightaway center field. He became much more aggressive at the plate last year. Twenty-one of his 55 hits went for extra bases.

He is a low ball hitter and looks for the fastball down. A breaking ball pitcher with a decent fastball up and in can get Castillo out. Carmelo is not the most patient of hitters, and that comes from not playing every day.

He has always had the physical package, but last year he gave the first indication that he was about to put it all together. His hitting has improved in every department and, with it, his confidence. He is still feeling his way, still finding out what he's capable of doing.

BASERUNNING:

Castillo gets out of the box fast. He doesn't bunt much, but can beat out his share of slow rollers and broken bat hits because of his speed. An oddity is that Castillo is not a threat to steal a base. With all his speed, he doesn't get a good jump and seems tentative running the bases. He stole one base last year.

FIELDING:

Castillo's arm strength is legendary. It has to be rated as one of the best

CARMELO CASTILLO
RF, No. 12
RR, 6'1", 185 lbs.
ML Svc: 2 years
Born: 6-6-58 in
San Pedro de Macoris, **DR**

1984 STATISTICS

AVG	G	AB	R	H	2B	3B	HR	RBI	BB	SO	SB
.024	87	211	36	55	9	2	10	36	21	32	1

CAREER STATISTICS

AVG	G	AB	R	H	2B	3B	HR	RBI	BB	SO	SB
.109	157	367	56	85	15	3	13	50	31	54	2

  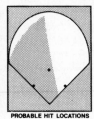

VS. RHP   VS. LHP   PROBABLE HIT LOCATIONS

guns in baseball even though he doesn't have pinpoint accuracy. Daring baserunners will challenge Castillo's arm only because he is erratic, but they won't do it often. Castillo used to be afraid of the fence, but last season he began to show more confidence in the outfield. He still has a problem charging ground balls and picking them up on the hop. He does not get a quick jump on balls hit in front of him.

OVERALL:

The Indians will give him more time against righthanded pitching in spring training; they want to see if Castillo can hit it consistently. Castillo was unhappy over his lack of playing time in the second half of last season.

Robinson: "He was a much better player in 1984 than ever before, and it is because he played more often. For him to help you, he has to get into at least 100 games."

PITCHING:

1984 was a non-season for Jamie "The Rat" Easterly. While jogging backward in preparation for spring training 1984, Easterly slipped into a hole and injured his back. That was the last anyone saw of The Rat until mid-June of last year.

Even then, the Indians activated him reluctantly. They wanted him to report to Triple A for a 20-day rehabilitation program at the start of the season. He felt that he was ready to pitch and refused to go.

It wasn't until Cleveland found themselves short of pitchers after trading Rick Sutcliffe and George Frazier to the Chicago Cubs that Easterly finally got the green light. By that time, he had lost his ranking as the Tribe's No.1 lefthanded reliever to Mike Jeffcoat.

Easterly throws hard and uses a fastball, a slider, a curve and a change. His out pitch is a fastball, but his slider is also wicked. He relies on those two pitches and tries to keep the ball down.

The Rat doesn't look like a pitcher. He says he's not fat, just short. His easy three-quarters motion fools people, because he throws between 87-88 MPH and is tough on lefthanded hitters.

Pitching almost strictly in long relief during the second half of the season, Easterly for the most part showed good control. That's a good sign because control has been Easterly's downfall over the years. When he loses his control, it seems to bother him in later innings.

Easterly has a good live arm and even started a game when the Indians were jammed with double headers in August. He can work with little rest and will take the ball when its offered. He has a good makeup for a reliever--nothing bothers him.

FIELDING:

He gets off the mound quickly on

JAMIE EASTERLY
LHP, No. 36
LL, 5'10", 180 lbs.
ML Svc: 7 years
Born: 2-17-53 in
Houston, TX

1984 STATISTICS

W	L	ERA	G	GS	CG	IP	H	R	ER	BB	SO	SV
3	1	5.68	26	1	0	69	74	31	26	23	42	2

CAREER STATISTICS

W	L	ERA	G	GS	CG	IP	H	R	ER	BB	SO	SV
18	29	4.59	242	29	0	461	508	268	235	237	261	14

bunts down the first base line and third base line. He has trouble with bunts between third and the mound. Easterly fields his position adequately and has a decent move to first, though he doesn't use it much.

OVERALL:

Easterly's good second half seemed to get him out of the Indians' doghouse. Used mostly in long relief, he'd like to challenge Jeffcoat as the team's left-handed stopper. If he stops running backward, he just might have a chance.

He is in the last year of a two-year contract. His first two years with the Indians were the best of his career, one that has been highlighted mostly by mediocrity. Whether he knows it or not, he may have found a home on the shores of Lake Erie.

Robinson: "Easterly is 18-29 lifetime, and that isn't too exciting. But through it all, he still has a very good arm. Everyone is always looking for a lefthanded pitcher and that's in his favor. I think he will help the Indians in 1985 more than he did in 1984."

PITCHING:

In one season and part of another, Steve Farr was 17-1 in the Indians' farm system. Then came the downside--the Indians called him to the big time last year when Rick Behenna went down with a rotator cuff injury.

The big time put the big hurt on him, as he finished 3-11 with a 4.58 ERA. By the end of the season, Farr was out of the starting rotation and pitching in long relief. Manager Pat Corrales says that's the role he'll have to fill if he is going to make the roster this year.

The righthanded Farr is a strikeout pitcher who leans on the fastball as his out pitch. Farr pitched well at first and lost some tough ballgames as the season progressed. Then he went on the disabled list with a shoulder injury and had control problems after being re-activated.

Farr throws between 88 and 89 MPH, but had trouble keeping his pitches down. He also fell behind in the count often and had trouble bouncing back from a bad inning. A rookie at 27 years old, Farr didn't know the strengths and weaknesses of the AL hitters, and it hurt him.

However, Farr has paid his dues with seven years in the minors. His overall composure on the mound is good. He throws a fastball, a curve, a slider, a forkball and a change and isn't afraid to use any of them, no matter what the situation. His overhand curve can be a monster. Last year he struck out eight Detroit Tigers in 6.1 innings relying on it.

FIELDING:

He has a good move to first and pays attention to runners. His throws to first follow no particular pattern, so runners have a hard time getting a good

STEVE FARR
RHP, No. 58
RR, 5'11", 190 lbs.
ML Svc: 1 year
Born: 12-12-56 in
Cheverly, MD

1984 STATISTICS

W	L	ERA	G	GS	CG	IP	H	R	ER	BB	SO	SV
3	11	4.58	31	16	0	116	106	61	59	46	83	1

CAREER STATISTICS

W	L	ERA	G	GS	CG	IP	H	R	ER	BB	SO	SV
3	11	4.58	31	16	0	116	106	61	59	46	83	1

jump. He was involved in a few close plays at first, and seemed to have some trouble covering the bag.

OVERALL:

Consistency is Farr's main problem. Last year he pitched either extremely well or extremely poorly. He battled all year and finally seemed to find his groove late in the season when he went to the bullpen.

Farr, so unemotional that Corrales said trying to read him was "like looking at a blank television screen," did not get much help last year. The Indians finished sixth the the AL East, and they seemed to play like a sixth-place team when he was on the mound.

Robinson: "Farr is a better pitcher than his record indicates, and I think he will have a winning record this year. He can help; he throws hard and strikes out people. I think he should get another chance. He was 13-1 in 1983 at Buffalo. I would chalk 1984 up to inexperience. I know he did a credible job in the pen, but I still think he's a starter."

HITTING:

Mike Fischlin looks like the Hunchback of Notre Dame at the plate. He crouches low over the plate, with his bat tapping the dirt in front of the catcher: he is known by baseball freaks from one AL stadium to another.

That in itself is amazing. Fischlin has made a living in the big leagues based on his talent as a utility infielder, but he will always be remembered for his peculiar batting stance and his struggle to be an adequate big league hitter.

He is a singles hitter and goes mostly to straightaway center but can go down either line due to decent bat control. He's a patient hitter, but a lack of playing time forces him out of his personality from time to time. He batted 133 times last year and struck out 20.

Bunting is a big part of Fish's game. He is especially adept when it comes to moving a runner into scoring position. He has enough speed to bunt for a base hit and can move a runner along with the hit and run.

Against righthanded pitchers, he likes fastballs on the inside of the plate from his hands down. His hitting zone against lefthanders covers the same location, only a little smaller. Pitchers with decent curves and off-speed pitches give Fischlin the most problems.

BASERUNNING:

Fischlin is aggressive on the bases. He always tries to go from first to third on a hit to right field. He gets out of the box fast and never loafs down the line. Once on base, Fischlin has the speed to steal, but doesn't take too many chances. He will slide hard to break up the double play.

FIELDING:

Fischlin played second, shortstop and third last year. During the last two months of the 1984 season, Fischlin be-

MIKE FISCHLIN
2B, No. 22
RR, 6'1", 165 lbs.
ML Svc: 4 years
Born: 9-13-55 in
    Sacramento, CA

1984 STATISTICS
AVG	G	AB	R	H	2B	3B	HR	RBI	BB	SO	SB
.226	85	133	17	30	4	2	1	14	12	20	2

CAREER STATISTICS
AVG	G	AB	R	H	2B	3B	HR	RBI	BB	SO	SB
.223	372	779	88	174	23	5	3	63	79	106	24

STRONG

VS. RHP

STRONG

VS. LHP

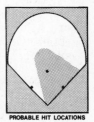

PROBABLE HIT LOCATIONS

came a starter in Cleveland's rotating second basemen sideshow. Fischlin would start, get lifted for a pinch-hitter--sometimes as soon as the second or third inning--and be replaced by Junior Noboa or Tony Bernazard.

Fischlin has a good arm and throws well. He turns the double play with no problem and charges grounders with authority. Making the deep throw from the hole at short or behind second is still his toughest play.

OVERALL:

Versatility has kept Fischlin in the big leagues for four seasons. He keeps himself sharp and always ends up starting somewhere when the season grows late.

Robinson: "I think you will see him playing for Cleveland next year and get the same kind of performance. Corrales says his job isn't to hit, it's to catch a ground ball and turn the double play."

HITTING:

It can be said now. Julio Franco can hit and hit and hit.

Some complained when he stopped pulling the ball to left field in 1984. He just shrugged and kept lining singles to right and center. When Franco finally stopped, he had 188 hits, the most by an Indian in 30 years.

Franco uses a closed stance and wraps the bat behind his right ear. He loves high fastballs and goes after the first pitch with abandon. Right and lefthanded pitchers can get him out with breaking balls away. Not an overly disciplined hitter, Franco will swing the bat before taking ball four.

Franco is an excellent bunter, but doesn't do it enough. His home run production slipped from eight in 1983 to three last season, but his average climbed (.273 to .286) and his RBIs were almost identical (80 to 79).

Personal goals motivate Franco. One of them is to hit .300. Another is to drive in 80 or more RBIs a year. Maybe that's why he's such a dangerous hitting threat with men in scoring position (.355).

BASERUNNING:

Franco gets out of the box quickly, but sometimes has a tendency to coast to first. Manager Pat Corrales yanked him for just such an offense last year, and Franco has been hustling ever since. His stolen bases dropped off from his rookie year (32 to 19), but he is always a threat to go. On the basepaths, he needs more experience. Julio likes to run until somebody tags him out.

FIELDING:

He led the league in errors last year with 36--he simply doesn't concentrate. He will make the hard play and then boot

JULIO FRANCO
SS, No. 14
RR, 6'0", 160 lbs.
ML Svc: 2 years
Born: 8-23-61 in
    San Pedro de Macoris, DR

1984 STATISTICS

AVG	G	AB	R	H	2B	3B	HR	RBI	BB	SO	SB
.286	160	658	82	188	22	5	3	79	43	68	19

CAREER STATISTICS

AVG	G	AB	R	H	2B	3B	HR	RBI	BB	SO	SB
.280	325	1247	153	349	47	13	11	162	72	122	51

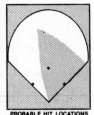

VS. RHP   VS. LHP   PROBABLE HIT LOCATIONS

the simple one.

Franco goes to his left as well as any shortstop in the league and has a strong arm that could be more accurate. He is good on the double play ball, whether he does it himself or feeds the second baseman. On fly balls to short left field and down the foul lines, he is seldom caught napping.

OVERALL:

After a slow start, Franco put together a consistent offensive performance. He even stopped arguing with official scorers . . . at least, he tried.

Robinson: "He is a player with a lot of offensive ability. What you saw in 1984 is what you'll get in 1985. I think you saw him at his best. He has a very good future in Cleveland."

HITTING:

The first thing one notices about Mel Hall's stance is his batting gloves flapping out of his back pockets. Hall carries three gloves in each pocket, with the fingers hanging down. When he runs, they sway in the breeze.

Hall uses a slightly closed stance. He is a fastball hitter with straight-away power and looks for the ball up over the plate. Hall is a free-swinger (57 strikeouts in 257 at-bats) who rarely gets cheated. He can pull the ball to right field.

Obtained along with Joe Carter from the Chicago Cubs, Hall came to the AL thinking he would tear it up. He was disdainful of American League parks, teams and pitchers--but he learned humility fast. Pitchers have the most success against Hall when they throw breaking balls down and on the outside half of the plate.

Hall was platooned with the Cubs, hardly ever facing lefthanders. The Indians used the same policy, but the change of leagues seemed to hurt Hall more than anything else. Hall is a streak hitter, and he never really got hot for the Indians.

He has better than average power and knows it. That's why he'll never stop swinging the bat--he realizes he can drive the ball in any park.

BASERUNNING:

Hall surprises you with his speed. He gets out of the box and down the line quickly. He is not much of a threat to steal, simply because he hasn't refined his techniques. There's no question he has the speed needed to steal bases. Hall runs the bases hard and will break up the double play. The fans love to watch his gloves flap in the wind at full speed.

FIELDING:

Hall was a pleasant surprise in the

MEL HALL
OF, No. 27
LL, 6'1", 185 lbs.
ML Svc: 2 years
Born: 9-16-60 in
Lyons, NY

1984 STATISTICS

AVG	G	AB	R	H	2B	3B	HR	RBI	BB	SO	SB
.257	83	257	43	66	13	1	7	30	35	55	1

CAREER STATISTICS

AVG	G	AB	R	H	2B	3B	HR	RBI	BB	SO	SB
.257	83	257	43	66	13	1	7	30	35	55	1

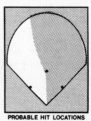

VS. RHP　　　VS. LHP　　　PROBABLE HIT LOCATIONS

outfield. Playing left field for the first time in his career, he showed an above average arm and a fine ability to go get the ball no matter where it was hit. His throws are on target, even from deep foul territory. He made several outstanding catches where his speed compensated for an initial mistake.

OVERALL:

The Indians are anxious to see what Hall can do in a full season. Said to have an attitude problem, the outspoken Hall nonetheless fits in well with the Indians. However, he did disappear for three days late in the season, and his irresponsibility is a concern to the team.

Robinson: "It was a shock for him to get traded. He will have a better year in every department in 1985. I don't know if he will be an everyday player, but I look for him to play in 130 games or so."

HITTING:

Mike Hargrove, the Human Rain Delay, stepped on the gas last year. He still went through all the motions--digging a hole in the box, leaning the bat against his leg, tightening his batting gloves, adjusting his helmet and wiping his face --he just did them faster.

Hitting instructor Bobby Bonds suggested picking up the pace because Mike was having trouble getting his bat cocked properly. The adjustment seemed to work in spring training, but Hargrove lost his first base job to Pat Tabler and his season went downhill.

Hargrove is an extremely patient hitter with a good eye and a great on-base percentage. He is a low ball, singles hitter with decent power to the gaps. He is not a home run threat.

Lack of playing time caused his average to slip to .267 last season. A lifetime .290 hitter, Hargrove is at the stage in his career where he feels he must play every day to be effective. He appeared in 133 games, but many of them were as a late-inning defensive replacement at first.

Hargrove likes off-speed pitches low and away in the strike zone. A fastball pitcher who can get ahead of him in the count can give him trouble. He is a much better hitter when he has the edge in the count. He hits righties and lefties equally well.

BASERUNNING:

Hargrove will never be mistaken for a shooting star. He has no speed to speak of, is never a threat to steal and seldom takes the extra base. The good thing is that Hargrove knows he's slow and doesn't take risks. He will go hard into second base to break up a double play.

FIELDING:

If the Indians had a one-run lead

MIKE HARGROVE
1B, No. 21
LL, 6'0", 195 lbs.
ML Svc: 11 years
Born: 10-26-49 in
  Perryton, TX

1984 STATISTICS

AVG	G	AB	R	H	2B	3B	HR	RBI	BB	SO	SB
.267	133	352	44	94	14	2	2	44	53	38	0

CAREER STATISTICS

AVG	G	AB	R	H	2B	3B	HR	RBI	BB	SO	SB
.290	1559	5280	752	1533	252	27	79	659	926	523	25

  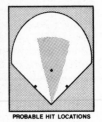

VS. RHP   VS. LHP   PROBABLE HIT LOCATIONS

late in a game last year, Hargrove went in at first base. He fields his position well and gets the most out of limited range. He turns the 3-6-3 double play well and is good at making diving stops on the foul line and at going to his right. Hargrove has a decent arm.

OVERALL:

Hargrove was not happy in Cleveland last year. He asked to be traded more than once. He feels he can play every day, but the Indians think differently.

Robinson: "He will probably get even less playing time this year than he did last year. Cleveland is making the change to a power team, and there is just no spot for him. He has to play a lot to really help a team."

PITCHING:

Neal Heaton drove his manager crazy last year. Corrales ripped him repeatedly in the press and threatened to send him to Triple A.

Heaton said that wasn't the way to handle him--and he was right. Toward the end of the season, the two finally came to an agreement. Still, it was a frustrating second season for this talented lefthander.

The major problem between the two was pitch selection. Corrales wanted Heaton to throw more off-speed pitches. Heaton kept going with his 88-89 MPH fastball. To make matters worse, the usually control-minded Heaton couldn't find the plate with any kind of pitch.

Heaton continually found himself behind in the count. He also showed a disturbing habit of allowing a big inning after getting two quick outs. He did not respond well to a bad inning.

Always confident, Heaton may have begun to doubt himself last season. Used to throwing hard and overpowering hitters, he had trouble adapting to his manager's orders, even though he has the ability to throw a curve, a slider and a change consistently for strikes.

After a splendid rookie season in which he pitched as a starter and reliever, the Indians expected very big things from Heaton last year. What they got was a 12-15 record--the second highest wins on the staff--but they wanted much more.

Control has always been his strength, but last year it wasn't there. Heaton's walks-to-strikeouts ratio was terrible (75-75), and he allowed 21 home runs, the most on the team. Heaton did have a slight elbow problem early in the year, but he absorbed much more punishment mentally.

FIELDING:

Heaton is a good all-around athlete

NEAL HEATON
LHP, No. 44
LL, 6'1", 205 lbs.
ML Svc: 2 years
Born: 3-3-60 in
   Jamaica, NY

1984 STATISTICS

W	L	ERA	G	GS	CG	IP	H	R	ER	BB	SO	SV
12	15	5.21	38	34	4	198	231	128	115	75	75	0

CAREER STATISTICS

W	L	ERA	G	GS	CG	IP	H	R	ER	BB	SO	SV
23	24	4.81	85	54	8	378	420	228	202	135	164	7

who fields his position well. He has a decent move to first base, but his deliberate windup allows good baserunners a chance to steal. He covers first base well.

OVERALL:

The Indians expect him to rebound from last year. What's more important, so does Heaton. Last season was the first time he's struggled as a pitcher at any level. Confusion and some slight mechanical problems were Heaton's main problems in 1984. The question this year is, Will he find equal time for his fastball and Corrales's demand for off-speed pitches? Heaton is a strong-minded man.

Robinson: "He will get better in 1985 because the team should be better. He has far too much talent not to win consistently and I look for him to turn it around. I would say he should finish better than .500--four or five games over .500. Overall, he was not able to make the pitches when he had to last year. He had control problems, but he has four good pitches and that should make him a winner."

HITTING:

As a hitter, Brook Jacoby progressed on a steady line his rookie year until he broke the hamate bone in his left hand in late August 1984 and went on the disabled list for the rest of the season. The righthanded hitting Jacoby began the year swinging for the fences and trying to pull everything to left field. It was not the best of moves.

Jacoby's average was below .200, and his home run production was minimal. Then he started to cut down on his swing and go up the middle: the strategy was right on target. Jacoby was hitting .365 for the month of August when the injury struck.

Brook uses a slightly closed stance and is notorious for swinging at the first pitch. He is a high ball hitter who likes to hit off-speed pitching. A pitcher with a good fastball down and in can get Jacoby out.

Jacoby had impressive power stats in Atlanta's minor league system, but was more effective as a singles hitter with the Indians last year. The Indians still think he can hit for power, and they believe he should be more relaxed in 1985 after putting on a strong showing in the second half of last year.

BASERUNNING:

Jacoby has average speed. He gets down the first base line well, but is not a big threat to steal. However, he did steal home twice last year on the front end of double steals. He goes hard to break up the double play and will take the extra base when he gets the chance.

FIELDING:

He played every game at third base for the Indians from spring training until the day he was injured. He is a

BROOK JACOBY
INF, No. 26
RR, 5'11", 175 lbs.
ML Svc: 2 years
Born: 11-23-59 in
   Philadelphia, PA

1984 STATISTICS

AVG	G	AB	R	H	2B	3B	HR	RBI	BB	SO	SB
.264	126	439	64	116	19	3	7	40	32	73	3

CAREER STATISTICS

AVG	G	AB	R	H	2B	3B	HR	RBI	BB	SO	SB
.258	141	457	64	118	19	3	7	41	32	77	3

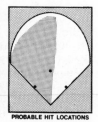

VS. RHP   VS. LHP   PROBABLE HIT LOCATIONS

steady, dependable fielder, but does not have great range. Anything Jacoby gets to, he can handle. He has a strong and precise arm. He does not guard the line particularly well and seldom dives for a ball.

OVERALL:

The Indians will experiment with him at second base during spring training this year. He also played as the emergency shortstop for a couple of innings in 1984. Although he didn't demonstrate overwhelming power, Jacoby overcame his slow start and was producing offensively when he was injured.

Robinson: "For a rookie, he did a nice job. He will be playing somewhere next year for the Indians--whether it is second or third. To me, it seems he has a long, lazy swing and that's the reason he hits off-speed stuff well."

PITCHING:

Mike Jeffcoat is a control pitcher who was used like a fine wine by the Indians last year. That is to say, he was used often, but always with discretion.

The lefthanded Jeffcoat appeared in 63 games, but only pitched 75.1 innings. He was definitely a situation pitcher. For the most part, he would enter a game against a lefthanded hitter, face one or two batters and exit.

A starter during his entire career in the minors, Jeffcoat went to the bullpen as a rookie last year, except for one start against Seattle. He was scheduled to start several other games early in the year but whenever his turn in the rotation arrived, so did the rain. It came as no surprise that the nickname "Raincoat" quickly followed.

Jeffcoat uses an overhand to three-quarters delivery. His three-quarters delivery is especially tough on left-handed hitters. Control is Jeffcoat's game, and when he's hot he has good command of his fastball, curve, slider and change. He throws his fastball between 87 and 88 MPH.

Another positive aspect of his role is his ability to throw double play balls. His fastball sinks, and hitters pound it into the ground. He rescued the Indians a number of times with his double play pitch, and Corrales didn't hesitate to use him with men on base.

Jeffcoat had a tough second half during which he lost his ability to get lefthanders out. Up and down in the bullpen frequently, Jeffcoat seemed to lose some zip on the ball. When that happened, his fastball straightened out and his pitches came up in the strike zone. He led the team with eight wild pitches while trying to stay in the strike zone.

MIKE JEFFCOAT
LHP, No. 46
LL, 6'2", 187 lbs.
ML Svc: 1 year plus
Born: 8-3-59 in
    Pine Bluff, AR

1984 STATISTICS												
W	L	ERA	G	GS	CG	IP	H	R	ER	BB	SO	SV
5	2	2.99	63	1	0	75	82	28	25	24	41	1

CAREER STATISTICS												
W	L	ERA	G	GS	CG	IP	H	R	ER	BB	SO	SV
6	5	3.11	74	3	0	107	114	41	37	37	50	1

FIELDING:

Jeffcoat is a good fielder and covers first base well. He has a good move to first, which, combined with his being lefthanded, helps to keep baserunners close. He gets off the mound quickly on bunts.

OVERALL:

Jeffcoat was frustrated over his lack of work in the second half, but still had a strong year, although his numbers are a little deceiving. The key for him is to keep the ball down, which he did most of the season. He also showed that he had the right mental makeup to pitch in relief.

Robinson: "He did a good job in relief. I see him being used in 1985 just the way he was in 1984--I don't expect him to pitch any more or any less. I think he proved that he can do the job."

PITCHING:

Don Schulze is one of the young, in-experienced rookie pitchers whom the Indians rushed to the big leagues in their extended spring training program. The Indians acquired Schulze as part of the Rick Sutcliffe trade on June 13, 1984; twelve days later, Schulze was in an Indian uniform.

Schulze simply needs more seasoning. He throws a fastball, a curve, a slider and a change-up. His out pitch is the fastball, but he needs at least one more year in the minors to learn how to control it.

Big and strong, Schulze has a compact, mechanical three-quarters delivery. When he's on and keeping the ball down, he looks like a smaller version of the Incredible Hulk. Brian Downing (California Angels--power hitter) hit him in the head with a line drive: Schulze barely blinked.

Most of the time, though, Schulze's emotions get the best of him on the mound. Always pressing, Schulze frequently seems overmatched against major league hitting. He throws 86 MPH and higher, but his pitches tend to flatten out when they aren't low.

Concentration is the key for him. He must control his temper while working. When he doesn't, he tries to overpower hitters and it doesn't work. This is another problem that probably could have been handled better in the minors, instead of during the Indians' on-the-job training sessions.

When Schulze pitched for the Chicago Cubs, they told him not to throw his curve. The Indians encouraged Schulze to start throwing it again, and he experienced some success with it. However, he still must become a more intelligent pitcher if he is to be successful.

Schulze spent time as a starter and reliever, but by the end the season he had worked his way into the starting rotation. That's where his future is, but

DON SCHULZE
RHP, No. 37
RR, 6'3", 225 lbs
ML Svc: 1 year plus
Born: 9-27-62 in
    Roselle, IL

1984 STATISTICS
W	L	ERA	G	GS	CG	IP	H	R	ER	BB	SO	SV
3	6	4.83	19	14	2	85	105	53	46	27	39	0

CAREER STATISTICS
W	L	ERA	G	GS	CG	IP	H	R	ER	BB	SO	SV
3	6	4.87	19	14	2	85	105	53	46	27	39	0

he still needs the important things that make a professional pitcher: composure, knowledge and experience.

FIELDING:

He is awkward off the mound because of his size, and can be bunted on. He takes his fielding seriously, but is average at best.

OVERALL:

When Schulze keeps his fastball and slider down, the ball explodes at the plate. The problem is keeping it down, and Schulze knows it.

He needs finesse and polishing. The competitive spirit is already there. In a game against Kansas City last year, he knew he had to pitch well or he would be sent back to the minors. He pitched seven strong innings and preserved his job. The rest of the package, however, is still missing.

Robinson: "He will get a full shot in 1985. I think he should have spent last year in the minors. He was in over his head in the majors. He might be able to pitch in the big leagues but, so far, is nothing great."

PITCHING:

First let's get the name straight: it can be Roy or Le Roy or Le Roy Purdy Smith III. The Indians' righthanded rookie pitcher answers to all three. But what you must call him is a fastball pitcher.

Smith was promoted from the Indians' Triple A club in Maine when Steve Farr went on the disabled list. The Indians gave him his first taste of the major leagues as a result of his going to the Florida Instructional League after the 1983 season and developing an off-speed curve.

Smith was once a promising prospect with the Philadelphia Phillies, but they soured on him when his velocity started to drop off. Smith came to the Indians in the John Denny deal of 1983, and it appeared the Indians had struck gold when Smith won his first two starts with the Tribe last season.

However, he showed a disturbing pattern that hounded him all season and eventually forced him to the bullpen: he gave up home runs in his first two starts and kept giving them up the rest of the season (14 in 86.1 innings).

A strikeout pitcher, Smith has a bad habit of getting the ball up in the strike zone, and his 88-90 MPH fastball gets turned around on him.

Smith wrestled with his control all season. His control is average at best. He also had problems pitching from behind in tight situations. Roy can throw hard, but his inexperience definitely hurts him.

Smith was sent to the bullpen because he stopped throwing his change-up/curve. Smith seemed to find himself in relief, allowing just one run in his last 8.1 innings. He allowed four earned runs in 13.2 relief innings.

ROY SMITH
RHP, No. 33
RR, 6'3", 200 lbs.
ML Svc: 1 year
Born: 9-6-61 in
Mt. Vernon, NY

1984 STATISTICS

W	L	ERA	G	GS	CG	IP	H	R	ER	BB	SO	SV
5	5	4.59	22	14	0	86	91	49	44	40	55	0

CAREER STATISTICS

W	L	ERA	G	GS	CG	IP	H	R	ER	BB	SO	SV
5	5	4.60	22	14	0	86	91	49	44	40	55	0

FIELDING:

Smith fields his position well. He keeps his eye on all runners and will throw to first to keep them close. His move to first is average.

OVERALL:

Smith showed some good signs last season: he throws hard, can strike out the hitters and has good overall poise. Roy is only 23 years old, but he's been pitching professionally since he was 18 and has an idea of what to do on the mound.

Although he had success in the pen, he is best suited to a starting role. If he can stay away from the long ball and throw his change-up/curve consistently for strikes, he could be a big help to the Indians.

Robinson: "I think you will see a better pitcher in 1985 in Roy Smith. He was rushed to the big leagues last year and got his feet wet. He does have some ability and could have a future with the Indians because he has a good live arm."

HITTING:

Pat Tabler remains the man without a position. The Indians gave him the first base job at the start of last season, then he split time between left field and first and finished the year at third base when Brook Jacoby went down with a hand injury.

The one constant was hitting. Tabler hit from the first of the year to the last. Batting righthanded with a squared stance, Tabler hit to all fields and even started to pull the ball to left field with power.

The Indians' coaching staff thinks that Tabler could become a home run hitter if he turned on more pitches. Pat, however, wants to be a high-average hitter. Last year, he had 10 home runs, a career high, and dreams of combining the two: power and average.

Tabler hit righthanded pitching better than lefties (.293 vs. .283) and likes fastballs out over the plate. Pitchers who keep the ball down on the outside part of the plate with curves and sliders have the best chance against him.

Tabler loves to hit with men on base. Last year he hit .310 with men in scoring position and a sizzling .556 (5 of 9), with 14 RBIs, in bases-loaded situations. He is a line drive hitter who goes to right field better than the opposition suspects.

BASERUNNING:

Tabler is not quick out of the box, but builds speed as he goes. He will take the extra base when the situation presents itself and doesn't mind breaking up a double play. Last year he stole three bases and will not make anyone forget Rickey Henderson.

FIELDING:

Tabler keeps getting ripped for his poor fielding, but he only committed seven errors last year while playing at

PAT TABLER
INF, No. 10
RR, 6'2", 195 lbs.
ML Svc: 2 years
Born: 2-2-58 in
    Hamilton, OH

1984 STATISTICS

AVG	G	AB	R	H	2B	3B	HR	RBI	BB	SO	SB
.290	144	473	66	137	21	3	10	68	47	62	3

CAREER STATISTICS

AVG	G	AB	R	H	2B	3B	HR	RBI	BB	SO	SB
.276	328	1089	142	301	51	11	18	145	122	171	5

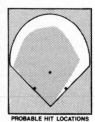

STRONG — VS. RHP   STRONG — VS. LHP   PROBABLE HIT LOCATIONS

three different positions. A shaky outfielder in 1983, Tabler worked hard and did a nice job in left field last year. He played well at third in place of Jacoby and did a solid job at first base, although Mike Hargrove replaced him for defensive reasons after the seventh inning in close games.

OVERALL:

Tabler wants one position to call his own and the Indians are going to try to find him one. He is an aggressive, all-out player who doesn't let one aspect of his game hurt the others. If he boots a ball in the field, he will make up for it at the plate.

Robinson: "He had another good year, and I think he will put even better numbers on the board next year. He can play anywhere and might end up at third base next year if Jacoby can make it at second base. To me, it appears that Tabler has found a home in Cleveland."

HITTING:

Andre Thornton is a righthanded power hitter who has made a living carrying the Indians on his thick shoulders for the last eight seasons. Last year was no different, as he hit 33 home runs and drove in 99 runs for Cleveland.

Thornton can go to right field when he wants to, but most of the time he looks for a low fastball he can pull over the left field fence. Pitchers have made a habit out of working around him. Last year, he drew 91 walks, 11 of them intentional.

Any pitcher in his right mind will pitch Thornton down and away with everything--especially breaking balls. Andre is a patient hitter and knows the strike zone well. He works out of a slightly open stance and has a quick, compact swing, unlike most power hitters.

He is a thunderous streak hitter who seldom gets frustrated by his slumps. Last year Thornton hit righthanders better than he did lefthanders. Against righties, Thornton hit 23 home runs and had 75 RBIs. Against lefties, he had 10 home runs and 24 RBIs.

Thornton didn't take as many pitches last year and that's because he had a better cast of players around him. It's ironic that when the Indians finally started looking like a power team, he turned free agent and seemed set on playing elsewhere.

BASERUNNING:

For a big man, Thornton gets out of the box and down the line quickly, especially if he has a shot at an infield hit. Based on pure skill, he is probably one of the best baserunners on the Indians. He will go from first to third in the right situation, always digs hard for doubles and stole six bases last year.

FIELDING:

Thornton can no longer play first

ANDRE THORNTON
1B, No. 29
RR, 6'2", 205 lbs.
ML Svc: 11 years
Born: 8-13-49 in
    Tuskegee, AL

1984 STATISTICS

AVG	G	AB	R	H	2B	3B	HR	RBI	BB	SO	SB
.271	155	587	91	159	26	0	33	99	91	79	6

CAREER STATISTICS

AVG	G	AB	R	H	2B	3B	HR	RBI	BB	SO	SB
.260	1285	4344	686	1131	215	22	214	736	754	684	40

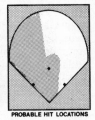

VS. RHP   VS. LHP   PROBABLE HIT LOCATIONS

base on a regular basis because it takes away from his hitting. However, he can do a nice job over a short period. He has limited range, but will dive for balls to his left and right and is good at blocking lows throws. He has a decent arm.

OVERALL:

The unmistaken leader on the Indians, Thornton says he will play for at least three more years. Unfortunately for the Indians, it probably won't be in Cleveland.

Robinson: "Thornton seems to be getting better with age (35). He had a big year in 1984, but I don't see him doing any better than that, though. He is really the leader of the Indians. His bat is still quick."

HITTING:

What a difference a year makes. In 1983, George Vukovich didn't look as if he could hit Triple A pitching, much less the kind being offered in the majors. If a pitcher threw him an off-speed pitch, Vukovich would swing until he fell down. And he'd miss it, too.

A lefthanded hitter, Vukovich learned to stay back on the breaking ball last year and stopped trying to pull every pitch to right field. He still has some problems with the breaking ball away, but he started to hit it to the left-center field gap in 1984.

A platoon player, Vukovich faced righthanded pitching and had his career-season. He led the Indians with a .304 average, with nine home runs and 60 RBIs.

Perhaps his success had something to do with manager Pat Corrales. Since Corrales took over as manager in 1983, Vukovich has hit .297 (152 of 512).

Vukovich uses a squared stance and stands fairly deep in the box. Basically a line drive hitter, Vukovich can hit home runs when he gets a fastball he can pull. Against righthanders, Vukovich likes the ball low and inside. Against lefthanded pitching--something he saw very little of last year--he likes the ball down and over the middle of the plate.

BASERUNNING:

Vukovich has average speed on the basepaths. He is aggressive on the bases and likes the headfirst slide. He will go hard into second to break up the double play. He is no threat to steal.

FIELDING:

Vukovich has a strong, accurate arm. Early in the 1984 season, runners tried to advance from first to third on him, but he put a stop to it quickly. He is an aggressive, heads-up fielder. Twice

GEORGE VUKOVICH
RF, No. 24
LR, 6'0", 198 lbs.
ML Svc: 4 years
Born: 6-24-56 in
Chicago, IL

1984 STATISTICS

AVG	G	AB	R	H	2B	3B	HR	RBI	BB	SO	SB
.304	134	437	38	133	22	5	9	60	34	61	1

CAREER STATISTICS

AVG	G	AB	R	H	2B	3B	HR	RBI	BB	SO	SB
.277	579	1168	121	324	54	10	19	158	97	154	7

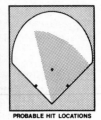

VS. RHP   VS. LHP   PROBABLE HIT LOCATIONS

last year Vukovich raced in to cover first base and second base on rundowns. Vukovich has good mobility, but seems to go to right-center better than to the foul line. He is not afraid of the fence and has decent jumping ability.

OVERALL:

On a young club such as the Indians, Vukovich seems like a veteran. But he is only 28 years old and is coming off his third full season in the bigs. He might be blossoming into a quality major leaguer.

Robinson: "I couldn't believe his final stats. He worked himself into the lineup and had a good year. I think he will be playing a lot next year and will have the same kind of season he had in 1984. Vukovich got his chance last year and was impressive in the way he took charge of his opportunity. I don't see him being sensational, just steady. That's plenty."

PITCHING:

If Tom Waddell did nothing else with the Indians last year, he left his mark by giving the nickname "The Undertow" to Clevand's version of "The Wave." Waddell made the observation after watching about 200 fans struggle with the wave on a cold September night at Cleveland Stadium.

The righthanded reliever is just as observant on the mound. A rookie last year, Waddell showed poise and savvy beyond his experience. He is a power pitcher who is helped greatly by his three-quarters delivery.

Waddell has decent control of four pitches: fastball, slider, curve and change. He went to the Florida Instructional League to work on a forkball to use against lefthanded hitters. Waddell had trouble with the forkball, but came up with a knuckler instead.

Drafted off the Atlanta Braves' minor league roster by the Indians, Waddell is 26 years old and more mature than most rookies. He has a good mental approach for a reliever and is most effective when he throws his 89 MPH fastball and keeps it low. When he gets the ball up, he's in trouble. He allowed 12 home runs in 97 innings last season.

Waddell developed an elbow problem just before the All Star break, and it hurt his delivery. He started throwing sidearm to take pressure off his elbow, and subsequently his pitches came up in the strike zone. An injection helped dissolve the bone chip in the elbow, and that's when the Indians stopped using him two or three days in a row. It turned out to be a good move. Pitching with at least a day's rest between appearances, Waddell put together a super second half of the season, going 5-2 with five saves and a 2.55 ERA.

Waddell doesn't like the Indians' strategy: he believes he can pitch every day—but he does not argue with success.

TOM WADDELL
RHP, No. 54
RR, 6'1", 190 lbs.
ML Svc: 1 year
Born: 9-17-58 in
Dundee, Scotland, U.K.

1984 STATISTICS													
W	L	ERA	G	GS	CG	IP	H	R	ER	BB	SO	SV	
7	4	3.06	58	0	0	97	68	35	33	37	59	6	
CAREER STATISTICS													
W	L	ERA	G	GS	CG	IP	H	R	ER	BB	SO	SV	
7	4	3.06	58	0	0	97	68	35	33	37	59	6	

FIELDING:

He uses one move to first base, and it is effective at keeping runners the close. He is not extremely quick off the mound, but he is still a decent fielder and works hard at it. He is good at directing traffic on infield flies and foul pops.

OVERALL:

Waddell is a bit of a comedian, and it helps his approach to the game. Never too high after a good performance or too low after a bad one, Waddell has the ability to make light of any situation.

Corrales used him mostly as a setup man last year, but he will probably get more save opportunities this year. He has good overall stuff and has performed well everywhere he's pitched.

Robinson: "I look for him to be a very good relief pitcher this year. He gained confidence as the year went on. In fact, he finished up with 23 scoreless innings. Not bad at all; keep your eye on this one."

HITTING:

Jerry Willard's first year in the big leagues opened his eyes. He started the season behind Ron Hassey. After Hassey was traded to the Chicago Cubs, Willard lost the starting job to Chris Bando, who simply took it away from him.

Willard still managed to hit 10 home runs and finally found his game, mentally speaking, in the last two weeks of the season, when Bando couldn't catch because of rotator cuff strain. Always an offensive player, Willard took his hitting problems behind the plate and it hurt his ability as a receiver.

Willard has a long lefthanded swing and is a sucker for any kind of breaking pitch. He is a free-swinger who can pull an inside fastball into the seats. Off-speed pitches and curveballs drive him crazy. He had 246 at-bats and 55 strike-outs last year.

Willard is a guess hitter and guessed mostly wrong last year. He hits out of a slightly closed stance and can't re-sist swinging at the first pitch. He is a dead pull hitter who looks for high fastballs on the inside part of the plate.

BASERUNNING:

As are most catchers, Willard is slow. He has average instincts on the bases and is definitely no threat to steal.

FIELDING:

Willard has a good arm and release point, but his work behind the plate needs polishing. The Indians got on him because of his work habits. They be-lieved that he did not practice hard enough when he wasn't in the starting lineup.

He has a tough time handling balls in the dirt and blocking wild pitches. Man-ager Pat Corrales is constantly remind-

JERRY WILLARD
C, No. 53
LR, 6'2", 195 lbs.
ML Svc: 1 year
Born: 3-14-60 in
  Oxnard, CA

1984 STATISTICS

AVG	G	AB	R	H	2B	3B	HR	RBI	BB	SO	SB
.224	87	246	21	55	8	1	10	37	26	55	1

CAREER STATISTICS

AVG	G	AB	R	H	2B	3B	HR	RBI	BB	SO	SB
.224	87	246	21	55	8	1	10	37	26	55	1

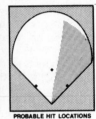

VS. RHP   VS. LHP   PROBABLE HIT LOCATIONS

ing him to "Catch the ball, Jerry!" Willard's rapport with the pitching staff improved as the season wore on.

OVERALL:

Willard got a taste of the major leagues as a rookie last year, and that should help him make some adjustments in 1985. Cocky and a bit abrasive, he had the starch taken out of him by a tough 1984 season. He has good power and all the tools to be a fine catcher, but he must work at developing those tools. He started to realize that at the end of last year.

Robinson: "All things considered, he got his rookie season under his belt and should be a better player in 1985. He should improve in all departments next season. Cleveland is a good spot for him: if he's got the talent, he will play. Look for him to share the catch-er's job with Chris Bando."

RICK BEHENNA
RHP, No. 32
RR, 6'2", 170 lbs.
ML Svc: 2 years
Born: 3-6-60 in
Miami, FL

PITCHING:

Rick Behenna came to the Indians late in 1983 from Atlanta with Brett Butler and Brook Jacoby for Len Barker. Behenna pitched well and was scheduled to be a starter in 1984.

However, Behenna injured his right arm late in spring training, and it never responded to treatment. He made three starts during the regular season before going on the disabled list May 15 with a torn rotator cuff. Behenna underwent surgery and began his rehabilitation program in the Florida Instructional League.

Behenna was throwing once a week in Florida under a 30-pitch limit. He was clocked at 89 MPH, but the Indians are keeping a close eye on him to prevent another blowout. Behenna is a power pitcher who relies primarily on a fastball and slider. That will make his comeback even tougher.

OVERALL:

The Indians are in desperate need of some starting pitchers. Medical reports say that Behenna's tear wasn't of a serious nature, but the jury is still out. He will go to spring training 1985, but he is still a long shot to make the club.

BRODERICK PERKINS
INF/OF/PH, No. 15
LL, 5'11", 180 lbs.
ML Svc: 5 years
Born: 11-23-54 in
Pittsburg, CA

HITTING, BASERUNNING, FIELDING:

Broderick Perkins is a good singles hitter with no power. He was lost in the Cleveland shuffle, and the Indians released him after the 1984 season ended. There were simply too many people in front of him.

The lefthanded hitting Perkins uses a closed stance. He can handle most pitches, but the fastball is his specialty. Perkins was rarely used last season (66 at-bats) except as a pinch-hitter and designated hitter. When he did get the chance, he failed to produce.

He has average speed, but is definitely no threat to steal. He does not run hard to first base.

Perkins is a liability in the outfield. The only position he can play is first base, and the Indians have Joe Carter, Mike Hargrove and Andre Thornton well in front of him.

OVERALL:

Perkins soured on Cleveland last year and his attitude deteriorated. In 1982, he led the NL with a .379 pinch-hitting average, and that may be his best role.

DETROIT TIGERS

PITCHING:

Sparky Anderson never forgets. And, like an elephant, he is loyal, too. He managed Milt Wilcox when they were both with the Cincinnati Reds and made sure that Wilcox found his way to Detroit. Doug Bair saved 28 games for Sparky in 1978 and when the Cardinals were looking to trade Bair in 1983, Anderson once again raised his trunk and trumpeted, "Go get him!"

Detroit got this righthanded reliever and he has not let them down. He may be the forgotten man in a bullpen that features Willie Hernandez and Aurelio Lopez, but before young Roger Mason came up in September, Bair had all of the saves that Hernandez and Lopez didn't-- all four of them.

Somebody has to do the dirty work and pitch the middle innings of games that get out of hand, and Bair is the man. He appeared in 47 games for Detroit in 1984. He did not have the 7-3 record that he had in 1983, but he was dependable.

He throws basically overhand but drops a bit to three-quarters at times. His main pitch is the fastball (88-90 MPH), which he uses for his strikeout pitch, but he does have an excellent slider that breaks sharply. When it breaks down and his fastball tails away from hitters, he is tough. He has a good overhand curve and change, but he is much more confident with the hard slider and fastball. Bair will use the big curve to righties when he is ahead in the count to set up the other hard stuff.

He can pitch in pressure situations and can pitch three or four times a week, but gets into trouble when his control is off. If he falls behind in the count, a batter can look fastball.

DOUG BAIR
RHP, No. 40
RR, 6'0", 180 lbs.
ML Svc: 9 years
Born: 8-22-49 in
Defiance, OH

1984 STATISTICS

W	L	ERA	G	GS	CG	IP	H	R	ER	BB	SO	SV
5	3	3.75	47	1	0	93	82	42	39	36	57	4

CAREER STATISTICS

W	L	ERA	G	GS	CG	IP	H	R	ER	BB	SO	SV
47	37	3.54	443	2	0	694	634	296	273	314	526	76

Bair allowed 10 homers in 93.2 innings, not a good ratio.

FIELDING:

Bair's move to first is average. His windup is quick but when he pitches from the stretch position he takes a very long time and runners will try to steal on him. He is working hard at releasing the ball more quickly with men on base and has begun to improve.

OVERALL:

When Ron Davis was with the Yankees, he used to say that Gossage got the saves and he got the "holds." Well, in Detroit, it is Bair who is doing the "holding."

Robinson: "He has an extremely tricky motion that keeps batters off stride. His fastball and curve are still good, and he followed up one winning year with another. He is a perfect guy for their staff and fits in well. He knows his job and does it."

PITCHING:

Juan Berenguer can drive a manager crazy. He might be the hardest thrower on the Detroit staff, but he simply cannot get the ball where he wants it often enough to be successful. Like Dennis Martinez of Baltimore, Berenguer can easily throw a two-hit shutout in one start and look like the return of Juan Marichal. Unlike Marichal, however, he can come back with four or five bad games in a row.

Everything he throws is hard--the fastball, the slider and the curve. He can keep them down and be effective, and he can throw the high inside fastball past most hitters. Batters do not like to dig in against him because he is the only one who has even the slightest idea of where the pitch will be.

He can be successful when he takes something off the curve or slider and moves his fastball around the edges of the plate, but he likes raw heat and keeps challenging batters. His fastball at times comes in too straight and he can be taken deep. He is hurt more often when he puts men on base and becomes too deliberate or when he gets his breaking ball up in the strike zone.

FIELDING:

He is big and burly and does not field his position well. He is not quick off the mound and has had trouble with bunts and chops. He does have an excellent move to first for a righthander. It is quick, fast and seemingly never expected by a runner.

JUAN BERENGUER
RHP, No. 44
RR, 5'11", 215 lbs.
ML Svc: 7 years
Born: 11-30-54 in
    Agualdulce, PAN

1984 STATISTICS

W	L	ERA	G	GS	CG	IP	H	R	ER	BB	SO	SV
11	10	3.48	31	27	2	168	146	75	65	79	118	0

CAREER STATISTICS

W	L	ERA	G	GS	CG	IP	H	R	ER	BB	SO	SV
23	32	3.89	106	69	5	476	399	234	206	243	344	1

OVERALL:

He has bounced around for seven years. Berenguer seemed to have put it all together in 1983 when he went 9-5 and had a 3.14 ERA. He was spotty last season so Sparky Anderson did not use him in either the Championship Series or the World Series . . . not a good sign for a power pitcher who is supposed to be able to start and relieve.

Robinson: "He was hot and cold all year long. He pitched in one game against the Orioles that I just couldn't believe: it was an important game for Detroit at the time and Juan pitched so well that he shut down the Orioles completely. There are so many other times, however, when he is not that sharp. I know that pitching coach Roger Craig gave him some confidence. He will be able to go as far as his control will take him."

HITTING:

Bergman is one of the few players in baseball who can bat .000 for a full season and still be of value to a team. In 1984, after spending parts of four years with the Astros and three with the Giants, Bergman happened to be of value to the Detroit Tigers.

But Bergman hit .273 points higher than .000 and gave Detroit an outstanding power year as the backup first baseman and pinch-hitter. He is a fastball hitter who likes the ball toward the inner half of the plate. He has trouble going the other way with pitches, particularly fastballs up and in. He rarely faces lefthanded pitchers and is a liability against them because he has trouble with breaking balls.

He is rated better than average as a clutch hitter and hit better than .300 with runners on base in 1983 with the Giants and in 1984 with Detroit.

BASERUNNING:

Usually, everybody runs in Sparky Anderson's scheme of things and Bergman is no exception. He is not particularly fast but gets a good jump from the box and from any base. He has learned how to run the bases, does not gamble but does not take foolish chances.

FIELDING:

Bergman is one of the best defensive first basemen in the league. He was never an everyday player because he cannot hit lefties, but his play around first leaves nothing to be desired. He can go either way, can handle errant throws and works well with pitchers when fielding grounders and flipping to first. He protects the line as well as any first baseman in the league. He plays first base when Darrell Evans is rested, and always replaces Evans in the late stages of regular season--or play-off--games. He saved Jack Morris's no-

DAVE BERGMAN
INF, No. 14
LL, 6'2", 180 lbs.
ML Svc: 9 years
Born: 6-6-53 in
Evanston, IL

1984 STATISTICS
AVG	G	AB	R	H	2B	3B	HR	RBI	BB	SO	SB
.273	120	271	42	74	8	5	7	44	33	40	3

CAREER STATISTICS
AVG	G	AB	R	H	2B	3B	HR	RBI	BB	SO	SB
.259	598	983	129	255	35	9	22	114	145	139	13

  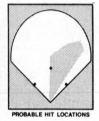

VS. RHP   VS. LHP   PROBABLE HIT LOCATIONS

hitter with two outstanding plays in the late innings in April 1984.

OVERALL:

He had his best offensive year ever and played in more games in 1984 than in any single year in the bigs. On June 4th, on national TV, he battled Roy Lee Jackson of the Blue Jays for 7 minutes and 13 seconds, through 13 pitches in the 10th inning with two men on base. On the 13th pitch he hit a three-run homer to win the game. "That was the greatest at-bat I have ever seen in the majors," Anderson said after the game. "Sparky tends to exaggerate," said Bergman, smiling.

Robinson: "He did a great job and got some very big hits for Detroit. I think he is a very underrated hitter, but I do think he will be a part-time player. He's a good, hard-nosed player with a good attitude, and Detroit seems the ideal team for him."

HITTING:

If you think any team in baseball drafted better than the Tigers did from 1974 through 1976, please let someone know. Detroit picked Lance Parrish, Jack Morris, Dan Petry, Lou Whitaker and Alan Trammell. Of course, they also picked Tom Brookens. Despite a succession of poor offensive and defensive years from him, the Tigers stayed with their utility infielder for five years and in 1984 this 1975 draftee paid back some dividends.

He remains an impatient hitter who rarely walks, but he made more contact in 1984 and improved his fielding immensely. He had always been the type of player to let his poor fielding affect his hitting, but he has changed. He is considered dangerous with men on base, although he is usually inserted into the lineup when a key player is injured or being rested, or late in a game that has already been won or lost.

He can hit low fastballs and will sometimes go the other way with men on base, but he has a tendency to swing too hard. He has trouble with breaking balls--anyplace--from righthanded pitchers but can hit the breaking ball from a lefty. He has trouble with hard sliders away and fastballs up and away from lefties.

Brookens is an excellent bunter who can bunt for a hit or for a sacrifice. He can bunt toward third or push the ball past the pitcher toward second. He led the team with eight sacrifice bunts in 1984.

BASERUNNING:

He will steal if you don't watch him, and will always be involved in a hit-and-run when on base if the situation calls for it. He is not overly aggressive, but when in a good frame of mind he is intelligent and will not hurt a team by making foolish mistakes.

FIELDING:

Brookens has several negative records for American League third basemen. Four

TOM BROOKENS
INF, No. 16
RR, 5'10", 170 lbs.
ML Svc: 6 years
Born: 8-10-53 in
  Chambersburg, PA

1984 STATISTICS

AVG	G	AB	R	H	2B	3B	HR	RBI	BB	SO	SB
.246	113	224	32	55	11	4	5	26	19	33	6

CAREER STATISTICS

AVG	G	AB	R	H	2B	3B	HR	RBI	BB	SO	SB
.246	673	1892	228	466	79	22	38	228	132	296	49

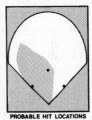

VS. RHP   VS. LHP   PROBABLE HIT LOCATIONS

errors in a game in 1980 tied one record, and 29 errors the same year led all third basemen in the league. Yet he continued to work hard and filled in well for Alan Trammell when the latter went down with the shoulder injury in mid-season. His range is limited at both short and third, but he has learned how to play the hitters and can now be counted on to make the necessary plays. Average arm, average in turning the double play, but much improved at third. He will dive either way to stop balls and can go back very well on pops.

OVERALL:

The Tigers stayed with him for five years, and he reduced his error total to 12 in 1984, so he must be doing something right.

Robinson: "He is a guy who can help a team because he plays so many positions. He can be a much better hitter if he stopped trying to jerk everything out of the park and go the other way more often. All he will wind up seeing is breaking balls away unless he starts to hit the other way."

HITTING:

Some players go about their business and are not distracted by anything. Others are always reading newspapers and finding something in print that bothers them. They either berate the writer or hide from anyone with a pad, pencil or tape recorder.

Prior to the World Series, one famous New York sportswriter wrote (when decribing the matchups): "Because of his experience and defensive skills, Graig Nettles is likely to start every game at third for San Diego. Detroit platoons a mediocre player like Marty Castillo with Darrell Evans when Evans isn't playing first base. Edge: Padres."

Castillo said nothing--except to hit .333 in the Series and win the third game with a homer.

Castillo is not a mediocre player. He can play third or catch. He is mediocre only if the word is synonymous with "a bit below average."

He is a high fastball hitter who tries to pull too much. Castillo does have occasional power but will not hit for a high average because he cannot handle the breaking ball. He goes up to home plate swinging the bat and does not draw many walks. He has trouble with righties who throw breaking balls, so he waits for the high fastball. Generally, he plays only against lefties unless he is catching.

BASERUNNING:

He gets out of the batter's box fairly well and has average speed. He has good instincts on the bases but does not take chances. He is not a threat to steal and the Tigers rarely play hit-and-run with him.

FIELDING:

Castillo is a decent catcher who knows enough to let a veteran staff call their own games. His arm is average but

MARTY CASTILLO
C/INF, No. 8
RR, 6'1", 190 lbs.
ML Svc: 4 years
Born: 1-16-57 in
    Long Beach, CA

1984 STATISTICS

AVG	G	AB	R	H	2B	3B	HR	RBI	BB	SO	SB
.234	70	141	16	33	5	2	4	17	10	33	1

CAREER STATISTICS

AVG	G	AB	R	H	2B	3B	HR	RBI	BB	SO	SB
.213	144	268	27	57	9	2	6	27	17	57	3

  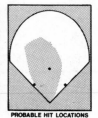

VS. RHP   VS. LHP   PROBABLE HIT LOCATIONS

accurate. At third, he committed only one error in 58 games in 1983. In 1984 he committed only seven errors in 70 games, playing at third (primarily) and behind the plate. His range at third is limited but he plays hard and tries to knock everything down. His arm is rated average to good.

OVERALL:

The World Series always showcases "mediocre" ball players. The Padres had their Kurt Bevaqua . . . and the Tigers had their Marty Castillo.

Robinson: "Average overall ability, but better in the field than people give him credit for. I doubt if he will ever hit that well. He is a perfect role player for the Tigers, and I look for him to perform this year as he did last year. I don't think he is an everyday player."

HITTING:

Darrell Evans is one-third of one of the toughest trivia questions now making the rounds: Who are the only three players to have hit more than 40 home runs in a single season while playing for the same team?

Henry Aaron, Davey Johnson and Darrell Evans (with the 1973 Atlanta Braves). That's three.

Evans gave the Tigers the extra lift they needed in 1984, filling in at first and third and as the DH. He did not hit for average but gave them leadership and a solid, all-around game. He struggled early, pressing and trying to hit homers every time up, but began making contact and the homers came.

He is a low ball, fastball hitter who bats from a square stance. He is extremely disciplined at home plate and has averaged close to 90 walks per season for 14 years. He will not chase bad pitches, but can be struck out by lefties with hard stuff in on his hands and breaking balls down and away.

He faced mostly righties in Detroit's scheme of things in 1984, and had to make some adjustments after 13 years in the National League. After playing in Candlestick Park and seeing the short porch in right in Tiger Stadium, Evans's eyes lit up early, but he began swinging too hard and trying to pull everything. Righties would give him the fastball away and turn it over, and Evans did not go the other way.

He is a good mistake hitter and if a pitcher gets the fastball or curve near the heart of the plate, it is gone.

BASERUNNING:

Evans is heady on the bases. He knows his limitations and will not take foolish chances. He will steal if he has to, but does not have good speed. He takes a bigger lead than most players and is always alert and aggressive when running the bases.

DARRELL EVANS
1B, No. 41
LR, 6'2", 195 lbs.
ML Svc: 14 years
Born: 5-26-47 in
    Pasadena, CA

1984 STATISTICS

AVG	G	AB	R	H	2B	3B	HR	RBI	BB	SO	SB
.232	131	401	60	93	11	1	16	63	77	70	2

CAREER STATISTICS

AVG	G	AB	R	H	2B	3B	HR	RBI	BB	SO	SB
.252	1984	6749	1116	1700	262	35	278	973	1204	1001	88

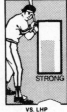

VS. RHP   VS. LHP   PROBABLE HIT LOCATIONS

FIELDING:

Better at first than third, Evans is extremely sure-handed despite a lack of range. He catches everything hit his way and will dive to knock balls down. He seems to be a "gamer" type of player, like Graig Nettles, who makes outstanding defensive plays in key situations.

OVERALL:

Detroit needed a mature, solid player who knew how to win. They avoided the free agent draft until Evans went free agent. Sparky Anderson called Evans on the phone and said one thing: "Sign with Detroit and you will get your chance to play in a World Series."

Robinson: "A power hitter coming to a new league always tries to pull everything from the start, and that is what Evans did. When he realized what was happening, he started to go the other way and that helped him. He hit 30 homers the year before, and if he plays enough in Detroit this year, he'll hit 30 again."

HITTING:

While playing with the Evansville Triplets in the American Association in 1983, Barbaro Garbey waved a bat menacingly at a fan who was taunting him.

For the first three months of his rookie season in 1984, Garbey waved that same bat at American League pitchers and was hitting well over .300. He finally cooled off a bit, but .287 is not that much of a drop when you are playing with a championship team and are the designated hitter against all lefthanders.

Garbey has a slightly open, straight-up stance and holds the bat high. He is a dead low fastball hitter who hits the ball to all fields. He does not have power and tends to get many hits on low liners or hard grounders. He does not get the ball in the air that much.

The book on most rookies the first time around the horn is to feel them out, see how they react to high, tight fastballs, then start throwing breaking balls away. Garbey, an aggressive and impatient hitter, swings but does not strike out a lot. He is a contact hitter.

Pitchers will throw the fastball past him, but it must be above the belt. A good breaking ball pitcher with control, who mixes in off-speed pitches, will give him trouble.

Garbey will swing at many first pitches, and when pitchers started to realize that, they would feed him the high hard one. If he swung and missed, he would then get breaking balls, but if they are in his hitting area, he can hit them and muscle them over the infield.

BASERUNNING:

Barbero is very aggressive on the basepaths and loves to run. He was caught seven times in 13 steal attempts and often runs when he shouldn't. He is, however, learning how to steal and how to run more intelligently.

BARBARO GARBEY
OF, No. 27
RR, 5'10", 170 lbs.
ML Svc: 1 year
Born: 12-4-56 in
Santiago, CU

1984 STATISTICS

AVG	G	AB	R	H	2B	3B	HR	RBI	BB	SO	SB
.287	110	327	45	94	17	1	5	52	17	35	6

CAREER STATISTICS

AVG	G	AB	R	H	2B	3B	HR	RBI	BB	SO	SB
.287	110	327	45	94	17	1	5	52	17	35	6

STRONG VS. RHP   STRONG VS. LHP   PROBABLE HIT LOCATIONS

FIELDING:

He can play first and the outfield, but defense is not his strong point. He is below average around the bag at first and has trouble with grounders. He does not move around enough to handle errant throws, and his arm is rated only average.

OVERALL:

He came to the U.S. from Cuba on the Freedom Flotilla in 1980. After signing with Detroit, he was severely beaned in the minors in 1981, but showed no fear when returning to the lineup.

Robinson: "He can hit and he did a great job with the bat for the Tigers. Finding a position might be a problem, so I believe he will play in about the same amount of games for the Tigers this year, and be used as a DH quite a bit. He is maturing fast, both on and off the field."

HITTING:

Kirk Gibson started hitting--and doing everything else right--after he hit something that wasn't a baseball. In 1983, he hit a guy in a bar who was heckling him.

The "next Mickey Mantle," as Gibson was once labeled by manager Sparky Anderson, was a platoon player who could do everything but hit lefties and field consistently. The fans booed him unmercifully in 1983. Gibson spent time thinking things over and went to the Pacific Institute in Seattle and learned many things about himself.

He didn't learn baseball there, but in the off-season he lost some weight, made a vow and played well in 1984.

He has a slightly open, straight-up stance, bat held high. In 1984 he stopped using only his powerful shoulders and arms and started shifting his hips properly to get his hands into play. He became a much better power and contact hitter. Playing every day, he became more patient at the plate and gained confidence. He was always a better high ball, fastball hitter than anything else, but he still chased balls out of the strike zone. In 1984, he looked more "zone" and began to hit the ball where it was pitched. He is still a pull hitter with power to all fields.

Lefties will feed him curves and sliders, low and away, mix in an off-speed pitch and spot the fastball away. Righthanded pitchers have stopped trying to throw the fastball past him and will try sinkers, sliders and junk away. He hit the low inside fastball against both lefties and righties much better in 1984 than he ever did in the past. He is an excellent bunter who now bunts when the occasion calls for it--instead of every time he is in a slump or has two strikes on him.

BASERUNNING:

His pure speed was finally turned into talent in 1984, when Gibson led the Tigers with 29 stolen bases. He is one of the most aggressive runners in baseball but cannot slide well. As a 6'3"

KIRK GIBSON
OF, No. 23
LL, 6'3", 210 lbs.
ML Svc: 5 years
Born: 5-28-57 in
Pontiac, MI

1984 STATISTICS

AVG	G	AB	R	H	2B	3B	HR	RBI	BB	SO	SB
.282	149	531	92	150	23	10	27	91	63	103	29

CAREER STATISTICS

AVG	G	AB	R	H	2B	3B	HR	RBI	BB	SO	SB
.273	492	1701	253	465	67	25	69	237	170	352	76

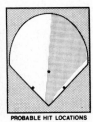

VS. RHP   VS. LHP   PROBABLE HIT LOCATIONS

ex-football player, he runs the bases like a linebacker chasing a quarterback. He runs hard at all times and is always a threat to steal.

FIELDING:

Gibson improved as a fielder, but he almost HAD to because he had less than a full season of minor league ball before reporting to the Tigers. Kirk has a good arm and is getting better and more accurate. He has trouble coming in on a ball, does not get the perfect jump but outruns balls hit anywhere.

OVERALL:

Gibson was the playoff MVP and leader of the team in game-winning hits (17) and had his biggest year in every single offensive category.

Robinson: "He was the first Tiger in history to hit at least 20 homers and steal at least 20 bases. He got everything together. He worked hard with Al Kaline in spring training and became a better outfielder. He finally realized the value of the word 'we' and he was a much better team player."

HITTING:

Some players demand to play every day. Some players are afraid to play every day because they would then have to face too many tough pitchers and their batting averages and self-esteem would take a drop.

And then there are players like Johnny Grubb, the Tigers' designated hitter against righthanded pitching in 1984. Grubb, due to a succession of injuries the past three years, saw less and less playing time, could not play the outfield but could always swing the bat. Ergo, he picked up the label of pinch-hitter/DH extraordinaire.

Grubb did just that, plus play much more in 1984 than he did in 1983. Knowing he would be in the lineup against only righties, Grubb made the most of his playing time. He became much more aggressive at home plate and swung for the long ball more often than not. He struck out twice as much in 1984 as he did in 1983, but he doubled his home run production.

He is a mature hitter who bats from a square, straight-up stance. He is an excellent low fastball hitter who generally has patience at the plate and looks for the fastball in a certain zone. He can also handle curveballs better than most hitters, but they must be in his power zone.

Pitchers are able to throw hard stuff past him up and in, but they must be careful. Grubb can be handled by pitchers with control who can keep the fastball and curve away. He will try to pull almost everything, so a pitcher who can turn the fastball over can get him to hit grounders to the right side. He will go the other way on occasion.

BASERUNNING:

Grubb is a smart baserunner with no speed to speak of. He will not steal or take chances on the bases but will go hard into second to try to break up double plays.

JOHN GRUBB
OF, No. 30
LR, 6'3", 180 lbs.
ML Svc: 13 years
Born: 8-4-48 in
Richmond, VA

1984 STATISTICS

AVG	G	AB	R	H	2B	3B	HR	RBI	BB	SO	SB
.267	86	176	25	47	5	0	8	17	36	36	1

CAREER STATISTICS

AVG	G	AB	R	H	2B	3B	HR	RBI	BB	SO	SB
.278	1206	3675	493	1022	181	27	79	386	478	489	29

  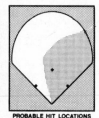

VS. RHP   VS. LHP   PROBABLE HIT LOCATIONS

FIELDING:

There was no room for Grubb, an outfielder by trade, to play in Detroit's outfield in 1984. He can play the outfield if he has to because he has a good arm and is fairly accurate with it. He is not spectacular but knows how to play the game.

OVERALL:

Grubb has the knack of winning big games, as he did with his extra-inning double in the American League Championship Series against the Royals. He had five game-winning RBIs in his limited playing time and came through with several key hits. He is not afraid to bat in pressure situations.

Robinson: "He is a part-time player and a good one. Injuries slow him down, but he's got some power and fits in well with Detroit playing against righthanded pitching. He can't play every day, but you are seeing him at his best right now."

PITCHING:

Popular music croons on and on about unrequited love and how it is always better the second time around. Willie Hernandez may know something about that. In seven years with the Chicago Cubs he was a .500 pitcher with 27 saves. In just one year with the Tigers, he saved 32 of his 33 possible chances, had a 9-3 record, won the AL Cy Young Award and MVP and became a millionaire. It was surely better for him the second time around.

The American League hitters had never seen him before and were not prepared to be impressed. Hernandez, however, had other ideas. Hitters stood in line to bat against him in the late innings, and one by one marched solemnly back to the dugout.

Hernandez can throw three-quarters to sidearm and does so to lefthanded hitters. He uses a top-notch screwball, a sinking fastball and a quick-breaking curve. He does not throw hard (his fastball is 85 MPH), but he does have outstanding control and he can spot the fastball in or out, up or down.

He does not give in to the hitters and is not afraid to throw his best pitch to their strength.

Hernandez was the short man on the championship Tigers and failed to save a game but once all season. He was untouchable all year, never wilted under pressure and never walked the key batter.

He uses the sinker/screwball/outside fastball to righthanders and the curve/screwball to lefthanded hitters. Batters do not know what is coming, and all of his pitches move. He allowed only six home runs in 140.1 innings.

FIELDING:

Hernandez is an excellent fielder who

WILLIE HERNANDEZ
LHP, No. 21
LL, 6'2", 180 lbs.
ML Svc: 7 years
Born: 11-14-54 in
Aguada, PR

1984 STATISTICS

W	L	ERA	G	GS	CG	IP	H	R	ER	BB	SO	SV
9	3	1.92	80	0	0	140	96	30	30	36	112	32

CAREER STATISTICS

W	L	ERA	G	GS	CG	IP	H	R	ER	BB	SO	SV
43	35	3.36	466	11	0	701	644	286	262	247	516	57

does not hurt himself on the mound and who is in perfect position after his release. Runners do not try to run on him.

OVERALL:

With the pennant-winning Philadelphia Phillies of 1983, Al Holland was the big man. After Detroit acquired Hernandez in March, Tony Perez told his old friend Sparky Anderson, "It was Willie who was the key man for the Phillies. He kept the team in the game until the ninth inning every time he was asked to." The Phillies traded Hernandez--and then disappeared from contention.

Robinson: "Sometimes I wonder about those who say that Willie doesn't throw hard. To me, it seems that he throws much harder than is the popular opinion. The hitters are always looking for a curve or the screwball, but Willie seems to just throw the fastball right by them. The change of leagues last season helped him, to be sure, but it was hardly the only factor in his success. He wanted to have that kind of season very badly--and he had it."

HITTING:

After hitting 23 homers in 1982 and 20 in 1983 and knocking in 180 runs in two years with Detroit, Larry Herndon slumped in the long ball department in 1984. When Ruppert Jones came up from Evansville in mid-season, Herndon was platooned and played only against left-handed pitching.

He has a quick bat that might be slowing down and stands deep in the box, square and upright. Righthanders will throw him hard stuff up and in, and curves and sliders away. He is a good low ball hitter who can hit either the curve or fastball if it is out over the plate. He can go the other way when he has to and will usually get a piece of the ball with men on base. He was always considered a good clutch hitter who became a better hitter when the game was on the line, but his platooning and his sudden lack of power left him more vulnerable to good pitching in 1984: his average dropped from .302 to .280.

He is not a good off-speed hitter, and lefties who keep the fastball up and the curve low and away and mix in something off-speed will give him trouble.

BASERUNNING:

Herndon is an excellent baserunner with good speed out of the box and on the bases. He will steal when he has to and is always on his way to two bases when he singles. He will take the extra base if the outfielder hesitates for just one second. He does something that every smart runner should do while running the bases--he cuts the bases beautifully and loses no ground when rounding any base he touches.

FIELDING:

Previously a below average left fielder, Herndon improved in 1984, cutting his error total from 15 to 3. He

LARRY HERNDON
OF, No. 31
RR, 6'3", 190 lbs.
ML Svc: 9 years
Born: 11-3-53 in
   Sunflower, MS

1984 STATISTICS

AVG	G	AB	R	H	2B	3B	HR	RBI	BB	SO	SB
.280	125	407	52	114	18	5	7	43	32	63	6

CAREER STATISTICS

AVG	G	AB	R	H	2B	3B	HR	RBI	BB	SO	SB
.278	1129	3753	479	1044	143	66	74	409	247	602	87

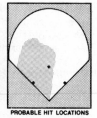

STRONG   STRONG

VS. RHP   VS. LHP   PROBABLE HIT LOCATIONS

catches what he gets to and is excellent at coming in on pops or short flies. He has some trouble going back and getting a good jump on a ball, but he has excellent speed and can catch up to balls other left fielders cannot. His arm is rated only average, but he has improved on his accuracy and on hitting the cut-off man.

OVERALL:

He is a tough, hard-nosed player who seeks no publicity and shies away from the press. He lets his actions on the field speak for themselves, and despite an off-year offensively he is the kind of player you want on your side.

Robinson: "His bat slowed down and pitchers took advantage of it. They threw a lot more fastballs past him last year than ever before. He has what they call warning track power."

HITTING:

Howard Johnson surprised his team, the fans and the opposition with his power and long ball ability in 1984.

The utility infielder, who plays third when Sparky Anderson makes one of his frequent lineup changes or pinch-hits for his third baseman late in a game, is a switch-hitter who has much more power batting lefthanded than righthanded. He batted .257 lefthanded and .224 righthanded. Ten of his twelve homers were from the left side.

He likes high fastballs and can hit for power if they are shoulder-level. He is aggressive and swings hard at everything, so he will have trouble with breaking balls down and away and off-speed pitches.

He has a square, wide stance and stands deep in the box. He is always ready for the high fastball, can go the other way if he has to but basically tries to pull everything. There is no definite pattern to his ability to be patient at the plate, but he will look at first pitches more often than not. He has a tendency to swing at bad pitches, but he did draw 40 walks in only 355 at-bats.

He is a good bunter either way and is called upon sacrifice.

BASERUNNING:

All signals were "go" for Johnson when he played in 1984. He tried 16 steals and was successful 10 times. He will run at the drop of a sign and is always a threat to steal.

FIELDING:

Johnson is considered a below average fielder at third. He has trouble with hard smashes and the in-between hops, but he does have decent range either

HOWARD JOHNSON
INF, No. 20
SR, 6'0", 175 lbs.
ML Svc: 1 year plus
Born: 11-29-60 in
Clearwater, FL

1984 STATISTICS											
AVG	G	AB	R	H	2B	3B	HR	RBI	BB	SO	SB
.248	116	355	43	88	14	1	12	50	40	67	10
CAREER STATISTICS											
AVG	G	AB	R	H	2B	3B	HR	RBI	BB	SO	SB
.262	197	576	77	151	19	1	19	69	63	107	17

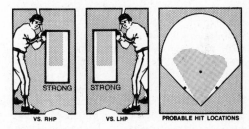

VS. RHP   VS. LHP   PROBABLE HIT LOCATIONS

way. His arm is rated average.

OVERALL:

He is another one of those players wearing a Tiger uniform who keeps coming at you from all directions. The knock on Detroit and their 35-5 start was that Anderson used his top nine players every day and the bench would not contribute as the year wore on. Johnson was one of the Detroit players who proved the critics wrong.

Robinson: "He was a much more aggressive hitter in 1984. He did have power in the minors, but it never showed in his limited playing time with Detroit. He'll have a better year this year, especially with the bat. I look for him to play a lot more this year but not every day."

HITTING:

And they say that a football takes crazy bounces! Ruppert Jones played out his option with the Padres after the 1983 season, was not signed, was invited to the Pirates' spring training camp-- and was released before the 1984 season began.

He went home, not feeling sad because he knew his phone would ring. But the postman and the phone did not ring once, let alone ring twice. Finally, in May, the Tigers asked him to go to their AAA Evansville club.

He did, proved he was still the player who was the number one selection by the expansion 1976 Mariners and reported to Detroit in mid-season. He won a game with a homer in his first game back and stayed along for the rest of the bubbly ride to the top.

He bats from a closed stance with an exaggerated crouch and looks for the fastball up and over the plate. He can get around on inside fastballs from righties but has trouble against left-handers who can throw breaking balls low and away. For that reason, manager Sparky Anderson used Jones only against righties, platooning him in left with Larry Herndon.

Jones has trouble with off-speed pitches if he is looking fastball but has learned to hit the fastball away to the opposite field. He becomes a much better hitter in the late innings with men on base because he knows he will get a fastball someplace. A pitcher must be careful in those situations with Jones. At other times he is an impatient hitter who tries for the long ball.

BASERUNNING:

Jones has excellent speed but does not get a good jump out of the batter's box when he swings too hard. He can steal if he has to but did not run in 1984. He takes more chances than most runners.

FIELDING:

Jones was always a center fielder but

RUPPERT JONES
OF, No. 22
LL, 5'10", 175 lbs.
ML Svc: 8 years
Born: 3-12-55 in
    Dallas, TX

1984 STATISTICS

AVG	G	AB	R	H	2B	3B	HR	RBI	BB	SO	SB
.284	79	215	26	61	12	1	12	37	21	47	2

CAREER STATISTICS

AVG	G	AB	R	H	2B	3B	HR	RBI	BB	SO	SB
.255	995	3441	479	876	169	31	101	435	393	610	124

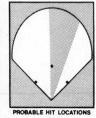

VS. RHP   VS. LHP   PROBABLE HIT LOCATIONS

had to play in left field with Detroit. He gets an excellent jump on a ball, is not afraid of fences (he was injured after crashing into a wooden fence in Oakland in 1980) and has a fair arm. Runners will run on him, but his arm is accurate and he generally keeps his throws low. He can go back on a ball as well as anyone.

OVERALL:

Jones had six game-winning hits in less than half a season and did everything asked of him. He won four different games for Detroit with late-inning home runs and saved two other games with spectacular catches.

Robinson: "Jones was a better hitter because he laid off the high fastball. What he gave Detroit was his best, and he can do it again for one very big reason--there has been a great amount of pressure put on him every place he has ever been. The Great Expectations were maybe a bit too great. He played in a much more relaxed manner in 1984 and he showed what he could do. He's a terrific hitter with good power."

HITTING:

Rusty Kuntz started playing professional baseball at the age of 22, older than most of the players who eventually make it to the big leagues. The Chicago White Sox waited patiently for him to develop, but disabling injuries in 1980 and 1982 eventually led to a trade to the Twins. In 1983 he played with the White Sox, the Twins . . . and Denver in the American Association. Detroit saw something they liked and acquired him in December of 1983.

Kuntz repaid the Tigers' confidence in him. He did everything asked of him, had the best full season of his pro career, hit better than anyone thought he would and played outstanding defense in the outfield.

He bats from an open stance with a slight crouch. Basically, he tries to pull everything, but he has no power. He is a contact hitter but an impatient hitter who will swing at the first pitch more often than not, particularly with men on base. He is a fair fastball hitter who likes the ball below the belt.

Pitchers can have success against him if they keep the fastball up and away and feed him curves and sliders low and away. He showed more aggressiveness at the plate in 1984 than ever before.

BASERUNNING:

Kuntz has good speed and good instincts on the bases. He is an aggressive runner who will take the extra base if the team needs it and tries not to make mental mistakes on the basepaths. He is not a threat to steal but takes a fairly long lead off first.

FIELDING:

It was his fielding that brought Kuntz to the big leagues in the first

RUSTY KUNTZ
OF, No. 15
RR, 6'3", 190 lbs.
ML Svc: 5 years
Born: 2-4-55 in
    Orange, CA

1984 STATISTICS

AVG	G	AB	R	H	2B	3B	HR	RBI	BB	SO	SB
.286	84	140	32	40	12	0	2	22	25	28	2

CAREER STATISTICS

AVG	G	AB	R	H	2B	3B	HR	RBI	BB	SO	SB
.239	272	436	75	104	23	0	5	38	58	98	12

VS. RHP

VS. LHP

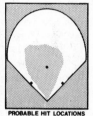

PROBABLE HIT LOCATIONS

place. He gets an excellent jump on the ball and can come in or go back very well. He has good range and knows how to play the hitters. His arm is rated good, as is the accuracy of his throws.

OVERALL:

Some players need a kick in the butt to produce. Others need a pat on the back. Kuntz falls into the latter class.

Robinson: "Sparky's confidence really helped him. He hit well in September, and overall he had what was obviously the best year of his life. He did an outstanding job for a part-time player and finally got the most out of his ability. I look for the same amount of playing time and the same production in 1985."

HITTING:

Most folks have come to think of "lemons" as things they'd rather not have to own. The Tigers feel much differently about their lemon. He may be the sweetest one in Detroit.

Chet Lemon stands deep in the box, almost on top of home plate, in a slight crouch and with a closed stance. Any hitting he does is a bonus for his team because he is now the best defensive center fielder in the league. In 1984, the Tigers got their bonus. Lemon made much more contact, did not stop swinging aggressively until the whole thing was over and lifted his average 32 points from the year before, when he was going for the long ball.

Lemon is an aggressive hitter who lunges toward the pitch and is often brushed back or hit by pitches. He is basically a high fastball hitter but has trouble with hard stuff in on his hands. Lefties and righties may try him up and away, but he can go the other way. Pitchers who have success against him will keep the ball down or use a variety of curves and sliders.

He is an excellent bunter who will bunt with two strikes, with men on base, with nobody out and any time you least expect him to.

BASERUNNING:

Lemon is one of the most aggressive runners in the league and will slide headfirst into any base and go hard into middle infielders while trying to break up double plays. He will always gamble on the basepaths and always try to take an extra base. Despite his speed, he is generally caught more than most runners because he will run through stop signs if he has a head of steam up.

FIELDING:

The only things that stop Lemon from catching everything hit to the outfield

CHET LEMON
OF, No. 34
RR, 6'0", 190 lbs.
ML Svc: 9 years
Born: 2-12-55 in
Jackson, MS

1984 STATISTICS

AVG	G	AB	R	H	2B	3B	HR	RBI	BB	SO	SB
.287	141	509	77	146	34	6	20	76	51	83	5

CAREER STATISTICS

AVG	G	AB	R	H	2B	3B	HR	RBI	BB	SO	SB
.282	1195	4230	633	1191	253	41	136	545	442	599	51

  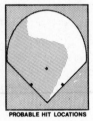

STRONG — VS. RHP   STRONG — VS. LHP   PROBABLE HIT LOCATIONS

are the left fielder, the right fielder and the fence. Nothing gets past him. He can come in and go back with the best, gets a tremendous jump on balls and committed only two errors in 1984. His arm is above average, but not as accurate as the best. All things considered, he is the most complete defensive center fielder in the league.

OVERALL:

He has matured and come into his own. He is a star, not a prima donna.

Robinson: "An outstanding outfielder. It was always said of him that he would run the bases until he found one where the ball was waiting for him, but he changed a lot in 1984. He is a much better fundamental player now. He came to play in 1984 and he played--all year long."

PITCHING:

Aurelio Lopez traveled a long way to stand on the mound for the World Champion Detroit Tigers. Many years ago, the manager of the Mexico City Diablos Rojas told Lopez that he couldn't make it in the Mexican League and would have to go to Sahuayo. Being sent to Sahuayo is a one-way ticket to Palookaville. Lopez bought his own ticket back.

Lopez went down, came back up to the Diablos, continued to rise and was with Kansas City briefly in 1974. He was sent back down for four years because he had assorted problems that were both physical and mental, but by 1978, Aurelio Lopez had had enough. This time, he stayed.

He throws smoke: a 90 MPH fastball that he mixes in with a slider, curve, change and screwball. He is effective against both left and righthanded hitters and will drop down from three-quarters to sidearm against righthanders and use the slider or curve. The straight change is just for show--Lopez uses the fastball or hard slider on the corners, usually down, for the strikeout pitch.

When he winds up or uses the stretch, his motion is herky-jerky and it seems that different parts of his portly body move at different times. The release is to his advantage because batters have a difficult time picking up the release of the ball.

He can pitch in long or short relief and is not bothered by men on base. At times he has control problems and when he does, he will come in with the fastball. If it comes in straight--and there are many times it does--batters can take him deep. In 1984 he allowed 16 homers in 137.2 innings, not a good ratio.

AURELIO LOPEZ
RHP, No. 29
RR, 6'0", 225 lbs.
ML Svc: 7 years
Born: 10-5-48 in
Pueblo, MEX

1984 STATISTICS												
W	L	ERA	G	GS	CG	IP	H	R	ER	BB	SO	SV
10	1	2.94	71	0	0	137	109	51	45	52	94	14

CAREER STATISTICS												
W	L	ERA	G	GS	CG	IP	H	R	ER	BB	SO	SV
54	25	3.37	337	9	0	707	600	288	265	279	517	80

FIELDING:

He has a big belly and looks as if he can't move around, but he can. He can get to chops toward first base and covers the bag well. His move to first is quick and effective, and he is not afraid to throw over four or five times in a row.

OVERALL:

Lopez was so disillusioned and troubled after arm trouble nearly ended his career several years ago that he seriously considered just retiring. Instead, he was lured back to the majors.

Robinson: "As good as he has been, last year was another perfect example of what it means to have a guy like Willie Hernandez on a team. I am sure that Lopez was helped mentally and had a lot of pressure taken off him because he wasn't the only man in the bullpen. Detroit has the perfect setup: he and Hernandez are a matched pair."

PITCHING:

When Jack Morris was 10-1 early in 1984, Baltimore catcher Rick Dempsey said that the Tigers' ace righthander would never win 20 games.

He was right . . . and wrong. Morris finished 19-11 and added a win against the Royals and two more in the World Series against the Padres. The last two wins were complete games--the only two that "Captain Hook" (Sparky Anderson) has allowed in 28 post-season games with both the Cincinnati Reds and the Detroit Tigers.

Morris might be the best righthander in the league. His windup exudes confidence. It is quick and powerful, and it seems as though his whole body is coming at you after his release. His fastball and slider are both clocked at 90 MPH or better, and he moves them in and out, pitching away from the batter's strength. If he has to, he will challenge a hitter and increase the velocity of his fastball. He usually busts it up and in to both left and righthanders.

His added forkball has made him more effective, as has the split-fingered fastball that all Tiger starters now use. It is a pitch that breaks down. He is a good control pitcher and when he has all four pitches working and mixes in a straight change, he is virtually unbeatable.

Because he challenges hitters, Morris can be taken deep. His is annually among the league leaders in home runs allowed. But he allowed only 10 in 1984, 10 fewer than in 1983.

He can pitch with men on base and is not fazed by any pressure situation. If anything, he tends to get lackadaisical when things are going too well. He is temperamental, calls his own game, but can get in trouble in the early innings if things are not going right--except in post-season play.

JACK MORRIS
RHP, No. 47
RR, 6'3", 190 lbs.
ML Svc: 7 years
Born: 5-16-55 in
   St. Paul, MN

1984 STATISTICS

W	L	ERA	G	GS	CG	IP	H	R	ER	BB	SO	SV
19	11	3.60	35	35	9	240	221	108	96	87	148	0

CAREER STATISTICS

W	L	ERA	G	GS	CG	IP	H	R	ER	BB	SO	SV
107	75	3.66	232	210	82	1597	1454	703	650	562	909	0

FIELDING:

He is one of the league's best fielders. Morris is cat-quick off the mound, handles bunts exceptionally well and has a good move to first. He knows what to do with the ball when he gets it and is in good position to handle balls hit back at him.

OVERALL:

Morris is moody: he did not get along with Anderson for four years, disagreed with pitching coach Roger Craig, argued with catcher Lance Parrish, sat alone on buses and planes when things were not going well, but . . . no pitcher in the league has won more games than he has since 1979 (103).

Robinson: "He is overpowering and can be better this year. Everybody knows he had struggles with himself and some of his coaches, but the chance to pitch in post-season play and do so well proves to me that Morris has gotten it all together. I have a feeling that he has come to the point where he won't let anything bother him anymore."

HITTING:

There seems little doubt that before Lance Parrish is through, he will break the all-time record for career homers (313 by Yogi Berra) by an American League catcher. In 1984 he broke his own single-season record of 32 by hitting 33.

His average slipped 30 points, but with everybody else on the team hitting, it didn't matter much. Parrish tried for the long ball and had his way. He is basically a high ball, fastball hitter and very few pitchers in the American League can get that pitch past him. He tries to pull and has enough power to muscle the ball out of the park even when he hits it down near his trademark.

He became less disciplined as a hitter in 1984, accounting for his career-high 120 strikeouts. Parrish will chase pitches out of the strike zone and will try to pull pitches on the outside portion of the plate. Righthanded pitchers will try to give him nothing but breaking balls down and away and mix in a sinking fastball. Lefthanders will try hard stuff up and away and sliders low and in.

He is a good clutch hitter, particularly against lefties. Occasionally, a pure power pitcher can get him with a high inside fastball because Parrish likes to have full extension of his arms and shoulders and does not like to get jammed. But a mistake is a home run when pitching to Parrish.

BASERUNNING:

Very few catchers have good speed and Parrish is no exception. He is an intelligent baserunner who knows his limitations, will not run the bases foolishly and will take the extra base rarely.

FIELDING:

He must be rated the top defensive catcher in the league. He was again at the top in throwing runners out and has the best throwing arm in the league: a

LANCE PARRISH
C, No. 13
RR, 6'3", 210 lbs.
ML Svc: 7 years
Born: 6-15-56 in Clairton, PA

1984 STATISTICS

AVG	G	AB	R	H	2B	3B	HR	RBI	BB	SO	SB
.237	147	578	75	137	16	2	33	98	41	120	2

CAREER STATISTICS

AVG	G	AB	R	H	2B	3B	HR	RBI	BB	SO	SB
.262	915	3397	460	889	168	21	162	540	255	674	20

  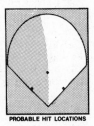

VS. RHP — STRONG   VS. LHP — STRONG   PROBABLE HIT LOCATIONS

veritable cannon, extremely accurate and a pitcher's best friend. He calls an excellent game and lets pitchers know exactly how he feels if they are doing something wrong. With his size and strength, when he talks, pitchers listen. He is outstanding at blocking pitches in the dirt and handling bunts and chops.

OVERALL:

He was the American League All Star catcher for the third straight year in 1984. He will probably be there again in 1985.

Robinson: "He had a long slump late in the year and his average suffered. I don't know if the drop in average bothered him that much because of his homer and RBI totals. He's basically a long ball hitter who likes to hit the ball as far as he can. He did have trouble with breaking balls away, but as far as power and defense, he's the best catcher in the league."

PITCHING:

One of these years, Dan Petry will win more games in a season than teammate Jack Morris. Most observers believe that Morris is the best righthanded pitcher in the league. Maybe he is, but over the last three years, Morris has a record of 56-40 and Petry is 52-28. Jack has won 17, 20 and 19 games, while Petry has won 15, 19 and 18. Morris may be winning more games, but Dan Petry loses a lot less.

Petry loses fewer games because he walks fewer batters and never lets anything bother him. He says, "Give me the ball," and goes outs and pitches, never missing a turn.

He uses a no-windup delivery and gets the ball to home plate very quickly. He puts a lot of effort into his windup and the image to the batters is that the ball will be fast--it is. Petry throws an 88 MPH fastball and a hard, sharp-breaking slider which is among the best in the league. He does not fool around with a change-up but uses a split-fingered fastball which acts like a change--at 85 MPH. He will pitch to spots and throw the slider low and in to both lefties and righties. The fastball runs in to a righthanded hitter and away from a lefthanded hitter. He can pitch under pressure and with men on base and he does not beat himself.

He has a tendency to get some of his pitches up in the strike zone and gives up more home runs than most pitchers. He did curtail that in 1984, when he allowed 21 homers, down from his 37 in 1983.

FIELDING:

He did not make an error in the en-

DAN PETRY
RHP, No. 46
RR, 6'4", 200 lbs.
ML Svc: 6 years
Born: 11-13-58 in
Palo Alto, CA

1984 STATISTICS
W	L	ERA	G	GS	CG	IP	H	R	ER	BB	SO	SV
18	8	3.24	35	35	7	233	231	94	84	66	144	0

CAREER STATISTICS
W	L	ERA	G	GS	CG	IP	H	R	ER	BB	SO	SV
78	51	3.52	173	170	37	1149	1068	499	450	438	608	0

tire 1984 season. He is flawless around the mound and cool on hard smashes hit back at him. He may be one step late in breaking from the mound on bunts but invariably gets the ball and the runner. He has a good move to first and runners will not run on him.

OVERALL:

You can call him "The Shadow" because nobody seems to know that he is in the big leagues. Everybody on the team seems to overshadow him, but he just might be better than Morris on a day in and day out basis. His .692 winning percentage was third best in the league. Only Mike Boddicker, Bert Blyleven and Morris won more games than Petry did.

Robinson: "He gave up a lot fewer homers this year and that helped him. He might have tailed off just a bit late in the year, but that did not detract from an outstanding year. His slider is probably the truest and best in the AL, and he can overpower the hitters."

PITCHING:

Dave Rozema throws everything but the kitchen sink to home plate. No matter, everything he throws sinks. He throws a fastball (at 84 MPH you really can't call it a fastball), a curve, slider and change.

At 6'4" and 200 pounds, he looks big on the mound and has a rapid windup and fairly forceful three-quarters to side-arm motion. That motion helps him because a batter simply cannot believe the ball takes a year to reach home plate.

Rozema is one of the best control pitchers in baseball, and in 1984 he walked only 18 batters in 101 innings. At times, however, his control is too good. Despite the breaking balls and off-speed pitches, batters know he will be around home plate and they always dig in on him. He allowed 13 home runs, a horrible total for the number of innings he pitched.

He understood several years ago that he would have to move batters off home plate and as a result started coming inside. He has caused at least three bench-clearing brawls by throwing near or at batters in the past three years. It seems ridiculous because he couldn't break a piece of balsa wood with his pitches.

Rozema is used as Detroit's spot starter, and split his time in 1984 between the bullpen and the starting rotation. He cannot pitch too often because he has a history of arm trouble. He is not bothered by either right or left-handed hitters because he generally keeps his pitches down. He gets much more than his share of strikeouts because he frustrates batters with his junk and will cause many of them to swing at breaking balls out of the strike zone.

DAVE ROZEMA
RHP, No. 19
RR, 6'4", 200 lbs.
ML Svc: 8 years
Born: 8-5-56 in
    Grand Rapids, MI

1984 STATISTICS

W	L	ERA	G	GS	CG	IP	H	R	ER	BB	SO	SV
7	6	3.74	29	16	0	101	110	49	42	18	48	0

CAREER STATISTICS

W	L	ERA	G	GS	CG	IP	H	R	ER	BB	SO	SV
57	46	3.38	208	128	36	1007	1006	436	378	233	401	10

FIELDING:

Rozema is not a good fielder, but he tries hard. His motion to first base has improved, but runners will run on him because they know it takes a half hour for the ball to reach home plate. He has trouble handling bunts.

OVERALL:

He has had outstanding success at Tiger Stadium in the past three years, but with the emergence of Juan Berenguer to go along with Jack Morris, Dan Petry and Milt Wilcox, Rozema is the fifth starter and will rarely start an important game unless one of the big four is injured.

Robinson: "I think he's starting to take the game more seriously because he knows he has to pitch well to stay on this team. Versatility is his key, and I can see him in the same role this year. He'll win some and lose some."

PITCHING:

A lanky lefthanded pitcher, Bill Scherrer is a specialty pitcher. More often than not, he will appear from the bullpen with the designated assignment of getting one crucial out against a lefthanded hitter--a task he performs with a three-quarters to sidearm motion and with high efficiency.

His tools include a particularly menacing curveball, a slider and a "sneaky" fastball. He backs lefthanders off the plate with the curve and then nails the corner with the fastball and slider.

Composed in pressure situations, Bill can work his way out of trouble by tantalizing the hitters with his breaking pitches. He rarely gives in. His problems in early 1984 were primarily because of an illness (an upper respiratory infection that stemmed from a bad case of the flu) and later a sprained ankle.

An intelligent pitcher, Scherrer uses his slim appearance as an aid. "People look at me and they say, 'This skinny guy can't get anybody out,'" Scherrer says, "so I throw them the junk and then slip a fastball up there. And a lot of times, I'll catch 'em off guard." For that reason and in that play, Scherrer often portrays the defeated, hapless stooge on the mound.

Scherrer is also capable of working in long relief but that does not appear to be his calling.

"I'm not a star," Scherrer said during the World Series, "I am a fill-in guy, the kind of pitcher who can hold

BILL SCHERRER
LHP, No. 34
LL, 6'4", 180 lbs.
ML Svc: 2 years
Born: 1-20-58 in
Tonawanda, NY

1984 STATISTICS

W	L	ERA	G	GS	CG	IP	H	R	ER	BB	SO	SV
2	1	4.18	54	0	0	71	138	35	33	14	31	35

CAREER STATISTICS

W	L	ERA	G	GS	CG	IP	H	R	ER	BB	SO	SV
5	5	3.40	114	2	0	180	168	73	68	47	95	45

them off until we can get to Willie Hernandez."

FIELDING, HITTING, BASERUNNING:

Scherrer is an agile and effective fielder. He is deceptively fast and gets off the mound very quickly fielding bunts. His move to first is adequate.

OVERALL:

Scherrer seems perfectly suited to Detroit, a team strong enough in starters and relievers to afford a specialty man such as Scherrer.

Campbell: "With the curveball and all the gangly arms and legs coming at the hitter, he gets a lot of people out. On a good ballclub, such as Detroit, he is a valuable pitcher to have around."

HITTING:

Dizzy Dean was once hit on the head by an infielder's throw and was rushed to the hospital. The next day the headlines blared: "X-rays of Dizzy's Head Show Nothing." In the off-season, Detroit's MVP shortstop Alan Trammell was also x-rayed for a shoulder and knee problem. The headlines should have read: "X-rays of Trammell's Knee and Shoulder Show Heart."

Trammell might be the pulse of the Tigers. If Dave Winfield had not decided to hit for average and Buddy Bell had not had a bunch of hits during the final weekend of the season, Trammell would have once again had the highest batting average of any American League right-handed batter, as he had in 1983.

His success recently has come about because of maturity and a stance change. He switched from an open one to a closed one, slight crouch, and now hits the ball wherever it is pitched. He murders fastballs low and in, slaps hard curves to the gaps, pulls low sliders and hits curves, sliders and fastballs away to the opposite field. Pitchers have become reluctant to pitch him hard stuff inside because he has added power and zip to his swing and can hit the long ball. Righthanded pitchers will try to throw him their best stuff up and in and hard sliders low and away. If they mix in a good straight change or a trick pitch they will have success with him. Lefties must throw him up and in and take something off the fastball, turn it over and keep it away. Trammell is an outstanding bunter and an excellent hit-and-run man and makes contact with two strikes.

BASERUNNING:

Trammell has outstanding instincts and is very aggressive on the basepaths. He gets an excellent jump out of the box and is one of the most fundamentally sound baserunners in the league.

ALAN TRAMMELL
SS, No. 3
RR, 6'0", 170 lbs.
ML Svc: 7 years
Born: 2-21-58 in
 Garden Grove, CA

1984 STATISTICS
AVG	G	AB	R	H	2B	3B	HR	RBI	BB	SO	SB
.314	139	555	85	174	34	5	14	69	60	63	19

CAREER STATISTICS
AVG	G	AB	R	H	2B	3B	HR	RBI	BB	SO	SB
.285	989	3452	516	985	160	28	56	372	379	391	110

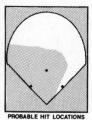

FIELDING:

He's the best at positioning himself for hitters, turning the double play and getting rid of the ball. A shoulder injury hampered him after the All Star break, but he still threw straight and picked up the speed of his release. Unlike most shortstops, Trammell throws everything overhand and his throws never take off, dip, dive, hook or fishtail.

OVERALL:

A good shortstop is a must for a championship team. Trammell is a good shortstop who picked up in almost every offensive category in 1984 and got better defensively.

Robinson: "If a ground ball is hit, he is the man you want it hit to. He might not be the best at any one particular phase of the game, but if you put everything together, he is the best composite shortstop around."

HITTING:

During the final three weeks of the 1984 season, manager Sparky Anderson rested his All Star second baseman to get him ready for the playoffs and World Series. As a result, Lou Whitaker's offensive totals were not as impressive as they were the year before, but Whitaker did not mind in the least.

At the plate, Whitaker is almost a mirror image of his DP partner Alan Trammell. From his square, straight-up stance he can pull the inside fastball and hit the outside fastball to left. He has become a much better hitter against lefties and hangs in until the last minute. Whitaker can hit a hanging curve, much like batting champ Don Mattingly.

He is a good leadoff batter who draws more than his share of walks. He will strike out more than the majority of leadoff men only because he is an aggressive hitter who does not like to be too defensive at the plate.

Lefthanders will try to throw him hard stuff and keep it down because he is an excellent high ball hitter. He can be fooled by an off-speed pitch. Right-handed pitchers will turn the fastball over to him and try to keep it down. Sinkerball pitchers give him the most trouble, and pitchers who can show him the fastball come back with a variety of breaking balls can get him out.

Whitaker is a good clutch hitter because he hits to all fields with men on base. He will pick and choose his spots when trying for the long ball but at times swings too hard.

BASERUNNING:

He had a few nagging injuries in 1984, and his stolen base production was off from his 17 thefts in 1983. He gets a good jump from the box, is aggressive on the basepaths and will always take the extra base.

FIELDING:

Whitaker has excellent range both

LOU WHITAKER
2B, No. 1
LR, 5'11", 160 lbs.
ML Svc: 7 years
Born: 5-12-57 in
New York, NY

1984 STATISTICS

AVG	G	AB	R	H	2B	3B	HR	RBI	BB	SO	SB
.289	143	558	90	161	25	1	13	56	62	63	6

CAREER STATISTICS

AVG	G	AB	R	H	2B	3B	HR	RBI	BB	SO	SB
.283	987	3512	527	993	146	35	52	376	433	449	76

  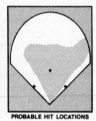

VS. RHP — VS. LHP — PROBABLE HIT LOCATIONS

ways and is very good at turning the double play. He can come in on a ball and has a quick release and a strong arm. He is very good at going back for short pops but is better going to his left toward the foul line than to his right into short-center. Hard hit short hoppers tend to give him trouble.

OVERALL:

In a league full of top-rate second basemen, Lou Whitaker does not have to take a back seat to any of them.

Robinson: "His average dropped from .320, but I don't think he's a .320 hitter. He'll give you the .290 and give you an excellent man in leadoff. He doesn't go into prolonged slumps because he can bunt and has speed. He's got a world of confidence and is very aggressive at the bat. I think when he stopped being a slap hitter and learned to turn on the ball and drive it he became a much better hitter."

PITCHING:

In October 1970, Milt Wilcox was a 20-year-old relief pitcher for the Reds and was managed by Sparky Anderson. Appearing in the World Series that year against the Baltimore Orioles, Wilcox was shellshocked in two appearances. In October 1984, Milt Wilcox was a 34-year-old proven starter for the Tigers and was managed by Sparky Anderson. Wilcox won game 3 of the World Series against the San Diego Padres. He has learned a lot in 12 years.

His motion hasn't changed. It is still the old-fashioned pump and his arms go up and down: he brings them back, brings them forward and throws the ball. His pitches always move down and are invariably checked by the home plate umpire. He has never been caught throwing anything illegal.

Wilcox has a fastball that comes in at 87 MPH, a forkball, curve and change. He has recently begun using a split-fingered fastball. He had no luck with a slider and junked it.

He can throw three-quarters and drop to sidearm against righthanded hitters. He will use the curve or split-fingered fastball to both set up and strike out hitters and will come up and in with his fastball. He is not afraid to pitch inside to both left and righthanded hitters (he led the Tiger staff with eight hit batsmen in 1984) but will usually keep the ball down and away to lefties. He has excellent control of his pitches and averages a walk every three innings.

Wilcox tends to pitch in streaks. He won his first six games in 1984, struggled in the middle and then came back to win six of his last seven in the regular season.

FIELDING:

He is a good, solid fielder in all

MILT WILCOX
RHP, No. 39
RR, 6'2", 215 lbs.
ML Svc: 12 years
Born: 4-20-50 in
Honolulu, HI

1984 STATISTICS

W	L	ERA	G	GS	CG	IP	H	R	ER	BB	SO	SV
17	8	4.00	33	33	0	193	183	99	86	66	119	0

CAREER STATISTICS

W	L	ERA	G	GS	CG	IP	H	R	ER	BB	SO	SV
118	102	4.02	374	265	73	1920	1866	951	858	728	1091	5

aspects of the game except when he gets too excited on the mound--then he jumps off the ground with both feet. Wilcox's move to first is one of the best in the league for a righthander: he is quick and tricky. Runners will not take too big a lead off first.

OVERALL:

Wilcox was part of a staff that led the league in ERA (3.49). He has always been labeled a .500 pitcher and is proof positive what a good mental approach means to a pitcher as well as a fierce competitive nature . . . but it sure helps to know that Willie and Aurelio are waiting to come in.

Robinson: "He is another guy who kept the ball in the park a lot better in 1984 than he did the year before. Milt is a smart pitcher who did away with the slider and began using a slow overhand curve to set up the hitters; he also was able to throw it for strikes."

DOUG BAKER
INF, No. 45
RR, 6'1", 190 lbs.
ML Svc: 1 year
Born: 4-14-60 in
Phoenix, AZ

HITTING, BASERUNNING, FIELDING:

Doug Baker is a utility infielder who was primarily a shortstop in the minors. He also played second, short and a little third in 1984. When Alan Trammell hurt his shoulder, Tom Brookens took over at short, but when Brookens hurt his leg, Baker took over and did well.

He is a switch-hitter who batted .197 lefty and .167 righty. He has a square stance, slight crouch, but obviously has trouble with fastballs and breaking balls. Pitchers can throw the ball by him and pitch him breaking balls down and away whether he is batting lefty or righty.

He has speed and managed three stolen bases in three attempts in his limited playing time in 1984.

Baker is rated good defensively, with good range and a better than average arm.

OVERALL:

He is the prime example of the old scout's famed line about a minor league prospect, "Good field, no hit."

Robinson: "He played fairly well at short in the games he appeared in. Unless Detroit finds another prospect in their system, he may be a utility player again this year."

DWIGHT LOWRY
C, No. 25
LR, 6'3", 210 lbs.
ML Svc: 1 year
Born: 10-23-57 in
Robeson Co., NC

HITTING, BASERUNNING, FIELDING:

When Casey Stengel made his first selection as manager of the expansion New York Mets, he chose Hobie Landrith over many other better and more widely known players. When asked why he chose Hobie Landrith, a catcher, he said (in so many words), "You'd have a wild pitch every pitch if there was nobody behind the plate." Well, what happens when Lance Parrish needs a break? SOMEBODY has to be behind the plate. Enter, Dwight Lowry.

Lowry is a lefthanded-hitting catcher. Generally, a team likes to have three catchers, but Marty Castillo was groomed as a catcher and he would be the third catcher in an emergency.

Lowry was a good contact hitter in the minors who did not strike out a lot but showed no power. He started several games for the Tigers when Parrish was rested but usually came into games to rest Parrish when they were either already won or lost.

He has no power and average speed. He has a fair arm. Runners have not as yet challenged him.

OVERALL:

He was the 26th man on the championship Tiger team, but as Stengel pointed out, somebody has to catch the pitches when the pitcher throws them.

Robinson: "The jury is still out on him. Parrish seems to catch every game. He may progress and have a future, but for the time being he's a backup."

SID MONGE
LHP, No. 42
SL, 6'2", 195 lbs.
ML Svc: 9 years
Born: 4-11-51 in
    Agua Prieta, MEX

PITCHING, FIELDING:

Sid Monge has done everything asked of him with the five major league teams he has pitched for in his 10-year career. He has started, pitched in both long relief and short relief and has been called in to face one or two lefthanded hitters. Today, he is the 10th man on a 10-man staff but can still pitch effectively.

Detroit picked him up in 1984 to give them another lefthander in the bullpen. For a team that once had no lefthanders, the Tigers now have three (Bill Scherrer and Cy Hernandez are the others).

Monge has lost something off his fastball but can still throw hard and to spots. He has always been bothered by control. At his best, he will spot the fastball and come back with curves and sliders, which he tries to keep low, and a very effective screwball. The screwball is used as an off-speed pitch to lefthanded hitters and as a strikeout pitch to righties.

He has a quick but average move to first and runners will run on him if he does not pay attention to them.

OVERALL:

He has a winning record in the majors and has been around. He knows how to pitch and has the stuff it takes. He seems suited to their staff.

Robinson: "He has got a good arm but he doesn't change speeds enough. He can get lefthanded hitters out, but he still has to change speeds so that the hitters will not just sit on his hard stuff."

KANSAS CITY ROYALS

HITTING:

After averaging 30 home runs a year for five years in the minor leagues, Steve Balboni finally got the chance to show his stuff in the big leagues.

He lived up to his advanced billing. He hit with power: his 28 home runs were the second highest total in Royals history. And he struck out, too, for a club record of 139. Balboni is the epitome of a power hitter. He can be pitched to—up and in with hard stuff and away with breaking pitches. He is so strong, however, that if he extends his arms and the pitcher makes a mistake, he will drive the ball a long way.

His strength is such that he can hit balls out of Royals Stadium (of all places) when he is off balance. At times he looks as if he just pushes deep drives with his strong forearms.

Balboni is definitely a streak hitter. He tied a major league record by striking out in nine consecutive plate appearances at Boston, and had stretches of 22 strikeouts in 12 games in late May and early June and 21 strikeouts in 10 games during August. Conversely, he went on home run binges of 10 in 14 games and six in 14 games.

When he is struggling, he is way out in front on pitches. When he is hitting, he keeps his hands back, even when his weight shifts. He will also drive balls to right field when he is going well, and has the power to hit the ball out of the park that way.

He fits well in the sixth spot in the lineup: when he is on a tear, he gives the team a big lift, but when he is struggling, he is not an immediate out in the heart of the order.

BASERUNNING:

Balboni's speed is below average, but not terrible. He is no threat to steal, but he can go from first to third or from second to home in decent time.

STEVE BALBONI
1B, No. 18
RR, 6'3", 225 lbs.
ML Svc: 4 years
Born: 1-16-57 in
Brockton, MA

1984 STATISTICS

AVG	G	AB	R	H	2B	3B	HR	RBI	BB	SO	SB
.244	126	438	58	107	23	2	28	77	45	139	0

CAREER STATISTICS

AVG	G	AB	R	H	2B	3B	HR	RBI	BB	SO	SB
.234	195	638	76	149	28	4	35	100	60	200	0

  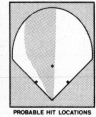

VS. RHP   VS. LHP   PROBABLE HIT LOCATIONS

FIELDING:

His size gives one the idea that he is a stone glove. That, however, is not accurate: he is average at first base. He is not afraid to go after balls to his right. He was considered a godsend by the other Royals' infielders because of the way he digs throws out of the dirt and adjusts to wide or high tosses.

OVERALL:

Balboni is as quiet personally as he is vocal with his bat. As long as he hits home runs, however, the Royals don't care if he ever hits the winter banquet circuit. He has a power hitter's makeup. He does not let the strikeouts bother him, knowing that it is only a matter of time before he gets his revenge.

Matthews: "Balboni strikes out a lot, and if you make good pitches you are going to get him out. Surprisingly, he has good power to the opposite field."

PITCHING:

Acquired by the Royals to be the righthanded power pitcher in the starting rotation, Joe Beckwith made only one start last season. He settled into the role of the setup man for bullpen ace Quisenberry. He seemed to adjust to the role in the second half of the season, compiling a 1.94 ERA during the final 10 weeks, and no longer talks about his desire to be a starting pitcher.

Beckwith has always relied primarily on an above average fastball (88-89 MPH), but he also has a decent slider, and last season he tried to throw a change-up, which got him in more trouble than it helped him. The key to his turnaround was the development of an off-speed breaking pitch, which he used as his out pitch in the second half of the season. It made his fastball, which has good movement, that much more effective.

He always has had pretty good control, and was better than ever in 1984, walking only 25 batters in 100.2 innings. He still maintained his ability to strike out hitters.

As a reliever, Beckwith can go right after hitters. He does not have to try to pace himself. When he starts to do that, he begins to have problems. He tends to be too careful, and gets himself in trouble when he gets behind in the count--hitters can then look for nothing but his fastball.

Beckwith has a three-quarters delivery. It is not very deceptive, which puts more pressure on Beckwith to make quality pitches.

FIELDING:

Despite the fact that the bulk of his big league time has been spent as a reliever, Beckwith has not developed a

JOE BECKWITH
RHP, No. 27
LR, 6'2", 200 lbs.
ML Svc: 4 years
Born: 1-28-55 in
    Auburn, AL

1984 STATISTICS
W	L	ERA	G	GS	CG	IP	H	R	ER	BB	SO	SV
8	4	3.40	49	1	0	100	92	39	38	25	75	2

CAREER STATISTICS
W	L	ERA	G	GS	CG	IP	H	R	ER	BB	SO	SV
17	14	3.19	165	5	0	308	305	128	109	36	79	2

good move to first base. It is merely average. He will throw over to keep runners close, but can be victimized by good basestealers. At times, he fields the ball and looks as if he does not know what to do next.

OVERALL:

Beckwith seems much more comfortable as a reliever than as a starter and has a good enough arm to flourish in that role. The big question, however, is his durability. He has not shown the ability to come back after working for a couple of innings. A manager has to be careful to use him only three times a week, and has to be careful not to loosen Beckwith up when he is not going to use him because that is just as draining on his arm as being in a game.

Matthews: "Beckwith became more of a breaking ball pitcher last season, and I suppose that is the influence of going to the American League from the National League. Joe had a very good second half. He was a key middle man and is not afraid to challenge hitters."

PITCHING:

There's nothing exceptional about Bud Black, but he is above average in every aspect of pitching--physically and mentally. His ability to blend many fine qualities allowed him to emerge as one of the top pitchers in the American League during 1984. He has command of four pitches: fastball, slider, curveball and change-up. He can throw all four pitches for strikes virtually every time he pitches. What makes him so hard for hitters is that he can change speeds on both his fastball and curve.

He will pitch inside to both right and lefthanded hitters and has excellent command of his pitches. In 1984, Black showed that he is a good strikeout pitcher.

When he is in trouble, Black will usually turn to his fastball, which will light up radar guns at close to 90 MPH. It has good movement. In the last three years, he has picked up five to six MPH on the fastball, a product of his physical maturity. Black has gained 20 lbs. since he left college.

It is easy to tell when Black is in trouble. He normally pitches down in the strike zone, but on those off days-- and they are rare--he gets his pitches up in the strike zone.

He has a very easy motion. It is a bit deceptive because it does not appear that he will throw as hard as he does.

FIELDING:

Black is well above average in every aspect of fielding as well. He has an excellent move to first (nine pickoffs in 1984). It is so good that when he came up with the Royals in 1982 he was called for a lot of balks, but since then he has established himself as a big

BUD BLACK
LHP, No. 40
LL, 6'2", 180 lbs.
ML Svc: 3 years
Born: 6-30-57 in
    San Mateo, CA

```
1984 STATISTICS
W  L  ERA  G  GS CG IP   H   R   ER  BB  SO  SV
17 12 3.12 35  35 8  257 226 99  89  64  140 0
CAREER STATISTICS
W  L  ERA  G  GS CG IP   H   R   ER  BB  SO  SV
31 25 3.59 83  73 11 507 479 222 202 144 238 0
```

league pitcher, and umpires are not as strict in their balk calls against him.

He moves off the mound very well, fields bunts well and does not get confused in tight situations. He is quick enough off the mound that if the batter does not make a good bunt Black can get the force at the lead base.

OVERALL:

Black proved himself to be a durable pitcher in 1984, his first full season in the big leagues. Not only did he finish tied for fifth in the AL with a 3.12 ERA, but he worked 257 innings and pitched at least seven innings in 27 of his 35 starts. He also showed that he could handle pennant race pressures, winning seven of his final nine decisions with a 1.98 ERA.

Matthews: "Black was one of the most consistent pitchers in the American League through the course of 1984. He was given the opening day assignment, and throughout the year reaffirmed his postion as the ace of the Royals' starting rotation."

HITTING:

The summer of 1984 was a summer of disappointment for George Brett. He missed the first 33 games of the season because of surgery on his left knee, and 23 of 24 games in late August/early September because of a pulled left hamstring. And even when he was healthy, he did not have the type of production that has marked his career.

It was as if, with a limited overall team offense, Brett tried to do too much. The pitch away, which in the past he had lined into the left-center field alley, more often than not became a fly ball to left. He did not have a consistent threat hitting behind him in the lineup, and was not as selective as he should have been to force good pitches.

Brett stands deep in the box, his bat at an angle to his body. He will kill low fastballs, but has shown the ability to handle most any pitch, having been forced to adjust because he has been thrown so many off-speed pitches over the years.

Brett is a situation hitter. With the game on the line in the late innings, he will pull the ball. Early in the game, or if a single will help, he is willing to go the other way. He normally is a patient hitter--he does not chase bad balls. He didn't do that in 1984, either, he just went after some strikes (with less than two strikes) that were not pitches he could drive.

BASERUNNING:

Once slightly above average in terms of speed, Brett is now just average. He remains above average as a baserunner. Once he hits the ball, he is always looking for a double or a triple, never satisfied with a single. He has cut down on his aggressiveness by design. He does not attempt to steal anymore, nor will he break up as many double plays as he used to.

FIELDING:

Brett is one of the more underrated third basemen in the game. He gets him-

GEORGE BRETT
3B, No. 5
LR, 6'0", 200 lbs.
ML Svc: 11 years
Born: 5-15-53 in
  Glendale, WV

1984 STATISTICS

AVG	G	AB	R	H	2B	3B	HR	RBI	BB	SO	SB
.284	104	377	42	107	21	3	13	69	38	37	0

CAREER STATISTICS

AVG	G	AB	R	H	2B	3B	HR	RBI	BB	SO	SB
.314	1462	5684	894	1783	362	103	163	865	512	394	131

  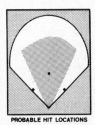

VS. RHP VS. LHP PROBABLE HIT LOCATIONS

self in trouble on routine plays, a victim of continued concentration lapses, especially with routine throws. He has excellent range for a third baseman, however, and a strong enough arm to make big throws. He continues to play third base because of the lifetime contract he signed with the Royals during the 1984 season, but would prefer to move to either first base or the outfield. He is a good enough athlete that he could make the transition.

OVERALL:

Brett's enjoyment of the game is obvious by the way he plays. The biggest problem is keeping him healthy. He has missed stretches of nine or more games with injuries ten times in the last six seasons.

Matthews: "Brett is one of the premier hitters in the American League. When he is healthy, he can rise to any occasion. The problem is, however, that he is injury-prone. He was hurt again in 1984, and everyone saw what it did to the Royals' offensive attack."

HITTING:

Given a chance to play every day, Onix Concepcion established himself as the Royals' regular shortstop during the summer of 1984. Struggling with a .192 average on July 18, he led all hitters in the American League with a second-half average of .370. It may be more than a coincidence that early in his struggle he was having to lead off because of the absence of Willie Wilson. He appears more comfortable hitting in the ninth slot.

He is a definite fastball hitter, and likes the ball up. He will chase balls up out of the strike zone, even over his head, and has trouble with pitches low and away. For a little guy, Concepcion has not yet made the adjustment to go with pitches. He tries to pull almost everything. He has shown signs of extra-base power, but needs to use all fields before he can take full advantage of what strength he has.

Concepcion is an excellent bunter and would help himself if he would try to bunt for a few more hits. He does a good job of getting the sacrifice bunt down. He also must learn to take more pitches and swing at a lot of first pitches. With his size and speed, he should be more willing to take a walk.

He is a better hitter on artificial surfaces. He has the speed to leg out hits, but also hits ground balls very hard: on the turf they speed through, but they are slowed down on grass fields.

BASERUNNING:

Concepcion has above average speed. He is a definite threat to steal a base, but should be more aggressive in that aspect. He will take the extra base--as a runner--but not when he is hitting.

FIELDING:

He is at the top of the class of AL

ONIX CONCEPCION
INF, No. 2
RR, 5'6", 180 lbs.
ML Svc: 3 years
Born: 10-5-58 in
Dorado, PR

1984 STATISTICS

AVG	G	AB	R	H	2B	3B	HR	RBI	BB	SO	SB
.282	90	287	36	81	9	2	1	23	14	33	9

CAREER STATISTICS

AVG	G	AB	R	H	2B	3B	HR	RBI	BB	SO	SB
.253	258	726	76	184	29	6	1	60	31	64	21

  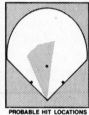

VS. RHP   VS. LHP   PROBABLE HIT LOCATIONS

shortstops with the glove. With a chance to play every day, he silenced critics who felt his range was just average, showing the ability to move well to both his left and right. He has an excellent arm: strong and accurate. Concepcion has also shown better than average ability as both a second baseman and third baseman during his days as a utility infielder, his strong arm again being his main asset.

OVERALL:

Before Concepcion can establish himself as a big league shortstop, he has to get past injury problems, which have haunted him throughout his career. He is a hard worker who never complains.

Matthews: "Concepcion has been injury-prone, which is a concern. When he was healthy, he had a solid year for the Royals, winning their shortstop job away from U.L. Washington."

PITCHING:

In 1984, Mark Gubicza's composure got a big test--and the rookie passed with flying colors. He was the Royals' hard-luck pitcher, but he never got down on himself or gave up. Not even when he saw the Royals being shut out in four of his first five losses, during which he gave up a total of six earned runs.

But then, with Gubicza's potential, there is no reason for him or anybody else to give up. He has a well above average fastball with good movement. He needs work on his other pitches, but don't forget that he has only four seasons of pro experience--and one of those was in short-season rookie ball and another was cut short at the midway point by tendinitis.

When he is throwing his slider for strikes, Gubicza is a tough ticket: witness the three-hitter of Oakland and four-hitter of Boston. Refining the slider and finding some type of change-up are his two major areas of concentration. What helps him is that he will cut the fastball.

When he is having trouble, it is because he is getting behind in the count, which stems from his inability to get that slider over. What he doesn't do is tire. When he has command of his pitches, he will have a slight drop in the middle innings, but by the end of the game he is as strong, if not stronger, than he was in the early innings.

His motion could eventually cause problems. He has a herky-jerky delivery, which creates fears that Gubicza could run into arm problems later on.

FIELDING:

For a big guy, Gubicza moves pretty well on the mound. He fields his position well, and does not get rattled by game situations. His move to first base

MARK GUBICZA
RHP, No. 23
RR, 6'6", 215 lbs.
ML Svc: 1 year
Born: 8-14-62 in
  Philadelphia, PA

1984 STATISTICS

W	L	ERA	G	GS	CG	IP	H	R	ER	BB	SO	SV
10	14	4.05	29	29	4	189	172	90	85	75	111	0

CAREER STATISTICS

W	L	ERA	G	GS	CG	IP	H	R	ER	BB	SO	SV
10	14	4.05	29	29	4	189	172	90	85	75	111	0

is average, but he is still young (22), and with some refinements, he could get better.

OVERALL:

Gubicza is big, but still has to improve his stamina over the course of a season (2-5, 5.52 ERA after July 29). It was only his second full season in pro ball, and he came into it after having had very little time off in the previous 12 months, having pitched all summer in the minor leagues in 1983, then in the Florida Instructional League and then, after only six weeks off, in the Royals' special program prior to spring training 1984.

He has shown, however, he is a definite power pitcher with real major league makeup. He was the first KC rookie since Dennis Leonard in 1975 to strike out more than 100 batters.

Matthews: "If Gubicza stays healthy, he is a power pitcher who has the potential to be one of the best power pitchers in the AL. He is not intimidated by hitters or situations. He challenges them."

PITCHING:

A control pitcher who mixes up his pitches, Larry Gura found himself out of control in 1984 and in trouble. He began the season as the veteran of the Royals' rotation, where he had worked regularly since 1977, but by the end of the year he was sitting (literally sitting) in the bullpen. He did not pitch between Sept. 1 and the Royals' clinching of the division title on Sept. 29, quite a change for the team's most consistent pitcher of the past half decade.

He has to have his control to be successful. His best pitch is his slider ("Slider" is even his nickname among his teammates). His fastball is not even average, but when he pitches well he spots the ball, moving it around and catching hitters off guard. He also has to have that type of pinpoint control with his curveball, change-up and screwball. That's what he lost in 1984, when he lost his stature as a top pitcher in the big leagues.

The scary part of the situation is that for the second year in a row, his walk-to-strikeout ratio (67 to 68) was well below the numbers he had maintained during the previous five years, when he was 76-46, striking out 438 and walking only 308.

Strangely, for a veteran pitcher with a lot of success, Gura is rattled when mistakes are made behind him. Instead of bearing down on the next hitter, he seems to give up.

FIELDING:

Gura has grumbled on several occasions about having not won the Gold

LARRY GURA
LHP, No. 32
LL, 6'1", 185 lbs.
ML Svc: 11 years
Born: 11-26-47 in
  Joliet, IL

1984 STATISTICS

W	L	ERA	G	GS	CG	IP	H	R	ER	BB	SO	SV
12	9	5.20	31	25	3	168	175	102	97	67	68	0

CAREER STATISTICS

W	L	ERA	G	GS	CG	IP	H	R	ER	BB	SO	SV
126	94	3.70	395	257	71	2021	1979	933	830	590	792	13

Glove. There's good reason for him to complain. He is an excellent fielder. He is quick around the mound and seems to be always in position to field. He comes up with the ball well, and gets rid of it in a hurry.

He has an excellent move to first base, and tries to mix up his throws to keep runners off guard. He does not want to develop a set pattern.

OVERALL:

If Gura can regain an aggressive style of pitching, he would seem able to regain his winning style. Physically, he is fine. He has always worked hard to keep himself in shape all year round and watches his diet closely.

Matthews: "At this stage in his career, it may be best for Larry to be in the bullpen. Over the past two seasons, he has done short stints there and has shown the kind of aggressiveness that is necessary for that role."

PITCHING:

A victim of a lack of work early in the season, Mark Huismann came back from the minor leagues in early July and became a big part of the Royals' bullpen. He has trained in the minor leagues as a stopper, and could eventually develop into that role in the big leagues. For now, however, Huismann will be called upon to be a middle reliever, setting the stage for Dan Quisenberry.

The bullpen is definitely his area of expertise. He has never made a start in five professional seasons, and does not have the command of enough pitches to give credence to such a move.

Huismann's main pitch is a hard, sinking fastball. He also has a curve, and has worked some with a forkball and a change-up. When he is in trouble, however, it is the fastball which Huismann turns to. It has average velocity (85-86 MPH), but the hard, sinking action makes it anything but an average pitch. That is how he was able to strike out 54 batters in 75 innings. And when he does not get strikeouts, he gets a lot of ground balls.

He has good control: he issued just 21 walks last season. The key to his game is to have that ball sinking. If he does not get enough work, however, he does not get the sink. The harder he throws, the straighter his fastball. That was his problem in the first two months of the season, which prompted his return to Omaha. At Omaha, he made 15 appearances in one month, did not allow a run, and when he came back to the Royals he appeared ready (3-1, 3 saves, 2.84 ERA).

He does have to keep his arm between three-quarters and over-the-top to get the sinking action. With his lanky body, he gives the hitters lots of arms and legs to look at during his delivery.

MARK HUISMANN
RHP, No. 38
RR, 6'3", 195 lbs.
ML Svc: 1 year plus
Born: 5-11-58 in
Littleton, CO

1984 STATISTICS
W	L	ERA	G	GS	CG	IP	H	R	ER	BB	SO	SV
3	3	4.08	38	0	0	75	83	38	34	21	54	3

CAREER STATISTICS
W	L	ERA	G	GS	CG	IP	H	R	ER	BB	SO	SV
5	4	4.54	51	0	0	105	112	58	53	38	74	3

FIELDING:

As a relief pitcher, Huismann needs to work on his pickoff move. So far, it is just average. He does throw over a lot--sometimes too much. He is a decent fielder. He does, however, seem to get flustered when he has too much time to make a throw.

OVERALL:

Overshadowed by the efforts of teammates Mark Gubicza and Bret Saberhagen, Mark Huismann's second-half record was just what the Royals had in mind when they unloaded Mike Armstrong prior to the 1984 season. He has a strong arm and the makeup necessary to work out of the bullpen.

Matthews: "Huismann's pitches have good movement. When he keeps the ball down, he is very, very tough because his pitches have good life. He can be a handful for hitters at times like that."

HITTING:

Dane Iorg is one of those hard-to-find bench players. He is a lefthanded hitter who has trained himself to handle the situation of long droughts between appearances, and he enjoys the pressure situations he gets called into.

He has a straight-up stance, and will use all the fields. If he is pitched inside, he will yank the ball to right field, and occasionally surprise the opposition with some power. He will line the pitch away to left field.

Iorg is basically a singles-doubles hitter who finds artificial surfaces well suited to his line drives. He is patient, willing to wait for his pitch. He knows his strike zone. He struck out looking only four times in 1984: three of those came during the same weekend in Chicago in early September when he was suffering from the flu.

He did have some trouble when he first joined the Royals in May of 1984, after having spent all his career in the National League. A good fastball hitter, Iorg had to adjust to the preponderance of off-speed and breaking pitches he was thrown. By the end of the year, he had regained his stature as a premier pinch-hitter.

Pitchers try to work Iorg by throwing him fastballs inside and off the plate, hoping he will chase the pitch. They have to be careful, however, because if they don't get it far enough inside he will put the ball in play.

BASERUNNING:

With below average speed, Iorg is not much of a threat on the bases. He is, however, a solid baserunner. He knows his limitations and will force as much out of himself as possible, but does not make stupid mistakes and get thrown out.

FIELDING:

As well as pinch-hitting and serving as a DH for the Royals, Iorg filled in

DANE IORG
OF, No. 19
LR, 6'0", 180 lbs.
ML Svc: 7 years
Born: 5-11-50 in
     Eureka, CA

1984 STATISTICS

AVG	G	AB	R	H	2B	3B	HR	RBI	BB	SO	SB
.255	78	235	27	60	16	2	5	30	13	15	0

CAREER STATISTICS

AVG	G	AB	R	H	2B	3B	HR	RBI	BB	SO	SB
.288	564	1383	129	398	90	9	11	195	95	137	5

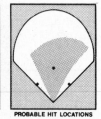

VS. RHP | VS. LHP | PROBABLE HIT LOCATIONS

at first and third and in the outfield. Third base was only an emergency move--he does not have quick enough reactions or a strong enough arm for much playing time in the hot corner. Iorg is an average first baseman, but does not move very well. His lack of speed hampers him in the outfield. He will catch what he can get to. He also does not have a very strong arm, but will throw to the right bases and hits cutoff men.

OVERALL:

Iorg is an ideal role player: he is versatile. He comes off the bench without problems, and he does not complain about his job.

Matthews: "Although the Royals look to Iorg to come off the bench and hit, he has surprised many people with his fielding. He has made some catches that really have been something. He is the kind of player that so many teams are looking for: versatile, hard-working and team-oriented."

PITCHING:

After bringing along a young pitching staff last year, the Royals have Danny Jackson as their pitching project for 1985. From the standpoint of pure ability, Jackson is the best of the bunch.

His future is as a starter, although he has seen limited work as a reliever in the big leagues and has done a good job out of the pen. But with his potential, the Royals envision more than long relief work for him.

He has a well above average fastball with good movement. His big pitch, however, is a slider, which he will run in hard on righthanded hitters. During his first two stints in the big leagues, he had trouble throwing the slider for strikes. In September, however, he came back to the Royals with his slider in working order, and made four impressive starts during the pennant race, even if he was only 1-1 in that span.

His motion is an easy one on his arm. He comes over the top, and likes to challenge hitters. There's enough movement on his pitches that, if he throws strikes, he can win the challenges. Like most young pitchers, he has to work on an off-speed pitch before he will be complete. He is affected by mistakes made by both his teammates and himself; there are times when his frustrations interfere with his composure on the mound. He is an intense competitor who has to learn to channel that intensity properly.

FIELDING:

Jackson is average as a fielder with a below average move for a lefthander. He was so dominating at the amateur and minor league levels that he never worked hard on doing the little things that are

DANNY JACKSON
LHP, No. 25
RL, 6'0", 190 lbs.
ML Svc: 1 year plus
Born: 1-5-62 in
San Antonio, TX

```
1984 STATISTICS
W  L  ERA   G  GS CG IP  H   R   ER  BB  SO SV
2  6  4.26  15 11 1  76  84  41  36  35  40 0
CAREER STATISTICS
W  L  ERA   G  GS CG IP  H   R   ER  BB  SO SV
3  7  4.45  19 14 1  95  110 53  47  41  49 0
```

required for him to be more than an average pitcher in the major leagues.

OVERALL:

Jackson has the potential. He just has to be pushed a bit to improve on the little things. At times, it seems as if he gets a little lazy, willing to rely on raw ability to get the job done, which is not good enough in the major leagues. He got married last winter, and became a father last summer, two things which he credits with helping him mature. He said that maturity has been carried over to the mound, and helped him improve his approach when he got the second chance in 1984.

Matthews: "Jackson has a lot of potential. The Royals are looking forward to some big things from him. He has grown up a bit over that last year or so, and appears to be ready to get serious on the mound. I can tell you one thing--his slider is already a serious pitch."

HITTING:

He began the season injured, but once he was healthy, Lynn Jones was one of the bigger surprises for the Royals. They had signed him for his defensive ability and his willingness to be an extra man.

A seldom-used offensive player with Detroit, Jones showed surprising pop with his bat. It was not home run power, mind you, but he did drive the ball well. He fits well into the No. 2 spot in the Royals lineup against lefthanded pitchers. He has good bat control and uses all the fields. He hits the ball as sharply to left-center as to right-center and is willing to give himself up to get the runner over.

Jones likes the fastball, especially up. He is solid against lefties, but when righthanders start throwing him breaking pitches, Jones's game breaks down. He has a slightly closed stance. For a player who has seen such irregular use, he has shown a good knowledge of the strike zone and has made good contact. In 748 career at-bats in the big leagues, he has whiffed only 66 times. He never struck out as many as 50 times in a full minor league season.

BASERUNNING:

Jones's speed is deceptive: he looks as if he is quick, but he is average, or slightly above, at best. He was a legitimate basestealing threat in the minor leagues, but since knee surgery early in the 1980 season, he has not shown the tendency to run.

Jones is a fundamentally sound player, and that includes his efforts on the bases. He gets the most out of his ability. He will go from first to third, and from second to home on singles. And he will go into second base hard in double play situations.

FIELDING:

Have glove, will play--Jones has made that his motto. He is one of the more

LYNN JONES
OF, No. 35
RR, 5'9", 170 lbs.
ML Svc: 6 years
Born: 1-1-53 in
    Meadville, PA

1984 STATISTICS

AVG	G	AB	R	H	2B	3B	HR	RBI	BB	SO	SB
.301	47	103	11	31	6	0	1	10	4	9	1

CAREER STATISTICS

AVG	G	AB	R	H	2B	3B	HR	RBI	BB	SO	SB
.269	349	748	96	201	25	5	7	81	59	66	13

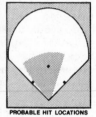

VS. RHP   VS. LHP   PROBABLE HIT LOCATIONS

solid outfielders in the AL. He does nothing flashy, has no blazing speed and does not have a cannon for an arm. But he does not make mistakes. He breaks well on balls, whether they are over his head or to his side. He comes up with balls smoothly, and he has a better than average arm in terms of strength and accuracy. He throws to the proper base and keeps his throws low enough to hit the cutoff man.

OVERALL:

Jones is one of those role players a good team has to have. He has been around and has accepted his fate as a backup player. He has not, however, grown lazy--he does all of the little things to help a team.

Matthews: "When a ball is hit to where Lynn Jones is playing, a manager can sit back and relax. He is as steady as they come in the field: he won't lose the ball or bobble the throw--he is invaluable in the field."

PITCHING:

At the end of the 1981 season, Mike Jones was the great hope of the Royals' future starting staff. He had above average major league pitches in his fastball and slider and was throwing the fastball consistently close to 90 MPH. All he had to do was get better command of the strike zone, and he would be one of the premier pitchers in the league, or so the Royals felt.

Then came that night in late December of 1981 when Jones's car skidded on ice, hit a tree and left him with a broken neck. There were fears at the time he would never walk again. Well, Jones is walking. It is unlikely he will ever become the pitcher once anticipated, but based on his progress in the last two years, he is going to be a solid major leaguer. Right now, his fastball is only average, 85 to 86 MPH. He also throws a slider and a curve. One of the biggest developments was that his injury forced Jones to learn HOW to pitch, not just simply rely on overpowering hitters.

He now will try to spot the ball. The problem Jones faces is stamina. By his own admission, he was gassed after four or five innings of work in 1984. That, however, should be overcome with another strong winter of work.

Remember, he did not pitch at all in 1982, and got in only half a season in 1983. What keeps the Royals optimistic is the fact that there was no damage done to his arm in the accident. He also showed glimmers of being in control with efforts like the eight-inning, one-hit start he made against Cleveland July 16.

Basically a starting pitcher in previous years, Jones has also filled the role of a swing man. The Royals are looking at him as a long reliever in 1985, but if he continues to make progress, he could force his way back into the rotation.

MIKE JONES
LHP, No. 17
LL, 6'5", 230 lbs.
ML Svc: 2 years
Born: 7-30-59 in
    Rochester, NY

1984 STATISTICS

W	L	ERA	G	GS	CG	IP	H	R	ER	BB	SO	SV
2	3	4.89	23	12	0	81	86	48	44	36	43	0

CAREER STATISTICS

W	L	ERA	G	GS	CG	IP	H	R	ER	BB	SO	SV
8	7	4.28	38	24	0	162	166	85	77	69	74	0

FIELDING:

Jones is not the smoothest moving pitcher around the mound. He is average, at best, at fielding his position. He does not get rattled in tight spots. His pickoff move is below average for a lefthanded pitcher.

OVERALL:

The fact that Jones was back in the big leagues last season says a lot about his determination to make it. He refuses to let adversity slow him down. He is an outstanding competitor who, obviously, is willing to put that extra effort into succeeding.

Matthews: "If Jones's fastball improves another four or five MPH, he will be tough. He has a lot of guts. Mike challenges hitters. When he has problems is when he gets behind in the count. You have to root for this fellow to make it back after what he has gone through."

PITCHING:

Charlie Leibrandt is a pitcher who defies his own scouting report. He is a case of on-paper-weak but in-game-strong. But we think we have got him here . . .

His fastball is below average from the standpoint of both velocity and movement. His curveball is average at best, and his slider is soft. He does have a decent change-up, but not anything to write home about.

So how did Charlie Leibrandt become one of the team's most consistent pitchers in 1984, giving them a big boost down the stretch, winnng four of his final five decisions, including the title-clincher at Oakland?

Determination. Intelligence. Command. Leibrandt has made adjustments to his pitching approach. He changes speeds very well and moves the ball around. Even though he is far from overpowering, he will set up the hitters and bust them inside with his fastball--even right-handed hitters.

When he starts to tire, he loses what movement he does have, and starts getting his pitches up in the strike zone. That is when it is time to get him out of the ball game.

He is an ideal fourth or fifth starter. He will give you six strong innings almost consistently, but rarely will he give you a complete game (none in 1984, but he did pitch eight innings four times). There are questions about whether he could work out of the bullpen. He does take a little while to get loose, but he has shown the ability to adapt to whatever has to be done and undoubtedly could make the adjustment if it became his role.

FIELDING:

There is nothing spectacular about

CHARLIE LEIBRANDT
LHP, No. 56
RL, 6'3", 200 lbs.
ML Svc: 3 years
sorn: 10-4-56 in
   Chicago, IL

1984 STATISTICS

W	L	ERA	G	GS	CG	IP	H	R	ER	BB	SO	SV
11	7	3.63	23	23	0	143	158	65	58	38	53	0

CAREER STATISTICS

W	L	ERA	G	GS	CG	IP	H	R	ER	BB	SO	SV
27	24	4.10	105	656	6	458	518	229	213	157	159	2

his fielding. He makes the routine plays, but does not move off the mound quickly enough to give himself a big boost. His move to first is very average, which, combined with a slow delivery to the plate, makes him susceptible to basestealers, despite the fact that he is lefthanded.

OVERALL:

Leibrandt's stock with the Royals was so low in the spring of 1984 that he pitched only two innings in an exhibition game before being sent to Omaha. Instead of sulking, Leibrandt responded by winning seven of eight decisions and compiling a 1.24 ERA, forcing the Royals to give him a chance. He may not be intimidating to hitters, but he is not intimidated by situations himself. He knows what he has to do, whether it be against one hitter or in his career.

Matthews: "Leibrandt has a good idea of what he is doing on the mound. He is proof that if a pitcher can hit spots, and has an idea of what he is trying to do, he can be effective."

NOTE: Dennis Leonard has not pitched since May 28, 1983, when he suffered a torn tendon below his left kneecap. He has since undergone four operations. The following report is based on his pre-surgery form.

DENNIS LEONARD
RHP, No. 22
RR, 6'1", 190 lbs.
ML Svc: 10 years
Born: 5-8-51 in
Brooklyn, NY

PITCHING:

Dennis Leonard's injury came on the heels of a broken finger, suffered when he was hit by a line drive, which limited him to just 21 games in 1982. If he does make the comeback, the Royals will be looking for the strong-armed power pitcher who was a dominant figure in the American League from his rookie campaign of 1975 through the strike year of 1981. He has never had any problems with his arm. He did not even have the normal stiffness the day after he pitched.

His comeback will create a strange feeling for Leonard because he will undoubtedly have to begin by working out of the bullpen. He has pitched in relief only five times in the big leagues, and only twice during his three years in the minor leagues.

Leonard is an overhand pitcher. His fastball--above average in terms of velocity and movement--has been his best pitch.

But he has a good, hard breaking pitch and was beginning to develop a pretty good change-up before the injury.

Leonard has always challenged hitters --he has better than a 2 to 1 strike-outs-to-walks ratio during his major league career. He comes inside on right-handed hitters with his fastball, and tries to keep it away from lefthanded hitters.

FIELDING:

The knee injury came about when Leonard's cleat caught in the turf as he

CAREER STATISTICS

W	L	ERA	G	GS	CG	IP	H	R	ER	BB	SO	SV
136	93	3.63	277	272	98	1992	1929	902	803	571	1208	1

went to field a routine ground ball. Do not get the wrong idea, however. Leonard is an excellent fielder. He has a smooth delivery, and gets in good position to field balls hit back to him.

Leonard has an average move to first base. He compensates for the move with a quick delivery to the plate.

OVERALL:

The subject of Leonard has become an uncomfortable one for the Royals to discuss. They watch him work out regularly only to suffer setbacks when another operation is required because the knee has not healed properly. The durability of the knee will remain a question even if he gets the go-ahead to return--until he pitches for an extended period and proves not only that it is strong but also that the problems will not affect his delivery and approach to the game.

Matthews: "Leonard was one of the most durable pitchers in the American League before being victimized by freak injuries over the past three seasons. He has a supple arm despite being such a hard-throwing pitcher."

HITTING:

There comes a time when hard work and the study of hitting give way to age. It seems that Hal McRae has reached that point at the age of 38. His all-out style has slowed down. McRae was one of the first players to accept and adapt to the role of being a designated hitter. Last year he opened the season in the DH role on a full-time basis, but hitting only .255 on June 16, he began platooning. The extra rest worked well. McRae raised his average to .303 by season's end.

He has always had trouble when pitchers jam him. In the past, McRae was able to fight that pitch off. In 1984, however, it became more of a problem, and McRae became so concerned about not being jammed that he no longer did what he had done so well. He became almost a pure pull hitter, instead of driving pitches away hard into right field. It made it easier for pitchers to work against him. He is still a patient hitter until he gets two strikes against him, and he is willing to wait for his pitch until he has to go after a strike.

He is a disciple of the Charlie Lau theory of hitting. He leans back in the box, and then moves his body into the pitch. Trying to compensate for his lack of quickness last year, he got himself into trouble by rushing his hands and not getting good extension.

BASERUNNING:

McRae was once the epitome of aggressiveness on the bases, but age has taken its toll on McRae's baserunning abilities. His speed is way below average. He still thinks aggression, but just can't deliver. He is no longer a threat every time he hits a single to stretch it into a double. The only time he tries to steal a base is on a missed hit-and-run.

HAL McRAE
DH, No. 11
RR, 5'11", 180 lbs.
ML Svc: 15 years
Born: 7-10-46 in
    Avon Park, FL

1984 STATISTICS

AVG	G	AB	R	H	2B	3B	HR	RBI	BB	SO	SB
.303	106	317	30	96	13	4	3	42	34	47	0

CAREER STATISTICS

AVG	G	AB	R	H	2B	3B	HR	RBI	BB	SO	SB
.293	1842	6588	872	1928	448	66	169	981	581	694	109

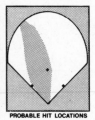

STRONG   STRONG

VS. RHP   VS. LHP   PROBABLE HIT LOCATIONS

McRae gets in trouble because he likes to play a wide-open style of baseball and tries to force opportunities which are no longer there.

OVERALL:

McRae remains a leader in the clubhouse. He responded well to part-time duties. There were no cries of a bruised ego--just the determination to do the best job possible. He is very good with the young players, and is willing to discuss hitting for hours at a time.

Matthews: "McRae is a hitter who adjusts well to a pitcher's patterns. His skills have obviously deteriorated. He still provides excellent pinch-hitting and leadership in the clubhouse."

HITTING:

The "Toy Cannon II," as Darryl Motley is known by his teammates, conjures up memories of Jim Wynn's small but muscular frame and his better than average power from left-center to right-center.

He is primarily a fastball hitter and likes the ball up and over the plate. Most of the time, he has trouble with off-speed pitches and breaking stuff away. When he is on a hot streak, however, Motley can get very hot and everything is fair game. He admits that he gets the feeling he can see the ball as soon as it leaves the pitcher's hand—such as during a 23-game stretch from mid-May to early June 1984: he hit in 20 of those games, going 33 for 90, with four doubles, two triples, five home runs and 21 RBIs.

When he struggles, it is that age-old problem of being too anxious. He will strike out a lot as he did in a nine-game streak in mid-August, when he swung and missed 12 times.

BASERUNNING:

Motley has slightly above average speed. He should be able to steal bases, but has not shown good instincts. He is sometimes picked off first even when he has no intention of trying to steal second. He needs to improve his concentration to avoid such incidents and to force extra bases, something he has the raw ability to do.

FIELDING:

He is not much more than an average fielder. While he was used mainly as a left fielder last year, he did play in both center field and right field as well. He moves decently, has enough range and has a strong enough arm. He does not, however, take advantage of his arm. He is slow getting rid of the ball, often taking four of five steps before he throws. He does not anticipate what runners might be going to do.

DARRYL MOTLEY
OF, No. 24
RR, 5'9", 196 lbs.
ML Svc: 1 year plus
Born: 1-21-60 in
    Muskogee, OK

1984 STATISTICS
AVG	G	AB	R	H	2B	3B	HR	RBI	BB	SO	SB
.284	146	522	64	148	24	6	15	70	28	73	10

CAREER STATISTICS
AVG	G	AB	R	H	2B	3B	HR	RBI	BB	SO	SB
.270	207	715	88	193	29	8	20	89	37	96	13

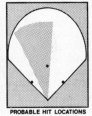

VS. RHP — STRONG   VS. LHP — STRONG   PROBABLE HIT LOCATIONS

OVERALL:

Two years ago, Motley was an outcast, being optioned to Detroit's Triple A team, but it seemed to give him a shot in the arm. Instead of giving up, he came to spring training early last year, and showed up early every day until the season was over, intent on reaching the potential the Royals foresaw when they selected him in the second round in June of 1978.

He went from the eighth outfielder on a team which planned to carry six to a leading role with the Royals with 144 games played in 1984. He is an outstanding athlete. (In high school, he held Danny Ainge to eight points in the Oregon State Championship game, the only time Ainge was held under double figures in his amateur basketball career.)

Matthews: "Motley had a productive year; he was a big, big surprise. He chipped in with some key hits, and was a very tough out at times."

HITTING:

The Royals acquired Jorge Orta in the hope he could finally adjust to the role of a pinch-hitter, something he had struggled with in past years. Well, they still don't know if Orta can do that job, because they wound up platooning him as the DH.

He has decent power for his size: 39 extra-base hits, including nine home runs and seven triples, in 403 at-bats. While his hits are mainly of the line drive variety, they are perfect for the big alleys and artificial surface at Royals Stadium.

Orta is a first-ball hitter, and, like so many players who grew up in Mexico, where the style of pitching is off-speed and breaking balls, he will jump on pitchers who do not challenge him with hard stuff. He has trouble with power pitchers who come up and in on him.

His short, quick swing keeps him from striking out much, although he does not take many walks, either. Don't get lulled into pitching him away, though-- he has been around long enough to know that he will stay around even longer by going with the pitch to left field.

BASERUNNING:

Orta is average, at best, in the speed department. He does not react well on the bases, and rarely tries to take the extra base. He will fool infielders, however: he breaks out of the batter's box and gets down the first base line in a hurry. It is as if he can smell a hit.

FIELDING:

He was a disaster at second base, and then was platooned in the outfield when Willie Wilson was suspended early last season. In the outfield, Orta was just adequate. He does not have a left fielder's arm, much less the arm to play in right field. He does, however, look more comfortable in right field chasing

JORGE ORTA
OF/DH, No. 3
LR, 5'10", 175 lbs.
ML Svc: 13 years
Born: 11-26-50 in
Mazatlan, MEX

1984 STATISTICS

AVG	G	AB	R	H	2B	3B	HR	RBI	BB	SO	SB
.298	122	403	50	120	23	7	9	50	28	39	0

CAREER STATISTICS

AVG	G	AB	R	H	2B	3B	HR	RBI	BB	SO	SB
.279	1518	5143	663	1437	228	60	115	650	452	646	117

VS. RHP   VS. LHP   PROBABLE HIT LOCATIONS

balls, possibly because they come off the bat in a manner similar to what he saw when he was a second baseman.

His primary role, however, is as a DH.

OVERALL:

Orta was acquired from Toronto because the Royals needed a lefthanded bat off the bench; he turned out to be more than they bargained for. As well as becoming a big part of their offense, Orta was a pleasant addition from an attitude standpoint. He works to keep himself in shape, showing no concern for how much work he is called on to perform. He adapts well, an outgrowth of his versatile athletic ability. (He was offered a basketball scholarship to UCLA, but had already signed to play pro baseball in his native Mexico.)

Matthews: "His best role is coming off the bench. He is an excellent team player, and the Royals got more productivity than they could have imagined when they picked him up."

HITTING:

Greg Pryor is a situation player, both in the field and at the plate. Basically a reserve, he saw an abnormal amount of playing time in 1984 and had one of his better years. He is an excellent hit-and-run man and a very good bunter, although his lack of speed does not allow him to bunt for hits.

A fastball, line drive hitter who uses the middle of the field, Pryor can surprise the opposition with his occasional power. All four of his home runs in 1984 came at Royals Stadium: a big park where pitchers have a tendency to get lazy against a player like Pryor. When they do that, he can sting them.

Pryor likes pressure situations. One of his home runs came with two out in the bottom of the ninth to beat Baltimore and Tippy Martinez. Another came with two out in the bottom of the 16th to beat Chicago and Bert Roberge.

Pryor makes good contact, averaging less than one strikeout per 10 at-bats throughout his pro career. Given a chance to play against righthanders last year because of injuries to George Brett, Pryor held his own, although he really struggled against hard breaking pitches from righthanders.

BASERUNNING:

He is an intelligent baserunner. He just does not have enough speed, however, to take advantage of his good instincts.

FIELDING:

He was originally a shortstop, but that would have to be Pryor's No. 3 position now. His range is limited, and his arm is average in terms of strength: a horrible combination on artificial surfaces.

His best spot is third base. He has quick reactions and good lateral movement. While his arm is not strong, it is

GREG PRYOR
3B, No. 4
RR, 6'0", 185 lbs.
ML Svc: 7 years
Born: 10-2-49 in
   Marietta, OH

1984 STATISTICS

AVG	G	AB	R	H	2B	3B	HR	RBI	BB	SO	SB
.263	123	270	32	71	11	1	4	25	12	28	0

CAREER STATISTICS

AVG	G	AB	R	H	2B	3B	HR	RBI	BB	SO	SB
.258	663	1657	189	427	78	9	13	136	93	159	10

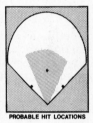

VS. RHP · VS. LHP · PROBABLE HIT LOCATIONS

extremely accurate--ideal for a third baseman who is not involved in as many bang-bang plays as a shortstop.

When Frank White missed 30 games at mid-season, Pryor platooned at second base as well, and left the impression that he could handle that spot on a fill-in basis. He was surprisingly adept at turning double plays.

OVERALL:

Pryor is the perfect extra man. He can play any of the four infield positions and has taken a stab in the outfield. He can sit for three weeks at a time, getting only one at-bat (which happened to him last season), and then step right in.

Matthews: "I think he is the best utility man in the league. He provides a lot of spark and is a good contact hitter. He does all of the little things that make a good ballplayer."

PITCHING:

Rest assured, Dan Quisenberry is in control when he is on the mound. He has walked only 23 batters in 268.1 innings over the last two seasons, and six of those have been intentional. Of course, he does not get a lot of strikeouts, either--only 89 in the last two years.

What he does get, however, is re-sults. He has saved 180 games in his five year career--and has 89 in the last two years, including a major league record in 45 in 1983, which was tied by Bruce Sutter in 1984.

He has done all that with a fastball which is in the low 80s, at its best. He mixes the fastball with a curveball, a slider and a knuckle curve--and the ability to change speeds on all his pitches from slow to slower. In 1984, he turned to the breaking pitches more, and made less use of the knuckleball, which he picked up during the Royals' tour of Japan after the 1981 season.

He has a resilient arm and the more he works, the better he feels. Because Quiz throws so few pitches in getting outs--he gets a lot of hitters on his first pitch or two--it is no big deal for him to work three innings. Manager Dick Howser will bring him in at the start of an inning, giving him a bit of breathing room, because Quisenberry is not a strikeout pitcher and can give up cheap hits on seeing-eye ground balls. If Quisenberry does not work on a par-ticular day, he normally will throw on his own because of the feeling that he works better with less rest.

He developed his famous submarine de-livery after his senior year at LaVerne (Calif.) College because of what he des-cribed as a "tired arm." He has never had a sore arm since. Being a top short reliever, he is obviously not bothered

DAN QUISENBERRY
RHP, No. 29
RR, 6'2", 180 lbs.
ML Svc: 5 years
Born: 2-7-54 in
   Santa Monica, CA

1984 STATISTICS

W	L	ERA	G	GS	CG	IP	H	R	ER	BB	SO	SV
6	3	2.64	72	0	0	129	121	39	38	12	41	44

CAREER STATISTICS

W	L	ERA	G	GS	CG	IP	H	R	ER	BB	SO	SV
36	26	2.51	360	0	0	635	595	196	177	84	205	180

by tight situations. In fact, if there is a time when he has trouble, it is when he has too big of a lead, and no challenge. It is tough for him to main-tain his concentration at times like that.

FIELDING:

Quisenberry does the little things to help himself in the field, like having a quick move to first. He does not give baserunners much of a chance to steal.

OVERALL:

There is nothing overpowering about Quisenberry, from his thin build to his less-than-fast fastball. But he com-bines his confidence on the mound with the ability to throw strikes to accumu-late overpowering results.

Matthews: "Quisenberry is the type of pitcher who goes after the hitters. He is one of the premier relief pitchers in the American League, the most consistent one in the last five years."

PITCHING:

After one year in the minor leagues, Bret Saberhagen proved he was ready to pitch in the big leagues. There were times of inconsistency, but down the stretch last season he pitched 16 shut-out innings in two starts against the contending California Angels.

He is looked upon as a member of the starting rotation in 1985, but he both started and relieved in his rookie season, and was one of the top men in the Royals' bullpen. He was 5-1 with a 2.32 ERA as a reliever. While he had ups and downs as a starter, he did have some big games, including the one in which he became the first pitcher to beat Detroit, when he threw six shutout innings at Tiger Stadium on April 19, and also the back-to-back efforts against California in September.

Saberhagen has a fastball which is around the major league average (85-87 MPH) but which has outstanding movement, a curveball, a slider and a change. When he can throw his curveball for strikes, it is his best pitch. Like most young players (he turns 21 years old this season), his problem is that he does not have consistent command of his breaking pitches, and that is why he gets in trouble as a starter--falling behind in the count and having to rely on the fastball to try to get outs.

He is aggressive and confident. He predicted his victory over Detroit, against whom he finished with a 3-1 record, the only pitcher other than the Orioles' Mike Flanagan to beat the world champs three times. He does not get down on himself after a bad game, but rather analyzes what went wrong, trying to figure out how to avoid the problems a second time.

FIELDING:

It is obvious he was a shortstop at one time because Saberhagen has excel-

BRET SABERHAGEN
RHP, No. 53
RR, 6'1", 160 lbs.
ML Svc: 1 year
Born: 4-13-64 in
   Chicago Heights, IL

1984 STATISTICS

W	L	ERA	G	GS	CG	IP	H	R	ER	BB	SO	SV
10	11	3.48	38	18	2	157	138	71	61	36	73	1

CAREER STATISTICS

W	L	ERA	G	GS	CG	IP	H	R	ER	BB	SO	SV
10	11	3.50	38	18	2	157	138	71	61	36	73	1

lent fielding skills. He has a quick little motion and is ready to field when he completes his follow-through. He has excellent range to both his left and his right, and is really good at coming up with bunts. He makes strong, accurate throws to the bases.

Saberhagen has an excellent pickoff move. He does not throw over a lot, but doesn't need to because it is obvious to runners that he can get the ball over there in a hurry, and they do not take liberties against him.

OVERALL:

A 19th-round draft choice in 1982 (as a shortstop at that) Saberhagen has shown an uncanny knowledge of how to pitch. He is the type of young pitcher teams build a staff around. He has good control, is a good competitor and has a live arm.

Matthews: "Bret has incredible poise for a rookie. He handles his job with maturity and confidence; he was especially impressive in the way he pitched in the American League Championship Series."

HITTING:

In the winter before the 1984 season, Pat Sheridan put himself on a weight training program. He'd better get back to the gym again. His stamina is as much of a question mark now as it ever was.

Given a chance to play every day, he started off strong, hitting .327 at the All Star break. But just as he did in 1983, he tailed off drastically in the final weeks of the season. He hit only .237 after the All Star break, and produced a miserable .216 in September, leaving him with a .196 average to show for the last two Septembers.

Sheridan is a fastball hitter who is anxious to swing at the first pitch. He prefers the ball away from him, and will try to hit it to left and left-center quite a bit. Being made into the No. 2 hitter in his platoon situation with Lynn Jones, Pat did have to learn a little more patience at the plate so that Willie Wilson could put his basestealing skills to use.

When he went into his late-season slump, pitchers were able to jam him. He also was chasing breaking balls down. When he struggles, he takes too many called strikes. He shows average power, but could show more power if he became more aware of yanking inside pitches.

BASERUNNING:

The physical ability is there--he is an above average runner. Concentration, however, is missing. He does not have an awareness of the opportunities to take the extra base. He has the makings of a good basestealer if he would just learn to read pitchers.

FIELDING:

This is where Sheridan's lack of concentration becomes an issue once again. There are times when he is outstanding in the field, whether it is in center or right. He breaks well on balls, moves into the gap quickly and has a strong

PAT SHERIDAN
RF, No. 15
LR, 6'3", 175 lbs.
ML Svc: 2 years
Born: 12-4-57 in
   Ann Arbor, MI

1984 STATISTICS

AVG	G	AB	R	H	2B	3B	HR	RBI	BB	SO	SB
.283	138	481	64	136	24	4	8	53	41	91	19

CAREER STATISTICS

AVG	G	AB	R	H	2B	3B	HR	RBI	BB	SO	SB
.277	250	815	107	226	36	6	15	89	61	156	22

  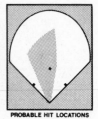

VS. RHP   VS. LHP   PROBABLE HIT LOCATIONS

arm. At other times, however, he looks as if he is sleepwalking. His arm is inconsistent, and the biggest problem is that he takes so long to get rid of the ball. He does not anticipate baserunning maneuvers. As a result, after he fields the ball, he has to come up and look before he sets himself and throws, giving a runner an extra five or six steps.

OVERALL:

In two big league seasons, Sheridan has yet to prove his contention that he can play every day. He does not show concentration over extended periods, and he has not proved that he is strong enough. He does have enough talent, however, to make him a viable platoon player.

Matthews: "It doesn't appear that he has a good idea of what is going on at times--you just have to wonder where the heck his head could be. Perhaps now that he has had a full year's experience he will stop being so distracted and get down to the task at hand."

HITTING:

Don Slaught's nickname is Yogi. Well, he is a catcher, but that is where the similarity ends. While Yogi Berra was a big power hitter with a top average, this Yogi is a contact hitter who tries to punch the ball up the middle or to right field.

Home runs are not his forte. He is, however, an excellent hit-and-run man. He seems to enjoy the concentration and contact required in that situation. He also likes to catch third basemen off guard by dropping a bunt down the third base line: he is an excellent bunter. Power pitchers are murder on him--but throw him breaking balls and off-speed pitches, and pay the price. Ask the Baltimore Orioles. While he was hitless against power-pitching Storm Davis, overall Slaught was 16 for 35 against their assortment of breaking ball pitchers. His bat is too slow to handle fastballs, however.

BASERUNNING

For a catcher, Slaught runs well--that is to say that he is average. He is, however, no threat to steal a base. Slaught will force things on the bases and likes to take the extra base. He likes contact around second base in double play situations.

FIELDING:

Slaught's strength in the minors was his defense. The question was whether he was going to have enough success with his bat to succeed in the majors. So far, however, he has been adequate as a hitter and inconsistent as a receiver.

The Royals' pitchers do like to throw to him. He works hard to get an idea of how to pitch hitters, and is considered capable in calling a game. He does not, however, ad lib as the game progresses. He follows the pre-game plan without deviation.

Slaught has average arm strength but

DON SLAUGHT
C, No. 7
RR, 6'1", 190 lbs.
ML Svc: 2 years
Born: 9-11-58 in
    Long Beach, CA

1984 STATISTICS

AVG	G	AB	R	H	2B	3B	HR	RBI	BB	SO	SB
.264	124	409	48	108	27	4	4	42	20	55	0

CAREER STATISTICS

AVG	G	AB	R	H	2B	3B	HR	RBI	BB	SO	SB
.283	250	800	83	226	46	8	7	78	40	94	3

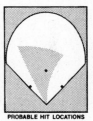

VS. RHP   VS. LHP   PROBABLE HIT LOCATIONS

an inconsistent release, which creates a lot of one-hop throws to second base and puts second baseman Frank White in danger of colliding with baserunners when he tries to stop the throws. It has become a mental thing: Slaught trying to hurry his throws more and more and getting wilder and wilder.

OVERALL:

After an injury-plagued career in the minor leagues, Slaught has avoided serious problems in back-to-back big league seasons. He still needs some work on his offense and his throwing, but he has shown the Royals enough to be their No. 1 catcher for now. He will never hit for power, but if he just hits for a solid average the Royals will be happy.

Matthews: "Slaught is a spray hitter who is good on the hit-and-run. He is really just an average catcher, but he is the best the Royals have at this point and will see most of the action behind the plate in 1985."

HITTING:

The Royals gave John Wathan a four-year contract prior to 1984, and then gave him a nice seat in the bullpen. He had the least active year of his career since his rookie season of 1977. Last season, he couldn't put anything together offensively.

A contact hitter and excellent hit-and-run man, Wathan basically likes fastballs up. He has a lot of problems with breaking balls away, and, with his struggle in 1984, found himself chasing that pitch even when it was out of the strike zone.

There is no power in Wathan's bat. He is a slap hitter who has to go to right field if he is going to enjoy any offensive success. In 1984, he tried to over-achieve during his limited appearances, and wound up pulling ground ball outs to the shortstop instead of flipping singles into right field.

BASERUNNING:

Wathan's baserunning is another aspect of his game which suffered, because he tried to do too much when he played. He had trouble getting on base the limited times he did play, and wound up trying to force things. As a result, he was only six for 12 in stolen bases, and was picked off three other times. He has better instincts than that; although his speed is only average, he should have a better ratio with his knack for thievery.

FIELDING:

A big part of Wathan's value is the fact that he can catch, play first base and either left field or right field. Defensively, first base is his best position, although he does not have enough power at the plate to earn a regular spot there. He handled 95 chances flawlessly at first in 1984. He has soft hands and excellent range and can scoop balls out of the dirt. He moves smoothly around the bag.

JOHN WATHAN
C, No. 12
RR, 6'2", 205 lbs.
ML Svc: 9 years
Born: 10-4-49 in
Cedar Rapids, IA

1984 STATISTICS

AVG	G	AB	R	H	2B	3B	HR	RBI	BB	SO	SB
.181	97	171	17	31	7	1	2	10	21	34	6

CAREER STATISTICS

AVG	G	AB	R	H	2B	3B	HR	RBI	BB	SO	SB
.264	800	2360	294	622	82	24	20	252	182	251	104

  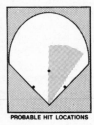

STRONG VS. RHP   STRONG VS. LHP   PROBABLE HIT LOCATIONS

As a catcher, Wathan is adequate. He is a good receiver, but his arm strength and accuracy are both below average. When he gets on a roll, he does have a quick release. He needs it to make up for his other problems.

He is very steady in the outfield. He has average range and an accurate arm.

OVERALL:

Wathan has plenty to offer a team. He is versatile, is a bat-control man and is a positive influence on his teammates. He also helps a team with his manner off the field. He is a quality person.

Matthews: "The proverbial good guy to have on a team. He does so many things well and should have all the confidence in the world. Last year, he was trying way too much at the plate; perhaps he wanted to prove too much in too little time. The results did not help him. This year, he should relax more and let his natural abilities come through for him."

HITTING:

Frank White has gotten better as he has gotten older. In the last three years, he has shown better than average power. After back-to-back seasons of 11 home runs (1982-83), he raised his career-high total to 17 home runs in 1984, despite missing 30 games with a pulled left hamstring.

He is a first-ball hitter who loves the fastball. He does have trouble when he gets behind in the count, becoming overly aggressive when he has two strikes against him, and chasing bad breaking pitches away. He has become very pull-conscious in the last three years, as exemplified by his 39 home runs from 1982 to 1984 after having hit only 48 (total) in his first eight big league seasons.

He is an outstanding bunter. He enjoys laying down sacrifice bunts. For some reason, however, he does not try to bunt for base hits.

BASERUNNING:

This is one area in which he has not gotten better as he has gotten older. White used to have above average speed, but is considered just average now. However, he has never been an aggressive runner or a basestealing threat. He was also one of the few Royals in the late 1970s who did not have a lackadaisical attitude about stretching singles into doubles--White always went for it.

FIELDING:

Well, he has won seven Gold Gloves, and while the honor has eluded him the last two years, he has not lost anything in the field other than votes from the AL managers and coaches. He plays the postion as well as ever. He has excellent range, a vital skill for playing on artificial surfaces. He has as good an arm as any second baseman. He has excellent hands. He plays hitters well,

FRANK WHITE
2B, No. 20
RR, 5'11", 170 lbs.
ML Svc: 11 years
Born: 9-4-50 in
Greenville, MS

1984 STATISTICS

AVG	G	AB	R	H	2B	3B	HR	RBI	BB	SO	SB
.271	129	479	58	130	22	5	17	56	27	73	5

CAREER STATISTICS

AVG	G	AB	R	H	2B	3B	HR	RBI	BB	SO	SB
.259	1503	4971	605	1289	252	49	87	540	229	625	152

VS. RHP   VS. LHP   PROBABLE HIT LOCATIONS

and he is smooth on the double play. He always seems to elude hard-sliding runners in time to get both outs. He is so good that he is often taken for granted.

OVERALL:

His veteran status has allowed White to emerge as a vocal member of the team. He defends his teammates consistently. White is willing to spend his time with the younger players to help them adjust to the major leagues. He is a durable player--his problem with the hamstring last year was only the second time in more than 11 years in the big leagues that White has been disabled.

Matthews: "White is still one of the premier second basemen in all of baseball. He should be helped by the new turf at Royals Stadium this year: we will see him move with even more speed and decisiveness because he will not have to worry about injuring himself on a worn-out and chewed-up surface."

HITTING:

The Detroit Tigers made no bones about it. In the American League play-offs last season, they knew that if they were going to beat the Royals they had to keep Willie Wilson off the bases because there are so many things he can do.

Wilson is a switch-hitter. He has a bit more power--in terms of driving the ball--from the right side. As a left-handed hitter, he is better off trying to slap at the ball, although in the final two months of 1984 he suddenly began to drive the ball deep batting lefthanded, too.

He is a good turf hitter. With his speed, he knows if he hits the ball on the ground he has a chance to beat it out. He goes to the opposite field well from both sides of the plate. Wilson likes the ball up from either side of the plate.

The best way to pitch him to to jam him with hard stuff and try to knock the bat out of his hands. He is a notorious first ball hitter, although he showed slightly better discipline in that regard last year. In spite of the fact that he missed the first 32 games of 1984, he walked 39 times--easily the highest total of his career.

Now, if he would just begin to bunt. With his speed, he could raise his average 10 or 15 points without any effort at all.

BASERUNNING:

Wilson's speed is the standard by which others are judged. He is aggressive, and is always looking for the extra base. Last season, he showed more of a willingness to steal with a left-handed pitcher on the mound. He was safe on 37 of 38 attempts with a righthanded pitcher working, and 10 of 14 against lefties.

FIELDING:

Minnesota manager Billy Gardner said that Wilson is so good that if the Roy-

WILLIE WILSON
CF, No. 6
SR, 6'3", 195 lbs.
ML Svc: 7 years
Born: 7-9-55 in
   Montgomery, AL

1984 STATISTICS

AVG	G	AB	R	H	2B	3B	HR	RBI	BB	SO	SB
.301	128	541	81	163	24	9	2	44	39	56	47

CAREER STATISTICS

AVG	G	AB	R	H	2B	3B	HR	RBI	BB	SO	SB
.305	970	3672	611	1119	131	69	17	270	189	470	393

VS. RHP   VS. LHP   PROBABLE HIT LOCATIONS

als had moved him from left field to center field in place of Amos Otis two years earlier they might have won two more titles. Wilson gets an outstanding jump on the ball going back and to his right side, sometimes having to slow down to make catches look routine on plays where he is actually robbing hitters of extra-base hits. His speed is a definite asset. He does have problems with balls hit in front of him, and takes a half step back at times. His arm is average, but because of the ground he covers, and how quickly he cuts off balls, he is able to compensate.

OVERALL:

Wilson left the drug scandal behind him when he returned to the Royals last season. After his six-week suspension at the start of the season, he was a new man. He seemed as if he had finally learned what baseball has to offer him.

Matthews: "He is the key to the Royals' offense. When he is on base, he sets up the whole batting order. When he is not, they spin their wheels."

BUDDY BIANCALANA
INF, No. 1
SR, 5'11", 160 lbs.
ML Svc: 1 year plus
Born: 2-2-60 in
Larkspur, CA

HITTING, BASERUNNING, FIELDING:

It is his hitting that will determine how much time Buddy Biancalana gets to play in the big leagues. A switch-hitter, he has shown some improvement at the plate, but it has been slow.

He has a very stiff stance from the left side, and he swings in a groove. He stunned some people last year when the ball met his bat when he was batting lefthanded. Righthanded, Biancalana is a little bit better hitter, but not by much. He looks more relaxed with a crouched stance. Either way, pitchers try to overpower him, jamming him with fastballs and then getting him to chance bad breaking balls away.

He has bunted for hits in the minor leagues, but did not try to do that last season. Despite his weak bat, Biancalana should be around for a few years because of his glove. He is primarily a shortstop with good range and a strong arm. He filled in at second base, along with Greg Pryor, when Frank White was hurt last season, and had no problems. He turned the double play well. During his stints in Omaha last year, he worked at third base.

Biancalana has excellent speed. He has been timid about trying to steal, although he has the physical ability which should allow him to become a good basestealer.

OVERALL:

Biancalana will at least be a major league utility player. If he can continue to make strides with the bat, he could develop into an everyday player at either shortstop or second.

BUTCH DAVIS
LF, No. 33
RR, 6'0", 185 lbs.
ML Svc: 1 year plus
Born: 6-19-58 in
Martin Co., NC

HITTING, BASERUNNING, FIELDING:

Talk about disappointments--talk about Butch Davis. He was supposed to be the Royals' everyday left fielder, but he wound up back in the minor leagues.

Davis is an aggressive hitter, but he became too aggressive for his own good in 1984 after a strong showing in the final six weeks of 1983. He was unable to even foul off breaking pitches, especially hard sliders.

Davis is a fastball hitter. When he is going well, he uses all fields and has outstanding power in the alleys to both left-center and right-center. He should be the prototypical artificial surface player--driving the ball well and running exceptionally well.

Davis has outstanding speed. He is a tad behind Willie Wilson from home to first, but he is as fast as anyone in the American League going from home to third. He is a good basestealer, but right now he relies on raw ability to get the job done. If he learns to read pitchers, he will get better.

Davis's future is as a DH. He is not bad on catching fly balls, although he will occasionally get a bad break. He outruns most of those mistakes. What he can't outrun is his arm. He may throw worse than anybody in the big leagues. He has to learn to get rid of the ball quickly, and throw to cutoff men to minimize that liability.

OVERALL:

Davis's stock fell so far that he was not even invited back when the rosters expanded in September. Reports from the minor leagues were that he was not even hitting the ball hard at that level.

LEON ROBERTS
LF, No. 16
RR, 6'3", 200 lbs.
ML Svc: 10 years
Born: 1-22-51 in
      Vicksburg, MI

HITTING, BASERUNNING, FIELDING:

Leon Roberts's career as a hitter was built around one year--1978 at Seattle, when he hit .301 with 22 home runs and 92 RBIs. It has been downhill since then, hitting rock bottom in 1984, when he was released by the Royals at the end of the season.

Roberts is a fastball hitter and likes the ball up. If he gets it there, he can drive it. Problem is, he did not get the pitch in that location very often. Roberts has problems when pitchers jam him with off-speed stuff, especially if they keep it down. He commits himself too quickly, and cannot hold up.

He can, and will, bunt for a base hit.

Despite his bulky appearance, Roberts runs well and runs hard. He will beat out a slow roller, and he will take the extra base. He definitely will take out middle infielders trying to complete double plays.

The sight of Roberts lumbering around is not a pretty one, but he does play hard and provides adequate defensive efforts in the outfield. He is not afraid of crashing into walls. His arm is average, but he somewhat makes up for it by anticipating what runners will be trying to do.

OVERALL:

Roberts has managed to hang around the big leagues for nearly ten years by working hard, not complaining and performing adequately if his team has to use him.

U.L. WASHINGTON
SS, No. 30
SR, 5'11", 175 lbs.
ML Svc: 7 years
Born: 10-27-53 in
      Stringtown, OK

HITTING, BASERUNNING, FIELDING:

Talk about quick turnabouts--talk about U.L. Washington. Three years ago, he was one of the better shortstops in the league. A year later, he was adequate. Last year, he was lucky to be around, and the only reason the Royals kept him was that they still owe him two seasons on his contract at $600,000 per.

A switch-hitter, he presents a threat from the right side, showing a little power and decent contact. From the left side, he is all mixed up. He tries to pull the ball but has a weak little swing and winds up hitting pop-ups. He likes the fastball up from both sides. He will bunt for a hit or sacrifice from both sides.

He used to be a good baserunner but is now average, at best. He appeared to beef up for the 1984 season, and the extra weight may have slowed him down.

A stiff player to begin with, he embarked on a weight-lifting program before the 1984 season, but the work made him even stiffer. His range was cut to average. He struggled to throw the ball all season, spending two stints on the disabled list and never looking fully healed.

OVERALL:

He found himself in several spots with Royals' management during the season, a surprising turn of events for the silent man in the clubhouse. He seemed to give up instead of accepting the challenge for the shortstop job which was presented by the emergence of Onix Concepcion.

MILWAUKEE BREWERS

HITTING:

Mark Brouhard, a husky Larry Csonka look-alike, is a platoon left fielder with the Brewers. He has tremendous power but does not play enough to put any big numbers on the board. He has a square stance, straight-up, and looks for and likes fastballs belt-high and toward the inside half of the plate. He has trouble with righthanded pitchers who will simply not give him that pitch. Righties, whom Brouhard does not face very often, will turn the fastball over and keep it away, because if it is near the plate, Brouhard will swing at it and try to pull it.

Lefthanders will use sliders low and in, keep their fastball away, show him the fastball out of the strike zone and use off-speed pitches on him. He never did walk much, but in 1984, opposing pitchers realized he could hurt them with one swing of the bat and kept the ball out of his power zone. He would much rather swing the bat than take a walk, but pitchers gave him some pitches he couldn't reach with a totem pole.

Because he saw less playing time in 1984 than he did in 1983, Brouhard tried to get two hits in every at-bat, an impossibility. He was impatient and swung at a lot of first pitches. He has a big swing and is a free swinger who can go into prolonged slumps. He will not bunt.

BASERUNNING:

Mark Brouhard looks like Larry Csonka and runs like him. He is always a threat to level an infielder if he throws a rolling block into second. He is absolutely no threat to steal. His last stolen base was in 1981.

FIELDING:

He platoons with Ben Oglivie in left, does not cover a lot of ground but tries

MARK BROUHARD
OF, No. 29
RR, 6'1", 210 lbs.
ML Svc: 5 years
Born: 5-22-56 in
  Burbank, CA

1984 STATISTICS

AVG	G	AB	R	H	2B	3B	HR	RBI	BB	SO	SB
.239	66	197	20	47	7	0	6	22	16	37	0

CAREER STATISTICS

AVG	G	AB	R	H	2B	3B	HR	RBI	BB	SO	SB
.258	267	802	97	207	33	5	24	91	48	158	2

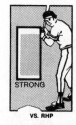

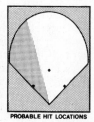

VS. RHP   VS. LHP   PROBABLE HIT LOCATIONS

hard for everything. He gets a fair jump on the ball and catches what he gets his hands on. He is rated average in arm strength and accuracy.

OVERALL:

Brouhard rarely makes waves, but then he rarely plays. He has spent more time between Vancouver (Triple A) and Milwaukee than American Airlines.

Robinson: "I think he is a better outfielder than people give him credit for. Maybe because he's not quick, people think he can't catch fly balls, but he does. He simply cannot play the way he has the past two years: in the lineup, out of the lineup, all over the place. He's got a quick swing and will strike out a lot but will hit the long ball and drive in runs--if he plays. I think he is the kind of player you can take a chance on."

PITCHING:

In 1984, for the first time since 1977, Mike Caldwell had a losing season. It was not only a losing season, it was a lost season and a loony season. He was voted the league's Pitcher of the Week on April 16th. Everything looked bright and sunny. Rollie Fingers was back and the Brewers had a new manager (Caldwell has always had the reputation of being tough to handle), and Caldwell was determined to improve on his 12-11 record of 1983.

From April 16th through the end of the season, Mike Caldwell managed only four wins. From May 9th through August 5th, he lost nine games in a row.

Caldwell has always been a streaky pitcher who wins in bunches and then loses in bunches, but in 1984 he just kept losing. He did poorly because the team and the bullpen fell apart. Another factor was his loss of velocity on his fastball. At his best, he could show the batters his fastball to keep them honest, and he usually had (and still does have) excellent control. He kept the ball down and away to both righties and lefties and was hurt only when he got the fastball up in the strike zone. His fastball does move, but not enough to hamper hitters anymore.

He throws three-quarters but drops to sidearm against many lefties and tries to keep his curve away from them. He has a sinker that is always very effective, but in 1984 batters did not seem to be fooled by it. They hit Caldwell to all fields because he simply lost a lot off the fastball and was always around the plate to both lefties and righties. He has always been accused of throwing a spitter, but nobody--especially the hitters--complained in 1984.

MIKE CALDWELL
LHP, No. 48
RL, 6'0", 185 lbs.
ML Svc: 13 years
Born: 1-22-49 in
Tarboro, NC

1984 STATISTICS

W	L	ERA	G	GS	CG	IP	H	R	ER	BB	SO	SV
6	13	4.64	26	19	4	126	160	76	65	21	34	0

CAREER STATISTICS

W	L	ERA	G	GS	CG	IP	H	R	ER	BB	SO	SV
137	130	3.81	475	307	98	2407	2581	1182	1020	597	939	18

FIELDING:

Caldwell is a good, solid fielder who knows what to do with grounders or bunts and knows what base to throw to. He is not afraid to throw to second or third on sacrifice bunts and is very accurate with his throws. Runners will run on him because of the off-speed pitches he throws. His move to first is rated average for a lefty.

OVERALL:

He is not talkative, is often moody but always tries his best on the mound. He is the kind of pitcher who will shock reporters by laughing after he loses a game and then by sulking when he wins another. He seems to be thinking of things other people cannot understand.

Robinson: "He has a good mental approach, but I think he is starting to doubt himself. He was in the Milwaukee rut in 1984. Hopefully, Bamberger will help him regain his past form. If not, it's going to be a long year and a big struggle for him."

PITCHING:

Some people can look at rookie Jamie Cocanower's 8-16 record in 1984 and scoff at it. The 6'4" starter-reliever can simply say: "Hey, don't knock me. LaMarr Hoyt was the Cy Young Award winner in 1983 and HE lost 18 games last season. I lost less than he did."

No pitcher, of course, likes to lose twice as many games as he wins, but Milwaukee had very few pitchers who did have winning records in 1984. Cocanower, had his control been better, might have been much closer to .500. However, he led the staff in negative statistics, aside from the 16 losses: he hit nine batters, uncorked 13 wild pitches and walked 78 batters.

He is a three-quarters pitcher who relies on hard stuff. His fastball has been clocked at 90 MPH, and he has a hard slider, a curve and a straight change. If his location is good, he is not bothered by righties or lefties. He will use the fastball to get ahead in the count, try the slider low and then throw the fastball or curve for the strikeout pitch. But he must be able to get the fastball over the plate more consistently. If he falls behind in the count, he is a bit reluctant to use too many curves, and batters can look for the fastball in a good spot.

He does have the ability to start batters off with a breaking ball. If he misses, he can overpower hitters with the fastball--IF he has his control. If he is having difficulty, the umpires will rarely give him (or any rookie) the benefit of the doubt on close calls.

JAMIE COCANOWER
RHP, No. 47
RR, 6'4", 190 lbs.
ML Svc: 1 year
Born: 2-14-57 in
Balboa Hts., CA

1984 STATISTICS

W	L	ERA	G	GS	CG	IP	H	R	ER	BB	SO	SV
8	16	4.02	33	27	1	174	188	99	78	78	65	0

CAREER STATISTICS

W	L	ERA	G	GS	CG	IP	H	R	ER	BB	SO	SV
8	16	4.02	33	27	1	174	188	99	78	78	65	0

FIELDING:

Cocanower is an average fielder in all respects, but he takes fielding seriously and has a fair move to first.

OVERALL:

Cocanower is not baseball-young: he is 28. But when teams talk to Milwaukee about possible trades, they will ALWAYS ask about the availability of Cocanower. Every team in the AL East wants him. One scout who asked not to be identified said he had the best young arm (despite his 28 years) in the league.

Robinson: "He most certainly does have a good arm. I think the Brewers may try to use him more in the bullpen to take the place of Fingers, if Rollie cannot come back. Cocanower seems to have the kind of arm that will allow him to pitch quite often out of the bullpen."

HITTING:

In 1974, Cecil Cooper hit .275 while playing for Boston. He hit .311 for Boston in 1975, .282 in 1976, and was traded to Milwaukee--where he hit .300 or better for seven straight years.

In 1984, Cecil Cooper hit .275.

It was his worst overall year. He started off by not hitting and could never get untracked. He did the exact same things he had done in the past, but, like 95% of the Brewers, he simply lost some of his drive, enthusiasm and aggressiveness. He played as if saying, "I'll save something for next year."

Cooper just couldn't hit the ball. He had the same crouched, open stance, weight back, and laid the bat softly off his belt, straight back. Several nagging injuries hampered his swing, and pitchers were able to throw more fastballs past him in 1984 than ever before. In addition, with no one behind him doing any hitting, pitchers were able to feed him breaking balls down and away, fastballs up and in and a lot of off-speed pitches, including forkballs and sinkers.

He has never drawn many walks and he did not do so in 1984, either. He swung at pitches out of his power zone and suffered a drastic drop in homers (down from 30 in 1983) and RBIs (down from 126 in 1983, which tied him for the league lead). Lefties ran the fastball in on him and kept sliders low and away. Cooper uses the whole field, but did not do it last year. It finally affected his batting average.

BASERUNNING:

A conservative runner with surprising speed when he gets under way, Cooper will not steal often but must be watched in critical situations. He knows when to try for the extra base.

FIELDING:

Smooth as a Mercedes diesel, Cooper is sure-handed and cat-quick around the

CECIL COOPER
1B, No. 15
LL, 6'2", 190 lbs.
ML Svc: 14 years
Born: 12-20-49 in
Brenham, TX

1984 STATISTICS

AVG	G	AB	R	H	2B	3B	HR	RBI	BB	SO	SB
.275	148	603	63	166	28	3	11	67	27	59	8

CAREER STATISTICS

AVG	G	AB	R	H	2B	3B	HR	RBI	BB	SO	SB
.305	1545	5926	859	1805	339	38	207	915	360	696	77

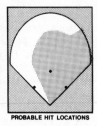

VS. RHP   VS. LHP   PROBABLE HIT LOCATIONS

bag. He is excellent at handling bad throws. He may have lost a step in covering ground, but he continues to play excellent positional first base. He is particularly adept at knowing what to do when he fields a grounder with a runner on first. He either steps on first and throws to second, or throws to second, whichever he thinks will get him the double play.

OVERALL:

He was a lifetime .308 hitter entering the 1984 season. Only George Brett (.316) and Rod Carew (.331) had higher lifetime averages in the AL. It makes one wonder if Cooper can bounce back at this stage of his career.

Robinson: "The year-long struggle he went through could have been caused by the poor start, the nagging injuries and the first prolonged slump of his career. He simply has to hit, and hit more home runs and drive in more runs for the Brewers. Personally, I think we will see Cecil bounce back this year."

PITCHING:

On July 23, 1984, Rollie Fingers, the all-time major league leader in saves (324) saved his 23rd game of the season for the Brewers. It was the 216th of his American League career.

He was through for the season a week later, suffering a herniated disc in his back. He had successfully conquered elbow problems, which had sidelined him for the entire 1983 season. But he was knocked flat on his back by the disc.

Fingers has outstanding control of five pitches--fastball, curve, slider, forkball and screwball. It would not make front page news if Fingers used each one of those pitches, in the exact order listed, to a particular batter. As a matter of fact, he can even reverse the order and throw all five.

He will nibble at corners, take something off, put something on, but always comes at a batter with the screwball or forkball in crucial situations. Left-handed and righthanded hitters are all the same to him. He has a big edge as a short relief man because of his outstanding track record. Batters know he will not wilt, that he will throw them something that moves on or near the corner. Occasionally, he will throw his fastball directly over the middle of the plate, and get away with it because the batter is gearing up for a breaking ball.

FIELDING:

He will never cost himself by throwing a ball away, by allowing a runner to steal on him in the late innings or by letting any slight defensive mistake either he or a teammate might make

ROLLIE FINGERS
RHP, No. 34
RR, 6'4", 200 lbs.
ML Svc: 16 years
Born: 8-25-46 in
   Steubenville, OH

1984 STATISTICS

W	L	ERA	G	GS	CG	IP	H	R	ER	BB	SO	SV
1	2	1.96	33	0	0	46	38	13	10	13	40	23

CAREER STATISTICS

W	L	ERA	G	GS	CG	IP	H	R	ER	BB	SO	SV
113	112	2.83	897	37	4	1645	1415	572	518	473	1275	324

bother him. Fingers has a good, crisp move to first and is always aware of who is where on the bases.

OVERALL:

It should come as no surprise that Willie Hernandez won both the Cy Young Award and MVP honors in the AL in 1984. Hernandez was the missing ingredient. In 1981, Fingers did the same thing for the Brewers and swept both awards. In 1984, immediately after it was announced he was through for the year, the Brewers lost 10 straight games (from July 29th to August 7th). By no means a coincidence.

Robinson: "With all he has been through, I have to question how effective he will be this year. What he's got going for him is the fact that he is a great pitcher, with savvy, and he does not have to be overpowering to win. He'll get anybody out with that forkball of his."

HITTING:

The Milwaukee second baseman, Jim Gantner, a solid performer for the past six years, does not like what has happened to the team that came within one game of winning the world championship in 1982: it finished fifth in 1983 and last (with the worst record in the American League) in 1984.

There is absolutely no reason why he should not be disenchanted with the franchise, but he did not let his feelings hamper his performance in 1984. Gantner hit from the same square stance and used the entire field. Basically, he is a line drive hitter who, in the past few years has learned to pull the ball more often. He is a high ball hitter and an impatient hitter. He will swing at anything round and anything that moves, but does not strike out very much. With two strikes he can make contact, although he will be a bit less aggressive.

Lefthanders who can throw him hard sliders or big overhand curves, toward the outside portion of the plate, can give him trouble. If he starts leaning, they will bust the fastball inside, but they must be careful. Gantner can handle that pitch with men on base, although he did not hit for power in 1984. He is now more of a gap hitter who can go to either right or left-center and can pull the ball down the right field line. Righthanders can use low sliders and curves, then take something off the fastball or turn it over and keep it away and down.

He is a very good bunter who usually bunts more in sacrifice situations than for a hit, and he is considered excellent at getting a runner home from third with one out or less.

BASERUNNING:

Gantner has good speed out of the box, nothing spectacular but nothing foolish. He knows how to run the bases and runs them hard.

JIM GANTNER
2B, No. 17
LR, 5'11", 175 lbs.
ML Svc: 7 years
Born: 1-5-54 in
        Eden, WI

1984 STATISTICS

AVG	G	AB	R	H	2B	3B	HR	RBI	BB	SO	SB
.282	153	613	61	173	27	1	3	56	30	51	6

CAREER STATISTICS

AVG	G	AB	R	H	2B	3B	HR	RBI	BB	SO	SB
.280	838	2851	329	797	115	18	28	285	182	234	39

VS. RHP   VS. LHP   PROBABLE HIT LOCATIONS

FIELDING:

Gantner is as solid as they come in the field. He is excellent at turning the double play and hangs in better than most second basemen when pivoting. He works well around second with Yount and has good range either way. He will dive, but he is not especially quick. He gets rid of the ball very quickly on slow rollers or after a diving stop.

OVERALL:

He was the perfect second baseman for the Brewers when they were the slugging Brewers. He didn't have to hit, but he did.

Robinson: "A solid year and he gives you his best. Gantner should do the same this year. From start to finish in 1984, he played as well as anyone on the team."

PITCHING:

Big, strong, young, husky and talented--and Moose Haas finished at 9-11 in 1984 after a league-leading percentage mark of .813 (13-3) in 1983.

Why should he have been any different than three-quarters of the Brewers in 1984? He had little offensive support and no bullpen to help him out. The Brewers' entire staff had 41 saves--Dan Quisenberry and Bruce Sutter each had more.

Haas is a power pitcher who once threw nothing but fastballs and hard sliders but who has learned to use and control a curve and split-fingered fastball. He can also keep batters off-stride with an excellent change.

He will challenge hitters by throwing his fastball (89 MPH) either up and in or low and away, and by throwing hard sliders to their weaknesses. He understands how to pitch and is now a pitcher as opposed to a thrower. He once had the reputation of falling apart if you stayed close to him for six innings, but now he battles each and every time he takes the mound. He is a deliberate, slow worker on the mound and takes more time than most pitchers with men on base.

He has good control of all his pitches, particularly the fastball and split-fingered fastball. He can be upset by a bad inning or a bad outing, but he had every right to be upset with the team that Milwaukee fielded in 1984.

FIELDING:

He is a good athlete and a better

MOOSE HAAS
RHP, No. 30
RR, 6'0", 170 lbs.
ML Svc: 8 years
Born: 4-22-56 in
  Baltimore, MD

1984 STATISTICS

W	L	ERA	G	GS	CG	IP	H	R	ER	BB	SO	SV
9	11	3.99	31	30	4	189	205	91	84	43	84	0

CAREER STATISTICS

W	L	ERA	G	GS	CG	IP	H	R	ER	BB	SO	SV
83	71	4.05	218	205	49	1381	837	669	621	383	722	2

than average fielder who can handle comebackers and bunts. He tends to worry too much about a runner on first and throws to first more often than most pitchers. At times he can make batters impatient, an edge for him, but at other times he is at a disadvantage because he loses some of his concentration.

OVERALL:

Haas stayed fairly healthy in 1984. In the past, injuries always followed him around. His ERA, on a team that finished ninth in the league in ERA (4.05), was lower than the team average, so his record is better than it appears.

Robinson: "I've always said he should be a winning pitcher and have more wins than he puts on the board. The way he throws, he should always have more wins than losses. He'll be a winning pitcher in 1985. Not a big winner, but a winning pitcher."

HITTING:

Dion James has hit better than .300 in each of his four minor league seasons, and if the 1984 season had lasted for one more week, he would have again hit .300 with the parent Milwaukee team. The Brewers didn't seem to know what to do with this rookie center fielder/right fielder until late July, when he was batting .245. They finally decided to play him someplace, almost every day, and he lifted his average 50 points.

James has a closed, straight-up stance and is basically a slap hitter with no power. He hits to all fields and prefers the fastball down so he can swing down and get hard grounders or low liners. He has outstanding speed and beats out many infield rollers. Most rookies tend to be impatient when they get their chance to show what they can do. But James split his walks and strikeouts fairly evenly.

Once they have seen him a few times, pitchers will feed him high fastballs and curves low and in on his hands. Lefthanders will use their sliders away, but James can slap those to left. A good control pitcher who moves the ball in and out, up and down, and takes something off the fastball, will give him trouble.

He is not prone to slumps, or at least was not in his rookie year, because he is a very good bunter who will bunt for a hit, and because he makes contact so often.

BASERUNNING:

James has good speed from the box and on the bases, but does not as yet have the knack for stealing or studying pitchers' moves. He stole 10 bases in 1984--but was also caught 10 times. He must be watched when on first base.

FIELDING:

His natural position is center, but

DION JAMES
OF, NO. 14
LL, 6'1", 170 lbs.
ML Svc: 1 year
Born: 11-9-62 in
        Philadelphia, PA

1984 STATISTICS

AVG	G	AB	R	H	2B	3B	HR	RBI	BB	SO	SB
.295	128	387	52	114	19	5	1	30	32	41	10

CAREER STATISTICS

AVG	G	AB	R	H	2B	3B	HR	RBI	BB	SO	SB
.295	128	387	52	114	19	5	1	30	32	41	10

  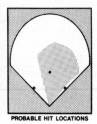

VS. RHP | VS. LHP | PROBABLE HIT LOCATIONS

his arm is only average. James covers a lot of ground, does not make many errors (three in 1984) but does not get a good jump on the ball. He will rely on his speed to catch up to balls hit in the gaps. He is much better coming in on the ball than he is going back. He does the same whether in right or in center.

OVERALL:

He will not be a power hitter, but he makes very good contact. There is no telling what he can bat if he plays all year.

Robinson: "I like him. He added speed and other dimensions to the club and puts the bat on the ball. His future looks bright."

PITCHING:

When Rollie Fingers missed the 1983 season, Pete Ladd stepped in and saved 25 games for the Brewers. It appeared as though he would be even better in 1984, when Fingers returned to action, but when Fingers went down in July with a herniated disc in his back, Ladd went from long man to short man in the bullpen . . . and the Brewers' suds went flat.

Ladd was hit hard, despite a herky-jerky motion which makes it tough for batters to pick up the ball and despite the fact that his fastball has been clocked at 90 MPH and better. Ladd throws everything hard, but is basically a one-pitch pitcher. His slider is almost as hard as his fastball, but it does not break as much as it should. Late in the year, when all else had failed, Ladd worked hard on perfecting a breaking ball that acted like a curve. He had trouble with that pitch, and the batters simply laid off anything that turned over and waited for the fastball. As fast as it is, it does not tail in or tail away--it is extremely straight.

He can obviously overpower many ping-pong hitters, but there are simply too many good fastball hitters in the American League, as he found out in 1984.

FIELDING:

Ladd is big and bulky, but surprisingly quick off the mound on bunts and slow rollers. After his release, he ends up in decent position to field balls hit back to him. He pitches from the stretch position at all times, so he is able to set himself up after the pitch. His

PETE LADD
RHP, No. 27
RR, 6'3", 240 lbs.
ML Svc: 3 years
Born: 7-17-56 in
Portland, ME

1984 STATISTICS

W	L	ERA	G	GS	CG	IP	H	R	ER	BB	SO	SV
4	9	5.24	54	1	0	91	94	58	53	38	75	3

CAREER STATISTICS

W	L	ERA	G	GS	CG	IP	H	R	ER	BB	SO	SV
18	28	4.18	124	1	0	170	148	88	79	68	134	28

move to first is average, and runners will go on him when he gets in trouble with the batter and forgets about who's on base.

OVERALL:

When George Bamberger was the pitching coach for the Baltimore Orioles, he developed pitchers who won more than 20 games a season 21 times. He helped the Brewers' pitching staff when he took over as manager in 1978. If anybody can straighten Ladd out, the man they call "Bambi" can.

Robinson: "He has a sinking fastball, but it seemed as though his fastball was as straight as a string in 1984. How else can you explain 16 homers given up in only 91 innings? He didn't get his breaking ball over, so batters--especially lefties--just sat and waited for their pitch. He simply has to be better than he was in 1984."

HITTING:

Who hits on this team, anyway? Charlie Moore is a fine defensive right fielder. Jim Sundberg is an excellent defensive catcher. Rick Manning might be the best defensive center fielder in the league. Therein lies most of this team's problems, aside from the disastrous injuries to Rollie Fingers, Pete Vuckovich, Chuck Porter and Paul Molitor . . . nobody hits.

Manning was one of the no-hitters of 1984--he started the season at .250 and stayed there throughout the year. He has the same stance he has always had, closed, wide and deep in the box. He is a high fastball hitter against both lefthanded and righthanded pitchers, but he swings down on the ball, has very little power and has trouble lifting the ball. He is basically a hard grounder and line drive hitter--when he hits the ball. He does make contact, does not strike out a lot, does not walk a lot and does not hit in the clutch very often.

Manning tries to use the whole field, but if a pitcher pitches him away, the defense plays him away and he usually hits that way, too. He has excellent speed and can bunt for a hit when he puts his mind to it. He gets many leg hits.

He hangs in fairly well against lefties but will have trouble with sliders low and away and with off-speed pitches. Righties will try to keep everything down to him. Although he does not have power, Manning caught enough mistake pitches to hit seven homers in 1984, only one less than his career-high of eight with the Indians in 1982--and he had 221 fewer at-bats in 1984 than he did in 1982.

BASERUNNING:

Manning has excellent speed all around the bases, starting from home plate. He will never hesitate to take the extra base, is very aggressive and is a threat to steal. He is a little too aggressive when it comes to stealing

RICK MANNING
OF, No. 28
LR, 6'1", 180 lbs.
ML Svc: 10 years
Born: 9-2-54 in
 Niagara Falls, NY

1984 STATISTICS

AVG	G	AB	R	H	2B	3B	HR	RBI	BB	SO	SB
.249	119	341	53	85	10	5	7	31	34	32	5

CAREER STATISTICS

AVG	G	AB	R	H	2B	3B	HR	RBI	BB	SO	SB
.260	1290	4713	593	1224	166	38	46	400	428	559	158

  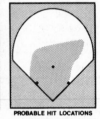

VS. RHP   VS. LHP   PROBABLE HIT LOCATIONS

and was thrown out seven times in 12 attempts in 1984.

FIELDING:

Manning covers more ground than the Pacific Ocean. He gets an excellent jump on the ball, has good speed coming in and will climb fences in any part of the park and get balls no other center fielder can. He cuts off hits, and by playing shallow he makes up for an average arm. He has a quick release, charges grounders like an infielder and has an accurate arm.

OVERALL:

A powerful offensive team can carry Rick Manning. Milwaukee may decide to go with Dion James, the outstanding rookie, unless Manning starts hitting in spring training and proves he can add punch.

Robinson: "I was really disappointed with him in 1984. It's just possible his best days with the bat are behind him. He can sure play center field, but he just has to hit to stay in the lineup day in and day out."

PITCHING:

Very few pitchers in the major leagues can do what Bob McClure does. He was a full-time starting pitcher in the minors, was converted to a full-time reliever in the majors, went back to a starter, back to a reliever, was used long, short, pitched to one or two batters . . . and finally did everything but run in the Boston Marathon in 1984.

Nobody, in truth, seems to know what to make of McClure. He is a devastating pitcher against virtually every power-hitting lefty in the league. When Reggie Jackson sees him come into a game, he looks toward the sky and says a little prayer that McClure will either hang a curve or throw the fastball straight.

McClure's fastball sinks, or at least it should in order for him to be effective. He can throw the 88 MPH fastball past many hitters, and when he faces lefties, he drops from three-quarters to sidearm and feeds then a sharp breaking ball. He has a slider and a change, but the change is really an off-speed curve. As a starter, he will use every pitch he has. As a reliever, he will rely on the fastball-curve, and in that regard is basically a two-pitch pitcher.

He is a frustrating pitcher for many managers because when his fastball moves and he gets his curve over, he can get anybody in the league out. But when his control is off, and when his fastball comes in belt-high, he can look like a Little Leaguer. At times, he can come into pressure situations and look as good as any reliever in the league. At other times, managers punch the side of a dugout or get right back on the phone and call the bullpen again.

FIELDING:

No one in baseball has a better pick-

BOB McCLURE
LHP, No. 10
SL, 5'11", 170 lbs.
ML Svc: 8 years
Born: 4-29-53 in
Oakland, CA

1984 STATISTICS													
W	L	ERA	G	GS	CG	IP	H	R	ER	BB	SO	SV
4	8	4.38	39	18	1	139	154	76	68	52	68	1

CAREER STATISTICS													
W	L	ERA	G	GS	CG	IP	H	R	ER	BB	SO	SV
40	41	3.88	321	72	12	758	733	366	327	345	347	31

off than McClure. It is the ultimate lefty pickoff move, and McClure is annually among the league leaders in pickoffs and balks. He can pick off a runner who is no more than three feet off the base. The rest of his fielding assets are just that--assets. He is quick off the mound and always alert on bunts.

OVERALL:

Some people claim McClure lacks the killer instinct. They say he can get pumped up for one or two batters and demolish them--then lose his desire.

Robinson: "I think his best role would be to stay in the bullpen and come in for a tough lefty. He is very good at that. And he can be valuable as a long or middle reliever. He has a tricky motion that helps him, but he must be able to get his fastball in the right location when facing righthanded batters."

HITTING:

They call it the "Tommy John Surgery" and that is what Paul Molitor had to undergo in 1984. He hurt his right arm in spring training, thought nothing of it, started the season--and destroyed the ligament in the arm. Doctors had to operate, remove the ligament and take another ligament from his lower back and ceate holes in his elbow to insert the new ligament. He played in only 13 games before the disastrous injury.

1984 was a lost year, but Molitor is a determined young man. He bats from a slightly closed stance and is (when healthy) a devastating high fastball hitter. Lefthanders or righthanders do not bother him because he can hit either the high fastball or the curve. He uses all fields but prefers to pull and often goes for the long ball. He has power to left and left-center.

Molitor is an extremely aggressive hitter with a good eye, but he can be caught by an unexpected pitch if the count is 3-1 or 3-2. Something off-speed, or low and away, will give him trouble, and when pitchers realize they cannot throw the fastball past him, they feed him nothing but curves. Pitchers will occasionally try to sneak the fastball past him, and he will swing at it even if it is above shoulder level.

Molitor is the best bunter on the team and one of the best in the league. He will bunt more often for base hits than in sacrifice situations, and corner infielders must always be ready.

BASERUNNING:

In a way, Molitor can thank the stars that the surgery was to his arm and not his leg. He is quick, fast and one of the best baserunners in the league. He will steal any time he gets on base, and very rarely stops at second on hits, whether they are to right field or left field. He knows the strength of outfielders' arms and will always gamble when running. He is a good slider with

PAUL MOLITOR
INF, No. 4
RR, 6'0", 175 lbs.
ML Svc: 7 years
Born: 8-22-56 in
St. Paul, MN

1984 STATISTICS

AVG	G	AB	R	H	2B	3B	HR	RBI	BB	SO	SB
.217	13	46	3	10	1	0	0	6	2	8	1

CAREER STATISTICS

AVG	G	AB	R	H	2B	3B	HR	RBI	BB	SO	SB
.291	765	3126	521	909	148	36	60	287	270	354	190

  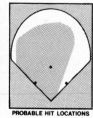

VS. RHP   VS. LHP   PROBABLE HIT LOCATIONS

great instincts.

FIELDING:

He can play second base, third base and center field. He is not the best third baseman in the league, but he tries hard, is quick and has good range. His arm (previously) was average but accurate. He goes to his left better than to his right at third base.

OVERALL:

It was a crying shame that he had to miss the 1984 season, after five outstanding years with the Brewers.

Robinson: "The Brewers missed him more than anyone else. He is the player who sets the tone of the game for Milwaukee. There is some talk that his recovery has not been what it should be, but he is so good that even if he is not 100%, he is a valuable cog in the Brewer machinery."

HITTING:

Most people agree that castor oil leaves a horrible taste in your mouth. Nonetheless, Charlie Moore would gladly have endured that rather than have the bitter taste left by his 1984 season.

He was a good major league catcher who became a good major league right fielder when the Brewers acquired Ted Simmons three years ago. He worked long and hard and with tremendous desire but Moore is basically a hard-nosed guy who doesn't hit for power. He fit in perfectly with a slugging Brew Crew. But when the sluggers turned to a poor few, the team had to sit Moore on the bench and use the young Dion James in right field. As a result, Moore had the worst offensive year of his career in 1984.

He has a slightly open, semi-crouched stance and stands in the middle of the box. He hit .284 in 1983, and accomplished that by not pulling everything and by using all fields. He is still a basic straightaway hitter who likes the ball low and hard. Any pitch above the belt will give him trouble, particularly high fastballs in on his hands.

He is an impatient hitter who does not draw walks but who manages to get his bat on the ball with two strikes and put it in play. He is also an excellent bunter who will sacrifice or bunt for a base hit.

In the trade, he is known as a player who is a pesky hitter, and seems to be able to drive in a runner from second with two out. Inactivity in 1984, however, saw him with no game-winning RBIs, an indication that he saw more wood on the bench than in his hands.

BASERUNNING:

Moore is very aggressive, very smart, will always gamble on the bases but will not steal unless the situation calls for it.

CHARLIE MOORE
OF, No. 22
RR, 5'11", 180 lbs.
ML Svc: 11 years
Born: 6-21-53 in
    Birmingham, AL

1984 STATISTICS

AVG	G	AB	R	H	2B	3B	HR	RBI	BB	SO	SB
.234	70	188	13	44	7	1	2	17	10	26	0

CAREER STATISTICS

AVG	G	AB	R	H	2B	3B	HR	RBI	BB	SO	SB
.265	1098	3342	382	887	152	35	32	331	285	367	42

  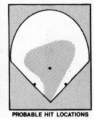

VS. RHP   VS. LHP   PROBABLE HIT LOCATIONS

STRONG   STRONG

FIELDING:

He can come in or go back, is not afraid of fences and cuts off balls down the line in right and in the right-center gap. Moore is sure-handed, and has an excellent and accurate arm.

OVERALL:

He can help almost any team in the majors because of his pride and desire. He cannot, however, sit on the bench after all he has accomplished. His problem was, and is, not having enough long ball power on a team that cries for it.

Robinson: "I think he would be better off on another team. I think Milwaukee has made up its mind to go with youth, and I really can't blame them. I look for Charlie to play even less in 1985."

HITTING:

Many baseball observers secretly believe that any team, regardless of how good they are, can suddenly go bad from one year to the next, particularly if their key players are over 30 years of age. The Brewers (like the Orioles) and Ben Oglivie seem to bear out that argument.

Oglivie was once again limited to fewer than 135 games in left field. The expression "nagging injuries" has followed him around for the past two seasons, and his include shoulder, rib and heel problems. To be effective, Oglivie must be completely healthy because he takes one of the hardest swings in the league.

He bats from a slightly closed, straight-up stance and looks fastball all the time. He can handle high curves, but has trouble with lefthanders who take something off the fastball and keep it away. He is a dead pull hitter and will try to pull everything. Lefthanders can also get him out with low sliders away and an occasional hard slider in on his hands.

Righthanders will keep their curves, sliders and sinkers low and on the outside portion of the plate. Oglivie stands close to home plate, so many pitchers try to jam him. He does have a quick bat, and, when healthy, can get around on hard stuff inside, although he has had more and more trouble with those pitches in the past two years.

He is not a good bunter. He is a better than average hitter with men on base.

BASERUNNING:

On the bases, Oglivie is fairly passive--no threat to steal--and does not have particularly good instincts. He does get out of the batter's box well except when he swings so hard that he loses his balance.

FIELDING:

An average left fielder with good

BEN OGLIVIE
OF, No. 24
LL, 6'2", 170 lbs.
ML Svc: 13 years
Born: 2-11-49 in
Colon, PAN

1984 STATISTICS

AVG	G	AB	R	H	2B	3B	HR	RBI	BB	SO	SB
.262	131	461	49	121	16	2	12	60	44	56	0

CAREER STATISTICS

AVG	G	AB	R	H	2B	3B	HR	RBI	BB	SO	SB
.271	1524	5226	713	1418	240	30	220	786	493	768	86

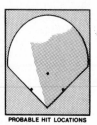

VS. RHP   VS. LHP   PROBABLE HIT LOCATIONS

speed and good range, Oglivie has good hands and catches what he catches up to. His arm is average and runners will run on him. He is not afraid of fences and will climb one if he has to.

He generally plays hitters the same way, rarely moving around regardless of whether the hitter is ahead or behind in the count or in a situation to pull the ball more.

OVERALL:

Oglivie seems to have leveled off, and his 1984 stats were almost a duplicate of his 1983 set. His best year was 1980, when he tied for the league lead with 41 homers, hit .304 and drove in 118 runs. Since then, it has appeared that he is going downhill.

Robinson: "I'm fairly certain that his best years are behind him. I think he'll have the same numbers this year that he has had the past two years. He is, however, a very aggressive player."

HITTING:

Ed Romero might be the most consistent home run hitter in the big leagues. If he can somehow play for another 15 years, he will end up with 20 homers--because in 1984 he hit his annual one. He has hit exactly one every year since 1980.

He obviously has no power, but Romero is a better than average contact hitter and is difficult to strike out. He bats from a slightly closed stance and is basically a high fastball hitter. He prefers the ball on the inside part of the plate. He played much more often in 1984 than ever before in his five years with Milwaukee and saw more righthanders than in past years. Righthanders are not afraid to challenge him up and in with fastballs. They will also use a lot of breaking balls and try to keep them down and away.

Romero got more playing time, but despite the fact that he has no power and is a singles hitter, he was not as patient as he should be at home plate. Lefties will show him the fastball away and come back with sliders and curves, mixed in with an occasional off-speed pitch.

He is a better than average hitter with men in scoring position and cannot be considered an automatic out. Pitchers who think he will roll over and hide are mistaken, and if they get the ball in the wrong place, Romero can find a hole to hit it into. He is an exceptionally good bunter who can bunt for a hit or in a sacrifice situation.

BASERUNNING:

Romero has good speed but does not steal. He is as aggressive as he can be, but not enough to frighten anyone. He has good instincts but will not gamble on the bases.

FIELDING:

He has fair range and is very good at

ED ROMERO
INF, No. 11
RR, 5'11", 150 lbs.
ML Svc: 4 years
Born: 12-9-57 in
   Santurce, PR

1984 STATISTICS

AVG	G	AB	R	H	2B	3B	HR	RBI	BB	SO	SB
.252	116	357	36	90	12	0	1	31	29	25	3

CAREER STATISTICS

AVG	G	AB	R	H	2B	3B	HR	RBI	BB	SO	SB
.259	323	866	101	224	38	0	5	78	60	72	6

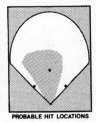

VS. RHP   VS. LHP   PROBABLE HIT LOCATIONS

turning the double play when he plays second, but is not as good at it when he plays short. Romero's arm is not strong, but it is accurate. He is average in coming in for slow rollers and when handling hard smashes, particularly at third. He had an off-year defensively in 1984.

OVERALL:

He has averaged a homer a year for five years; another amazing statistic is that for a player with decent speed, Romero has not hit a triple in five years.

Robinson: "He will get less playing time if Molitor returns this year. I do not think he is an everyday player, but he is good to have on your club because he can fill in almost anyplace and can even play the outfield. He knows his role, accepts it and even likes it."

HITTING:

Kids in the playgrounds are always yelling, "Come on, Joey, a walk is just as good as a hit." Bill Schroeder had better not hear them say that or he is liable to tear up their playing surface. He might be the only major leaguer in history to have more homers than walks in parts of two seasons.

Schroeder simply loves to swing the bat. He has an extremely wide, slightly closed stance and takes a long swing at everything he sees. It is a case of hit-or-miss. Fastballs up are what he looks for and hits, but both righthanders and lefthanders can jam him so he cannot extend his arms and use the big swing. Righthanders will have success against him if they throw the fastball away, then use nothing but breaking balls low and away or low and in.

He has trouble hitting lefties because they will give him fastballs away and he tries to pull them. Once ahead in the count, good lefties can feed him sliders and curves and try to keep them low.

BASERUNNING:

Schroeder has very little speed and is no threat to steal, take a big lead or scare a pitcher. He does, however, run everything out and is aggressive on the basepaths. He cannot be expected to take too many extra bases.

FIELDING:

He did not show his best when he relieved Jim Sundberg behind the plate when the latter was injured, but Bill does have the tools to work with. His arm is considered better than average and fairly accurate, but runners tested him in 1984. His release is good and he learned a lot about calling games in the

BILL SCHROEDER
C, No. 21
RR, 6'2", 200 lbs.
ML Svc: 2 years
Born: 9-7-58 in
   Baltimore, MD

1984 STATISTICS

AVG	G	AB	R	H	2B	3B	HR	RBI	BB	SO	SB
.257	61	210	29	54	6	0	14	25	8	54	0

CAREER STATISTICS

AVG	G	AB	R	H	2B	3B	HR	RBI	BB	SO	SB
.237	84	283	36	67	8	1	17	32	11	77	0

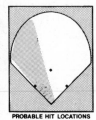

VS. RHP   VS. LHP   PROBABLE HIT LOCATIONS

61 games he managed to get in during the past season.

OVERALL:

Simple arithmetic--if you add up his at-bats, walks, homers and strikeouts in the past two seasons, and project them for a full year, Schroeder would get up 566 times, walk 22 times, hit 34 homers and strike out 154 times.

Robinson: "To me, he was a surprise, and I'm sure the Brewers were pleasantly surprised as well. He had only two fewer homers than Yount for the team high. He's following his minor league history: a lot of home run power and a lot of strikeouts. But he did show he could be a factor in the catching department this year, and Milwaukee can use him for added power. Look for him to play more this season."

HITTING:

About all that can be said for Ted Simmons, once one of the best switch-hitters in baseball, is that in 1984 he was consistent. He hit .223 lefthanded, .218 righthanded . . . and .221 overall. His average dropped and incredible 87 points from 1983's .308.

All of the basics are still there, but basically Simmons's bat slowed to a crawl. Always an aggressive hitter who drew very few walks and struck out very few times, Simmons was usually fed off-speed pitches to neutralize his natural affinity--either way--for hitting fastballs. Whatever success pitchers had against him in the past came from throwing him high curves when he batted lefty and low curves when he batted righty. They did that, and always tried to keep it away from the inside part of the plate.

In 1984, pitchers were happily surprised to find they could still throw junk and off-speed pitches to Simmons, but could also throw the fastball past him--particularly on the inside, where he once murdered everything.

In 1983, after two poor years with the Brewers (adjusting to American League pitching after 11 seasons of averaging .298 with the Cardinals), Ted started to use all fields and make contact. He was content to go the other way with pitches that gave him trouble. In 1984 he couldn't do much of anything, because pitchers kept their breaking balls low and their fastballs in on his hands whether he was batting righty or lefty.

BASERUNNING:

Simmons is considered a liability on the bases. He has no speed but always runs hard and plays aggressively on the basepaths. He will, however, make mental mistakes. He is never a threat to steal except if the first baseman plays behind him and the pitcher rarely looks over to check on him.

TED SIMMONS
C, No. 23
SR, 6'0", 200 lbs.
ML Svc: 15 years
Born: 8-9-49 in
    Highland Park, MI

1984 STATISTICS

AVG	G	AB	R	H	2B	3B	HR	RBI	BB	SO	SB
.221	132	497	44	110	23	2	4	52	30	40	3

CAREER STATISTICS

AVG	G	AB	R	H	2B	3B	HR	RBI	BB	SO	SB
.288	2086	7741	974	2226	435	45	226	1247	750	616	18

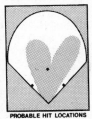

VS. RHP   VS. LHP   PROBABLE HIT LOCATIONS

FIELDING:

The Brewers began using Simmons as a designated hitter two years ago when they realized his arm had lost some zip and he had lost some quickness behind the plate. Runners were running on him, and he was having trouble with many pitches in the dirt. They started using him at first, where he tried his best, but he does not have good range and his arm is still only average. He was their full-time DH in 1984, with an occasional game at first and third.

OVERALL:

Simmons bears an amazing similarity, as far as statistics go, to Toby Harrah of the New York Yankees. Both have been All Stars in the past and have had solid seasons year-in and year-out. Both batted incredibly poorly in 1984.

Robinson: "His talent is eroding. Simmons just has to be better than 1984. I look for him to rebound unless his advancing age becomes too much of a factor."

HITTING:

Jim Sundberg has so many defensive records that when a new catcher comes into the league, people invariably ask: "Is he as good as Jim Sundberg?"

Very few catchers are. However, hitting is not a strong point for Sundberg, although after 10 years of squatting in the blazing Arlington sun with the Texas Rangers, the cooler Milwaukee air helped Sundberg take a deep breath and start hitting in 1984. Before he hurt his back in August and was disabled, he was among the team leaders in batting average, doubles, triples, homers, RBIs and game-winning hits. From the mid-.280s prior to the back problems, Sundberg after returning to play fell to a .261 average.

He is not a power hitter but can go deep on occasion. He does have gap power and can go to the opposite field when he puts his mind to it. He will pull more often than not, but is an excellent hit-and-run batter who can hit behind the runner. At times he swings at everything he sees, and at other times he takes pitches.

His stance is slightly open and upright, and he likes the fastball up. Pitchers can get him out by throwing the ball in on his hands, to tie him up, and feeding him off-speed and breaking pitches down and basically on the outside part of the plate. He is a much better bunter than most catchers in the league. He was not considered better than average as a clutch hitter in his 10 years with Texas, but was vastly improved when it came to hitting with men on base in 1984 prior to the back problems.

BASERUNNING:

Sundberg will not steal but knows how to run the bases and how to take orders from the third or first base coach. He does not gamble while running the bases but is alert and watches how outfielders play base hits both in front and behind him.

JIM SUNDBERG
C, No. 8
RR, 6'1", 192 lbs.
ML Svc: 11 years
Born: 5-18-51 in
   Galesburg, IL

1984 STATISTICS

AVG	G	AB	R	H	2B	3B	HR	RBI	BB	SO	SB
.261	110	348	43	91	19	4	7	43	38	63	1

CAREER STATISTICS

AVG	G	AB	R	H	2B	3B	HR	RBI	BB	SO	SB
.254	1508	4794	499	1216	208	30	61	502	606	753	19

  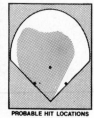

STRONG   STRONG
VS. RHP   VS. LHP   PROBABLE HIT LOCATIONS

FIELDING:

He has won six Gold Gloves. He has an outstanding arm and an excellent release, but he does need help from his pitching staff in keeping runners close. He is cat-quick on bunts and chops.

OVERALL:

At one point in his career, while with the Rangers, Sundberg said that baseball wasn't everything, that a family and a future were important to him. It almost seemed as though Sundberg did not enjoy the tension and pressure of day-in, day-out, win-at-all-costs baseball. Yet he does his job.

Robinson: "He would have had the best year of his career if he had not gotten hurt. His defense has always overshadowed his offense, but he was going pretty well in all areas in 1984 before the injury. The change of scenery did him a world of good. I think he'll pick up again in 1985."

PITCHING:

Don Sutton needs only 20 more wins to reach the magical 300 mark, something that will automatically qualify him for the Hall of Fame. In addition, he holds a record that no other pitcher does--in 1984 he struck out 143 batters, giving him 19 straight years with 100 or more strikeouts.

Sutton had a winning record in 1984 with the worst team in the American League. When Milwaukee started suffering the summer slump, Sutton kept his marbles in one bag and won eight of 10 decisions. He knows how to pitch.

He knows how to pitch because he has one of the best curveballs in the league and will use it anytime, anyplace, anywhere and to either righties or lefties. He has lost something off the fastball, but he seems (people claim) to throw fastballs that sink quite unexpectedly. They may or may not be wet, but it is a cinch they will be scuffed up and occasionally cut up.

He does not give in to hitters. He allows more than his share of home runs (a team high 24 in 1984), but that stems from the fact that he is always around home plate with his excellent control and that hitters know it.

He cannot go nine innings, but if he could, he would have won almost 20 games in 1984. His bullpen deserted him and blew many leads in games he should have had in the "W" column.

FIELDING:

Sutton has a big windup, is fairly

DON SUTTON
RHP, No. 20
RR, 6'1", 190 lbs.
ML Svc: 19 years
Born: 4-2-45 in
    Clio, Al

1984 STATISTICS

W	L	ERA	G	GS	CG	IP	H	R	ER	BB	SO	SV
14	12	3.77	33	33	1	212	224	103	89	51	143	0

CAREER STATISTICS

W	L	ERA	G	GS	CG	IP	H	R	ER	BB	SO	SV
280	218	3.14	655	638	173	4568	4238	1765	1593	1164	3208	0

quick, throws over the top, but has a tendency to fall to one side of the mound after delivery, leaving him vulnerable to balls hit back at him. He is a good, solid fielder in every other respect. He has an excellent move to first and throws there more than most pitchers do because runners know he throws many curves and will try to steal on him.

OVERALL:

He is 40 years old and was 8-13 with an eight-game losing streak in 1983 with Milwaukee. In 1984 he proved he could still pitch, and the Brewers renewed his option year. They still need him.

Robinson: "If he ever gets help from the bullpen, he'll win his 15-17 games. For six or seven innings he'll keep you in the game as well as any pitcher."

PITCHING:

What Tom Tellman does best is what Willie Hernandez did best when he was with the Phillies--set up a game and leave it to the ace to finish it off. For two straight years, Tellman kept the Brewers in ballgames that could have gone either way.

He throws overhand to three-quarters with a forceful motion toward home plate, and uses all his pitches--fastball (87 MPH), curve, slider and change. He is good at his job because he keeps his pitches low, changes speeds and throws strikes. He does not become rattled with men on base and will always throw his pitches low in order to induce grounders and possible double plays.

He is not overpowering enough to be a strikeout pitcher, so he must use finesse, move the ball around and hit his spots. He keeps his fastball low and away to lefties, can turn the fastball over and will keep his breaking balls on the outside corner to righties. He is tough to hit a homer off because the ball never comes in straight and directly over the heart of the plate.

FIELDING:

He takes his fielding seriously and tries his best, but is rated average in most aspects of fielding. He has a decent move to first and keeps his eyes on potential stealers.

OVERALL:

Tellman was 9-4 in 1983 and 6-3 in

TOM TELLMAN
RHP, No. 42
RR, 6'4", 184 lbs.
ML Svc: 2 years
Born: 3-29-54 in
    Warren, PA

1984 STATISTICS

W	L	ERA	G	GS	CG	IP	H	R	ER	BB	SO	SV
6	3	2.78	50	0	0	81	82	28	25	31	28	4

CAREER STATISTICS

W	L	ERA	G	GS	CG	IP	H	R	ER	BB	SO	SV
15	7	2.80	94	0	0	180	177	62	56	66	76	12

1984. His ERA was under 3.00 both years in a total of 99 games. He has done everything asked of him except replace Rollie Fingers as the man who comes in to clean the table.

Robinson: "He was one of the few bright spots on the staff and did his job. It appears, however, that he will be a so-called second-stringer unless Fingers can't make it back or the Brewers lose Fingers in the free agent draft. He's put together two fine years, despite the fact that Milwaukee used Pete Ladd instead of him late in many games. I think he'll be called on a bit more this year to pitch in important games."

PITCHING:

It has taken Rick Waits almost two years to understand the difference between starting and relieving. He was a starter with Cleveland for seven years before tearing up his knee in 1982, and in June of 1983 he was traded to Milwaukee. The latter used him as a spot starter and reliever, but decided he was to be their lefthanded ace out of the bullpen in 1984.

He never reached the rank of ace and managed only three saves in 46 relief appearances.

He does have a good fastball (87 MPH) and is tough on lefthanded hitters. He has an effective fastball that he turns over to lefties, and it acts almost like a screwball to righties, but he has trouble keeping his pitches down in the strike zone. He will move his fastball around and try to keep his slider low and in to righties, but he has problems with location. The Brewers did not use him much after July last year.

He did not get into games that meant a lot, but the way the Brewers were sledding downhill from July on, very few games really amounted to anything.

Waits does have a curve and change, but does not get them over the plate as much as he would like. He relies on hard stuff, but his slider and fastball seem to come in at the same speed. He can pitch under pressure when he has control and confidence, but he had neither in 1984.

FIELDING:

Waits is tall and lanky and has a good reach. The knee has slowed him down, but he takes his fielding seriously and is better than adequate. He

RICK WAITS
LHP, No. 36
LL, 6'3", 195 lbs.
ML Svc: 10 years
Born: 5-15-52 in
Atlanta, GA

1984 STATISTICS

W	L	ERA	G	GS	CG	IP	H	R	ER	BB	SO	SV
2	4	3.58	47	1	0	73	84	32	29	24	49	3

CAREER STATISTICS

W	L	ERA	G	GS	CG	IP	H	R	ER	BB	SO	SV
76	90	4.18	293	190	47	1378	1447	704	640	551	635	7

has a fair move to first for a lefty, but runners will try to run on him.

OVERALL:

He can always point out that in 1979 and 1980, as a starter, he won back-to-back home openers with the Indians, something only Hall of Famer Bob Feller had ever accomplished. He can also point out he defeated the Yankees on the last day of the 1978 season in Yankee Stadium, forcing the famous Fenway playoff. What else he can point to is the fact that he might have finally learned how to be a relief pitcher.

Robinson: "He's got a rubber arm, is successful against lefties but has to vary speeds and learn how to get right-handed hitters out better. I have a feeling he doubts if he will ever be a winning pitcher again. He will also have to change his pitching philosophy this year. Don't ask me why, but I feel deep down he'll be a much improved relief pitcher this year."

HITTING:

There was gloom and doom in the land they call Milwaukee last year. The only bright spot in a miserable season was a young man named Robin Yount.

Yount maintains his wide stance, slightly closed, deep in the box, and rarely takes his eye off the ball. He follows it from the pitcher's hand until it crosses home plate and has a superb batting eye. He looks fastball--up anyplace--and can pull the high fastball, hit it straightaway or hit it into right-center. He has the ability to inside-out the ball, to hit an inside fastball to right field.

Yount is one of the best breaking ball hitters in the league, particularly curves up and sliders belt-high. He will pull those pitches or hit them into the left-center field gap. Lefthanders will try the fastball low and away then come back with hard sliders at the knees and in. Righties will try to throw curves and sliders, low and away. Both types of pitchers will take something off the fastball, although Yount is a better than average off-speed hitter.

He can bunt for a hit--usually toward third--but with Milwaukee's ping-pong offense in 1984, Yount had to swing the bat. There were very few hot hitters for Milwaukee all year long, so pitchers had the luxury of toying with Yount and trying to give him pitches that he could not take deep. He is an excellent clutch hitter and will hit the ball wherever it is pitched with men on base.

BASERUNNING:

Yount is an extremely intelligent runner with better than average speed. He led the Brewers with 14 stolen bases. He will steal in key situations and will

ROBIN YOUNT
SS, No. 19
RR, 6'0", 170 lbs.
ML Svc: 11 years
Born: 9-16-55 in
  Danville, IL

1984 STATISTICS

AVG	G	AB	R	H	2B	3B	HR	RBI	BB	SO	SB
.298	160	624	105	186	27	7	16	80	67	67	14

CAREER STATISTICS

AVG	G	AB	R	H	2B	3B	HR	RBI	BB	SO	SB
.286	1549	6049	885	1727	323	72	129	713	424	651	142

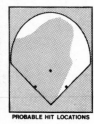

VS. RHP | VS. LHP | PROBABLE HIT LOCATIONS

invariably take the extra base. He is one of the top baserunners in baseball. He has good speed from home plate.

OVERALL:

He is so good that when people speak of Alan Trammell or Cal Ripken as premier shortstops, they compare them to Yount. He led the Brewers in everything but disappointment in 1984.

Robinson: "A good year for Robin despite some problems with his shoulder that hampered his throwing and a bit of back trouble. He has leveled off but has one solid year after another. If the back and shoulder don't give him trouble, he'll have another good year this year, especially with his attitude--which is great."

BOBBY CLARK
OF, No. 25
RR, 6'0", 190 lbs.
ML Svc: 4 years
Born: 6-13-55 in
Sacramento, CA

HITTING, BASERUNNING, FIELDING:

Bobby Clark was once a highly regarded outfielder in the California Angel chain, but he could not crack their All Star outfield of Reggie Jackson (when he played), Juan Beniquez, Fred Lynn and Brian Downing. He was doomed to sit on the bench unless someone got hurt, but no one did. After three years they finally traded him to Milwaukee, but Clark once again rode the bench.

He has a square, straight-up stance and likes pitches up in the strike zone. He is an impatient hitter who will swing at the first pitch and try to pull everything. He could become a better hitter if he tried to go the other way, but he lays off pitches on the outside portion of the plate becuase of his penchant for pulling the ball. Pitchers will try to keep everything down to him, and feed him curves, sliders and sinkers down and basically away.

He has fair speed, but does not steal. He was caught five of six times in 1984--he is not considered a threat to steal. He is an aggressive baserunner who takes an average lead.

Clark is an excellent defensive outfielder who rarely makes mistakes. He has a good arm and is accurate with his low throws. He goes back on a ball extremely well and gets an excellent jump on balls hit into the gap. He can play any outfield position.

OVERALL:

Outfielders are supposed to hit. Clark doesn't.

Robinson: "He has yet to prove he is an everyday player, and I doubt that he ever will. I think you have seen his best. His role will be the same this year: play once in a while, fill in here and there, in and out of the lineup."

ROBERT GIBSON
RHP, No. 40
RR, 6'0", 195 lbs.
ML Svc: 2 years
Born: 6-19-57 in
Philadelphia, PA

PITCHING, FIELDING:

Bob Gibson was used as both a starter and a reliever in 1984, but a mysterious virus started affecting both his body and his pitching ability last summer. He began getting shelled by every team he faced but didn't say anything because he was striving to make the team. When Brewer management found out, they sent him to Vancouver--with orders to see several doctors first.

Once he got rid of the virus, he came back to Milwaukee stronger than ever and had an excellent September. Control has always been a problem for him, but he has an excellent fastball, decent curve and slider. He can shut a team out despite allowing five or six walks. He uses the fastball to either righties or lefties and has a lot of confidence in it. He tries to keep all his pitches down, and when he does, he is effective. Lack of control of the breaking ball leaves him in tough spots and he must come back with the fastball. He is working on an off-speed pitch and used it well late in the year.

He is rated no more than average in fielding ability, but tries his best and takes his work seriously, because he wants to be the best he can in all areas and stay with the Brewers.

OVERALL:

He was 2-3 in September but should have been 4-1. He threw a two-hit shutout against the Orioles and combined on a shutout with Ray Searage against Toronto on the final day of the season. Quite possibly a case of all's well that ends well.

Robinson: "He will make this team in 1985 and will start and relieve. Everybody knows what Milwaukee needs--arms."

ROY HOWELL
INF, No. 13
LR, 6'1", 194 lbs.
ML Svc: 10 years
Born: 12-18-53 in
    Lompoc, CA

HITTING, BASERUNNING, FIELDING:

You can't blame Roy Howell for the year the Brewers had in 1984, but then again, you can't blame Milwaukee for the year Howell had in 1984.

He bats from an upright, closed stance and looks for nothing but the fastball. He likes them low and toward the middle of the plate. Because he has had so much trouble with lefthanded pitching in the past few years, Howell played only against righties, as an occasional DH, occasional pinch-hitter and occasional third baseman.

Righties will keep the ball away from him, throw him a high inside fastball every so often and use breaking balls on the corners. He is not a good off-speed hitter and has become more impatient with each succeeding year, trying to get the most out of his minimal number of at-bats.

He is not fast on the bases and will never steal a base. He does not have good insticts on the bases and will rarely scare a pitcher or middle infielder when sliding to break up a double play or an outfielder by trying to take the extra base.

He has limited range at third, an ordinary arm and average release and is not as sure-handed as he should be.

OVERALL:

Robinson: "His talent seems to be fading and I believe his best days are behind him. He doesn't play the field, can DH sometimes and pinch-hit sometimes. If he has any value to a team it will be as a pinch-hitter. I tend to think he won't be in the big leagues in 1985--or at least he'll be lucky to be in the big leagues in 1985."

WILLIE LOZADO
INF, No. 26
RR, 6'1", 170 lbs.
ML Svc: 1 year
Born: 5-12-59 in
    Brooklyn, NY

HITTING, BASERUNNING, FIELDING:

Willie Lozado is yet another young infielder the Brewers brought up late in the season last year. He can play third base or second base and was used at both spots. (Milwaukee had six different players taking turns at the hot corner last year.)

He has a straight-up stance and looks to pull everything. He does not have power but is a good line drive hitter and can drive the ball into the gap in left-center. He makes contact and is a good hit-and-run man for a young player.

He hit .271 in 43 games after the Brewers called him up. Pitchers did not have a line on him so they used the old standard--fastballs up and in, curves low and away. Lozado can hit the fastball if it is not up, and can drive it if it is near the middle of the plate or below the belt. He is a good low ball hitter.

Lozado has no definite pattern on the bases but has good instincts and may try a delayed steal if you do not watch him. He was thrown out three times in three steal attempts. He is considered average in speed and in fielding ability.

OVERALL:

Lozado appears to be a role player, but if his hitting picks up he may play more than people expect this year.

Robinson: "He made contact, a good sign for a rookie. He might turn out to be one of the pesky hitters who beats you if you sell him short."

CHUCK PORTER
RHP, No. 43
RR, 6'0", 188 lbs.
ML Svc: 2 years
Born: 1-12-56 in
Baltimore, MD

PITCHING, FIELDING:

Chuck Porter happened to be the best pitcher on the Brewer staff in 1984-- until he ruptured a ligament in his pitching arm in July. He was 5-1 with a 1.70 ERA before he hurt his arm. He kept pitching and finished 6-4 before the extent of the injury was made known. Like Paul Molitor, he had to have a ligament removed and put into his right arm, the "Tommy John surgery," and was lost to the Brewers for the rest of the year.

He is a three-quarters pitcher with a good sinking fastball, a slider, a curve and a change. He is successful against both righties and lefties because he keeps the ball down and has good velocity (87 MPH) on his fastball. He can pitch with men on base and does not get rattled. Like most sinker pitchers, he gets into trouble when his pitches are above the knees and in the strike zone. He has outstanding control and is always around home plate.

He is considered an average fielder. He does not pay too much attention to runners unless he knows it is an obvious steal situation.

OVERALL:

Year after year, the Brewers lose a key pitcher to either a rotator cuff injury or a ruptured ligament. In Porter's case, it is particularly sad because he worked hard for eight years in the minor leagues before getting his chance in 1983 and again in 1984.

Robinson: "He was good before he got hurt. I think his fastball improved and he was giving it his best shot because he knows he must do his best to stay on the staff. If he can overcome that injury, he has a chance to be a starter this year."

PETE VUCKOVICH
RHP, No. 50
RR, 6'4", 220 lbs.
ML Svc: 9 years
Born: 10-27-52 in
Johnstown, PA

PITCHING:

Pete Vuckovich went from Cy Young in 1982 to Sayonara in 1983-1984.

He has been unable to rebound from the dreaded rotator cuff injury he incurred in March of 1983 and has been lost for two full years. He did come back late in the 1983 season, but seemed to be pushing the ball to the plate, in obvious discomfort. At his best and in his prime, he was an extremely competitive pitcher who loved to stare at batters and try to intimidate them. At times he even spit at home plate. If he pitched in 20-degree weather, he would refuse to wear the long undershirt that most pitchers would be afraid to leave the parking lot without.

He throws from three-quarters to overhand and relies on a good fastball that moves and one that he spots effectively. He knows how to pitch and is not afraid to use the fastball, overhand curve, wide-breaking slider, sinker and off-speed pitch (which many batters believed was wet).

Vuckovich always gives up a lot of hits, but never quits and is always tougher with men on base. He almost has to be, because when he was 32-10 in 1981 and 1982, there were always men on base.

He is a professional fielder with no more than adequate range off the mound but with a good move to first.

OVERALL:

When Milwaukee was on top, Vuckovich was one of the key men who helped get them there and stay there. Milwaukee is now at rock-bottom . . . as is the man they have counted on in the past, Pete Vuckovich.

Robinson: "I really don't think he'll make it back."

MINNESOTA TWINS

HITTING:

Darrell Brown is one of those pesky contact hitters who'll drive pitchers crazy, especially on artificial surface, by getting not only his line drive hits but any number of bloopers and excuse-me grounders as well.

A strong fastball hitter when the ball is out over the plate, Brown does not have the strength to fight off the inside hard stuff. Pitchers generally try to jam him. He is a hard man to strike out; when he does chase a bad pitch, odds are it's a hard slider.

Brown is an up-the-middle hitter from either side of the plate. His major flaw at this point remains his poor pitch selection. If it doesn't bounce, he'll probably get wood on it. That makes him a good hit-and-run man and a tough man to double up, because he runs well. This also makes him more of a threat with men in scoring position.

What Brown has lacked so far in his career is consistency. Instead, he tends toward hot or cold streaks, both of which can be awesome in their scope.

He is a good bunter.

BASERUNNING:

Much as he is at the plate, Brown is undisciplined on the bases. He has the speed and maybe even the instincts but still lacks great judgment. He still challenges the wrong arms now and then, though last season when he had the chance he made things happen as often as not.

Lack of playing time hurts his game, and often it will show up in a mistake on the bases when Brown tries to force something he shouldn't.

FIELDING:

Brown's speed makes him a better center fielder than he would be otherwise because he lacks a great arm and still doesn't know the hitters that well. He

DARRELL BROWN
CF, No. 26
SR, 6'0", 180 lbs.
ML Svc: 2 years
Born: 10-29-55 in
    Oklahoma City, OK

1984 STATISTICS

AVG	G	AB	R	H	2B	3B	HR	RBI	BB	SO	SB
.273	95	260	36	71	9	3	1	19	14	16	4

CAREER STATISTICS

AVG	G	AB	R	H	2B	3B	HR	RBI	BB	SO	SB
.274	210	591	82	162	15	6	1	44	25	47	9

  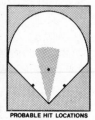

VS. RHP   VS. LHP   PROBABLE HIT LOCATIONS

can get to almost anything, however, has good hands and charges the ball well. When he looks bad, it's usually on the faster surfaces when he'll pull up and play the kangaroo-hop. Better baserunners challenge him.

OVERALL:

He is a good contact hitter and a fair defensive player and has lots of speed. He may find himself cast in the fourth outfielder role much of his career. He has no power, doesn't really hit for a great average and isn't brilliant defensively. He can do a lot of things well, though nothing spectacularly. If he wants to play, he'll have to cut down on fundamental mistakes and hone the skills he does have.

Matthews: "Lack of playing time has not allowed him to express the skills he has, but he will become a more valuable role player with further experience."

HITTING:

Along about mid-season last year, Tom Brunansky was putt-putting along toward another so-so year with fair numbers in the power and RBI categories but nothing to build a franchise around. Then . . he got aggressive.

He stopped waiting for perfect pitches and started hitting the way he did in the Angels' minor league system when he was graded their best prospect in years. The result? He had career highs in every department that counted and became a legitimate threat every time up.

Slumping or not, Brunansky looks for the fastball, though when he is slumping he can be made to look dreadful chasing a bad one. When he is more selective, when he makes a pitcher use the strike zone, Brunansky is far more effective.

He gained a reputation last year for his ability to kill "cripple" pitches, mistakes that he would have let pass earlier in his career. He is more selective with runners on base and showed the capacity to trade power for contact in RBI situations, even going to right and right-center in certain situations.

The artificial surface doesn't really help Tom much. His hits are either line drives or long gone.

Over the second half of the season, he helped to carry the Twins to within a few victories of a division title by hitting consistently for power, production and a fair average. Now THAT is what the teams in the American League are going to have to expect over a full season from him.

BASERUNNING:

Brunansky has decent speed and good instincts and will slide hard in breaking up a double play. He'll run hard all the time, go for the extra base and seems to genuinely love running the bases. He is rarely a threat to steal, will challenge an outfielder's arm and, on occasion, try to force throws.

FIELDING:

A better than average arm and good

TOM BRUNANSKY
OF, No. 24
RR, 6'4", 205 lbs.
ML Svc: 3 years
Born: 8-20-60 in
West Covina, CA

1984 STATISTICS

AVG	G	AB	R	H	2B	3B	HR	RBI	BB	SO	SB
.254	155	567	75	144	21	0	32	85	57	94	4

CAREER STATISTICS

AVG	G	AB	R	H	2B	3B	HR	RBI	BB	SO	SB
.248	444	1605	229	398	75	6	83	219	197	300	8

VS. RHP

VS. LHP

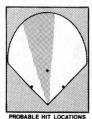

PROBABLE HIT LOCATIONS

speed make him a good outfielder, though he is not yet a great one, in part because of silly mistakes. His errors are as likely to come when he takes his eye off a routine ball as when he has made a physical mistake. He takes pride in playing defense but just hasn't put as much effort into it as he has into his hitting.

OVERALL:

All of his flashes of brilliance came together for a few months last year, and Brunansky had the kind of year many had predicted he could. No one doubts his home run potential, but it is his consistency that is questioned. He needs to improve defensively to become an all-around player. Still, no one can complain about his bat in the lineup.

Matthews: "Tom has really begun to develop into a solid big league player. With an everyday job, he developed the confidence and showed the home run and RBI production that he possesses. He is now a key man in the Twins' offense."

PITCHING:

Though he went into the 1984 season all of 27 years old, John Butcher bore the burden of a "big potential/small result" label that had followed him throughout his career.

What followed was the best year of Butcher's up-and-down career, and it may have come for the ever-so-simple reason that from opening day on he was in the starting rotation. Given that job, John proved he deserved it and was a big reason the Twins contended for the American League West title.

A big man on the mound, Butcher's strengths are cut-and-dried--he throws hard, his ball moves and he's not afraid to come inside on anybody. He relies on a slider that breaks in a hurry, a sinker that some have considered "dampened" a time or two and a fastball he'll throw from a number of release points, including three-quarters.

For much of his career Butcher seemed hesitant to go with his sinker on artificial surfaces, but though ground balls did squirt through at the Dome last season, the sinker became a big part of his success.

Pitching inside, especially to right-handed hitters, became a necessity for Butcher since the natural break on most of his pitches is away from righthanders, and if it doesn't come in, batters can have a field day. On the other hand, because of the way his pitches naturally break, lefthanded hitters are not always at ease.

Butcher's battles have almost always been with his control, and not just in base-on-balls problems, either. When his control is lacking (or when he's tired), Butcher's pitches are usually wild high, and if he's working there he's usually hittable. For the first time in his ca-

JOHN BUTCHER
RHP, No. 32
RR, 6'4", 190 lbs.
ML Svc: 3 years
Born: 3-8-57 in
  Glendale, CA

1984 STATISTICS

W	L	ERA	G	GS	CG	IP	H	R	ER	BB	SO	SV
13	11	3.44	34	34	8	225	242	98	86	53	83	0

CAREER STATISTICS

W	L	ERA	G	GS	CG	IP	H	R	ER	BB	SO	SV
24	27	3.67	101	62	13	505	524	226	206	149	226	6

reer, however, Butcher began to believe last year that being hittable isn't the same as being beatable.

FIELDING:

Though he has improved his fielding, if for no other reason than being a starter forced him into it, Butcher is no Gold Glove on the mound. He has good hands, but his motion leaves him in poor position to field balls hit toward the left side. He will throw both to first and second base when he senses liberties are being taken. He has good concentration.

OVERALL:

Butcher took a quantum leap in his career last season and, should he find consistency, could remain the mainstay of the Twins pitching rotation. He won some very big games last year.

Matthews: "Like so many of the Twins, Butcher realized in 1984 that he had the talent and ability to pitch in the big leagues. He is now a solid starter."

NOTE: John Castino underwent back surgery last season that sidelined him for all but a handful of at-bats and could potentially end his major league career. What follows is a scouting report based on his pre-surgery form.

HITTING:

When he is healthy, John Castino is a combative player, a man who will adjust to pitchers and try to outthink them. He can foul off a pitcher's best pitch or, if necessary, hit it to any part of the park.

Gifted with a great natural swing, Castino is one of the better two-strike hitters on the Twins because he will change his approach once he is behind in the count. He will spray the ball to all fields, though occasionally he can overpower a high fastball. He has average power and his swing is best-suited to parks with artificial surfaces.

Aggressive at the plate, Castino will guess along with a pitcher on the first pitch and cut loose if he guesses right. He has excellent bat control and can bunt. Hard sliders give him trouble, but then hard sliders give everyone trouble —including pitchers who throw too many of them.

Castino has few exploitable weaknesses at the plate.

BASERUNNING:

Injuries have limited his basestealing ability over the years but haven't stopped Castino from wreaking havoc on the bases. Coming in on the double play, few players slide harder than Castino and few will go from first to third on a hit more frequently. He runs with abandon and is backed up by good instincts.

FIELDING:

Originally a third baseman, Castino moved to second base in 1983 but the pain in his back stopped him cold last season. Neither position figures to help

JOHN CASTINO
2B, No. 2
RR, 5'11", 178 lbs.
ML Svc: 6 years
Born: 10-23-54 in
    Evanston, IL

1984 STATISTICS

AVG	G	AB	R	H	2B	3B	HR	RBI	BB	SO	SB
.444	8	27	5	12	1	0	0	3	5	2	0

CAREER STATISTICS

AVG	G	AB	R	H	2B	3B	HR	RBI	BB	SO	SB
.278	666	2320	293	646	86	34	41	249	177	298	22

  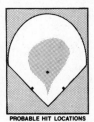

VS. RHP   VS. LHP   PROBABLE HIT LOCATIONS

his back problems, especially playing on an artificial surface.

Castino's defense is marked by the same competitiveness he shows at the plate. He will do anything to stop a ball and is simply unable to "baby" himself to protect an injury. He has a strong arm and is fearless in the face of an oncoming baserunner. Castino is rock-solid defensively, though he does not have the range of some quicker infielders. He has good hands.

OVERALL:

Castino has long been regarded as a tough out at the plate and a tough man in the field. He is a competitor who makes his team better whenever he plays. The problem has been his inability (because of his injuries) to play often enough.

Matthews: "The final week of the 1984 season was a nightmare for the Twins, but the entire 1984 season was a nightmare for John Castino."

PITCHING:

Ron Davis endured an identity crisis last season, finding himself a power pitcher uncertain of his power and searching for solutions he never really found as the season wore on.

Davis's fastball had always been his No. 1 pitch, a 92 MPH buzzsaw that set up a hard slider and anything else he chose to tinker with over the years. At it's best, his fastball explodes on hitters at the plate.

So what happened? Last year Davis went through a typical late-inning relief slump and decided, or maybe just believed what he read, that his fastball had lost a few feet. So he went to the slider as his out pitch, overthrew his pitches and walked far more batters than was his style and had among the worst ERAs in modern short-relief history.

His extra-high ERA, however, was more the result of blow-up innings (a walk, a hit, a home run) than a day-in and day-out ineffectiveness. Davis's unwillingness to challenge anyone and everyone with his fastball surprised the hitters even more than his own teammates, for that has long been his reputation.

Many suspect that Davis simply had a season in which he never found a groove, complicated by a stubborn resistance to advice that he pitch any way other than the way he chose to. Davis seems incapable of working carefully to a batter, and every pitch he throws has as much behind it as he can muster.

Bad year or not, Davis is still no fun for hitters to see marching out of the bullpen. When he's right, the fastball seems to rise, and Davis has never been particular about precisely where the ball goes within the strike zone. You don't find many batters digging in against him.

FIELDING:

When Davis is pitching well, few

RON DAVIS
RHP, No. 39
RR, 6'4", 195 lbs.
ML Svc: 6 years
Born: 8-6-55 in
Houston, TX

1984 STATISTICS
W	L	ERA	G	GS	CG	IP	H	R	ER	BB	SO	SV
7	11	4.55	64	0	0	83	79	44	42	41	74	29

CAREER STATISTICS
W	L	ERA	G	GS	CG	IP	H	R	ER	BB	SO	SV
42	38	3.51	337	0	0	569	529	236	222	209	438	103

balls come back toward him, except little ones, and he holds his own with them. He has quick hands, though he's not particularly quick coming off the mound. His delivery often leaves him in a distinctly non-fielding position. He has an average move to first, which is made a little better by the speed of his throws.

OVERALL:

Anyone capable of throwing a hard fastball/slider combination as well as Davis remains a potential 25-save short relief man--and Davis has both those pitches. What he lacked last season, control and confidence, are correctable flaws.

Matthews: "Ron had some excellent outings but is still dogged by some inconsistencies and the occasional ill-timed home run ball. His better outings brought him 29 saves, but his bad days shoved his ERA to a way-too-high 4.55. He still has the demeanor and the pitches to remain one of the AL's top relief pitchers."

HITTING:

The problem that American League pitchers have with Dave Engle is that he doesn't try to overpower pitches, does not try to pull and doesn't chase many bad balls. Hitters who do all those things usually increase their chances at the plate considerably--and Engle does.

Though he really doesn't have home run power at this point, he can drive the ball well to both alleys, and that is part of his strength. Engle hits well from left-center to right-center, and the majority of his hits are up the middle of the field.

Engle could probably hit between 12 and 18 home runs a year if he was less disciplined, but he has become a heady hitter at the plate, especially with men in scoring position. He seems intent on spraying the ball around.

A better hitter on artificial surface, Engle is a good bunter with fine bat control perfect for his role in the lineup. Off-speed pitches are still a weakness, and many pitchers try to move fastballs in on his hands.

He has cut down on his swing which used to be a very full one.

BASERUNNING:

Like a lot of men not gifted with speed, Engle seems to know what to do on the bases--except that he doubts his own ability to do it. As a result, he can appear uncertain at times. He is not aggressive, and while he runs hard, his lack of speed and lack of confidence do not make him much of a threat on the bases. He is also slow to first.

FIELDING:

Engle's problems behind the plate have been largely due to inexperience: an understandable reluctance to look bad. The result has been that runners test him often and frequently with suc-

DAVE ENGLE
C, No. 20
RR, 6'3", 210 lbs.
ML Svc: 4 years
Born: 11-30-56 in
San Diego, CA

1984 STATISTICS

AVG	G	AB	R	H	2B	3B	HR	RBI	BB	SO	SB
.266	109	391	56	104	20	1	4	38	26	22	0

CAREER STATISTICS

AVG	G	AB	R	H	2B	3B	HR	RBI	BB	SO	SB
.270	369	1199	151	324	63	11	21	129	77	120	2

VS. RHP   VS. LHP   PROBABLE HIT LOCATIONS

cess. An outfielder for most of his career, Engle can play a number of positions, and, given his choice, catching would be at the bottom of the list.

Still, he is willing to try even at the expense of his pride. He has a strong if erratic arm and still hurries his throws to second.

OVERALL:

A good hitter, especially against lefthanders, Engle has shown a desire to play any position and accept any role in order to stay in the major leagues. He deserves the opportunity.

Matthews: "Until the 1983 season, Dave had performed as a catcher only during high school. He really put his nose to the grindstone to learn the position. He still has some trouble with his release and accuracy, but began to improve a bit in 1984. I give him a lot of credit for sticking with it."

PITCHING:

It is a tough adjustment for a young pitcher to make when he had always been told he had to throw soooooo hard to get to the big leagues--only to learn that an 86 MPH fastball is considered an average pitch up there. It is also a bit of a shock. Reality and his own misconceptions about the majors hit Pete Filson in the face last season. He tried to adjust but had mixed results.

On the positive side, Filson has a good off-speed pitch and a pretty fair breaking ball. On the negative side, when he gets behind in the count, he too often relies on that fastball.

Filson's over-the-top motion makes him slightly less effective pitching to lefthanded batters than some southpaws are: you don't often see hitters bailing out against him. But his breaking pitch is good enough to keep them honest, just the same.

To this point in his career, Filson seems unable to make the full transition from high school power pitcher to a soft-tossing lefthander like Geoff Zahn or Tommy John. He'll use his breaking pitches and change-ups, just not always in the right spots.

Used primarily in long relief last year, Filson was the kind of pitcher who nonetheless had good success going one time through a batting order, mixing his speeds well and keeping hitters out in front. When he made mistakes, it was as often a matter of location as of pitch selection: if Filson throws a fastball, curve or change-up in the strike zone, he's in trouble. When he works corners, his stuff makes hitters pursue pitches that aren't strikes.

FIELDING:

Though he is sound mechanically, Pete

PETE FILSON
LHP, No. 23
SL, 6'2", 195 lbs.
ML Svc: 3 years
Born: 9-28-58 in
  Darby, PA

1984 STATISTICS												
W	L	ERA	G	GS	CG	IP	H	R	ER	BB	SO	SV
6	5	4.12	55	7	0	118	106	56	54	54	59	1
CAREER STATISTICS												
W	L	ERA	G	GS	CG	IP	H	R	ER	BB	SO	SV
10	8	4.09	86	18	0	220	210	102	100	91	118	2

is an average fielder at best with a just-to-let-you-know-I'm-here move to first. If he picks someone off, the runner's asleep. He's not aggressive in pursuit of either runners or ground balls.

OVERALL:

Filson has the potential to join the growing list of off-speed major leaguers who have had success. First, his control must improve, and he must decide once and for all if he can live with the label "junk pitcher." To do that, all he has to do is realize that that term was created by batters driven crazy by their inability to hit that particular brand of pitching.

Matthews: "It appears that Pete is suffering from the effects of misguided advice during his formative years. The Twins are high on his future as an off-speed pitcher, but Filson has some bad habits that he still can't break."

HITTING:

Pitchers did not say much after Gary Gaetti's 1983 season, a year in which he hit 21 home runs and 30 double-sackers and had a .245 average. When guys swing for the fences and forsake contact for pure power, they are going to get those extra-base hits. They are also going to leave lots of holes in their swing--and Gaetti has plenty of 'em. And just the way a fly will find his way into the house, the pitchers have found all of the holes in Gaetti's bat.

The 1983 situation was that, given the power he showed, many pitchers worked him carefully, and Gaetti can just blister mistake pitches. In 1984, more and more pitchers went right after him, pounding him with inside fastballs and making him wave at off-speed breaking stuff outside.

Because he can be jammed, Gaetti will sometimes pull the ball, making him not only a pull hitter but one who is very susceptible to change-ups.

When he does make contact, however, he makes very hard contact. Last season, however, too many of his hits stayed in the park--he did not show his usual power. The artificial surface makes him a better hitter simply because even his ground balls are hard, usually have top-spin and get through the infield quickly.

Last year was a battle for confidence for Gaetti, a year in which he was productive but had a major dropoff in home runs. He is going to have to adjust, something he hasn't always done. He is not a patient or disciplined hitter. It works against him.

BASERUNNING:

Gaetti runs the bases like a linebacker gone wild. No one slides harder or takes out more infielders in double play situations. He creams catchers the way Mr. T would.

His baserunning philosophy seems to be to get there--at any cost, regardless of how it looks. He has the instincts of a good baserunner but is trapped inside

GARY GAETTI
3B, No. 8
RR, 6'0", 193 lbs.
ML Svc: 3 years
Born: 8-19-58 in
Centralia, IL

1984 STATISTICS

AVG	G	AB	R	H	2B	3B	HR	RBI	BB	SO	SB
.262	162	588	55	154	29	4	5	65	44	81	11

CAREER STATISTICS

AVG	G	AB	R	H	2B	3B	HR	RBI	BB	SO	SB
.246	473	1706	199	419	84	11	53	230	135	315	18

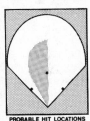

VS. RHP   VS. LHP   PROBABLE HIT LOCATIONS

the legs of an average one.

FIELDING:

As a third baseman, Gaetti uses the biggest glove in the majors. He calls it "his chest." He will get in front of anything and play the carom if he can't catch it cleanly. He has a strong arm that sometimes misfires, and those misfires are rarely within reach of the first baseman. He does not have great range or reflexes. Gaetti is from the Butch Hobson School of Infielders, whose motto is, "Who cares how it looks, was he safe or out?"

OVERALL:

Gaetti is the throwback-type of player who plays hard, wants to win and wants to have fun doing it. He is a fierce competitor and loves to be considered a power hitter, but if he wants to see it here, he'll have to darn the holes in his swing.

Matthews: "Gary has a great attitude and will quite likely have a fine year in 1985. There are several teams that would love to have him."

HITTING:

Mickey Hatcher continued to be among the American League's toughest batters to strike out last season, proving once again that he's a solid major league hitter who has discipline, bat control and extra-base-hit power.

Perhaps the toughest thing about him is that he adjusts to being pitched any given way quickly. Getting him out easily on a certain pitch in one at-bat may not help much the next time he's up. Hatcher has 15-20 home run power but seems to disregard that, choosing instead a contact hitter's approach, including a short, compact swing that produces line drives rather than long fly balls. Some believe that was a decision he made because he was playing so many games on an artificial surface. At this point he is a more dangerous hitter on turf simply because he does make constant, solid contact.

An excellent fastball hitter regardless of the count, Hatcher can be had with good breaking pitches--though they have to be good ones. He has a good eye but will rarely take a base-on-balls. He has a knack for fouling off pitches that are just out of the strike zone.

A very competitive hitter, Hatcher has proven to be more effective with men on base, to be a man capable of driving the ball up either alley or down either base line. A spray hitter, Hatcher must be played straightaway because he'll use all fields.

Given his bat control, Hatcher is a fine hit-and-run man at the plate, an above average bunter who will bunt for base hits and an unselfish hitter who will go to the right side consistently in situations requiring that he move a runner over.

BASERUNNING:

Hatcher has been compared to a young pup on the basepaths: a man who runs tirelessly, ears back and tongue out, enjoying every step. He has good instincts, average speed and a genuine, unstoppable enthusiasm for baserunning

MICKEY HATCHER
OF, No. 9
RR, 6'2", 195 lbs.
ML Svc: 5 years
Born: 3-15-55 in
Cleveland, OH

1984 STATISTICS											
AVG	G	AB	R	H	2B	3B	HR	RBI	BB	SO	SB
.302	152	576	61	174	35	5	5	69	37	34	0

CAREER STATISTICS											
AVG	G	AB	R	H	2B	3B	HR	RBI	BB	SO	SB
.282	531	1782	183	502	92	13	22	189	83	133	6

that makes him not only a good baserunner but one who'll gamble.

FIELDING:

Hatcher has worked hard everywhere a team has tried him. He has improved his defense a little. As an outfielder, he has a fair arm, fair instincts and the charming ability to turn what appears to be disaster, like a momentarily lost fly ball, into an exciting out. The Metrodome ceiling has given him some very tense moments. Whatever Hatcher's defensive flaws, his overwhelming enthusiasm on the field helps make up for them.

OVERALL:

Hatcher still has that Little League love for suiting up and playing. He has proved he can hit .300, and his natural electricity has made him a team sparkplug and favorite.

Matthews: "Hatcher had his best big league season in 1984. He was uncanny in the clutch, has a positive influence on his teammates and is fun to watch. He is a very versatile player."

HITTING:

Kent Hrbek continued to make life miserable for American League pitchers in 1984, improving his numbers across the board--even though his numbers have always been very good indeed.

At his best, Hrbek has the ability to foul off great pitches, hit good pitches solidly and crush mistakes. Though he is a fine fastball hitter, he adjusts quickly to off-speed pitching. If pitchers try to pitch him strictly with off-speed stuff, he inevitably goes deep.

Hrbek's best qualities at the plate may be his short power stroke and the discipline in a smallish ballpark not to try to pull everything. Pitch Hrbek away and he'll go to left field or up the middle. A mature power hitter, Hrbek has faith that home runs will come often enough when he puts the ball in play. He has been right in his first three full-time big league seasons.

Hrbek likes to get full arm extension, and his natural strength allows him to "miss" some balls and still hit them out, especially at home in the Dome.

At this point in his career, the big battle Hrbek must fight is his weight. Twice in two seasons he's added a little too much and paid for it with a loss of bat quickness. As he has shed the weight over the course of the year, his numbers have always responded.

Pitchers who have had the most success against Hrbek are those who have used their complete arsenal in beating him, keeping him slightly off stride by featuring everything they've got. He makes a man pay for mistakes, however.

BASERUNNING:

Hrbek is aggressive but slow and even slower with additional weight early in the season. He'll take anybody out going into second, however, and makes few mistakes once on the basepaths. Hrbek is ranked among team leaders in doubles, triples and home runs the past three seasons, an indication that he is hardly an all-or-nothing power hitter.

KENT HRBEK
1B, No. 14
LR, 6'4", 229 lbs.
ML Svc: 3 years
Born: 5-21-60 in
  Minneapolis, MN

1984 STATISTICS

AVG	G	AB	R	H	2B	3B	HR	RBI	BB	SO	SB
.311	149	559	80	174	31	3	27	107	65	87	1

CAREER STATISTICS

AVG	G	AB	R	H	2B	3B	HR	RBI	BB	SO	SB
.301	454	1673	242	503	98	12	67	290	181	247	8

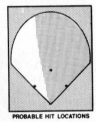

VS. RHP — VS. LHP — PROBABLE HIT LOCATIONS

FIELDING:

Quite simply, he is among the best defensive first basemen in the league. Hrbek will dive for anything, scoop up low throws with anyone and may have one of the most effective stretches around. He has good, soft hands and a strong arm that he is not afraid to use. Hrbek is not the kind of fielder to take liberties with. He will throw to second on a sacrifice bunt and has good instincts. He is quick if not fast, a necessity on artificial turf.

OVERALL:

Hrbek appears to be solidifying his All Star credentials as a complete player and star. He seems only to require self-discipline at the dinner plate--not home plate.

Matthews: "He is developing into one of the top hitters in baseball. He is also becoming one of the team's leaders. He has the physical tools to continue to be a star."

HITTING:

A fine minor league hitter, Tim Laudner discovered the old adage in his first few big league seasons: major league pitching puts you into slumps. However, he is still a good fastball hitter, especially on inside fastballs.

Laudner's power is considerable, but so is his vulnerability both to off-speed pitches and down and away fastballs and sliders. He is not a disciplined hitter, nor is he especially patient at the plate. Pitchers getting ahead of him in the count have a sizable advantage since he can be made to pursue most anything. All that said, Laudner can turn on an inside pitch and drive it a long way, though his tendency is to try and turn on most any pitch.

If a pitcher has the expert control to work only outside, fine. But when he comes inside, it has to be good. Few fastballs are too fast, and those up in the strike zone are his favorites.

In the second half of 1984, Laudner appeared to be making some adjustments at the plate, using more of the field, if not all of it, and even improving his batting eye. Though the raw ability still appears to be raw, there are many who believe he'll become a much better hitter. To do so, he'll have to shorten his strike zone and stretch his patience.

BASERUNNING:

Not unlike many young catchers, Tim has more enthusiasm than speed and tends to run the bases like a pulling guard. He is not especially fast but is murder on anyone getting in the way. He is an aggressive runner but rarely gets the chance; Laudner is living proof that to break up a double play you still have to get to second base in time. He doesn't.

TIM LAUDNER
C, No. 15
RR, 6'3", 212 lbs.
ML Svc: 3 years
Born: 6-7-58 in
     Mason City, IA

1984 STATISTICS

AVG	G	AB	R	H	2B	3B	HR	RBI	BB	SO	SB
.206	87	262	31	54	16	1	10	35	18	78	0

CAREER STATISTICS

AVG	G	AB	R	H	2B	3B	HR	RBI	BB	SO	SB
.218	256	779	92	170	46	2	25	91	70	218	0

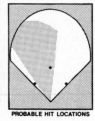

VS. RHP   VS. LHP   PROBABLE HIT LOCATIONS

FIELDING:

Laudner improved as a catcher in 1984, but that was hardly unexpected. Until last year, he was borderline terrible, and at his best he remains below average.

Laudner isn't quick behind the plate, has a so-so arm and can be run on. His pitch selection improved vastly last year and, with experience, his overall defense may follow. A good catching coach might know where to start here.

OVERALL:

Matthews: "At this point in his career, Tim is just a backup catcher. He should improve at most phases of his game, especially offense."

PITCHING:

Rick Lysander is the kind of pitcher who can pitch himself into and out of jams--his own or someone else's--and has a knack for getting double play ground balls at the most appropriate times. That alone is testament to a sinker that often acts as a spitter does, with its sharp, downward break.

Lysander throws his sinker often, and though it may be his No. 1 pitch, especially in double play situations, he'll mix a fair slider and average fastball in, too. When batters worry about his sinker, the fastball has enough zip to surprise them.

This is not to say he is a power pitcher or anything close to it. Rick is more of a magician on the mound, a man who lives by sleight of hand and by keeping hitters off balance. When he's mixing his pitches and his control is good (meaning he's pitching low, low, low), he can be very effective.

When he's tired or hasn't got his control, his sinker comes in too low to be a strike. When that happens, he is in trouble. Like most sinkerballers, if Lysander absolutely has to throw a strike with his secondary pitches, he's vulnerable.

Lysander tries to work the corners, both inside and out, with all his pitches, and that can be both an advantage and a disadvantage. Because his stuff isn't overpowering, impatient hitters can be lured by it even when the location isn't where they want it. On the other hand, he has to fight tendencies to be too fine--never give the hitter anything too good to hit.

The key to any sinkerball pitcher's success is to make the sinker look so good the hitters can't resist it. When Lysander's sinkers look good, they usu-

RICK LYSANDER
RHP, No. 19
RR, 6'2", 188 lbs.
ML Svc: 2 year
Born: 2-21-53 in
    Huntington Park, CA

1984 STATISTICS

W	L	ERA	G	GS	CG	IP	H	R	ER	BB	SO	SV
4	3	3.65	36	0	0	56	62	23	23	27	22	5

CAREER STATISTICS

W	L	ERA	G	GS	CG	IP	H	R	ER	BB	SO	SV
9	15	3.80	102	4	1	194	218	99	82	74	85	8

ally are. The result can be a couple of outs in a hurry.

FIELDING:

Lysander's biggest defensive asset is his mental approach to the game. Not only is he always ready to field, he's always aware of the game situation. If he makes an error it'll almost always be a physical one. He will throw often to first if he feels he has to, but his move is not likely to cause great concern to better baserunners.

OVERALL:

A valuable situation pitcher, he is a man who can come into a game in a spot where a ground ball is needed and, in most cases, produce it. As with any pitcher who lives by keeping the ball in play, however, Lysander's ground balls don't always go where he'd like them to.

Matthews: "All managers would like a sinkerball relief pitcher who can produce double play grounders. Lysander fills that role for the Twins."

HITTING:

Last year, Kirby Puckett made the Twins, seized center field and became a very dangerous major league leadoff man.

At the top of the order, Puckett has all the dimensions required: speed, bat control, the threat of the bunt and a willingness to take a walk. He is pesky and has a little pop in his bat, especially on artificial turf, where hard-hit line drives go to the wall. He is also very aggressive, and outfielders who play cautiously will find that he moves up an extra base as fast as anybody.

He is a good hitter, period. Puckett won't overpower the best fastballs but will get wood on them. Once a ball is in play, his speed makes things happen. Puckett can still be fooled by good off-speed pitches--but fooling him and getting him out aren't always the same.

He will bunt to both third and first. Infielders have to play him honestly. His exceptional bat control makes some pitchers complain about his "clinkers, rollers and seeing-eye grounders," but many of them are by Kirby's design. On turf, Puckett can hit pool cue shots with the best of them--intentionally. He has tailored his game to the role he plays and the park in which he plays it.

BASERUNNING:

Among the best baserunners on the Twins, Puckett is fast. He is quick off the bag and likes to run and keep going. He slides hard, plays hard and has earned the respect of pitchers, catchers and infielders with his hard but clean plays.

Give Puckett too big a lead at first and he's gone. Pitchers have to pay attention to him. Give him a hole and he will score from first on a long single.

FIELDING:

Puckett makes up for an average arm in center by playing balls exceptionally

KIRBY PUCKETT
CF, No. 34
RR, 5'8", 175 lbs.
ML Svc: 1 year
Born: 3-13-61 in
Chicago, IL

1984 STATISTICS

AVG	G	AB	R	H	2B	3B	HR	RBI	BB	SO	SB
.296	128	557	63	165	12	5	0	31	16	69	14

CAREER STATISTICS

AVG	G	AB	R	H	2B	3B	HR	RBI	BB	SO	SB
.296	128	557	63	165	12	5	0	31	16	69	14

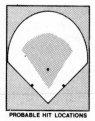

VS. RHP   VS. LHP   PROBABLE HIT LOCATIONS

well, getting himself in position to throw and getting a great jump on balls hit in front of him. He has marvelous outfield speed.

His range in center is a definite plus for both the right fielder and left fielder. He is a take-charge player out there: if he can reach it, it's his. He shows no fear of fences, has very good hands and makes few bad throws.

OVERALL:

Puckett grabbed opportunity by the horns in 1984 and shook a great year out of it. Puckett's attitude seems as solid as his ability. He could be a factor as a leadoff hitter for years to come.

Matthews: "Kirby Puckett is one of the American League's exciting newcomers. He figures to improve with experience, as he works hard at his game. He sets the tempo for the Twins offense and will be more effective as he learns more about the strike zone. He has a great attitude."

PITCHING:

In part because it has taken him a long time to reach the majors, Ken Schrom burst onto the scene as an unknown quantity and then surprised AL batters not only with his pitching but also with his savvy. He showed up in a Twins uniform knowing how to pitch and took it from there.

Injuries decimated his season last year. When he was healthy, he was the proverbial odd-man-out, the one pitcher on the staff who never seemed to get runs in low-scoring games. Nonetheless, the Twins look at Schrom as a steady 15-game winner based on the caliber of his pitches and the depth of his study of batters' flaws.

Schrom has an average fastball that will peak just under 90 MPH, good breaking pitches that he can change speeds with and an exceptional change-up he will throw at any point in the count. He is the kind of pitcher who breaks bats, not with power pitching but by fooling hitters and keeping them off balance.

Schrom is no great experimenter on the mound. If he finds a weakness, the hitter must prove he can defense that flaw or Schrom will exploit it in each and every confrontation.

He will also vary his delivery, moving from overhand to near-sidearm, a disturbing ability since he seems willing and able to throw all his pitches from any point of release. Again, Schrom makes changes after thinking things through.

The most glaring weakness in his game is control, a problem magnified by the fact that Schrom won't give in when he is behind hitters. Thus, at times, he walks batters who might better be challenged.

KEN SCHROM
RHP, No. 18
RR, 6'2", 195 lbs.
ML Svc: 2 years
Born: 11-23-54 in
      Grangeville, ID

1984 STATISTICS												
W	L	ERA	G	GS	CG	IP	H	R	ER	BB	SO	SV
5	11	4.47	25	21	3	137	156	75	68	41	49	0

CAREER STATISTICS												
W	L	ERA	G	GS	CG	IP	H	R	ER	BB	SO	SV
22	19	4.20	81	49	9	379	397	196	177	155	150	1

FIELDING:

Schrom is a fine fielder around the mound: sure-handed, quick and usually in good position. His weakness, to say the least, is his move to first. He has none that threatens a runner, and his rather deliberate delivery to the plate too often means runners get big jumps on a catching crew that has enough problems nailing runners when it has the chance. Schrom has to work on keeping runners close.

OVERALL:

If arm problems don't derail his progress, Schrom's return to the rotation this season could be a big boost for the Twins. He's a very heady pitcher.

Matthews: "Schrom suffered through an injury-plagued 1984 season, and he has hopes that 1985 will turn out like 1983, when he was the Twins' best pitcher. He is a finesse type of hurler who seems to have a good idea behind every pitch he throws."

PITCHING:

Among the taller pitchers ever to play the game, Mike Smithson presents a formidable challenge on the mound, a man whose 6'8" frame comes at a hitter from what often seems considerably less than the reported distance between the rubber and home plate.

What makes the perception all the more difficult is that Smithson will send any number of pitches spinning toward the batter, choosing from a fastball, breaking ball, slider, sinker and a change. He will throw his breaking ball whether he's ahead or behind in the count.

What make his breaking pitches so effective are his fastball and hard slider. The fastball has good velocity and the slider freezes righthanded hitters. When he adds the slow breaking pitch, he can seem to have an unfair advantage and simply dominate a ball game.

So why doesn't Smithson dominate more often? Lack of experience, for one thing; last season, he gained some and became far more consistent as the season wore on. Over the years, in various roles and situations, he has pitched brilliantly, only to fall prey to a bad inning that inevitably was blamed on his lack of concentration.

More and more last season, however, Smithson grew into the role of starting pitcher and showed the endurance and desire to finish what he started. He's a pitcher who usually starts out rocky and then settles in. Batters are often lulled in the first two innings, only to find themselves facing a stronger pitcher in their later at-bats.

Because of his height and delivery, all of Smithson's pitches appear to be sinking simply because he's throwing

MIKE SMITHSON
RHP, No. 34
LR, 6'8", 215 lbs.
ML Svc: 2 years
Born: 1-21-55 in
Centerville, TN

1984 STATISTICS
W	L	ERA	G	GS	CG	IP	H	R	ER	BB	SO	SV
15	13	3.68	36	36	10	252	246	113	103	54	144	0

CAREER STATISTICS
W	L	ERA	G	GS	CG	IP	H	R	ER	BB	SO	SV
28	31	3.90	77	77	23	522	530	241	226	138	303	0

down in the strike zone. The effect on hitters can be immense. Smithson gets a lot of his strikeouts on pitches batters chase out of the strike zone.

FIELDING:

Mike suffers the dilemma of most tall pitchers, a lanky delivery that takes its time unfolding and leaves Smithson open to better base runners. Though he is quick, he has trouble getting grounders that hug the ground up the middle. His good hands and good instincts help, as does his competitiveness.

OVERALL:

Smithson is a pitcher who is continuing to progess. Last year he gave indications that he is learning to control not only his pitches but himself.

Matthews: "Mike is developing into one of the most imtimidating pitchers in the league. His breaking ball can be devastating. He improved both physically and mentally in 1984."

HITTING:

A baby-faced hit man, Tim Teufel lists among his strengths an ability to put wood on most anything and some surprising extra-base pop. He's a streak hitter who is very good when he's hot and no automatic out when he's not.

Another of the Twins who has benefited from the artificial surface of the Metrodome, Teufel has exceptional bat control and uses the entire field. He is a good hit-and-run man and a good fastball hitter.

Like so many youngsters, Teufel displayed weaknesses early in the year that were a result of his inexperience with pitchers. He was often surprised by pitches he didn't expect or didn't know the pitcher had. As the year progressed, he became a tougher out.

Teufel's power is up the alley with line drives, though once in a while he will muscle up on an inside pitch and drive the ball. He seems content just to hit within his limitations and he is a stronger hitter for it.

Teufel will bunt and will show the bunt to make the third baseman come in on him. He is a smart, aggressive young hitter who has to be kept off balance at the plate.

BASERUNNING:

He is a good, solid baserunner, though he lacks great speed. He knows the fundamentals of when to run and where to run and won't run into an out often.

Teufel gets a good jump off the bases and has good instincts once the ball gets past the infield. He will take an extra base any time he senses the opportunity.

FIELDING:

Teufel's bat got him to the majors;

TIM TEUFEL
2B, No. 11
RR, 6'0", 175 lbs.
ML Svc: 1 year plus
Born: 7-7-58 in
　Greenwich, CT

1984 STATISTICS

AVG	G	AB	R	H	2B	3B	HR	RBI	BB	SO	SB
.262	157	568	76	149	30	3	14	61	76	73	1

CAREER STATISTICS

AVG	G	AB	R	H	2B	3B	HR	RBI	BB	SO	SB
.268	178	646	87	173	37	4	17	67	78	81	1

VS. RHP　　VS. LHP　　PROBABLE HIT LOCATIONS

he is just a little above average as an infielder. Turf doesn't give anyone much range on hard-hit balls, but Teufel has good hands, a strong arm and an improving knowledge of hitters. He turns double plays well at second and is a good clutch fielder.

OVERALL:

He showed lots of ability and even more potential last season. He could be one of those Twins products who comes up, takes a while getting acclimated and then takes off.

Matthews: "Teufel was part of the triple play that Rick Cerone of the Yankees hit into last season, but it was probably his highlight as a fielder. But at the plate, he shows a lot more promise. He has impressed just about everyone with his ability to hit a whole lot of pitches and get himself on base."

PITCHING:

Ever since making it to the major leagues, Frank Viola has been expected to be too great too often. As far as the impatient were concerned, he was merely good. Last year, however, he was what everybody hoped he could be.

Three years ago, Gene Mauch called him "one of the best young lefthanders in the league"--that was before he proved to be one of the best pitchers in the league, period. Viola has great stuff, good control, an idea of what he wants to do in every situation and, suddenly, total confidence.

Viola has four major-league-caliber pitches and the control to throw each for a strike. His fastball is in the 90 MPH range and he can make it do tricks-- running in or out depending upon his grip.

He has a big curveball with which he changes speeds, a straight change-up and a slider that breaks sharply down. In fact, nearly everything Viola throws stays down, a necessity since so many of his games are pitched in the generous Metrodome.

Viola's stuff goes beyond the ability to get outs; he can flat out embarrass good hitters with it. He has chalked up nearly everyone a time or two by getting a third-strike swing in which the hitter is so off stride he staggers.

The next step in his development (and hitters aren't looking forward to this one) is learning how to win without his best stuff. When Viola is on, nobody is going to hit him hard. When he's not, when his pitches come up or his control is off, he has to show the ability to adjust. That's still not always the case.

As it is, Viola is the Twins' No. 1 starter and a man coveted by every team he encountered. He's the kind of pitcher who prevents long losing streaks for his team by keeping them in the game every time he goes out.

Frank Viola is now a very solid

FRANK VIOLA
LHP, No. 16
LL, 6'4", 209 lbs.
ML Svc: 3 years
Born: 4-19-60 in
Hempstead, NY

```
1984 STATISTICS
W  L  ERA  G  GS CG IP  H   R   ER BB  SO  SV
18 12 3.22 35 35 10 257 225 101 92 73  149 0
CAREER STATISTICS
W  L  ERA  G  GS CG IP  H   R   ER BB  SO  SV
29 37 4.45 92 91 17 593 619 319 293 203 360 0
```

pitcher with the chance to be among the very best.

FIELDING:

Viola improved his move to first base last year, though it's still just above average, at best. His entire game improved last season when he avoided his past tendency to pitch and then leave it up to the rest of the Twins--or the gods.

Maturity seems to have given Viola the notion that he can control games not only with his arm but with his glove and his head. He has gone about the business of doing that.

OVERALL:

Viola was a big winner for a team that wasn't the big winner last season. On a superior team he might have had a 24-win record with the way he pitched. Viola keeps his team in every game he pitches, and when he is at his best, he can completely keep the opposing team out of the game.

Matthews: "Viola has a chance to be one of the top pitchers in the majors. He has progressed to the point now where he must learn how to win even when he doesn't have his best stuff."

HITTING:

In pro ball for 14 years, Washington has always been a contact hitter with .275 potential who hits better when playing every day but rarely has had that opportunity in the majors.

The reason is simple enough. When phenoms come up, Washington sits down. But Washington has survived any number of power-hitting phenoms and remains a proven journeyman hitter who will do anything to help a team win.

A good fastball hitter, Washington rarely tries to overpower a ball, instead lining topspin hits to left field or up the middle and using his speed. The less he plays, the less patience he has at the plate. He can be induced to chase balls out of the strike zone. He is not a strong off-speed pitch hitter.

Washington is, however, a battler at the plate, and with his bat control, he is not only a fine hit-and-run man but also the kind of hitter who will foul off a number of good pitches in any given at-bat. He can't be taken for granted.

If a pitcher makes mistakes to Ron, they are most dangerous when they are mistakes on the inner half of the plate. Keep the ball away and you can control Washington.

BASERUNNING:

Washington's once above average speed has been diminished somewhat, but he remains cat-quick and ambitious on the bases. He goes from first to third as well as anyone on the team. His speed down the first base line is still very good for a righthanded hitter. He will steal if he is ignored at first but is not a constant threat to go.

FIELDING:

Give Washington a glove for most any

RON WASHINGTON
SS, No. 38
RR, 5'11", 160 lbs.
ML Svc: 3 years
Born: 4-29-52 in
New Orleans, LA

1984 STATISTICS											
AVG	G	AB	R	H	2B	3B	HR	RBI	BB	SO	SB
.294	88	197	25	58	11	5	3	23	4	31	1

CAREER STATISTICS											
AVG	G	AB	R	H	2B	3B	HR	RBI	BB	SO	SB
.266	344	1068	113	284	38	15	12	94	44	176	19

VS. RHP VS. LHP PROBABLE HIT LOCATIONS

position and though he may not make it Golden, he will do the job for you. He has played shortstop, outfield, third base and even briefly caught in the Twins organization. He has been consistent everywhere. Washington may not have the range to make great plays, but he will make good ones. He has a good arm, good quickness and lots of intensity.

OVERALL:

Washington is reaching the point at which he may be a fourth infielder/outfielder kind of player. He has the personality to accept that role and even to excel in it.

Matthews: "Washington always seems to get the job done. He is very valuable because of his versatility."

PITCHING:

When Ron Davis struggled last season, the Twins went more and more frequently to Len Whitehouse. He showed the ability and personality required to be a short reliever.

Whitehouse certainly has the pitches for it: a 90+ MPH fastball that he can make do tricks, a couple of breaking pitches and a straight change. While he has tinkered with a No. 2 and No. 3 pitch for a couple of seasons, his reliance in tight spots is and probably will remain No. 1--his fastball.

This lefthander's fastball can come in either over-the-top or, against left-handed batters, from a three-quarters delivery. Since he can make the ball move in or out by changing his grip, few lefthanders dig in against him. When Whitehouse's fastball is moving, it is sharp.

Controlling his fastball, or not controlling it, has been a factor not only for opposing batters but for Whitehouse as well. His walks-to-strikeouts ratio isn't very impressive yet but probably will be more so with experience. When Whitehouse walks a batter, he is not being too cautious--rather, he just does not have his control.

One of the things coaches like about his late-inning attitude is that he does go right after hitters.

The Twins hope to bring him along slowly, using him for an inning or so to set up Davis, or better still, using him against a predominantly lefthanded line-up in the late innings before bringing in Davis to face the righthanded hitters. While that didn't happen last year, Len responded with some good games and some bad ones, but learned from the experience.

He has the arm to be a very good short man; whether he works on his pitches and his control will determine whether he becomes one.

LEN WHITEHOUSE
LHP, No. 22
LL, 5'9", 175 lbs.
ML Svc: 2 years
Born: 9-10-57 in
Burlington, VT

1984 STATISTICS

W	L	ERA	G	GS	CG	IP	H	R	ER	BB	SO	SV
2	2	3.16	30	0	0	31	29	11	11	17	18	1

CAREER STATISTICS

W	L	ERA	G	GS	CG	IP	H	R	ER	BB	SO	SV
9	4	4.25	92	1	0	108	107	52	51	63	64	3

FIELDING:

Whitehouse still spends far more effort releasing the ball than trying to field anything that might come back at him, but he has improved his fielding with experience. A fine natural athlete, he still has the tendency to rely solely on innate ability and not on fundamentals. His move to first is quick and he will use it. He is not easy to run on because of both his move and his fastball. His motion to the plate quickens with runners on base.

OVERALL:

A gifted young pitcher, Whitehouse still needs to come up with a solid second pitch he can throw for strikes. He must learn more control of the pitches he throws.

Matthews: "Whitehouse seems to have pretty good stuff. He will challenge hitters and has a chance to become a dependable reliever."

HOUSTON JIMENEZ
SS, No. 1
RR, 5'7", 144 lbs.
ML Svc: 1 year plus
Born: 10-30-57 in
    Mexico City, MEX

HITTING, BASERUNNING, FIELDING:

Owner of one of the naturally smaller strike zones in baseball (he's only 5'7"), Houston Jimenez diminishes even that with a crouched stance, and many pitchers in the league believe he looks as hard for walks as for base hits.

Jimenez is basically unaggressive at the plate, at best a contact hitter without power who is better on turf than on natural surfaces. He is a better off-speed hitter than fastball hitter, attributable to his years in the Mexican Leagues. Pitchers tend to go right after Jimenez with fastballs and hard sliders, pitches with which he has little success.

He is a good, quick baserunner without much aggression. Jimenez made it to the majors on the strength of his fielding. He's spider-quick, has a strong arm and good hands but doesn't make anyone forget the better infielders in baseball.

OVERALL:

At best, he is a pesky low-in-the-order hitter who'll make the most of somebody's bad control or get on base with ground singles and bloops. Jimenez ultimately appears to be a utility infielder. He is strong on defense and weak at the plate.

Matthews: "Jimenez is a solid defensive player. He must have a better idea at the plate to become a good all-around player."

RANDY BUSH
DH, No. 25
LL, 6'1", 184 lbs.
ML Svc: 2 years
Born: 10-5-58 in
    Dover, DE

HITTING, BASERUNNING, FIELDING:

Once again, Randy Bush got the most out of his ability and attitude, filling a number of spots for the Twins in a utility role.

He is one of those young players who got into the majors because he could hit anyone's fastball. But the lefthanded-hitting Bush soon learned that he could not handle most anyone's best breaking or off-speed pitches. That, and the fact that he doesn't have a No. 1 position, defensively, have given the 26-year-old Bush a role as a pinch-hitter and DH.

He has fair power, especially on fastballs in, and can turn on a ball very well. He is predominantly a line drive hitter who has difficulty with change-ups.

As a baserunner, Bush is one-base-at-a-time. His instincts on the bases begin and end with checking with his coaches. He is not aggressive, not fast, and is rarely used as a pinch-runner.

Bush's best defensive spot is first base, but nearly everyone in baseball has a No. 1 first baseman. He can play in the outfield, but his range is limited and so is his arm. Bush's strengths have been his simple out-and-out persistence--he may get beat, but he won't quit. That, and his gift for clutch hits should keep him in the majors.

MIKE WALTERS
RHP, No. 30
RR, 6'5", 195 lbs.
ML Svc: 2 years
Born: 10-18-57 in
St. Louis, MO

PITCHING, FIELDING:

Mike Walters is a pitcher who has stayed in professional baseball and made it to the majors on the strength of his unorthodox delivery. His delivery borders on submarine style and that makes him a good candidate for long relief. It has been his role, and he has met it with varying results.

Given the opportunity to work with any regularity, Walters can be effective, especially if limited to one time through a batting order. But that has not been the way it's worked out, and Walters suffers when he is not used often. His control vanishes.

Walters has a mid-80s fastball and a sinker that, given his delivery, rarely reaches the batter's thighs.

He is quick coming off the mound and has good hands and good reflexes, though not much of a move to first base.

Walters needs to pitch to find out how good he is. That hasn't happened yet.

OVERALL:

As of now, Walters remains one of those pitchers on the fringe; a man with an unusual delivery who has been both successful and ineffective in big league appearances. He will probably remain the 10th man on a 10-man staff.

Matthews: "Tough on most hitters when they see him for the first time. He is marginal at this point."

AL WILLIAMS
RHP, No. 28
RR, 6'4", 184 lbs.
ML Svc: 4 years
Born: 5-7-54 in
Pearl Lagoon, NIC

PITCHING, FIELDING:

The rap against Al Williams throughout his career has been that he has winning stuff and a rather lackadaisical attitude. That, combined with annual injuries that sideline him, have made him a .500 pitcher over the course of his career.

Williams has a fine curveball (one of the better curves around) and a mid-80s fastball that he spots. He's also thrown a change-up for years, though it hasn't been effective. At times, the curve has caused him more trouble than any other pitch.

What coaches have questioned is his tendency to try and pitch high (in the "power pitcher" zone) without power pitcher stuff. A good curve is tough to hit no matter where it's thrown, but Williams's second and third pitches must be low if he is to be effective at all.

His delivery sends him off the mound in a position not designed to field balls hit back up the middle, and a good many of them aren't, for precisely that reason. He's also vulnerable to bunts on the third base side.

Williams seems to concentrate so hard on simply staying in the majors that he doesn't make the adjustments needed to keep him there and to make him a winner. With his stuff, he can win, but he can't do it challenging the better hitters strength-for-strength. He has to use more finesse.

OVERALL:

Williams has the potential to win in the majors, and it may be that over his career he simply hasn't responded to the coaching he's been given in the Twins organization. Now, apparently, he will get a chance to respond to coaching in another organization.

Matthews: "Al has been a mystery to many people. He has never put together a solid, consistent season. He will pitch very well, then disappear for a few outings."

NEW YORK YANKEES

HITTING:

Don Baylor and Dave Winfield seem to have traded years in 1984. Winfield's home run and RBI totals dropped while his average soared, and Baylor's average dipped while his home run and RBI numbers went through the roof.

Baylor is one of the toughest players in either league. He stands as close to the plate as possible, almost sitting right on it. His arms and hands actually border the inside edge of the plate. Once again, Baylor led the league in getting hit by pitches. He won't even flinch or rub the spot that got hit-- ever. You try that.

Baylor began to pull the ball much better this season. Pitchers realized that he can hammer the ball if he extends his arms out over the plate; they tried jamming him, but Baylor added some bat speed last year and just about got them all.

Lefthanders will throw him sliders low and in and take something off the fastball when they have two strikes on him. Righthanders send him curves, either low or away. Baylor can hit the low pitch, but is a much better high ball hitter. It is difficult to throw a fastball past him, so he will rarely see a belt-high fastball with men on base.

Baylor hits to all fields with men in scoring position. He will not bunt for a base hit, but can bunt to move runners along if called upon to do so.

BASERUNNING:

Baylor is one of the hardest sliders in baseball and will knock a middle infielder over with everything he's got.

He is a smart baserunner and knows the strengths and weaknesses of various outfielders and will always take the extra base if the situation calls for it. He is also smart enough to know that if he does stretch a single into a double late in the game, the next batter may be intentionally walked, so he will sacrifice the extra base. That is something

DON BAYLOR
DH, No. 25
RR, 6'1", 205 lbs.
ML Svc: 13 years
Born: 6-28-49 in
Austin, TX

1984 STATISTICS

AVG	G	AB	R	H	2B	3B	HR	RBI	BB	SO	SB
.262	134	493	84	129	29	1	27	89	39	67	1

CAREER STATISTICS

AVG	G	AB	R	H	2B	3B	HR	RBI	BB	SO	SB
.267	1770	6484	978	1733	303	26	261	994	613	764	277

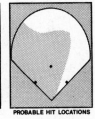

VS. RHP — STRONG · VS. LHP — STRONG · PROBABLE HIT LOCATIONS

he learned from his former teammate Frank Robinson.

FIELDING:

Baylor does not like being a DH, and while he can still play the outfield, his arm never fully recovered from an early football accident. He might see some more action in right field and can still play first base in a pinch.

OVERALL:

Don Baylors are few and far between. Any team should be grateful to have one. He plays hard all the time and does not get moody if he is in a slump. He also knows that a pat on the back of a slumping teammate goes a long way.

Robinson: "I think that Don has finally accepted the fact that he is a DH, even though I'm sure he feels he might have played someplace in the field. I think his DH-adjustment is now complete and he will be around for a few more years doing a solid job."

PITCHING:

Marty Bystrom simply cannot get through a season without suffering an injury. He exploded onto the National League scene in 1980 with a shutout of the Mets while he was with Philadelphia, won five straight games and helped the Phillies into the World Series.

He has spent time on the disabled list every year since, and when the Yankees acquired him in June of 1984 to replace Shane Rawley, he was again disabled with arm, shoulder and elbow problems. He is a power pitcher who throws the fastball, curve, slider and change, but can be considered a combination of curveball and power pitcher. His fastball has been clocked at 90 MPH, but he uses it primarily to jam both left and righthanded hitters and keep them off the plate.

His strikeout pitch is the curve or slider. He can spot the slider on the corners. In the American League for the first time in his career, Bystrom did not get the low strike from umpires, as he did while with the Phillies.

Bystrom throws three-quarters to overhand, depending on how his arm feels, and uses a variety of speeds to keep batters off balance. When he is healthy and in full command of the four pitches, he is tough to beat.

He is not afraid to throw the breaking ball in any situation, regardless of the count. He has the edge because he generally keeps batters on their toes with his inside fastballs. His change can be effective, but he must learn to disguise it better. He was able to dominate many AL batters when he finally pitched in 1984, because they had not seen him before and did not know what to expect with two strikes. He will throw everything but the change-up when trying for the strikeout.

MARTY BYSTROM
RHP, No. 50
RR, 6'5", 200 lbs.
ML Svc: 4 years
Born: 7-26-58 in
   Coral Gables, FL

1984 STATISTICS

W	L	ERA	G	GS	CG	IP	H	R	ER	BB	SO	SV
2	2	2.97	7	7	0	39	34	16	13	13	24	0

CAREER STATISTICS

W	L	ERA	G	GS	CG	IP	H	R	ER	BB	SO	SV
22	20	3.95	65	60	4	337	344	171	148	117	206	0

FIELDING:

Bystrom's move to first is average, and he must learn--as Jay Howell did--to cut down on his leg kick to prevent runners from getting a big jump. He could be better off the mound on bunts and choppers, and could be faster when covering first on grounders to the right side.

OVERALL:

Bystrom did not like leaving Philly to go to New York. He said so in no uncertain terms. He has pitched under pressure in both leagues and should easily have a good year this season if he stays healthy.

Robinson: "Obviously he has to stay healthy and be in the right surroundings. When both these factors are in place, he can help a team. In terms of his career, this will probably be a pivotal year."

HITTING:

Rick Cerone had his third consecutive year of batting under .230 and his third consecutive year of non-productivity. His offense suffers in direct proportion to his playing time.

Cerone was somewhat content starting off last season in a platoon role, but he lost even that when Butch Wynegar won the full-time job because he caught Phil Niekro's knuckleball so well.

Cerone saw only sporadic play and changed his stances monthly. He wound up by standing deep in the box with his bat held higher than he had ever held it before. He began to make better contact with the ball late in the season, but usually hit the ball right at somebody.

Righthanders will try the fastball away as well as the curveball low and in. Cerone's lack of playing time made him have a rough time with off-speed pitches from both left and righthanders. In the past, Rick could handle the high fastball, but he had trouble with even that last season.

He is still considered a better than average clutch hitter who can get a runner home from third when he plays frequently. This new slightly closed stance also enabled him to pull inside pitches and to slap the ball to right on belt-high pitches over the plate or toward the outside corner

BASERUNNING:

Cerone is not fast out of the box and is no threat to steal. He still runs aggressively, but became extremely tentative last year. He did not take as many chances (true, he did not have as many). He will not take anything but a short lead.

FIELDING:

He retains his agility and can handle the knuckleball better than he has been given credit for. When he is playing

RICK CERONE
C, No. 10
RR, 5'11", 185 lbs.
ML Svc: 10 years
Born: 5-19-54 in
Newark, NJ

1984 STATISTICS

AVG	G	AB	R	H	2B	3B	HR	RBI	BB	SO	SB
.208	38	120	8	25	3	0	2	13	9	15	1

CAREER STATISTICS

AVG	G	AB	R	H	2B	3B	HR	RBI	BB	SO	SB
.238	694	2298	229	548	103	12	36	261	154	237	3

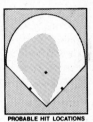

VS. RHP   VS. LHP   PROBABLE HIT LOCATIONS

contentedly, Cerone has a better than 50% chance of throwing out potential basestealers and blocking pitches in the dirt. When he is not playing regularly, his head does not seem to be in the game. His throwing suffered when he incurred a severe elbow problem, and it hampered his ability to make strong, accurate throws.

OVERALL:

Cerone is a battler, but his Yankee situation could leave no winner. He is a player who would relish the chance to play every day and could offer a young pitching staff quality direction from a major leaguer who knows big-time pressure.

Robinson: "I doubt he will ever reach the plateau he was at in 1980 when he had a great year. Injuries have slowed him down, and I believe that big ball-park (Yankee Stadium) psyched him out."

PITCHING:

The Atlanta Braves gave the New York Yankees two gifts last season. One was Phil Niekro and the other was Joe Cowley. Cowley spent eight years in the Atlanta minor league system seeing only infrequent and brief appearances with the parent club. He came to the Yankees and knew that it was his last shot. The Yankees were 11-0 in games that Cowley started and he ripped off eight straight wins in August and September.

He is not an overpowering pitcher and relies on sinkers and sliders to get ahead of the hitters. He has an excellent curveball which he throws from either three-quarters or sidearm to right-handed hitters. He uses his curve as his strikeout pitch. He is not afraid to throw a breaking ball in any situation regardless of the count, regardless of the number of men on base and regardless of the score.

On occasions, Cowley will throw five or six consecutive breaking balls or sinkers to righties. If he catches them leaning, will bust his fastball on the inside. His fastball is clocked at only 85-88 MPH, but looks much faster after the breaking balls. If he gets ahead of lefthanded batters, he will waste a fastball away, trying to catch the outside corner, and if he misses, will come back with the curve. Many of his strikeouts (he has a high strikeout-per-innings-pitched ratio) are on called third strikes to batters who are unfamiliar with his variety of pitches.

He enjoys pitching in bigger ball-parks, particularly Yankee Stadium, where he was unbeaten. If his sinker/slider combo is working, he will get ground balls, but when he falls behind and gets his pitches up, he gives up the long ball. A big park helps keep long flies inside the fences, and the improved Yankee outfield was helpful to him after the All Star break.

JOE COWLEY
RHP, No. 38
RR, 6'5", 210 lbs.
ML Svc: 2 years
Born: 8-15-58 in
Lexington, KY

1984 STATISTICS

W	L	ERA	G	GS	CG	IP	H	R	ER	BB	SO	SV
9	2	3.56	16	11	3	83	75	34	33	31	71	0

CAREER STATISTICS

W	L	ERA	G	GS	CG	IP	H	R	ER	BB	SO	SV
10	4	3.93	33	19	3	135	128	61	59	47	98	0

FIELDING:

He is a superb fielder for a big man and has a perfect follow-through after release. He is almost never out of fielding position, and covers first as well as Phil Niekro. He keeps runners close, has a good move to all bases, and is excellent on choppers and bunts.

OVERALL:

He was 10-3 with the Clippers as a starter, and better than that when the Yankees bought his contract in July. He was not considered a rookie because he pitched more than 50 innings with Atlanta in 1982, but he enjoyed the Yankees' efforts to make him a successful major league starter. He did not let them down.

Robinson: "He is no flash in the pan, not by a long shot. His fastball is not overpowering, but he keeps going after the hitter. He has an idea of what he's going to do on the mound. He won in 1984 and should win again in 1985."

HITTING:

If Brian Dayett had come close to what he accomplished in the minors (Star of Star Award, 35 homers, 108 RBIs in 1983), he would have been a cinch to patrol left field for the Yankees in 1985. As things turned out, Dayett came to the Yankees in June 1984, played every day at first but was eventually used only against lefthanded pitchers. He never could regain the stroke he had in the minors, but he did show occasional power.

Dayett has a closed stance and bats from a slight crouch. He has a quick bat but gets fooled with off-speed pitches from both righties and lefties. He does not strike out a lot and makes contact quite often. Despite his ability to hit fastballs, he can be struck out by fastballs up and in or low and away.

Lefties will try to jam him with hard stuff and throw the curve on the outside corner when they are ahead in the count. Righties (when he faces them) will throw the curve low and away and the fastball up and in. Dayett is basically a pull hitter who does not go the other way as often as he should.

BASERUNNING:

He is a miniature Don Baylor on the basepaths, extremely aggressive and alert. Dayett is fundamentally sound on the bases and knows how to run them. He always watches the third base coach when he is trying to go from first to third or when trying to stretch a double into a triple. He slides hard into every base, and will not hesitate to knock over any catcher blocking home plate.

FIELDING:

The entire Yankee ballclub points to Dayett as a prime factor in shoring up their early-season porous defense. Bobby Meacham and Mike Pagliarulo patched up short and third, and Dayett gave them a

BRIAN DAYETT
OF, No. 62
RR, 5'10", 180 lbs.
ML Svc: 1 year
Born: 1-22-57 in
New London, CT

1984 STATISTICS

AVG	G	AB	R	H	2B	3B	HR	RBI	BB	SO	SB
.244	64	127	14	31	9	0	4	23	9	14	0

CAREER STATISTICS

AVG	G	AB	R	H	2B	3B	HR	RBI	BB	SO	SB
.237	75	156	17	37	9	1	4	28	11	18	0

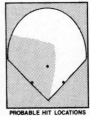

VS. RHP   VS. LHP   PROBABLE HIT LOCATIONS

a left fielder who could track balls down and who could stop runners from taking extra bases and running at will.

Not fast, Dayett gets an excellent jump and is extremely quick. At Yankee Stadium, he threw out three runners trying to stretch singles into doubles on balls hit inside the third base line. He has one of the best arms in the league, can go either way, but is a bit better at going back on a ball than he is at coming in.

OVERALL:

He is the "Rocky" of the team. His time may have past because of the six years in the minors, but he has proved to be a hustler and a fighter who should find a job with some major league team.

Robinson: "He has been around the minors for a while and must prove that he can play in the majors. Outstanding power, but I think he tries to pull too much in Yankee Stadium and that hurts him. He can swing the bat and play defense, but that may not be enough."

HITTING:

Veteran infielder Tim Foli was re-signed to playing backup baseball with the Yankees in 1984, but a spring training injury slowed him down, contract problems annoyed him and at least one coach on the team bothered him. As a result, he was never fully utilized. He was told twice that he would be traded and once that he would be released. He had his bags packed. He stayed, however, until the bitter end, when he asked for a trade.

He was played sparingly, but after overcoming his slow start was very helpful to the Yankee infield. He hit better than .400 with men on base while playing second, short and third late in the season, committing only three errors in the late stages of the season.

He bats from a virtually square stance, slight crouch, and can hit the ball wherever it is pitched. There is no definite "book" on Foli. He is a good bad ball hitter and can hit outside pitches to right and inside pitches over the third baseman's head, chop down on high pitches and golf low pitches. He is no threat to hit the long ball, but has excellent bat control and is a good hit-and-run man.

Pitchers will try to get him out with high hard stuff and off-speed curves. Lefthanders will also throw him up and in then turn the fastball over and try to hit the outside corner. Despite a lack of speed, Foli can and will bunt for a base hit toward either first or third, and is an outstanding bunter when called upon to sacrifice.

BASERUNNING:

Foli seems to delight in sliding hard into middle infielders on teams that have players who slide hard into him when he is playing second or short. He is a smart runner who knows his limitations. He will take the extra base if he is sure he can make it or if he knows the limitations of an outfielder's arm. He is no threat to steal.

TIM FOLI
SS, No. 2
RR, 6'0", 175 lbs.
ML Svc: 14 years
Born: 12-8-50 in
    Culver City, CA

1984 STATISTICS

AVG	G	AB	R	H	2B	3B	HR	RBI	BB	SO	SB
.252	61	163	8	41	11	0	0	16	2	16	0

CAREER STATISTICS

AVG	G	AB	R	H	2B	3B	HR	RBI	BB	SO	SB
.251	1677	6010	575	1508	241	20	25	499	261	397	81

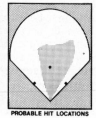

STRONG VS. RHP   STRONG VS. LHP   PROBABLE HIT LOCATIONS

FIELDING:

Foli has good range and a good arm. What he lacks in range, he makes up for by playing position baseball, that is, cheating a few steps either way depending upon the pitcher and the batter. He can still turn the double play from either second or short, and is not afraid to make an unorthodox throw from either second or third, throwing to a base a runner might not expect. He has an accurate arm.

OVERALL:

Foli's bitterness at unfair treatment by the Yankees will not allow him to take another chance on packing and unpacking his bags once a month this year. He will make sure he stays with his new team.

Robinson: "He'll give you an average job wherever he plays. He knows how to play the game and won't hurt you with mental mistakes. He does what it takes, and will always give you his best."

PITCHING:

It might have been that old sophomore jinx with Ray Fontenot last year: he was 8-2 as a starter in 1983, but 5-8 in 1984.

He has no fastball but does have an excellent sinker, a fair curve and a good slider. He is working on a change-up. He starts righthanded hitters off with the sinker, always low and away. He will continue to turn the ball over and keep it away from righties. With men on base, Fontenot will try to keep his pitches low in order to induce grounders. When he became the third starter (after injuries to Ron Guidry, Shane Rawley and John Montefusco), Ray began to throw too hard. His ball stayed up and he was hit hard. In order for Ray to be effective, he must have a "tired arm" like Tommy John, Larry Gura or Geoff Zahn: his ball must sink.

He is a methodical worker on the mound and has an easy, fluid motion. He throws three-quarters to sidearm. Ray also had control problems in 1984 and seemed a bit too upset when he did not get the calls on close pitches. He will use his curve and slider more often against lefthanded hitters, and can be effective when he keeps both pitches low and away.

He let too many things distract him early in the year, was shuttled back and forth as an emergency starter and long relief man in the bullpen and felt generally unwanted. When he saw the young Yankee pitchers come up from Columbus and produce, he dug down and became effective as the fifth Yankee starter.

FIELDING:

Fontenot is a good fielding pitcher with a better than average move to first base. He is in good fielding position

RAY FONTENOT
LHP, No. 57
LL, 6'0", 175 lbs.
ML Svc: 2 years
Born: 8-8-57 in
    Lake Charles, LA

1984 STATISTICS
W	L	ERA	G	GS	CG	IP	H	R	ER	BB	SO	SV
8	9	3.61	35	24	0	169	189	77	68	58	85	0

CAREER STATISTICS
W	L	ERA	G	GS	CG	IP	H	R	ER	BB	SO	SV
16	11	3.52	50	39	3	266	290	118	104	83	112	0

after his release and normally does not hurt himself on the mound. At times, he is a step slow in covering first base and must work to improve that aspect of his game. Runners will go because he does not have a fastball, but his good move to first enabled him to pick off several unsuspecting runners in 1984.

OVERALL:

He has overcome arm and shoulder troubles and is of the same ilk as Ron Guidry. He considered 1984 a lost year and must be able to prove that his two full years with New York will enable him to crack the starting rotation in 1985.

Robinson: "It appears that Fontenot is a two-pitch pitcher. If he doesn't get both pitches over, he can get into trouble. When he keeps the sinker and slider low, he can work the corners; he will get hit if he gets his pitches too high. Late in the year, he started coming inside and that impressed me because it will keep the hitters from digging in."

HITTING:

Hitting is just about all that Oscar Gamble has left, now that his sense of humor and fielding privileges have deserted him. He languished on the bench with injuries in 1984 and decided that the New York media were the cause of his plight.

Gamble can still hit, however, and is particularly dangerous in Yankee Stadium. He is a power-hitting lefty with the severest crouch in baseball. His stance is wide open, with his back foot and his hands virtually on the inside portion of the plate.

It is difficult to throw a belt-high fastball past Gamble. He constantly looks for fastballs toward the inner portion of the plate, and will look to go deep with those pitches. Despite his reduced playing time, Gamble annually leads the league in homers per at-bats. It has been projected that Gamble, if he had more than 500 at-bats per season, would average 35-40 homers.

Lefthanders will try curves low and away but must be careful not to hang one high. Righthanders will occasionally try to sneak an inside fastball past him, and if they get ahead in the count will try the fastball away or something off-speed. Gamble is considered a dangerous batter with runners on second and third, and will often drive a sacrifice fly off a tough pitcher on any pitch he sees. He cannot bunt, either for a base hit or in sacrifice situations.

BASERUNNING:

Gamble is faster than people think, gets a good jump from the box, will make infielders hurry their throws on chopping ground balls. He has good instincts on the basepaths and will take the extra base. He will steal if he's left alone at first. He is aggressive, but not that much of a threat when it comes to sliding hard.

OSCAR GAMBLE
OF/DH, No. 17
LR, 5'11", 177 lbs.
ML Svc: 16 years
Born: 12-20-49 in
  Ramer, AL

1984 STATISTICS

AVG	G	AB	R	H	2B	3B	HR	RBI	BB	SO	SB
.184	54	125	17	23	2	0	10	27	25	18	1

CAREER STATISTICS

AVG	G	AB	R	H	2B	3B	HR	RBI	BB	SO	SB
.268	1514	4354	636	1165	183	31	196	646	576	524	47

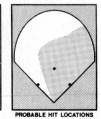

VS. RHP · VS. LHP · PROBABLE HIT LOCATIONS

FIELDING:

He was once a capable outfielder--not pretty, but able to catch 99% of the balls he could reach. While his arm is powerful, he was not used in the field in 1984.

OVERALL:

His usual good nature makes him hard to dislike, but he did become sullen and morose in 1984. He was once a favorite of Manager Yogi Berra and several important members of the Yankee hierarchy, but he seemed to sense he was not wanted in the new youth movement of 1984 and showed his bitterness.

Robinson: "Oscar can swing the bat with the best of them, and if he gets enough at-bats, he will hit his share of homers. I was a bit surprised to hear about his negative attitude because Yankee Stadium is such a good park for him. If he plays in a good frame of mind, he hit some home runs."

HITTING:

Before last year's All Star break, Ken Griffey was hitting .252 with zero homers. Two months later, he had lifted his average to .288 and put seven homers next to his name. Griffey did not change his stance, but did see more playing time in both left field and right field. His annual knee problems in spring training were followed by his annual pulled muscle problems, and he did not hit as the season headed into July.

He has a slightly closed stance, with a slight crouch, and holds the bat at shoulder level. When he started playing against righthanded pitchers, his timing and confidence came back. He started using all fields, waited very well on off-speed pitches, and could pull the fastball or curve for homers or dump outside pitches into left and center. With men on base, Griffey looks for the ball away to slap it to left, but is intelligent enough to guess pitching patterns and pull an inside pitch.

He raised his average because he began hitting righties and kept his balance against lefties. He slaps southpaw curves to center. Pitchers were able to get him out when he looked to pull, and they would take something off the fastball or turn it over and spot it on the outside corner. On those occasions, he hit easy pops and grounders. With a runner on first and the first baseman holding the bag, Griffey will shoot for the hole between first and second.

BASERUNNING:

Griffey is quick out of the box and runs with short, fast steps. He hustles on grounders and on the bases, but has obviously lost a few steps because of his leg injuries. He made several base-path mistakes simply because he was unhappy on the bench. In a contented state of mind, Griffey is a typical National League runner--not afraid to slide hard into any base.

KEN GRIFFEY
OF/1B, No. 33
LL, 6'0", 200 lbs.
ML Svc: 12 years
Born: 4-10-50 in
Donora, PA

1984 STATISTICS

AVG	G	AB	R	H	2B	3B	HR	RBI	BB	SO	SB
.273	120	399	44	109	20	1	7	56	29	32	2

CAREER STATISTICS

AVG	G	AB	R	H	2B	3B	HR	RBI	BB	SO	SB
.302	1412	5198	846	1569	265	66	90	580	524	532	167

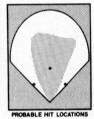

VS. RHP   VS. LHP   PROBABLE HIT LOCATIONS

FIELDING:

He has lost quite a bit in the outfield. Left field at Yankee Stadium is difficult to play because of the tremendous amount of ground to cover, and Ken cannot track down balls in left-center or deep down the line. His arm is still not a strong one, and runners will take extra bases on him. He is accurate on short throws, but a long throw will see the ball tail off as it nears the base.

OVERALL:

Because the younger Yankee team made such excellent strides last year, Ken Griffey may decide to accept a platoon spot in 1985 with a team that looks as if it can win. He had planned on playing first base last season, but with the emergence of Don Mattingly, Griffey was off the case.

Robinson: "What you've seen is what you'll get. He won't hit homers or drive in runs, but will hit his .300. Finding a position for him is a problem."

PITCHING:

Some people are calling it the "Cy Young Jinx." Ever since Ron Guidry won the Cy Young Award in 1978, every other AL pitcher to win it has had either a serious ailment or an inexplicably bad subsequent year. Starting in 1979, it hit Mike Flanagan, Steve Stone, Rollie Fingers, Pete Vuckovich and LaMarr Hoyt. The jinx took its time, but 1984 was Guidry's turn.

He was disabled in August with a rib injury and could have taken the year off (he was even left at home on one West Coast swing), but came back to pitch in relief and as a starter. He is a competitor through and through, and you can never sell him short.

He throws fewer fastballs now than in his prime, but it is his lean frame that really dictates that move. He uses his fastball early in the count, and will come back with curves and sliders to both left and righthanded hitters. If he can get by the first five innings with finesse pitches (he is working on a straight overhand change and an off-speed, almost sidearm, curve), he will use his fastball and hard slider when he gets in trouble after the fifth inning. He will get beat by the long ball, but it will always be against his fastball or slider. He will not throw anything but the heater and the slider. He will get beat with his best.

Guidry got off to a poor start in 1984 for several reasons. The team was not set defensively, and no one knew how Dave Righetti would fare in the bullpen. In addition, relievers Armstrong and Murray were disabled, Jay Howell was feeling his way, and no one seemed able to hold a Guidry lead. When things fell into place, Guidry proved he could still pitch, and did so until his August injury.

RON GUIDRY
LHP, No. 49
LL, 5'11", 162 lbs.
ML Svc: 10 years
Born: 8-28-50 in
 Lafayette, LA

1984 STATISTICS
W	L	ERA	G	GS	CG	IP	H	R	ER	BB	SO	SV
10	11	4.51	29	28	5	195	223	102	98	44	127	0

CAREER STATISTICS
W	L	ERA	G	GS	CG	IP	H	R	ER	BB	SO	SV
132	62	3.16	270	233	77	1767	1585	677	621	500	1367	4

FIELDING:

There are no better fielding pitchers than Guidry. He is the fastest pitcher off the mound, fields bunts before the catcher or corner infielders can get there, is next to an infielder on foul pops and often beats runners to first on high chops to his left. He is in perfect fielding position after his release and very few balls get past him. His move to first is average, but he will throw over six or seven times in a row, and often picks runners off who do not expect that many throws to first.

OVERALL:

He is as good as the team is. If the Yankees are good in 1985, Guidry will win 20 games again.

Robinson: "Ronnie seems to have lost some of his concentration on the mound. He has lost something off his fastball-- not that much, but just enough to make it important that he concentrate on every hitter. He'll have to start pitching to better spots, because unless he has mastered another pitch, he will still throw hard stuff, and batters will be looking for it."

HITTING:

For thirteen years, Toby Harrah played almost every day. He had a streak of 467 consecutive games heading into the 1983 season. He was stopped by a broken hand. It all came to a screeching halt in 1984, his first season with the Yankees.

Harrah was the odd man out all year, but did wind up playing third against lefthanded pitching late in the season. His stance is an extremely wide one, closed and deep in the box. With runners on base, Harrah will look to hit the ball to right field or up the middle. When he is playing regularly, he can hit the fastball, and will swing at anything close to the plate with two strikes to score or advance a runner.

Because of his limited playing time in 1984, Harrah did not get the close calls from the umpires on some pitches despite his excellent batting eye. He was caught looking at pitches that were low and inside. He will hit the curve the other way and pull the fastball. Off-speed pitches gave him more trouble than usual, because he was basically rusty all year. A chipped bone in his hand also hampered his swing, and when he was just about ready to play every day, Mike Pagliarulo was brought up from the minors.

BASERUNNING:

In the past, he had been a threat to steal, but not any longer. In 1984, he stole just three bases. Toby played and ran hard, but his mind was usually in a state of confusion because of his uncertain situation. As a result, he made several baserunning blunders. In one game, he tagged up from second on a ball that hit the right field fence and he only advanced one base. In the proper surroundings, Harrah is a hard-nosed runner who will take out infielders on potential double plays and take the extra base if the fielder doesn't charge the ball.

TOBY HARRAH
INF, No. 11
RR, 6'0", 180 lbs.
ML Svc: 14 years
Born: 10-26-48 in
Sissonville, WV

1984 STATISTICS

AVG	G	AB	R	H	2B	3B	HR	RBI	BB	SO	SB
.217	88	253	0	55	9	4	1	27	42	28	3

CAREER STATISTICS

AVG	G	AB	R	H	2B	3B	HR	RBI	BB	SO	SB
.266	1934	6717	974	1784	271	37	179	834	996	755	225

  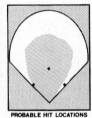

VS. RHP — STRONG   VS. LHP — STRONG   PROBABLE HIT LOCATIONS

FIELDING:

Despite his plight, Harrah is a solid fielder. Any errors he made were magnified because the Yankee Stadium fans booed him constantly. He is not fast, but has quick, sure hands. He knows how to play the hitters and is very accurate on throws to second or first. Any trouble he had was going to his left because he was unsure of the range of shortstop Bobby Meacham.

OVERALL:

Harrah refused all interviews late in the year, except to complain.

Robinson: "It is almost inconceivable that Toby Harrah had such a low home run and RBI total. He has always been an offensive threat; how one can fall so flat on his face in just one year is hard to believe. He's not through, not by a long shot, and will surely help someone, somewhere."

PITCHING:

The Yankees did not seem to know what to do with this pitcher who throws a 95 MPH fastball and has a sharp overhand curve and a crackling slider. Jay Howell received advice from Jim Palmer, went to the bullpen . . . and was outstanding. He pitched an extraordinary number of innings out of the bullpen and kept his strikeouts well above his number of innings pitched for most of the year.

The big righthander throws three-quarters and at times straight overhand. In the past, he would use his curve to both righties and lefties in order to set up his fastball, but Jim Palmer also helped Howell out here with a little advice. He told Jay what other coaches had also directed--that he use his fastball to set up his curve. Howell delighted in the future Hall of Famer's advice and did exactly that. He challenged every batter he faced with the fastball, then he used the curve or slider as his out pitch; it resulted in many strikeouts.

Lack of control can be a problem for Howell, particularly if his curve is missing the plate. He gets help because his fastball moves and batters will often swing at bad pitches when they are ahead on the count and are looking for the fastball. He adjusted to the bullpen after starting for the past two years because he realized he did not have a change-up and simply could not get by with all hard stuff. Late last season, he began to work on a change and if he masters it, could become one of the top relievers in the league.

FIELDING:

He could be a better fielder. His follow-through is good, but he is a bit

JAY HOWELL
RHP, No. 50
RR, 6'3", 205 lbs.
ML Svc: 2 years
Born: 11-26-55 in
  Miami, FL

1984 STATISTICS

W	L	ERA	G	GS	CG	IP	H	R	ER	BB	SO	SV
9	4	2.69	61	1	0	103	86	33	31	34	109	7

CAREER STATISTICS

W	L	ERA	G	GS	CG	IP	H	R	ER	BB	SO	SV
14	12	4.58	101	21	2	238	248	129	121	92	202	7

slow on reacting to grounders hit back at him and on bunts in unexpected situations. He has some trouble throwing to second on potential double play grounders. In previous seasons, he had difficulty taming his high leg kick, and runners would take off at will against him when he started or relieved. He learned to cut the kick in half while playing winter ball and became better in 1984 at keeping runners close.

OVERALL:

The Yankees expect to keep Righetti in the bullpen and are counting on him and Jay Howell to give them late-inning one-two punch.

Robinson: "Howell seems to have found himself in the bullpen. Having Righetti in the pen with him takes some heat off Jay, but it takes nothing away from the heat of his fastball and the confidence in his curve. It seems that the Yankees have suddenly duplicated what they had with Ron Davis and Goose Gossage."

HITTING:

Steve Kemp made a remarkable recovery after a near-fatal accident in September 1983 when he was struck in the face with a batted ball and almost lost his eyesight. Doctors told him it might take a year for the sight in his eye to come back, but Kemp hit close to .300 for much of the 1984 season. His average began to suffer only when he pulled a hamstring and started to swing too hard in almost every at-bat late in the season.

After tinkering with four or five different stances, Kemp reverted to the stance that saw him have six productive years with the Tigers and the White Sox. It is a wide stance, closed, with the bat held at shoulder level and constantly moving.

Kemp strides into every pitch and pitchers pitch him up and in or low and in. When he looks for the pitch inside, he is waiting for a fastball, so pitchers can get him out by throwing curves low and away or off-speed pitches away. He began swinging so hard late last season that he could not handle pitches he was once able to hammer.

He is a situation hitter who formerly disdained the long ball, but would sacrifice an at-bat with a runner on second to move him over a base. An extremely intense hitter, Kemp wore down as the 1984 season wore on. He began trying to pull outside pitches with men on base instead of going to center or left.

He can inside-out the ball when he puts his mind to it. He bunted better in 1984 than in the past, but he is still no threat to bunt for a hit.

BASERUNNING:

He continues to run the bases as he always has--hard, fast and furious. He hustles on every ball hit, both from the batter's box and when on base. He does not have blazing speed, but will always try to take the extra base. His various leg injuries slowed his ability to run the bases quite a bit in 1984.

STEVE KEMP
OF, No. 21
LL, 6'0", 190 lbs.
ML Svc: 8 years
Born: 8-7-54 in
  San Angelo, TX

1984 STATISTICS

AVG	G	AB	R	H	2B	3B	HR	RBI	BB	SO	SB
.291	94	313	37	91	12	1	7	41	40	54	4

CAREER STATISTICS

AVG	G	AB	R	H	2B	3B	HR	RBI	BB	SO	SB
.281	1047	3770	559	1060	166	23	127	610	550	536	30

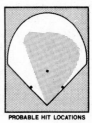

VS. RHP   VS. LHP   PROBABLE HIT LOCATIONS

FIELDING:

The whispers are that Kemp may have lost his left field job. His arm is not strong and runners take extraordinary chances against him, often going from first to third on hits to left and never stopping at third on singles to left when they are on second. He can cover a lot of ground, but does not get a good jump on the ball. Kemp is not afraid of fences.

OVERALL:

Kemp never quits. If his eyesight can return to 100%, he might return. The team will sacrifice on defense but he can make up for it with his offensive production. He is a good team player who likes to win.

Robinson: "The jury is still out: the team isn't sure about his eye yet. He plays hard, but may be interested in a change of scenery."

HITTING:

At the age of 23, Don Mattingly must be considered the finest young lefthanded hitter in baseball. It took him a year of servitude at first base and as a platoon outfielder, but Mattingly can now be considered the equal of Wade Boggs--or vice versa.

His stance is virtually square to the plate. It is a wide stance, and he does occasionally open it up a bit against certain lefthanded pitchers. Observers point out that although he is a few inches shorter than Hall of Famer Stan Musial, he has the same broad sloping shoulders that Musial had and swings the bat in much the same manner. It is an extremely quick bat, and a pitcher simply cannot throw a fastball past him.

Junkball pitchers, who seem to bother many free-swingers, can give Mattingly trouble by showing him the fastball away before nibbling at the outside corner with curves and assorted garbage. Despite Mattingly's excellent eye and knowledge of pitchers' patterns, he will occasionally try to pull an outside pitch and wind up hitting a grounder to first or second. Those occasions are rare.

With men on base, he becomes twice as difficult to handle because he will not try for the long ball but will hit the ball wherever it is pitched. His home run total was amazing, but Mattingly has a decided edge. He will poke a single to left, line a single to center, drive a grounder past third; when the pitchers think he is not looking inside, they will try to come in with a fastball or slider. Mattingly simply eats those situations up and comes up with the long ball.

When his bat does slow down, he is a bit vulnerable to hard sliders, low and in, and off-speed pitches away.

BASERUNNING:

He has excellent, sound judgment from any base. Mattingly is not gifted with exceptional speed but will still go from

DON MATTINGLY
OF/1B, No. 46
LL, 5'11", 185 lbs.
ML Svc: 2 years
Born: 4-20-61 in
Evansville, IN

1984 STATISTICS

AVG	G	AB	R	H	2B	3B	HR	RBI	BB	SO	SB
.343	153	603	91	207	44	2	23	110	41	33	1

CAREER STATISTICS

AVG	G	AB	R	H	2B	3B	HR	RBI	BB	SO	SB
.322	251	894	125	288	59	6	27	143	62	65	1

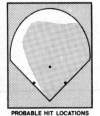

VS. RHP VS. LHP PROBABLE HIT LOCATIONS

first to third when outfielders do not hustle, and will tag from first or second on long flies. His baserunning mistakes occur about once a year.

FIELDING:

He is the best fielding first baseman in the league because of his ability to turn the 3-6-3 double play and his excellent range to both left and right. He catches pops in short right and is always aware of what bases opposing runners are on. Eddie Murray might have a slight edge, but that is debatable. Don Mattingly should win a few Gold Gloves.

OVERALL:

Robinson: "How in the world could anyone expect Don to come so far so fast? A batting title at his age is really something. He has virtually no flaws as a player and teams can't find a way to defense him. His own defensive play is excellent. Get used to him."

HITTING:

After an abrupt dismissal to Columbus in April of 1984, Bobby Meacham vowed to return to the Yankees and make it. He did so--in a very big way.

He changed his batting stances both righty and lefty and now hits almost the same either way. The stances are open, and he stands with less of a crouch. The weight is on the back foot (the Piniella theory), but Meacham bends his back leg batting righty or lefty. His front foot seems to barely touch the ground, as though he were dipping it into a pool to test the temperature of the water. A complete flop as a righthanded hitter in the latter stages of 1983, Meacham began making contact from that side in 1984 and batted higher from the right side than from the left. His power is from the left side.

He has the ability to hit off-speed pitches when behind in the count, and garnered more than his share of 1-2 or 0-2 hits in 1984.

Pitchers will try to throw him hard stuff away early in the count, and then come back with curves, low and in. Bobby is a better low ball hitter than high ball hitter, and with his added confidence can now pull the ball much better. He still, however, will hit the pitch away to the opposite field.

BASERUNNING:

He is the fastest of the Yankees who have reins on them. He stole eight straight bases when called up late in 1983 but had trouble reaching that figure for virtually the entire 1984 season. If given the green light, Meacham can steal second or third with ease. He can go from first to third as well as any runner in the league, but is still prone to rookie mistakes on the basepaths. He is not as aggressive as he could be when sliding while attempting to break up double plays.

BOBBY MEACHAM
INF, No. 20
SR, 6'1", 175 lbs.
ML Svc: 2 years
Born: 8-25-60 in
  Los Angeles, CA

1984 STATISTICS

AVG	G	AB	R	H	2B	3B	HR	RBI	BB	SO	SB
.253	99	360	62	91	13	4	2	25	32	70	9

CAREER STATISTICS

AVG	G	AB	R	H	2B	3B	HR	RBI	BB	SO	SB
.251	121	411	67	103	15	4	2	29	36	80	17

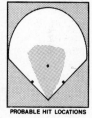

VS. RHP   VS. LHP   PROBABLE HIT LOCATIONS

FIELDING:

He improved so much that he had to be seen to be believed. His range is outstanding and he is superb at coming in on a ball. His arm is strong, but his throws are often off the mark. Most of his troubles came when he threw too soon, too late or off the wrong foot. He worked hard throughout the season to correct that. When asked who had the best stuff on the Yankees in 1984, first baseman Don Mattingly quipped, "Bobby Meacham."

OVERALL:

Robinson: "The knock on the Yankees during the first half of the season was their poor defense. If anybody on the team helped mold that defense together and soldify the infield, it was Bobby Meacham. He was THE most important defensive player the team had in Part Two of the season. He came back from the minors and tried more than 100%."

PITCHING:

One National League scout (who asked not to be identified) said that John Montefusco's unnatural pitching motion would someday lead to rib injuries. He was right. Montefusco suffered the rib injury early in 1984 and was hurt in a car crash a week later. He came back after a rehabilitation program in the minors, but was of no help to the team until late August.

He releases the ball from three-quarters, but has his arm far away from his body and puts added strain on his chest. He suffered a sprained sternum in his third start. When healthy, he starts most batters off with sliders, usually pitched low. He has an excellent sharp-breaking slider and a curve that breaks down when he releases it from an almost overhand motion. He will use the overhand curve as an out pitch to lefthanded hitters, and a slider or cut fastball away to righthanders.

Montefusco has excellent control and averages about 2.2 walks per nine innings. His motion is not smooth but herky-jerky, a benefit to him because it keeps many batters off stride. He has several off-speed pitches he will use in certain situations, but with men on base will go fastball, slider, curve--in any combination.

He still does not get as many low strikes as he did while pitching in the National League, but he came back strong after the injury and the team seemed to win when he pitched.

FIELDING:

Adequate in all areas, except a bit slow in handling bunts. He is quick on

JOHN MONTEFUSCO
RHP, No. 24
RR, 6'1", 192 lbs.
ML Svc: 10 years
Born: 5-25-50 in
   Long Branch, NJ

1984 STATISTICS

W	L	ERA	G	GS	CG	IP	H	R	ER	BB	SO	SV
5	3	3.58	11	11	0	55	55	26	22	13	23	0

CAREER STATISTICS

W	L	ERA	G	GS	CG	IP	H	R	ER	BB	SO	SV
85	83	3.53	291	243	32	1631	1583	717	639	506	1076	5

grounders and knows what base to throw the ball to. He has a quick pickoff move to first and is not afraid to throw to first five or six times in a row to keep a runner close.

OVERALL:

Montefusco has a guaranteed contract. He is a bit arrogant and totally sure of himself. At this stage, the Yankees should count on him to be the veteran righthanded starter to go along with Phil Niekro and young Joe Cowley. He is aware of the youth movement, so despite his brashness, he knows he will have to produce--quickly--in 1985.

Robinson: "He's a tough pitcher with a deceptive motion. He isn't afraid to let batters know he has the ball in his hand. His good riding fastball has won in the past, and can win again if he stays healthy."

HITTING:

The lean Omar Moreno found himself platooned last season and did not like it. He was benched for a month, and when he began taking extra batting lessons from coach Lou Piniella he was hitting .225. His hitting immediately picked up, but the Yankees had brought up Vic Mata from the minors and Moreno was again platooned.

He bats from a slight crouch, with a severely closed stance. His front foot faces the third base coach, and he peeks over his right shoulder while looking at the pitcher. Moreno changed in one respect in 1984--instead of hitting off his front foot, he began to switch the weight to his back foot and step into the ball. He still picks up his front foot slightly as the pitch approaches, and is invariably ahead of the pitch, which leaves him extremely vulnerable to off-speed pitches.

Most teams play him to hit to the opposite field and pitch him the same way, but they are not afraid to come inside because Moreno has very little power. He did manage to hit several homers when he learned the weight shift, but he did not hit consistently when he was platooned after the All Star break. He improved his average from .225 to .265, but seemed to lose interest when he hit well one day and found himself on the bench the next.

He is an outstanding bunter and prefers to push the ball between the pitcher and the shortstop. When he does, he cannot be thrown out because he is just so fast. He seems able to make contact in the middle two innings and in clutch situations, but can be struck out with curves and low fastballs in key spots late in games.

BASERUNNING:

Most of his salary is based on speed, yet the Yankees put a rein on him. He had 449 stolen bases coming into the 1984 season, but he had his lowest stol-

OMAR MORENO
OF, No. 22
LL, 6'3", 185 lbs.
ML Svc: 8 years
Born: 10-24-52 in
　　　Puerto Armuelles, PAN

1984 STATISTICS

AVG	G	AB	R	H	2B	3B	HR	RBI	BB	SO	SB
.259	117	355	37	92	12	6	4	38	18	48	20

CAREER STATISTICS

AVG	G	AB	R	H	2B	3B	HR	RBI	BB	SO	SB
.254	1206	4497	632	1140	148	77	30	343	362	784	469

VS. RHP　　　VS. LHP　　　PROBABLE HIT LOCATIONS

en base totals last year since 1976. It bothered him and he said so. He has blazing speed, from the box and on the bases, but did not make full use of it in 1984. Many times he would dare an outfielder to throw him out while heading for the next base, slow up a hair-- and find the ball waiting for him.

FIELDING:

Outstanding jump on the ball and tremendous range, yet Moreno shies away from fences and often dives for a ball instead of knocking it down. He has an ordinary arm, but generally keeps it low when throwing to the cutoff man, as he should. Runners will run on him, so he plays much closer to the plate than most center fielders.

OVERALL:

Robinson: "His status has suffered. A guy with speed like his only stealing 20 bases is hard to take. He had several lapses because he was unhappy."

PITCHING:

In spring training of 1984, many Yankee insiders claimed that if 45-year-old Phil Niekro did not win between 13 and 15 games, the team couldn't win the Eastern Division title. He had 16 wins before he injured his ribs and back during a brawl with the California Angels in September, but the Yankees still could not stop the Tigers. Had he kept up his earlier pace, Niekro would have been the oldest man to win 20 games and be a virtual cinch for the Cy Young Award.

None of the American League teams had ever seen his knuckler before, but they all saw plenty of it last season. He had outstanding success during his first time around the league, and when batters tried to sit and wait for a flat knuckler, he fooled them by using curves, sliders and what was left of his fastball to catch a corner.

He will not give in to a batter and will throw his best pitch of the day--whether it be the knuckler or slider--in any situation. He did not get as many called strikes as he would have liked. When he fell behind in the count in games that he lost, he sometimes came in with a pitch that was too fat.

He showed outstanding control and had more strikeouts than some people expected he might get. When he enjoyed a lead, he would come in with a floating knuckler, resembling a folly floater or a "lob." He was extremely tough with men on base and in late innings. He never quit on himself.

FIELDING:

Niekro proved that he can field in the American League as well as he did for his 18 years in the National League. He is one of the best fielding pitchers

PHIL NIEKRO
RHP, No. 35
RR, 6'2", 195 lbs.
ML Svc: 20 years
Born: 4-1-39 in
    Blaine, OH

1984 STATISTICS
W	L	ERA	G	GS	CG	IP	H	R	ER	BB	SO	S
16	8	3.09	32	31	5	215	219	85	74	76	136	0

CAREER STATISTICS
W	L	ERA	G	GS	CG	IP	H	R	ER	BB	SO	S
284	238	3.19	771	625	231	4834	4437	2002	1714	1528	3048	2

even in his new league. He knows what to do with the ball when he gets it, always covers first and backs up bases, is cat-quick off the mound and throws as much as any pitcher to first to keep runners close. Runners will, of course, try to steal on the master, but Niekro has several different stretch positions and makes it very difficult for a runner to get a good jump.

OVERALL:

The Yankees got their money's worth from Niekro. He knew the team gambled when they signed him and he was determined to prove their faith in him. While the Braves wound up building a statue for him in Atlanta, they would have been much better off with the man himself.

Robinson: "He got off to an unusual start but struggled a bit late in the year. He should be able to give the Yankees another productive year in 1985 because he takes such good care of himself and because the knuckleball doesn't take that much out of his arm. He is a pro."

HITTING:

Mike Pagliarulo seems to be the next Graig Nettles. He was brought up from the minors, was shoved into a game and responded with three hits. The Yankees liked his defense and his surprising ability to adjust to major league pitching. He stayed for the entire second half and played against righthanders, enjoying success at Yankee Stadium with its short right field porch.

He is almost a mirror image of his tutor, Lou Piniella. Mike's stance is square with a slight crouch, deep in the box, bat held at shoulder level. The weight shift is noticeable. His weight is on his back foot, and he is learning to swivel his hips and legs into the proper hitting position. He can inside-out the ball to left field and will go that way if pitchers pitch him that way, but his main strength lies in his power to right and right-center. For just about the entire second half of the season, more than half his hits were for extra bases.

When he is unsure of a pitcher, Mike can look awkward and be fooled by off-speed pitches. His swing is then more of a lunge. When he gets too anxious, he will try to pull everything and will pop up or hit easy grounders. When they get two strikes on him, pitchers will try to jam him with hard stuff low. He has shown that he can hit lefthanded pitching, and he hangs very tough at the plate against southpaws. Although he does not have good speed, he can bunt toward third if the situation arises.

BASERUNNING:

Pagliarulo is an extremely intelligent runner, very aggressive and a "fear nothing" type of player. He does not have good speed but runs hard. Fielders cannot take him for granted when he is on base, and must make certain to cut balls off in the gap or he will take the extra base.

MIKE PAGLIARULO
3B, No. 57
LR, 6'2", 195 lbs.
ML Svc: 1 year
Born: 3-15-60 in
   Medford, MA

1984 STATISTICS

AVG	G	AB	R	H	2B	3B	HR	RBI	BB	SO	SB
.239	67	201	24	48	15	3	7	34	15	46	0

CAREER STATISTICS

AVG	G	AB	R	H	2B	3B	HR	RBI	BB	SO	SB
.239	67	201	24	48	15	3	7	34	15	46	0

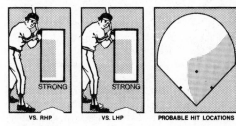

VS. RHP   VS. LHP   PROBABLE HIT LOCATIONS

FIELDING:

He was hitting .212 when the Yankees brought him up in July--it was his glove that they were after. They got it.

Pagliarulo can go to his right or left and has even made some of Nettles's patented diving plays in the hole to his left. He has a strong, accurate arm and can come in very well on bunts and make all the plays. If anything, easy grounders hit directly at him are the ones that he sometimes bobbles.

OVERALL:

Pagliarulo could be the Yankee third baseman for the next ten years. He has the knack of feigning runners who come to third, making believe that no throw is coming. He has a lightning-like swipe tag. He will do anything to win.

Robinson: "He really impressed me. He reminds me of Graig Nettles and his lefty power makes him a Yankee natural. He has already learned to take advantage of the Stadium's quirks. Great future."

HITTING:

Willie Randolph worked hard throughout the 1984 season. His diligence paid off because he stayed near .300 for much of the year.

He understood early on that the infield of the Yankees was really none at all. No one seemed to have any idea of who was going to play where. For Willie to be effective, he has to be in the lineup every day (with slight rests now and then) and know the people around him. Once Mattingly and Meacham were settled in, the team felt some sanity, and a comfortable Randolph justified his status in the field and at bat.

He retains his slightly closed stance as the leadoff batter and still steps directly into every pitch. For that reason, he can hit for power to right and right-center. He will not swing at bad pitches because he tries to draw as many walks as possible, but will be struck out with two strikes on him if he guesses fastball and gets a curve.

Pitchers will try to jam him and get him to take a close pitch on the outside corner when they have two strikes on him. Righties with sharp curves give him trouble. He can still hit high pitches with power, but has trouble with low breaking pitches from either a righty or a lefty. He did not hit in the clutch as well as he had in past years, despite his good average.

BASERUNNING:

Like many Yankees, Randolph did not steal as often in 1984 as he had in the past. Manager Yogi Berra simply does not like steals, but does use many hit-and-runs. Randolph is a smart and aggressive baserunner who will always try to stretch a single into a double and a double into a triple. He will slide headfirst into any base most of the time.

He will force fielders to hurry their throws when he is trying to beat out a grounder or get to first before a double play can be turned.

WILLIE RANDOLPH
2B, No. 30
RR, 5'11", 166 lbs.
ML Svc: 10 years
Born: 7-6-54 in
   Holly Hill, SC

1984 STATISTICS

AVG	G	AB	R	H	2B	3B	HR	RBI	BB	SO	SB
.287	142	564	86	162	24	2	2	31	86	42	10

CAREER STATISTICS

AVG	G	AB	R	H	2B	3B	HR	RBI	BB	SO	SB
.274	1210	4522	746	1238	180	51	29	361	695	359	201

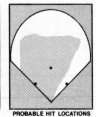

VS. RHP   VS. LHP   PROBABLE HIT LOCATIONS

FIELDING:

He is still acknowledged to have the widest range of any second baseman in the league, can and will dive for balls hit to his left or right and is the best at turning the double play. Randolph can be counted on to field any tough shots in crucial situations. He has a strong arm on relays.

He has come to criticize the rock-hard Yankee Stadium infield, an infield which seems to lead to more bad hops than other infields.

OVERALL:

Randolph is a mature pro who must be left alone, and must be rested when he starts to wear down.

Robinson: "As usual, he is steady. He gets things going, draws a lot of walks and gets on base. I think he gets a little overlooked, but you've got to have him there."

PITCHING:

Dennis Rasmussen, a 6'7" lefthanded starter, appears to be the prototype power pitcher. Despite an outstanding fastball clocked at 90 MPH, he is basically a breaking ball pitcher. He will start off righthanded hitters with a big overhand curve, and if he gets ahead in the count will stay with the breaking ball, pitching to corners. He may turn a fastball over to a power pull hitter, but is not afraid to come inside. When behind in the count or in trouble because of control problems, he is prone to give up the long ball. Had he pitched a full season (based on innings pitched and homers allowed in his starts in 1984), he would have allowed close to 30 homers, a very high number.

Rasmussen throws basically three-quarters with a kind of slingshot arm delivery, similar to John Montefusco. He is very effective when he gets his curve and slider over the plate. He spots his fastball to both left and righthanded hitters, and will use it as a strikeout pitch if he thinks a batter is not set up for it.

Although American League batters saw him for the first time, they appeared to be able to catch up to him in the later innings when his stamina seemed sapped. He led the staff in wild pitches, and was hurt by control problems with men on base in the late innings of many of his starts.

FIELDING:

He has a good move to first and keeps runners close, but is slow coming off the mound. He is in good fielding position after his release, but does not

DENNIS RASMUSSEN
LHP, No. 45
LL, 6'7", 230 lbs.
ML Svc: 1 year
Born: 4-18-59 in
Los Angeles, CA

1984 STATISTICS

W	L	ERA	G	GS	CG	IP	H	R	ER	BB	SO	SV
9	6	4.57	24	24	1	147	127	79	75	60	110	0

CAREER STATISTICS

W	L	ERA	G	GS	CG	IP	H	R	ER	BB	SO	SV
9	6	4.57	24	24	1	147	127	79	75	60	110	0

move well when fielding grounders or bunts.

He works hard on his game and is trying to become a solid fielder, particularly when covering first on grounders to the right side.

OVERALL:

Rasmussen figures prominently in the Yankees' plans. They really wanted him: they traded for him (Tommy John), traded him away (John Montefusco) and went right back after him in the Nettles trade. He listens to pitching coach Mark Connor and is a rapid learner. Yankee management always spends extra time in grooming lefthanded starters, particularly for Yankee Stadium, where they can strangle lefty power hitters.

Robinson: "I like him. I was impressed by what he did, especially in the minors. He showed a lot of moxie. He moved the ball around, and he could be the real sleeper. He definitely has the stuff to win some games."

PITCHING:

The successful transition of Dave Righetti from a starter to a reliever has set traditional pitching theory into a spin. Managers all over baseball are scrutinizing their staffs hoping to find a young flamethrower who can become a bullpen stopper.

After a shaky start, Righetti joined the league leaders in saves. He proved not only that he has the stuff to do it but, perhaps more important, that he is the stuff that heroes are made of. He was not happy, yet he did not moan and gave the team everything he had.

Righetti shelved his change-up, used his curve sparingly and came at the hitters with his 93 MPH fastball and hard slider. It was no secret what he would throw, but his fastball rises and his slider breaks sharply, making it difficult for batters to make contact even if they know what is coming.

There was a control problem and it hurt him in several games. He did not give in to the hitter, but walked many of them in key situations early in the year. Righetti admitted to lacking the "killer instinct" when he got onto the mound and usually walked or allowed a hit to the first batter.

He was not used every day earlier in the season because no one knew how well his arm would stand up, and NO ONE wanted to take the chance. He still throws the same way he did as when he was a starter, three-quarters, and has that same motion that deceives so many hitters. He throws almost effortlessly, particularly from a windup, but the ball explodes as it nears the plate.

Location is a bit of a problem for him, and some hitters can just poke at the pitch when it appears on the outside corner or beat him with bloops to the opposite field.

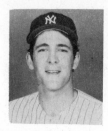

DAVE RIGHETTI
LHP, No. 19
LL, 6'3", 198 lbs.
ML Svc: 5 years
Born: 11-29-58 in
   San Jose, CA

1984 STATISTICS												
W	L	ERA	G	GS	CG	IP	H	R	ER	BB	SO	SV
5	6	2.34	64	0	0	96	79	29	25	37	90	31

CAREER STATISTICS												
W	L	ERA	G	GS	CG	IP	H	R	ER	BB	SO	SV
38	29	3.15	146	76	13	618	513	245	216	260	524	32

FIELDING:

Dave is a better than average fielder with a good move to first. He actually has two moves: one is the standard lefty move; in the other, he steps quickly off the rubber and flips the ball to first using only his arm. No other part of his body moves. It is very effective. However, because Righetti now comes into games with such a specific role, that is, to get the hitter, he can lose track of the baserunners.

OVERALL:

Righetti would love to be a starter, but understands his new role and will stay in the pen.

Robinson: "At first, I did not like the move the Yankees made with Dave. But the more you look at it, well, it has to be the best move they made all year. He had an outstanding season. When you consider the importance of a Righetti or Hernandez of the Tigers in the bullpen, you can easily see why a manager would want one of them before he'd take a 20-game winner."

PITCHING:

Toward the end of the 1984 season, a reporter asked lefty starter/reliever Bob Shirley if there were any good points about his 1984 season. "Yes," he said, "I was the only pitcher who stayed healthy all year. I must be the most valuable pitcher around here. They have been saving me for two years. I wonder what for?"

It was the truth. Shirley was supposed to be in the starting rotation with Billy Martin's 1983 Yankees, fell into disfavor and was thereafter placed in virtual mothballs. In 1984, he knew he would be in the bullpen, considering the additions of Montefusco and Niekro, but the Dave Righetti move to the bullpen left Bob in no-man's land. He was the "designated pitcher." He never really knew what his job was or how to prepare for it.

He pitches quickly with a short, compact windup and delivery. He hides the ball well from batters. His fastball is live and moves. Shirley uses it well when he mixes it with his short, snappy slider and overhand curve. He uses the latter two pitches as his out pitches to lefthanded hitters, and will throw the fastball up and away to righties when ahead in the count.

He keeps the ball low with men on base, but gets hurt when a lack of pitching time sees him lose his control and location. He must pitch regularly to be effective, and when used in several long relief spots late in the year, performed well.

FIELDING:

Shirley is a good fielder with a perfect follow-through after his release.

BOB SHIRLEY
LHP, No. 29
RL, 6'1", 185 lbs.
ML Svc: 8 years
Born: 6-25-54 in
Cushing, OK

1984 STATISTICS												
W	L	ERA	G	GS	CG	IP	H	R	ER	BB	SO	SV
3	3	3.38	41	7	1	114	119	47	43	38	48	0

CAREER STATISTICS												
W	L	ERA	G	GS	CG	IP	H	R	ER	BB	SO	SV
61	85	3.74	332	147	14	1175	1175	563	488	455	658	13

He is very much like a little lefthander of years ago, Bobby Shantz, and is quick off the mound when fielding bunts and choppers. He has a "balk" move to first, but is rarely called on it. As a result, he picks off more than his share of runers and keeps potential basestealers very close to the bag. He covers first base on grounders to the right side as well as most pitchers.

OVERALL:

He has been around and does not let adversity bother him. He has pitched and won crucial games in the past, but in 1984, was used in games that were either already won or lost when he appeared on the scene.

Robinson: "I think he'd rather be a starter, but he is used in all kinds of situations. We've probably seen his best. He's a .500 pitcher who can help a team if used properly, but it appears he'll be number eight or nine on a ten-man staff."

HITTING:

With the exception of Dave Kingman, Dave Winfield has the widest stance in baseball. At 6'6", Winfield is a menacing figure, and in 1984 it was a unanimous opinion that no one in baseball hit harder line drives than Winfield.

His weaknesses remain the same: righthanded pitchers feed him a steady diet of curves, low and away, and occasionally try to bust the fastball up and in. Lefthanders try slow curves on the outside corner, or hard sliders down and in.

Winfield had a fantastic year because the Yankees started putting men on base in front of him and pitchers could not take the chance of walking him or pitching around him. In addition, he had at least 20 hits when he simply threw his bat at an outside pitch and dumped the ball into the outfield.

His high batting average came about because he had already proved that he could hit homers in Yankee Stadium and did not have to prove it again. He decided to go for average--and he did. He hit near .350 in all types of situations. Had he begun the season a little quicker at home plate, he might have made a serious run for the Triple Crown. As he raised his average from .270 to .370 (before tailing off a bit), Dave hit everything pitched to him, to every field, and hustled out many ground balls that became hits instead of outs.

BASERUNNING:

He does not get a good jump out of the box because his hard swing leaves his weight shifting away from home plate. When he gets in gear, he can be rated with the fastest players in the game. Two bases are always his goal when he is on first or second. He will slide hard into any base and breaks up many potential double plays. Infielders do not relish tangling with him.

DAVE WINFIELD
RF, No. 31
RR, 6'6", 220 lbs.
ML Svc: 12 years
Born: 10-3-51 in St. Paul, MN

1984 STATISTICS

AVG	G	AB	R	H	2B	3B	HR	RBI	BB	SO	SB
.340	141	567	106	193	34	4	19	100	53	71	6

CAREER STATISTICS

AVG	G	AB	R	H	2B	3B	HR	RBI	BB	SO	SB
.289	1655	6089	940	1761	288	60	255	1016	662	838	170

  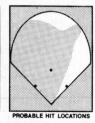

STRONG   STRONG   VS. RHP   VS. LHP   PROBABLE HIT LOCATIONS

FIELDING:

He was the best left fielder the Yankees had had in many years. He is their best center fielder, but found his rightful place in right field over the past two years. He catches everything in sight, can leap over fences, gets an excellent jump on balls hit either way, and when he doesn't get a good jump, he simply outruns balls. His height is a tremendous asset on balls hit over his head. Very few runners challenged him in 1984: his arm must be rated as the best in the American League.

OVERALL:

Brash, cocky, arrogant and highly paid . . . and why not, he is arguably the best overall player in the AL.

Robinson: "I've always said that he is the best player on the team. He plays excellent defense, hustles, hits and does it all. He does not strike out much for such an aggressive hitter. What more can they expect from him?"

HITTING:

Wynegar seems to have finally won the full-time catching job for the Yankees. His ability to catch Niekro's knuckler and his own switch-hitting were big factors in his three-year battle with Rick Cerone.

He now bats virtually the same way from either side of the plate, from a slight crouch and in a slightly open manner. His lefthanded stance resembles that of George Brett, with his weight back and bat held near shoulder level. He has an excellent batting eye when batting lefthanded and hits with more power from the left side, but hits for a better average from the right side.

He is a better high ball hitter than low ball hitter either way, and with men on base pitchers will keep the ball low because he is always a threat to hit into double plays because of his lack of speed. Pitchers will try hard stuff away or try to slip a low slider in on his hands, then use an off-speed pitch to get him to swing while off balance. He is a much better fastball hitter left-handed and has the power to reach the seats, but is more of a gap hitter that way. He loses many extra-base hits because he cannot run, and will settle for a single on a ball hit either down the right field line or in the right-center gap.

If he gets his pitch with men on base, he is a tough out. He did, however, hit much better with men on in 1983 than he did in 1984.

BASERUNNING:

He can be ignored when on base, will never steal and will rarely take the extra base. He is the second slowest runner in the league, a close photo finish with Willie Aikens.

FIELDING:

He is the best--or close to it--low ball catcher in the league and has

BUTCH WYNEGAR
C, No. 27
SR, 6'0", 194 lbs.
ML Svc: 9 years
Born: 3-14-56 in
York, PA

1984 STATISTICS

AVG	G	AB	R	H	2B	3B	HR	RBI	BB	SO	SB
.267	129	442	48	118	13	1	6	45	64	36	1

CAREER STATISTICS

AVG	G	AB	R	H	2B	3B	HR	RBI	BB	SO	SB
.261	1080	3680	440	960	151	13	52	432	514	345	10

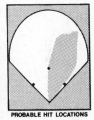

VS. RHP   VS. LHP   PROBABLE HIT LOCATIONS

proved he can handle knucklers. He also calls a much better game now. He has learned to go with a pitcher's strength. Niekro credited him with calling for sliders and curves when opposing batters expected knucklers, and he worked well with the aging master.

He has a quick release and can be expected to throw out runners with ease if pitchers keep the runners close. His throws to third are extraordinarily accurate. He still tends to avoid collisions at home plate when handling throws from the outfield, but is not afraid to block the plate if the ball reaches him in time.

OVERALL:

He is injury-prone, and for that reason, the Yankees enjoyed the luxury of having Rick Cerone on the same team.

Robinson: "He beat out Cerone because he did the things he's always done--be steady behind the plate and have a good eye at bat. He is tough with men on base and is a good, consistent player."

MIKE ARMSTRONG
RHP, No. 36
RR, 6'3", 206 lbs.
ML Svc: 4 years
Born: 3-7-54 in
Glen Cove, NY

PITCHING:

Mike Armstrong did very little pitching for New York in 1984. He hurt his elbow in spring training and was lost to the team for half the year. When he came back, he found that the bullpen job of long relief and spot pitcher to righties had gone to Jay Howell.

He is a power pitcher who drops from three-quarters to sidearm against righty batters and is very effective when healthy. He uses a sinking fastball and hard slider. He has been working on a forkball to give him an off-speed pitch.

Armstrong usually throws hard to right or lefthanded hitters. When he gets ahead in the count, he can be very tough on righthanders because of his delivery. Against lefties, he will throw the slider low and away or low and in, but he must be careful to stay ahead in the count and not get his pitches high in the strike zone.

His elbow problems seemed behind him when he returned to pitch, but he now feels that he must rehabilitate his entire body in order to stay free from injuries and prove effective in 1985.

He has a big motion toward the plate and runners will try to steal on him. His follow-through tends to leave him off balance. Balls hit back through the middle may get past him because he is not in position to knock them down.

OVERALL:

Young Yankee arms like Kelly Faulk and Clay Christiansen are being touted for this season as bullpen righthanders. Armstrong must rebound and stay healthy, or he is in trouble.

REX HUDLER
2B, No. 56
RR, 6'1", 180 lbs.
Born: 9-2-60 in
Tempe, AZ

HITTING, BASERUNNING, FIELDING:

In the words of one Yankee official, "It took him six years to grow up, but now that he has, he is the best second baseman in baseball."

That player is Rex Hudler, New York's number one pick in the 1978 draft. Most observers claim that Hudler is indeed the best defensive second baseman in the minors, and might be better than most in the majors. National Leaguers will of course disagree, but Hudler's ability to turn the double play, his strong arm and his excellent range make him the logical choice to be the next Yankee second baseman when and if Willie Randolph is through.

He has a square stance, slight crouch with the bat held high. He will hit to right field more than most righty batters. He has little power, but after his six-year maturation process Hudler managed to hit better than .300 for the past two years with the Triple A team.

Hudler has good speed and stretches ordinary singles into doubles. He will also steal a base any time he is given the green light.

OVERALL:

Like many Yankees, he has paid his dues and now at the age of 24, Hudler has his chance not only to make the Yankees but to make it with five of his ex-teammates in the minors.

VIC MATA
OF, No. 24
RR, 6'1", 165 lbs.
Born: 1-6-64 in
　Harbor City, CA

HITTING, BASERUNNING, FIELDING:

Everybody asked, "Where did he come from?" when the New York Yankees brought up center fielder Vic Mata from the minors in July. The 24-year-old Mata had already played six and a half years in the Yankee minor league system: he was a stranger to the fans, not to the organization.

Mata bats from a straight-up stance and has a very quick bat. He can hit for power when he gets a fastball on the inside corner, and can manage to put his bat on the curveball. He hit .500 in his first 32 Yankee Stadium at-bats, including his first major league home run in August. A hand injury suffered in a melee with the Angels sidelined him for much of September, but the Yankees know he can hit major league pitching.

He does not have excellent speed, but is a good bunter with a good jump from the batter's box. He will bunt in any situation imaginable.

Mata's strength is his outfield play. He gets an excellent jump on balls hit in the gap, and comes in or goes back with ease. He has a strong arm, but one that is not as accurate as it should be. On throws to third, he sometimes throws directly into the sliding runner.

OVERALL:

When he was in the minors, he was told "to hustle or else." He responded in spring training of 1984, played outstanding baseball with the Clippers and impressed the Yanks.

DALE MURRAY
RHP, No. 48
RR, 6'4", 205 lbs.
ML Svc: 9 years
Born: 2-2-50 in
　Cuero, TX

PITCHING:

Dale Murray has been itching to pitch for the past two years, but a bad back caused by a sciatic condition has disabled him constantly. The Yankees acquired Murray from the Blue Jays after the 1982 season because he was the best short relief man in the Jays bullpen and had always been effective against the Yankees.

At his best, Murray throws a hard slider and effective sinker. He keeps both pitches low and away and is a tough pitcher to hit homers off. But the move to New York bothered him both mentally and physically, and he was never able to be the man the team needed to get out tough righty batters. A lot of his problems stemmed from spring training of 1983, when then-manager Billy Martin used him to pitch four innings in an exhibition game. Murray was hurt shortly thereafter and was lost for most of 1983. Injuries again plagued him in 1984, despite his short stints of appearing very effective.

He pitches from the stretch with or without men on base, has an extremely quick release and can be effective when he keeps his two pitches down.

A lack of pitching time saw him get his pitches up where they could be hit. The team brought him along slowly after his rehabilitation program in July.

OVERALL:

Murray would like to go out a winner, does not grumble or cry, but simply cannot help the team when hurt. He embarked on a strenuous body strengthening program in the 1984-85 off season in hopes that he may earn his salary and help the team.

OAKLAND A'S

HITTING:

Bill Almon abandoned his crouched stance four years ago and has been hitting with a straight-up style ever since. He likes the fastball up and over the plate, which is hardly unusual. Righthanders try to work him low and away with breaking pitches, while left-handers usually have good luck pitching him down and in. Teams play him slightly to pull, a strategy he will occasionally defy by going to right field.

Almon seems to be going for more power as he nears the final stages of his career. Traditionally when he drove the ball, it was for doubles up the alley. But in 1984, despite his lowest at-bat total in four years, he set a personal high with seven homers. Almon is a notorious streak hitter, and it's wise to let him play until he cools off. He can play first base, second base, shortstop or the outfield for short periods of time without hurting the team.

Almon is a good situation player in that he'll bunt the ball or play the hit-and-run with dexterity. If he had a problem last season, with so few opportunities, it was that he became impatient at the plate and was vulnerable to pitches that he could previously drive.

BASERUNNING:

Almon was used as a pinch-runner in the wake of his surprisingly strong 1983 season (26 steals, including 20 in his first 25 attempts), but he may be slowing down a little. Although he is an intelligent baserunner, Almon stole just six bases and was caught six times. He plays it aggressively when breaking up the double play.

FIELDING:

Erratic defense has kept Almon from

BILL ALMON
INF, No. 34
RR, 6'3", 190 lbs.
ML Svc: 8 years
Born: 11-21-52 in Providence, RI

1984 STATISTICS

AVG	G	AB	R	H	2B	3B	HR	RBI	BB	SO	SB
.223	105	211	24	47	11	0	7	16	10	42	6

CAREER STATISTICS

AVG	G	AB	R	H	2B	3B	HR	RBI	BB	SO	SB
.257	957	2790	314	717	108	23	23	239	186	505	107

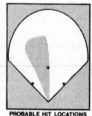

VS. RHP   VS. LHP   PROBABLE HIT LOCATIONS

being one of the game's better middle infielders--so much so that he rarely gets a chance at shortstop or second base. His strong suits now are the outfield, where he is fundamentally sound in all phases, and first base.

OVERALL:

Almon will never be the player he was expected to be out of college: he was the nation's No. 1 draft pick out of Brown University in 1974--but he has established himself as one of the top utility players in baseball. A down season in 1984 hasn't tarnished his fine reputation.

Matthews: "Almon is a guy who has always done a lot of things pretty well, and he has the proper temperament for bench roles. I think any team would like to have him."

PITCHING:

Keith Atherton entered the 1984 season with a live fastball and very little to back it up. The result was a disappointing year that erased the memory of his fine rookie showing.

As an unknown quantity in 1983, Keith rolled up some quality numbers, including a 2.78 ERA. That was before the AL got to know him. Last year he gave up an alarming number of home runs—six of them during one four-inning stretch—and became an inviting target.

Atherton is a power pitcher who uses a three-quarters delivery, occasionally throwing sidearm. His fastball has been clocked around 92 MPH, making him effective against righthanded hitters, but he has yet to develop the sharp-breaking slider or off-speed pitch he needs to get lefthanders out. Reports also indicate that his fastball lacks movement, that it comes in too straight. His slider is only average, and he doesn't have enough confidence in his change-up to throw it all the time.

And in the end, confidence (or the lack of it) was his biggest problem. Even in a low-pressure situation—he was used as a setup man for Bill Caudill—he failed to produce consistently for the A's last year.

By mid-season, Atherton had lost his reputation as an aggressive competitor. Although he has good control and likes to challenge hitters, he tried to be too fine and often found himself behind in the count. The A's wanted to see him "bust" more hitters inside, then work

KEITH ATHERTON
RHP, No. 55
RR, 6'4", 200 lbs.
ML Svc: 2 years
Born: 3-20-54 in
Newport News, VA

1984 STATISTICS

W	L	ERA	G	GS	CG	IP	H	R	ER	BB	SO	SV
7	6	4.33	57	0	0	104	110	51	50	39	58	2

CAREER STATISTICS

W	L	ERA	G	GS	CG	IP	H	R	ER	BB	SO	SV
9	11	3.72	86	0	0	172	163	73	71	62	98	6

the outside corners to keep them off balance.

FIELDING:

Atherton handles his position well. He is quick on plays in front of him, seldom makes an errant throw and has an above average pickoff move to first.

OVERALL:

Atherton doesn't have the Lee Smith-type of fastball and can't make a living on what he does have. Until he adds a little variety to his repertoire, he'll find it tough in the big leagues.

Matthews: "You hate to see a control pitcher get behind the hitters; it does not speak well for a guy's character. Atherton has the ability, but it takes hard work, too."

HITTING:

Bruce Bochte took a one-year break from the game in 1983, and it showed at the plate when he returned from his "retirement" last season. Although he solidified his reputation as a contact hitter, he never had an extended hot streak and became a master of the one-for-four game.

Bochte's style, however, has not changed. He is still a slashing, yet patient, hitter with no clear weakness, able to drive any pitch in any location. Defenses generally play him honestly, giving him credit as a line drive hitter who uses the entire ballpark. He hits righthanders consistently well, but has problems against lefthanders with sweeping, sharp-breaking curveballs. He hit just .241 against lefties and was platooned at first base much of the year.

Batting out of a crouch, Bochte is an intelligent hitter who will take two or three pitches in order to be able to sit on the one he wants. He seldom bunts because of his lack of speed, but is a valuable hit-and-run man with his ability to place the ball. Occasionally he will jump on an inside fastball and hit it out of the park.

BASERUNNING:

Bochte is a fine natural athlete (he played basketball in college), but despite his strong and lean build, he's one of the slowest runners in either league. To compound his problems, his fierce swing finds him lurching toward the catcher on his follow-through, slowing his baserunning time to first base. He is definitely not a threat to steal.

FIELDING:

Although he looks awkward at times,

BRUCE BOCHTE
1B, No. 20
LL, 6'3", 200 lbs.
ML Svc: 9 years
Born: 11-12-50 in
Pasadena, CA

1984 STATISTICS

AVG	G	AB	R	H	2B	3B	HR	RBI	BB	SO	SB
.264	148	469	58	124	23	0	5	52	52	59	2

CAREER STATISTICS

AVG	G	AB	R	H	2B	3B	HR	RBI	BB	SO	SB
.284	1276	4402	538	1249	220	19	80	555	539	536	37

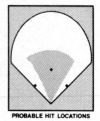

VS. RHP   VS. LHP   PROBABLE HIT LOCATIONS

Bochte is an accomplished first baseman at playing tough hops on well-hit balls. Range is a problem on balls hit to either his left or right, and his throwing --only average at best--has been hampered by shoulder problems.

OVERALL:

He has always been a thinking-man's type of player who places the team ahead of salaries or personal goals. Although he still feels that baseball's business side has made it a dehumanizing game, he seems grateful to be involved again and will accept any role assigned to him.

Matthews: "With a year under his belt in this second go-round, it will be interesting to see how well he can hit in 1985. He is a very fine hitter and should be back to his .280 form."

PITCHING:

It's hard to imagine a more one-sided deal than the one Oakland pulled off in the winter of 1983. They sent a minor league outfielder named Rusty McNealy to Montreal for Ray Burris--who then became the unquestioned ace of their pitching staff.

Burris reported to camp in the best shape of his life (he's been known to do 500 sit-ups a day) and pitched superbly from start to finish. He is a control pitcher who blends finesse with power, using a wide variety of pitches to outsmart the hitters in crucial situations. Opponents batted just .244 against him last year, as his hits-per-inning ratio would indicate.

Although his basic delivery is three-quarters, Burris will come sidearm or over-the-top to keep the hitters off balance. He has a conventional fastball, around 88 MPH, and a cut fastball that he turns over against lefthanded hitters. His slider and change-up are both rated above average, and he mixes his pitches beautifully.

Burris is a first-rate competitor. At times, it seems he's more comfortable with two runners on and nobody out, just for the sheer enjoyment of meeting a challenge. He tends to throw a lot of pitches and sweats profusely (he wears long sleeves even in the hottest weather), but he's invariably good for seven strong innings, if not more.

FIELDING:

Burris is quick off the mound and

RAY BURRIS
RHP, No. 48
RR, 6'5", 210 lbs.
ML Svc: 11 years
Born: 8-22-50 in
   Idabel, OK

1984 STATISTICS
W	L	ERA	G	GS	CG	IP	H	R	ER	BB	SO	SV
13	10	3.15	34	28	5	211	193	84	74	90	93	0

CAREER STATISTICS
W	L	ERA	G	GS	CG	IP	H	R	ER	BB	SO	SV
93	114	4.04	418	262	41	1912	2003	963	858	667	942	4

handles any play that comes his way. Although he has only an average move to first base, he's persistent in keeping runners close to the bag. He doesn't like anyone taking liberties with him.

OVERALL:

Burris once said, "A pitcher's arm is like a woman. Take good care of it, and it will take care of you." That's the way he's approached his career, and look at the results--Burris seems to be getting better with age.

Matthews: "A tough guy. He just battles and battles, mixing up his pitches as well as anybody. He gives you a good effort physically and mentally, and perhaps most important, he can adapt to things. That's going to keep him in the big leagues another four or five years."

HITTING:

Indications grow stronger every season that Jeff Burroughs, once one of the most feared hitters in baseball, is near the end of the line. He has even lost his knack for pinch-hitting, his finest ability, which made him so valuable to the A's two years ago.

At his best, in the mid-1970s, he was that rarest of combinations: a man who could hit with power yet patience, with prodigious RBI production yet a respectable average. He was known for his keen batting eye and his knack for waiting on the pitch he wanted.

Last season, Burroughs often looked confused at the plate. In one stretch, he was struck out looking five straight times--three times to end the game.

Both left and righthanded pitchers change speeds on him and work the outside corner, away from his vaunted power, with considerable success.

Despite his decline, Burroughs still hasn't met a fastball he doesn't like. Batting out of a straight-up stance, he has a smooth, powerful swing that has always been rated among the purest in baseball. His bat speed and eye-hand coordination still make him a long ball threat, although it seems apparent he needs to play more often. Coming off the bench once every five nights isn't cutting it for him.

BASERUNNING:

Burroughs knows his limitations on the bases, so he seldom embarrasses himself. But he not only lacks speed, he's also been putting on weight over the years. The fact that he hasn't stolen a base in three years tells the story.

FIELDING:

Burroughs was a decent outfielder in

JEFF BURROUGHS
DH, No. 3
RR, 6'0", 200 lbs.
ML Svc: 14 years
Born: 3-7-51 in
  Long Beach, CA

1984 STATISTICS											
AVG	G	AB	R	H	2B	3B	HR	RBI	BB	SO	SB
.211	58	71	5	15	1	0	2	8	18	23	0
CAREER STATISTICS											
AVG	G	AB	R	H	2B	3B	HR	RBI	BB	SO	SB
.261	1604	5345	702	1394	221	17	234	854	97	1099	16

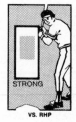  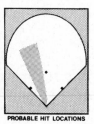

VS. RHP   VS. LHP   PROBABLE HIT LOCATIONS

his day, overcoming his lack of range with good instincts, but he's strictly a pinch-hitter/designated hitter type of player now. It's unlikely he'll be asked to start in the field again.

OVERALL:

At 34 years old, Burroughs cannot be considered finished--not with his distinguished record. But the cold facts show that Burroughs didn't produce a single homer or RBI after June 12. If he doesn't bounce back this season, who would want that kind of production?

Matthews: "It's never pleasant to see someone's skills erode. I thought Jeff would be much more effective as a pinch-hitter, but he is still good for a vintage performance every now and then."

PITCHING:

The A's knew they were getting a talented reliever in Bill Caudill, but they couldn't have forseen what he'd mean to the club. Caudill set a club record with 36 saves and became the A's first top-flight reliever since Rollie Fingers.

There is no real mystery to Caudill: everyone knows that he throws exclusively fastballs, yet he consistently holds the upper hand. It's not so much his velocity--he throws around 90 MPH, a slight dropoff from his flamethrowing days with the Chicago Cubs--but rather it is his location that gets the hitters. Caudill throws hard to spots, and that's what makes him so effective. He can make the ball sink or rise, and he will throw in a slider or a change-up just to give hitters something extra to think about.

Caudill uses a three-quarters delivery and pitches out of a stretch--even with nobody on base. Interestingly, he's only an average pitcher in a one-sided game, but he's almost unhittable with the game on the line. "That's when the adrenaline starts flowing," he says. "I kick into a different gear."

Whether he's ahead in the count or behind, Caudill sticks to his swashbuckling style. With a few exceptions--say, an Eddie Murray or a Jim Rice--he refuses to pitch around hitters, and he detests the intentional walk.

The A's were worried that Caudill was putting on too much weight last season, but he finished the season with an impressive run of nine saves in his last 11 appearances. The league hit just .218 against him for the year.

BILL CAUDILL
RHP, No. 36
RR, 6'1", 210 lbs.
ML Svc: 6 years
Born: 7-13-56 in
   Santa Monica, CA

1984 STATISTICS

W	L	ERA	G	GS	CG	IP	H	R	ER	BB	SO	SV
9	7	2.71	68	0	0	96	77	30	29	31	89	36

CAREER STATISTICS

W	L	ERA	G	GS	CG	IP	H	R	ER	BB	SO	SV
29	42	3.53	332	24	0	553	488	238	217	235	534	89

FIELDING:

Caudill is trying to improve his ability to hold runners on, but he's vulnerable in that category. He is also a bit slow to the plate, so baserunners usually challenge him. Occasionally, he will throw runners off balance by making a snap throw to first as he's coming off the stretch.

OVERALL:

Caudill is unquestionably the best power-pitching reliever in the American League, and he thrives on work. As long as he's saved for the eighth and ninth innings, he can be effective five to six days a week.

Matthews: "A pure strikeout pitcher. He just says, 'Here comes the fastball. Try to hit it.' Caudill is the type who can turn a good team into a World Series contender."

PITCHING:

When Chris Codiroli enters the clubhouse in street clothes, somebody invariably cries out, "Anyone call for a cab?" This rail-thin pitcher resembles anything but a professional athlete--until he takes the mound.

A sidearming righthander with a wicked fastball and slider, Codiroli led the A's with 12 wins as a rookie in 1983. But last season was a disaster from the beginning of spring training, when he was told that he would have to fight for a starting job. That seemed to hurt his confidence, and it was late September before he hit his stride.

Codiroli's fastball has been clocked around 89 MPH, and he's very tough on righthanded hitters. Lefthanders find him more inviting, because his slider tends to break more across the plate than down. He occasionally throws a change-up, but he has abandoned the curveball that got him into so much trouble last season. The slider **is his out pitch.**

Codiroli was demoted to the minors twice during the year, and he says he learned two things from the experience: one was to pitch more aggressively and the other was to work faster. By winning four out of his five major league decisions, Codiroli got back in the club's good graces. A lot of people think he's too thin, but he insists he's at his best that way.

FIELDING:

Codiroli is slow to the plate, but

CHRIS CODIROLI
RHP, No. 23
RR, 6'1", 160 lbs.
ML Svc: 2 years
Born: 3-26-58 in
     Oxnard, CA

1984 STATISTICS

W	L	ERA	G	GS	CG	IP	H	R	ER	BB	SO	SV
6	4	5.84	28	14	1	89	111	67	58	34	44	1

CAREER STATISTICS

W	L	ERA	G	GS	CG	IP	H	R	ER	BB	SO	SV
19	18	4.86	68	48	8	311	335	190	168	110	134	2

he has an above average pickoff move and throws to first base often. He has cut down on his tendency to make wild throws to the bases after fielding bunts or ground balls.

OVERALL:

If Codiroli can get into the third inning unscathed, he's a commanding pitcher who stays on top of the hitters. A rough start tends to shake his confidence, and when he starts to finesse the hitters, he gets into more trouble. It appears that all he needs is a set job in the rotation--a role that eluded him in 1984.

Matthews: "A lot of people like this guy. He has a chance to be a really good pitcher; it is a matter of concentration and getting his head together. The raw talent is there."

PITCHING:

Tim Conroy has always been described as a pitcher with great potential, but he may be running out of time. At 25 years old, Conroy has yet to establish himself as a consistent pitcher in the big leagues.

Talent isn't the problem. He throws a 94 MPH fastball and has a devastating curveball that, when it is on, dives sharply below the knees at the last moment. Despite Conroy's unsightly ERA, the AL hit just .235 against him last year.

On certain days, Conroy gets by on sheer "heat." He pitched an eight-inning one-hitter against Texas one afternoon, throwing 95% fastballs. But such performances are exceptions; Conroy's curve is wildly erratic, and he becomes a different pitcher, not nearly as aggressive, when he can't get it over.

Over the last two years, he has probably led the league in one-bounce curveballs off the catcher's shinguards.

The A's spent all of last season debating Conroy's role. He was given three shots at the starting rotation, each time losing out because of inconsistency. Most people see Conroy as a dominant short reliever in time, but it won't happen until he finds his control.

FIELDING:

Conroy is only an average fielder, perhaps due to his occasional lapses of concentration. He doesn't have a particularly good move to first base, although

TIM CONROY
LHP, No. 24
LL, 6'1", 185 lbs.
ML Svc: 2 years
Born: 4-3-60 in
 Monroeville, PA

1984 STATISTICS

W	L	ERA	G	GS	CG	IP	H	R	ER	BB	SO	SV
1	6	5.32	38	14	0	93	82	58	55	63	69	0

CAREER STATISTICS

W	L	ERA	G	GS	CG	IP	H	R	ER	BB	SO	SV
10	18	4.42	84	39	4	285	256	166	140	188	198	0

he can be effective with a snap-throw from the hip.

OVERALL:

Conroy will be in the big leagues as long as he can throw that world-class fastball, but one wonders if his career was ruined by Charlie Finley. The A's owner called him up directly out of high school in 1978, an experience that destroyed his confidence.

Matthews: "Conroy might become one of those 'What might have been' cases. His career went backward because he had been in the majors before he ever saw a minor league mound, and he's been fighting his way back ever since. People haven't given up on him as a front-line starter, but this will be a critical year."

HITTING:

The second-year jinx struck Mike Davis in a big way last season, to the point where it baffled everyone--fans, writers, the Oakland management and scouts all over baseball. Mike Davis was simply too talented to be that bad--but he was, hitting around .200 most of the season and in the .175 range with runners in scoring position.

Oddly enough, the pressure should have been off him last year. After hitting a solid .275 in 1983 in the demanding role of batting behind speedster Rickey Henderson, Davis was dropped to sixth in the order. But, as some scouts have pointed out, Davis saw more fastballs behind Henderson, from pitchers trying to get the ball home as soon as possible. In his new role, Davis saw an array of off-speed and breaking pitches and never adjusted; by mid-season, his confidence was shot.

Davis is still known as a dead fastball, first ball hitter. There are those who believe his stance (very closed, with his knees bent) needs adjusting, and he definitely needs work on handling the low and away curveball from left-handed pitchers. He became a defensive hitter last season instead of the aggressive, slashing type he'd been the previous season. Because he is quick, powerful and just 25 years old, most people expect him to bounce back.

BASERUNNING:

For an athlete so gifted, Davis had the basestealing statistics (14 for 23) of an ordinary player. He has good speed out of the box and kicks into a higher gear from first to third, but has yet to grasp the nuances of baserunning. He made some key mistakes last season and showed he hadn't learned the pickoff moves of opposing pitchers. He is only adequate in breaking up the double play.

MIKE DAVIS
RF, No. 16
LL, 6'3", 185 lbs.
ML Svc: 3 years
Born: 6-11-59 in
  San Diego, CA

1984 STATISTICS

AVG	G	AB	R	H	2B	3B	HR	RBI	BB	SO	SB
.230	134	382	47	88	18	3	9	46	31	66	14

CAREER STATISTICS

AVG	G	AB	R	H	2B	3B	HR	RBI	BB	SO	SB
.257	353	1015	131	261	49	8	19	126	69	166	52

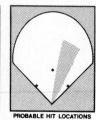

VS. RHP   VS. LHP   PROBABLE HIT LOCATIONS

FIELDING:

Davis's 1984 season was so dismal that it eventually affected his fielding. He made an alarming 12 errors and had trouble establishing the proper angle on cutting off balls in the alley. Still, Davis has Gold Glove potential in the outfield. He runs, charges ground balls and throws with the best.

OVERALL:

This is a critical year for Davis. He has been known as a player with the tools of an All Star, but now he has to prove it.

Matthews: "When you've got a guy this good, a bad season has to be a matter of mental attitude and concentration. Chalk it up as an off-year, and start over again."

HITTING:

Mike Heath's style has changed drastically over the last two years. Once a dead pull hitter who left himself vulnerable to the low and away pitches, he has adopted an off-field stroke under the tutelage of Carney Lansford.

On occasion, it works. Heath is much more adept at the hit-and-run and he can drive the ball with authority to right-center field. But his new stroke is a one-armed effort that leaves him in an awkward follow-through, his bat pointing straight into the air. One scout called it "the worst-looking swing in America. There's no way it has to be that exaggerted."

Aesthetics aside, Heath has become a more complete hitter, still capable of ripping the fastball down the left field line or out of the park. He is hitting the long ball more consistently than ever (his 13 homers and 64 RBIs were personal highs). He is also an accomplished bunter. One glaring statistic: he hit .309 against lefthanded pitching but just .213 against righthanders. Despite his new style, he still has trouble with breaking balls on the outside corner.

BASERUNNING:

Heath runs better and more aggressively than most catchers in baseball, an extension of his all-out style of play. But, curiously, Heath has a habit of not running out routine ground balls. He claims that needless hard running is a risk to his lower back (a recurring injury), but the Oakland management needed a better answer: he was benched for a spell last year for not running them out.

FIELDING:

With his strong arm and quick re-

MIKE HEATH
C, No. 2
RR, 5'11", 190 lbs.
ML Svc: 5 years
Born: 2-5-55 in
Tampa, FL

1984 STATISTICS

AVG	G	AB	R	H	2B	3B	HR	RBI	BB	SO	SB
.248	140	475	49	118	21	5	13	64	26	72	7

CAREER STATISTICS

AVG	G	AB	R	H	2B	3B	HR	RBI	BB	SO	SB
.250	620	2094	215	524	84	13	34	234	121	261	25

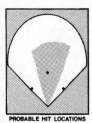

STRONG
VS. RHP

STRONG
VS. LHP

PROBABLE HIT LOCATIONS

lease Heath is challenged only by the best basestealers. He is extremely agile around the plate, which helps him on bunts and popups, and he blocks the ball well. Aggressive and intense, he will stand up to anyone as he blocks the plate. If he has a weakness, it might be his temper. Although he calls a smart game, not all pitchers find him easy to work with.

OVERALL:

He may not be the perfect ballplayer, but he brings a refreshing blend of talent and aggressiveness to the game.

Matthews: "There aren't many catchers who can bunt, steal, play the hit-and-run and throw people out the way Heath can. He has to be regarded among the best in the league."

HITTING:

Rickey Henderson has reached a pivotal point in his career. With his amazing raw ability, he can, with very little effort, continue to be a top-flight player. But Henderson's motivation has come under question, and there are those who wonder if he will ever fulfill his staggering potential.

Pitchers have found that Henderson has few weaknesses as a hitter, so intimidation has become a familiar weapon. Henderson aggravates pitchers with his deep-crouch stance and tendency to argue calls, and he's seeing more and more fastballs around the chin. That sets him up for the sharp breaking balls away, and when Rickey isn't fully concentrating, that's the way to get him out.

At his best, though, Henderson is a marvel. Whether it's an inside fastball or a hanging curve, he'll drive the ball (occasionally up to 420 feet) with his surprising power. But because he is so conscious of hitting the ball to all fields, he has the discipline to wait on outside pitches, even the best ones, and drive them to right field. He has a keen batting eye and always ranks near the top in walks.

Henderson was told to hit for more power at the beginning of last season and it confused him. Around June, given the freedom to hit his own way, he became the type of all-around hitter everyone recognized from past years.

BASERUNNING:

Henderson rarely takes the time to study pitchers' moves, and he still gets picked off too often by lefthanders-- even those with ordinary moves. Despite it all, he's the unquestioned king of the basestealers, a tribute to his sheer confidence and speed. He also steals third base more often than anybody. When he is healthy and has a patient No. 2 hitter behind him, Henderson is almost a cinch for 100-plus steals.

RICKEY HENDERSON
OF, No. 35
RL, 5'10", 195 lbs.
ML Svc: 6 years
Born: 12-25-58 in
  Chicago, IL

1984 STATISTICS
AVG	G	AB	R	H	2B	3B	HR	RBI	BB	SO	SB
.293	142	502	113	147	27	4	16	58	86	81	66

CAREER STATISTICS
AVG	G	AB	R	H	2B	3B	HR	RBI	BB	SO	SB
.291	791	2916	586	850	129	29	51	271	520	416	493

  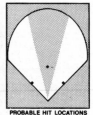

STRONG · VS. RHP   STRONG · VS. LHP   PROBABLE HIT LOCATIONS

FIELDING:

No left fielder covers more ground, and though Henderson's hands aren't the softest around, he's good for several spectacular catches a year. Thanks to hard work, his footwork and mechanics are excellent. Shoulder problems have reduced his throwing from excellent to average.

OVERALL:

Watching Henderson over the last two years, the A's were convinced he didn't always put out to the maximum. Even below par, Henderson has star ability--but he's capable of so much more.

Matthews: "When he applies himself and has his total concentration, he is one of the most dominant offensive forces in baseball. I can't imagine a more perfect leadoff man."

HITTING:

Before the 1984 season even started, Donnie Hill had problems with his right eye (a corneal abrasion) and his throwing arm. That set the tone for a disappointing year that left the young shortstop's career in doubt.

Like many switch-hitters, Hill has two different styles. Lefthanded, he likes the ball low and has a tendency to pull. Pitchers throw him fastballs up and curveballs away. Righthanded, he likes the fastball up and uses the whole field, but hasn't come close to establishing himself (.146 righthanded last year compared to .262 lefthanded). Pitchers are not afraid to challenge him because he seldom hits for the extra base, let alone the home run.

Either way, Hill is a first ball, fastball hitter. He is aggressive and it is always an event when he walks or strikes out (in one stretch last year, he went seven weeks between walks). He needs to hit the breaking balls and offspeed pitches more often to convince people that he is ready for the big leagues. He handles himself well on the hit-and-run but seldom bunts.

BASERUNNING:

The consensus on Hill is that he's more of an athlete than a student of the game. Reports say his mind tends to wander and that his concentration is not what it should be. This is borne out by his basestealing numbers (two attempts, one steal), a regrettable record in light of the fact that he has above average speed. He cannot be counted on to break up the double play with hustle.

FIELDING:

Hill is a fluid, graceful shortstop

DON HILL
SS, No. 25
SR, 5'10", 160 lbs.
ML Svc: 2 years
Born: 11-12-60 in
     Pomona, CA

1984 STATISTICS
AVG	G	AB	R	H	2B	3B	HR	RBI	BB	SO	SB
.230	73	174	21	40	6	0	2	16	5	12	1

CAREER STATISTICS
AVG	G	AB	R	H	2B	3B	HR	RBI	BB	SO	SB
.247	126	332	41	82	13	0	4	31	9	33	2

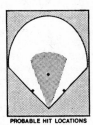

VS. RHP   VS. LHP   PROBABLE HIT LOCATIONS

with good range, especially to his right side. He has sure hands and a strong, accurate arm when healthy (he expects to enter the 1985 season at full strength). But again, concentration is a problem. Hill has very little idea of the opposing hitters' tendencies, and he found there was much to learn from the sagacious Joe Morgan, his infield partner in Oakland last year.

OVERALL:

Matthews: "He's more of a steady player than a spectacular one. So far, he hasn't appeared ready to be a full-time player--and he certainly had the opportunity in Oakland. This will be an important season for him."

HITTING:

The sporting public saw Dave Kingman at his finest last year. He was hungry: the A's were the only team to offer him a contract--and he became a more disciplined hitter than ever before. Remarkably, he never went more than two games without a hit until early September. He also played from June 12 on with a torn ligament in his left knee, an injury that required a brace for support.

Not that Kingman has turned into Rod Carew. He is still a free, powerful swinger and a dead pull hitter, which leaves him vulnerable to anything on the outside corner. Righthanders continue to get him out with curveballs, but they had better be good ones; Kingman is a notorious mistake hitter who can drive any pitch when he gets his arms extended. Similarly, any pitcher throwing a fastball would be advised to get it inside--way inside.

Kingman didn't hit a single home run to right field last season. Not surprisingly, teams played him to pull, and some used an exaggerated shift with three infielders on the left side. He gets most of his power on low or waist-high pitches, so a high fastball will work if it is timed correctly. If there was any change in Kingman's style last year, it was that he often abandoned his power stroke to simply make contact for base hits. That showed up in his average, which was in the .275-.280 range much of the year.

BASERUNNING:

Kingman may look awkward, but he's a hustling, intelligent baserunner who seldom gets caught in the wrong place. Even last year, with his tender knee, he stole two bases when teams failed to hold him on first. He will also run hard to break up the double play.

DAVE KINGMAN
DH, No. 10
RR, 6'6", 215 lbs.
ML Svc: 13 years
Born: 12-21-48 in Pendleton, OR

1984 STATISTICS

AVG	G	AB	R	H	2B	3B	HR	RBI	BB	SO	SB
.268	147	549	68	147	23	1	35	118	44	119	2

CAREER STATISTICS

AVG	G	AB	R	H	2B	3B	HR	RBI	BB	SO	SB
.237	1639	5544	765	1316	205	25	377	1025	513	1576	79

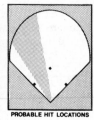

VS. RHP   VS. LHP   PROBABLE HIT LOCATIONS

FIELDING:

Kingman readily admits that the DH is perfect for him. Playing the outfield only subjects him to mistakes that hurt the team and the inevitable abuse from the fans. He can throw--some remember Kingman as an intimidating pitcher at USC--and he can play first base in a pinch, but all things considered, he shouldn't be playing the field.

OVERALL:

Matthews: "He doesn't have the greatest reputation, but Kingman keeps his head in the game and does extreme damage when he's hot. He's the type of player who can carry a team for three weeks at a time."

PITCHING:

Bill Krueger is still trying to come back from a fateful night in June of 1983 in Arlington, Texas. That's when he tore a muscle in his forearm, ruining a season that had him contending for Rookie of the Year.

Krueger was decidedly tentative last spring, concerned about throwing too hard and re-injuring his arm: he spent the first month in the Pacific Coast League. Although he eventually became a regular member of the A's rotation, he was painfully erratic and failed to convince anyone he had made it all the way back.

Krueger is an outstanding athlete who played basketball at Portland State and didn't start pitching until his junior year. He pitches with a smooth, over-the-top motion and has all the basic pitches: a fastball (around 87 MPH), a curveball that breaks straight down when it's on, and a straight change-up. His cut fastball, a trademark of the Oakland pitchers, is inconsistent but can be an effective pitch breaking away from righthanded hitters. Because he is not overpowering, Krueger needs to have at least two pitches working to get past the early innings.

The A's feel that Krueger, an earnest and conscientious type, sometimes worries too much for his own good. They would like to see him become more of a competitive pitcher because he has the stuff to be dominant.

FIELDING:

Krueger is a hard worker and a good

BILL KRUEGER
LHP, No. 32
LL, 6'5", 205 lbs.
ML Svc: 2 years
Born: 4-24-58 in
McMinnville, OR

1984 STATISTICS
W	L	ERA	G	GS	CG	IP	H	R	ER	BB	SO	SV
10	10	4.75	26	24	1	142	156	95	75	85	61	0

CAREER STATISTICS
W	L	ERA	G	GS	CG	IP	H	R	ER	BB	SO	SV
17	16	4.25	43	40	3	252	260	149	119	138	119	0

fielder, but he has difficulty holding runners on. Manager Jackie Moore admitted that the word is out on this weakness, and Krueger was sent to the Instructional League to work on it.

OVERALL:

Krueger has the physical makeup of a front-line starter in the big leagues. If he develops mental toughness to go with it, the A's will have a valuable property.

Matthews: "You have to be impressed just watching a good athlete like Bill, but he hasn't tapped his potential. That is pretty much the story of all the young Oakland pitchers."

HITTING:

The 1984 season was a struggle for Carney Lansford, particularly the first half, but like the professional hitter he is, Lansford finished at an even .300 --the fourth straight year he's reached or cleared that figure.

Lansford's biggest problem was hitting fourth or fifth in the order and being expected to drive in runs. He admitted being uncomfortable in that role, and when he took over the A's cleanup spot due to Dave Kingman's injury, he was woefully inadequate with runners in scoring position.

By late summer, Lansford was batting second behind Rickey Henderson and enjoying the role. He's more of a spray hitter than a long ball threat and is able to hit line drives to any spot in the ballpark. Opposing pitchers speak highly of Lansford and his discipline; while other hitters are being mowed down by tough curveballs, Lansford waits on the pitch and drives it with authority.

Although Lansford hits well to the opposite field, he uses a one-armed stroke on outside pitches and occasionally looks bad. There were reports that he wasn't as patient at the plate as always, and his strikeout total (62) was his highest in four years. Still, he is known as one of the league's toughest hitters, an honor he should uphold for years to come.

BASERUNNING:

After a one-sided victory that featured one of his better hitting performances, Lansford was seen muttering to himself because he'd been thrown out at home plate. That's how seriously he takes his baserunning. Although he does not run particularly well and seldom steals, he has a knack for the daring and the unexpected. He'll also go out of his way to break up a double play.

CARNEY LANSFORD
3B, No. 4
RR, 6'2", 195 lbs.
ML Svc: 7 years
Born: 2-7-57 in
San Jose, CA

1984 STATISTICS

AVG	G	AB	R	H	2B	3B	HR	RBI	BB	SO	SB
.300	151	597	70	179	31	5	14	74	40	62	9

CAREER STATISTICS

AVG	G	AB	R	H	2B	3B	HR	RBI	BB	SO	SB
.295	890	3486	503	1028	178	24	81	445	262	446	90

VS. RHP

VS. LHP

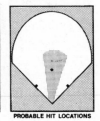

PROBABLE HIT LOCATIONS

FIELDING:

Although he doesn't have speed, he has quickness, a necessity for a third baseman. He is good at diving for balls hit to either side and consistently picks up ground balls. His arm is strong but not always accurate; many of his errors come on poor throws.

OVERALL:

At 28 years old, Lansford is at the peak of his abilities, and despite a career-long tendency to get hurt, he managed to play in 151 games last year.

Matthews: "Lansford is a good hitter, a smart baserunner, a solid fielder, and has a great attitude no matter what the circumstances. Every scout likes this guy."

PITCHING:

There are two ways of looking at Steve McCatty. On the one hand, he is only a shadow of his former self, a power pitcher destroyed by a sore arm. On the other hand, he is still a competitive starter--which is more than one can say for Mike Norris, Matt Keough, Rick Langford and Brian Kingman, the other members of Oakland's "Five Aces" who burned out under then-manager Billy Martin.

McCatty was disheartened by the loss of his fastball, a pitch he used to blow by the best hitters in baseball, but he adjusted. He works the corners with curves and sliders, blending in a fastball that now checks in around 85 MPH. Occasionally, he can finesse his way through a game. More often, though, he is hit hard. Just check his home run total (24) and his hits-per-inning statistics.

McCatty still uses a three-quarters delivery, and while he doesn't have much confidence in his change-up, he'll throw it effectively at times. Although he lacks the tools of intimidation, he still pitches inside and won't back down from anybody. That became apparent last year when he willingly tangled with the Yankees' Dave Winfield after hitting him with a pitch.

FIELDING:

He is prone to putting on weight, but he is a better athlete than he might appear and fields his position well. He's

STEVE McCATTY
RHP, No. 54
RR, 6'3", 205 lbs.
ML Svc: 7 years
Born: 7-21-58 in
Detroit, MI

1984 STATISTICS

W	L	ERA	G	GS	CG	IP	H	R	ER	BB	SO	SV
8	14	4.76	33	30	4	179	206	101	95	71	63	0

CAREER STATISTICS

W	L	ERA	G	GS	CG	IP	H	R	ER	BB	SO	SV
59	59	3.87	191	152	44	1102	1077	525	474	479	505	5

vulnerable to the stolen base, however, because he's slow getting the ball to the plate and has only an average pickoff move.

OVERALL:

The Oakland A's were heading toward a youth movement and low-budget contracts over the winter, and that was bad news for McCatty. He gets a lot of respect for his guile--much like Texas's Frank Tanana, another fallen arm--but he'll never be the dominant pitcher he was.

Matthews: "There's nothing tougher than making the transition from power to finesse. It's kind of a sad story. It was not that long ago that he was one of the best pitchers around. Now you have to wonder if he's reached the end of the line."

HITTING:

For the first time in his career, Dwayne Murphy has a role he can live with. First it was hitting second behind Rickey Henderson, a self-sacrificing task that he detested. Then it was hitting fourth, where too much power was expected of him.

By the end of last season, Murphy was hitting third--and flourishing. He set personal highs with 33 homers and 93 runs scored while keeping his average at a respectable level. He is one of the game's most feared hitters, if not the most consistent.

Murphy's right in there in style with Reggie Jackson and Steve Kemp and it results in some tape-measure home runs. Murphy has often experimented with a more compact swing, but he's a long ball man at heart; invariably he goes back to the big stroke. It's cost him a few base hits on the drag bunt, a skill he has mastered but seldom tries any more.

As a result, Murphy is more of a pull hitter than ever before. He doesn't go with the off-speed pitch for base hits to left field, as he did earlier in his career, and defenses play him accordingly. He is a dead fastball hitter, high or low, and has problems against left-handers with wide-breaking curveballs. Some teams try to jam him low and inside, but changing speeds is the best way to get him out.

BASERUNNING:

Murphy has chronic problems with his feet, a condition he'll have to live with as long as he plays. That leaves him with few chances to use his speed and baserunning knowledge. He runs basically to take the opposition by surprise.

FIELDING:

Murphy has some stiff competition in

DWAYNE MURPHY
CF, No, 21
LR, 6'1", 180 lbs.
ML Svc: 7 years
Born: 3-18-55 in
Merced, CA

1984 STATISTICS

AVG	G	AB	R	H	2B	3B	HR	RBI	BB	SO	SB
.256	153	559	93	143	18	2	33	88	74	111	4

CAREER STATISTICS

AVG	G	AB	R	H	2B	3B	HR	RBI	BB	SO	SB
.250	881	2976	448	743	90	14	116	430	496	619	88

VS. RHP   VS. LHP   PROBABLE HIT LOCATIONS

center field--Chet Lemon, Gary Pettis and Willie Wilson, to name a few---but he's widely considered the class of the American League. He plays shallow, yet tracks down drives to the fences, and he uses an average arm to the utmost with accuracy and good judgment. Murphy is particularly good at charging ground balls and coming up throwing.

OVERALL:

Some observers feel that Murphy's big swing deprives him of becoming a complete ballplayer, but there isn't a team that wouldn't want him around.

Matthews: "It is a pleasure to watch an outfielder with such great instincts. He's also a team leader, which makes him even more valuable."

HITTING:

The switch-hitting Tony Phillips continues to be a better hitter from the right side (.307, as compared to .245 lefthanded last season), but at least he has realized that he isn't a power hitter. Until last season, Phillips hit out of a deep crouch that saw him uppercutting at the ball and hitting a lot of needless fly balls.

As a righthanded hitter, Phillips bats straight-up and teams play him conventionally. Because he likes the fastball out over the plate, he sees a lot of breaking pitches on the outside and off-speed pitches below the knees. From the left side, he uses a more open stance, and teams give him the middle, shading him toward the two holes.

In either case, Phillips is a line drive and ground ball hitter with very little power, getting most of his extrabase hits on pulled drives down the lines. For a player who considers himself a contact hitter, he still strikes out too much. He bunts well toward first or third, and defenses have to respect that.

BASERUNNING:

Despite his remarkable quickness, he doesn't do much damage on the bases. He stole just 10 bases last year and was caught six times. In Phillips's defense, he's had enough trouble finding a position, let alone a spot in the lineup, and hasn't had the time to read the pitchers' moves. He has the potential to steal 30-40 bases a year.

FIELDING:

Moving from shortstop to second base did wonders for Phillips's career. While he came to the majors as a highly touted shortstop, his arm was only slightly

TONY PHILLIPS
2B, No. 18
SR, 5'10", 160 lbs.
ML Svc: 2 years
Born: 11-9-59 in
  Atlanta, GA

1984 STATISTICS

AVG	G	AB	R	H	2B	3B	HR	RBI	BB	SO	SB
.266	154	451	62	120	24	3	4	37	42	86	10

CAREER STATISTICS

AVG	G	AB	R	H	2B	3B	HR	RBI	BB	SO	SB
.253	342	944	127	239	38	8	8	80	102	181	28

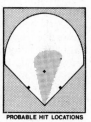

VS. RHP   VS. LHP   PROBABLE HIT LOCATIONS

better than average and he had a maddening tendency to bobble the routine play. At second base, his quickness is a noticeable asset and he isn't asked to make so many tough throws. He still needs work on the double play pivot with a runner bearing down on him.

OVERALL:

Phillips's raw ability has drawn rave reviews since he signed his first contract. Now, at age 25, he's looking to become a full-time player for the first time.

Matthews: "Everybody likes him better at second base. You have to wonder why he doesn't steal more often, but he is still finding himself as a ballplayer. The big thing now is to cut down on his errors (29 last year)."

PITCHING:

Chuck Rainey has always been an intelligent student of the game. Unfortunately, he's one of the guys in the pitching coach's classroom who can be intimidating, in that he tries to know as much as the guy running the mound corps. As a result, there is a conflict between the teacher and the know-it-all who doesn't always produce good grades. That led to Rainey's departure from the Cubs to Oakland last July.

With the Cubs in 1984, Rainey lacked consistency. In his defense, he literally didn't know from one day to the next what he was going to be doing. A few of his early-season starts were rained out, forcing him to start the following day or miss a start altogether. Oakland, however, may have found a place for him in their bullpen.

Although he mixes slider and fastball fairly well, Rainey failed to come to grips with the fact that a pitcher has to be a low ball pitcher at Wrigley Field or he will pay a steep price.

Rainey's slider is still tough to hit when it's working, but it wasn't working very often in Chicago. At Wrigley Field, Rainey needed a lot of runs behind him early. Otherwise, it was a shaky proposition that he would last very long.

FIELDING:

His cerebral side comes out on the

CHUCK RAINEY
RHP, No. 30
RR, 5'11", 195 lbs.
ML Svc: 5 years
Born: 7-14-54 in
   San Diego, CA

1984 STATISTICS

W	L	ERA	G	GS	CG	IP	H	R	ER	BB	SO	SV
5	7	4.30	17	16	0	88	102	55	42	38	45	0

CAREER STATISTICS

W	L	ERA	G	GS	CG	IP	H	R	ER	BB	SO	SV
42	34	4.39	123	104	10	639	695	356	312	270	290	1

mound. He fields his position very well, seeming to anticipate situations better than most pitchers. Now that he's back in the American League, he can cancel his bat order. He wasn't much of a hitter, anyway.

OVERALL:

Perhaps one of the most intelligent players in the game, Rainey also tends to over-analyze the situation.

Snider: "He's still a little of this and a little of that. He pitched up way too much."

PITCHING:

When the A's signed Lary Sorensen as a free agent, they were expecting a .500 pitcher who would work a lot of innings and keep games close until the late stages. That had been his history over a seven-year career that included one All Star selection. But they got considerably less.

Sorensen opened the season with a win, then went on an eight-game losing streak and never recovered. He wound up allowing 240 hits in 183.1 innings, a horrifying ratio, and never lasted more than a month in the starting rotation.

The problem was Sorensen's sinker, the pitch that had made him a respectable starter over the years. He couldn't get it around the knees consistently, and Sorensen doesn't have the type of fastball (around 85 MPH) to dominate the hitters.

His slider, normally an effective pitch for him, was also inconsistent. As a result, Sorensen's pitches found too much of the strike zone, and the league hit a resounding .316 against him.

Around mid-season, Sorensen began experimenting with a knuckleball during idle moments in the bullpen. He used it effectively at times, and he may need that pitch in the future. Although he's always been a starter, Sorensen may find himself pitching relief unless he is able to bounce back from 1984.

FIELDING:

Sorensen has more agility than the average pitcher, but he put on too much

LARY SORENSEN
RHP, No. 38
RR, 6'2", 200 lbs.
ML Svc: 8 years
Born: 10-4-55 in
      Detroit, MI

1984 STATISTICS

W	L	ERA	G	GS	CG	IP	H	R	ER	BB	SO	SV
6	13	4.91	46	21	2	183	240	117	100	44	63	1

CAREER STATISTICS

W	L	ERA	G	GS	CG	IP	H	R	ER	BB	SO	SV
87	92	4.12	266	227	69	1589	1794	805	727	363	505	3

weight last year and it affected his mobility. He'll make the plays he can get to, and he holds runners on with a quick move to first base.

OVERALL:

The A's released Sorensen despite the fact that they were short of veteran pitchers. That didn't say much for his performance; he needs to re-discover the control of his sinker for a return to form. In Sorensen's defense, he took a stand-up attitude toward his demise and never made excuses. He still has the utmost confidence in his ability.

Matthews: "This guy has to keep the ball down to be effective. You won't see him walk or strike out too many people. You have to remember that he has never played with a really good team. Sometimes that can subconsciously affect your performance."

PITCHING:

Mike Warren pitched a no-hitter as an Oakland rookie in September of 1983, and it got him a lot of attention. Looking back, though, the A's feel it might have been the worst thing that could have happened.

It all seemed so easy that day against the White Sox, but as Warren discovered last season, it isn't. He lasted only 10 starts in the rotation, lost his confidence, and spent the rest of the season on a roller coaster. He was optioned to the minors twice and didn't approach his peak form until September.

Warren falls somewhere between a power pitcher and a control pitcher. His best pitches are a slow curve and a high-velocity slider, which makes him very tough on righthanded hitters. He also throws what one scout called a "mystery pitch," a change-up that looked like a forkball but came to the plate more slowly. But he throws a lively fastball when he's right, and he can fire it high in the strike zone and get away with it.

At his best, Warren is an effortless worker who impresses everyone with his natural athletic ability. He will throw any pitch at any time, even when he's behind in the count. But the A's found him of little value when he got down on himself. The key to this young pitcher is confidence.

FIELDING:

The long-armed Warren has a slow de-

MIKE WARREN
RHP, No. 43
RR, 6'1", 195 lbs.
ML Svc: 1 year plus
Born: 3-26-61 in
Inglewood, CA

1984 STATISTICS												
W	L	ERA	G	GS	CG	IP	H	R	ER	BB	SO	SV
3	6	4.90	24	12	0	90	104	52	49	44	61	0
CAREER STATISTICS												
W	L	ERA	G	GS	CG	IP	H	R	ER	BB	SO	SV
8	9	4.59	36	21	3	155	155	85	79	62	91	0

livery to the plate, and his pickoff move is only average, so he's vulnerable to the stolen base. Otherwise, he does not hurt himself defensively.

OVERALL:

Warren went almost four months between starts for the A's, and his bullpen performances were sporadic. It seems evident that he's a starting pitcher; but he'll have to prove his worth with more consistent effort.

Matthews: "Like so many of the Oakland pitchers, he is young, inexperienced and very hard to evaluate. He's pitched a couple of great games, and I agree, maybe the no-hitter hurt him in the long run. But if Warren can ever establish himself as a starter, he'll be a guy to watch."

PITCHING:

It was late June of 1984 before Curt Young got his chance to pitch in the major leagues. Two months later, he was 6-1 with a 2.54 ERA and was clearly the most impressive of the A's pitching prospects. Although his performance fell in the final month, he left a big impression on the American League.

Appropriately, Curt Young looks young --maybe 17 or 18 years old--and his build is so slight, you wouldn't give him much chance of getting people out. But he throws a fastball close to 90 MPH and isn't afraid to pitch inside. He keeps hitters off balance with a slider (his best pitch), straight change-up and occasional curve.

Young handled many of the league's better clubs, including Detroit, Baltimore and Minnesota during the season. Invariably, the opposition said the same thing: he has a great combination of control and a live, moving fastball. He seldom gets knocked out of a ballgame. Young has also shown the ability to shake off a bad inning and come back strong, his confidence unshaken.

FIELDING:

Young has the lefthander's advantage when it comes to holding runners on, but his move is just ordinary. He does have a fairly quick delivery, however, and handles himself well on bunts, slow grounders and throws to the bases.

CURT YOUNG
LHP, No. 29
RL, 6'1", 180 lbs.
ML Svc: 1 year plus
Born: 4-16-60 in
        Saginaw, MI

1984 STATISTICS

W	L	ERA	G	GS	CG	IP	H	R	ER	BB	SO	SV
9	4	4.06	20	17	2	108	118	53	49	31	41	0

CAREER STATISTICS

W	L	ERA	G	GS	CG	IP	H	R	ER	BB	SO	SV
9	5	5.00	28	19	2	117	135	70	65	36	46	0

OVERALL:

While most people were talking about the Warrens, Conroys, Codirolis and Kruegers, Curt Young came from relative obscurity to steal the show. Among this stable of young talent, he seems to be the only one with a starting spot assured for 1985. The A's have considered the possibility of Young working short relief--who wouldn't like a lefthander with his stuff in that role? But that move will come later, if at all.

Matthews: "He doesn't look very tough, but he's got guts, talent and a presence on the mound. He keeps the pace going, so infielders like playing behind him, and he handles himself like a professional. Now the league knows him; this season will be a big test."

JIM ESSIAN
C, No. 19
RR, 6'1", 187 lbs.
ML Svc: 10 years
Born: 1-2-51 in
Detroit, MI

HITTING, BASERUNNING, FIELDING:

Jim Essian is the ideal backup catcher--an intelligent veteran who handles pitchers expertly and never complains about his status. He doesn't hit much, but he has more defensive savvy than many of the game's big names.

At the plate, Essian is basically a pull hitter, which often works to his disadvantage. He'll hit the long ball to left field occasionally, but has trouble with any type of pitch away--especially against righthanded pitchers as his .213 average would attest (he hit .346 vs. lefties). To his credit, Essian seldom strikes out and has a good idea of the strike zone. On the bases, he recognizes his limitations and seldom takes foolish chances.

For a catcher with only an average arm, Essian commands respect. His snap-throw release is among the quickest in baseball, and while runners consistently challenge him, they often get burned. In terms of calling pitches and having a rapport with his pitchers, Essian is first-rate. He generally draws raves from young pitchers trying to work out their problems.

OVERALL:

Essian has proved to be a valuable addition to the many teams he's played for over the years.

Matthews: "He's very smart defensively; has a really good feel for the game. He knows how to set up hitters within the context of pitchers' abilities. He's never been a good hitter, which is why you don't see him playing regularly."

STEVE KIEFER
INF, No. 28
RR, 6'1", 180 lbs.
ML Svc: 1 year
Born: 10-18-60 in
Chicago, IL

HITTING, BASERUNNING, FIELDING:

In the spring of 1984, many felt that Steve Kiefer was the A's most impressive shortstop. Now, with a year of Triple-A seasoning, he will take a shot at the regular job.

As many observers have noted, Kiefer moves with the easy grace of a born ballplayer. Although his range and throwing arm are only average by major league standards, he gets the job done with natural ability. He has sure hands and moves well to make the difficult plays on either side of him.

At the plate, Kiefer has a long, looping swing that produces too many strikeouts--but in a manner reminiscent of Robin Yount, he drives the ball deep to all fields. Kiefer has a history of extra-base power. In his very first at-bat in the big leagues, he ripped an opposite-field triple off Chicago's Floyd Bannister. Like many young players, his biggest weakness is making contact with the down and away breaking pitch.

Reports indicate that Kiefer is above average in bunting ability, speed, base-stealing and the hit-and-run. He will take his chances on the bases and breaks up double plays aggressively.

OVERALL:

If Kiefer continues to hit for power, he'll be a valuable addition. The A's haven't had a decent shortstop since Bert Campaneris, so Kiefer doesn't have to be Cal Ripken--just dependable.

RICK LANGFORD
RHP, No. 22
RR, 6'0", 185 lbs.
ML Svc: 7 years
Born: 3-20-52 in
Farmville, VA

NOTE: Rick Langford is still in the rehabilitation process from surgery on his right elbow in August 1983. He claims to be ready to pitch without pain for the first time in two years. The following report is based on his pre-surgery form.

PITCHING, FIELDING:

Arm problems have left Langford's career in serious doubt, but one thing hasn't changed: his remarkably competitive nature. At a time when everyone was writing him off, Langford worked diligently to get back into shape, and now he's poised for a comeback.

If Langford is able to pitch, he'll look familiar: over-the-top delivery, an average but tailing fastball (around 82 MPH), sinkers and sliders around the knees, and a cut fastball that he turns over against lefthanded hitters. The key will be if Langford has the old snap on his breaking balls. If he has to rely on the fastball, his career will be over.

Langford is a fast worker and a true professional. He holds runners on first base with a good pickoff move, fields his position well and never loses his composure. Control has always been one of his strong points, and he was throwing strikes even in his rock-bottom years of 1983-84.

OVERALL:

Matthews: "Rick Langford was a superb finesse pitcher who always had a good idea of what he wanted to do with every pitch. Because he didn't throw hard, he had a lot of guys thinking, 'That was a comfortable 0 for 4,' but it is the results that count. If anybody can make this kind of comeback, it's Rick Langford."

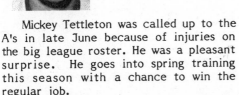

MICKEY TETTLETON
C, No. 57
SR, 6'2", 195 lbs.
ML Svc: 1 year
Born: 9-16-60 in
Oklahoma City, OK

Mickey Tettleton was called up to the A's in late June because of injuries on the big league roster. He was a pleasant surprise. He goes into spring training this season with a chance to win the regular job.

One of the few switch-hitting catchers around, Tettleton has very little power despite his impressive build. He's a line drive hitter who can spray the ball around from both sides of the plate. In his limited exposure last season, he appeared to be vulnerable to breaking pitches and often looked overanxious at the plate.

The A's would be satisfied with a .250 average from Tettleton, because defense is his strong suit. He was known as a wild, temperamental player at Oklahoma State (where he also played football), but at 24 years old, he is now a calm, mature presence behind the plate. Many of the A's best late-season pitching performances came when Tettleton was catching.

Tettleton has good game-calling instincts, a strong arm, agility, and rapport with his pitchers. His speed is below average, and he has yet to attempt a stolen base in the big leagues.

OVERALL:

Built along the lines of San Diego's Terry Kennedy and the Cubs' Jody Davis, Tettleton fits the modern-day mold of a catcher. His hitting is suspect, but his defensive ability seems to be beyond question.

SEATTLE MARINERS

PITCHING:

Salome Barojas is basically a power pitcher who has the three main pitches: a fastball, a hard slider and a sweeping curve. In two and a half years with the Chicago White Sox, he was used exclusively as a reliever in 137 appearances.

With Seattle, however, his ability to throw three pitches led to his being moved into the starting rotation. The switch to starting appeared to help him. He was 6-4 with a 3.89 ERA in the second half, when 14 of his 15 appearances came as a starter. Starting allows him to overcome some problems with command. He can afford to walk a batter and work his way out of the jam.

His delivery is basically overhand, but he drops down occasionally. Barojas is very deliberate on the mound, something which he must improve if he stays in the starting rotation. It keeps him from getting into a smooth rhythm.

The hard slider is his best pitch, with the fastball (slightly above the major league average of 86 MPH) as his second best pitch. He will usually go to the slider when he is in trouble, but the fastball is tough on righthanders because it tails in on them. The fastball is a sinking type of pitch, and at times it sinks enough that there have been allegations that Barojas has put something extra on the ball.

Pressure doesn't bother him. He showed signs in 1982 of becoming a solid reliever by posting 21 saves. The following year, however, his arm was a bit tired, having pitched all winter in his native Mexico, and it took him a while to get straightened out. He has a resilient arm, which was why he was counted on as a reliever with the White Sox. He appeared in 113 games during his two full years with them after six years of pitching in his native Mexico.

What Barojas does not have is resounding command. Control difficulties have hounded him throughout his career. His strikeouts-to-walks ratio is usually

SALOME BAROJAS
RHP, No. 30
RR, 5'11", 175 lbs.
ML Svc: 3 years
Born: 6-16-57 in
Cordova, MEX

1984 STATISTICS
W	L	ERA	G	GS	CG	IP	H	R	ER	BB	SO	SV
9	7	4.15	43	14	0	134	136	70	62	60	55	2

CAREER STATISTICS
W	L	ERA	G	GS	CG	IP	H	R	ER	BB	SO	SV
18	16	3.52	156	14	0	327	302	137	128	138	149	35

close. Only once, in 1980 at Reynosa, has he come close to striking out twice as many hitters as he has walked: 82-49.

FIELDING:

Self-defense is about the only reason Barojas seems to care about fielding balls hit back at him. He doesn't move well on the mound and doesn't react quickly, being willing to let someone else worry about fielding. He also does not seem to be too interested in holding baserunners, which is a bit surprising in light of his experiences as a relief pitcher. He is the type of pitcher that running teams take advantage of.

OVERALL:

The most common complaint about him deals with his consistency, or rather the lack of it. Just look at his starting appearances with the Mariners: he won his first four decisions and finished the season winless in his last 6 starts (three losses and three no decisions).

Matthews: "He has always had decent stuff, but his control problems keep him from really blossoming. If he could master the strike zone, he could blossom into a major league pitcher."

PITCHING:

A one-time phenom in the Oakland organization, Dave Beard has failed to phenomenate. He is a relief pitcher whose problem is that he has not consistently provided relief. He certainly has not shown anywhere near the type of command or assortment of pitches that would make a manager think about returning him to a starting role. He has not been a starter for four years.

He comes straight over the top: there is no deception. Hitters have no reason to fear what he's going to throw. From a velocity standpoint, Beard has an outstanding fastball, clocking consistently in the lower 90 MPH range. The ball moves fast, but that's it. It comes in straight, and the hitters have few problems with it.

Beard does experience short stretches during which he begins to look like a legitimate stopper. He keeps his slider under control, which keeps hitters from sitting on the fastball. If he could throw the slider over more often for strikes, it would be his best pitch. As a short reliever, if he could throw the other two pitches, he wouldn't need an off-speed pitch--good thing--he doesn't have one.

His pitching strategy is quite simple: challenge hitters. When he is pitching well, Beard doesn't have to worry about getting behind. When he is behind in the count, he struggles because his slider is not in the strike zone and hitters will feast on the fastball.

FIELDING:

Beard is the stereotype of the big

DAVE BEARD
RHP, No. 36
LR, 6'5", 215 lbs.
ML Svc: 4 years
Born: 10-2-59 in
   Atlanta, GA

1984 STATISTICS												
W	L	ERA	G	GS	CG	IP	H	R	ER	BB	SO	SV
3	2	5.80	43	0	0	76	88	56	49	33	40	5

CAREER STATISTICS												
W	L	ERA	G	GS	CG	IP	H	R	ER	BB	SO	SV
19	18	4.62	161	2	0	257	249	147	132	115	180	30

pitcher. He is not at all fluid moving around the mound. His move to first base is very average, and he takes a long time getting the ball to home plate. It all adds up to a field day for baserunners when Beard is on the mound.

OVERALL:

The elbow injury which forced him on the disabled list late last June has forced the Mariners to wonder. Beard pitched only 25 times after the injury, and his record was less than impressive: zero wins, no losses or saves but a whole lot of ERA (8.49). For a pitcher who was supposed to fill Bill Caudill's shoes, Beard never got past the laces.

Matthews: "His control is decent when he's got it. Lack of control was even more of a problem for him early in his career but improved as he gained experience. A few years ago it looked as if he would be one of the fine power-type relief pitchers in the league, but he regressed."

PITCHING:

Jim Beattie has become an enigma. He shows signs of being one of the best starting pitchers in the AL, but at the end of the season he always seems to come up lacking.

He uses an over-the-top delivery. When you see Beattie start dropping down, it is because he is getting lazy-- and at that point, he is headed for trouble. The same holds true for his pace on the mound. When he works quickly, he enjoys good results. When Beattie starts walking around the mound and shaking off signs, he usually does not hang around very long.

There is nothing wrong with his assortment of pitches. He has an above average fastball, consistently better than 88 MPH and normally better than 90 MPH. It has good movement on it. He likes to come inside on righthanded hitters but stays away from lefties. His big pitch, however, is one of the best hard-breaking sliders in the majors.

When Beattie is pitching well, he is ahead in the count, throwing his fastball and slider for strikes. It is no secret when Beattie is in trouble: he is like a fighter holding on too long. He is a good competitor, but he seems to come up just short.

Consider that since August of 1983, he has thrown 18 complete games and lost six of them, despite a 1.85 ERA.

Is he a hard-luck pitcher or just not capable of getting the big out?

FIELDING:

Beattie works hard on his fielding, and despite his size Beattie moves well around the mound, an outgrowth of his basketball abilities (he was a starter at Dartmouth during his college days).

JIM BEATTIE
RHP, No. 45
RR, 6'6", 220 lbs.
ML Svc: 6 years
Born: 7-4-54 in
Hampton, VA

1984 STATISTICS

W	L	ERA	G	GS	CG	IP	H	R	ER	BB	SO	SV
12	16	3.41	32	32	12	211	206	86	80	75	119	0

CAREER STATISTICS

W	L	ERA	G	GS	CG	IP	H	R	ER	BB	SO	SV
47	75	3.88	176	160	30	1038	1024	492	448	414	591	1

His big problem is holding runners on base. He has a slow, deliberate move to the plate and a very average move to first. What he has done to help himself is develop a short-step move to the plate which he mixes into his delivery when a basestealing threat is on base.

OVERALL:

The Mariners thought enough of him a year ago to sign him to the first long-term contract inititated by owner George Argyros.

While he wasn't the dominating pitcher the Mariners kept expecting, Beattie appeared to be shaking the nagging injuries which have haunted him throughout his career. His 32 starts were a career-high.

Matthews: "He has an excellent slider, as quick as any in the American League. He has the type of ability which makes him a threat to pitch a two- or three-hit shutout every time out. He is the type who can be flirting with a no-hitter when he has his excellent stuff."

HITTING:

Barry Bonnell is a National Leaguer at heart. He likes the fastball, especially up. He will pull the ball but also is capable of driving it into both of the alleys. He is not a power hitter although he will pick up a few more home runs than normal because of Seattle's Kingdome.

Bonnell was a strict pull hitter until two years ago, when he began to go the other way. Given his lack of legitimate power, he will only help himself by becoming more aware of the opportunities presented to him for hitting the ball to right field.

If you make a mistake with the fastball, Bonnell will make you pay for it. He can, however, be pitched to. Pitchers like to show him the fastball in, off the plate, moving him back, and then try to get him out with breaking stuff down and away. He does not chase too many bad pitches, however, so they have to stay close.

Bonnell has a closed stance and stands deep in the batter's box. He is never in a hurry to hit. He likes to take the first pitch.

BASERUNNING:

Bonnell has above average speed, and he makes good use of it. He is an excellent baserunner and gets a good jump out of the box. He is capable of stealing a base, especially if pitchers ignore him at first.

FIELDING:

He can play all three outfield positions although he is better off in left or right. He gets a good jump on the ball off the line. He has a strong and accurate arm and rarely throws to the wrong base. The respect for his arm is established enough that he does not get many assists, because runners do not challenge him very often.

Originally a third baseman, Bonnell

BARRY BONNELL
OF, No. 9
RR, 6'3", 200 lbs.
ML Svc: 8 years
Born: 10-27-53 in
Milford, OH

1984 STATISTICS

AVG	G	AB	R	H	2B	3B	HR	RBI	BB	SO	SB
.264	110	363	42	96	15	4	8	48	25	51	5

CAREER STATISTICS

AVG	G	AB	R	H	2B	3B	HR	RBI	BB	SO	SB
.274	911	2906	409	796	133	24	55	341	222	355	63

  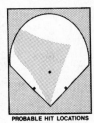

VS. RHP   VS. LHP   PROBABLE HIT LOCATIONS

played a bit there for the Mariners in 1984. He does not have the best range or reactions; Bonnell will make the routine plays but not much more.

OVERALL:

He is an excellent extra player on a team. He has a good attitude, works hard and can do a lot of little things, from playing in the outfield to pinch-running to pinch-hitting.

A manager has to be careful: too much exposure to righthanded pitchers takes its toll on Bonnell. Despite his size, he is not durable, which makes platoon usage ideal for him.

Injuries added to his problems in 1984. He had only 72 at-bats in August and September because of a pinched nerve in his neck. This is not expected to be a lingering problem.

Matthews: "He is a solid fourth or fifth outfielder. He will not embarrass you defensively. Barry will provide you with some big hits from time to time."

HITTING:

An outstanding athlete with great natural instincts, Phil Bradley forced his way into the Seattle outfield.

Bradley stands close to the plate in a slightly closed stance, hands held slightly apart, and chokes up on the bat. A power hitter during his days at the University of Missouri, he has made the adjustment to becoming a contact hitter in professional baseball.

Bradley is extremely comfortable in the No. 2 spot in the batting order, where he has to be disciplined and can take advantage of his ability to spray the ball. He also is an excellent bunter for base hits as well as in sacrifice situations. He led the Mariners with 11 sacrifice bunts in 1984. He will take a pitch to allow a man on base to steal.

He is not afraid of being behind in the count. As with most inexperienced players (he has played less than four full years of pro ball), he is mainly a fastball hitter. He likes the ball down but has worked hard at hitting all types of pitches. Pitchers try to jam him with fastballs because he is not very strong.

Teams have to play him straightaway because he does not try to pull the ball. Interestingly, Bradley hit .354 against righthanded pitchers and only .208 against lefties.

BASERUNNING:

Bradley is a definite asset on the bases. He anticipates situations well. He has above average speed and makes good use of it. He can take the extra base, and he is a very good basestealer.

FIELDING:

Bradley is a solid outfielder. His best position is center field, but he is also above average in left field. The one weakness is his throwing arm, which shows the residual effect of a high school football injury. His throwing is slightly below average but has improved since he underwent surgery after the

PHIL BRADLEY
OF, No. 29
RR, 6'0", 175 lbs.
ML Svc: 1 year plus
Born: 3-11-59 in
Bloomington, IN

1984 STATISTICS

AVG	G	AB	R	H	2B	3B	HR	RBI	BB	SO	SB
.301	124	322	49	97	12	4	0	24	34	61	21

CAREER STATISTICS

AVG	G	AB	R	H	2B	3B	HR	RBI	BB	SO	SB
.296	147	389	57	115	14	4	0	29	42	66	24

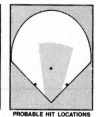

VS. RHP   VS. LHP   PROBABLE HIT LOCATIONS

1981 season. He makes up for some of the deficiency by getting rid of the ball quickly and by always throwing to the correct base. He hits cutoff men accurately.

When it comes to catching balls or running them down in the gaps, Bradley is outstanding. He plays a shallow center field, breaking back very well. He also breaks well to both his left and right.

OVERALL:

He applies himself to the task at hand. He has proven that just by playing in the major leagues despite the skeptics. The more he plays, the better he appears to be. Given a chance to be a regular in the second half of 1984, he hit .349 during the final 11 weeks.

Matthews: "Bradley is an outfielder who does not have a lot of power. He is primarily a line drive, contact type of hitter. Obviously, as he matures he will become a pretty decent outfielder."

HITTING:

Al Cowens has become a study in offensive inconsistency. His career was written off in both 1981 and 1983, but he came back after both seasons with strong showings for the Mariners, raising his average 74 points from 1983 to 1984, when he also drove in 78 runs, the second highest total of his career.

Cowens has a very closed stance. He did back off the plate some in 1984. That would seem to make it harder for him to handle outside pitches, but he compensated for it by looking for the ball away.

Cowens has been a good fastball hitter. Pitchers will change speeds on him and then try to jam him with fastballs, which is why he moved off the plate last year.

He is a streak hitter, and it is easy to tell when Cowens is in the midst of a good streak. When he is hitting well, he lines balls in the alley. When he pulls balls deep and foul, he is struggling and jumping at the ball. That is when off-speed pitches are impossible for him to handle. Cowens will take a lot of pitches. He will bunt when the opportunity presents itself and has the speed to beat out a bunt for a base hit.

BASERUNNING:

Once a well above average runner, Al still has good speed. He is a threat to steal a base. He reads pitchers well and gets a good jump when he is going to steal. He is a very aggressive runner. Cowens likes to take the extra base and will barrel into middle infielders.

FIELDING:

Cowens has always been one of the better defensive outfielders in the AL, and he won a Gold Glove in 1977. He is so smooth in the outfield that at times it looks as if he is not putting a full effort into his job. He judges balls very well although there were times in 1984 when he looked a little lost in right field.

He does not have the rifle arm that was his trademark in younger years--arm

AL COWENS
OF, No. 16
RR, 6'2", 200 lbs.
ML Svc: 11 years
Born: 10-25-51 in
  Los Angeles, CA

1984 STATISTICS
AVG	G	AB	R	H	2B	3B	HR	RBI	BB	SO	SB
.277	139	524	60	145	34	2	15	78	27	83	9

CAREER STATISTICS
AVG	G	AB	R	H	2B	3B	HR	RBI	BB	SO	SB
.272	1434	5000	640	1359	240	63	94	642	356	585	119

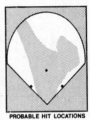

STRONG   STRONG   PROBABLE HIT LOCATIONS
VS. RHP   VS. LHP

problems over the last couple of seasons have bothered him. Cowens is still a solid thrower because of his accuracy. He always throws to the right base, and never misses the cutoff men.

OVERALL:

Cowens's biggest problem is trying to live up to the expectations of his 1977 season, when he was the runner-up to Rod Carew as the AL MVP. Instead of that being considered a career year, it has been held up as a standard for him to match again. He has not come close. Those expectations, plus the problems of adjusting after being hit in the face by a pitch from Ed Farmer in 1979, have created disappointments. Cowens, however, seems to have found the proper environment in Seattle for his return to being a solid player. He has become a leader in the Mariner clubhouse. He also has shown he can handle righthanded pitchers, hitting for a better average against them than against lefthanders in his three years with the Mariners.

Matthews: "Cowens had a nice comeback and has done well in the role that they gave him as the elder statesman."

HITTING:

With only one year of major league experience, Alvin Davis is emerging as a classic hitter. He has a classic stance, pretty much straightaway, and holds his bat in a cocked position.

There were times in 1984 when teams thought they had him figured out, but it did not work for long. He was supposed to be a dead fastball hitter. As a result, he was shown a steady diet of breaking pitches, especially off-speed. He calmly adapted to them, and the pitchers paid the price. The only way to get him out consistently is to throw him fastballs up and in. They had better be way in, barely on the corner of the plate. If not, he will do damage.

Davis had always shown the ability to drive the ball, but in 1984, for the first time in his baseball career, he became a legitimate power threat with the Mariners. Enjoying the short fences of the Kingdome, he drove the ball out of the park to both left and right fields.

He is an extremely disciplined hitter. He will hit the ball to any field, and he will not chase bad pitches. He will take the walk before he will be fooled. Davis's 97 walks were the fifth highest total ever for an AL rookie. His knowledge of the strike zone is excellent has been compared to that of a young Ted Williams.

BASERUNNING:

He is slightly below average in speed and not much of a threat to steal bases. He is, however, a very smart player and despite not having good speed is a very good baserunner. He will take the extra base if it is available but does not take stupid chances. He plays hard. Second baseman beware.

FIELDING:

Davis is as solid with the glove as he is with the bat. He has soft hands. He moves well around first base. He makes the play on throws in the dirt

ALVIN DAVIS
1B, No. 61
LR, 6'1", 190 lbs.
ML Svc: 1 year
Born: 9-9-60 in
Riverside, CA

1984 STATISTICS

AVG	G	AB	R	H	2B	3B	HR	RBI	BB	SO	SB
.284	152	567	80	161	34	3	27	116	97	78	5

CAREER STATISTICS

AVG	G	AB	R	H	2B	3B	HR	RBI	BB	SO	SB
.284	152	567	80	161	34	3	27	116	97	78	5

VS. RHP

VS. LHP

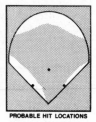

PROBABLE HIT LOCATIONS

more often than not and has good judgment on what balls to go after and when to cover first.

OVERALL:

In one year, Davis established himself as one of the more feared hitters in the American League. With his discipline, mental make-up and dedication he should get even better. His enjoyment of playing is obvious by the way he carries himself on the field. He always has a smile. But then, with his ability, he should be smiling.

Matthews: "What a good-looking hitter. Watching him operate at the plate, you wouldn't consider the fact he is a first-year player. He has such a good idea of what he is doing. He sorts out the pitches that are just beyond the strike zone or that he can't handle. He just waits and waits. Once he gets a pitch he can handle, he doesn't make many mistakes. He has the potential to be one of the fine players in the American League."

PITCHING:

As desperate as Toronto has been for a lefthanded pitcher, the Blue Jays did not even protect Dave Geisel a year ago, allowing him to go to Seattle for a mere $25,000. The Blue Jays, however, got the better end of the deal. Geisel, a lefthander whose primary function in the big leagues has been as a reliever, has not proved to be of any value to the Mariners.

Geisel has an easy motion; there is nothing deceptive about the way he throws or what he throws. His best pitch is a fastball, but he also has a slider, curve and change, none of them being exceptional. The fastball doesn't do much. His lack of deception makes it extremely tough for him to get righthanded hitters out and limits the length of his outings.

Geisel keeps hanging around because clubs hope he will get lefthanders out. However, that is all it is--a clasped-hands and look-to-the-sky hope.

He can give managers headaches, retiring the first batter he faces less than half the time. That's a big problem for the role he is supposed to fill: come in, get the lefthanded hitter out, and sit down.

Geisel showed some signs in 1984 of overcoming one major problem--walks. He gave up only nine while striking out 28 in 43.1 innings with the Mariners. If he can maintain a ratio like that, he will give himself a better chance of succeeding.

The best thing he has going for him is that he is lefthanded. Teams are always looking for a lefthander out of the bullpen. What he has to overcome is his propensity for taking a batter or two to get into the groove of the game--because his job is usually over by the time he faces a couple of hitters.

FIELDING:

He doesn't do the little things to

DAVE GEISEL
LHP, No. 37
LL, 6'3", 205 lbs.
ML Svc: 4 years
Born: 1-18-55 in
Windber, PA

1984 STATISTICS												
W	L	ERA	G	GS	CG	IP	H	R	ER	BB	SO	SV
1	1	4.15	20	3	0	43	47	22	20	9	28	3

CAREER STATISTICS												
W	L	ERA	G	GS	CG	IP	H	R	ER	BB	SO	SV
5	5	3.70	119	8	0	180	174	81	74	82	127	8

help himself out of jams as a reliever, like field bunts exceptionally well and hold runners. His move to first is only average, but he is lefthanded, which does give him a slight edge.

OVERALL:

Obviously, clubs see potential. He has been around since 1975, but he has yet to show results. Only once in 10 pro seasons has he had an ERA lower than the 3.78 mark he compiled at Midland of the Class AA Texas League back in 1974. The Mariners gave him a quick look as a starter three times last year, but having worked as a situation reliever since 1979. Geisel doesn't have the stamina needed to be a regular in the rotation.

Matthews: "Geisel is the type of guy who retires three or four hitters in one relief appearance and next time gives up two hits and a walk and doesn't get anybody out. He is the type of pitcher who has good stuff, but because of inconsistency, and possibly his concentration, he has not been able to be much of a factor as a big league pitcher."

HITTING:

The first first-round draft pick in Mariner history, David Henderson appears to be on the verge of becoming a solid everyday player. He had his first commendable half season in the final part of 1984, hitting .353, the fourth highest post-All Star average in the American League.

He has a spread stance at the plate but holds his bat almost straight up. He has pretty good power to all fields, a nice attribute in a park with Kingdome dimensions. It has only been the last two years, under the guidance of Al Cowens, that Henderson has realized just how much damage he can do by hitting the ball to the right of second base.

He likes fastballs up in the strike zone, even a bit out of it. Pitchers can throw him fastballs, but they had better throw them way in on the fists. He has trouble when pitchers change speeds although he is getting better about laying off breaking balls in the dirt. He has a quick bat and commits himself swiftly. If he is fooled, the third baseman and shortstop should beware: Henderson has a tendency to let go of the bat in an ill-fated effort to check his swing. His impatience and bad judgment make him a horrible risk to hit-and-run.

Patience is not a big part of his game. He is a hacker. He does not get cheated. Henderson will bunt for a hit (he cannot sacrifice bunt) but not as much now as he did when he first came up. He realizes he is going to make it big by driving in runs, not by getting on base.

BASERUNNING:

Despite knee surgery after the 1980 season, Henderson still has better than average speed. He does not make good use of it, however. He does not have good baserunning instincts and does not get a good jump for stealing bases.

FIELDING:

It is a waste of his ability to play

DAVE HENDERSON
CF, No. 42
RR, 6'2", 210 lbs.
ML Svc: 3 years
Born: 7-21-58 in
  Dos Palos, CA

1984 STATISTICS

AVG	G	AB	R	H	2B	3B	HR	RBI	BB	SO	SB
.280	112	350	42	98	23	0	14	43	19	56	5

CAREER STATISTICS

AVG	G	AB	R	H	2B	3B	HR	RBI	BB	SO	SB
.258	412	1284	156	331	67	6	51	159	99	240	18

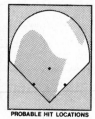

VS. RHP   VS. LHP   PROBABLE HIT LOCATIONS

him anywhere but in center field. He glides back with ease on fly balls over his head. In his first few years, he had problems on balls in the gap, trying to cut them off too quickly. In 1984, however, he seemed to improve on that aspect. He has a strong arm, but it is not always accurate. He will miss cut-off men often enough for runners to challenge him.

OVERALL:

Concentration is Henderson's key. If he can maintain his concentration and put his natural abilities to full use, he will become a solid everyday player with good power. So far, however, he has been a tease. He will go through streaks during which he is in the upper echelon of the league's hitters and then regress to sub-par play.

Matthews: "When Henderson is in a groove, he is a tough out. He is fairly tough to pitch to, especially in the Kingdome, where he can use his power to the opposite field."

HITTING:

Artificial surface has been a godsend for players like Steve Henderson. He likes to chop the ball and hits it hard enough to take advantage of the way the artificial turf gives a ground ball extra momentum.

He stands on top of the plate and usually hits the ball from the left of second base to right field. He fights off the pitch in on his fists with an inside-out swing that limits his power to doubles instead of home runs. He is a fastball hitter and likes the ball up. If you get a fastball up in the middle of the plate, he will pull it but not much else. Pitchers try to change speeds on him, but he usually makes contact of some type.

He is big enough and strong enough, it would seem, to pull the ball more often and hit more home runs, but he is satisfied with hitting for an average and sacrificing power.

He does like to bunt. He is good at sacrificing and if he catches the third baseman back is not afraid to drop the ball down in an attempt to pick up a hit.

BASERUNNING:

Henderson does have slightly better than average speed, but the only time it is obvious is when he is going from first to third. He slips when he swings and is late getting out of the box. He does not read pitchers well or get a good jump, which keeps him from stealing as many bases as he would seem capable of.

FIELDING:

Give Henderson an "A" for effort: he is fearless. He will run over bullpen mounds and into outfield fences. He will never fail because of a failure to try. Unfortunately, he does not get a good jump on fly balls, and he has a tendency to make what seem like careless errors.

His arm is a sore subject. He is way

STEVE HENDERSON
OF, No. 5
RR, 6'1", 188 lbs.
ML Svc: 7 years
Born: 11-18-52 in
  Houston, TX

1984 STATISTICS											
AVG	G	AB	R	H	2B	3B	HR	RBI	BB	SO	SB
.262	109	325	42	85	12	3	10	35	38	62	2
CAREER STATISTICS											
AVG	G	AB	R	H	2B	3B	HR	RBI	BB	SO	SB
.281	901	3105	414	873	144	46	62	380	349	605	78

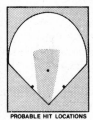

VS. RHP   VS. LHP   PROBABLE HIT LOCATIONS

below average when it comes to throwing. Normally, he does not try to fool himself. He gets rid of the ball quickly and hits the cutoff man. On occasion, however, he tries to throw out a runner on his own, and it is a wasted effort.

OVERALL:

He is a decent player and would make a nice extra outfielder for any team or a righthanded-hitting DH for a team on artificial surfaces. However, that is not good enough for most baseball people. They look at his size and tools and wonder why he has never become a dominating player.

His enthusiasm is contagious; he does not sulk. He always hustles and he is very good with young players, trying to help them cope with the mental aspects of big league baseball.

Matthews: "Henderson is the epitome of the guy everybody thought had unlimited potential but never lived up to it. He has never hit with the power people expected or stolen bases the way he did when he was young."

HITTING:

Despite his solid build and rugged appearance, Bob Kearney does not appear to have the stamina necessary to catch every day and produce offensively. He tired drastically in the second half of 1984, hitting only .193, including a club-record 0-for-36 slump during September.

Kearney is a first-ball hitter--or at least swinger. The outfield plays him slightly to pull. While he will hit the ball in the gap, he does not make much effort to go to right field. As strong as he looks, he has limited power, best suited to the Kingdome, which is where he hit all seven of his home runs.

He likes fastballs in, up or down--it doesn't seem to make any difference. Righthanded pitchers should try to keep everything down and away from him. Left-handers can dazzle him with off-speed breaking pitches, and they did a good enough job to limit him to a .168 average in 1984. He will bunt along third.

BASERUNNING:

If you don't pay attention to him, he will steal a base although he has below average speed. He was successful on seven of 12 attempts in 1984. He loves contact and is very aggressive in attempting to break up double plays.

FIELDING:

Kearney's arm is average to just above average. He does, however, have one of the quickest releases in the AL, which makes him a threat to throw out baserunners. He was the only catcher to gun down Kansas City's Willie Wilson twice last year.

One big problem: in his haste to throw out basestealers, Kearney is willing to sacrifice his game-calling. He will call for all fastballs with a baserunning threat on first or second.

He gets in definite ruts with pitch

BOB KEARNEY
C, No. 11
RR, 6'0", 180 lbs.
ML Svc: 2 years
Born: 10-3-56 in
San Antonio, TX

1984 STATISTICS

AVG	G	AB	R	H	2B	3B	HR	RBI	BB	SO	SB
.225	133	431	39	97	24	1	7	43	18	72	7

CAREER STATISTICS

AVG	G	AB	R	H	2B	3B	HR	RBI	BB	SO	SB
.231	266	800	79	185	38	1	15	80	43	132	8

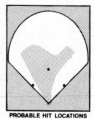

VS. RHP   VS. LHP   PROBABLE HIT LOCATIONS

selection. Trying to prove he could mix up pitches last season, he began calling for the hard-throwing Mariner staff to send hitters a preponderance of off-speed breaking pitches. He does not seem to be able to adjust to the developments of a game. He has one plan of how to pitch hitters and doesn't alter.

OVERALL:

Kearney doesn't have the mental concentration or physical stamina to be a regular catcher. He does have enough attributes, however, that he would fit in nicely as a platoon catcher, which is why the Mariners were searching during the winter for a lefthanded-hitting catcher.

Matthews: "He has an average arm but one of the quickest releases of any catcher in the league. He likes to throw to first base quite a bit. He did nothing last year to prove he is going to be a consistent big league hitter."

PITCHING:

If there are any doubters about Mark Langston as a power pitcher, they are the hitters who haven't faced him yet. In his rookie season, the Mariner left-hander became only the fourth rookie in American League history to strike out 200 batters in a season and, along with Dwight Gooden of the New York Mets, only the 11th rookie in major league history to lead a league in strikeouts.

He comes at hitters over the top but hides the ball well and does not give away his pitches.

Langston has an explosive fastball that appears to rise on hitters and is consistently in the 90 MPH range on the radar gun. Tiger coach Dick Tracewski compares it to the fastball of his former Dodger teammate, Hall of Famer Sandy Koufax. Whoa . . . who IS this guy?

He is a young pitcher who is able to throw two types of curveballs--a hard one and an off-speed one he developed during his rookie year, thanks to former pitching coach Frank Funk. Funk felt Langston needed some type of an off-speed pitch, and the results would seem to bear out Funk's belief. Armed with the new pitch in the second half of the season, he was 11-3 with a 2.98 ERA after the All Star break, en route to the most wins by a rookie lefthander in the big leagues since Gary Peters won 19 with the Chicago White Sox in 1963.

Langston gets his strikeouts with his breaking pitches, setting up hitters with the off-speed pitch and then throwing the hard breaking ball. The combination of curveballs makes his lively fastball even more devastating.

Langston is young and he is strong; he is the only member of the Mariner staff to make every scheduled start in 1984 and enjoyed a club record of 17 victories. He shows no weakness at this time.

FIELDING:

Langston is one of the better-field-

MARK LANGSTON
LHP, No. 43
RL, 6'2", 177 lbs.
ML Svc: 1 year
Born: 8-20-60 in
San Diego, CA

1984 STATISTICS												
W	L	ERA	G	GS	CG	IP	H	R	ER	BB	SO	SV
17	10	3.40	35	33	5	225	188	99	85	118	204	0

CAREER STATISTICS												
W	L	ERA	G	GS	CG	IP	H	R	ER	BB	SO	SV
17	10	3.40	35	33	5	225	188	99	85	118	204	0

ing pitchers in the league. He gets off the mound in a hurry and is always in position to field when he completes his follow-through. He has a compact motion and a good delivery to the plate. His move to first is only average, but being lefthanded and getting rid of the ball in good fashion helps him keep runners honest.

OVERALL:

He keeps in the game well, paying attention to hitters even when he is not pitching, looking for an edge that will help him. He is a willing learner and picks up new ideas, like that off-speed breaking ball, in a hurry.

He is at a stage at which he needs some subtle refinements to become one of the best pitchers in the league. His strong second half shows he made the adjustments that were necessary to make it big in the big leagues.

Matthews: "He was easily the best rookie pitcher of the American League. His future is unlimited. He's the type of power pitcher who can excite the fans. Seattle would do well to hang on to him."

HITTING:

Don't try to get too cute with this guy. Orlando Mercado will surprise you. He is supposed to be a dead fastball hitter: the book on him is that he likes the fastball up or down. From the standpoint of average, that is very true. But he generates his power off breaking pitches. He also shows signs of learning to have patience with off-speed offerings.

His body has filled out over last couple of years, and Mercado now looks as if he is going to have some power. He is a definite pull hitter, which has been one of his big problems in making the adjustment to the big leagues.

He has a spread stance, bent at the middle, and has a big sweeping swing. That is where the breaking balls come in. If you throw him good ones, he cannot make any adjustment; but then if you throw him a good fastball inside, he cannot get around on it quickly enough. He needs to cut down the stroke if he wants to make a home in the big leagues.

BASERUNNING:

He has a body which gives the appearance of speed--but there is none. He is below average in speed. He is above average, however, in instincts. He will take the extra base but is not much of a threat to steal.

FIELDING:

Fielding is his strength. Pitchers love to throw to him. He gives a steady, low target. He moves well behind the plate, and he works exceptionally hard to call a good game. He enjoys catching a win more than he enjoys hitting a home run.

He has an arm that is well above average, but it is wasted. His footwork on throwing to second base on stolen base attempts in constantly getting

ORLANDO MERCADO
C, No. 2
RR, 6'0", 180 lbs.
ML Svc: 2 years
Born: 11-7-61 in
    Arecibo, PR

1984 STATISTICS

AVG	G	AB	R	H	2B	3B	HR	RBI	BB	SO	SB
.218	30	78	5	17	3	1	0	5	4	12	1

CAREER STATISTICS

AVG	G	AB	R	H	2B	3B	HR	RBI	BB	SO	SB
.198	105	273	16	54	14	3	2	27	18	44	3

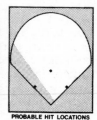

VS. RHP   VS. LHP   PROBABLE HIT LOCATIONS

mixed up, and he winds up taking forever to get rid of the ball. When he does get rid of it, he has no idea where it is headed. It is, however, just a mechanical problem so he should be able to overcome it.

OVERALL:

He should become a solid catcher in the next two years. He has an outstanding makeup and works hard. He is intelligent. He was signed at the age of 15, and Seattle has had patience in bringing him along. They have remembered that he had never worn a catcher's glove before he signed with them.

Matthews: "He likes fastballs in, either up or down. You have to keep the ball away and breaking stuff down and away. He has a good arm, but it is very erratic."

PITCHING:

Paul Mirabella is a middle reliever with an impressive fastball. He can be tough on lefthanded hitters with the fastball--as long as he is pitching on a minor league mound. Once he gets up to the parent club, he loses it. At the minor league level, he is a power pitcher with a good strikeout-to-walk ratio, but he appears to be intimidated in the majors. He just can't seem to throw a strike when he is in the bigs.

He seemed to be coming around in the first half of 1984 (3.18 ERA) but went backwards in the second half. He has to realize he has good enough stuff to get hitters out and not be intimidated. He has to challenge them, throw strikes and take his chances. When he does, he gets hitters out.

PAUL MIRABELLA
LHP, No. 52
LL, 6'2", 196 lbs.
ML Svc: 4 years
Born: 3-20-54 in
Bellville, NJ

1984 STATISTICS
W	L	ERA	G	GS	CG	IP	H	R	ER	BB	SO	SV
2	5	4.37	52	1	0	68	74	39	33	32	41	3

CAREER STATISTICS
W	L	ERA	G	GS	CG	IP	H	R	ER	BB	SO	SV
11	24	4.93	156	31	3	316	346	205	173	161	163	7

FIELDING:

There is nothing exceptional about Mirabella as a fielder. He is average in every aspect, including his move to first. But like other lefties, facing the runner gives him a slight advantage.

OVERALL:

He went to spring training with the Mariners as a non-roster player and appeared ready to finally take advantage of his natural ability. He had a strong spring and did not allow an earned run in his first nine relief appearances. He also went through a stretch in July during which he retired 27 of 30 batters.

But old habits are hard to break, and by the end of the season it was the same mediocre results as in previous years, even though his 52 appearances were more than he had ever made in a big league season. Mirabella has to learn to carry the intense concentration he has over the course of an entire season, not just for a week or two at a time.

Mirabella has shown he can pitch against the best with success, having finished each game of the Mariners' three-game sweep of the world champion Detroit Tigers in late May.

Matthews: "Mirabella is a journeyman type of pitcher. He is in the major leagues only because of the fact he is lefthanded."

PITCHING:

Mike Moore was the No. 1 draft pick in the country in June of 1981 because he had such a promising right arm. He still has the arm, but the promises have yet to be realized.

Moore has an overpowering fastball which is consistently around 94 MPH. The movement on his fastball will be good enough, considering its velocity, once he develops other pitches he can throw for strikes when he wants to.

Moore's slider is still inconsistent. On the days he throws it for strikes, he turns in performances like 12 strikeouts against Kansas City on Sept. 8. Those days, however, are in the minority. Just check his club record 17 losses in 1984.

His change-up is his outstanding pitch, especially in light of how hard he throws it. But he is hesitant to use it. When he does, it is unhittable, but he still remembers those days at Oral Roberts University when the change-up was the only pitch collegiate hitters could hit off him. He has to make the pitching adjustment to the big leagues, where hitters sit on his fastball.

He has good arm action in his motion and has worked on smoothing out the remainder of his delivery. When Moore originally came up to the Mariners in the spring of 1982, he caught his glove against his left leg when he followed through. He has abbreviated that and is working to totally eliminate the catch, which will help him with consistency.

What Moore has is durability. The longer he is in a game, the stronger he seems to get. He will frequently throw harder in later innings—that is, if he is still pitching in later innings.

MIKE MOORE
RHP, No. 25
RR, 6'4", 205 lbs.
ML Svc: 3 years
Born: 11-26-59 in
Eakly, OK

1984 STATISTICS

W	L	ERA	G	GS	CG	IP	H	R	ER	BB	SO	SV
7	17	4.97	34	33	6	212	236	127	117	85	158	0

CAREER STATISTICS

W	L	ERA	G	GS	CG	IP	H	R	ER	BB	SO	SV
20	39	5.02	84	81	10	484	525	293	270	224	339	0

FIELDING:

For a big guy Moore moves around the mound well. He does not get flustered fielding bunts and makes strong, accurate throws. He has a slow delivery but keeps runners honest with a jump move to first which borders on a balk.

OVERALL:

The million-dollar arm has yet to pay big dividends. It's a bit puzzling because Moore is a willing student for his pitching coaches. He also is an excellent competitor. Part of his problem in 1984 was a strained forearm muscle, which forced him to miss two starts in mid-May, but he was over that in the second half of the season when he managed only three wins in 14 decisions.

Matthews: "Mike was a disappointment this year, but I still think a lot of teams would like to take a chance on him. He could explode and become a very fine pitcher."

PITCHING:

Talk about gifted, then talk about Edwin Nunez, who in the last year and a half has begun making the transformation from a starter into a relief pitcher. The Mariners look at the second half of 1984 and have to feel the move has been a success. Not only did he have seven saves but he had a 2.89 ERA to show for 28 appearances.

It's not that Nunez could not be a starter, but he is so intimidating from both a physical and an ability standpoint and his arm bounces back so quickly that the Mariners feel he can fill their bullpen void. He could also return to the starting rotation later in his career.

He throws a 90+ MPH fastball that moves, and he has a wicked slider. Nunez can throw a curve and is still working on a change-up. When the Mariners will let him, Nunez will uncork a knuckleball.

What makes his assortment of pitches seem even better is that he has an assortment of delivery points as well, ranging from straight over the top to sidearm. In his abbreviated big league exposure, he also has made it clear that he is not the least bit afraid to come inside on hitters.

He is definitely a power pitcher, averaging better than two strikeouts for every walk he has issued in the big leagues as well as in the minor leagues.

FIELDING:

Don't be deceived by the big body-- he is quick off the mound. Nunez has good reactions and seems to enjoy the challenge of fielding. He does have a big leg kick, which makes him a target

EDWIN NUNEZ
RHP, No. 30
RR, 6'5", 235 lbs.
ML Svc: 1 year plus
Born: 5-27-63 in
Humacao, PR

1984 STATISTICS													
W	L	ERA	G	GS	CG	IP	H	R	ER	BB	SO	SV
2	2	3.18	37	0	0	68	55	26	24	21	57	7

CAREER STATISTICS													
W	L	ERA	G	GS	CG	IP	H	R	ER	BB	SO	SV
2	2	3.18	37	0	0	68	55	26	24	21	57	7

for potential basestealers. The thieves, however, had better be careful. He has an excellent spinning move to first base and throws the ball hard.

OVERALL:

The biggest problem Nunez faces is that people don't realize he won't even turn 22 years old until May 27, 1985. He is so big and has so much talent that scouts and managers tend to think of him as much older. He also has had to adapt to his size. When the Mariners signed him back in 1979, he only weighed 160 pounds; and then came the growth years for the Puerto Rico native who was just 16 years old when he debuted.

The only adjustment Nunez has to make is controlling his temper. He gets too emotional when things go poorly for him.

Matthews: "With his size he can be a pretty intimidating force on the mound. He is the type of pitcher who can come in and get a strikeout in a relief situation."

HITTING:

Ken Phelps could have been around the big leagues a couple of years before he finally arrived in 1984. To do that, however, he would have had to be willing to pinch-hit, and, at the time, he refused to make the mental adjustments necessary to being a part-time player.

Phelps stands on top of the plate with a slightly closed stance and uses a surprisingly short bat for a power hitter. Phelps is the prototypical left-handed hitter: he likes the ball down. He is not, however, a fastball hitter. Even an average fastball up--in or out--ties him up. He has trouble just fouling hard stuff off.

Throw him a breaking ball and forget it, especially if you try to get it inside. He is a very good breaking ball hitter. When he gets his pitch, he will drive it a long way (24 home runs in 290 at-bats, for an AL-leading home run every 12.1 at-bats).

What hurts him as a pinch-hitter is that he is very selective at the plate. He takes way too many pitches--including third strikes. At one stretch he took 11 consecutive pitches in three consecutive pinch-hit at-bats, nine of them for called strikes.

He turned his career around in 1982 at Wichita of the Class AAA American Association. He finally began going with pitches instead of trying to pull everything.

In a park the size of the Kingdome he can do plenty of damage to left field as well as right field.

BASERUNNING:

It is a good thing he can hit the ball out of the park because he is not going to leg out any hits. He definitely clogs up the bases. He does not take the extra base and is no threat to steal.

FIELDING:

He prides himself as a good first

KEN PHELPS
INF, No. 44
LL, 6'1", 205 lbs.
ML Svc: 3 years
Born: 8-6-54 in
    Seattle, WA

1984 STATISTICS

AVG	G	AB	R	H	2B	3B	HR	RBI	BB	SO	SB
.241	101	290	52	70	9	0	24	51	61	73	3

CAREER STATISTICS

AVG	G	AB	R	H	2B	3B	HR	RBI	BB	SO	SB
.233	185	451	63	105	13	2	31	68	75	116	3

  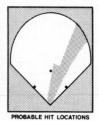

VS. RHP   VS. LHP   PROBABLE HIT LOCATIONS

baseman, but in reality Phelps is very average defensively. He has a below average arm. He uses a very small first baseman's glove, which might account for his problems with scooping balls out of the dirt.

OVERALL:

Given a chance to play on a platoon basis in the big leagues for the first time last year, Phelps certainly showed he could hit home runs. He also showed he could be pitched to: 51 RBIs on 24 home runs. If he will finally accept the backup role, he will be around for a few years because he is a definite offensive threat.

Matthews: "Phelps's best role is coming off the bench and providing the type of pinch-hitting that can tie a game with one swing of the bat."

PITCHING:

Last year was supposed to be Mike Stanton's year to emerge as the key man in the bullpen. Instead, it was another summer of Stanton teasing the Mariner management.

It became more evident than ever that Stanton's best spot is as the No. 2 man in the bullpen, where he has someone to back him up, easing the pressures. Oh, he's got the ability. He has as good an assortment of stuff as any pitcher on the Seattle staff. He throws a hard sinking fastball, consistently in the low 90 MPH range. He also has a good hard slider that has an abnormally big break, but Stanton has a tendency to fall in love with it and throw it too many times in succession. What he doesn't have is any type of off-speed pitch, which is why he has made his living as a reliever.

Whether he is working as the setup man in the late innings or as the stopper, there is nothing tricky about his approach--he tries to go after hitters.

There is no book on Stanton in pressure situations: either he overpowers hitters or they overpower him. He goes through streaks: one earned run in May last year and no earned runs in 11 appearances from May 24 to June 22. But then there were the final 10 weeks of the season during which he did not register a save. Of course, part of the problem is a tender right shoulder, which limited him to only two appearances in the month of September.

Stanton does not use a windup even with the bases empty. At times, he seems to almost short-arm the ball.

FIELDING:

He gets himself in position to field

MIKE STANTON
RHP, No. 46
RR, 6'2", 200 lbs.
ML Svc: 5 years
Born: 9-25-52 in
St. Louis, MO

1984 STATISTICS

W	L	ERA	G	GS	CG	IP	H	R	ER	BB	SO	SV
4	4	3.54	54	0	0	61	55	28	24	22	55	8

CAREER STATISTICS

W	L	ERA	G	GS	CG	IP	H	R	ER	BB	SO	SV
12	19	4.41	242	3	0	343	351	184	168	153	275	29

but is so hyper that he is not a very good fielder--he gets flustered. He also does not hold runners on. That is a big problem for a reliever, especially one like Stanton who does not get rid of the ball to the plate in a hurry.

OVERALL:

So much talent yet so little consistency. Another problem for Stanton is his continually stiff shoulder, which limits his usage. He is rarely able to pitch on consecutive days. In fact, if he even warms up one day, he can't pitch the next day. If a manager tries to use him more than three or four times in a week, his shoulder will sideline him for an extended period.

Matthews: "His slider is actually more of a slurve, a big breaking slider. Righthanded hitters had success going the other way and up the middle with Mike, but if they try to pull that sinking fastball or slider all they get are ground ball outs."

PITCHING:

Bob Stoddard found himself in the bullpen for the Mariners for most of 1984, which means trouble. He does not warm up quickly and he does not challenge hitters. And he does not have an arm which bounces back quickly.

If Stoddard is going to be a successful major league pitcher, he is going to have to find a manager who will let him start and will stay with him in the rotation long enough to let him get in a groove.

Stoddard has a good assortment of pitches. His fastball is average to slightly above average (84 to 87 MPH). Stoddard also throws a slider, a curve and a change-up. The change-up is his best pitch. He does not telegraph it, and it has good movement. He also has been experimenting with a screwball in his continuing effort to improve.

Without overpowering ability, he has to work the ball around in the strike zone and try to hit the corners. He is intentionally wild at times in trying to set up hitters. He may not overpower hitters, but he is not afraid to come inside with a strike or a purpose pitch.

Stoddard does not get shaken easily. He will bounce back from mistakes (his own or his defense's) and make quality pitches.

The biggest thing he has going for him is a desire to excel.

His problem is that he is just a little short on ability. He could overcome that if he found that perfect manager who would stay with him and allow him to work his way out of jams--because he will always be in a jam with his style of pitching.

FIELDING:

One of Stoddard's strengths is his fielding ability. He is in good position when he finishes his delivery. He anticipates well and is quick in fielding bunts and making plays. He is a good

BOB STODDARD
RHP, No. 34
RR, 6'1", 200 lbs.
ML Svc: 2 years
Born: 3-8-57 in
San Jose, CA

1984 STATISTICS

W	L	ERA	G	GS	CG	IP	H	R	ER	BB	SO	SV
2	3	5.13	27	6	0	79	86	51	45	37	39	0

CAREER STATISTICS

W	L	ERA	G	GS	CG	IP	H	R	ER	BB	SO	SV
16	24	4.01	76	43	5	357	351	178	159	122	172	0

enough fielder that he can gamble on getting force plays.

Stoddard has an excellent move to first. It is so good that he will work with other pitchers on pickoff moves during training camp. He will throw over many times and is also one of the few pitchers who has been able to perfect the fake-to-third-and-throw-to-first move. Even players who are well aware of this aspect of Stoddard's repertoire find themselves having to scramble to get back to base.

OVERALL:

Stoddard is not the type of pitcher who makes a good impression. He has to battle to survive. There's nothing pretty about him.

He will, however, give you more than a normal effort. He studies hitters and keeps his own charts, making notations when he is pitching as well as when others are pitching. He knows he needs every edge he can find to survive.

Matthews: "He is the solid type of pitcher every staff needs. Stoddard is a thinking man's pitcher. He does a lot of little things well but doesn't overpower anybody."

HITTING:

The Mariners acquired Gorman Thomas in the hope that he would provide them with a legitimate long ball threat in the middle of their lineup. Instead, the nagging shoulder problem which had been bothering Thomas for two years was finally diagnosed as a torn rotator cuff, and he spent the summer of 1984 trying to repair the problem.

Thomas is the classic home run hitter. When he makes contact, he drives the ball. When he doesn't drive the ball, he strikes out a lot, including an American League season record 175 times (1979).

He has a better idea of the strike zone than his strikeout total would indicate. Thomas is not afraid to take a walk. The only time he did not get at least 73 bases on balls in his big league career was during the strike-shortened 1981 season, when he also had his only sub-100 strikeout season.

Thomas is mainly a fastball hitter, but if a pitcher hangs a curve or gets it up Thomas will drill it. He is a guess hitter, and will sit on the pitch he expects. Lefthanders try to throw him sliders low and either in or away. They know better than to get the ball over the plate. He will surprise some with an occasional bunt attempt if the situation calls for it.

BASERUNNING:

He was an aggressive and good baserunner but has been slowed the last few years by knee surgery. The aggressiveness he shows at the plate is also evident when he runs the bases. If you want to turn a double play, you'd better watch out for him. He plays to win and will do anything within his power to obtain the result.

FIELDING:

Again, injuries have taken their toll on Thomas. Before he lost some of his

GORMAN THOMAS
OF, No. 20
RR, 6'3", 200 lbs.
ML Svc: 9 years
Born: 12-12-50 in
Charleston, SC

CAREER STATISTICS

AVG	G	AB	R	H	2B	3B	HR	RBI	BB	SO	SB
.231	1164	3770	554	871	185	11	219	646	527	1081	44

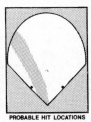

STRONG vs. RHP   STRONG vs. LHP   PROBABLE HIT LOCATIONS

speed and his arm was hurt, he was one of the better center fielders in baseball. He was fearless going after fly balls. Physical ailments, however, have taken his range away and also limited the strength of his arm. If he returns in 1985, he will have to make the transition to either left field or DH.

OVERALL:

The Mariners wanted more than his bat when they acquired Thomas. They wanted his inspirational leadership and were hoping that his gung-ho approach to the game would set a good example for their young kids.

Matthews: "For a period of a few years he was one of the premier power hitters in the game. It would have been fun to see how he would have done in the Kingdome had he played there in 1984. If he comes back this year, it will be interesting to see what kind of year he can have even at this stage of his career in that small park."

PITCHING:

After spending his first two major league seasons as a reliever, Vande Berg found himself bouncing between the rotation and bullpen in 1984. It led to a disaster. He is best suited as the left-handed short man in the bullpen. Just take a look at April and September, when he was used exclusively out of the pen. Try a 2-0 record, 2 saves and 1.10 ERA to show for 19 appearances.

He throws a slightly better than average fastball--86 to 88 MPH. He also has a good slider and a sweeping curveball. He has been dabbling with a screwball for an off-speed pitch. Ed's big pitches are the breaking pitches, which are especially tough on lefthanded hitters.

His windup and delivery don't look so deceiving, but he has a little flick of his glove just before he throws the ball which seems to distract hitters a bit. He also haunts lefthanded hitters with a three-quarters to sidearm delivery.

What he has to do to be effective is throw strikes. His pitches are tough to hit because they have so much movement, but if he is wild, hitters will lay off them. He has to make hitters swing.

He does have a durable arm. Even with 17 starts last year he made 50 appearances, after averaging 73 appearances-- and only 70 innings--in each of his two previous big league seasons. He can get loose with just a handful of pitches and can loosen up three or four times during a game without it appearing to bother him.

FIELDING:

Vande Berg is an excellent fielder. A wiry body gives him good movement around the mound. He has good reactions and does not get flustered in pressure situ-

ED VANDE BERG
LHP, No. 32
RL, 6'2", 175 lbs.
ML Svc: 3 years
Born: 10-26-58 in
 Redlands, CA

1984 STATISTICS

W	L	ERA	G	GS	CG	IP	H	R	ER	BB	SO	SV
8	12	4.76	50	17	2	130	165	76	69	50	71	7

CAREER STATISTICS

W	L	ERA	G	GS	CG	IP	H	R	ER	BB	SO	SV
19	20	3.77	196	17	78	270	278	129	113	104	180	17

ations. He can get the force at third on a bunt if the bunt is not perfect.

He does have a bit of a leg kick in his delivery out of the stretch but has a good move to first. He will catch some runners off guard with a quick throw to first from the hip.

OVERALL:

Confidence is the key to Vande Berg. His belief in himself has taken a beating in the last two years and hit bottom in 1984 when he was used as a starter then as a reliever. He finally asked to remain in the bullpen. He has to be aggressive or else he begins hanging the slider and curveball and becomes a very mediocre pitcher. When he goes after hitters, his breaking pitches are as good as those of anybody in the American League.

Matthews: "He has not made any great strides in the last year or two. He was most effective his first year, but he appears to have leveled off since that strong rookie season. He still has shown enough, however, to make him interesting to most teams."

PITCHING:

The sophomore jinx lives in the case of Matt Young. Hailed as one of the top young lefthanders in baseball in 1983, he wound up spending part of 1984 in the minors. A congenital back problem did play a part in his struggle, forcing him on the disabled list ahead of his being sent to the minor leagues.

Just how much the back had bothered him became obvious when he went 6-0 with a 1.51 ERA in six starts at Salt Lake City before returning to Seattle in September last year and compiling a 2.38 ERA in six starts and allowing three earned runs in his final 23 innings.

Young throws a fastball and a slider and occasionally will take a little off the slider but really has no consistent off-speed pitch. He will try to run the slider down and in on righthanded hitters. His fastball has above average velocity. He will turn the thing over from time to time, and it is his best pitch. There is so much natural movement on it that his teammates don't like to play catch with him. He has a rather jerky motion which, combined with his back problem, creates fears about an arm injury in the not-too-distant future. He also lands awkwardly on his right (front) foot, which can create consistency problems.

When he is struggling, it is because he is having trouble throwing strikes. He has to stay ahead of hitters to win. What he has to remember is that harder is not better. Young finds he has better command of his pitches and better results against hitters when he lets up a little on his pitches. The movement is better along with the ability to keep the pitch in the strike zone.

MATT YOUNG
LHP, No. 40
LL, 6'3", 205 lbs.
ML Svc: 2 years
Born: 8-9-58 in
Pasadena, CA

1984 STATISTICS

W	L	ERA	G	GS	CG	IP	H	R	ER	BB	SO	SV
6	8	5.72	22	22	1	113	141	81	72	57	73	0

CAREER STATISTICS

W	L	ERA	G	GS	CG	IP	H	R	ER	BB	SO	SV
17	23	4.16	55	54	6	316	319	167	146	136	203	0

FIELDING:

Young has a long way to go in his fielding. He doesn't have too much trouble fielding balls, but he does have some problems throwing them--especially on easy plays. For a lefthander, his move to first base is horrendous. It is an area where he needs major improvement.

OVERALL:

When Young returned to the majors in September, he appeared to be returning to the style of pitcher which made him such a hit in 1983--he threw hard and threw strikes. He has to take care of himself and keep his concentration at an optimum level. If he does that, he has shown he has the natural ability to neutralize the hitters.

Matthews: "Last year he didn't look anything like the pitcher of two years ago--he looked as if he had an arm problem. He was such a good-looking pitcher in his rookie year but will have to change some things to make it again."

AL CHAMBERS
OF, No. 47
LL, 6'4", 217 lbs.
ML Svc: 1 year plus
Born: 3-24-61 in
    Harrisburg, PA

HITTING, FIELDING:

Al Chambers coils at the plate like Dave Parker, but without the results. Chambers is a dead low fastball hitter. Breaking pitches are trouble for him, and lefthanders are enough of a problem that the Mariners only let him bat against a lefty once in 1984.

He is a pull hitter, trying to drive every pitch out of the park. Unfortunately, he does not succeed often. He has never hit more than 20 home runs in a professional season and more than 13 only once. This is not very impressive, considering he has spent the last three years at Salt Lake City, where the light air makes home runs even easier to hit.

For a big man, Chambers has good speed. He is average as a baserunner, however, and does not take advantage of his speed. He can steal a base when he wants to.

Chambers will have to hit to make it in the big leagues. He certainly is not going to get his chance with his glove. He is not even close to average. He does not judge fly balls well and has trouble catching them when he does get to them. His arm is below average even for a left fielder.

OVERALL:

Chambers has not shortchanged himself on effort. In fact, at the lower minor league levels, the Mariners had to keep him away from the park during the early afternoon because they were afraid he might burn himself out. However, the results have not been there.

JIM PRESLEY
INF, No. 19
RR, 6'1", 180 lbs.
ML Svc: 1 year
Born: 10-23-61 in
    Pensacola, FL

HITTING, FIELDING:

Jim Presley took some time to get squared away in the big leagues, but once he made the adjustments he made other teams pay the price. Presley had six of his 19 home runs and 16 of his 36 RBIs during his 90 September at-bats. He is a pull hitter with a bit of a sweeping swing. Just the same, he likes the ball up and in, and he is quick enough with the bat to be able to handle such a pitch. He is definitely a fastball hitter.

Pitchers change speeds on him effectively. He has to become more patient on breaking balls. He commits himself too quickly, especially on hard sliders, which leaves him with no chance of adjusting.

Presley has very average speed, but he will, however, steal a base if the pitcher forgets about him. He averaged 11 stolen bases a year in four full minor league seasons. He is an average baserunner. A silent type, he will make noise breaking up double plays.

Presley is also average with the glove. He does not have very good lateral movement. His first step is slow. He is sure-handed, however, and will catch what is hit at him. And he does have a strong although sometimes erratic arm.

OVERALL:

Presley will go as far as his bat can carry him. He is good enough at third base if he continues to hit with the type of power he has shown. If not, he is not going to hang around as a defensive replacement.

Matthews: "Presley has some potential. With his power, he has a chance to be a pretty good third baseman."

ROY THOMAS
RHP, No. 49
RR, 6'6", 215 lbs.
ML Svc: 14 years
Born: 6-22-53 in
Quantico, VA

PITCHING, FIELDING:

Roy Thomas has bounced between the bullpen and the starting rotation during his 14-year professional career. His main duty in the big leagues has been out of the bullpen as a long reliever.

He has a good assortment of pitches: a hard sinker, an average slider, a big-breaking curve and a so-so change. The slider is his best pitch but has a tendency to flatten out.

He has a big, wild motion which keeps him from finding consistency. He appears to be looking at third base when he delivers the ball to the plate. Righthanded hitters don't enjoy facing him at all, but lefthanded hitters pick up Thomas's breaking pitches pretty well. That's a big part of his problem: the inability to get lefties out, and when teams see him enter a game, they get all of their lefthanded wood in the lineup.

With his wild delivery to the plate, Thomas still gets in decent position to field, but his move to first base is only average. He takes a long time to get rid of the ball to the plate, giving runners another break.

OVERALL:

Obviously, the ability is there. He has hung around pro ball since 1971, when the Philadelphia Phillies made him the sixth player taken in the June draft. But the ability hasn't surfaced. In 14 years of pro ball, he has spent only slightly more than three years in the majors--only one was a full season. His career has taken him through six organizations.

TEXAS RANGERS

HITTING:

Every winter for the past few years, the Rangers have thought about trading Buddy Bell. And every summer, they've been glad they haven't.

Bell is one of the best third basemen in baseball, and in 1984 he had his best season in several years. Part of the reason for his success is that the Rangers added some offense to their lineup in 1984, and pitchers didn't find it as easy to pitch around Bell as they had in the past.

Another reason for Bell's fine 1984 season was that he was healthy for most of the year. In the past, he had both knee and back problems.

Even when Bell's back is healthy, he hits out of a full upright stance and prefers fastballs up and in. He appears to have trouble getting his arms out to hit low, outside pitches, and pitchers should throw him breaking balls there, changing speeds and mixing in an occasional fastball in on the fists.

Bell does not have a lot of power and does not strike out often--he makes contact with the ball and hits line drives to all fields. He will go to right field with pitches that are up in the strike zone.

He is not often asked to bunt and is pretty good on the hit-and-run.

Bell leads by example and is one of the most respected players on the team. He rarely lets his emotions show, but beneath his calm exterior is a fierce competitor.

BASERUNNING:

Bell has average speed and has lost a step since the beginning of his career. He always hustles on the bases, and is difficult to pick off first because he studies pitchers' moves carefully and takes only a moderate lead. He is not a threat to steal. His biggest weakness is that he can be a little overaggressive at times, and will get thrown out while trying to take the extra base.

BUDDY BELL
3B, No. 25
RR, 6'2", 185 lbs.
ML Svc: 13 years
Born: 8-27-51 in
   Pittsburgh, PA

1984 STATISTICS

AVG	G	AB	R	H	2B	3B	HR	RBI	BB	SO	SB
.315	148	553	87	174	36	5	11	83	63	54	2

CAREER STATISTICS

AVG	G	AB	R	H	2B	3B	HR	RBI	BB	SO	SB
.286	1827	6940	886	1987	335	45	147	850	592	618	43

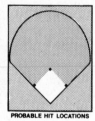

VS. RHP   VS. LHP   PROBABLE HIT LOCATIONS

FIELDING:

Bell is one of the best at his position and has the Gold Gloves to prove it. Last season, he was able to play a step closer to the line than he could in the past because both of the Rangers' young shortstops have good range. The presence of Curtis Wilkerson and Jeff Kunkel at short enabled Bell to cover his own position with more confidence, and as a result not many balls got between him and the line. He goes to his right better than to his left and has sure hands, excellent reflexes and a strong arm. Not many can dive, knock a ball down and throw a runner out as well as he can.

OVERALL:

Matthews: "Bell is simply one of the most solid players in the league. If last season is any indication of the effect of his increasing age, he should have a few more good years left."

PITCHING:

There are some knowledgeable baseball people who think that this is the year that Danny Darwin will become one of the winningest pitchers in baseball.

Of course, a lot of knowledgeable baseball people thought that would be the case last year. And the year before that. And the year before that.

While he has never quite lived up to the lofty expectations others have had for him, he continues to add pitches to his arsenal. Darwin has lost some velocity on his fastball since his first few years in the majors, but he still has an above average fastball. He throws three-quarters or even lower at times. He also has a sweeping slider and last year continued to work to perfect a forkball and a change-up. He blends finesse and power with the stress on finesse as he approaches the age of 30.

He uses the fastball or the change as his out pitch.

Since Darwin has been bounced back and forth between the starting rotation and the bullpen throughout his career, he is still learning how to prepare himself mentally between starts. His concentration level during games is sometimes a problem: he appears easily distracted.

FIELDING:

Darwin has good range, gets off the mound quickly and covers first well on a ball hit to his left, but overall he is only an average fielder. He doesn't get the ball to the plate very quickly and has an average move to first; as a result, he can be run on.

DANNY DARWIN
RHP, No. 44
RR, 6'3", 190 lbs.
ML Svc: 6 years
Born: 10-25-55 in Bonham, TX

1984 STATISTICS

W	L	ERA	G	GS	CG	IP	H	R	ER	BB	SO	SV
8	12	3.94	35	32	5	223	249	110	98	54	123	0

CAREER STATISTICS

W	L	ERA	G	GS	CG	IP	H	R	ER	BB	SO	SV
53	50	3.58	217	90	21	838	793	378	333	291	544	15

OVERALL:

Labels stick--especially in major league baseball circles. Once the label "utility" has been applied to a player, it is hard to shake, and that can be bad. Once a pitcher is labeled "middle reliever," that is pretty much what he will be doing. Likewise, once the word gets out that a player--especially a pitcher--has "potential," it could take years before the inner circle will allow themselves to be proved wrong. Danny Darwin seems to be a case of the latter: his name always comes up when the Rangers talk trade.

Matthews: "Darwin is a valuable pitcher to have on the staff because he has both started and pitched out of the bullpen. He has pretty good stuff and seems to be getting a better idea of what he's doing on the mound."

HITTING:

When Earl Weaver managed the Orioles, he always liked the flexibility of having a lefthanded batter who could also catch. The Rangers have such a player in Marv Foley, but Weaver is nowhere in sight.

Foley was signed as a minor league free agent in November 1983 and came to spring training in 1984 as a non-roster player. He wasn't expected to make the team, but impressed the right people with his aggressive style at the plate.

Foley likes to jump on the first pitch and tries to pull everything. Because of that, he looks for fastballs up and in. He is an impatient hitter, and pitchers have had success with change-ups and breaking balls outside. He is not a good bunter and doesn't have good bat control, making him unsuitable for hit-and-run plays or hitting behind the runner.

While he doesn't hit for a high average, Foley does have some power. Five of his first nine hits in 1984 were home runs. After that, his production fell off dramatically, but he was routinely used in clutch situations as a pinch-hitter. He did not, however, show himself to be a dangerous clutch hitter.

Foley relies on pitchers to make mistakes. If they make their pitches, he is probably not going to be able to eek out much of a hit.

BASERUNNING:

He has barely average speed and is not a threat to steal or to take the extra base. Foley knows his limitations and doesn't take foolish chances. He is a hard-nosed baserunner who will break up a double play.

MARV FOLEY
C, No. 59
LR, 6'0", 195 lbs.
ML Svc: 5 years
Born: 8-29-53 in
  Sanford, KY

1984 STATISTICS

AVG	G	AB	R	H	2B	3B	HR	RBI	BB	SO	SB
.217	63	115	13	25	2	0	0	19	15	24	0

CAREER STATISTICS

AVG	G	AB	R	H	2B	3B	HR	RBI	BB	SO	SB
.224	203	419	37	94	10	0	6	51	41	61	0

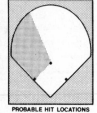

VS. RHP   VS. LHP   PROBABLE HIT LOCATIONS

FIELDING:

As a catcher, Foley has a strong arm but doesn't get rid of the ball quickly enough. On top of that, his throws are not always accurate. However, he calls a good game and will block the plate. He always hustles and does a good job of getting out from behind the plate to field a bunt.

OVERALL:

It appears that Foley can show good hitting abilities for very short periods of time. He can turn it on, but then something just turns it off. His future is limited.

Matthews: "Foley has been around. He's an aggressive player who makes the most of his limited talents."

PITCHING:

Charlie Hough is far from a natural athlete, but he has won a lot of games for Rangers teams that have been mediocre or worse in the past three years.

There are two reasons for that. The biggest reason, of course, is that he throws a knuckleball, one of only two pitchers in the American League who do. And secondly, few players study their craft the way Hough does. His goal is to be a manager or a general manager someday and is preparing himself now.

Although Charlie throws the knuckler most of the time, he will also throw a below average fastball or a little slider when he is behind in the count. But now and then, he will throw his fastball or slider when he thinks the hitter is expecting the knuckler.

He has a great mental makeup and does not let what happened with the previous hitter or in the previous game bother him.

Hough tends to go in streaks. His usual pattern is to have problems early in the year when it's cold and wet, get hot when the weather does, then level off during the last month or so of the season.

Like most knuckleballers, his success is directly tied to his control. When the pitch is not working too well, it dances out of the strike zone. He gets behind in the the count, and hitters can sit on the fastball and slider. When the pitch is working, he finds a groove in the middle--well, it looks like the middle--of the plate and can dominate the game.

FIELDING:

Hough has developed one of the better

CHARLIE HOUGH
RHP, No. 49
RR, 6'2", 190 lbs.
ML Svc: 13 years
Born: 1-5-48 in
   Honolulu, HI

1984 STATISTICS

W	L	ERA	G	GS	CG	IP	H	R	ER	BB	SO	SV
16	14	3.76	36	36	17	266	260	127	111	94	164	0

CAREER STATISTICS

W	L	ERA	G	GS	CG	IP	H	R	ER	BB	SO	SV
100	89	3.55	542	126	44	1688	1452	746	665	746	1096	61

righthanded moves to first in baseball, one that borders on a balk. He also holds runners on well, which helps compensate for his slow delivery to the plate and the fact that the knuckleball is a diffcult pitch for a catcher to handle. Hough is always among the league leaders in picking runners off first.

OVERALL:

In a few years, Hough will be ready to look for a manager's job somewhere in the major leagues. He has been studying the game all the while he has been watching the hitters flail away at his fickle knuckler.

Matthews: "Charlie Hough is a typical knuckleballer in that, when it's working and he can get it over, nobody is going to abuse him much. He pays attention to details and can help himself."

HITTING:

When the Rangers made Jeff Kunkel the third player in the nation to be picked in the June 1983 draft, they expected him to get to the majors quickly. He made it even faster than the Rangers expected, being called up a year later.

The Rangers front office was bitterly divided on the issue of whether or not Kunkel should be called up, and those who voted against the move looked smarter than those who were in favor of it.

While he has great tools, he struggled last year. Fortunately, he has a good mental makeup and was able to handle the frustrations. He has been around baseball all his life--his father, Bill, is an American League umpire.

Last season, Kunkel had trouble with all kinds of pitches. He was overmatched by fastballs and showed little ability to handle major league breaking pitches. Still, the Rangers believe he will come around. "There are some players you say will make it IF certain things happen. There are other players who you know will make it no matter what happens," said one Rangers official. The Rangers feel that Kunkel is in the latter mold.

He has little power, but should develop some as he gets older and stronger. He strikes out a lot, but should eventually be a good contact hitter.

The Rangers haven't given up on him. They think he is their shortstop of the future. It is just the present that gives him trouble.

BASERUNNING:

Kunkel is a smart player and applies his abilities on the bases. He has good speed, but his talent is unrefined. As he gains more experience and confidence, he should have the potential to steal 30 or 40 bases a year. In time, the Rangers project him to be an excellent runner.

FIELDING:

By reputation, Kunkel is an above average fielder with excellent range, soft hands and a strong arm. He didn't

JEFF KUNKEL
SS, No. 20
RR, 6'2, 180 lbs.
ML Svc: 1 year
Born: 3-25-62 in
  West Palm Beach, FL

1984 STATISTICS

AVG	G	AB	R	H	2B	3B	HR	RBI	BB	SO	SB
.204	50	142	13	29	2	3	3	7	2	35	4

CAREER STATISTICS

AVG	G	AB	R	H	2B	3B	HR	RBI	BB	SO	SB
.204	50	142	13	29	2	3	3	7	2	35	4

  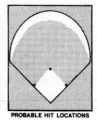

VS. RHP   VS. LHP   PROBABLE HIT LOCATIONS

show any of these reported skills after he was called up last season. Quite the opposite, he moved stiffly in the field. That could have been because he was pressing, or it may have been because he was still bothered by back problems that forced him to miss the first several weeks of the season. Just as his hitting and baserunning should improve, so his fielding should as well. He has the physical tools and the Rangers are counting on Kunkel to come through.

OVERALL:

Kunkel seems to have handled the pressures and criticisms well. If he has the abilities that the Rangers think he has and his father's plugged ears, a new star may rise in the west.

Matthews: "He is a classic case of a young player being rushed and brought to the majors too soon. What he needs more than anything is experience. When he gets that, he still has a chance to become a first-rate major league player."

PITCHING:

The Rangers were counting on a young pitcher to make a splash last year, and one did. The Rangers thought it would be Allen Lachowicz, but it wasn't. Partly because Lachowicz came down with elbow problems, lefthander Mike Mason had his chance to shine.

Mason got off to a hot start and was the Rangers' best pitcher for the first half of the season until a tired arm slowed him down. He pitched in winter ball in 1983-84 and by June of 1984, he had thrown over 250 innings in one year. He spent some time in the bullpen and had mixed success after the All Star break, but he is being counted on heavily for 1985.

Mason has an above average fastball with good movement and a good curve. He has been equally effective against both right and lefthanded batters. His most outstanding trait is the poise he showed as a rookie. The Rangers didn't score many runs for him, but he never let it bother him.

His curve breaks down sharply and he isn't afraid to throw it when he is behind in the count. Mason sets up hitters with his fastball, which he usually throws on the corner, and uses his sinker and slider as his out pitches.

While his fastball has been clocked in the low 90s, he needs to change speeds and move the ball around to be effective. He showed surprising composure and command of his pitches for a rookie.

He was used briefly in the bullpen at mid-season in hopes that it would give his arm a rest, but he is better suited to being a starter.

MIKE MASON
LHP, No. 16
LL, 6'2", 205 lbs.
ML Svc: 1 year plus
Born: 11-21-58 in
 Faribault, MN

1984 STATISTICS

W	L	ERA	G	GS	CG	IP	H	R	ER	BB	SO	SV
9	13	3.61	36	24	4	184	159	78	74	51	113	0

CAREER STATISTICS

W	L	ERA	G	GS	CG	IP	H	R	ER	BB	SO	SV
10	17	3.90	45	28	4	217	190	98	94	66	130	0

FIELDING:

Mason is an above average fielder with sound mechanics in fielding bunts and covering first. He has an average move to first and needs to become more aware of holding runners on because he has a slow motion when throwing to the plate.

OVERALL:

For a young pitcher to have his kind of poise on the mound could be one of the little signals that indicate that Mason is here to stay. He will be carrying a large load on his back in 1985-- good thing he has that kind of maturity . . . he is going to need it.

Matthews: "Mason came out of nowhere for the Rangers last year and should continue to improve. The most impressive thing about him is that he knows how to pitch and can win when he doesn't have his best stuff."

PITCHING:

When the Rangers traded for Dickie Noles last July, they were not sure whether they had a starter or a reliever, a good pitcher or an average one. Now, after having several months to watch him pitch, they still don't know.

Noles was inconsistent all year. He would have one good outing followed by a bad one. Part of the reason may have been the way he was used. He was shuttled back and forth between the bullpen and the starting rotation.

He has a good arm and is basically a power pitcher. He throws a good fastball, a slider and a curve and is very aggressive about pitching inside and keeping hitters off the plate. He is a strong competitor, but has calmed down off the field in the last couple years.

A lack of consistency has hurt him throughout his career. The book on Noles is that, if you can't beat him, there is at least a chance he will find a way to beat himself.

FIELDING:

One of the ways Noles hurts himself is with his fielding. He doesn't do a good job with the glove and does not hold runners on well. Improvement in all areas of his defense would make him a better pitcher.

DICKIE NOLES
RHP, No. 36
RR, 6'2", 190 lbs.
ML Svc: 4 years
Born: 11-19-56 in
  Charlotte, NC

1984 STATISTICS

W	L	ERA	G	GS	CG	IP	H	R	ER	BB	SO	SW
2	3	5.21	18	6	0	57	60	38	33	30	39	0

CAREER STATISTICS

W	L	ERA	G	GS	CG	IP	H	R	ER	BB	SO	SW
23	36	4.37	148	79	3	573	590	318	278	231	316	6

OVERALL:

Noles's career has been undistinguished in the past few years. He has been called a headhunter and excitable, though he has not shown that much lately. What he has to do--soon--is pitch.

Matthews: "Control difficulties, both on and off the field, have prevented him from becoming a real good pitcher in the past. He sometimes seems to fight himself and appears to be his own worst enemy."

HITTING:

For years the Texas Rangers had a reputation for giving up too quickly on players, for not having the patience to let them develop properly. With Pete O'Brien, the Rangers have had patience, and in his second year with the club, it paid off.

O'Brien was one of the most improved hitters in baseball last year. He did everything the Rangers could have expected him to do, and more. He hit with some power and was at his best with runners in scoring position.

One of the biggest reasons for O'Brien's good year was that he stopped chasing balls out of the strike zone. He made the pitcher throw him his pitch. He likes fastballs up, and before last year he would swing at high outside pitches; last season he waited to get a pitch up and in. Pitchers try to keep everything down on him, which is a little unusual for a lefthanded hitter.

He is supremely confident, which allowed him to get through his slump in good shape. He was a streak hitter when he first came to the majors and still is to some extent, but is much more consistent now than he used to be. Still, when he's hot, he can carry a team for a week or more at a time.

He has quick hands and is difficult to fool. He stands back in the batter's box and waits until the last moment to commit himself. O'Brien likes to use the whole field, but most of his power is to right field when he can pull the ball.

BASERUNNING:

O'Brien has good but unrefined speed. Although he is improving, he could probably steal more bases if he concentrated on it. He is an aggressive runner who will break up a double play and try to take the extra base.

FIELDING:

The feeling is that O'Brien will have to clear some space on his mantel for

PETER O'BRIEN
1B, No. 9
LL, 6'1", 198 lbs.
ML Svc: 2 years
Born: 2-9-58 in
   Santa Monica, CA

1984 STATISTICS

AVG	G	AB	R	H	2B	3B	HR	RBI	BB	SO	SB
.287	142	520	57	149	26	2	18	80	53	50	3

CAREER STATISTICS

AVG	G	AB	R	H	2B	3B	HR	RBI	BB	SO	SB
.260	316	1111	123	289	54	8	30	146	117	120	9

VS. RHP   VS. LHP   PROBABLE HIT LOCATIONS

the Gold Gloves he will win someday. Although he appeared to have concentration lapses in the field occasionally last season, he still has all the tools to be one of the best fielding first basemen in the league.

He has an average arm, but he is not intimidated by sharp ground balls and turns the first-to-second-to-first double play as well as anyone. He has pretty good range, especially to his right, and has excellent hands.

OVERALL:

He is smooth at first and has ever-increasing power at the plate. The Rangers must continue to urge him on if they are to contend in the West.

Matthews: "O'Brien is just beginning to emerge as a big leaguer. He will have a lot of pressure on him in 1985. There are some who think that his 1984 performance was just a fluke. O'Brien's challenge this year will be to prove that he can be consistent and that he really is as good as his hype."

HITTING:

Larry Parrish was in his usual early-season slump last year, but broke out of it in Chicago's Comiskey Park when he hit 18 home runs in one night. Actually, 16 of them were in a pre-game contest. But two of them came in the game, and Parrish was off and running to his best season ever, the first time in his career he has driven in 100 runs in a season.

While still considered a streak hitter, he has developed more consistency over the past two years. He has a slightly closed and upright stance and almost tucks his head under his shoulder to remind him to stay in on the ball.

He likes to swing at the first pitch, although he is patient when he gets behind in the count. He likes the ball up and out over the plate. Pitchers try to keep it down on him. He will go through stretches in which he tries to pull the low, outside pitch and can look bad, but those spells seem to get shorter each year. In 1984, he showed power to the opposite field, more so than he had in previous seasons.

Parrish is the kind of hitter who gets better with runners in scoring position or with the game on the line. While he isn't often asked to bunt, he can handle the hit-and-run.

He is a clubhouse leader. Nothing seems to bother him, and it is impossible to tell whether he is hot or slumping by the way he conducts himself. One negative is that he doesn't hit as well playing DH as he does when he is in the field. He's the type of hitter who can carry a team for a while--as he has often done with the Rangers.

BASERUNNING:

With barely average speed, Parrish is not much of a threat to run, but he does what he can. He will break up a double play and is not often caught trying to do more than what he's capable of. He plays within his limits.

LARRY PARRISH
OF, No. 15
RR, 6'3", 215 lbs.
ML Svc: 11 years
Born: 11-10-53 in
  Winter Haven, FL

1984 STATISTICS

AVG	G	AB	R	H	2B	3B	HR	RBI	BB	SO	SB
.285	156	613	73	175	42	1	22	10	42	116	2

CAREER STATISTICS

AVG	G	AB	R	H	2B	3B	HR	RBI	BB	SO	SB
.267	1396	5019	629	1338	292	29	165	604	367	903	24

VS. RHP   VS. LHP   PROBABLE HIT LOCATIONS

FIELDING:

Parrish's most outstanding defensive feature is his arm. Few, if any, right fielders have a better one. He has improved every year as an outfielder after spending most of his career as a third baseman. He filled in nicely at third when Bell missed several games with injuries last year. In the outfield, he still has some trouble coming in on a fly ball. He lacks range, but is reasonably sure-handed once he gets there. Occasionally, he will make a fielding error that a more experienced outfielder wouldn't.

OVERALL:

If he can get hot for a good portion of 1985 and the rest of the team hits as well, fans will have good reason to go to Arlington Stadium this year.

Matthews: "He thrives on the RBI situation and isn't afraid to come up with the game on the line. At those times, he is even more dangerous than usual."

HITTING:

Mickey Rivers is the type of hitter who could roll out of bed in the middle of January, step to the plate and slap a single to right.

He doesn't have the speed he used to when he could ignite a rally by beating out an infield grounder and then stealing second. But Rivers has made the transition from superstar to supersub and can still do things to help a team.

He bats from a deep crouch and could draw plenty of walks if he wasn't such a free swinger. In fact, he is known as one of the best bad ball hitters in baseball. The usual pattern is to start him off with a fastball inside and then try to get him to swing at a breaking ball in the dirt outside.

While he would rather pull the ball, he will hit a ball where it is pitched and can go to all fields. He has almost no power anymore, but can still bunt for a hit. He has surprising bat control for a free swinger and can handle the hit-and-run.

Rivers is consistent. He doesn't go into long slumps. He is at his best leading off an inning, or in the later innings with the winning run in scoring position. He is used mostly as a DH or pinch-hitter now, but has emerged as something of a team leader.

BASERUNNING:

Rivers is no longer a threat to steal. While he's lost a step, he still has the speed, but rarely takes the initiative. He can, however, take the extra base. He does not often attempt to break up a double play. Rivers has been troubled by various muscle pulls in his legs over the past couple years which cut down on his effectiveness.

FIELDING:

Rivers doesn't put a glove on much

MICKEY RIVERS
OF, No. 17
LL, 5'10", 162 lbs.
ML Svc: 15 years
Born: 10-30-48 in
Miami, FL

1984 STATISTICS

AVG	G	AB	R	H	2B	3B	HR	RBI	BB	SO	SB
.300	102	313	40	94	13	1	4	33	9	23	5

CAREER STATISTICS

AVG	G	AB	R	H	2B	3B	HR	RBI	BB	SO	SB
.295	1467	5629	785	1660	247	71	61	499	265	471	266

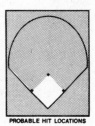

VS. RHP   VS. LHP   PROBABLE HIT LOCATIONS

anymore. When he starts, it's usually as the DH. Otherwise he's a pinch-hitter and leaves the game at the end of the inning. On the rare occasions that he plays the outfield, he still covers a lot of ground, but his arm is below average. He can still throw out an occasional runner who has taken a foolish chance, though.

OVERALL:

He has had a long and productive career. He has found a way to continue to produce and provides a veteran's point of view to the young club.

Matthews: "He can still bother you when he gets on base. He hasn't changed much over the past several years."

HITTING:

Just when Billy Sample thought his career was coming together, it fell apart again in 1984. Sample had always said he could live up to the Rangers' expectations if only he played every day. In 1983, he did (play) and did (have a good year). He thought he was secure.

But last year, he went back to being played on an irregular basis, and his production fell off dramatically.

He likes fastballs up and in. Sample can hit to all fields, but his power is strictly as a pull hitter. He gets a lot of extra-base hits because he will pull the ball into the corner. He has extremely quick hands and a good knowledge of the strike zone, which makes him hard to fool.

He doesn't strike out often. Sample makes good contact for an aggressive hitter. Because of his aggressiveness, pitchers sometimes have success throwing him breaking balls low and away. He will chase bad pitches.

Sample has a tendency to get down on himself when he's in a slump. A guess hitter, he has better success against pitchers he knows. He is a pretty good clutch hitter and can bunt and hit-and-run. A smart player, he will do the little things.

BASERUNNING:

A pulled hamstring in spring training 1984 kept Sample from being as aggressive on the bases as early in the year as he would have liked, and he never seemed to find the groove. When he is healthy, he is a legitimate threat to steal. Sample needs to attempt it more often than he has in the past. He is a smart, hard-nosed runner who will break up a double play and take the extra base almost every chance he gets.

FIELDING:

While he still has the reputation he

BILLY SAMPLE
OF, No. 5
RR, 5'9", 175 lbs.
ML Svc: 7 years
Born: 4-2-55 in
  Roanoke, VA

1984 STATISTICS

AVG	G	AB	R	H	2B	3B	HR	RBI	BB	SO	SB
.247	130	489	967	121	20	2	5	33	29	46	18

CAREER STATISTICS

AVG	G	AB	R	H	2B	3B	HR	RBI	BB	SO	SB
.270	675	2177	1230	587	111	9	39	201	172	194	92

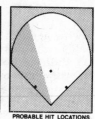

VS. RHP   VS. LHP   PROBABLE HIT LOCATIONS

was tagged with a long time ago, that of a below average fielder, he has worked hard to become a pretty good outfielder. He is not afraid to go into the wall to catch a fly and is excellent at going to the line to cut off a ball before it gets into the corner. He has an average arm, but has a quick release and hits the cutoff man well.

OVERALL:

One of the most determined hitters in the game, Sample steps up to the plate and really wants to hit the ball. Some players wonder if they will hit; Sample has no doubts.

Matthews: "He had a disappointing year in 1984, but injuries and lack of playing time may have contributed to that. He is a solid player who could be at the crossroads of his career now."

PITCHING:

Dave Schmidt believes in his slider, his change-up and himself . . . and not necessarily in that order.

It's a good thing, too, because he has had to overcome more than his share of obstacles over the past few years. There was elbow surgery in 1982 and a hyperextended elbow in 1983. Then there was a bitter contract negotiation in 1984, after which he was told, "We resent paying you this much money."

But Schmidt's confidence is his most outstanding feature, and he had a good season in 1984 despite being used in long, short and middle relief. He just shrugged and got people out.

He has the potential to be a stopper out of the bullpen. Not only does he thrive on pressure situations, but he gets a lot of ground ball outs and throws strikes. He should continue to improve.

FIELDING:

Schmidt is not quick to the plate, but helps compensate for that with a pretty decent move to first. He also isn't afraid to throw to first six or seven times in a row to keep a runner close. He's an above average fielder.

DAVE SCHMIDT
RHP, No. 24
RR, 6'1", 185 lbs.
ML Svc: 3 years
Born: 4-22-57 in
Niles, MI

1984 STATISTICS

W	L	ERA	G	GS	CG	IP	H	R	ER	BB	SO	SV
6	6	2.56	43	0	0	70	69	30	20	20	46	12

CAREER STATISTICS

W	L	ERA	G	GS	CG	IP	H	R	ER	BB	SO	SV
13	16	3.13	121	9	0	259	260	106	90	70	157	21

OVERALL:

Sheer confidence can get one over a lot of hurdles. With the help of a good slider, Schmidt is doing well in spite of his critics, his injuries and his unsettled role on the staff.

Matthews: "He'll challenge the hitters, and is the type of pitcher who likes to throw strikes and see what happens. Schmidt is a come-at-them type of pitcher, who knows his limitations and pitches within them. Since he can also be a spot starter, he is a valuable pitcher to have."

HITTING:

The question about Donnie Scott is a little like trying to decide whether the chicken or the egg came first. In his case, it goes like this: Did he hit below expectations because he didn't play every day? Or did he not play every day because he hit below expectations?

When he was called up from the minors at mid-season, it was assumed that the Rangers wouldn't have brought him up unless they expected him to replace Ned Yost as their everyday catcher.

For a few weeks, Scott played behind the plate most of the time and did fairly well. Then, gradually, his innings and his batting average began to drop; it is hard to tell which started first.

A switch-hitting catcher, Scott likes fastballs in as a lefthander and fastballs down and away when hitting right-handed. Like many young players, he has trouble with big league breaking balls, and that's what he saw most of the time.

He bats from a slightly hunched-over stance and has a good knowledge of the strike zone. He is only average as a bunter and, because he had some trouble making contact, was not reliable on the hit-and-run. He has shown the ability to hit to the right side to move a runner over from second with nobody out.

An aggressive hitter, Scott must learn patience at the major league level. He is prone to getting himself out more than making the pitcher get him out.

BASERUNNING:

Scott is not a good runner. He has below average speed and is not a threat to steal. He has to learn some fundamentals and improve his lead-taking techniques to avoid getting picked off. He is prone to being thrown out trying to take the extra base.

FIELDING:

At this point of his career, defense

DONNIE SCOTT
C, No. 12
SR, 5'11", 185 lbs.
ML Svc: 1 year plus
Born: 8-16-61 in
   Dunedin, FL

1984 STATISTICS

AVG	G	AB	R	H	2B	3B	HR	RBI	BB	SO	SB
.221	81	235	16	52	9	0	3	20	20	44	0

CAREER STATISTICS

AVG	G	AB	R	H	2B	3B	HR	RBI	BB	SO	SB
.218	83	239	16	52	9	0	3	20	20	44	0

VS. RHP   VS. LHP   PROBABLE HIT LOCATIONS

is Scott's strongest point. He has a strong, accurate arm and was successful throwing runners out from his first day in the majors. He is not intimidated even by the best runners, calls a good game and generally handles his position well.

OVERALL:

Scott's value to the club may be as a backup catcher, but in the event that Ned Yost does not adjust better this year than he did in 1984, Scott may become the first-stringer.

Matthews: "With the problems the Rangers were having at the catcher's spot, Scott had a chance to establish himself as a starter but didn't do it. He has the potential to be an excellent defensive player, but whether or not he'll hit enough is still a question."

HITTING:

When Bill Stein is healthy, he is one of the best pinch-hitters in the AL. His biggest problem in 1984 was that he was not healthy all year. He suffered a badly sprained wrist in spring training and was never at 100% for the rest of the season.

Stein's trademark is his aggressiveness at the plate. "Since I am probably only going to have one at-bat, I have to get my swings in," he once explained. "I can't let myself get cheated."

He will swing at the first offering most of the time--and the pitchers know it. He prefers the ball up and in. Stein is a contact, line drive hitter who will hit the ball to all fields, but also has occasional power.

His greatest strength is his temperament: he is well suited to pinch-hitting. He handles pressure situations well and seems to thrive when a hit is needed to keep a rally alive or drive in an important run.

BASERUNNING:

Stein is a better than average baserunner, which may come as a surprise to some people. Because of the situations he usually finds himself in during a game, he often has a runner in front of him, or the percentages dictate against a steal attempt. Given the opportunity, though, he can steal a base. He is basically a conservative runner. He won't try to take the extra base unless he's absolutely sure he can make it, and he is difficult to pick off first because he takes such a short lead.

FIELDING:

He is the type of player who makes lineup-juggling in the late innings a lot easier for a manager. He has played

BILL STEIN
INF, No. 1
RR, 5'10", 170 lbs.
ML Svc: 11 years
Born: 1-21-47 in
    Battle Creek, MI

1984 STATISTICS

AVG	G	AB	R	H	2B	3B	HR	RBI	BB	SO	SB
.279	27	43	3	12	1	0	0	3	5	9	0

CAREER STATISTICS

AVG	G	AB	R	H	2B	3B	HR	RBI	BB	SO	SB
.268	915	2732	263	731	119	17	43	299	185	408	16

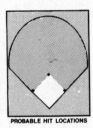

STRONG   STRONG

VS. RHP   VS. LHP   PROBABLE HIT LOCATIONS

third base, second, first and the outfield for the Rangers. He has an above average arm and pretty good range. Stein will make the routine play. When he is at second base, he makes the double play pivot reasonably well.

OVERALL:

When he steps up to the plate, he knows that he may get the chance at four or five pitches. He doesn't mind--in fact, Stein seems to like that kind of challenge. He usually manages to hit at least one of those pitches and get on base.

Matthews: "When he is healthy, he is a tough out, especially when the game is on the line. His versatility is another plus. He is the kind of player every team has to have."

PITCHING:

In his first start of the year, Dave Stewart gave up five runs and didn't survive the second inning.

And then things really started to get bad.

He had trouble throwing strikes. And when he did get the ball across the plate, it was usually hammered. After the All Star break, he seemed to smooth out some of his problems, but never could really seem to break the spell. "It was just one of those years. It was a real learning experience," Stewart said, and much to his credit, he did not get down on himself through it all.

When he was traded to Texas from the Los Angeles Dodgers in August 1983, the Rangers converted him to a starter and he blossomed into a star. He has above average velocity, around 95 MPH, and a good curve. There are times when his pitches don't have much movement, though, and that's usually when he gets hit hard. He is working on a change-up and a forkball, but he doesn't have the confidence to use either as an out pitch yet.

Control was his biggest problem in 1984. He not only walked batters and got behind in the count, but he also had trouble pitching to spots within the strike zone. That resulted in his giving up a lot of home runs. However, he has the physical ability and the mental makeup to bounce back.

FIELDING:

Stewart has a big windup and is slow

DAVE STEWART
RHP, No. 31
RR, 6'2", 200 lbs.
ML Svc: 4 years
Born: 2-19-57 in
    Oakland, CA

1984 STATISTICS

W	L	ERA	G	GS	CG	IP	H	R	ER	BB	SO	SV
7	14	4.73	32	27	3	192	193	106	101	87	119	0

CAREER STATISTICS

W	L	ERA	G	GS	CG	IP	H	R	ER	BB	SO	SV
30	29	3.72	164	50	5	518	488	234	214	200	307	15

getting rid of the ball to the plate. Because of that, he needs to pay more attention to the baserunners: when he does throw to first, nobody in baseball guns it over there harder. He is an above average fielder.

OVERALL:

Building a major league pitching arsenal takes some time. It will also cost some mistakes. Stewart had his troubles last year but earned respect by not despairing.

Matthews: "It seems that he is becoming a little more of a pitcher and less of a thrower. He has shown the ability to be a top starter and reliever, but needs to become much more consistent."

PITCHING:

In baseball slang, some pitchers are a "a comfortable 0 for 4." That is, batters don't mind facing them. They feel comfortable and confident at the plate. But when the game is over, they realize they haven't had any hits. The expression could have been invented for Frank Tanana.

Before he hurt his arm, Tanana was the kind of pitcher batters hated to face. He had a wicked curve and one of baseball's best fastballs. Now, he has made the full transition from total power pitcher to pure finesse pitcher. His fastball is below average and he rarely throws it for strikes. The speed of his curve could be timed by an hourglass instead of by a radar gun.

Despite that, he is an experimenter on the mound and uses every pitch there is: he has a slider, a change-up and a forkball. He can throw most of them with three or four different motions.

A student of the game, Tanana normally tries to jam righthanders with his fastball and keep his breaking stuff away from lefthanders. He sometimes throws his breaking ball to set up his fastball, the opposite pattern from what most pitchers use.

FIELDING:

Tanana is a pitcher who will help himself with his fielding. His move to first is deceptive, almost a hesitation

FRANK TANANA
LHP, No. 28
LL, 6'3", 195 lbs.
ML Svc: 12 years
Born: 7-3-53 in
     Detroit, MI

1984 STATISTICS												
W	L	ERA	G	GS	CG	IP	H	R	ER	BB	SO	SV
15	15	3.25	35	35	9	246	234	117	89	81	141	0
CAREER STATISTICS												
W	L	ERA	G	GS	CG	IP	H	R	ER	BB	SO	SV
135	130	3.26	343	328	116	2354	2180	973	852	650	1647	0

throw. He is a very tough pitcher for a runner to get a jump on, even though his motion is slow and the ball takes a long time to get to the plate.

OVERALL:

Any pitcher who throws a curveball as slow as Tanana has to be smart--one wrong pitch to one wrong batter and it's bye-bye, Frank. That has not happened too often, however. He knows both himself and the opposition and uses the information to his advantage.

Matthews: "Tanana is very bright. He has made the transition from power to finesse as well as anybody ever has. He thinks his way through a game. Every pitch has a purpose."

HITTING:

Gary Ward's 1984 season has to be considered in two parts. In the first half, he was not aggressive at the plate, didn't hit for power or average, didn't drive in many runs and struck out a lot.

In the second half, though, Ward became the kind of slugger the Rangers had hoped he would be when they got him from the Minnesota Twins. He lifted his average and starting hitting homers and driving in runs.

Like most power hitters, Ward likes fastballs in. He is a first ball hitter with good power to all fields. In the first few months of the season, Ward seemed to shy away from inside pitches and breaking balls. He later admitted that he was still thinking about being beaned late in the 1983 season. He also had enjoyed playing for the Twins, and the trade to the Rangers had shaken him up.

Once he adjusted, though, he began to hit the ball hard. He began hanging in on the breaking pitches and emerged as one of the more dangerous bats in the Rangers' lineup. He is an aggressive player who earned the respect of his teammates by the way he handled his early-season slump. When Ward is going well, he won't give in to the pitcher and can carry a club for a week or two.

A classic streak hitter, his usual pattern is: start slow/finish fast. In 1984, however, his start in 1984 was slower than usual.

BASERUNNING:

Ward is a good baserunner, especially for a big man. He has good speed and knows how and when to take the extra base and how and when to steal. He is aggressive in all phases of his game, including running the bases.

FIELDING:

Ward had all kinds of trouble in the

GARY WARD
OF, No. 32
RR, 6'2", 207 lbs.
ML Svc: 4 years
Born: 12-6-53 in
  Los Angeles, CA

1984 STATISTICS

AVG	G	AB	R	H	2B	3B	HR	RBI	BB	SO	SB
.284	155	602	97	171	21	7	21	79	55	95	7

CAREER STATISTICS

AVG	G	AB	R	H	2B	3B	HR	RBI	BB	SO	SB
.284	572	2145	313	610	101	27	72	298	170	355	33

  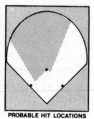

VS. RHP   VS. LHP   PROBABLE HIT LOCATIONS

beginning of the season, partly because he played both left field and center field in an unfamiliar stadium. In the middle of the season, Ward was the DH quite a bit, but his fielding, like his hitting, improved as the season continued. He has a good arm, and is fundamentally very sound in the field.

OVERALL:

Ward is a solid ballplayer, dependable both at the plate and in the field. He took a while to become adjusted to being with the Rangers, but should be fresh and tough right from the start in 1985.

Matthews: "It's hard to say how much getting hurt had bothered him, but he came on strong at the end of the season. He is a proven hitter and has always been the kind of batter who will drive in runs. He's just a solid, all-around player."

HITTING:

After Curtis Wilkerson went practically 0 for April, there were those who were ready to concede that the rookie was overmatched by big league pitching.

Wilkerson, however, was not one of them. As the weather warmed up, so did his bat. And when the season ended, he had had a more than respectable offensive year.

As the year went on, he became more aggressive at the plate. He likes to swing at the first pitch and prefers fastballs up and over the plate. He can be jammed, and seems to have trouble with breaking stuff down. He has little power, but makes pretty good contact and can line a ball into the corner or the alleys for extra bases. He has slightly more power batting righthanded than lefthanded, but will bunt for a hit from both sides. He also has good bat control and will hit behind the runner and execute the hit-and-run.

Wilkerson has a good attitude and still has room to improve. If he does, he can be a top-quality middle infielder.

BASERUNNING:

He has above average speed and is always a threat to steal. He will probably be even more of a threat after he learns the pitchers and develops more confidence in his abilities. While he will make rookie mistakes, most of them are misjudgments.

FIELDING:

Wilkerson was the seventh opening day shortstop the Rangers have had in eight years. He vowed to be the last one for a long time. That may not be the case, however. He was moved to second base at mid-season to make room for yet another

CURT WILKERSON
SS, No. 19
SR, 5'9", 158 lbs.
ML Svc: 1 year plus
Born: 4-26-61 in
Petersburg, VA

1984 STATISTICS

AVG	G	AB	R	H	2B	3B	HR	RBI	BB	SO	SB
.248	153	484	47	120	12	0	1	26	22	72	12

CAREER STATISTICS

AVG	G	AB	R	H	2B	3B	HR	RBI	BB	SO	SB
.243	169	519	54	126	12	1	1	27	24	77	15

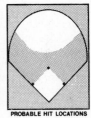

VS. RHP   VS. LHP   PROBABLE HIT LOCATIONS

shortstop, rookie Jeff Kunkel. At either position, Wilkerson has the potential to become an excellent fielder. He has good range and a strong arm. He will make the spectacular play but, like many young players, has trouble on routine grounders right at him.

OVERALL:

Wilkerson's future will be determined by his glove. If his bat can just keep up with big league pitching, the Rangers will be happy. The team may be on its way to gaining not just defensive respectability, but real strength.

Matthews: "Wilkerson is a young and much-improved player. It will be interesting to see how much better he can get. If he keeps up his current pace, he could be one of the best in a few years."

HITTING:

George Wright was on the verge of be-coming one of the best center fielders in baseball last year, but then spent more time trying to recover from injur-ies than playing baseball.

A switch-hitter, he prefers to pull the ball when he can and likes fastballs up and in. Pitchers have had some suc-cess changing speeds on him, and he has difficulty with low, outside breaking balls. Sometimes a fastball can sneak by him, but only if it's at the knees. If it's up, Wright will make the pitcher pay for his mistake. It is also impor-tant to change speeds on him. He is al-most fanatical about working out with weights and taking extra batting prac-tice, and as he gets stronger he should add even more power.

The injuries left him in low spirits for much of the year; he has a hard time sitting and watching while others play. As he matures, he should get better and better. He will bunt for a hit, usually pushing the ball toward third base.

BASERUNNING:

When he is healthy, Wright is a speedy and dangerous baserunner. He is always a threat to steal. He takes a long lead no matter how many times a pitcher has thrown to first, but rarely gets picked off. If anything, he may be too aggressive on the bases, but he can also make things happen with that style of play.

FIELDING:

The Rangers put a wraparound score-board around the Arlington Stadium bleachers last year. That cut down the wind that usually blows in from right, and as a result, balls carried a lot more than they ever had before.

GEORGE WRIGHT
CF, No. 26
SR, 5'11", 180 lbs.
ML Svc: 3 years
Born: 12-12-58 in
Oklahoma City, OK

1984 STATISTICS

AVG	G	AB	R	H	2B	3B	HR	RBI	BB	SO	SB
.243	101	383	40	93	19	4	9	48	15	54	0

CAREER STATISTICS

AVG	G	AB	R	H	2B	3B	HR	RBI	BB	SO	SB
.264	413	1574	188	415	67	15	38	178	86	215	11

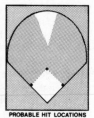

VS. RHP   VS. LHP   PROBABLE HIT LOCATIONS

Still, Wright plays as shallow as anyone in the league. He has outstanding range and a strong arm. There was some thought of moving him to right, but the experiment was shelved after a short trial.

OVERALL:

A recovered George Wright is a happy George Wright, and a happy George Wright is crucial to the Rangers. He will be chomping at the bit to get back into the lineup in 1985, and if Texas is lucky, he will try to make up for lost time.

Matthews: "When injuries interrupted him, he was on his way to becoming one of the best. He has great natural talent and works hard to improve it, which is a great combination."

HITTING:

It was bad enough for Ned Yost that he had to come to the Rangers and replace popular veteran Jim Sundberg. It was bad enough that manager Doug Rader said that Texas had gotten Yost because they thought he was better than Jim Sundberg. It was bad enough that, when he arrived, Yost found out he had been assigned Sundberg's old number, 10.

But what really got the 1984 season off to a rocky start for Yost was that, in the second game of the regular season, the Cleveland Indians stole six bases off him.

He never seemed to live that down and became sensitive to criticism, both real and imagined. After failing in his first chance to be an everyday starting catcher in the big leagues last year, his goal will be to try to start 1985 anew.

Yost always seems to look for, and swing at, a high inside fastball. He is impatient at the plate and pitchers can take advantage of that with breaking pitches, change-ups and even fastballs out of his hitting area.

He doesn't walk much and is prone to prolonged slumps. He will hit a home run occasionally, but is not considered dangerous with runners on base and can be pitched to under any circumstance.

BASERUNNING:

Yost has pretty good speed for a catcher and is aggressive on the bases. He does not ordinarily present a threat to steal. He will do what he can to help the team, including slide hard to break up a double play.

FIELDING:

He has a strong arm, but a slow release and not much accuracy. The Rangers were convinced when they traded for him that his problems were mechanical, but now they're not so sure. Having the Indians steal the six bases didn't help

NED YOST
C, No. 10
RR, 6'1", 190 lbs.
ML Svc: 4 years
Born: 8-19-55 in
Eureka, CA

1984 STATISTICS

AVG	G	AB	R	H	2B	3B	HR	RBI	BB	SO	SB
.182	80	242	15	44	4	0	6	25	6	47	1

CAREER STATISTICS

AVG	G	AB	R	H	2B	3B	HR	RBI	BB	SO	SB
.212	214	594	53	126	15	4	16	64	21	115	5

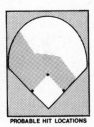

VS. RHP   VS. LHP   PROBABLE HIT LOCATIONS

any. With Yost behind the plate, the number of passed balls increased sharply, indicating that he wasn't blocking pitches that Sundberg might have. However, he is agile behind the plate, gets out to field bunts well and has good range on pop fouls.

OVERALL:

It is difficult to imagine Yost being compared to Sundberg. You have to wonder what impressions the Rangers were basing their moves on. In 1983, the year they were looking at, Yost had the second worst fielding percentage in the league. It was unfair from the start to consider him an adequate replacement.

Matthews: "He played tight all year, maybe because he was replacing Sundberg and maybe because he was pressing too hard to do well in his first chance to be a full-time starter. At any rate, he still has to prove he can do the job."

JIM ANDERSON
C/INF, No. 14
RR, 6'0", 180 lbs.
ML Svc: 6 years
Born: 2-23-57 in
    Los Angeles, CA

HITTING, BASERUNNING, FIELDING:

When he started his pro career, Jim Anderson expected to become one of the best shortstops in baseball. And, with his infectious confidence, he may have even convinced some other people.

Remaining unconvinced, however, were most of the managers Anderson played for. So he decided to try the next best thing. He decided to become a good player at as many different positions as he could find.

Since then, Anderson has played sec-ond base, third base, outfield and even catcher. In the process, he's made himself a valuable addition to the team because of his versatility.

Hitting is another story, though. He didn't do enough of it and, as a result, spent part of the 1984 season in the minors. Anderson is a slap hitter with little power. He tries to put the ball in play and use the whole field. He likes fastballs up and in and has trouble with breaking pitches down and away, partly because he bats out of an upright stance.

He has good hands and an above average arm from shortstop. Anderson has slightly above average speed on the bases, and plays well within his limits.

OVERALL:

Matthews: "His versatility makes him an asset to a team, but he has to prove he can hit well enough not playing every day to become more valuable."

ALAN BANNISTER
INF/OF, No. 7
RR, 5'11", 175 lbs.
ML Svc: 10 years
Born: 9-3-51 in
    Buena Park, CA

HITTING, BASERUNNING, FIELDING:

When the Rangers traded for Alan Bannister early last season, there was one question that everybody asked: Why?

Bannister quickly answered the question, not with anything he said, but by the way he played. A versatile veteran, he can fill in at any infield position except shortstop and better yet, he can do it well even if he has been sitting on the bench for several games.

Bannister isn't known for having power, but he helped beat the Minnesota Twins last season with a home run. He made all the plays in the field. Simply, he did everything he was asked to do and did it well. Only a sprained wrist that caused him to miss several weeks kept him from contributing even more.

Bannister does the little things that can help a team win. He is a good bunter, makes contact and hits behind the runner when necessary. A contact, line drive hitter, he's usually aware of what the pitcher is trying to accomplish and won't play into his hands. He prefers pitches on the inside of the plate.

While he has limited range, he makes up for it by playing hitters well and by getting a good jump on the ball. He has a below average arm. A smart runner despite average speed, Bannister won't hurt the team when he's on the bases.

OVERALL:

Matthews: "Bannister is a smart guy. He thinks his way through a game pretty well. Because of his versatility and the fact that he can pinch-hit, he's a good type of player to have on a team. He can do a lot for you."

BOBBY JONES
OF/1B, No. 6
LL, 6'1", 170 lbs.
ML Svc: 2 years
Born: 10-11-59 in
  Elkton, MD

HITTING, BASERUNNING, FIELDING:

Bobby Jones is an example of persistence that paid off. He signed his first pro contract in 1967, but it wasn't until 18 years later that he spent his first full year in the majors. In between, he served a stint in Vietnam, played for two years in Japan and was released by the California Angels.

Jones has developed the ability to be a steady performer even though he plays irregularly. He can handle fastballs up and in. A seasoned veteran, he is not often fooled by off-speed pitches, but good breaking stuff can give him a problem. He is a patient hitter who makes the pitcher get him out.

After all these years, his attitude is perfectly suited to the long baseball season. He doesn't get too high when things are going well or too low when he is in a slump.

Jones is a savvy hitter who can bunt and hit-and-run and will do the little things that can help a team.

He has only average speed, but knows how to run the bases. He can steal a base if the pitcher lets him get a jump. He can take the extra base if an outfielder does not pay attention.

In the outfield, Jones is also a steady performer. He makes the routine play and has a slightly above average arm. He will hit the cutoff man or throw to the right base and rarely makes a mental mistake that will hurt the team.

OVERALL:

Matthews: "While not outstanding in any category, Bobby is a solid player. It would have been interesting to see what he could have done if he had gotten a chance to play regularly in the big leagues when he was younger."

ODELL JONES
RHP, No. 21
RR, 6'3", 174 lbs.
ML Svc: 5 years
Born: 1-13-53 in
  Tulare, CA

PITCHING, FIELDING:

Just when it looked as if Odell Jones would have to start looking for another line of work, Rangers pitching coach Dick Such watched him shagging flies in the outfield one day. Jones was throwing the balls back to the infield with an easy, underhanded motion that reminded Such of the Kansas City Royals' submariner Dan Quisenberry.

A few weeks later, just before the All Star break, Jones tried out his new delivery. It was successful early, but less so as the season went on. Jones's career is back at the crossroads.

Jones relied on a straight overhand fastball for most of his career, but indifferent success and some arm problems convinced him to experiment. He became a short reliever in 1983, and for a while that seemed to be the answer. However, he struggled last year. He still throws an overhand fastball and a sweeping slider.

Jones has a slow delivery to the plate and sometimes doesn't concentrate enough on holding runners close to first. As a result, he is easy to run on. He also does not end his follow-through in the classic position to field and has trouble fielding bunts and covering first on a ball hit to the left side.

OVERALL:

Matthews: "While he has had some success in the past and could develop as a submariner, the jury is still out."

DAVE TOBIK
RHP, No. 41
RR, 6'1", 190 lbs.
ML Svc: 7 years
Born: 3-2-53 in
    Euclid, OH

PITCHING, FIELDING:

Dave Tobik started last season as the Rangers' bullpen stopper. He ended it in the minors.

It wasn't that he was consistently bad: he was consistently inconsistent.

A finesse pitcher, Tobik's control has to be perfect for him to be effective. He throws a decent change-up, but his best pitch is a forkball. He tends to throw it too low and bounces it in the dirt with runners on base.

Tobik doesn't hold runners on well and has a deliberate motion to the plate. He is average at fielding bunts, backing up bases and covering first.

OVERALL:

Matthews: "Tobik has been effective at times, but hasn't shown enough consistency. If he is used properly, he can help some teams."

WAYNE TOLLESON
2B, No. 3
SR, 5'9", 160 lbs.
ML Svc: 3 years
Born: 11-22-55 in
    Spartanburg, SC

HITTING, BASERUNNING, FIELDING:

Wayne Tolleson has shown streaks of brilliance, but the Rangers are convinced that his lack of size means he tires easily and cannot be an everyday player.

A starter during the second half of 1983 and the first half of 1984, Wayne reacted in typical fashion when told the team wanted him to be a utility player. "Then I will try to become the best utility player I can," he said.

A switch-hitter, Tolleson bats from a slightly closed stance. He is strictly a fastball hitter who likes the ball up where he can handle it. He will swing at the first pitch. He has a little more power from the right side than the left, and most teams will shade him to left when he's batting lefthanded. But his biggest skills as an offensive player are bunts and hit-and-run situations that take advantage of his superior bat control.

He has above average speed and is a threat to steal when on base. Pitchers must always be aware of him. Despite his small size, he is scrappy on the bases.

In the field, he has an adequate arm but pretty good range and gets rid of the ball quickly and accurately. He stays in well on the double play.

OVERALL:

Matthews: "Tolleson is a tough player who has surprised some people over the years. He has handled his demotion with determination, which is what the team would have expected."

TORONTO BLUE JAYS

PITCHING:

The Atlanta Braves have now realized they made a mistake in letting Phil Niekro and Joe Cowley go to the New York Yankees. Jim Acker is another former Brave farmhand. He had a very good year in his rookie year with the Blue Jays in 1983, but slacked off in 1984, so the jury is obviously still out on this big, hard throwing relief pitcher.

He was a starter until the Jays put him in the bullpen in 1983, and he will stay in the pen. He throws from over the top and has an excellent fastball. He is difficult to hit homers off because he throws what baseball people call a "heavy ball." In addition, he keeps the fastball and slider low. He does not have a good curve, but as a reliever, relies on the fastball and hard slider. Occasionally, he will throw a straight change.

He can be effective when he keeps the pitches down and away, but he is not afraid to come inside to either lefties or righties with hard stuff, usually up. If his location is off, he can be hit, and he gave up more than a hit an inning in 1984.

He comes at batters and will use the fastball with two strikes, or the slider down and away. Although he does not walk many batters, he will come in with too many fat pitches, particularly when behind in the count.

FIELDING:

He is a good athlete and a good fielder who fielded his position flawlessly in 1983. He saw more action in 1984 and backed up bases very well. He has a good move to first, but he is not

JIM ACKER
RHP, No. 31
RR, 6'2", 210 lbs.
ML Svc: 2 years
Born: 9-24-58 in Freer, TX

1984 STATISTICS

W	L	ERA	G	GS	CG	IP	H	R	ER	BB	SO	SV
3	5	4.38	32	3	0	72	79	39	35	25	33	1

CAREER STATISTICS

W	L	ERA	G	GS	CG	IP	H	R	ER	BB	SO	SV
8	6	4.34	70	8	0	170	182	91	82	63	77	2

as accurate as he should be on throws to first when holding a runner or fielding a bunt. He tries his best as a fielder and after his release winds up in good position to field comebackers.

OVERALL:

He had a great time as a rookie in 1983, going 5-1 as a starter and reliever. When the Jays got Dennis Lamp, it was obvious Lamp was to be the main man out of the pen, and Acker was shuffled back in the pack. Either through ineffectiveness or inactivity, Acker did not have many save opportunities and was not used in many critical games. It could have an effect on his confidence.

Robinson: "It seems he has the ability to shake off a bad outing and he knows his role with the Jays. He is probably pitching as well as he can. He just might be a borderline major leaguer who can help the Jays as a middle inning reliever."

HITTING:

Willie Aikens has a closed stance with a slight crouch and looks for fastballs above the belt and close to the inside part of the plate. Before his drug problems, which sent him to prison, Aikens had four productive years with Kansas City. He has power and looks to hit the long ball. If he gets a fastball up an in, he can hit it out of any park in the league; but in 1984, after his ordeal and a late start, he never got untracked with the bat. His timing was off and pitchers were able to throw the fastball by him. He did manage 11 homers in 234 at-bats, but was helped by the short fences in Exhibition Stadium.

Lefthanded pitchers (whom he rarely faces) will throw him curves away and in the dirt. Aikens has a tendency to chase bad pitches. Righthanders will turn the ball over and keep it away, but Aikens can go to left field if he has to. He hit well in post-season play while with the Royals, and must be considered a threat with men on base.

Toronto gave him a second chance in baseball after acquiring him from the Royals in the off-season. Given the job of DH against certain righthanders, he hit less than .200 for much of the year. He was, however, one of the few Blue Jays who hit well in September.

BASERUNNING:

It usually takes a home run to score Aikens from first base or, quite possibly, three singles. He is without doubt the slowest major league runner, and will never steal or advance more than one base at a time.

FIELDING:

Aikens has defensive shortcomings at first base. His range is limited and his arm is average. He does not stretch well or reach too far for throws from the infielders, but now that he is a DH, it is

WILLIE AIKENS
INF, No. 24
LR, 6'2", 220 lbs.
ML Svc: 6 years
Born: 10-14-54 in
Seneca, SC

1984 STATISTICS

AVG	G	AB	R	H	2B	3B	HR	RBI	BB	SO	SB
.205	93	234	21	48	7	0	11	26	29	56	0

CAREER STATISTICS

AVG	G	AB	R	H	2B	3B	HR	RBI	BB	SO	SB
.271	762	2472	299	671	124	2	109	410	316	438	3

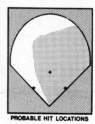

VS. RHP   VS. LHP   PROBABLE HIT LOCATIONS

doubtful that he will play much first base.

OVERALL:

Aikens has a chance to help a team because he has played with a winner and can pinch-hit. He can also be a productive DH. His future seems to be up to him. He is a decent person who did not speak to the press for several years because he had a severe speech problem, yet he tried his best to overcome that and was quite popular with both the Royals and the Blue Jays players.

Robinson: "He is now a DH against righthanded pitchers, and that should indeed be his cup of tea. He has got a good park to hit in, and I think that the best thing for Aikens and all others concerned is to forget that there ever was a 1984. His attitude is good and I know that he will work his hardest to try to have a year like he did with the Royals a few years ago."

PITCHING:

Doyle Alexander was never mentioned as a candidate for the Cy Young Award in 1984, but if he had won his last start on the last day on the season, he would have been 18-5 and had a 10-game winning streak. They are difficult figures to overlook. Alexander did not win his last start, but still finished with the highest winning percentage (.739) in the league.

He does not have a good curveball but does have an excellent sinker, slider and change. His fastball is spotted in and out, up and down, and can surprise batters who see nothing but off-speed pitches and an occasional knuckler. He is not afraid to throw his 84 MPH fastball directly over the heart of the plate if he has a batter set up.

He is now one of the best control pitchers in the league and will not let walks beat him. He has control of every pitch he throws and knows the strengths and weaknesses of every batter in the league. He usually hits the outside corner with a sinker or slider, then starts throwing sinkers and sliders up and down in the strike zone. He is a deliberate pitcher and gets tougher with men on. He can release any of his four pitches from overhand or three-quarters, giving him a wide assortment of release points and making it difficult for the batter to know how a certain pitch will break.

FIELDING:

He has been around and knows how to field. He is not fast off the mound, but covers first well and backs up the

DOYLE ALEXANDER
RHP, No. 33
RR, 6'3", 190 lbs.
ML Svc: 14 years
Born: 9-4-50 in
Cordova, AL

1984 STATISTICS												
W	L	ERA	G	GS	CG	IP	H	R	ER	BB	SO	SV
17	6	3.13	36	35	11	261	238	99	91	59	139	0

CAREER STATISTICS												
W	L	ERA	G	GS	CG	IP	H	R	ER	BB	SO	SV
132	115	3.70	397	300	71	2219	2170	1009	912	699	918	3

proper base with men on. He winds up in perfect fielding position after release and fields his position very well. He fields bunts well and makes accurate throws to the proper base. He does not let fielding beat him. With men on base, he is not afraid to throw six or seven times to first base to keep a runner close.

OVERALL:

The Yankees gave up on him, but in 1983 he won his last seven games for the Jays. In 1984 he was tied for third in innings pitched, tied for fourth in starts, tied for sixth in wins and tied for eighth in earned run average. What more could he have done to prove the Yankees wrong and the Jays right?

Robinson: "He must be good because everyone counted him out and now all he does is win. He doesn't overpower anybody, changes speeds and gets batters out. He's amazing."

HITTING:

Just when Barfield thought he would become the fourth Jay player to play every day--along with Willie Upshaw, Lloyd Moseby and Damaso Garcia--along came George Bell, and Barfield joined the Platoon Parade. He did raise his average from .253, but his homers and RBIs dropped significantly. He played right field against lefties, with Bell playing left, but sat against righties, with Bell playing right.

Barfield stands deep in the box, stance slightly closed, feet spread apart. Despite the fairly wide stance, Barfield takes a big step toward the pitch as it approaches home plate. Pitchers can throw hard stuff to him, but they must be careful to keep it in and up. He gets around very well on fastballs and prefers them low. Once a notorious pull hitter, Jesse has learned to go with the pitch and has outstanding power to both left and right-center.

Like most power hitters, Barfield sees a lot of curves and sliders, low and away, and off-speed pitches. He has long arms and can reach some of those pitches, and he improved his average, despite seeing less playing time, by going the other way. He will, ordinarily, try to pull a fastball that he thinks he can hit for a homer. He cut down his strikeout total (from 110 to 81) and drew a few more walks (35 to 22) and is obviously learning to be more patient. He is known as a streak hitter who can hit anything in sight when he is hot, but does suffer slumps and dry spells.

BASERUNNING:

He is fast enough out of the box and on the basepaths. He also ran more on the basepaths in 1984 and stole eight of 10 bases. He does not frighten opposing pitchers, but will steal when he has to and will take the extra base. He also runs hard and is aggressive.

JESSE BARFIELD
OF, No. 29
RR, 6'1", 190 lbs.
ML Svc: 3 years
Born: 10-29-59 in
   Joliet, IL

1984 STATISTICS

AVG	G	AB	R	H	2B	3B	HR	RBI	BB	SO	SB
.284	110	320	51	91	14	1	14	49	35	81	8

CAREER STATISTICS

AVG	G	AB	R	H	2B	3B	HR	RBI	BB	SO	SB
.257	402	1197	170	308	43	8	61	184	103	289	15

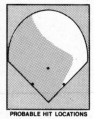

STRONG · VS. RHP   STRONG · VS. LHP   PROBABLE HIT LOCATIONS

FIELDING:

No one in baseball has a stronger arm than Barfield. It is a cannon. He charges grounders well and has a quick release. He must, however, try to hit his cutoff man more. He can go to his left or right and is not afraid to dive either way. He gets a decent jump on a ball, but has a bit too much trouble with grounders coming his way.

OVERALL:

He is still young, something many people seem to forget, and he is still learning this game.

Robinson: "He has some talent but did not play every day because of long dry spells as a hitter. To have a great year he will have to play more, but his attitude is good and he does many good things for you. If he plays more, he'll come back up in homers and RBIs."

HITTING:

There was weeping and moaning in the streets of Toronto when Barry Bonnell was traded away in December 1983, but the sorrow turned to joy when Blue Jays fans got a look at George Bell.

He started swinging in spring training and never stopped until the season was over. He set club records in doubles with 39 (third in the league) and in extra-base hits with 69, tying him for fourth in the league.

Bell uses a closed stance, stands deep in the box and keeps his weight on his front foot. As the pitcher is winding up, Bell shifts the weight to his back foot and hurls everything he has at the pitch. He is truly a player who does not get cheated at the plate; he swings at everything he sees.

Because of his trigger-like mechanics at the plate, it is difficult to throw a fastball by him. He usually hammers anything that is hard, up and in.

Pitchers seem to be having trouble setting up a book on him. Those who have had a degree of success throw the fastball low and away, as well as off-speed curves and sliders. Bell can hit the high curve, but will have trouble with the straight change or a series of breaking balls on the outside part of the plate.

Bell is not up there to walk and will swing hard at everything he sees, regardless of the count.

BASERUNNING:

He is an all-out aggressive player with above average speed. He is still, however, learning to run the bases. He takes a long lead at first to distract the pitcher, and does a good job of it. He is not a good slider, but runs hard into every base.

FIELDING:

Bell played in left field against lefthanded pitchers and in right field

GEORGE BELL
OF, No. 11
RR, 6'1", 185 lbs.
ML Svc: 2 years
Born: 10-21-59 in
    San Pedro de Macoris, DR

1984 STATISTICS

AVG	G	AB	R	H	2B	3B	HR	RBI	BB	SO	SB
.292	159	606	85	177	39	4	26	87	24	86	11

CAREER STATISTICS

AVG	G	AB	R	H	2B	3B	HR	RBI	BB	SO	SB
.278	258	881	109	245	46	9	33	116	33	130	15

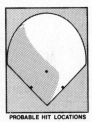

STRONG VS. RHP   STRONG VS. LHP   PROBABLE HIT LOCATIONS

against righthanded pitchers: it is not an easy thing to do. He is fast, covers a lot of ground and has a good arm. He is learning how to come in and go back on balls better than he does, but he still makes some mental and physical mistakes in the outfield. His throws are strong, but not as accurate as they should be.

Bell needs to work on fielding ground balls, although he is picking up the tricks and foibles of artificial surfaces.

OVERALL:

Bell had a steady year. At various points in the season, he had a 10-game hitting streak, an eight-game streak and a dozen streaks of four or more games. He got his big chance last year and did everything in his power to keep the job.

Robinson: "George starts swinging in the hotel lobby and never stops. This young man is no flash in the pan . . . he is just a good hitter."

PITCHING:

Jim Clancy went from a 15-game winner in 1983 to a 15-game loser in 1984. Only four pitchers in the league with at least 13 decisions had a higher ERA than Clancy's 5.12. . .but no pitcher in the league started more games than Clancy (36).

He is a definite, bona fide enigma because he is 6'4" and 203 lbs. and throws a fastball that has been clocked at better than 92 MPH and a hard slider that many teams claim is the best in the league. He has been told he needs another pitch, so he has recently worked on a forkball . . . which may or may not be a mistake.

Clancy throws from three-quarters and is similar to teammate Dave Stieb in that he does not give in to batters. He will throw the fastball up and in to righties and throw the slider at the heart of the plate when he would rather place it on the outside corner. Despite the excellent slider, Clancy has trouble changing speeds with it. He will throw it in any situation, regardless of the count, but because it is so fast and because it does not always break as much as it should, batters can hit it.

He had control problems in 1984 and completed only five games. For a team without a strong bullpen, that is not a good way to try to be a .500 pitcher. Clancy pitched every fifth day, all year long, but had a tremendous amount of trouble in the early innings in many games. He was hit hard and often. When manager Bobby Cox tried to stay with him, he had to keep his fingers crossed that Clancy would not start getting wild. In one game in August, Clancy walked nine White Sox batters--in six innings.

FIELDING:

He has worked hard on perfecting his

JIM CLANCY
RHP, No. 18
RR, 6'4", 203 lbs.
ML Svc: 7 years
Born: 12-18-55 in
Chicago, IL

1984 STATISTICS

W	L	ERA	G	GS	CG	IP	H	R	ER	BB	SO	SV
13	15	5.12	36	36	5	219	249	132	125	88	118	0

CAREER STATISTICS

W	L	ERA	G	GS	CG	IP	H	R	ER	BB	SO	SV
79	96	4.20	222	220	57	1420	1425	741	662	587	747	0

move to first and has tried to pitch more quickly in order to keep his fielders on their toes, but runners will run on him. He still has trouble handling bunts and could improve his fielding in general.

OVERALL:

He is the senior Jay player. He says, "Give me the ball," does not miss a turn, but seems to be going backward while the team is going forward.

Robinson: "I have to believe it was just one of those years. How in the world can a guy who throws so hard and has so much stuff pitch that bad? He MUST be better than 13-15 and a 5.12 ERA. I'm not saying the year was bad with 13 wins, but he is a better pitcher than giving up more than five runs a game. It's just possible his fastball is a bit too straight when it comes in. If the Jays can't make a deal for an ace reliever, they might try him in the bullpen, even though I think he is best as a starter. They've tried just about everything else with him."

PITCHING:

Between 1974 and 1980, Bryan Clark played with 11 minor league teams. He never gave up, persevered and finally came up to the Seattle Mariners in 1981. He started and relieved and went 7-10 in 1983 with a pitiful team. He got his "break" in December of 1983 when the up-and-coming Blue Jays traded outfielder Barry Bonnell to the Mariners and acquired him.

The Jays needed a lefty, whether as a reliever or as a starter. Clark was their idea of the man.

Clark did neither in 1984, gained a bit too much weight, was sent to the minors (Syracuse) and wound up pitching in only 20 games for the Jays. It is a shame, because Clark has one of the best sliders in the big leagues. Lefties simply cannot hit it because he throws it hard and usually in good spots. It does not dip as much as Ron Guidry's, for example, but it breaks late. Clark's fastball is upwards of 88 MPH, so it would appear that he would be perfect as a short relief man to come in to get out lefties. As a starter, Clark fiddled with a curve and change, neither of which was effective. Clark has trouble controlling his curve, and the Jays were forced to send him down to the Chiefs with a simple bit of advice: "Throw strikes!"

The lefty power pitcher had difficulty throwing strikes all year and that got him in trouble. He had six wild pitches in only 45.2 innings and averaged a walk every two innings.

FIELDING:

He is a deliberate worker who doesn't throw to first as often as he should.

BRYAN CLARK
LHP, No. 35
LL, 6'2", 185 lbs.
ML Svc: 4 years
Born: 7-12-56 in
Madera, CA

1984 STATISTICS

W	L	ERA	G	GS	CG	IP	H	R	ER	BB	SO	SV
1	2	5.91	20	3	0	45	66	33	30	22	21	0

CAREER STATISTICS

W	L	ERA	G	GS	CG	IP	H	R	ER	BB	SO	SV
15	19	3.93	127	34	4	415	422	213	181	207	219	2

Runners will run on him because he takes his time getting the ball to home plate. His move to first is slightly above average. His follow-through does not leave him in a good position to field grounders hit to either side of him.

OVERALL:

Clark just might have arm or elbow problems that are bothering him, but he seems to be able to pitch any time he is asked. He was hit too hard and too often in 1984 for everything not to be right.

Robinson: "I think you have seen his best. He surely takes the game seriously because he knows this might be his last hurrah, but I doubt if he'll get any better. Toronto wants him to make it because they need a lefthander. If Clark does make it, he will be the number 9 or 10 man on the staff."

HITTING:

When things went bad for Dave Collins in the past, he would head to the nearest gymnasium to work out AFTER the ballgame. He needed a place to run off his excess energy. With the Blue Jays in 1984, Collins used the baseball field to let off his excess energy and had a superb year.

He batted over .300 both left and righthanded and tied for the league lead in triples with 15. His power is from the left side, but he hit very well from the right side last season, going 23 for 64 and posting a .359 average.

Collins has no long ball power, but has foul line and gap power. He hits to all fields and likes to swing down on pitches while playing on artificial turf to utilize his blazing speed. That speed enables him to stay away from prolonged slumps because he can push or drag a bunt, batting either way, and outrun throws to first on simple grounders.

He is a better breaking ball hitter batting lefthanded and also a better low ball hitter from this side. Batting righthanded, Collins likes the fastball up. Pitchers will try to keep the ball up and away from him batting either way and keep breaking balls low. He is not a good off-speed hitter because he tends to be impatient and swing a lot. If he stayed back a bit and was not so aggressive at the plate, he would be able to hit the off-speed stuff the other way. He is one of the best bunters in the league, for either a hit or a sacrifice.

BASERUNNING:

He gets from home to first as fast as anybody and has an edge when he bats lefthanded and gets the extra two steps. Infielders must play him shallow because if he puts a bunt in the right spot he cannot be thrown out. He finished second in the league in stolen bases with 60 and will take the extra base anytime,

DAVE COLLINS
LF, No. 10
SL, 5'10", 175 lbs.
ML Svc: 10 years
Born: 10-20-52 in
Rapid City, SD

1984 STATISTICS

AVG	G	AB	R	H	2B	3B	HR	RBI	BB	SO	SB
.308	128	441	59	136	24	15	2	44	33	41	60

CAREER STATISTICS

AVG	G	AB	R	H	2B	3B	HR	RBI	BB	SO	SB
.278	1132	3686	516	1023	137	44	27	288	349	508	313

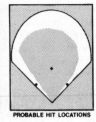

VS. RHP — VS. LHP — PROBABLE HIT LOCATIONS

anyplace, anywhere. He is a good slider who has perfected the stand-up slide and often confuses umpires who cannot tell that his feet are on the bag.

FIELDING:

Collins has excellent range and is much more confident in the outfield when playing every day. He catches up to balls with sheer speed. Sure-handed when he gets to a ball, he has a bit of trouble on liners right at him. His arm is accurate but average, and runners will run on him.

OVERALL:

Robinson: "He cannot play any better than he did in 1984. They can't keep this man out of the lineup because he is an igniter. If he plays every day in 1985, he'll steal 80 bases and there's no telling what else he might do."

HITTING:

Fernandez has a closed stance and stands straight up, looking to hit the ball hard and far. He does not have that much power, but the power he does generate comes from the left side. He reminds observers of teammate Alfredo Griffin in that he is a switch-hitting shortstop, but he is three inches taller and five years younger and seems to be the shortstop of the future.

He hits straightaway, and has some power to the gaps in left-center and right-center. He is an extremely aggressive hitter who likes eye-high fastballs batting either righty or lefty. Pitchers who think he cannot handle hard stuff are burned by Fernandez, and pitchers who have not seen him and try to throw him up and in are also surprised. He should be thrown breaking balls low and away and off-speed pitches because he strides rapidly into the ball and can be off balance if he is looking fastball.

His power is lefthanded, and all three homers came from the left side. He can bunt, but seemed more intent on swinging in 1984. He is an impatient hitter who will also chase bad pitches, like Griffin.

BASERUNNING:

He is aggressive and quick out of the box, but he did not steal in 1984. He did have excellent minor league stolen base totals, and must learn the moves of different pitchers in order to utilize his quickness. He appeared a bit timid about taking too many chances on the basepaths in 1984, a not uncommon failing in rookies.

FIELDING:

He is an incredible fielder who can come in on a ball as well as any shortstop in the league. He can throw off

TONY FERNANDEZ
SS, No. 1
SR, 6'2", 165 lbs.
ML Svc: 1 year plus
Born: 8-6-62 in
    San Pedro de Macoris, DR

1984 STATISTICS

AVG	G	AB	R	H	2B	3B	HR	RBI	BB	SO	SB
.270	88	233	29	63	5	3	3	19	17	15	5

CAREER STATISTICS

AVG	G	AB	R	H	2B	3B	HR	RBI	BB	SO	SB
.270	103	267	34	72	6	4	3	21	19	17	5

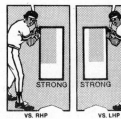

VS. RHP   VS. LHP   PROBABLE HIT LOCATIONS

his right foot or his left foot and can get steam on throws from deep in the hole. His arm is outstanding and might be the best in the league. He is extremely acrobatic, and reminds scouts of a young Ozzie Smith or Garry Templeton. His arm helps him save errors, but he must learn to be a bit more accurate when he makes stops in the hole, behind the bag, or when turning the double play.

OVERALL:

He is too good a fielder and hitter (with a potential of .275-.280) to sit on the bench.

Robinson: "Toronto has to find a place for him. He's as smooth as glass and has something very few young infielders have--tremendous instincts and anticipation. He is an extraordinary talent who can run, hit and dazzle defensively."

HITTING:

They always tell young hitters to stand any way that makes them feel comfortable. Damaso Garcia is a perfect example. His stance is unique: his feet are almost together in the batter's box and his toes point toward one another. He stands virtually square to home plate, but changes a bit on different pitchers and can stand either slightly open or slightly closed.

He swings down on the ball and swings at everything he sees. He is one batter who truly fits the description of "hitter"--he has walked only 40 times in more than 1,150 at-bats over the past two years.

Garcia is an impatient hitter who managed to get his bat on the ball for a surprising number of leg, broken-bat and bloop hits. He is a high fastball hitter, although lefties will try to throw him the fastball up and away. They will also try to turn the ball over to him and take something off a pitch. Offspeed pitches give Garcia trouble.

Righthanded pitchers try to jam him or throw sliders away, but he strides into the pitch and can muscle an inside pitch to left or slap one a few inches off the ground to right or right-center.

There is no one best way to pitch to him, but pitchers should definitely try to avoid throwing a strike when they are ahead in the count: instead, send him something off-speed and off the plate. Like most Blue Jays, Garcia did tail off toward the end of the 1984 season.

BASERUNNING:

Because he strides into pitches and hits the other way quite a bit, Garcia is halfway to first after hitting the ball. He is one of the fastest men out of the box and extremely quick to first. He has learned how to steal and finished sixth in the league in stolen bases with 46. He is very aggressive on the basepaths and always thinks in terms of two bases, not one. Many of his doubles

DAMASO GARCIA
2B, No. 7
RR, 6'0", 175 lbs.
ML Svc: 5 years
Born: 2-7-57 in
    Moca, DR

1984 STATISTICS

AVG	G	AB	R	H	2B	3B	HR	RBI	BB	SO	SB
.126	152	633	79	80	32	5	5	46	16	46	46

CAREER STATISTICS

AVG	G	AB	R	H	2B	3B	HR	RBI	BB	SO	SB
.250	663	2627	334	658	126	22	18	190	87	219	159

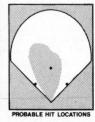

STRONG | STRONG |
VS. RHP | VS. LHP | PROBABLE HIT LOCATIONS

would be singles for everyone else. He is a threat to steal any base at any time if he is given the green light.

FIELDING:

Garcia has outstanding range on grounders and pops to the infield. He might have the most range of any second baseman in the league, has an excellent arm, turns the double play as well as anybody and is marvelous at coming in on high chops and drag bunts. His release is quick and his throws are accurate.

OVERALL:

Damaso is another player the Yankees let get away. He is a star in a league that has a bushel full of good second basemen.

Robinson: "Toronto may not keep Garcia because they are loaded with Fernandez and Griffin. They might do well to convert one of them into a third baseman and break up the Iorg/Mulliniks duo."

PITCHING:

Jim Gott pitched on complete game in 1984--a two-hit shutout of the California Angels on July 3rd. It was his only complete game in 12 starts, as the Jays shifted him from spot starter to bullpen duty. Toronto is now seriously considering making one of their young flame-throwing starters into a full-time reliever, as the Yankees did with Dave Righetti, and they just might do it with Gott--if they had more confidence in him. In May, he threw 21 consecutive scoreless innings as a starter, then tailed off after the July shutout.

Like Jim Clancy, Gott is a puzzlement. He throws overhand to three-quarters and has a big sweeping curve, sharp slider, 92 MPH fastball and straight change. His problem has always been inconsistency, and he may become better if he heeds Jim Palmer's advice. Palmer told Yankee reliever Jay Howell to throw fastballs to get ahead in the count, then come back with the curve. Gott has a tendency to throw the curve early in the count, then come back with the fastball. Problem is, most pitchers throw the fastball for strikes 70% of the time and the curve only 30% of the time. When Gott falls behind with the curve, he must come in with the fastball, and good major league hitters can hit a fastball--unless it belongs to Nolan Ryan.

Gott is effective when he keeps the fastball and slider low and in to righties and lefties. When he gets his pitches up he is in trouble. His fastball also has a tendency to come in straight, so he must learn to turn it over and keep it away from lefties and righties.

FIELDING:

Gott is not a particularly good

JIM GOTT
RHP, No. 38
RR, 6'4", 210 lbs.
ML Svc: 3 years
Born: 8-3-59 in
Hollywood, CA

1984 STATISTICS
W	L	ERA	G	GS	CG	IP	H	R	ER	BB	SO	SV
7	6	4.02	35	12	1	109	93	54	49	49	73	2

CAREER STATISTICS
W	L	ERA	G	GS	CG	IP	H	R	ER	BB	SO	SV
21	30	4.50	99	65	8	422	422	233	211	183	276	2

fielder, and he has problems with runners who will steal on him. He tends to forget they are on base when he is struggling with his control. His move to first is average, and he is not quick off the mound.

OVERALL:

His hobbies include karate, opera and ballet. They should include learning to throw strikes when coming out of the bullpen.

Robinson: "Inconsistency plagues him. He has been at a standstill for several years now. In fact, 1984 was a disappointment despite his winning record. He continues to have the best overall stuff on the team, but that is of little help if he can't get his pitches over the plate. Toronto must hope that he can find the key. If he does, watch out; but I don't think he will. He has been around too long to change his style now--but he really has a great arm."

HITTING:

Griffin came to life with the bat late in the year, when he realized that rookie Tony Fernandez was so good that his shortstop job was in jeopardy after five years. He is a switch-hitter who stands with legs spread extremely wide, with a closed stance and in a severe crouch. He bats basically the same both ways, choking up six inches on the bat and hits the ball where it is pitched. He will swing at just about anything near the plate, and has even swung at pitches over his head and in the dirt. He simply refuses to walk to first and considers a walk a personal insult. He walked four times in 419 at-bats last season, a major league record.

When batting lefty he can hit fastballs low and in. Batting righty he likes fastballs up and in. His power (that is, whatever power he has) is lefthanded, and he is a better hitter from the left side of the plate as well. He will go the other way against hard throwers, often sticking his bat out just to make contact. Pitchers will try hard stuff on the corners early in the count, then come back with low curves or sliders on the corners. He will bunt in any situation and is an excellent bunter, for hits and to advance runners. His strikeouts-to-at-bats ratio is good (33 in 419 at-bats) and he can be counted on to make contact. He is not considered dangerous in the clutch, and is often a defensive hitter with men on base.

BASERUNNING:

Griffin has outstanding speed out of the batter's box and corner infielders will play much closer to the plate with him at bat than any other player on the team. He stole 11 bases in 1984 but could steal more if he learned to study pitchers' moves. He tends to be a bit passive when it comes to sliding hard and breaking up double plays, but will always try to go from first to third and stretch a single into a double.

ALFREDO GRIFFIN
SS, No. 4
SR, 5'11", 165 lbs.
ML Svc: 6 years
Born: 3-6-57 in
Santo Domingo, DR

1984 STATISTICS

AVG	G	AB	R	H	2B	3B	HR	RBI	BB	SO	SB
.241	140	419	53	101	8	2	4	30	4	33	11

CAREER STATISTICS

AVG	G	AB	R	H	2B	3B	HR	RBI	BB	SO	SB
.249	904	3200	352	798	119	50	13	221	139	286	78

VS. RHP   VS. LHP   PROBABLE HIT LOCATIONS

FIELDING:

He is a good fielder with good range and a fair arm who makes many simple errors. He can reach balls other shortstops cannot, but makes too many errant throws. He turns the double play well, but tries to avoid contact when coming across the bag or when applying the tag to potential basestealers.

OVERALL:

He is lean, small, but pesky. He always seems to get a hit when you least expect it and make a big play in the field when you least expect it.

Robinson: "Griffin has performed well for Toronto, but Fernandez cannot be kept out of the lineup. The Jays may try to make Griffin a third baseman (see report on Damaso Garcia) if they consider breaking up the Mulliniks-Iorg connection. Griffin can also play second if he had to."

HITTING:

Garth Iorg managed his first and only homer of the year over the Labor Day Weekend in 1984, so that speaks for his power--or lack of it. Nothing changed for Iorg in 1984 except for one rather important statistic--he stopped hitting and struggled all year. His average dropped almost 50 points from 1983. He was still platooned at third base with Rance Mulliniks, and played only against lefthanded pitching. He has a square stance but exaggerates his weight shift, with all the weight on his back foot, and bats from a slight crouch. He tends to lunge at pitches and looks for fastballs from the belt and above. He will not see those pitches with men on base, and pitchers will throw him hard stuff away and off-speed pitches in any location.

Iorg is an impatient hitter who only drew five walks in 247 at-bats. Some people claim that when a batter takes too many pitches, he tends to lose his aggressiveness at the plate, but Iorg could be more selective. His hits are hard grounders or low liners and he has trouble getting the ball in the air.

When he is hitting, he will go with the pitch to center and right-center, but in 1984 he tried to pull too much. He has trouble with breaking balls, even high ones, and saw many more breaking balls in 1984 than he had in previous years. He can bunt and will push a bunt to third in an effort to get a hit.

BASERUNNING:

He was plagued by several nagging injuries and did not run as much as he had in the past, although he is not a fast runner. He does not get a good jump out of the box but is aggressive on the basepaths.

GARTH IORG
3B, No. 16
RR, 5'11", 170 lbs.
ML Svc: 6 years
Born: 10-12-54 in Arcata, CA

1984 STATISTICS

AVG	G	AB	R	H	2B	3B	HR	RBI	BB	SO	SB
.227	121	247	24	56	10	3	1	25	5	16	1

CAREER STATISTICS

AVG	G	AB	R	H	2B	3B	HR	RBI	BB	SO	SB
.258	541	1525	153	393	73	14	6	127	52	173	15

  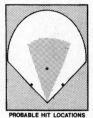

VS. RHP   VS. LHP   PROBABLE HIT LOCATIONS

FIELDING:

He is not spectacular, but he gets the job done with an average and accurate arm. He can go to his right better than to his left and knows how to play on artificial surfaces. He is not particularly quick coming in for bunts and can be bunted on.

OVERALL:

Toronto is starting to bring up young infielders to challenge the guard--Iorg may have heard the footsteps.

Robinson: "An off year for him. He struggled as a platoon player playing only against lefties, and this year is pivotal for him. He and Mulliniks have given the Jays great mileage at third the past three years, but I have a feeling Iorg will play less in 1985."

PITCHING:

The Blue Jays did not exactly lie down and die last September, but their bullpen was not sharp enough to keep them from posting a losing record in the last month of the season. Despite tying for the team-lead in saves with 10, Roy Lee Jackson lost something in that final stretch.

Earlier in the year, Jackson had a consecutive scoreless inning streak of 16.2 innings, but before the season was over, his ERA was heading toward 4.00. He can pitch every day and can pitch in long or short relief. He has a crackling fastball and a sharp slider. He releases the ball from a three-quarters motion and gets his whole body behind the ball. When he is pitching in long relief, he will use a curve and change; but when he pitches in key situations, he will come in with his fastball and his slider.

Jackson can be effective when his fastball moves in on a righthanded hitter and away from a lefty, and when he keeps his slider low and away. His control is good, but he must always remind himself of location. He gets hurt when he gets his pitches up, and in 1984, he gave up more home runs than he had in the past. If he is tired or does not get his fastball to move, he will be hit hard and taken deep. When Jackson is in gear, he will sink the fastball and keep it away from the batters, making him extremely effective. With men on base, however, he tends to get the fastball in the wrong place--a bit too high.

FIELDING:

It has taken some time, but Jackson is beginning to improve as a fielder. He has a quick move to first and throws there often. At times, it seems as if he is paying more attention to the runner

ROY LEE JACKSON
RHP, No. 25
RR, 6'2", 205 lbs.
ML Svc: 5 years
Born: 5-1-54 in
    Opelika, AL

1984 STATISTICS

W	L	ERA	G	GS	CG	IP	H	R	ER	BB	SO	SV
7	8	3.56	54	0	0	86	73	40	34	31	58	10

CAREER STATISTICS

W	L	ERA	G	GS	CG	IP	H	R	ER	BB	SO	SV
26	30	3.85	230	16	1	461	442	218	197	174	291	30

than to the batter. He is quick off the mound on bunts and chops.

OVERALL:

Jackson is a good relief pitcher. But for the second year in a row, the Blue Jays have been unable to come up with a true stopper in the bullpen. They chased the Tigers all year, and had second place all to themselves for most of the season. They were challenged for that spot in September by both the Yankees and the Red Sox, and the Jays almost blew it in the end. In 1984, Jackson had a record of 7-8--far too many decisions for a relief pitcher. Jackson is good, but he is not the stopper the Jays need.

Robinson: "He doesn't seem to have the same good stuff every time he takes the mound. He needs to be sharp in every game. In 1985, Jackson will probably be hot and cold again in the bullpen. One good thing about him is that he is not afraid to pitch as often as he is asked to, in both long and short relief."

HITTING:

You can call this man Cliff, or you can call him C.J, or you can call him Country, but never call him late to home plate. In 1984, Cliff Johnson belted his 19th career pinch-hit home run and set an all-time record with that blast. He seems to be the man they invented the DH rule for; he never did like to play first base or catch. His livelihood is now strictly made as a pinch-hitter and DH, and he is very good at it.

He has a slightly closed stance and has been crouching and holding his bat lower and lower each year. Baseball people will always tell you that as the years creep up, a batter should hold his bat lower to generate more bat speed, but Johnson's bat has not lost any.

Johnson loves fastballs, "Good old country hardball," as Johnson likes to call it, and stands fairly close to the plate. He is very dangerous with men on base and when he gets the fastball near the middle of the plate on in. Lefthanders will try to throw low sliders and fastballs away, but Johnson can handle any breaking ball above the belt.

Righthanders may try to move him off the plate early in the count, and come back with sharp sliders or off-speed pitches down and away. He can be struck out with a straight change if he is looking fastball, because he rarely goes to right field and continually tries to pull the ball. He knows that his penchant for high fastballs sees him swing at many bad pitches, so he has become more selective at the plate.

BASERUNNING:

Despite a lack of natural speed, he hustles down the line and on the bases. He will go from first to third when the situation calls for it, and is a terror when it comes to knocking over infield-

CLIFF JOHNSON
DH, No. 44
RR, 6'5", 225 lbs.
ML Svc: 11 years
Born: 7-22-47 in
San Antonio, TX

1984 STATISTICS											
AVG	G	AB	R	H	2B	3B	HR	RBI	BB	SO	SB
.304	127	359	51	109	23	1	16	61	50	62	0
CAREER STATISTICS											
AVG	G	AB	R	H	2B	3B	HR	RBI	BB	SO	SB
.258	1156	3240	456	836	159	8	168	578	470	600	9

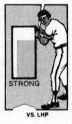

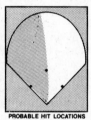

VS. RHP   VS. LHP   PROBABLE HIT LOCATIONS

ers and catchers. He would just as soon throw a rolling block at a defensive player as slide.

OVERALL:

He takes forever to get set and steps in and out of the box as though he were testing the water in a bathtub and frequently annoys pitchers who get fidgety. Some of them throw right at him, but that is a big mistake because it might cost them a limb or a long ball. There have been occasions when the bat has suddenly slipped out of his hands.

Robinson: "A very good year indeed for Cliff Johnson, and it would have been even better if Toronto had not used Aikens as the DH for so many games. If Cliff had played every day, I think he would have led the Jays in home runs and RBIs and still manage to hit over .300."

PITCHING:

Would the Detroit Tigers have won everything last season without Willie Hernandez? Would Hernandez have tilted the balance of power toward Toronto if he pitched for them? The questions are, of course, moot ones. The Jays are overloaded with righty relief pitchers, and Jimmy Key and Bryan Clark are their only lefties in the pen. Clark did not help the Jays—Key did.

Key has a lot of moxie for a 23-year-old rookie and pitches with confidence. He also pitches quickly and does not fiddle or dawdle while on the mound. He gained a lot of confidence early in the year, struggled in the middle of the year in the midst of a big league pennant race, but finished strong in September, picking up three saves to give him 10, tying him for the team lead with Roy Lee Jackson.

He has a fastball, a curve, a slider and a change, and is not afraid to start righties off with the curve, which he will throw low and in or outside and break it over the corner. His fastball is quick and gets to home plate before batters realize it. He is very effective against lefties because he will throw the curve away and the slider low and away. When he learns to take something off the fastball and turn it over, he will be a better pitcher. His 63 mound appearances, all in relief, were a team high and tied him for eighth in the league, so it is obvious the Jays have confidence in him.

FIELDING:

He is quick and fast off the mound

JIMMY KEY
LHP, No. 27
RL, 6'1", 175 lbs.
ML Svc: 1 year
Born: 4-22-61 in
Huntsville, AL

1984 STATISTICS

W	L	ERA	G	GS	CG	IP	H	R	ER	BB	SO	SV
4	5	4.65	63	0	0	62	70	37	32	32	44	10

CAREER STATISTICS

W	L	ERA	G	GS	CG	IP	H	R	ER	BB	SO	SV
4	5	4.65	63	0	0	62	70	37	32	32	44	10

but makes rookie mistakes when throwing to bases on bunts. His move to first is a good one, but he tends to concentrate on the batter. He gets an edge in keeping runners close because his stretch and release are quick.

OVERALL:

They say a man with one eye is king in the land of the blind. Key has two eyes, is young, throws hard and is the only reliable lefty the Jays had in their pen in 1984.

Robinson: "He ran hot and cold in 1984. He was tough early in the year because the hitters didn't know him. They caught up to him later. He throws strikes and has poise for a youngster. I think he will help the team in 1985 because Toronto needs a lefty reliever and he now has a full year under his belt."

PITCHING:

It was an expensive gamble that did not work. The Jays, realizing they could not contend without a strong man out of the bullpen, signed Dennis Lamp as a free agent and gave him half of the Labatts brewery. After a few months of trying to be THE MAN, Lamp realized he couldn't do it and the beer went flat.

He can be very effective against both lefties and righties because he has a sinker that sinks, a slider that sinks and a fastball that sinks. A sinker is the toughest pitch for a hitter to hit, and Lamp had extraordinary success with it with the White Sox in 1983. In 1984 it didn't sink enough. In addition, Lamp went from natural grass to artificial surface, and batters could pound the sinker into the almost billiard-table-like surface and manage to get on base.

Lamp is an aggressive pitcher who comes at batters, but in 1984 his control went awry. He pitched to a lot of 3-2 counts even when he started an inning. His fastball has been clocked at 87 MPH, and when he has that pitch working, and mixes in a small curve, he is effective against righties. Against lefties he must rely on hitting spots and getting the ball over the plate. In 1983 he walked only 29 batters in 116 innings. In 1984 he walked 38 hitters in 85 innings.

He has pitched in pressure situations, but it appeared as though he found a different kind of pressure up north. Usually a tough pitcher to hit the long ball off because of his sinker, he allowed nine homers in 85 innings in 1984--not a good percentage.

FIELDING:

Lamp has a deliberate move to home

DENNIS LAMP
RHP, No. 53
RR, 6'3", 210 lbs.
ML Svc: 7 years
Born: 9-23-52 in
Los Angeles, CA

1984 STATISTICS

W	L	ERA	G	GS	CG	IP	H	R	ER	BB	SO	SV
8	8	4.55	56	4	0	85	97	53	43	38	45	9

CAREER STATISTICS

W	L	ERA	G	GS	CG	IP	H	R	ER	BB	SO	SV
61	70	3.89	303	154	21	1174	1275	578	507	361	492	29

plate and runners will steal on him. He has a good move to first for a righty, but sometimes forgets to throw over. He is generally slow off the mound when covering first or backing up the bases, and needs improvement in his fielding.

OVERALL:

He got a ton of money from Toronto. He had no saves in September 1984 and his ERA went from 3.71 in 1983 to 4.55 last season. He was also used in two starts in September. The Jays were trying to get their money's worth.

Robinson: "He was too hot and cold to be number one and lost that job to several other relievers. I think he can help Toronto this year, but I don't think he'll be the stopper they wanted. I look for him to pitch in relief this year, long and short. He must be able to pitch in spots more effectively to be better."

PITCHING:

A pitcher who finished 13-8 with a team that came from the cellar three years ago to second place in 1984 should feel elated, right?

Wrong!

Luis Leal won eight of his first 10 games as the Jays chased the Tigers all spring and summer, but faltered badly late in the year and lost five games in a row from August 29th through September 18th. He always was--and still seems to be--an extremely streaky pitcher. Leal might be the type of pitcher who simply dislikes late season cold weather, because he falters late in the year. In hot weather he is virtually unbeatable.

He has a crackling fastball and slider, good curve and change and uses them all. When he has control and confidence in all four pitches, Lamp is tough. When he falls behind, to either righties or lefties, he has a tendency to come in with a hard slider or fastball, but if the pitches do not move as they should, batters can go deep on him. He led the Jays staff in the dubious distinction of homers allowed (27) in 1984.

He throws from three-quarters, and is able to make his fastball move in and out, a big plus when he is in the proper groove. He can throw the overhand curve, an effective pitch to a righty, and can keep the slider low and away to both lefties and righties, another plus. When his control is off, or he is bothered by something, he gets distracted and loses some of his concentration.

FIELDING:

He has a sort of Luis Tiant move to

LUIS LEAL
RHP, No. 48
RR, 6'3", 215 lbs.
ML Svc: 5 years
Born: 3-21-57 in
   Barquisimeto, VEN

1984 STATISTICS												
W	L	ERA	G	GS	CG	IP	H	R	ER	BB	SO	SV
13	8	3.89	35	35	6	222	221	106	96	77	134	0
CAREER STATISTICS												
W	L	ERA	G	GS	CG	IP	H	R	ER	BB	SO	SV
48	52	4.01	150	137	27	879	886	430	392	296	458	1

first base. His move is quick and fast, and he does keep runners close when he puts his mind to it. Runners will run on him if he starts getting in trouble and is thinking of the next pitch to the batter rather than watching the runner. His fielding is average.

OVERALL:

It's tough for a player to go through an entire month with no success, as Leal did in September. The Jays were virtually out of the chase by then, but Leal did not win a game after August 25th. To have 13 wins in August and finish with 13 is not good--in any league.

Robinson: "He still seems to be getting better, despite the finish. He does get in trouble when he starts nibbling at corners, but he is trying to keep after the hitters more than he did in the past. He is gaining confidence and is a better all-around pitcher. He'll win more games this year."

HITTING:

Buck Martinez and Ernie Whitt are the two catchers platooned by the Blue Jays. They share the eighth position in the batting order, and are weak hitters with a little bit of pop in their bats. In 1984, the Jays were in second place from the opening bell and could not be taken lightly, so pitchers started to concentrate a bit more on every batter in the order.

Martinez's average dipped 30 points, but he did not play regularly and pinch-hit quite a bit. His home run total was cut in half from 1983, but he did drive in many key runs. Martinez is the type of hitter who is better against the better pitchers, much like Baltimore's Rick Dempsey.

He has a slightly closed stance and looks for fastballs from the middle of the plate on in. He is a pull hitter who does not got to right field enough, and pitchers will try to keep the fastball away and the breaking ball down. A control picher who can move the ball around in the strike zone and not give Martinez a pitch he can pull is effective against him.

He rarely swings at the first pitch and is a patient hitter who looks for a "cripple" or a mistake pitch, but he does not walk much. He tries to make as much as he can out of his limited at-bats. Martinez is extremely effective with a runner on third and less than two out, and will get the ball to the outfield, somehow, to get the runner home. He led the Jays in sacrifice flies last year.

BASERUNNING:

Martinez will not steal a base. He hasn't taken one in 14 years and won't do it this year, either. He is, however, smart and doesn't make mistakes.

BUCK MARTINEZ
C, No. 13
RR, 5'11", 190 lbs.
ML Svc: 13 years
Born: 11-7-48 in Redding, CA

1984 STATISTICS											
AVG	G	AB	R	H	2B	3B	HR	RBI	BB	SO	SB
.220	102	232	24	51	13	1	5	37	29	49	0
CAREER STATISTICS											
AVG	G	AB	R	H	2B	3B	HR	RBI	BB	SO	SB
.231	926	2484	221	573	117	10	52	295	200	382	5

  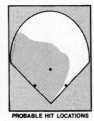

STRONG   STRONG

VS. RHP   VS. LHP   PROBABLE HIT LOCATIONS

FIELDING:

Martinez earns his money when he puts on the "tools of ignorance" behind the plate. He is far from ignorant. He knows the strengths and weaknesses of the pitching staff and calls a heady game.

He is quick to field foul pops. He has a good release and is accurate with his throws.

OVERALL:

Martinez is heading into his 15th year in the big leagues. He is doing something right.

Robinson: "He is a good receiver who gave the staff a lot of confidence. His future seems secure on the Blue Jays because of his experience and his good rapport with the staff. He is a good handler of pitchers who is not afraid to speak his mind."

HITTING:

Lloyd Moseby dropped off a bit in average last season, but he improved his all-around game. His stance varies slightly from square to closed, but it is a wide stance, with a slight crouch, and with the bat held low below his chest. He is a fastball hitter who looks for that pitch all the time and will swing at anything hard if it is from the belt to the ankles.

A dead pull hitter in the past, he has learned to hit the fastball to center and left-center. He has a fairly good eye at the plate, led the team in walks but also struck out more than he had in the past.

Playing center field every day, Moseby faced more lefthanded pitchers last season and saw more breaking balls. Lefthanded pitchers will throw the fastball up and away and then come back with a variety of hard sliders low and away. Both left and righthanders use the straight change or off-speed pitch when setting him up, and will try to spot the fastball away or hit a corner with the curve for the out pitch. He is a free swinger.

Moseby is a good bunter, especially for a big man. He can do it for a base hit or to advance a runner. The artificial turf in Toronto helps him. He has become more of a "hitter" with men on base; he tries to make contact rather than hit the ball out of the park. He tied with teammate Dave Collins for the league lead in triples with fifteen.

BASERUNNING:

Moseby is a fast runner and has finally learned to run the bases and to steal. He finished seventh in the league with 39 stolen bases and will go from first to third on anything hit to the outfield. He is a threat to steal anytime he is on base, and he will break up the double play with a hard slide.

LLOYD MOSEBY
CF, No. 15
LR, 6'3", 205 lbs.
ML Svc: 5 years
Born: 11-5-59 in
Portland, AR

1984 STATISTICS

AVG	G	AB	R	H	2B	3B	HR	RBI	BB	SO	SB
.280	158	592	97	166	28	15	18	92	78	122	39

CAREER STATISTICS

AVG	G	AB	R	H	2B	3B	HR	RBI	BB	SO	SB
.263	670	2385	332	628	119	34	63	314	211	484	92

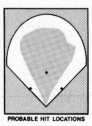

VS. RHP   VS. LHP   PROBABLE HIT LOCATIONS

FIELDING:

Moseby has a good arm and is improving year by year in center field. He has become more confident in his ability, but must still get a better jump on balls hit over his head. He must try to take charge a bit more in center. His natural speed helps him to catch up to balls hit in the gaps.

OVERALL:

Lloyd hit well in September, but did not hit any home runs after September 2nd. He is, however, determined to improve the other aspects of his game.

Robinson: "He is a very good player who just might win a batting title or the MVP award before too long. His future is very bright."

HITTING:

When the Blue Jays visited the Yankees in early September 1984, many Yankee players called Rance Mulliniks "George."

It was a play on words--they likened him to KC's hitting machine: George Brett.

Mulliniks changed his stance slightly in 1984 and had a much more positive and aggressive attitude at the plate. It is now a basically square stance, with his weight on the back foot and an extremely loosey-goosey type swing. He lays the bat on his shoulder, takes a short, quick stroke and uses his wrists much more. He raised his average above .330 in September, and would have finished behind the top three hitters in the league had he had enough plate appearances to qualify.

He is basically a fastball, straightaway hitter with the ability to pull inside pitches and slap outside pitches to left. Too many pitchers make the mistake of trying to throw the fastball past him on the inside, but Mulliniks can and does get around on those pitches. He is also a better high ball hitter than a low ball hitter, and can handle any type of pitch above the belt. He does not play against lefties--an obvious advantage--and righties who have success against him will try fastballs away and sliders low and in or low and away.

He did not try for the long ball in 1984. In 1983, he hit 10 homers, a career-high, but in 1984 he made slight changes in his weight shift and was determined to hit the ball where it was pitched, and to hit it hard and low in the gaps.

BASERUNNING:

He is a smart baserunner, but he will not steal, gamble or take chances on the bases. He gets a good jump from the box but does not have enough speed to get many leg hits.

RANCE MULLINIKS
3B, No. 5
LR, 6'0", 170 lbs.
ML Svc: 7 years
Born: 1-15-56 in
Tulare, CA

1984 STATISTICS

AVG	G	AB	R	H	2B	3B	HR	RBI	BB	SO	SB
.324	125	343	41	111	21	5	3	42	33	44	2

CAREER STATISTICS

AVG	G	AB	R	H	2B	3B	HR	RBI	BB	SO	SB
.264	576	1574	190	416	102	11	22	172	169	226	8

VS. RHP — STRONG | VS. LHP — STRONG | PROBABLE HIT LOCATIONS

FIELDING:

He has an average arm, but he is a third baseman who knows how to play the hitters. He is very good on artificial turf, can knock down hard smashes in the hole, and is better at going to his right (over the bag) than he is at going to his left. He knows where to throw the ball when he gets it and has an accurate arm.

OVERALL:

He does not look for headlines and expects no glory. He is platooned with Garth Iorg, knows he will leave the game or be pinch-hit for when a lefty comes in and is the prototype team player.

Robinson: "If he hasn't made a believer out of people yet, he never will. You look at his performance in 1984 and you fully expect the same thing in 1985. At this point, it would be a mistake to play him every day, because he gives the team his maximum effort in what he does."

PITCHING:

Who was the pitcher who won the 1983 All Star Game?

Who was the pitcher who lost the 1984 All Star Game?

That is correct--Dave Stieb, proving that it's not whether you win or lose, it's just nice to be an All Star.

Stieb is an All Star pitcher, and had he not suffered blisters on his pitching hand and some tough luck in September, would have won 20 games and led the league in strikeouts and ERA. He is an overpowering pitcher with excellent control who matures day by day, week by week and year by year. At one time he was strictly power--fastball (94 MPH) and slider (92 MPH)--but he has added a short curve and straight change. He is a power-against-power pitcher who will not give in to a hitter's strength. If a hitter is a good low ball, fastball hitter, and Stieb has that pitch working for him on a given day, he will come right at the batter with that pitch and challenge him.

He tries to keep the hard stuff low and in to both righties and lefties, and will tinker with a change or wrinkle while setting a batter up for the "K." He gets the majority of his strikeouts on the hard fastball or slider.

Stieb is not a bigger winner because he has trouble in the early innings of many games. If the team is not hitting and Stieb gives up a few runs early in the game, he is in obvious difficulty. But he is learning how to keep the team in the game and not let one or two bad innings or outings bother him.

FIELDING:

A natural athlete who was once an outfielder, Stieb is one of the best

DAVE STIEB
RHP, No. 37
RR, 6'1", 185 lbs.
ML Svc: 5 years
Born: 7-22-57 in
  Santa Ana, CA

1984 STATISTICS

W	L	ERA	G	GS	CG	IP	H	R	ER	BB	SO	SV
16	8	2.83	35	35	11	267	215	87	84	88	198	0

CAREER STATISTICS

W	L	ERA	G	GS	CG	IP	H	R	ER	BB	SO	SV
81	67	3.30	186	184	76	1389	1228	556	509	448	775	0

fielding pitchers in the league. He can stab hot smashes through the box, cover the first base and third base foul lines and make a strong throw after fielding a slow chop. He covers first base perfectly on balls hit to the right side and is always alert on the mound. His move to first has improved.

OVERALL:

For starters (no pun intended), he led the league in innings pitched, has averaged better than 30 starts a year for the past five years, was second in stikeouts and ERA, tied for fourth in starts, tied for fifth in winning percentage (.667), tied for ninth in complete games and shutouts and tied for 10th in wins. All this despite a poor month of September. He lost the ERA title to Mike Boddicker on the last weekend of the season.

Robinson: "He's getting even better. This year he will win 20 games because he's ready for it. He is a tough competitor, knows he is good and has a world of confidence."

HITTING:

In 1984 Willie Upshaw was upstaged. The undisputed offensive leader of the Jays in 1983, Upshaw slumped in the "big three" of homers, RBIs and batting average.

He is a powerful lefthanded hitter who stands deep in the box, with a closed stance and a slight crouch. He is always ready to swing the bat and is poised like a snake ready to strike when he sets himself at home. He loves low fastballs and likes to pull them, but he does have the ability to go the other way if the situation calls for it.

He is a better than average bad ball hitter who will make contact on the first pitch if it happens to be a fastball anywhere near the plate. He can also handle hard sliders, can pull them or slam them to center, but has trouble with off-speed pitches. Righties will try to work him hard and away, and come back with sliders or curves on the outside. Lefthanders can get the high fastball past him, but they must be extremely careful, particularly in parks with short dimensions, because Upshaw does have power to left-center and center. A pitcher with no hard stuff at all will give him trouble, because he is an impatient, aggressive hitter who likes heat, not junk. If he knows he will see nothing but change-ups, he is annoyed. He saw many more breaking balls in 1984, and that may have accounted for his power shortage. He did, however, cut down on his strikeouts and he tried to make contact with men on base.

FIELDING:

He worked hard on his fielding and cut down from 21 to 14 errors at first base. He is learning to knock down errant throws and to position himself more against various batters. At one time, he followed in the footsteps of former first baseman John Mayberry and played every batter on the line, deep

WILLIE UPSHAW
1B, No. 26
LL, 6'0", 185 lbs.
ML Svc: 5 years
Born: 4-27-57 in
Blanco, TX

1984 STATISTICS											
AVG	G	AB	R	H	2B	3B	HR	RBI	BB	SO	SB
.278	152	569	79	158	31	9	19	84	55	86	10

CAREER STATISTICS											
AVG	G	AB	R	H	2B	3B	HR	RBI	BB	SO	SB
.271	662	2124	306	575	96	27	73	295	206	338	35

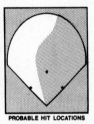

VS. RHP | VS. LHP | PROBABLE HIT LOCATIONS

behind the bag. He has also been able to knock down hard smashes on artificial turf, and keep the ball in play.

BASERUNNING:

He is exceptionally quick out of the batter's box and much faster than people think. He will beat out grounders if infielders misjudge his speed. He can run and is very aggressive on the bases.

OVERALL:

Some pitchers did not think the Blue Jays were for real in 1983 and may have subconsciously let down against Upshaw and his teammates. In 1984, everyone knew they were for real and buckled down against all Jay hitters. Upshaw had 19 homers on September 2nd--and 19 homers when the season ended.

Robinson: "His attitude, like his future, is good. He'll have a solid year this year, but he has to keep in mind that he's going to see a lot of breaking balls."

HITTING:

Ernie Whitt had the lowest batting average of his career last season in large part due to a series of nagging injuries. He did keep up his excellent homers-to-at-bats ratio, pounding 15 in only 315 at-bats.

Whitt is platooned with Buck Martinez behind the plate and usually plays against righthanded pitching. Whitt is a high fastball hitter with a good eye, and he likes to pull most pitches. He does have good success against hard throwers, can jerk the high fastball out or slash it up the middle. He does not go to left field as often as he should, and in 1984, his average suffered because of it.

He has a closed stance and bats straight up, but late last year, when his average dropped 20 points, Whitt began laboring at the plate and used only his arms and shoulders to swing the bat. He looked like a rusty gate.

Pitchers will show him the fastball away, then come back with changes or curves, either down and away or down and in.

As catchers go, he is a better bunter than most. In 1984, however, Whitt was never thinking bunt--rather, the long ball was heavily on his mind.

BASERUNNING:

Whitt has been around for a long time and knows how to run the bases. He knows the outfielders' strengths and weaknesses. On occasion, he may try to sneak from first to third, but will rarely try it if he knows that the outfielder has a cannon for an arm.

FIELDING:

With solid skills in all aspects of the catching position, Whitt is a take-charge kind of player who handles a young staff well. He is adept at foul pops and has a quick release and an accurate arm, yet runners will run on him.

ERNIE WHITT
C, No. 12
LR, 6'2", 200 lbs.
ML Svc: 6 years
Born: 6-13-52 in
Detroit, MI

1984 STATISTICS

AVG	G	AB	R	H	2B	3B	HR	RBI	BB	SO	SB
0.238	124	315	35	75	12	1	15	46	43	48	0

CAREER STATISTICS

AVG	G	AB	R	H	2B	3B	HR	RBI	BB	SO	SB
0.243	565	1496	163	364	67	7	51	203	166	213	10

VS. RHP

VS. LHP

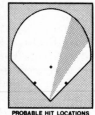
PROBABLE HIT LOCATIONS

Actually, it is not Whitt that the runners are going on; rather, they are taking their chances against the Toronto starters who do not pay attention to anyone on base.

Whitt is good at handling low balls and is a catcher who stands firm in blocking the plate. He is quick to field bunts and choppers. Whitt had only four errors in the 124 games he appeared in last season.

OVERALL:

He is certainly no spring chicken and spent time on the disabled list last year. The Jays need him to be physically sound.

Robinson: "Ernie can do more than one thing well. He calls a good game, can DH or pinch-hit and always gives a professional effort. If he hits for average, it will be to his advantage because he does have some pop in his bat, and the home runs will come."

RICK LEACH
INF, No. 7
LL, 6'0", 195 lbs.
ML Svc: 4 years
Born: 5-4-57 in
  Ann Arbor, MI

HITTING, BASERUNNING, FIELDING:

Steve Garvey, John Stearns and Kirk Gibson are three former outstanding college football players who have made their mark in major league baseball. Rick Leach, starting quarterback for the Michigan Wolverines in two Rose Bowls, has never made it.

He is now a pinch-hitter and is used sparingly at first and in the outfield. He did manage to hit .261 last season as a pinch-hitter and part-timer, 25 points higher than his lifetime batting average. He has a closed, straight-up stance and looks for fastballs, belt-high or higher, on the inside part of the plate. He has no power, but will try to pull the inside fastball. Righties (he only faces righties) will throw him hard stuff away and breaking balls down. They will also use off-speed pitches and trick pitches--knuckler, palmball and forkball--against him.

He has less than average speed and will not steal or take chances on the basepaths. He has had injuries throughout his career and cannot throw very well. In the outfield, runners will run on him. At first base, he can handle low throws in the dirt, has fair range, but has trouble with bunts.

OVERALL:

Leach was released by Detroit in spring training of 1984 and could not share in the team's championship after parts of three years with them. He went to Syracuse, the Jays' AAA team, and in May came to Toronto, where he was used as a pinch-hitter.

Robinson: "He's a borderline major leaguer who may be able to help some team filling in at first or in the outfield, but more so as a pinch-hitter swinging the bat. His attitude, despite what he has been through, is fantastic. His future is as a pinch-hitter."

THE
NATIONAL LEAGUE

ATLANTA BRAVES

PITCHING:

For the third straight year, Len Barker is a physical question mark—more so now than ever because he underwent off-season surgery on his troublesome right elbow. A power pitcher, he is ineffective at less than full velocity. Although possessing a good curveball, his forte is the fastball, which he throws 90+ MPH from a three-quarters to overhand delivery. When he is throwing his fastball for strikes, his slow, sharp-breaking curve can be a devastating complement to it. He also throws a slider.

Because of his large size (6'4", 230 lbs.) and his unorthodox, very high leg kick, Barker can be a threatening sight on the mound, especially to righthanded hitters.

The Braves continue to count on Len as one of their starting pitchers, but his future depends solely on his physical condition. He and the Braves hope the off-season surgery will cure his elbow woes and enable him to retrieve the form that once made him one of the better pitchers in the American League. The Braves sent three players to Cleveland for Barker in August 1983, and they now await a return on that investment.

FIELDING, HITTING, BASERUNNING:

Barker's liability as a fielder is the high leg kick which characterizes his delivery to the plate. This can be an inviting feature for opposing baserunners when Barker elects not to pitch out of the stretch, because it gives them too good a jump on him. It also affects Barker's positioning on the fol-

LEN BARKER
RHP, No. 39
RR, 6'4", 230 lbs.
ML Svc: 8 years
Born: 7-7-55 in
    Fort Knox, KY

1984 STATISTICS
W	L	ERA	G	GS	CG	IP	H	R	ER	BB	SO	SV
7	8	3.86	21	20	1	126	120	59	54	38	95	0

CAREER STATISTICS
W	L	ERA	G	GS	CG	IP	H	R	ER	BB	SO	SV
70	66	4.19	217	165	35	1204	1151	613	561	459	906	5

low-through. On the other hand, when he is pitching from the stretch, Barker delivers the ball quickly to the plate. He generally does not throw to first base very often. Otherwise, he is an adequate fielder.

As a hitter, Barker is the prototypical American Leaguer, a victim of all those years in the minors and the AL, where the designated hitter rule kept him from batting. As a baserunner, well . . . he rarely gets there.

OVERALL:

Obviously, his effectiveness has been curtailed by his arm problems. But he is a good competitor and he wants to pitch. His desire to succeed increases the likelihood of a comeback.

Campbell: "I would consider him certainly a key to the Braves moving back in a position to contend for the NL West championship in 1985."

PITCHING:

As in 1983, Steve Bedrosian was awesome in the early months of 1984, and as in 1983, he tapered off in the later months, losing his arm strength, much of his velocity and much of his effectiveness.

The season ended with Bedrosian pronounced physically sound, but there was no doubt that he once again had been unable to hold up under the grueling workload of a short reliever. Thus, the question has to be asked: Should Steve be a starter or a reliever? It is a question the Braves must ponder and answer in 1985.

In the months of April, May and June and during some of July, he is an overpowering relief pitcher, one of the hardest throwers in the game. He has the kind of fastball (95+ MPH at times) that hitters cannot get around on even when they know it is coming. He also has a crisp slider that breaks down and away from righthanded batters, a particularly effective pitch which he also throws very hard. Bedrosian has still not developed a major league change-up, and needs something off-speed to round out his repertoire. He pitches three-quarters to overhand.

FIELDING, HITTING, BASERUNNING:

Opposing baserunners can take liberties with him. His best asset defensively is that he gets the ball to the plate in a hurry, simply because he throws it hard. Otherwise, he has an average move to first, and runners tend to break his concentration at times. He sometimes gets rattled on bunts and other fielding plays.

Like most pitchers who have been used

STEVE BEDROSIAN
RHP, No. 32
RR, 6'3", 195 lbs.
ML Svc: 3 years
Born: 12-6-57 in
    Methuen, MA

1984 STATISTICS

W	L	ERA	G	GS	CG	IP	H	R	ER	BB	SO	SV
9	6	2.37	40	4	0	83	65	23	22	33	81	11

CAREER STATISTICS

W	L	ERA	G	GS	CG	IP	H	R	ER	BB	SO	SV
27	24	2.93	189	9	0	365	282	126	119	156	327	41

primarily as short relievers, Bedrosian rarely gets opportunities as a hitter and baserunner. That is just as well because he is weak in both areas.

OVERALL:

In each of the past two seasons, his first and second in the big leagues, Bedrosian has had impressive stretches and unimpressive stretches. Now he is at something of a crossroads, and the Braves must decide whether to keep him in the bullpen or start him. Since he has buckled under the burden of short relief the last two years, there is a case to be made for starting him.

Campbell: "One thing you don't want is for your short relief pitcher not to be able to pitch well in August and September. I would not be surprised to see the Braves make him a starter in 1985. It's either that or keep him in the bullpen and only use him twice a week, a tough thing to do."

HITTING:

In 1983, Bruce Benedict experienced one of the biggest offensive turnarounds in the league, keeping his average above .300 most of the year and finishing at .298. But in 1984, Benedict experienced another turnaround, this time going the other way ending up at .223. He is hard to figure.

He was using the same stance that served him so well the year before. It is a closed stance that has Benedict deep in the box concentrating on hitting everything up the middle or to right-center. But in 1984, pitchers consistently got him out with fastballs in on his hands and sliders down and away.

He is a high ball hitter who likes the pitch out over the plate. The best way to defense him is to position fielders toward the middle and shallow, taking away the alleys and cutting off a lot of singles that otherwise would fall in. This alignment will give up the occasional double, however.

BASERUNNING:

For someone who looks reasonably athletic, Benedict is incredibly slow. You will almost never see him go from first to third on a single, and you cannot count on him scoring from second on a single. As for stealing a base, forget it.

FIELDING:

His defensive skills, once promising, have deteriorated significantly. He throws very poorly to second base, last season throwing out under 20% of the runners who attempted to steal on him. He has mechanical problems, often appearing totally out of synch, stumbling

BRUCE BENEDICT
C, No. 20
RR, 6'1", 195 lbs.
ML Svc: 6 years
Born: 8-18-55 in
   Birmingham, AL

1984 STATISTICS

AVG	G	AB	R	H	2B	3B	HR	RBI	BB	SO	SB
.223	95	300	26	67	8	1	4	25	34	25	1

CAREER STATISTICS

AVG	G	AB	R	H	2B	3B	HR	RBI	BB	SO	SB
.256	655	2019	164	516	71	5	16	197	232	172	11

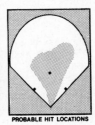

STRONG · STRONG

VS. RHP · VS. LHP · PROBABLE HIT LOCATIONS

over his own footwork, trying to throw sidearm. He also has a problem when it comes to blocking the plate; he seems to prefer avoiding physical contact.

OVERALL:

Once upon a time, in 1981, Benedict threw very well. Once upon a time, in 1983, he hit very well. But in 1984, he didn't do either very well, making 1985 a big question mark.

Campbell: "I would consider him an erratic catcher. As far as blocking the plate, I have never been impressed. He is not a blood-and-guts type of player."

PITCHING:

The 1984 season marked a revival for Rick Camp's career. After pitching splendidly for the Braves as a short reliever in 1980 and 1981, he floundered as a starter, spot starter, short reliever, middle reliever and long reliever throughout the 1982 and 1983 seasons. But in 1984, he got a full-fledged opportunity as a starter and by the end of the season had established himself as the team's No. 2 starter behind Rick Mahler.

Camp's best pitch is a sinker, which induces a lot of ground ball outs. He also throws a very good slider. When he is at his best, he has his sinker and slider working in tandem. He can use the down-and-in sinker and the down-and-out slider as his out pitches.

Camp's other pitches, the fastball, curve, and change, are merely something to show the hitters. He rarely throws a ball faster than 85-87 MPH, so movement and location are crucial.

FIELDING, HITTING, BASERUNNING:

Camp has a good move to first and, unlike some Braves pitchers, does not tend to forget the baserunners. He is able to concentrate on the runner without giving in to the batter and has a better than average move to first base. This ability comes from his years as a short reliever. Camp fields his position well.

Camp is a notoriously bad hitter. In

RICK CAMP
RHP, No. 37
RR, 6'1", 198 lbs.
ML Svc: 7 years
Born: 6-10-53 in
    Trion, GA

1984 STATISTICS

W	L	ERA	G	GS	CG	IP	H	R	ER	BB	SO	SV
8	6	3.27	31	21	1	148	134	59	54	63	69	0

CAREER STATISTICS

W	L	ERA	G	GS	CG	IP	H	R	ER	BB	SO	SV
52	43	3.29	348	63	5	813	840	348	297	274	358	54

fact, his ineptness as a hitter is fodder for a lot of jokes among his teammates. He is a good natural athlete, so he probably could hold his own on the bases. But he never gets there.

OVERALL:

Camp, because of elbow troubles, was a physical question mark going into 1984, but he now is regarded as sound. Still, with a new manager leading the Braves, it is not clear whether Camp will be used as a starter or reliever in 1985.

Campbell: "He is a very competitive guy. I think he is the kind of guy you can put out there and depend on for six or seven strong innings. He gives you that consistently."

HITTING:

Until last season, one word had always summarized Chris Chambliss as an offensive player: consistent. But all of a sudden, Chambliss plummeted.

At 35 years old, he was no longer the steady run producer who always seemed to maintain a .280 average, 20 homers and 80 RBIs. He had a terrible second half—totally non-productive—and there is reason to wonder if he is finished as a regular player.

When he's on, he is a high ball hitter who likes the ball out over the plate so he can get his arms extended. He has power straightaway. He bats with a closed stance, standing toward the back of the box. He can be vulnerable to off-speed pitches if they are kept down. Throughout his career, he has not been an effective hitter against left-handed pitching. The best way to get him out has always been with breaking balls away and fastballs riding in on the fists.

BASERUNNING:

The best thing Chambliss does as a baserunner is slide tough, especially when there is a play to be broken up. He does not have good speed and is no threat to steal or do anything else adventurous on the bases.

FIELDING:

His fielding has slipped about as much as his hitting. Yes, he still has the same sure hands at first base, but his range has diminished considerably. He also does not react as quickly to the batted ball anymore. He's always had only an average throwing arm. One attribute still going for him as a defensive player is that he knows hitters and can play situations very well.

OVERALL:

The Braves seem to have written Chris out of their future--at least in any

CHRIS CHAMBLISS
1B, No. 10
LR, 6'1", 221 lbs.
ML Svc: 14 years
Born: 12-26-48 in
Dayton, OH

1984 STATISTICS

AVG	G	AB	R	H	2B	3B	HR	RBI	BB	SO	SB
.257	135	389	47	100	14	0	9	44	58	54	1

CAREER STATISTICS

AVG	G	AB	R	H	2B	3B	HR	RBI	BB	SO	SB
.279	1976	7278	883	2031	377	42	180	937	599	960	43

VS. RHP

VS. LHP

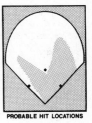

PROBABLE HIT LOCATIONS

type of prominent role. He may be back as a lefthanded pinch-hitter in 1985, but the Braves appear to be committed to young Gerald Perry as their starting first baseman. If there is a market for the high-salaried Chambliss, the Braves are sure to deal him.

Campbell: "The last half of 1984 may have indicated that all of a sudden the bells began to chime for Chambliss, who had been one of the most productive players in the big leagues for the last 10 years. He had an awful second half from an offensive standpoint. What happened, I don't know. I thought his weight was up. But when someone is going badly, you start looking for reasons, and most of the time it's just old age creeping up. Chambliss has probably worn out his welcome in Atlanta. I'd be very surprised if he is wearing a Braves uniform by the time the season starts."

PITCHING:

Strictly a reliever, Jeff Dedmon received much acclaim during the months preceding the 1984 season as a valuable addition to the Braves staff. But his 1984 season was undistinguished.

He opened the season in the big leagues, pitched very well for the first few weeks, then pitched poorly for a few weeks, then was sent to the Richmond, Virginia, farm club. He returned to the major leagues late in the season and pitched erratically--good at times, bad at times.

His repertoire resembles that of teammate Rick Camp. His best pitch is a heavy, sinking fastball, and he also throws a reasonably sharp slider. When both pitches are working, he has the stuff to be a very good relief pitcher in the big leagues. But obviously, he didn't have them working with great regularity last season or he would not have made the trip back to Richmond.

There should be a verdict on his future in 1985.

FIELDING, HITTING, BASERUNNING:

He knows how to hold runners on base, the result of working with coach Johnny Sain in the minor leagues, and he fields his position competently.

Used primarily as a long and middle reliever in 1984, he rarely got a chance to bat. But like most young pitchers who came through a minor league system

JEFF DEDMON
RHP, No. 49
LR, 6'2", 200 lbs.
ML Svc: 1 year plus
Born: 3-4-60 in
Torrance, CA

1984 STATISTICS												
W	L	ERA	G	GS	CG	IP	H	R	ER	BB	SO	SV
4	3	3.78	54	0	0	81	86	39	34	35	51	4

CAREER STATISTICS												
W	L	ERA	G	GS	CG	IP	H	R	ER	BB	SO	SV
4	3	4.24	59	0	0	85	96	45	40	35	54	4

that uses the designated hitter, he looks uncomfortable and futile at the plate.

OVERALL:

Perhaps because the Braves had such high expectations of him, they were disappointed with him last season. But he could benefit from the change of managers and get a good second shot.

Campbell: "He appears cool as a cucumber to me. I remember the first time I saw him. He came into a game at San Diego with 40,000 people in the stands, the bases loaded, one out and Steve Garvey batting. He got a double play ball and walked off the field like that's the way it was supposed to be."

PITCHING:

The veteran Terry Forster has reached a very definite crossroads in his career. Last season was a total waste for him, most of it spent on the disabled list with a hamstring injury. His biggest problem, however, is his weight.

The Braves say Forster got up to 255 pounds last season, 30 to 40 pounds heavier than he should be. It is reasonable to think that his recent injuries are related to his weight.

If he can get his weight under control, he still has the qualities of a good relief pitcher. He is an extraordinary competitor who never scares. He relishes game-on-the-line situations, is experienced and knows the hitters.

He has a good sinker, a good hard slider and good control. Additionally, he is a lefthander--and lefthanded short relievers are precious commodities. If Forster is to help the Braves in 1985-- indeed, if he is to prolong his career, he will have to lose weight and hope that enables him to stay injury-free.

FIELDING, HITTING, BASERUNNING:

He is a fair fielder, but his weight slows him in coming off the mound, fielding bunts or covering first base. He does not have a good move to first base at all. In fact, his method of holding runners on base is generally to step off the rubber and toss the ball to the first baseman.

Forster is, and has always been, an extraordinary hitter for a pitcher, with a career average of over .400. But he is also a lucky hitter, as he acknowledges. Most of his hits seem to be roll-

TERRY FORSTER
LHP, No. 51
LL, 6'4", 255 lbs.
ML Svc: 14 years
Born: 1-14-52 in
Sioux Falls, SD

1984 STATISTICS

W	L	ERA	G	GS	CG	IP	H	R	ER	BB	SO	SV
2	0	2.70	25	0	0	26	30	9	8	7	10	5

CAREER STATISTICS

W	L	ERA	G	GS	CG	IP	H	R	ER	BB	SO	SV
48	61	3.28	527	39	5	1004	938	414	366	412	726	121

ers, bloopers, pop flies or soft liners that find an opening. It all looks the same in the box score, though. On the bases, Forster lumbers more than he runs.

OVERALL:

As a pitcher, he is competitive and determined, and he's going to need to use those qualities in controlling his weight. The Braves are looking for him to bounce back productively.

Campbell: "I just think that a major league pitcher in his 30s, especially one with a history of injuries, has to take care of himself physically. Otherwise, injuries will keep cropping up. If Forster has good years left, he's going to have to go on a good diet and maintain it during the season. He may think he needs weight for strength, but in my opinion, the extra weight can cause injuries to the lower extremities."

PITCHING:

Gene Garber is no longer the pitcher who saved 30 games for the Braves in 1982, when the Atlanta bullpen statistically was the best in baseball. But he still is a competent relief pitcher.

His 1984 season was up and down. There were times when he had difficulty getting anyone out, but there also were stretches when he appeared virtually unbeatable. The real Garber is somewhere in between, but he does not have the consistency that he used to have.

That probably is because he doesn't hit the good spots as much now. He never was a "stuff" pitcher, always relying on location and change of speeds more than anything. He has an excellent change-up, (it has always been his best pitch), but he probably has lost a little off his fastball, which reaches the plate in the low 80s. That enables hitters to sit on it and get to him if he makes a mistake on the change-up or breaking stuff.

As always, Garber delivers with an unorthodox, back-to-the-plate motion. He is a thinker on the mound, not a thrower. He must have movement and location to get hitters out.

FIELDING, HITTING, BASERUNNING:

His unorthodox delivery is an invitation for opposing baserunners to steal second and, sometimes, third. He tries to compensate by throwing to first base very often. He is a quick, alert fielder who comes off the mound well despite a herky-jerky motion.

GENE GARBER
RHP, No. 26
RR, 5'10", 165 lbs.
ML Svc: 12 years
Born: 11-13-47 in
   Lancaster, PA

1984 STATISTICS											
W	L	ERA	G	GS	CG	IP	H	R	ER	BB	SO	SV
3	6	3.06	62	0	0	106	103	45	36	24	55	11

CAREER STATISTICS											
W	L	ERA	G	GS	CG	IP	H	R	ER	BB	SO	SV
77	88	3.31	723	9	4	1218	1139	531	448	359	815	169

He rarely gets an opportunity to bat, being a short reliever. But when he does get to the plate, Garber appears to thoroughly enjoy himself and never lets the pitcher off easy. He runs a lot before games, but has no speed.

OVERALL:

Garber's best quality as a relief pitcher is his competitiveness; he does not scare. He is much like teammate Terry Forster in this regard. But, unlike Forster, Garber does not have a weight problem.

Campbell: "Gene is a battler who does not have as good stuff as he used to, but still good enough to make the Atlanta pitching staff. At one time, that bullpen was the best in baseball, and I suspect it will still be pretty darn good in 1985."

HITTING:

The problem with Bob Horner is not what he does at the plate. The problem is getting him there.

Once again in 1984, an injury struck Horner down. This time, he re-broke a bone in his right wrist, the same bone that ended his 1983 season. The question continues to be asked, "Can Bob Horner ever play a full season without a crippling injury?"

Despite all the injuries, Horner has had five seasons with 20 or more homers and three seasons with 30 or more. He is a mature, disciplined hitter who has unusual patience. He crowds the plate, making himself most susceptible to hard stuff inside. He is a pull hitter who will hit any type of pitching mistake out of the park. He is one of the most exciting streak hitters in the game.

BASERUNNING:

He runs in degrees of slowness, depending largely on fluctuations in his weight. He does not get a good jump off first base, but he does show some aggressiveness when trying to break up a double play.

FIELDING:

Horner's strength as a fielder is the accuracy of his throwing arm. His arm is not exceptionally strong, but he rarely throws balls away.

He has extremely limited range in the field, not reaching many balls to his left or right. On the exceedingly routine plays, Horner is reliable; he has good hands and plays hitters well.

BOB HORNER
3B, No. 5
RR, 6'1", 220 lbs.
ML Svc: 7 years
Born: 8-6-57 in
Junction City, KS

1984 STATISTICS

AVG	G	AB	R	H	2B	3B	HR	RBI	BB	SO	SB
.274	32	113	15	31	8	0	3	19	14	17	0

CAREER STATISTICS

AVG	G	AB	R	H	2B	3B	HR	RBI	BB	SO	SB
.282	689	2571	414	724	113	4	161	476	235	360	12

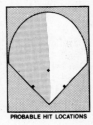

VS. RHP STRONG VS. LHP STRONG PROBABLE HIT LOCATIONS

OVERALL:

The Braves keep thinking and talking of Horner in terms of a 50-homer season and a Triple Crown. But there are more and more doubts as to whether he will ever play a full season.

Campbell: "The big question, not only in Atlanta but in just about every other city where baseball fans reside, is, 'Will Bob Horner ever play a full year?' You get very suspicious of injuries like a re-broken bone in his wrist; it almost reminds you of basketball's Bill Walton and his notorious foot problem."

HITTING:

Glenn Hubbard is a tough, intelligent clutch hitter who performs best with men on base. One of the shortest players in the majors, he has good upper-body strength. He has excellent timing and is particularly good in hit-and-run situations.

He is a dead high ball hitter who hits to the alleys and surprises you occasionally with a home run. He is an exceptional bunter. He is vulnerable when pitched inside and when fed breaking balls away.

BASERUNNING:

He is small but slow--in other words, not a basestealing threat. What he does have going for him as a baserunner are good instincts and aggressiveness. He breaks up double plays as well as anyone on the Braves team.

FIELDING:

You would have to search hard to find someone who turns the double play better than Glenn Hubbard. He is not the smoothest-looking second baseman around, but he makes the plays.

He has an awkward throwing motion, but makes good throws. Hubbard's range is limited, but occasionally he will surprise you by coming up with a ball that looked like a hit. He does this by positioning himself for hitters and defensive situations very well.

GLENN HUBBARD
2B, No. 17
RR, 5'8", 169 lbs.
ML Svc: 6 years
Born: 9-25-57 in
   Hahn AFB, GER

1984 STATISTICS

AVG	G	AB	R	H	2B	3B	HR	RBI	BB	SO	SB
.234	120	397	53	93	27	2	9	43	55	61	4

CAREER STATISTICS

AVG	G	AB	R	H	2B	3B	HR	RBI	BB	SO	SB
.246	770	2726	336	670	126	17	50	280	288	285	24

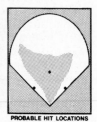

VS. RHP   VS. LHP   PROBABLE HIT LOCATIONS

OVERALL:

He has made himself a player through hard work. He may have peaked, but only because he has already coaxed the maximum out of his modest ability.

Campbell: "If the Braves management is looking for even more from him, I think 1985 will be a make-or-break year for him."

HITTING:

Randy Johnson will never hit for power, which makes him less than ideal as the backup third baseman on a team that so often loses its starting third baseman, Bob Horner.

But he can get hot and drop in a lot of singles and doubles. While filling in first for Horner and later for Ken Oberkfell last season, Johnson indeed got hot a few times. He is a spray hitter who uses all fields; he rarely hits the ball down either line, so the best defensive alignment against him is to yield the lines and bunch toward the middle.

He is a high ball hitter who is most vulnerable against inside pitches. He doesn't get fidgety if he is not in the lineup, a much-needed characteristic of a good pinch-hitter.

BASERUNNING:

His speed is no better than average, but he has worked hard at the game and has good instincts on the bases. He won't steal a base, but he will take the extra base when it is prudent to do so.

FIELDING:

For a few games at a time, Johnson is an adequate fielder. But over a longer stretch, his weaknesses are exposed.

He does not play the bunt well and has only average range. Johnson has some difficulty with anything other than routine plays. In addition to third base, he has had experience at second, which might be his better defensive position.

RANDY JOHNSON
INF, No. 6
RR, 6'1", 190 lbs.
ML Svc: 3 years
Born: 6-10-56 in
    Escondido, CA

1984 STATISTICS

AVG	G	AB	R	H	2B	3B	HR	RBI	BB	SO	SB
.279	91	294	28	82	13	0	5	30	21	21	4

CAREER STATISTICS

AVG	G	AB	R	H	2B	3B	HR	RBI	BB	SO	SB
.267	204	484	55	129	21	0	6	53	47	52	5

STRONG   STRONG

VS. RHP   VS. LHP   PROBABLE HIT LOCATIONS

OVERALL:

His skills are not commensurate with his playing, say, 100 games a year. But as a second utility infielder, as a righthanded pinch-hitter, as a 25th man on the roster, he can contribute.

Campbell: "He is a solid player, not spectacular at any phase of the game but a guy who'll go out there and do a decent job."

PITCHING:

Without any question, Rick Mahler was the Braves' most pleasant surprise last season. The year before, manager Joe Torre decided Mahler could not pitch in the big leagues and banished him to the minors. Mahler would have been traded by the Braves long before the opening of the 1984 season except for the intervention of team owner Ted Turner, who astutely ordered the team not to deal any more pitchers.

In any case, the unwanted Mahler gradually forced his way to the top of an ineffective, injury-riddled staff and by the end of the season was the team's No. 1 starter. He even converted Torre, who by the end of the season was starting him every fourth day.

Mahler, who pitches from an overhand delivery, is a breaking ball pitcher. That is why Torre did not like him at first; Torre prefers power pitchers.

Mahler throws an 86 MPH fastball that sinks, but his out pitches are a change-up, a slow curve and a slider.

He has one of the best curveballs in the league. When he throws it, he has a powerful follow-through that makes it appear that he's throwing a 95 MPH fastball. But instead, the curve floats to the plate and away from the hitter. Mahler can throw to spots, and he can out-think the hitter. He's a pleasure to watch if you enjoy guile.

FIELDING, HITTING, BASERUNNING:

He keeps a watchful eye on baserunners at first and has an adequate move.

RICK MAHLER
RHP, No. 42
RR, 6'1", 202 lbs.
ML Svc: 4 years
Born: 8-5-53 in
Austin, TX

1984 STATISTICS

W	L	ERA	G	GS	CG	IP	H	R	ER	BB	SO	SV
13	10	3.12	38	29	9	222	209	86	77	62	106	0

CAREER STATISTICS

W	L	ERA	G	GS	CG	IP	H	R	ER	BB	SO	SV
30	26	3.60	138	76	15	580	577	257	232	187	285	2

Overall, he fields his position competently.

Mahler's 1984 season was a success as a hitter, too. Despite not batting much in the minors, he knows what he is doing as a hitter.

OVERALL:

For the Braves, he brings to mind the cliche that says the best trades often are the ones never made. One reason Torre was fired after the 1984 season was that his judgment on pitchers frequently was quesionable: Mahler, Phil Niekro, Joe Cowley, Larry McWilliams. Mahler, meanwhile, is firmly entrenched.

Campbell: "You have to admire him. He doesn't have all that much natural ability, and he's had a lot more downs than ups in his career. But he's made himself a good big league pitcher."

PITCHING:

The National League's rookie pitcher of the year in 1983, Craig McMurtry fell dramatically in 1984. For the most part, he did not look like the same pitcher.

McMurtry is a control pitcher. He throws a fastball, slider, sinker and curveball, but he throws none of them with such distinction that he can afford to lose his location and groove. In 1984, unlike 1983, he was not in a groove.

His most visible shortcoming was in the first inning: almost one third of the runs against him were scored in the first inning. So often, it seemed, he'd be down 4-0, 5-0 before getting the first three outs of the game. Since he prepared for games just as he had done the year before, when he won 15 games, the best guess is that McMurtry's first inning problem became psychological and compounded itself.

He throws from a three-quarters motion and can be especially tough on righthanders, whom he likes to jam on the hands with hard stuff. The Braves continue to see him purely as a starting pitcher, although he fell into the bullpen for a month amidst last season's hard times.

FIELDING, HITTING, BASERUNNING:

He is tall and rangy and has a smooth delivery, putting himself in good fielding position. He reacts quickly to a

CRAIG McMURTRY
RHP, No. 29
RR, 6'5", 195 lbs.
ML Svc: 2 years
Born: 11-5-59 in
Temple, TX

1984 STATISTICS

W	L	ERA	G	GS	CG	IP	H	R	ER	BB	SO	SV
9	17	4.32	37	30	0	183	184	100	88	102	99	0

CAREER STATISTICS

W	L	ERA	G	GS	CG	IP	H	R	ER	BB	SO	SV
24	26	3.65	73	65	6	407	388	186	165	190	204	0

batted ball. He has a very good move to first base, something he picked up from ex-teammate Phil Niekro.

He can run all right, but he can't hit. So he never gets to use whatever baserunning skill he might have.

OVERALL:

The Braves can only hope McMurtry goes into the 1985 season with his confidence restored. If so, there is no physical reason he cannot be the pitcher who won 15 games as a rookie.

Campbell: "I don't believe in the sophomore jinx. You either have a good year or a bad year, and McMurtry did not have a solid year in 1984."

PITCHING:

A year ago, Donnie Moore was described as a "role pitcher, a journeyman who is not much more than a 10th man on a staff." For most of his career before 1984, that description fit Donnie Moore snugly. But in 1984, he became substantially more.

While fellow relievers Terry Forster, Gene Garber and Steve Bedrosian had assorted difficulties, Moore emerged as the Braves' No. 1 reliever for much of the season. Spotting his pitches well and throwing slightly harder than in the past, he came through in clutch situations.

He has a basic repertoire of fastball (86-88 MPH), curve, slider and change-up. He throws from three-quarters and has a very durable arm. He'll pitch hurt, too, as he showed in 1984. His role might revert to middle and long relief in 1985, and then again it might not. In either case, he figures to go to spring training more secure than at any point in his career.

FIELDING, HITTING, BASERUNNING:

He has always had a decent move to first base, and he appeared to refine it somewhat last season. He does not forget about baserunners. He's quick off the mound and plays the bunt very well.

DONNIE MOORE
RHP, No. 31
LR, 6'1", 185 lbs.
ML Svc: 5 years
Born: 2-13-54 in
  Lubbock, TX

1984 STATISTICS

W	L	ERA	G	GS	CG	IP	H	R	ER	BB	SO	SV
4	5	2.94	47	0	0	64	63	27	21	18	47	16

CAREER STATISTICS

W	L	ERA	G	GS	CG	IP	H	R	ER	BB	SO	SV
24	23	4.17	261	4	0	421	471	220	195	122	252	28

He has the bat of a short reliever, which is to say he isn't a hitter. He has above average natural speed, but doesn't get a chance to flaunt it very much.

OVERALL:

Throwing hard, keeping the ball moving and often coming inside, Moore was no fluke in 1984. His challenge now is to duplicate the performance. He's determined, confident--a professional.

Campbell: "Even in bad years, a team has a pleasant surprise or two. In 1984, Donnie Moore definitely was a pleasant surprise for Atlanta."

HITTING:

What more can be said about Dale Murphy? Although he failed to win a third consecutive Most Valuable Player award last season, he did nothing to diminish his standing as one of the truly phenomenal hitters in the game.

His statistics should be viewed with the knowledge that he played with Bob Horner on the disabled list and Chris Chambliss non-productive. For the two previous years, those players had hit around Murphy in the batting order.

In 1984, he had uncharacteristic trouble hitting with runners in scoring position, and he still would like to cut down on his strikeouts.

Murphy bats from a slightly closed stance while standing off the plate. However, he continues to have some trouble with inside pitches and perhaps should move farther off the plate, in the style of Mike Schmidt. Occasionally, Murphy will chase inside pitches, especially if they are up, and he will go fishing for down and away sliders and curveballs. He also tends to become a defensive hitter when he has two strikes on him.

But if you throw him a fastball out over the plate, or if you fall behind in the count, Murphy is a devastating hitter. He uses all fields, but his forte is driving the ball to right and right-center. He is a streak hitter, and when he's hot, forget all of the above--he'll hit everything.

BASERUNNING:

Murphy is known as a hitter, but he is also one of the best baserunners in the game. He isn't blessed with exceptional speed, but he is blessed with unteachable baseball instincts. In 1983, he became only the sixth player in baseball history to hit 30 homers and steal 30 bases in the same season. He always knows when to run; he almost never makes a mistake on the bases.

DALE MURPHY
CF, No. 3
RR, 6'5", 218 lbs.
ML Svc: 7 years
Born: 3-12-56 in
Portland, OR

1984 STATISTICS

AVG	G	AB	R	H	2B	3B	HR	RBI	BB	SO	SB
.290	162	607	94	176	32	8	36	100	79	134	19

CAREER STATISTICS

AVG	G	AB	R	H	2B	3B	HR	RBI	BB	SO	SB
.275	1038	3787	606	1040	153	23	200	628	452	812	112

  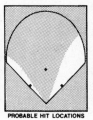

VS. RHP   VS. LHP   PROBABLE HIT LOCATIONS

FIELDING:

He is a very good center fielder, but he might eventually be moved to right because of his powerful throwing arm. He covers a lot of ground because he reacts quickly and accurately to the batted ball, and then moves in long, graceful strides. He almost never misjudges a ball or throws to the wrong place.

OVERALL:

If he is not the best all around player in baseball, he definitely is in the running. And he is just as good off the field as on.

Campbell: "He truly is one of the greats in this game, not just as a ballplayer, but as a human being. If he gets ahead in the count, it's time for the pitchers to duck."

KEN OBERKFELL
3B, No. 24
LR, 6'1", 185 lbs.
ML Svc: 7 years
Born: 5-4-56 in
  Highland, IL

HITTING:

The Braves acquired Ken Obkerfell to replace the injured Bob Horner in the lineup, but there was no way Oberkfell could replace Horner as a hitter. Not that Oberkfell is a bad hitter, but he is an altogether different type of hitter than Horner.

While Horner is a run producer, Ken Oberkfell is not. He does not hit well with runners in scoring position and is not suited for the No. 6 spot in which the Braves frequently used him. His value as an offensive player is in starting and sustaining rallies, not capping them.

He is a singles and doubles type of hitter with .290-.300 credentials, a straightaway line drive hitter. He likes the ball up and over the plate. He is not as good a hitter against pitchers season, who change speeds cleverly, and pitchers should also try to jam him while keeping the ball down. He should be defensed toward the middle of the diamond, giving him the lines.

1984 STATISTICS											
AVG	G	AB	R	H	2B	3B	HR	RBI	BB	SO	SB
.269	100	324	38	87	19	2	1	21	31	27	2

CAREER STATISTICS											
AVG	G	AB	R	H	2B	3B	HR	RBI	BB	SO	SB
.288	774	2508	316	722	126	29	12	220	280	175	46	2

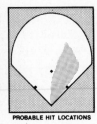

VS. RHP   VS. LHP   PROBABLE HIT LOCATIONS

BASERUNNING:

He has decent speed but is not a great basestealing threat, though he is not a liability on the bases, either. He has the speed of a solid No. 2 hitter.

FIELDING:

As a third baseman, he is average at best. He was originally a second baseman, but a knee injury forced him to third.

OVERALL:

Presuming that Bob Horner is healthy at the start of next season, Oberkfell will be a utilityman if he is with the Braves.

Campbell: "I think that on a good ballclub, Oberkfell could be a valuable player. He would give you a good bat coming off the bench, and he could fill-in in a couple of spots without embarrassing you."

PITCHING:

Pascual Perez quickly has become known as one of the most volatile and controversial pitchers in the game. That is partly because of his off-the-field troubles with the law, partly because of his difficulty in getting to the ball-park on time and partly because of his hot dog antics on the field.

He was in a Dominican Republic jail when last season opened, facing drug charges. He joined the Braves in May after being found guilty of a misdemeanor, fined and released. He had an up-and-down season, certainly not as impressive as his 1983 season.

He pitches mostly from a three-quarters motion, occasionally dropping to sidearm. His best pitch is a lively, 90 MPH fastball that rides in on left-handed batters and sinks for righties. He also has a good slider, curve and change. Overall, he is tougher on righties than lefties. A weakness is concentration lapses that lead to home runs.

Although he throws hard, his control is good, and he is probably more of a control pitcher than a power pitcher. He loves to come inside on hitters, and that gets him into trouble sometimes, as in last year's brawl with the Padres.

FIELDING, HITTING, BASERUNNING:

He is a good natural athlete--quick, fast, strong. He uses those qualities as a fielder. He comes off the mound very quickly and always is in position for a bunt or other batted ball. He has a better than average move to first base.

PASCUAL PEREZ
RHP, No. 27
RR, 6'2", 163 lbs.
ML Svc: 3 years
Born: 5-17-57 in
Haina, DR

1984 STATISTICS

W	L	ERA	G	GS	CG	IP	H	R	ER	BB	SO	SV
14	8	3.74	30	30	4	211	208	96	88	51	145	0

CAREER STATISTICS

W	L	ERA	G	GS	CG	IP	H	R	ER	BB	SO	SV
35	28	3.58	98	89	13	603	613	275	240	153	371	0

His most memorable experience as a hitter came in the infamous San Diego game last year in which three Padres pitchers threw at him. Normally, he likes to take his cuts, but isn't really a threat at the plate. He has good speed, so he can move on the bases when he gets there.

OVERALL:

The biggest rap against Perez has nothing to do with the way he throws the baseball. His on-the-field showmanship rubs a lot of people the wrong way. As a pitcher, though, Perez figures to be in the Braves' starting rotation again in 1985.

Campbell: "As for his hot dog mannerisms and general demeanor, that's going to continue to keep him in hot water. I think it would be a lot better for baseball if he'd change some of his habits, but I don't guess he's going to."

HITTING:

The Braves feel that Gerald Perry is now capable of contributing the type of offense that Chris Chambliss contributed consistently until last year. So, Perry is projected as the Braves' starting first baseman for 1985.

Like Chambliss, he is a lefthanded hitter with good power, especially to the opposite field. He has a quick bat and is aggressive at the plate. He hangs in well against lefthanded pitching; in fact, he figures to hit lefties better than Chambliss ever did. He is a high ball hitter. Pitchers might have better success against him if they keep the ball down and inside--jam him with fastballs.

BASERUNNING:

He has above average speed and, with experience, should become a basestealing threat along the lines of a Dale Murphy. He is tough and aggressive on the bases, too.

FIELDING:

Interested in getting his bat into the lineup last spring, the Braves attempted to convert Perry to left field. He looked like a player who had never been there before in his life, which, of ·course, he hadn't. But at first base, Perry is comfortable and polished.

He has good range, a good first-base arm and good hands. The only drawback is his height (5'11"), though it is not a very significant factor in his case.

GERALD PERRY
INF, No. 28
LR, 5'11", 172 lbs.
ML Svc: 2 years
Born: 10-30-60 in
Savannah, GA

1984 STATISTICS

AVG	G	AB	R	H	2B	3B	HR	RBI	BB	SO	SB
.265	122	347	52	92	12	2	7	47	61	38	15

CAREER STATISTICS

AVG	G	AB	R	H	2B	3B	HR	RBI	BB	SO	SB
.275	149	386	57	106	14	2	8	53	66	42	15

  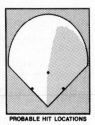

VS. RHP   VS. LHP   PROBABLE HIT LOCATIONS

OVERALL:

He will get his chance in 1985. He is confident, almost cocky at times, and he thinks he is ready.

Campbell: "Since the Braves didn't really contend for the National League West championship last season, this is the natural time to move a young guy into the lineup."

HITTING:

Rafael Ramirez looked like a very good hitter, especially for a shortstop, throughout the 1983 season and during the first half of the 1984 season. But in the second half of the 1984 season, Ramirez did virtually nothing at the plate, hitting under .200.

In fact, his decline as a hitter was perhaps the biggest disappointment of the Braves' season. He appeared to lose all discipline at the plate; pitchers frequently got him to chase the fastball up and the breaking ball down. It also appeared questionable at times whether Ramirez was totally concentrating at the plate.

In good times, he is a high ball hitter and extremely aggressive. He hits line drives to all fields, and he has power that can turn a mistake into a home run.

BASERUNNING:

Ramirez has good speed and can be an asset on the bases. However, he does not have good enough speed to run on all catchers, and the Braves perhaps sent him too often. He is aggressive on the bases.

FIELDING:

He has always been an erratic fielder, capable one minute of making a brilliant play and equally capable the next of botching a routine play.

The Braves generally have tolerated his inconsistency in the field, but they got down on him late in 1984. One flaw

RAFAEL RAMIREZ
SS, No. 16
RR, 6'0", 181 lbs.
ML Svc: 4 years
Born: 2-18-59 in
    San Pedro de Macoris, DR

1984 STATISTICS											
AVG	G	AB	R	H	2B	3B	HR	RBI	BB	SO	SB
.266	145	591	51	157	22	4	2	48	26	70	14

CAREER STATISTICS											
AVG	G	AB	R	H	2B	3B	HR	RBI	BB	SO	SB
.271	599	2294	254	622	81	16	23	189	124	247	66

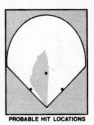

VS. RHP   VS. LHP   PROBABLE HIT LOCATIONS

in Ramirez's defensive game is that he often makes wild throws even when he does not have a play. He does, however, have exceptional range.

OVERALL:

At the moment, he is a mystery. The Braves at one time thought of him as their long-term shortstop, but they are now thinking of trading him in their search for pitching.

Campbell: "I thought he showed great improvement in 1982 and 1983, but he really took a step backward in 1984."

HITTING:

If you want power hitting from your catcher, Alex Trevino does not fill the bill. But he is a solid line drive hitter who, at times, can contribute to an offense. He is a streak hitter.

Im ediately after being dealt from the Reds to the Braves last season, Trevino went on a tear with the bat, but predictably, he cooled down in the following months.

He likes high balls, and he likes to hit the opposite way, to right field. The way to get him out is to jam him inside, especially with hard stuff. He can be overpowered.

BASERUNNING:

He has extraordinary speed for a catcher; in fact, he may be the fastest catcher in the National League. One reason for this is his size; he is unusually slight for a catcher. Unlike most catchers, he does not have heavy legs to slow him down.

FIELDING:

The biggest question is his durability behind the plate. Because of his size, it is extremely doubtful whether he could catch more than 110-120 games a season. He is difficult to measure defensively. On the one hand, he has just about the quickest release of any catcher in the National League, a release reminiscient of the late Thurman Munson. But on the other hand, Trevino's throws are often are wild, landing nowhere near second base. After his trade from the Reds to the Braves, Trevino began throwing more accurately, but it remains to be seen if that transformation will last.

Overall, he is a good receiver, but because of his size, he is not enthusiastic about blocking the plate.

ALEX TREVINO
C, No. 29
RR, 5'10", 165 lbs.
ML Svc: 7 years
Born: 8-26-57 in
Monterrey, MEX

1984 STATISTICS

AVG	G	AB	R	H	2B	3B	HR	RBI	BB	SO	SB
.243	85	272	36	66	16	0	3	28	16	29	5

CAREER STATISTICS

AVG	G	AB	R	H	2B	3B	HR	RBI	BB	SO	SB
.250	526	1517	144	380	58	7	5	141	114	172	13

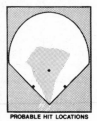

VS. RHP   VS. LHP   PROBABLE HIT LOCATIONS

OVERALL:

In Trevino and Benedict, the Braves have two small catchers who, they hope, can add up to an asset at the position. It is a difficult situation, though, because neither can feel secure about playing time. Since both are righthanded batters, a strict platoon system is impossible. They are very similar players, both offensively and defensively. Given what they have, all the Braves can do is play the hot hand.

Campbell: "The Braves have an interesting situation with their two catchers. Eventually, Atlanta will have to choose one of them as their everyday backstop. Of the two, Benedict and Trevino, I think that it is Trevino who has found a home in Atlanta."

HITTING:

Claudell Washington remains an enigma to the Braves. In the first half of last season, he virtually carried the team, playing possibly the best half season of his life. But in the second half, he was a non-entity.

A lefthanded hitter, Washington has great strength to right-center and center field. He likes the fastball out over the plate and belt high, so that he can extend his arms. He has trouble with breaking pitches, and he can be retired with fastballs running in on him.

Washington strikes out a lot, does not bunt often and is a typical streak hitter. When he is hot, pitchers should exercise great care.

BASERUNNING:

Washington is a good basestealer, but he is not a good overall baserunner. He steals bases with his pure speed, and after a decade in the big leagues, he still hasn't lost more than a half step.

But when it comes to the mental side of running the bases, Washington is less talented; he tends to have lapses of concentration. He has been known to run into foolish outs at foolish times.

FIELDING:

Most outfielders are generally consistent in the field, good or bad. But not Washington.

Some days, he is a very good outfielder; some days he is a very bad outfielder. He can make spectacular plays at the fence, and he can botch routine plays. The explanation seems to be that his concentration comes and goes.

In the past, he has had an above average throwing arm, but he did not demonstrate that arm at all in the 1984 season.

OVERALL:

Washington is in a precarious situa-

CLAUDELL WASHINGTON
OF, No. 15
LL, 6'0", 195 lbs.
ML Svc: 10 years
Born: 8-31-54 in
    Los Angeles, CA

1984 STATISTICS

AVG	G	AB	R	H	2B	3B	HR	RBI	BB	SO	SB
.286	120	416	62	119	21	2	17	61	59	77	21

CAREER STATISTICS

AVG	G	AB	R	H	2B	3B	HR	RBI	BB	SO	SB
.279	1313	4818	664	1345	245	55	104	592	385	851	246

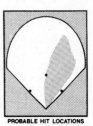

VS. RHP   VS. LHP   PROBABLE HIT LOCATIONS

tion with the Braves. If he starts the 1985 season as he ended the 1984 season, it is unlikely he will hold a starting job for very long.

He has just one year remaining on the free-agent contract he signed with the Braves, and there is a chance the team will try to shop him around. It is also unlikely that the Braves will try to retain Washington beyond the end of his contract. He has produced for the Braves at times, but his inconsistency has become bothersome to the team. With young outfielders like Brad Komminsk and Milt Thompson on the way, this is the time for the Braves to create a vacancy.

Campbell: "Washington is a streak hitter--when he gets hot, you'd better watch how you pitch to him. When he is cold, he is very, very cold. He will have to look for a team that is willing to accept the good with the bad."

AL HALL
OF, No. 2
RR, 5'11", 155 lbs.
ML Svc: 1 year plus
Born: 3-7-59 in
    Birmingham, AL

HITTING, BASERUNNING, FIELDING:

A year ago, the Braves thought Albert Hall could develop into the same type of offensive player as Brett Butler, who had been dealt to Cleveland. However, Hall did not show much at all in his first big league season, failing convincingly when he was given a chance to claim the starting left field job.

As a hitter, he seemed overmatched, both from the left and right sides of the plate; he never really drove the ball anywhere. As a defensive player, he could cover a lot of ground in the outfield, but he judged fly balls erratically and displayed only an average arm. His greatest value was as a baserunner. He had better speed than anyone else on the team and contributed as a pinch-runner. But, with other players coming along, that alone won't assure him a roster spot for long.

OVERALL:

Unless he shows more skills in spring training than he showed during last season, Hall's first season with the Braves will probably be his last.

BRAD KOMMINSK
OF, No. 7
RR, 6'2", 205 lbs.
ML Svc: 2 years
Born: 4-4-61 in
    Lima, OH

HITTING, BASERUNNING, FIELDING:

Since Brad Komminsk came into the organization, the Braves have regarded him as a can't-miss prospect, "the next Dale Murphy." He struggled mightily last year, though, in his first significant exposure to the big leagues, hitting under .200 for most of the season.

He appears to have some holes in his swing and will have to make some adjustments before he can hit major league pitching successfully. Good sliders and hard stuff in on the fists still trouble him; in fact, just about everything troubled him last season.

He has the tools. He has power in his bat. He has the speed to steal 30 or so bases. And he has the ability to be an above average outfielder, although his arm might never be better than average.

OVERALL:

Whenever he's ready, Komminsk will be a starter in the outfield, whether it means taking over in left or supplanting Claudell Washington in right.

Campbell: "He is the Braves' great hope of the future. When you have a player with this much promise, you just have to go through some growing pains with him. I think the Braves made up their minds to suffer with him last year. I suspect the guy is going to be a very good big league player some day. How soon? That is the question mark."

RUFINO LINARES
OF, No. 25
RR, 6'1", 190 lbs.
ML Svc: 3 years
Born: 2-28-55 in
San Pedro de
Macoris, DR

HITTING, BASERUNNING, FIELDING:

Rufino Linares made it to the big leagues with a one-dimensional game--he can hit, period. But it's debatable how long that one attribute will keep him there. He is a very aggressive hitter; he hits high pitches best, but he swings at anything and everything. He is an undisciplined line drive hitter who hits to the alleys with extra-base power. A smart pitcher should get him out.

No other aspect of his game merits praise. He is a very erratic, downright dangerous defensive player; he can and does play the most routine of fly balls into adventures. He has a very weak throwing arm, as well. As a baserunner, he has good speed, but that is offset by his lack of sound instincts and his own failure to concentrate.

OVERALL:

Because of his potential as a hitter, the Braves have been tempted from time to time to give him a shot as a starting outfielder. The experiment never lasts long.

Campbell: "I'd say his best value to a team is as a righthanded pinch-hitter and maybe an occasional fill-in in the outfield."

JERRY ROYSTER
INF, No. 1
RR, 6'0", 165 lbs.
ML Svc: 10 years
Born: 10-18-52 in
Sacramento, CA

HITTING, BASERUNNING, FIELDING:

Jerry Royster's greatest asset is his versatility--his ability to play second base, shortstop, third base and the outfield with roughly comparable efficiency. He is an aggressive hitter. He does not hit consistently for either power or average, but he has a history of getting hot for a couple of months at a time.

He is a dangerous hitter when he is ahead in the count 2-0 or 3-1, but he is not a good hitter when he is behind in the count. To get him out, throw fastballs in and change speeds; he likes to brace himself for one speed.

Royster isn't outstanding defensively at any one position, but he does an adequate job everywhere he plays. Sometimes he is overly aggressive in the field and takes too many chances. He has a good throwing arm but unreliable hands. He has a tendency of diving futilely for balls which he should be able to reach staying on his feet.

As a baserunner, Royster has lost a step or two recently. He holds the all-time Atlanta record for stolen bases, but then the Braves have never been much of a running franchise.

OVERALL:

After years of resisting the label, Royster now prides himself as a utility man. He actually can ignite a team for a few weeks at a time when he is playing well.

Campbell: "I think he can be a pretty good utility player, someone valuable to several different clubs in the major leagues."

CHICAGO CUBS

PITCHING:

Rich Bordi had a right to be upset in late September when the Cubs left him off the 25-man playoff roster. He had filled in as a spot starter and in long relief, winning some starts that the Cubs had virtually conceded. He had done a good job out of the bullpen.

Bordi uses primarily a fastball and a breaking ball and showed good control of both in 1984. However, he did give up the long ball on too many occasions. Opponents took him so deep that more than once even HE turned around to watch his mistake sail onto Waveland and Sheffield Avenues.

Bordi does not dwell on his misfortunes too long. He is able to bounce back from bad innings and bad outings. He accepts the starter-today, reliever-tomorrow and who-knows-after-that role in stride. He was used as a starter for the first time in his major league career with surprisingly good results.

On another team, Bordi might easily fit into the starting rotation and could probably be trusted with the ball every four or five days. On the Cubs, he might have to battle to get even the fifth spot in the rotation. That doesn't seem to bother him, but because good long relievers are hard to find, perhaps his place for now should be the bullpen.

FIELDING, HITTING, BASERUNNING:

Bordi is not to be taken too seriously at the plate. In the field, the tall righthander has improved his glove work, but could be a bit quicker covering first and a bit more polished coming off the mound to field bunts and grounders.

RICH BORDI
RHP, No. 42
RR, 6'5", 210 lbs.
ML Svc: 2 years
Born: 4-18-59 in
  S. San Francisco, CA

1984 STATISTICS

W	L	ERA	G	GS	CG	IP	H	R	ER	BB	SO	SV
5	2	3.46	31	7	0	83	78	37	32	20	41	4

CAREER STATISTICS

W	L	ERA	G	GS	CG	IP	H	R	ER	BB	SO	SV
5	2	3.46	31	7	0	83	78	37	32	20	41	4

Bordi hasn't been on base enough to enable anyone to make an adequate judgment of his baserunning abilities. Because of his role, Bordi can expect to be lifted for a pinch-runner if he gets on base, especially if it's late in the game.

OVERALL:

There are role players and there are star players: baseball is full of both of them. Many of today's stars were role players for many seasons before they enjoyed recognition. Bordi's best bet is to continue to pitch well and bide his time. It is going to be difficult for a young pitcher to shine on a staff that includes Smith, Sutcliffe, etc.

Snider: "He has a pretty good breaking ball and good control. Bordi is probably not one of the four or five the Cubs would use, but he's a good middle man."

HITTING:

After tearing up the American Association by hitting .358 at Iowa, Thad Bosley was promoted to the big leagues again in late June. A 28-year-old outfielder, Bosley suffered through the indignities of being a non-roster player in spring training and being sent back to Iowa before coming back to become one of the most reliable bats off the Cubs' bench for the second year in a row.

Most of Bosley's action was as a pinch-hitter, late-inning substitute, or second-game-of-a-double-header type of player. Nonetheless, he showed the makings of a clutch hitter by being a very steady pinch-hitter.

Bosley tends to be patient at the plate but will swing at the first pitch when it's up. Before 1984, Bosley was known as a spray hitter but pulled the ball more after he was called up again. That doesn't mean he's turned into a power hitter. Bosley's power is occasional, nothing more.

BASERUNNING:

Bosley has adequate speed and stole five bases in the relatively few opportunities he had. He doesn't need a long lead at first and is fairly dependable in hit-and-run situations.

FIELDING:

Seeing limited action in left and right fields, Bosley still handled both well. He has no trouble coming in on the ball although balls that force him to back pedal sometimes cause him problems.

THAD BOSLEY
OF, No. 20
LL, 6'3", 175 lbs.
ML Svc: 5 years
Born: 9-17-56 in
Oceanside, CA

1984 STATISTICS

AVG	G	AB	R	H	2B	3B	HR	RBI	BB	SO	SB
.296	55	98	17	29	2	2	2	14	13	22	5

CAREER STATISTICS

AVG	G	AB	R	H	2B	3B	HR	RBI	BB	SO	SB
.294	98	170	29	50	6	3	4	26	23	34	6

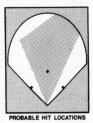

VS. RHP   VS. LHP   PROBABLE HIT LOCATIONS

OVERALL:

As long as he's a Cub, Bosley will have to resign himself to a life on the bench. If he were with another team, such as a non-contender in the National League or even one of the contenders in the American League West, Bosley would have a good chance to play every day.

Snider: "He will never be a superstar because he doesn't have that kind of power, but he won't hurt his team at the plate or in the field. He continues to strike out too often, however."

HITTING:

Age may have finally caught up with Larry Bowa: In 1984, he had one of his worst years ever. Stubbornly a switch-hitter, Bowa was abysmal from the left side and just barely a decent singles hitter from the right side. Unfortunately, he saw more righthanders than lefthanders, meaning he hit from the left side more often.

At first, Bowa had trouble seeing the ball and took to wearing glasses, a notion he later abandoned. Then he blamed his lack of playing time. That might have been part of the answer. Bowa had a decent September when he was left alone and told he would play every day.

A lack of patience at the plate is one of his problems. Even choking up on the bat didn't help him as much as he'd have liked it to. From the left side, Bowa tends to pull the ball, but can hit it up the middle and/or to the opposite field. As a righthander, he pulls the ball toward left field half the time or swings late and hits to the opposite field.

Usually a good bunter, Bowa's skills in that department showed signs of erosion in 1984. When the game was on the line, he was lifted for a pinch-hitter.

BASERUNNING:

On the bases, it was a different story: Bowa stole 10 bases, his high-water mark as a Cub. Now that he's been around for 15 years, Bowa relies more on his smarts to tell him when the time is right to steal. He wasn't very good at breaking up double plays, though.

FIELDING:

Thanks to a Wrigley Field ground crew that keeps the infield grass high, Bowa's lack of range doesn't show up as much at home as it does on the road, especially in one of the many parks that have an artificial surface. He simply can't get to balls as well as he used

LARRY BOWA
SS, No. 1
SR, 5'10", 155 lbs.
ML Svc: 15 years
Born: 12-6-45 in
Sacramento, CA

1984 STATISTICS

AVG	G	AB	R	H	2B	3B	HR	RBI	BB	SO	SB
.223	133	391	33	87	14	2	0	17	28	24	10

CAREER STATISTICS

AVG	G	AB	R	H	2B	3B	HR	RBI	BB	SO	SB
.261	2161	8204	972	2141	253	95	15	510	459	547	313

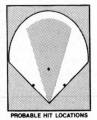

VS. RHP   VS. LHP   PROBABLE HIT LOCATIONS

to. He still has a strong arm, and his throws tend to be accurate, although he no longer can give a clinic on how to play shortstop.

Teamed with Ryne Sandberg, the Cubs have one of the best double play combinations in the majors, but it's Sandberg who's carrying the load for pulling off the twin killings.

OVERALL:

Bowa openly sulked when he was put on the bench for non-production at the plate, even mentioning that he might be better off somewhere else. As no other shortstop is ready to step in immediately, Bowa can count on being around to have a hand in grooming his likely successor, Shawon Dunston.

Snider: "In spite of his problems at the plate, when the game's on the line, Larry still wants to beat you. He plays his position with his knowledge of the hitters in his back pocket all the time. He's still the quarterback out there."

PITCHING:

Warren Brusstar became a streak pitcher in 1984 despite the fact that he was one of the Cubs' sharpest relievers during June and August. In those months, his ERA was under 2.00. Brusstar had his slumps during which he was ineffective, though it seldom cost the Cubs a ball-game. He remained one of the Cubs' most called-upon middle relievers, a role he will probably retain as long as he is in the majors.

Even with his slumps, Brusstar maintains his reputation as a control pitcher. He throws a fastball, a curve and a slider. When it is effective, his slider is still his out pitch. His breaking stuff, when going well, appeared to be much improved last season.

Not a fireballer, he relies on his ability to move the ball around rather than blow it by hitters. Brusstar does not lose much effectiveness when he is behind in the count; he is an above average pressure pitcher. When Brusstar has a bad game, it is usually clear that he is going badly right from the first pitch. He will get hit early.

His only injury last season was a pulled rib cage muscle early in the year. He missed two weeks and came back showing no ill effects.

FIELDING, HITTING, BASERUNNING:

On the mound, Brusstar takes his own fielding seriously and doesn't make

WARREN BRUSSTAR
RHP, No. 41
RR, 6'3", 200 lbs.
ML Svc: 6 years
Born: 2-2-52 in
 Oakland, CA

1984 STATISTICS

W	L	ERA	G	GS	CG	IP	H	R	ER	BB	SO	SV
1	1	3.11	41	0	0	63	57	23	22	21	36	36

CAREER STATISTICS

W	L	ERA	G	GS	CG	IP	H	R	ER	BB	SO	SV
24	13	3.06	289	0	0	409	389	148	139	145	239	43

sloppy throws or fail to cover first. He has a good move to first.

Brusstar went 1-for-5 at the plate last season, prompting more than one National League pitcher to begin taking him seriously. However, for a pitcher, Brusstar is not the best of baserunners.

OVERALL:

Snider: "He's still a good guy to have around and had a pretty fair year last season. His breaking pitches can be effective when he's got them going well. Brusstar always seems to get the job done."

HITTING:

While his fellow infielder Larry Bowa shows his age everywhere, Ron Cey shows his only in the field. Cey showed no signs of succumbing to age at the plate, having had one of his best years in 1984. This is a player who will be 37 years old when he arrives at spring training this season.

Cey provided power for the Cubs in 1984. He went into prolonged slumps and was in danger of seeing his batting average fall under .200 at various points in the season. Nonetheless, he stuck with his compact swing and open stance.

Cey was hit by a pitch June 23, giving him a sore right wrist for the rest of the season. Later, he jammed his left wrist while diving for a foul pop-up. Despite those handicaps, Cey still showed the ability to hit to all fields, although he generally is a pull hitter.

Cey is a patient hitter who is flustered only when he sees pitches high and inside. That may stem from his frightening beaning by a Goose Gossage fastball in the 1981 World Series. However, Cey's judgment may actually be impaired. He had numerous beefs with home plate umpires and the arguments always had one thing in common: Cey thought the pitch was either too high or too inside. Because of his wrist problems last season, Cey had an additional handicap when faced with outside pitches--he was unable to get around on them as he once had.

Somehow, he managed 25 homers and 97 RBIs, both team highs. The former was to Cey's credit. The latter was due to the fact that teammates were frequently on base when Cey connected.

BASERUNNING:

Cey stole three bases last year, all by the element of surprise. They don't call him "Penguin" for his short stature alone. He tries to get a good running lead and keep the momentum going once he starts his waddle toward second. If pitchers merely pay attention to him,

RON CEY
3B, No. 10
RR, 5'9", 185 lbs.
ML Svc: 12 years
Born: 2-15-48 in
Tacoma, WA

1984 STATISTICS

AVG	G	AB	R	H	2B	3B	HR	RBI	BB	SO	SB
.240	146	505	71	121	27	0	25	97	61	108	3

CAREER STATISTICS

AVG	G	AB	R	H	2B	3B	HR	RBI	BB	SO	SB
.263	1786	6302	859	1659	283	19	277	1029	888	1031	23

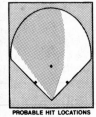

STRONG   STRONG   PROBABLE HIT LOCATIONS
VS. RHP   VS. LHP

they can keep him from stealing. But once the ball is in play, Cey is still very good at breaking up the double play, relying on aggressiveness more than speed to get the job done.

FIELDING:

Cey has no range whatsoever, even though he tries to make it appear as if he does. His belly flops to his right and left simply turn base hits into doubles in the corner, as Cey tends to hit the dirt rather than stop the ball and keep it in the infield. His arm strength and reactions continue to be suspect. Apart from his excessive diving and glove skills hampered by injuries, Cey did remain strong in covering bunts. He is not surprised or fooled very often.

OVERALL:

Snider: "Ron did a heck of a job this year even though he hit .240. He didn't seem to be swinging well. He was popping the ball up and favoring his wrists. But he's a gamer. Ron is going to drive in quite a few runs to win games for you."

HITTING:

Henry Cotto was as much a long shot to win a spot on the Cubs' roster as the team was to win the National League East. And it was just as surprising to see Cotto, taken north primarily because of his glove and speed, come through with his bat.

Cotto is a light-hitting outfielder who may not be taken lightly if he learns the virtue of patience at the plate and masters the art of taking the pitch to the opposite field. When young Cotto gets a hit, it's almost always a single to left. Nonetheless, the kid put together a 17-game hitting streak. However, he's not going to repeat that feat if he continues his 1984 ways. Cotto has got to stop swinging at bad first pitches and has to make the right fielder do something besides yawn out there.

BASERUNNING:

Cotto has the natural tools to become a basestealing threat but needs some help on his lead, jump and ability to read pitchers before he can be given the green light.

FIELDING:

Cotto's job on the 1984 Cubs seemed to be replacing defensive liability Gary Matthews in the late innings with the game on the line. Cotto took over in left field and earned a salute for his fine job in covering that turf. But he also showed that he can play a decent center field, as he subbed for Bob Dernier at times and did no worse than the Cubs' regular center fielder.

Cotto is blessed with a strong arm, something opposing baserunners discovered the hard way when they forgot that

HENRY COTTO
OF, No. 28
RR, 6'2", 180 lbs.
ML Svc: 1 year
Born: 1-5-61 in
Bronx, NY

1984 STATISTICS

AVG	G	AB	R	H	2B	3B	HR	RBI	BB	SO	SB
.274	105	146	24	40	5	0	0	8	10	23	9

CAREER STATISTICS

AVG	G	AB	R	H	2B	3B	HR	RBI	BB	SO	SB
.274	105	146	24	40	5	0	0	8	10	23	9

  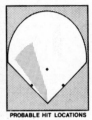

VS. RHP — STRONG   VS. LHP — STRONG   PROBABLE HIT LOCATIONS

it was Cotto, not Matthews, out there in left field. While he has no trouble coming in or going to his left, Cotto does hesitate going to his right on balls hit toward the left field corner.

OVERALL:

Like teammate Thad Bosley, Cotto's career could skyrocket if he were in the American League West. Teamed with speedsters at the top of the order, Cotto could provide a team with a mercury-fast 9-1-2 combination.

Snider: "He's a good outfielder with great speed and had some key base hits. I liked the way he went after the ball in short center field. That showed me something."

HITTING:

The upper-cutting Jody Davis had already proven himself a long ball hitter. In 1984, he simply upheld that reputation while proving to be more of a clutch hitter than previously thought.

No longer was Davis a streak hitter—he was hot the first half of the season and cold after that, primarily a result of being overused. His batting average dropped 32 points after the All Star break, when he started forcing his swing more. When he's hot, Davis has the ability to carry a team

During his slump, Davis stuck with a closed stance, feet spread wide and deep in the box. He opens up as he swings, a motion that allows him to be the pull hitter that he is. Pitchers can get an edge on him by keeping the ball down and by changing speeds. By keeping the ball down, pitchers prevent Davis from having much of an upper-cut on the ball, thereby keeping it inside the park.

Also during his slump, Davis seemed to be less patient, becoming more of a first-pitch hitter than he normally is. Overall, Davis showed more ability to hit to the opposite field, though half the time he'll end up pulling the ball. His power is still primarily to left and left-center.

BASERUNNING:

Davis stole five bases in 1984, the first five of his career. He was holding back before the running game came to Wrigley Field. He simply became more aggressive on the basepaths than he had been. No longer can Davis be counted on to stay put at first.

FIELDING:

Bullpen coach Johnny Oates turned Davis back into a respectable big league catcher in 1984. The key was convincing Davis that defense and calling a good game behind the plate had priority over his achievements at the plate, no matter

JODY DAVIS
C, No. 7
RR, 6'3", 210 lbs.
ML Svc: 4 years
Born: 11-12-56 in
Gainesville, GA

1984 STATISTICS											
AVG	G	AB	R	H	2B	3B	HR	RBI	BB	SO	SB
.256	150	523	55	134	24	2	19	94	47	99	5

CAREER STATISTICS											
AVG	G	AB	R	H	2B	3B	HR	RBI	BB	SO	SB
.262	487	1631	166	427	80	7	59	251	137	312	5

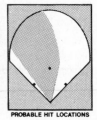

VS. RHP   VS. LHP   PROBABLE HIT LOCATIONS

how loud the crowd chanted "Jo-Dee, Jo-Dee." Davis went from being one of the worst to an above average catcher in 1984.

Baserunners will challenge his arm, but many of them paid the price last season. Even though Davis has a tendency toward making rushed, high throws that sail into center field, coach Oates did succeed in speeding up Davis's release by working on the catcher's footwork.

OVERALL:

Cubs pitchers, who came from far and wide during 1984, respected Davis almost immediately. He knows how to call a good game, even though a previous regime came close to shattering his confidence by repeatedly second-guessing him.

Snider: "His average dipped, but he was tired last season. His clutch base hits brought the club back. Davis wants to beat you and wants to do it by playing good, hard-nosed baseball."

HITTING:

The Philadelphia Phillies tried everything they could think of in an attempt to get Bob Dernier to develop into a major league hitter. Like Greta Garbo, Dernier just wanted to be left alone. That proved to be the best method, as the Cubs did just that while allowing him to find his niche in 1984.

Dernier had never done anything left-handed, but the Phillies tried to turn him into a switch-hitter. That was one of the Philadelphia experiments that failed.

A natural contact hitter, Dernier tends to pull the ball. He has little ability to take the pitch to the opposite field. That may be his key weakness at the plate. Ironically, Dernier tends to like his pitches toward the outer half of the plate. Although he is now more patient at the plate, Dernier occasionally will swing at the first pitch. However, he proved to be an ideal lead-off man and was able to get on base via a clean base hit to left, a bunt single or walk.

While he showed some rare glimpses of power, Dernier knows his limitations well enough not to try swinging for the fences, especially when Ryne Sandberg follows him in the order. When he does connect, a Bob Dernier homer is a line drive shot.

BASERUNNING:

Dernier is the best the Cubs have on the basepaths. He has excellent speed as well as superb acceleration and is always a definite threat to steal. But when Dernier gets on base, the opposing pitcher then has to worry about pitching to Sandberg. Because of that, Dernier couldn't help but improve on his already fine basestealing skills. If Sandberg follows with a single, it's a sure bet that Dernier will quickly put himself in third gear and be on his way toward third base safely.

BOB DERNIER
OF, No. 22
RR, 6'0", 160 lbs.
ML Svc: 3 years
Born: 1-5-57 in
Kansas City, MO

1984 STATISTICS
AVG	G	AB	R	H	2B	3B	HR	RBI	BB	SO	SB
.278	143	536	94	149	26	5	3	32	63	60	45

CAREER STATISTICS
AVG	G	AB	R	H	2B	3B	HR	RBI	BB	SO	SB
.263	407	1138	196	299	46	7	8	69	118	150	127

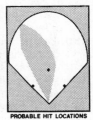

STRONG   STRONG

VS. RHP   VS. LHP   PROBABLE HIT LOCATIONS

FIELDING:

No one has ever played center field for the Cubs the way Dernier has. He covers for both his left fielders and right fielders, as he can outrun balls hit to left and right-center with ease. He dives for and gets balls hit in front of him and has no trouble going back. On a scale of 1 to 10, Dernier rates a nine in the field: he needs Andre Dawson's arm to get a 10.

OVERALL:

Chicago picked Philadelphia's pocket last season and found two of their own keys: one was Dernier and the other was Matthews.

Snider: "Bob got a chance to play in Chicago, and a lot of times that's all a guy needs. Maybe he's not a .300 hitter, but that trade was a steal for the Cubs."

HITTING:

Poor health and Bill Buckner were the only two things preventing Leon Durham from having the kind of year he had in 1984 sooner. First, Buckner was traded, allowing Durham to take his natural position at first base. Then, Durham went the rest of the season relatively injury-free, as all he suffered was a jammed shoulder near the All Star break.

Durham started the season wearing contact lenses and started off 1 for 11. He went back to glasses and finished with a career-high 23 homers with 96 RBIs and a .279 batting average. Along the way, he became less of a spray hitter and more of a pull hitter. More often than not, Durham took the pitch to right but seemed to have an easier time of it trying to hit to the opposite field than up the middle.

Leon suffered from a lack of patience at times and swung at bad pitches, but then he likes just about all pitches except change-ups and off-speed pitches.

Some pitchers have Durham's number, but Atlanta's Pascual Perez isn't one of them. Durham eats him and his fastball up. When Perez isn't pitching, however, he is not the best man to have at the plate in the clutch.

During 1984, Durham showed signs of being a streak hitter. He rebounded from a slow start and got torrid, carrying the club in the process. When he cooled off, pitchers struck him out with more and more consistency.

BASERUNNING:

They call Durham "The Bull," but perhaps that's a misnomer. He is one of the quicker Cubs, and this is a team that became downright fast with Bob Dernier, Henry Cotto and Thad Bosley around. Still, Durham became more conservative on the basepaths this season. His history of pulled hamstrings, right and left, probably hinders his enthusiasm for 30-yard dashes. As far as basestealing goes, Durham still needs work on his lead. He is extremely aggressive in

LEON DURHAM
OF, No. 10
LL, 6'2", 210 lbs.
ML Svc: 5 years
Born: 7-31-57 in
Cincinnati, OH

1984 STATISTICS

AVG	G	AB	R	H	2B	3B	HR	RBI	BB	SO	SB
.279	137	473	86	132	30	4	23	96	69	86	16

CAREER STATISTICS

AVG	G	AB	R	H	2B	3B	HR	RBI	BB	SO	SB
.285	568	1980	312	564	110	29	75	318	246	354	89

  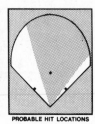

VS. RHP — VS. LHP — PROBABLE HIT LOCATIONS

breaking up the double play and throws caution to the wind.

FIELDING:

Durham didn't make anyone forget Bill Buckner at first base. He did turn in a fair season there, and his comfort there carried over to the plate.

Durham's range is limited, especially to his right, giving Ryne Sandberg more ground to cover. The deficiency isn't noticeable when the Cubs are at home or on natural turf, but it can show up on artificial surfaces. However, Durham showed the ability to turn doubles into outs. If the Cubs find a better first baseman, he could always return to left field.

OVERALL:

Snider: "He's a class guy, a great guy to have in the lineup. He's not in awe of anybody or anything. He's been a pretty good hitter over the years."

PITCHING:

After spending six and a half years with the Boston Red Sox, whose home field is Fenway Park, Dennis Eckersley had the right stuff to make a living in Wrigley Field, another ballpark that favors hitters over pitchers. Or did he?

Eckersley was a tough-luck pitcher all season. Although he didn't have nearly as good a record as teammate Rick Sutcliffe, he pitched as well as the ace did on a few occasions. For some reason, the Cubs never got runs for Eckersley the way they did for the other starters, and the righthander was short-changed on days when he had his best stuff.

His stuff? An 85 MPH fastball, curve, sinker and slider. In other words, a full arsenal. He learned the National League and by late in the season had learned the hitters fairly well —at least the ones who were apt to wait on his fastball and slider and park them in the seats when Eckersley fell behind. His out pitch was the fastball. His slider can stand some improvement. His sinker could also use some fine-tuning. It could become his most effective weapon in Wrigley Field.

Eckersley is nothing but a control pitcher. He no longer is able to blow it by hitters, and he knows that. The back and arm problems that took the steam out of his fastball are gone. At least he suffered no recurrences in Chicago.

FIELDING, HITTING, BASERUNNING:

With his three-quarters delivery,

DENNIS ECKERSLEY
RHP, No. 43
RR, 6'2", 190 lbs.
ML Svc: 10 years
Born: 10-3-54 in
    Oakland, CA

1984 STATISTICS
W	L	ERA	G	GS	CG	IP	H	R	ER	BB	SO	SV
10	8	3.03	24	24	2	160	152	59	54	36	81	0

CAREER STATISTICS
W	L	ERA	G	GS	CG	IP	H	R	ER	BB	SO	SV
130	106	3.59	309	293	91	2060	1959	893	822	549	1340	3

Eckersley still has an above average move to first. Runners do steal on him more than on most pitchers, but he makes an effort to keep them in check. As a fielder, Eckersley ranked as one of the Cubs' poorest. One reason is his delivery, which leaves him in an awkward position to field anything hit his way. His throws to first do tend to stray.

Having spent his entire career in the American League, Eckersley was not taken seriously as a hitter. He doesn't get cheated, going to the plate and taking his hacks. As a baserunner, Eckersley is fair for a pitcher.

OVERALL:

Snider: "He came over and did what the Cubs thought he could do. He won more than he lost. He knows the league now, and that's what hurt him earlier. He's a good competitor."

PITCHING:

George Frazier didn't get his chance to live down his dubious claim to fame: losing a record three games in the 1981 World Series. He might, though, if he sticks around with the Cubs, a team as intent on getting there as Frazier is of redeeming himself.

Frazier also has a reputation of loading up the ball and was shaken down a few times by National League umpires after being traded to the Cubs in mid-season. He was never caught, so the official verdict at this time stands as not guilty.

Frazier throws a fastball, a curve and a forkball that appears to lack any rotation. He also has a rubber arm, making him ideally suited to the demands of middle relief. It's an area where he thrived, particularly in August and September last year. On days when George doesn't have it, a gopher ball will sail out of the park during his first inning of work.

He throws three varieties of curves: an overhand one, one at three-quarters and one at sidearm. They all have their own varying degrees of break. His overhand curve has the sharpest downward break, the three-quarters curve has a flatter break, while his sidearm curve is unpredictable.

FIELDING, HITTING, BASERUNNING:

Frazier would do well in a fielding derby among the Cubs' pitchers. He is fundamentally sound, from fielding bunts in front of or to either side of the mound to stopping high smashes up the middle to covering first base. He has a

GEORGE FRAZIER
RHP, No. 43
RR, 6'5", 205 lbs.
ML Svc: 7 years
Born: 10-13-54 in
 Oklahoma City, OK

1984 STATISTICS
W	L	ERA	G	GS	CG	IP	H	R	ER	BB	SO	SV
9	5	4.75	59	0	0	108	98	49	57	40	82	4

CAREER STATISTICS
W	L	ERA	G	GS	CG	IP	H	R	ER	BB	SO	SV
20	25	3.73	260	0	0	439	402	194	182	160	279	19

quick move to first and will throw there often, depending on the baserunner. His quick move means that runners will have to wait for him to throw his off-speed stuff before they try to steal on him.

Frazier learned his lessons well in the St. Louis Cardinals organization. He didn't embarrass himself at the plate last year, getting two singles in seven at-bats when the Cubs had to leave him in the game.

OVERALL:

Frazier is haunted by his losing record in the World Series. That is unfair because he is a better pitcher than that. He longs for the opportunity to become known as something--anything--else.

Snider: "I think he tends to overthrow the ball. He might give hitters too many pitches to hit. But I like his makeup."

HITTING:

Ron Hassey took an immediate liking to the National League after being traded by the Cleveland Indians. Unfortunately, his playing time was reduced to zero when he turned a knee while racing toward first base after making a play behind the bag.

Hassey likes to hit fastballs and can expect to see a lot more of them in the National League than he did in the American League. He likes to see the low fastball, though fastballs up and in or fastballs and curves on the outside corner befuddle him. He is a patient hitter who will wait for a pitcher to make a mistake.

He still has some sock in his bat, proved to be a clutch hitter in the few opportunities he had with the Cubs but wasn't around long enough to be tracked during a slump.

Hassey will hit to the right side although last season he did manage a few to the opposite field: they were accidents.

BASERUNNING:

Hassey is another lumbering catcher. He isn't a threat to steal, and can be a threat to break up a double play only when he can get down to second in time.

FIELDING:

Hassey can catch as well as play first base. He's a much better catcher, to be sure, and should stay there. He injured himself at first base and before falling down in a heap, looked very awk-

RON HASSEY
C, No. 9
LR, 6'2", 195 lbs.
ML Svc: 7 years
Born: 2-27-53 in
   Tuscon, AZ

1984 STATISTICS
AVG	G	AB	R	H	2B	3B	HR	RBI	BB	SO	SB
.333	19	33	5	11	0	0	2	5	4	6	0

CAREER STATISTICS
AVG	G	AB	R	H	2B	3B	HR	RBI	BB	SO	SB
.274	540	1574	160	431	75	4	28	212	185	159	8

  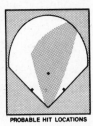

VS. RHP   VS. LHP   PROBABLE HIT LOCATIONS

ward at that position.

Having been a starter at Cleveland, Hassey still knows how to call a good game and can still nail a baserunner, but with Jody Davis and Steve Lake around, Hassey's catching is limited to bullpen duties--not a promising future.

OVERALL:

Even if Hassey's healthy, it will be difficult for him to gain much playing time with the Cubs, playing behind Jody Davis. His fine defensive skills may erode after spending too much time on the bench.

HITTING:

They don't call Richie Hebner the "Hackman" for nothing. When Hebner goes up to the plate, he goes up there hacking, and when he's healthy, he can still connect. He'll swing at the first pitch, second pitch, third pitch, or whichever one strikes his fancy. He isn't fussy.

He is a pull hitter and will often chase bad pitches, living up to his nickname. During his injury-plagued 1984 season, Hebner didn't get the chance to take as many hacks as he would have liked.

Another one of the Cubs' walking wounded, Hebner was one of the team's biggest contributors off the bench before tendinitis in his right shoulder set him down. The maladies prevented him from hitting as well down the stretch as he was capable of doing.

BASERUNNING:

Hebner is still capable of breaking up a double play, but if he gets a pinch-hit late in the game when it's on the line, a pinch-runner is strongly recommended. Hebner does not run well and is no threat to steal.

FIELDING:

At the start of the season, the Cubs thought they had themselves a utility man who could play first and third bases as well as some outfield. By the time the season ended, Hebner was not even working out in the field. When he did play, he displayed his best abilities at third base, which was his original position in the majors. He makes throws from third better than Ron Cey can. Hebner

RICHIE HEBNER
INF, No. 2
LR, 6'1", 195 lbs.
ML Svc: 16 years
Born: 11-26-47 in
  Boston, MA

1984 STATISTICS

AVG	G	AB	R	H	2B	3B	HR	RBI	BB	SO	SB
.333	44	81	12	27	3	0	2	8	10	15	1

CAREER STATISTICS

AVG	G	AB	R	H	2B	3B	HR	RBI	BB	SO	SB
.277	1825	6024	855	1668	268	57	210	968	680	726	38

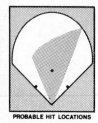

VS. RHP   VS. LHP   PROBABLE HIT LOCATIONS

actually looks more comfortable at third than he did at first base, where the Pirates had pegged him.

Unfortunately, the Cubs found out that Hebner, because of his shoulder problems, could only play first--if that --by the time the season ended.

In the outfield, Hebner is a liability.

OVERALL:

Hebner's future lies in the return of his shoulder.

Snider: "Richie is a veteran player and can still come off the bench and get a hit for you, but he may have no future at all if his shoulder doesn't heal."

HITTING:

When you're playing behind ironman Jody Davis and miss a good chunk of the season with hepatitis, maybe it's excusable to go up to the plate and start hacking at the first pitch. It may be why Steve Lake hasn't proven to be a consistent major league hitter. Lake is a notorious first pitch hitter, or rather, swinger. If he were more patient at the plate, he would pick things up immeasurably. Lake finally began to temper his enthusiasm at the plate late in the season. It was so late in the year, however, that he could not help his .222 average.

For the first time in his career, Lake showed some long ball potential, belting two home runs in 1984. One of them was a wind-aided blast at Wrigley Field, the other was at Pittsburgh's Three Rivers Stadium, which is a truer test of home run power.

Lake is a pull hitter with little, if any, ability to take it to the opposite field. In the future, if he continues to improve in the patience-at-the-plate department, he might prove to be more valuable to a team as something other than a backup catcher.

BASERUNNING:

With just 12 hits and two of them home runs, there isn't much evidence in on Lake's baserunning ability. He has more speed than most catchers, though.

FIELDING:

The Cubs have a secret: they do not start their best defensive catcher. Jody Davis may be the starter, but Steve Lake is a full notch above Davis as a defensive catcher. He could nail more baserunners than Davis and will guard the

STEVE LAKE
C, No. 16
RR, 6'1", 190 lbs.
ML Svc: 2 years
Born: 3-14-57 in
Inglewood, CA

1984 STATISTICS

AVG	G	AB	R	H	2B	3B	HR	RBI	BB	SO	SB
.222	25	54	4	12	4	0	2	7	0	7	0

CAREER STATISTICS

AVG	G	AB	R	H	2B	3B	HR	RBI	BB	SO	SB
.245	63	139	13	34	8	1	3	14	2	13	0

  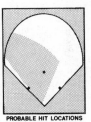

VS. RHP   VS. LHP   PROBABLE HIT LOCATIONS

plate with more authority.

Pitchers, especially Steve Trout, seem to place full confidence in Lake's ability to call a game. His release is quicker than Davis's and opponents would be wise to think twice about stealing against him, especially if they would not do it with Davis behind the plate.

OVERALL:

Obviously, Lake's problem is his bat. Things like swinging at the first pitch and hacking away are coachable traits—if Lake wants to be taught. Davis is a much stronger hitter, and unless Steve picks up at the plate he will be wasting his excellent defensive skills.

Snider: "He doesn't seem to have any problem behind the plate."

HITTING:

Looks can be deceiving, as far as Gary Matthews is concerned. He steps into the batter's box waving his hands as if he is holding a magic wand or a 34" toothpick, making circles above the plate. He looks a tad impatient, but in reality Matthews is anything but. He drew 103 walks last season while batting third in the Cubs' lineup. Leon Durham and Keith Moreland came up after him in the order.

Matthews got his fair share of brush-back pitches last season and was hit often because he leans so far over the plate. When he finds a pitch to his liking--and that could be anywhere from the first pitch to the fifth--he has the ability to take it to any field. For the most part, he is a pull hitter; but at times it seems as though he thrives on poking the ball to the opposite field. Breaking balls down and away give him trouble.

Primarily a line drive, contact hitter, Matthews can hit the ball with power to left, center or right. He is best when he is simply trying to put the ball in play. He was also the best clutch hitter on the Cubs, leading the league in game-winning RBIs.

In 1984, Matthews seemed to become a more disciplined hitter even though he still showed his trademark aggressiveness at the plate. With a handful of sluggers following him in the order, it made sense for him to strive for the high on-base percentage he finally recorded. The fact that he drew so many walks is testament to his increased discipline or to the opposing pitcher's forgetfulness as to who was to follow (the latter, however, is doubtful.)

BASERUNNING:

When he takes off, Matthews leaves his helmet rolling in the dust. He will often take the chancey move of stretching a single into a double. He is very

GARY MATTHEWS
OF, No. 34
RR, 6'3", 190 lbs.
ML Svc: 12 years
Born: 7-5-50 in
San Fernando, CA

1984 STATISTICS
AVG	G	AB	R	H	2B	3B	HR	RBI	BB	SO	SB
.291	147	491	101	143	21	2	14	82	103	97	17

CAREER STATISTICS
AVG	G	AB	R	H	2B	3B	HR	RBI	BB	SO	SB
.286	1724	6318	976	1806	287	50	197	869	802	969	178

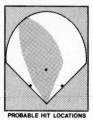

STRONG VS. RHP   STRONG VS. LHP   PROBABLE HIT LOCATIONS

good at breaking up the double play. He will be 35 years old this summer, but he runs as if he is just pushing 30.

FIELDING:

After bordering on atrocious at times, Matthews can come up with an occasional acrobatic diving or tumbling catch. The Cubs were smart enough to put Henry Cotto in as a defensive replacement for Matthews late in the game. Matthews is not to be trusted in left field when the game is on the line. He has trouble backing up and going to the corner. His arm is average.

OVERALL:

Snider: "He might have slowed up a little in the field, but he knows how to get on base. He is a good mistake hitter and a pretty good guess hitter as well."

HITTING:

A lot of baseball people thought that Keith Moreland had his career-year in 1983. He surprised just about everyone and topped that in 1984, even though he started the season platooning with Mel Hall in right field, seeing only left-handed pitching.

It was a shame because Moreland hits left and righthanders about the same. Against righthanded pitching, Moreland hits to the opposite field a bit more, making him an even more dangerous threat at the plate. However, Moreland is still basically a pull hitter.

The pitchers who have the best success against Moreland, who is an aggressive hitter and one who loves the sight of the fastball, are the ones who throw him sinkers and pitches that are low.

Moreland's aggressiveness at the plate makes him an impatient hitter. He gives the pitchers the opportunity to quickly get ahead in the count.

As he has been in previous years, Keith was a study in consistency in 1984. He did not go into any prolonged slumps, and played the same before and after the All Star break. The only change was his 180 degree shift in attitude once Mel Hall was traded to Cleveland and Moreland had the right field job on a full-time basis.

BASERUNNING:

Moreland is smart enough not to challenge anyone to a footrace. He is a smart baserunner, though, and is seldom caught looking foolish on the basepaths.

He may be the best man that the Cubs have for breaking up the double play. When Moreland goes in to second, he has been compared to a runaway beer truck.

FIELDING:

Another big surprise last year was his improvement in playing the field. He didn't play quite as badly as many people thought he would. Quite the contrary: he was rather good, considering that he

KEITH MORELAND
OF, No. 6
RR, 6'0", 200 lbs.
ML Svc: 6 years
Born: 5-2-54 in
Dallas, TX

1984 STATISTICS

AVG	G	AB	R	H	2B	3B	HR	RBI	BB	SO	SB
.279	140	495	59	138	17	3	16	80	34	71	1

CAREER STATISTICS

AVG	G	AB	R	H	2B	3B	HR	RBI	BB	SO	SB
.283	570	1909	217	541	82	10	57	292	174	247	5

  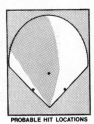

VS. RHP   VS. LHP   PROBABLE HIT LOCATIONS

spent half the time battling the sun in Wrigley Field. (At the Cubs' home field, the sun sets directly in front of the right fielder's eyes late in the game.) He lost a few that way, but caught what he was able to see.

Moreland's arm quickly won the respect of opposing baserunners and he was fast enough afoot to run down balls hit to the right field corner. He is not as quick to his right, but then Bob Dernier is there next to him to back Keith up or to make the play himself.

OVERALL:

His 1983 scouting report read: "At best, his arm is mediocre . . . (it) is erratic. He has no range . . ."

1985: a nice, big change.

Snider: "He improved as an outfielder and was more disciplined at the plate last season. Moreland went to right field more, too. He has a good arm and with him, the Cubs were able to let Mel Hall go."

PITCHING:

Rick Reuschel may have come to the end of the line in late September when he was left off the Cubs' 25-man playoff roster. It may be an omen of things to come for him this spring at the Cubs' training camp--if he gets there. He openly displayed hostility toward manager Jim Frey, clearly hinting that he will be pitching somewhere other than with the Cubs in 1985.

Never the owner of a blazing fastball, Reuschel struggled more often than he succeeded in 1984 when he was tried briefly as a starter and then sent back to the bullpen. He wasn't fooling very many hitters and his sinker wasn't working often enough to save him. Instead of setting up the hitters, Reuschel was often getting treated like a batting practice pitcher.

Reuschel always has believed in getting hitters to beat his pitch into the ground rather than trying to strike them out. In 1984, Reuschel had a tough time doing either. It didn't matter whether he was a starter or a reliever, Reuschel struggled. If he does have any future at all, it is as a mop- up man in the bullpen.

The hitters were driving his pitches up and out.

FIELDING, HITTING, BASERUNNING:

Reuschel remained one of the team's better-fielding pitchers despite his

RICK REUSCHEL
RHP, No. 47
RR, 6'3", 235 lbs.
ML Svc: 12 years
Born: 5-18-49 in
Quincy, IL

1984 STATISTICS

W	L	ERA	G	GS	CG	IP	H	R	ER	BB	SO	SV
5	5	5.17	19	14	1	92	123	57	53	23	43	0

CAREER STATISTICS

W	L	ERA	G	GS	CG	IP	H	R	ER	BB	SO	SV
139	131	3.48	370	354	68	2361	2440	1031	912	673	1389	3

massive size. (Dropping 30 lbs. did not have any noticeable effect.) His moves remained cat-like on the very few driblers bounced back to the mound. Reuschel always has been a decent hitter for a pitcher, but got few opportunities to prove it in 1984.

His move to first is still decent and he holds runners in check.

OVERALL:

Snider: "Rick has had some wonderful years. He looks like he'd be real nice to go up and hit against. He has to rely on the sinker, and on it being out of the strike zone."

PITCHING:

When Dick Ruthven looks back on 1984, he'll be thankful just for the chance to have finished the season. Midway through the year, it looked as though Ruthven's season, if not his career, was over. He underwent shoulder surgery in late May to relieve pressure on an artery caused by a muscle pressing on a blood vessel. Prior to the operation, Ruthven's arm went numb before the fourth inning. He was able to go the distance once in a while or at least go long enough to get to the ace of the bullpen, Lee Smith.

After a rehabilitative assignment, Ruthven returned to the starting rotation and had some good outings that prompted some hope. Unfortunately, he was not the same pitcher in the second half of the season that he was in the first half, which included the starting assignment on opening day. Not only was his control gone, but he was being hit hard when he did get the ball into the strike zone.

Whether Ruthven regains his spot in the Cubs' starting rotation remains to be seen. He was a member of the five-man rotation until the post-season, when he was sent to the bullpen and told he'd be used in long relief. That may be where his future lies, if he can continue to make progress on the comeback trail. Regardless, the operation has carved a few miles off his fastball and has hindered his ability to put the ball where he wants to.

FIELDING, HITTING, BASERUNNING:

Jim Frey had so much confidence in

DICK RUTHVEN
RHP, No. 44
RR, 6'3", 190 lbs.
ML Svc: 11 years
Born: 3-27-51 in
Sacramento, CA

1984 STATISTICS

W	L	ERA	G	GS	CG	IP	H	R	ER	BB	SO	SV
6	10	5.04	23	22	0	126	154	75	71	41	55	0

CAREER STATISTICS

W	L	ERA	G	GS	CG	IP	H	R	ER	BB	SO	SV
119	120	4.12	329	317	71	2010	2040	1017	920	724	1116	1

Dick Ruthven's hitting ability that he sent him to the plate as a pinch-hitter once in 1984. Ruthven hit .159 last year, 25 points lower than his lifetime mark.

Ruthven takes his defense seriously and was flawless last year. He still has a good move to first and gets off the mound in time to cover first base or to field balls hit in front of the mound. He is still an above average fielder.

OVERALL:

Snider: "His performance for the Cubs after his return from surgery was more promising than the team had expected. While it is doubtful that he will be the same pitcher he was, Ruthven has a competitive spirit and will do whatever it takes to come back. However, he may have to realize that his days as a full-time starter are over."

HITTING:

A very unselfish, unassuming player, Ryne Sandberg blossomed into The Franchise on national television in 1984. During spring training last season, manager Jim Frey took Sandberg aside and told him that he could become a home run hitter. Sandberg must have believed him because he immediately started pulling the ball, and the rest is MVP candidate history. Before their little chat, Ryne had been content to make contact and put the ball in play. From here on in, however, Sandberg will be making contact with the ball and putting it over the fence.

Sandberg did not change much in his routine at the plate. He pumped iron during the off-season, and it was the added strength along with Frey's words that helped him to hit a career high of 19 home runs. Sandberg did not turn into an exclusive pull hitter; he hits to all fields.

Curves down and away continued to give him trouble and he started to show signs of fatigue late in the season. He began to swing at bad pitches. Pitchers might try to crowd him with fastballs and breaking balls down and by changing speeds.

BASERUNNING:

With Bob Dernier added to the team, Sandberg not only had his leadoff partner from his minor league days with the Phillies back with him, but he also had the team's leading basestealing threat in front of him. Sandberg got on and stole 32 bases himself.

He studies the pitches well and gets a good jump. If he took a bigger lead, he would do even better as a thief.

FIELDING:

Sandberg was headed for another Gold

RYNE SANDBERG
2B, No. 23
RR, 6'2", 185 lbs.
ML Svc: 3 years
Born: 9-18-59 in
  Spokane, WA

1984 STATISTICS

AVG	G	AB	R	H	2B	3B	HR	RBI	BB	SO	SB
.314	156	636	114	200	36	19	19	84	52	101	32

CAREER STATISTICS

AVG	G	AB	R	H	2B	3B	HR	RBI	BB	SO	SB
.282	483	1910	313	538	94	28	34	186	139	271	101

  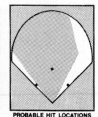

VS. RHP   VS. LHP   PROBABLE HIT LOCATIONS

Glove year in 1984. Larry Bowa had shown him the double play ropes during the previous season, and Sandberg simply polished his act to an even shinier luster. He seems able to get to everything, deep to his left and up the middle.

OVERALL:

Snider: "How many superlatives can you write about Ryne Sandberg? He is one of those ballplayers you just love to watch. I have a Gold Pass and can get into any ballpark free, but I would pay to watch Ryne Sandberg play. I know that he is only going to get better, and that's exciting."

PITCHING:

For the second season in a row, Scott Sanderson couldn't stay healthy. This time it was recurring back spasms that sent him into traction in June. But Sanderson went to Class A on rehabilitative assignment, and bounced back--at least for a while. The back problems flared up again without warning. While on the mound, Sanderson would feel the shooting pains and know that it was time to leave for the training table.

It is an unfortunate injury because when he is completely healthy, Sanderson borders on dazzling. He won four of his first five decisions before the first wave of spasms hit. Besides a fastball that can hover in the low 90s, Sanderson has mastered the art of changing speeds and throws a slow curve in addition to his 1984 invention, the palmball. He had moderate success with his new pitch.

Sanderson is not afraid to challenge the hitters. A nice guy off the mound, he can be a tough customer and was thrown out of a game against the Mets for throwing a retaliatory pitch.

Wrigley fans expecting a nice afternoon at the ballpark can forget about an early dinner when Sanderson is pitching. He is a slow worker, from the time it takes him to deliver the pitch to the number of throws to first to keep the runners there.

His delivery is over-the-top and his fastball comes in very true with little movement. When hitters connected, they often took it very deep. Sanderson worked on trying to make his fastball move away from lefthanders. He has trouble with righthanded hitters because

SCOTT SANDERSON
RHP, No. 21
RR, 6'5", 198 lbs.
ML Svc: 6 years
Born: 7-22-56 in
Dearborn, MI

1984 STATISTICS

W	L	ERA	G	GS	CG	IP	H	R	ER	BB	SO	SV
8	5	3.14	24	24	3	140	140	54	49	24	76	0

CAREER STATISTICS

W	L	ERA	G	GS	CG	IP	H	R	ER	BB	SO	SV
64	52	3.31	173	160	27	1022	978	417	376	264	679	2

he has difficulty throwing his slow curve consistently. Sanderson also has a palmball, but it isn't going to set the world on fire yet.

FIELDING, HITTING, BASERUNNING:

Sanderson hit just .119 in 1984, nothing to write home (or here) about. Once on the bases, he is slow and awkward.

Sanderson must make frequent throws to first to keep runners honest because his leg kick gives them a better than average chance to steal. Sanderson was a better than average fielder.

OVERALL:

Snider: "He's a willing worker, and even though he had that back problem, he should get better. I wish he could come up with a Carl Erskine change-up, maybe a split-fingered fastball."

PITCHING:

On several occasions in 1984, Lee Smith proved to Wrigley Field fans and to the baseball world that bullpen aces and Rolaids candidates are human, too. The only one he didn't prove it to was himself. The man with a fastball that approaches the high 90s and can still reach 100 MPH has to learn that he is not, and is not expected to be, Superman.

When Smith comes in from the bullpen, hitters should expect fastball, fastball, fastball--even though Smith has been trying to take a little off the fastball to get hitters off balance. The similarities between himself and Goose Gossage are that they're both big, menacing, imposing figures on the mound, both have the same mean stare and look of disdain and both were faulted in 1984 for failing in save situations in an increasing number of times. The difference is that Gossage is able to blow off the steam, Smith is not.

Hitters go to the plate with the idea that it's power versus power. Some succeeded and became instant heros, as Smith is usually in there when the game is on the line. Although his rates of saves in save-situations dropped last year, Smith is most effective in that role. When there is no save to be had, Smith becomes just another thrower.

FIELDING, HITTING, BASERUNNING:

Arthroscopic knee surgery did not

LEE SMITH
RHP, No. 46
RR, 6'6", 220 lbs.
ML Svc: 4 years
Born: 12-4-57 in
    Jamestown, LA

1984 STATISTICS

W	L	ERA	G	GS	CG	IP	H	R	ER	BB	SO	SV
9	7	3.65	69	0	0	101	98	42	41	35	86	33

CAREER STATISTICS

W	L	ERA	G	GS	CG	IP	H	R	ER	BB	SO	SV
20	28	2.81	265	6	0	410	351	143	128	158	343	80

prevent Smith from upholding his reputation as a decent fielder at best. He may actually be overrated as a fielder. Everyone remembers the smash by Pete Rose that went off his glove for a game-ending out, a scene in the Cubs' highlight film. As a hitter, Smith is harmless.

OVERALL:

Snider: "He has a tendency to overthrow. Like Gossage, he's really not a pitcher. I haven't seen anybody yet who can get every hitter out."

PITCHING:

Tim Stoddard can sure handle rejection. He was cast off by the Baltimore Orioles and Oakland A's in a matter of a few months before the Cubs decided he was the man to replace Bill Campbell as Lee Smith's set-up man. He responded well, posting a career-high 10 wins while pitching in Wrigley Field.

Still, in too many of his outings, Stoddard looked like a pitcher in search of control. He was trying to harness a 90 MPH fastball and a hard slider. When his control was absent, it was obvious right from the start, and hitters would hit him and hit him hard as soon as he entered the game. At other times, he was dazzling to the point of competing with Smith for the distinction of being the team's relief ace--at least for the day. Unlike Smith, Stoddard rebounds well after bad outings.

Although there were rumors that Tim was not physically sound, he showed no arm or knee problems in 1984. Had there been any real problems, they would have been immediately evident because he is a power pitcher. His only problems stemmed from not being able to control his fastball, curve or slider, and making mistakes with them. He would benefit from developing a better off-speed pitch.

FIELDING, HITTING, BASERUNNING:

Stoddard probably had better moves to

TIM STODDARD
RHP, No. 49
RR, 6'7", 250 lbs.
ML Svc: 6 years
Born: 1-24-53 in
    East Chicago, IL

1984 STATISTICS

W	L	ERA	G	GS	CG	IP	H	R	ER	BB	SO	SV
10	6	3.82	58	0	0	92	77	41	39	57	87	7

CAREER STATISTICS

W	L	ERA	G	GS	CG	IP	H	R	ER	BB	SO	SV
29	20	3.70	288	0	0	406	373	179	167	198	336	64

the hoop as a member of the 1974 North Carolina Wolfpack than he does off the mound and to first. He is not the most agile of fielders on the mound and is shaky on bunts in front of him. He made it to first base when he had to.

Stoddard can hit, but he's not the fleetest on the basepaths.

OVERALL:

Snider: "He's a workhorse, but I wish he had a little more control. He makes too many mistakes. But he's not afraid out there. It doesn't matter what he did yesterday."

PITCHING:

As most baseball fans are aware, Rick Sutcliffe was unbeatable after being traded to the Cubs last June. What we don't know is whether he can continue to master the National League.

A good part of Sutcliffe's success is his herky-jerky delivery that keeps batters off stride, especially if they're trying to keep their eye on the ball. "Don't even try to watch the ball," warns Al Oliver, a lifetime .300 hitter.

Sutcliffe's motion appears to contain two hitches. He keeps the ball behind his back until the last possible moment. Then, he unleashes a 90 MPH fastball, curve or slider toward the plate. The curve and the slider will break differently depending on whether he releases them from a three-quarters or a straight over-the-top delivery.

Although his fastball still has some zip, he isn't in Dwight Gooden's range, for example. Sutcliffe has made his mark because of his phenomenal pinpoint control. He often succeeds at playing with the corners. He uses the slider as his out pitch and will challenge hitters with his hard stuff and his intimidating presence.

Umpires' decisions rarely ruffle his feathers; nor do his own or his teammate's errors. Sutcliffe simply comes back and throws his hard stuff again. More often than not, it got him out of a jam.

Hitters, take heart. History is on your side. Cy Young Award winners in recent years have had sub-par seasons after winning the famed plaque. If Rick does not fall victim to the bewitched year, the hitters will have to figure out a way to hit him on their own.

FIELDING, HITTING, BASERUNNING:

He ranks among the best-fielding

RICK SUTCLIFFE
RHP, No. 40
RR, 6'6", 215 lbs.
ML Svc: 7 years
Born: 6-21-56 in
    Independence, MO

1984 STATISTICS

W	L	ERA	G	GS	CG	IP	H	R	ER	BB	SO	SV
16	1	2.69	20	20	7	150	123	53	45	39	155	0

CAREER STATISTICS

W	L	ERA	G	GS	CG	IP	H	R	ER	BB	SO	SV
69	41	3.67	188	129	29	1015	932	466	414	413	652	6

pitchers in the game. He covers bunts well, gets over to first in time and has good pickoff moves to both first and second. He will throw to first often to keep runners in check.

Against the Mets late in the season, Larry Bowa was walked intentionally to get to Sutcliffe, who was hitting 11 points higher at the time. Although he didn't get the respect he deserved as a hitter, Sutcliffe didn't forget the batting lessons he learned while in the Los Angeles Dodgers organization. He even has occasional power.

If Sutcliffe has a fault, it is that he tends to be nonchalant on the bases --he could use the rest.

OVERALL:

Snider: "His philosophy and outlook on the game have changed completely. It is great to see the guy have the kind of year he did, but it'll be very difficult for him to come back and have the same kind of year again."

PITCHING:

Credit the birth of his first child, or credit pitching coach Billy Connors, but Steve Trout finally grew up in 1984. Trout always had good stuff, but until last year carried a bad attitude with him to the mound. It nearly put him out of baseball.

He is now virtually assured of a roster spot, if not a spot in the starting rotation in spring training 1985.

He finally had the year of his career, paying off all of the promise that was previously only talk and paper. He worked hard to become a pitcher instead of a thrower. He led the team with six complete games and in those, he showed a tendency to get stronger as the game wore on--an exciting quality.

He used to throw a spitter when he was with the crosstown White Sox but has abandoned it. He went back to his fastball and an excellent curve and was able to change speeds better than he did in previous seasons.

Assuming Trout is re-signed by the Cubs, the lefthander can look forward to a bright future with them after posting career highs in wins, ERA and strikeouts.

Trout found a measure of consistency in his curveball, something else that had been missing in years past. He has been drilled by pitching coach Connors to think, "control, control, control." It appears that Trout got the message.

FIELDING, HITTING, BASERUNNING:

Trout had a little more trouble at the plate than he did in 1983, his first season in the National League.

Being a lefthander aids his otherwise good move to first. However, he ranked

STEVE TROUT
LHP, No. 34
LL, 6'4", 189 lbs.
ML Svc: 6 years
Born: 7-30-57 in
Detroit, MI

1984 STATISTICS

W	L	ERA	G	GS	CG	IP	H	R	ER	BB	SO	SV
13	7	3.41	32	31	6	190	205	80	72	59	81	0

CAREER STATISTICS

W	L	ERA	G	GS	CG	IP	H	R	ER	BB	SO	SV
60	61	3.89	81	141	26	992	1087	503	429	325	453	4

as one of the worst fielders on the Cubs' pitching staff. A reason for that is his delivery leaves him too low to the ground to recover adequately. He did spend time trying to correct what he could in order to improve his fielding.

As a baserunner, Trout doesn't take it very seriously--neither should the opposition.

OVERALL:

There were many people in baseball who would have given up on Steve Trout a few years ago. He had a fly-by-night attitude and was a bit exasperating for the management. He found strength and maturity somewhere. He seems to have finally settled in to becoming a pitcher who will let his arm play ball and not his head.

Snider: "He went from a thrower to a pitcher. His attitude's changed. Instead of just letting the ball go, he knows what he's doing. Hitters couldn't sit back against him."

HITTING:

Gary Woods continued to be used more for his glove than his bat last season. He got half as many trips to the plate as he did the year before, and then only in pinch-hit situations.

When Woods did start, it was against lefthanded pitchers, particularly Steve Carlton and Pittsburgh's fine pitcher Larry McWilliams. For quite unknown reasons, Woods hits both of them (especially Carlton) very well. Two of Woods's three homers last season came off Larry McWilliams.

When he does go up to the plate, Woods tends to be a very patient hitter. He also splits between pulling the ball to left and stroking it to the opposite field. Overall, he is more than adequate for bench duty and was a fairly reliable clutch hitter, considering that he spent most of his time in the batter's box as a pinch-hitter.

BASERUNNING:

Woods has average speed and is still a threat to steal a base. He will mix it up trying to break up the double play.

FIELDING:

Woods's primary value to his team is his glove. He won't get the opportunity to play every day for the Cubs. He can play all three outfield positions well. He has no major difficulty in either coming in on the ball or back pedaling, but he is certainly no threat to take over Bob Dernier's job.

His best position may be a toss-up between center field and right field. But that's not all . . . during spring

GARY WOODS
OF, No. 25
RR, 6'2", 190 lbs.
ML Svc: 5 years
Born: 7-20-53 in
    Santa Barbara, CA

1984 STATISTICS

AVG	G	AB	R	H	2B	3B	HR	RBI	BB	SO	SB
.235	87	98	13	23	4	1	3	10	15	21	2

CAREER STATISTICS

AVG	G	AB	R	H	2B	3B	HR	RBI	BB	SO	SB
.243	444	950	106	231	45	4	13	106	72	166	22

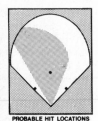

STRONG (VS. RHP) STRONG (VS. LHP) PROBABLE HIT LOCATIONS

training a few years back, he tried his hand at catching and was good enough to be considered as the Cubs' emergency catcher.

Last spring, he also got a taste of playing second base and did not look bad there either. But Woods is not going to replace Ryne Sandberg, oh no. Nonetheless, the journeyman gloveman is good to have around, and he did not commit any errors last season.

OVERALL:

Like many other 1984 Cubs players, Woods could get a lot more playing time for a team of lesser quality.

JAY JOHNSTONE
OF, No. 21
LR, 6'1"190 lbs.
ML Svc: 19 years
Born: 11-20-45 in
Manchester, CT

HITTING, FIELDING, BASERUNNING:

Jay Johnstone was doing an adequate job for the Cubs as a pinch-hitter against righthanded pitchers when all of a sudden the Cubs went out and got Davey Lopes as the player to be named later for Chuck Rainey. Johnstone found himself relegated to the ranks of an honorary coach, which kept him in uniform in September during the National League Championship Series.

Some wondered why the Cubs cast aside Johnstone, who had proven there was some life left in his bat, while others wondered how the 38-year-old Johnstone had wrangled almost another year of major league service time out of the Cubs. Johnstone remained a streaky hitter, giving skeptics and boosters evidence depending on whether he was hot or cold.

Johnstone wasn't on base long enough to dispel the notion that he had become conservative on the basepaths.

Fly balls were becoming an adventure for the outfielder, and his arm is no longer what it used to be. In his latest stints in the outfield, Johnstone seemed to be having increased difficulty going back for fly balls.

OVERALL:

He may have outlived his usefulness to the Cubs. But Johnstone has been cut loose by more than one team during his 19-year-career, and it wouldn't be surprising to find him on a major league roster on opening day. He wouldn't make the best designated hitter, but he could provide bench help for some team.

DAVE OWEN
INF, No. 19
SR, 6'1", 175 lbs.
ML Svc: 1 year
Born: 4-25-58 in
Cleburne, TX

HITTING, BASERUNNING, FIELDING:

Dave Owen will not be confused with his brother, Spike, a Seattle infielder. A Cub utility infielder, Dave is the lighter-hitting of the two.

Although he showed some ability to come through with a clutch single or two, Owen still has a long way to go before he can consistently hit big league pitching. He is a switch-hitter, and so far he has not shown which is his better side. The Cubs shipped him back and forth between Triple A ball and Wrigley Field all season, so he was not really around long enough to get an in-depth look.

Owen is a dependable pinch-runner, showing that he learned his lessons in that area well while he was down on the farm. He has some speed, but probably would benefit from a longer lead off first.

When he spelled the slumping Larry Bowa at shortstop, Owen was inconsistent. At times he looked rusty, even at the Triple A level. At other times, Owen appeared to be a smooth fielder. He demonstrated good range, particularly to his left, and that made some people think that he could take over the job on a temporary basis and make the aging Bowa expendable.

OVERALL:

Unless he develops into a hitter, Owen is destined to be a utility player at best, for the rest of his big league career. He has the proper attitude and appears willing to work at becoming a major leaguer for good.

CINCINNATI REDS

HITTING:

Dann Bilardello is still a player in search of himself at the plate. After a good start last season, he tailed off into his old tendencies and found himself back in the minor leagues.

An aggressive hitter who likes the fastball up and over the plate, Dann is primarily a pull hitter. He can go deep on occasion. More often, however, he tends to get behind in the count. When he does deliver, it is usually a line drive to left or left-center.

Bilardello uses a slightly closed stance and seems vulnerable to a pitcher's basic attack: breaking balls away and fastballs in. The safest route may be to work Bilardello tight. He doesn't have great bat speed.

As a hitter, confidence seems to be a problem for Bilardello. Consequently, he is not particularly dependable in clutch or hit-and-run situations. The same holds true for his ability to move runners over or hit deep flies for a sacrifice. Bilardello can bunt but is an unlikely candidate to bunt for a base hit.

BASERUNNING:

Bilardello has no speed. He is not a threat to steal or to take a risky extra base. He is aggressive on the bases and generally shows good judgment and good awareness of game situations. He is a baserunner who pays close attention to his base coaches. A sturdy sort, he will go hunting for the pivot man on a double play.

FIELDING:

Bilardello has a strong, accurate arm and a quick release. He likes the challenge presented by baserunners and must

DANN BILARDELLO
C, No. 11
RR, 6'0", 185 lbs.
ML Svc: 2 years
Born: 5-26-59 in
     Santa Cruz, CA

1984 STATISTICS

AVG	G	AB	R	H	2B	3B	HR	RBI	BB	SO	SB
.209	68	182	16	38	7	0	2	10	19	34	0

CAREER STATISTICS

AVG	G	AB	R	H	2B	3B	HR	RBI	BB	SO	SB
.227	177	480	43	109	25	0	11	48	34	83	2

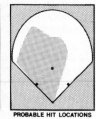

STRONG — VS. RHP   STRONG — VS. LHP   PROBABLE HIT LOCATIONS

be tested with some discretion. He has a good rapport with his pitchers, though some question his ability to call a good game.

He gets out quickly on bunts and foul pop-ups behind the plate.

OVERALL:

Scouts say Bilardello is qualified for a backup position in the big leagues but not for a starting role.

Campbell: "He's a take-charge guy with a very positive attitude but he has some obvious deficiencies. He has a lot of spunk but not a lot of ability. If you have a solid lefthanded hitting catcher, Bilardello is still the kind of player who will have some value as a platoon player."

PITCHING:

"You have to like Brownie," says Cincinnati pitching coach Jim Kaat. What's not to like? He does so many things right.

Here's another young pitcher the Reds are counting on for 1985 and not without just cause. Browning came up late in the season and proved himself a winnner.

Browning doesn't have great stuff, but he makes up for it with intelligence and location. An overhand/three-quarters pitcher, Browning mixes his pitches well and changes speeds effectively.

The screwball is his out pitch and it makes him tough against both righthanded and lefthanded hitters.

Though Browning has limited major league experience, his composure on the mound is noteworthy. He doesn't scare and has the ability to get a something extra on a pitch when he has to.

He is one of those pitchers who has a bit of Houdini in his soul, displaying a particular knack for getting out of a jams. Browning works quickly on the mound.

FIELDING, HITTING, BASERUNNING:

Browning is an average fielder with a fair move to first. He handles the bunt well and is aware as a fielder. He isn't much of a hitter but is reliable on the bases.

TOM BROWNING
LHP, No. 12
LL, 6'1", 180 lbs.
Born: 4-28-60 in
   Casper, WY

1984 STATISTICS
W	L	ERA	G	GS	CG	IP	H	R	ER	BB	SO	SV
1	0	1.57	3	3	0	23	27	4	4	0	5	14

CAREER STATISTICS
W	L	ERA	G	GS	CG	IP	H	R	ER	BB	SO	SV
1	0	1.57	3	3	0	23	27	4	4	0	5	14

OVERALL:

Browning is a "gamer" in the truest sense. He loves baseball. He was scheduled for a Saturday start in Houston last September; on Friday, his wife gave birth to a baby girl--Browning flew home on Friday, returned to Houston on Saturday afternoon and started that night. "I wanted to pitch," Browning said, a little bleary-eyed after his travels. His outing was typical: seven innings, six hits, one run.

HITTING:

After a 1983 season which most saw as his swan song, Cedeno came up with a new attitude and a new life. At the season's end, Reds' player-manager Pete Rose had nothing but praise for Cedeno. Rose feels that Cedeno may have been the most complete player in the league for the last six weeks of the season.

Much of Cedeno's improvement showed at the plate. He hit with power, for average and in the clutch. He was the the Cedeno of old.

With a slightly closed stance, Cedeno preyed on pitches up. His particular pleasure is a fastball or hanging slider about waist-high and over the plate. But any pitch between the knees and letters could be a problem for opponents.

Cedeno also showed a renewed skill to go with the pitch when the situation required, and he produced some opposite-field power. He is still, however, a pull hitter but one who is now less likely to wait on his pitch. He will reach outside and flick the pitch off to right.

Pitchers will try to drive Cedeno off the plate and get their strikes on the outside corner. That's the best tactic. Anything on the plate could be trouble.

Cedeno can bunt and bunt for hits. He proved himself adept, once again, in team hitting: sacrifice flies, right-side grounders and hit-and-run plays.

BASERUNNING:

Despite his age, Cedeno is still quick on the bases. He is aggressive and sure and he knows when to gamble. Of all the impressive things about Cedeno's play in 1984, his stolen bases and his tendency to turn singles into doubles with heads-up baserunning were perhaps more remarkable than anything else. Nowadays, he runs the bases like a kid.

FIELDING:

Cedeno was rejuvenated as a left

CESAR CEDENO
OF, No. 28
RR, 6'2", 190 lbs.
ML Svc: 15 years
Born: 2-25-51 in
  Santo Domingo, DR

1984 STATISTICS

AVG	G	AB	R	H	2B	3B	HR	RBI	BB	SO	SB
.276	110	380	59	105	24	2	10	47	25	54	19

CAREER STATISTICS

AVG	G	AB	R	H	2B	3B	HR	RBI	BB	SO	SB
.286	1858	6936	1041	1983	418	58	190	921	641	883	535

  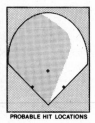

VS. RHP   VS. LHP   PROBABLE HIT LOCATIONS

fielder last season, making sparkling throws and daring catches. His arm isn't what it was, but he gets the job done with hustle, a quick release and good game awareness.

At first base, he is adequate. It's obvious Cedeno is still not wholly comfortable there.

OVERALL:

Much of Cedeno's progress seems a result of a stress management program he took during the winter of 1983. In any case, Cedeno is once again a productive player. Few are now saying he's through. Maybe his best days are gone, but there are still some good ones left.

Campbell: "He went through a remarkable transformation. The stress management program and the confidence Rose showed in him gave him a new lease on life. He can still be a productive player."

HITTING:

Here's another player who came alive after Pete Rose became player/manager of the Reds in mid-August 1984. Lackadaisical through most of 1984, Concepcion showed some of his old skills. Suddenly, an at-bat by him did not always result in a fly ball to right field off a lazy swing.

Concepcion still uses an upright, slightly closed stance and stays way off the plate. He does not appear to be as vulnerable to the inside pitch as he once was. He appears to have gained bat speed as well as aggressiveness. He prefers the ball up and away but can adjust to hit a pitch that is low and away.

His best power is to center and right-center, but he can drive the ball to left on occasion. A good guess hitter, Concepcion is a consistent situation hitter and is at his best with runners in scoring position. Though not as often as he has in the past, Concepcion will find a way to score the run. He can bunt but doesn't like to.

A pitcher's best tactic is to work Concepcion low and away. Like most aspects of his performance, his offensive play depends on his attitude. His teammates feel that he can do just about anything he wants to but that he lacks the desire to push himself to do the things he can.

BASERUNNING:

Despite his age, Concepcion is still quick on the bases. He was more aggressive on the basepaths last season than in recent years and promises 35 stolen bases in 1985. He doesn't make mistakes and when he takes a chance the odds are generally in his favor. He's shrewd on the bases and operates with a good knowledge of opponents skills. He knows who to challenge.

DAVE CONCEPCION
SS, No. 13
RR, 6'1", 180 lbs.
ML Svc: 15 years
Born: 6-17-48 in
Aragua, VEN

1984 STATISTICS

AVG	G	AB	R	H	2B	3B	HR	RBI	BB	SO	SB
.245	154	531	46	130	26	1	4	58	52	72	22

CAREER STATISTICS

AVG	G	AB	R	H	2B	3B	HR	RBI	BB	SO	SB
.268	2055	7376	849	1976	333	44	90	831	614	1029	285

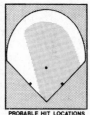

VS. RHP | VS. LHP | PROBABLE HIT LOCATIONS

FIELDING:

Concepcion's once outstanding range at shortstop has lessened, but not appreciably. He positions himself well and still has extremely quick hands. His arm is still strong and accurate. He continues to be quick and daring on the double play pivots. Concepcion, still the master of the one-hop AstroTurf throw, will also be used at third base from time to time. At third, he is very good.

OVERALL:

If Concepcion makes good on all the promises of 1984, he may be a candidate for Comeback Player of the Year. As of now, he's a competent player approaching the end of a brilliant career.

Campbell: "He seems to be a guy who gets the sac fly when you need it and drives in the key run. He's a competent shortstop . . . but not the productive player he once was."

HITTING:

A coming superstar? Brilliant? Perhaps the next Henry Aaron? Such statements were commonplace about Eric Davis last September when he went on a power binge, hitting seven homers in 10 games, including four in three games.

Davis uses the standard power hitter's stance--upright and a bit closed--and goes hunting for the high pitch. Extremely aggressive at the plate, Davis takes a vicious swing. Generally, he is an all-or-nothing hitter who frequently strikes out, again typical of power hitters.

Somewhat weak in his knowledge of the strike zone, Davis demonstrates power to all fields. He will hit towering shots to left and is capable of poking the ball out to the opposite field. Nothing he hits is cheap.

Davis appears to be a natural, but he needs discipline at the plate. Still, pitchers will work him carefully: jamming him and then going away. At this stage of his career and with an obvious taste for the long ball, Davis can be fooled by changing speeds and good breaking balls.

He looks like one who will be strong in the clutch, but it's still too early to call. Added experience will make him a better situation hitter.

He can bunt and has the speed to bunt for base hits, but with his power he is seldom called on to do so.

BASERUNNING:

Davis has great speed. Some project him as a Bobby Bonds type of player--one who can hit 30 homers and steal 30 bases. He uses his speed well rather than recklessly. Off season knee surgery may slow him down some, though the surgery was termed "minor."

FIELDING:

Davis has great range and a very strong arm. He makes the tough chance

ERIC DAVIS
OF, No. 55
RR, 6'2", 165 lbs.
ML Svc: 1 year
Born: 5-29-62 in
    Los Angeles, CA

1984 STATISTICS

AVG	G	AB	R	H	2B	3B	HR	RBI	BB	SO	SB
.224	57	174	33	39	10	1	10	30	24	48	10

CAREER STATISTICS

AVG	G	AB	R	H	2B	3B	HR	RBI	BB	SO	SB
.224	57	174	33	39	10	1	10	30	24	48	10

  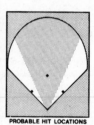

VS. RHP / VS. LHP / PROBABLE HIT LOCATIONS

routine. Given the level of his skills, Davis still works hard at his game. He is aware of what's going on in the game and rarely makes a poor judgment. There are no gaps here.

OVERALL:

All the tools and all the talent seem to be present in Eric Davis. Time, his surgery and experience will be the determining factors.

"I'm confident Eric will be one of the superstars of this game," said Dave Parker, "I just wish I had 10% of his future."

Campbell: "He has worlds of potential but still has a long way to go. If the Reds had a good ballclub, I think they would like to send him to Triple A to cut down on his strikeouts, but given the power he showed in September I don't think they can afford that luxury."

HITTING:

"Potential" remains the key word surrounding Nick Esasky, but making contact remains the essential problem. In many opinions, his failure to make consistent contact is tarnishing what was once seen as a promising career.

One of the more powerful hitters in baseball, Esasky does not put the bat on the ball often enough to be a genuine offensive threat. He is easily fooled and doesn't adjust his swing. Too often he looks for the perfect pitch and he is frequently behind in the count. Consequently, he is forced into a position of swinging at a pitch he doesn't like or ends up taking a called third strike.

Proponents of Esasky's potential—many say he is suffering the same problems experienced by Mike Schmidt and Dale Murphy at similar points in their careers—say he needs to be in the lineup every day and needs more time to become accustomed to major league pitching.

Critics say he's had enough time, doesn't hit the breaking pitches and isn't aggressive enough at the plate.

Esasky uses a straight up, closed stance and waits for the pitch out over the plate. A strict pull hitter, he oscillates between being overly anxious at bat and too willing to wait for his pitch. Confidence became a real problem in 1984. Good breaking balls usually send Esasky back to the bench with his bat in his hand.

BASERUNNING:

He's got a great home run trot, if only he got to use it more. Otherwise, he is an average baserunner. He is not a threat to steal or to take risky extra bases. He has a slow first step.

FIELDING:

Esasky has limited range at third and

NICK ESASKY
3B, No. 12
RR, 6'3", 200 lbs.
ML Svc: 2 years
Born: 2-24-60 in
  Hialeah, FL

1984 STATISTICS

AVG	G	AB	R	H	2B	3B	HR	RBI	BB	SO	SB
.193	113	322	30	62	10	5	10	45	52	103	1

CAREER STATISTICS

AVG	G	AB	R	H	2B	3B	HR	RBI	BB	SO	SB
.228	198	624	71	142	20	10	22	91	79	202	7

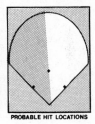

STRONG vs. RHP   STRONG vs. LHP   PROBABLE HIT LOCATIONS

is inadequate at first. He's not good defensively: his arm is average, his hands are below average. He has to hit to make it.

OVERALL:

Many now question whether or not he will ever come around.

Campbell: "In the long run, I suspect Esasky's going to end up being the odd man out. He's had two years to prove himself and hasn't done it. He strikes out one of every three times at bat, and unless you are going to hit 35 to 40 homers, that's no good. He's got to improve on making contact. Looks like his only chance is to go to a club that has a shortage of infielders and can take a chance on playing him everyday."

HITTING:

Surprise! Tom Foley can hit. He hit well enough last season to force club officials into considering trading Dave Concepcion.

Given the opportunity, Foley demonstrated himself to be a good clutch hitter with surprising power. He was frequently used as a pinch-hitter late in the 1984 season and came through regularly.

Foley is a well-disciplined spray hitter whose power is to right field. Offered an inside pitch, Foley will beat you. Foley is a heady hitter with an improving knowledge of the strike zone. He likes the ball up and over the plate. You can get him out by working him low and/or away. He thrives on mistakes and knows his role in the line-up.

He can bunt and bunt for base hits. He needs experience in situational hitting. Foley will often swing at a bad pitch when the situation calls for a fly ball or a right-side grounder.

BASERUNNING:

He is smooth and quick and can take an extra base now and again. Fast enough to get the extra base, Foley is also smart on the bases. He is not flashy and is usually fundamentally sound.

FIELDING:

Foley has good range around short-- greater to his left than his right. He has extremely quick feet and hands and is agile on the double play. His arm is strong and true. He can also play second but is much more comfortable at short.

TOM FOLEY
INF, No. 10
LR, 6'1", 175 lbs.
ML Svc: 2 years
Born: 9-9-59 in
    Columbus, GA

1984 STATISTICS

AVG	G	AB	R	H	2B	3B	HR	RBI	BB	SO	SB
.253	106	277	26	70	8	3	5	27	24	36	3

CAREER STATISTICS

AVG	G	AB	R	H	2B	3B	HR	RBI	BB	SO	SB
.240	174	375	33	90	12	4	5	36	37	53	4

VS. RHP

VS. LHP

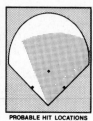

PROBABLE HIT LOCATIONS

OVERALL:

Foley is an improved player who seems bent on finding a place in the major leagues. His talent is such that the Reds are forced into making a decision on him.

Campbell: "He's a gifted infielder. He gives the Reds a good one-two tandem with Concepcion, allowing them the luxury of going with the hot guy or a platoon situation. He may want more playing time this season, however. He seems capable of playing every day and may not be satisfied platooning."

PITCHING:

Though short in stature, John Franco was big and tough during his rookie season of 1984. This lefthanded short reliever demonstrated the confidence and the cool necessary for his assignment. A power pitcher with a fastball in the 85-90 MPH range, Franco comes over-the-top and at the hitters. He doesn't dawdle when he is handed the game. The only variance in his delivery is an occasional drop to a three-quarters motion, although this doesn't appear to have any direct relation to the pitch thrown.

Franco's best pitches are his fastball, curve and screwball. It is a combination which makes him nearly as effective against righthanded hitters as he is against lefthanders. He will sometimes throw a change-up, but not very often. When he needs the out--which is very often in his role--he will go to the fastball or screwball. He will get you with the screwball, but more often, he will utilize that pitch to set up the hitter for his fastball (which he will throw inside). If he can get the fastball in consistently, he will get his outs. Most righthanded hitters look for the screwball away and they end up being jammed.

Franco's control of both his emotions and his pitches gives him an edge in tight situations. Like several young Reds' pitchers, Franco does not seem to let one bad pitch or one bad outing alter his next attempt. At this point in his career, Franco's greatest strength appears to be his composure. His greatest weakness is his limited knowledge of the opposing hitters.

JOHN FRANCO
LHP, No. 52
LL, 5'10", 175 lbs.
ML Svc: 1 year
Born: 9-17-60 in
Brooklyn, NY

1984 STATISTICS

W	L	ERA	G	GS	CG	IP	H	R	ER	BB	SO	SV
6	2	2.62	54	0	0	79	74	28	23	3	36	55

CAREER STATISTICS

W	L	ERA	G	GS	CG	IP	H	R	ER	BB	SO	SV
6	2	2.62	54	0	0	79	74	28	23	3	36	55

FIELDING, HITTING, BASERUNNING:

Franco needs to polish his move to first. It is somewhat deliberate, and as a result, runners will often take some liberties with him. He does not throw over to first base a great deal; rather, he prefers to concentrate on the hitter. He is quick, agile and dependable in the field.

OVERALL:

Franco just does not scare--and that kind of confidence is an absolute must for a short reliever. Given this, and his excellent command of all of his pitches, Franco looks like a pitcher who is only going to get better.

Campbell: "With all of the problems that the Los Angeles Dodgers have, it is hard to believe that they let Franco get away (the Reds purchased him from LA in the winter of 1983). I bet they wish they had him now because he looks like he's going to be a great one."

HITTING:

Brad Gulden is a tenacious, bulldog type of player. Reporters covering the team gave him the nickname "Rockpile." Scouts say he is simply a backup catcher pressed into a starting role.

Gulden is not an accomplished hitter. He has some power to right field but more often than not flares the outside pitch into shallow left. He can take the inside pitch deep, but not with much consistency. Gulden's long balls are generally mistakes on the part of the pitcher.

Gulden likes the ball away and is thereby vulnerable to the inside pitch. He can bunt and has the necessary discipline to succeed in hit-and-run situations, moving runners over and producing the fly ball when needed.

Gulden will occasionally come through in the clutch, but by no stretch of the imagination is he a consistent clutch hitter.

BASERUNNING:

Not blessed with great speed, Gulden goes all-out on the bases. He is not a basestealing threat, but he is not a player to be ignored either. On a double play ball, he turns into a linebacker. He's the kind of player who will take a wall out if asked to. Give him the base path or he will take it. Given his spirit, however, he isn't reckless.

FIELDING:

Gulden handles pitchers relatively well. It was this skill which put him in the No. 1 slot with the Reds last season. His arm leaves something to be desired, however. It is neither strong

BRAD GULDEN
C, No. 4
LR, 5'11", 180 lbs.
ML Svc: 2 years
Born: 6-5-56 in
New Ulm, MN

1984 STATISTICS

AVG	G	AB	R	H	2B	3B	HR	RBI	BB	SO	SB
.226	107	292	31	66	8	2	4	33	33	35	2

CAREER STATISTICS

AVG	G	AB	R	H	2B	3B	HR	RBI	BB	SO	SB
.206	165	413	43	85	14	2	5	42	43	56	2

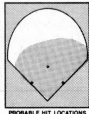

VS. RHP   VS. LHP   PROBABLE HIT LOCATIONS

nor accurate. His throws to second are often short or wide. Baserunners will take liberties--they are often blatantly dismissive. He's tough behind the plate, though, sacrificing his body to pitches and baserunners.

OVERALL:

Gulden is a journeyman: spirited, plucky, a team player. His spirit has probably lengthened his stay in the big leagues. With his skills he could survive at no other position.

Campbell: "He's spunky, a plugger but error-prone. He's not blessed with great ability . . . a stop-gap player who isn't going to set the world afire."

PITCHING:

Tom Hume's career has fallen on hard times and is on the line. His velocity is down and his pitches are up. He is nicknamed "Boom-Boom" Hume--that is "Boom-Boom" as in long balls, base hits, anything but outs.

Hume has a classic overhand delivery. He complained last season that he was not used correctly, citing his employment as a short man, long reliever, middle man and spot starter. The fact of the matter is that Hume was not effective enough in any assignment to hold a position.

The sinkerball, once his out pitch, has lost its bite. The slider, which was the mask for the sinker, doesn't get the job done and his fastball has lost its zip. More troublesome than all this is that Hume, formerly strong on location, seems to have has lost that too. His pitches often creep up into the hittable zones and often are hit.

What is most perplexing about his fall is that at times, though too few, Hume exhibits flashes of his old brilliance.

After becoming the Reds' player/manager, Pete Rose offered these words, "I really don't know what's wrong with Tommy. I wish I did. I faced him when I was with Montreal (earlier in the 1984 season) and he threw me some nasty cheese. Other times, well, I just don't know."

Many believe Hume has lost confidence in his ability, a process that began two years ago after he injured a knee which ultimately required corrective surgery. Whatever the cause of his problems, Hume is now a very mediocre middle reliever who, at times, comes out strong and then visibly unravels as the hits start to fly.

TOM HUME
RHP, No. 47
RR, 6'1", 185 lbs.
ML Svc: 8 years
Born: 3-29-53 in
Cincinnati, OH

1984 STATISTICS
W	L	ERA	G	GS	CG	IP	H	R	ER	BB	SO	SV
4	13	5.65	54	8	0	113	142	83	71	14	41	59

CAREER STATISTICS
W	L	ERA	G	GS	CG	IP	H	R	ER	BB	SO	SV
48	61	3.89	390	48	5	827	863	397	357	245	384	141

FIELDING, HITTING, BASERUNNING:

Hume remains a sure fielder and baserunner, though not fleet afoot. He can put the bat on the ball and can bunt when called upon. His move to first is average.

OVERALL:

Hume is one of the most well-liked people in the game. His work habits draw widespread respect. Consequently, many agonize with him in his fight--and clearly it's a fight, one visible in his every gesture on and off the field--to regain his past successes. But facts are facts.

Campbell: "His career is definitely on a downhill slide. Unless he comes up with a trick pitch, his control improves dramatically or his velocity returns-- well, his career has really seen better days. His injuries have taken their toll. He's a quality performer and if somebody gives Tom Hume a chance in 1985, he has got to have a good year to keep from looking for other work."

HITTING:

Wayne Krenchicki is an impressive specialty player who has proven he can hit with power, in the clutch and for average against righthanded pitchers. Against lefties, he is, admittedly, in trouble.

Krenchicki has a Charlie Lau stance reminiscent of that used by George Brett. The bat is high, his weight is back. He stays deep in the box and hits to all fields. For the most part, he hits to center and right-center. His power, however, is to right. His weakness is inside, hence his difficulty with lefthanders.

He likes the fastball thigh-high and out over the plate. His bat is surprisingly quick given his stance and he will occasionally turn on an inside fastball. Breaking pitches in give him fits.

Like Concepcion, Krenchicki is a good two-strike hitter. He generally puts the bat on the ball and is dependable. A hard worker and one who is always in the game, Wayne hits well as a pinch-hitter. He is one who rises to the occasion. He is a good bunter.

BASERUNNING:

Krenchicki is not fast but he can steal a base. He can move from first to third on a single. But, as is the case with his hitting, he knows his limitations. He won't hurt his team on the bases.

FIELDING:

Krenchicki can play all infield positions but is best suited and most comfortable at third. A product of the Baltimore organization, Krenchicki can

WAYNE KRENCHICKI
INF, No. 15
LR, 6'1", 175 lbs.
ML Svc: 6 years
Born: 9-17-54 in
Trenton, NJ

1984 STATISTICS

AVG	G	AB	R	H	2B	3B	HR	RBI	BB	SO	SB
.298	97	181	18	54	9	2	6	22	19	23	0

CAREER STATISTICS

AVG	G	AB	R	H	2B	3B	HR	RBI	BB	SO	SB
.274	359	669	70	183	29	3	9	76	56	89	5

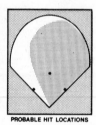

VS. RHP   VS. LHP   PROBABLE HIT LOCATIONS

do a pretty good Brooks Robinson routine. He is quick and has good reflexes. At short and second he is limited in range. At first, he is adequate. His arm is strong and accurate and he has a quick release.

OVERALL:

A dependable utility, specialty player, Wayne is one of the more productive utility infielders in the game.

Campbell: "He's a valuable player, a good guy to have around. He can play several positions and is a good pinch-hitter. He is one of those players-- all you have to do is wind him up."

PITCHING:

There are some who believe that, given some kind of continuity, Andy McGaffigan could be a quality pitcher. Cincinnati was his third club of the 1984 season, and the story there was much the same as it has been. He worked in all relief capacities and made an occasional start. He was good at times, bad at times and enters the 1985 season wearing the "journeyman" label. A lack of consistency is his problem.

McGaffigan is a hard sinker/slider pitcher who uses both a three-quarters and an overhand delivery. He has an occasional excellent outing. The problem is that those excellent performances are too few in number. Some suggest that he needs to change speeds better and more often to keep hitters off stride with the fastball and breaking ball. His fastball is in the 86-89 MPH range.

McGaffigan is composed on the mound whether he's enjoying one of his better outings or faced with a bad one. He is also one who willingly accepts the role he is assigned and exerts his energies on fulfilling that assignment instead of wishing for another.

His biggest asset is his breaking pitches. That's where he will get his outs, most of those coming on ground balls. However, when hitters start lifting the ball on him, Andy is usually in for a bad time. That usually signals some difficulty with the breaking pitches and the fastball just does not have enough sting to keep him out of trouble.

FIELDING, HITTING, BASERUNNING:

McGaffigan is lean, flexible and quick in fielding his position. He is

ANDY McGAFFIGAN
RHP, No. 28
RR, 6'3", 190 lbs.
ML Svc: 2 years
Born: 10-25-56 in
    West Palm Beach, FL

1984 STATISTICS

W	L	ERA	G	GS	CG	IP	H	R	ER	BB	SO	SV
3	6	3.52	30	6	0	69	60	28	27	4	23	57

CAREER STATISTICS

W	L	ERA	G	GS	CG	IP	H	R	ER	BB	SO	SV
7	15	3.84	79	22	0	218	201	99	93	47	122	59

"in the game" defensively and rarely makes an errant decision. His move to first is average.

McGaffigan takes his cuts as a hitter but he is not a base hit threat. An adequate bunter, he is quick on the bases but reserved in his advancement. No gambles taken.

OVERALL:

McGaffigan has been around and around, but some still believe he can be a quality pitcher.

Campbell: "The Reds should give him a chance to win a place in their starting rotation. If it doesn't work out, then it looks like he will be best suited to long relief. It looks to me like Andy would have better success if he developed a good straight change or a slow curve. That would enhance his other pitches."

HITTING:

Eddie Milner is a starter, a "rabbit," a contact hitter who will spray line drives throughout the park. He likes the fastball over the plate but can handle breaking pitches.

Milner is disciplined at the plate and shows good awareness of the strike zone.

Primarily a No. 1 or No. 2 hitter, Milner battles pitchers. He is not a cheap out. His power, occasional though it may be, is to right and right-center. Defenses will bunch the middle of the field on Milner, hoping to cut off the extra-base hit in the alley.

In the No. 2 slot, he demonstrates good two-strike ability and will pull the ball to right. As a lead-off man, he'll take the outside pitch to the opposite field.

Milner can bunt and has the speed to turn an apparent sacrifice into a base hit.

He seems vulnerable on pitches down, but will chase them and sometimes connect with one when the situation calls for it. Milner's game is on-base percentage. When he performs with reasonable success, he will, at times, come up with the clutch hit. He seems to have a flair for the dramatic.

BASERUNNING:

Milner is fast and smart and a definite threat to steal a base. There are those who believe that he could steal just about as many as he wanted if his on-base percentage were to go up or if he were a leadoff man on a consistent basis. He uses his speed wisely.

EDDIE MILNER
CF, No. 20
LL, 5'11", 170 lbs.
ML Svc: 5 years
Born: 5-21-55 in
  Columbus, OH

1984 STATISTICS

AVG	G	AB	R	H	2B	3B	HR	RBI	BB	SO	SB
.232	117	336	44	78	8	4	7	29	51	50	21

CAREER STATISTICS

AVG	G	AB	R	H	2B	3B	HR	RBI	BB	SO	SB
.255	390	1253	183	319	55	15	20	94	161	151	80

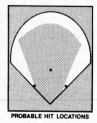

VS. RHP   VS. LHP   PROBABLE HIT LOCATIONS

FIELDING:

Milner is a reliable center fielder with outstanding range. He can "go get 'em" with nearly anyone in the league. His arm is not very strong and not always accurate, but he compensates for it with alertness and good game awareness.

OVERALL:

Milner is nothing spectacular--just a solid center fielder who will hit .260 on a regular basis. He was hobbled in 1984 by hepatitis.

Campbell: "Eddie's not going to overwhelm you anywhere, he is just a steady and solid performer."

HITTING:

Maybe Ron Oester will put together a complete season someday. So far, however, he hasn't. This switch-hitter turned it up in the last half of last season and saved what began as a disastrous performance.

A player who some say has yet to reach his peak as a big leaguer, Oester is a switch-hitter who is demonstrably better lefthanded than he is righthanded. Ironically, he is a natural righty. As a lefthander, Oester drives the ball into the alleys. When he is hot, line drives are his forte. Defenders will bunch the middle on him. He likes the ball out over the plate and has trouble when pitchers work him in. That is true from both sides of the plate. He is more consistent as a lefty and demonstrates more power. When he takes one out of the park, it's to dead right or down the line.

As a righthander, Oester is a spray hitter. He'll loft the ball more, make contact less often and strike out more. Breaking balls trouble him more from the right side.

Oester is capable of coming up with the clutch hit, but he has yet to earn the label of "proven clutch hitter." As a bunter and a situation hitter, he is generally reliable. He will put the bat on the ball.

BASERUNNING:

Oester is not blessed with great speed and last year he was bothered by a knee injury. He will take a base now and then, but it will be a "surprise" theft. He is tenacious on the bases, but his "gamer" instincts sometimes override good judgment. He is susceptible to making rash moves, infrequent as they may be, that will take his club out of an inning.

FIELDING:

Developed as a shortstop, Oester has

RON OESTER
2B, No. 16
SR, 6'2", 185 lbs.
ML Svc: 5 years
Born: 5-6-56 in
    Cincinnati, OH

1984 STATISTICS											
AVG	G	AB	R	H	2B	3B	HR	RBI	BB	SO	SB
.242	150	553	54	134	26	3	3	38	41	97	7
CAREER STATISTICS											
AVG	G	AB	R	H	2B	3B	HR	RBI	BB	SO	SB
.261	675	2319	266	605	100	21	30	206	193	381	22

VS. RHP   VS. LHP   PROBABLE HIT LOCATIONS

good range and an extremely strong arm. When Oester is the cutoff man on a throw from the outfield, baserunners had best proceed with caution. He is agile on the double play pivot, strong on ground balls to his left. But here again, he is subject to inexplicable breakdowns, as if he suffered from lapses in concentration.

OVERALL:

Is there such a thing as being too intense? Oester's performance often leads to this question. A quality player whose skills are sometimes overtaken by his anxiousness to excel, Oester has a tendency to let the bad moments stay with him.

Campbell: "He can get down on himself and he can be temperamental: he kicks a lot of dirt. He's getting to an age when he should overcome that. Ron is a player with obvious skills who possibly hasn't reached his potential."

PITCHING:

Another Cincinnati utility pitcher, the lefthanded Bob Owchinko seems most effective in a long relief role. One who survives on guile and good location, Owchinko is a change-of-speeds artist who is blessed with a durable arm.

His repertoire is basic major league: a tailing fastball, slider, change-up, curve and slow curve (slurve). Often, Owchinko is at his best when he has good command of the slurve. When he does, he will use that pitch to set up the others --particularly the slider--for outs. He has average big league velocity on his fastball (85 MPH) and average stuff, but location is still his key to a good performance. When his location is off, he will get hurt and he will often get hurt by the long ball. While pitching in Oakland, for instance, Owchinko was given the nickname "The Human Batting Tee."

On his good days, Owchinko is the kind of pitcher who will have hitters fighting with themselves--insisting they should be able to "hit this guy" but, all the while, unable to get the job done.

When Owchinko is on, look for a lot of foul balls as well as hitters being way out in front of the pitch. When he is off, the outfielders have a busy day.

FIELDING, HITTING, BASERUNNING:

Owchinko is adequate in the field and has an average move to first, but nei-

BOB OWCHINKO
LHP, No. 32
LL, 6'2", 195 lbs.
ML Svc: 7 years
Born: 1-1-55 in
Detroit, MI

1984 STATISTICS

W	L	ERA	G	GS	CG	IP	H	R	ER	BB	SO	SV
3	5	4.12	49	4	0	94	91	47	43	10	39	60

CAREER STATISTICS

W	L	ERA	G	GS	CG	IP	H	R	ER	BB	SO	SV
36	60	4.30	272	101	10	874	920	455	418	331	463	65

ther is his strong suit. He will keep baserunners honest, but is slow afoot. He will not save base hits whether they are well-placed bunts or shots up the middle. His business is pitching.

As a hitter, Owchinko is a victim of his slowness. Consequently, he is careful. He doesn't want to take away a possible run that his team could use.

OVERALL:

Campbell: "He is a guy who can wear many hats. Basically, I think that he was a good acquisition for the Reds--he still has pretty good stuff. One of the things that Bobby does very well is to change speeds. I think that he can be a pretty effective pitcher in a long relief role or even as a spot starter."

HITTING:

Dave Parker is a pro as well as a proven clutch hitter and RBI man. Before the 1984 season started, many felt that Parker was through. He proved he wasn't.

Parker covers the plate with the wingspan of a Boeing 727. There are few holes in his strike zone. He takes the outside pitch to left and left-center, drives the "fat" pitch and can turn on the inside pitch. Parker's power, which has been lessened to a degree by time, is to right and right-center. Though the home run is still a part of his game, he is far more apt to beat an opponent with a double into the alley or a line single. He is the kind of hitter who is either starting something with a base hit or trying to find a way to get a run across.

Pitchers will attack Parker with an inside game. Those who get him out consistently are those who work him inside with hard stuff. When this is happening, watch Parker stare at the pitcher, trying to intimidate him. The inside pitch is a dangerous one to throw to Parker, however: if he is looking for the inside fastball, this is the pitch he will line into the seats.

Parker is a good situation hitter with the skills to produce what his team needs: right-side grounder, sac fly, etc. Nine times out of 10, Parker will make contact. Eight times out of 10, he will make something happen.

BASERUNNING:

Time and bad knees have slowed him down some. He'll still try to steal a base but his efficiency rate is about 50%. What he's lost in speed, however, he seems to make up for with good instincts and good knowledge of opposing fielders.

Parker uses his size—he's built like a defensive end—as a tool on the bases. Infielders and catchers pay him respect.

DAVE PARKER
OF, No. 39
LR, 6'5", 230 lbs.
ML Svc: 11 years
Born: 6-9-51 in
Jackson, MS

1984 STATISTICS

AVG	G	AB	R	H	2B	3B	HR	RBI	BB	SO	SB
.285	156	607	73	173	28	0	16	94	41	89	11

CAREER STATISTICS

AVG	G	AB	R	H	2B	3B	HR	RBI	BB	SO	SB
.303	1457	5455	801	1652	324	62	182	852	387	866	134

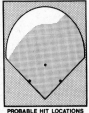

VS. RHP   VS. LHP   PROBABLE HIT LOCATIONS

FIELDING:

Instincts and knowledge of the parks and his opponents makes up for any speed lost to age and injury. If he reaches a ball he catches it and he often reaches some that appear to be out of his range. He continues to be bothered by balls hit around his knees and ankles. His arm is still strong and accurate. It is not, however, the ray gun it once was. Nevertheless, baserunners pay great attention to him.

OVERALL:

This is a player "who came to play." Healthy or injured, he gives his best. Parker has led his critics to concede there are several more productive years ahead in his career.

Campbell: "He certainly rebounded in 1984. He took off an awful lot of weight, although that is something he will have to constantly watch. He plays hard. His professionalism really helped the young Reds."

PITCHING:

For a while in 1984, Frank Pastore looked as though he would rebound from a bad season to achieve what many--especially the Reds' executives--had always hoped for him. But he was hit on his pitching arm by a line drive and the old problems returned. Pastore was very hittable, very erratic, and very, very mediocre. Pastore is another whose best years appear to be behind him.

In 1979 and 1980, Pastore was much like Tom Seaver. His stock-in-trade was the good, exploding fastball, the good slider and change. But the operative word is "was." This pitcher's promise has, for some reason, departed. His fastball no longer has its zip and the overhand breaking ball no longer has its bite. The straight change is there, but without the complementing pitches its usefulness is extremely limited.

He still has the same classic Seaver motion, over-the-top with the accentuated hip and leg drive, but that's about it. Each outing is a struggle: Pastore looking for an out pitch, Pastore looking for the strike zone . . .

He often ends up aiming his pitches and he is often hit hard. His greatest difficulty seems to be control. Just as often, Pastore seems to be caught on the mental treadmill produced by failure. One hit leads to another and another to a walk, as Pastore tries to pitch around trouble.

Some suggest injury (tendinitis in his pitching hand and later the line drive to his right arm) is part of his problem. Others say that, like Tom Hume, Pastore has lost confidence in his ability because of his continued failures. Still others think he may have pitched too much, too hard, too early in his career and has nothing left. All, however, are faced with the same set of facts. Pastore does not get outs.

FIELDING, HITTING, BASERUNNING:

Pastore is a good fielder and has one

FRANK PASTORE
RHP, No. 35
RR, 6'3", 210 lbs.
ML Svc: 6 years
Born: 8-21-57 in
Alhambra, CA

1984 STATISTICS

W	L	ERA	G	GS	CG	IP	H	R	ER	BB	SO	SV
3	8	6.52	24	16	1	98	110	74	71	10	40	53

CAREER STATISTICS

W	L	ERA	G	GS	CG	IP	H	R	ER	BB	SO	SV
43	56	4.34	170	132	21	882	915	456	425	231	481	57

of the quicker moves to first among righthanders in the National League. Though bulky in build, he covers first well and gets off the mound quickly to field bunts. He can hit, though he is not a sure bunter. On the bases, he is slow but fundamentally sound, not reckless and not dense. He is "in the game" in the field even if he is losing it on the mound.

OVERALL:

There are many who have suggested that Pastore's greatest problem is his tendency to become overly involved in "mental games" and overly attentive to "mechanics." Former Reds' manager John McNamara once went to the mound and upon hearing Pastore complain about his mechanics screamed, "Forget the mechanics, Frank, just throw the damned ball!"

Whatever the cause, Pastore has more problems than just mechanics.

Campbell: "I think his problems are velocity and location. He has a tendency to get the ball up in the strike zone a lot, and that's where the hitters make their money. He probably needs a change of scenery. He is still young, and I hesitate to say that he is through."

HITTING:

A great career winds down. Termed by many as "one of the best RBI men ever to play the game," Tony Perez is now at the point in his career at which he is best utilized as a pinch-hitter or designated hitter.

Still a total pro at the plate, Perez battles to make up for a loss in bat speed. He covers the plate well and has few holes in his strike zone. He knows pitchers and knows how most work. He is usually two pitches ahead and even when fooled can get the bat around in time to foul a pitch off and begin the maneuvering anew.

The most productive attack against Perez seems to be to outthink him. A safe bet is to work him down and away or in on the fists.

His power, though lessened, is from left to right-center. He still has the power to take one out to straightaway center, but that is a rare occurrence.

More often, he will line a pitch into the alley. The remarkable thing about Perez is that with increasing age he has shown increasing willingness and ability to go with the pitch. The pitch delivered low and away can end up as a base hit down the right field line.

He is an exquisite situation hitter.

BASERUNNING:

Perez was once known as the "Cuban Comet," but time and hundreds upon hundreds of games have taken Perez's speed. He is not a threat to steal or to take the extra base. More often than not, Perez is replaced by a pinch-runner.

FIELDING:

Perez is adequate at first base. His hands and reflexes have slowed. His arm

TONY PEREZ
1B, No. 24
RR, 6'2", 210 lbs.
ML Svc: 21 years
Born: 5-14-42 in
      Camaguey, CU

1984 STATISTICS

AVG	G	AB	R	H	2B	3B	HR	RBI	BB	SO	SB
.241	71	137	9	33	6	1	2	15	11	21	0

CAREER STATISTICS

AVG	G	AB	R	H	2B	3B	HR	RBI	BB	SO	SB
.279	2628	9395	1233	2621	485	78	371	1590	878	1820	49

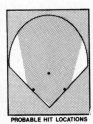

VS. RHP   VS. LHP   PROBABLE HIT LOCATIONS

is accurate but not very strong. He will not blunder in the field, but neither will he prevent a base hit by picking off a ground ball in the hole between first and second.

OVERALL:

Perez can still contribute but in the specific role of pinch-hitter.

Campbell: "Perez is a total professional who can still be one of the most competitive hitters you'll see. If his salary demands are reasonable, he can come back because he is a player who can help a club in a pinch-hitting role. I don't know, though, if that's something Tony wants to accept."

PITCHING:

Ted Power is a pitcher who found his niche in 1984 and was one of the few bright spots in the Reds' pitching picture. After an impressive spring, he was installed as the No. 1 righthanded reliever in short situations. He went on to lead the league in appearances.

In Power's case, the name says it all. A native of Guthrie, Oklahoma, Power goes after hitters with all the energy of a plains twister. His chief tools are a good fastball and slider. He will also mix in an off-speed curve and a change just to keep hitters off balance. Power can be as good as anybody around. He challenges the hitters with everything he's got.

Power made three significant changes in his delivery which led to his success. He shortened his motion, moved to an overhand delivery and concentrated on leg-drive. It took a while for these changes to become ingrained, and still--at times--Power will slip back into old habits. When his arms go well above his head or when he slides into a three-quarters delivery, he will have trouble.

A no-nonsense, down-to-business worker on the mound, Power makes the hitter go for his pitch. His battle plan is basic: breaking ball away and fastball in and always keep the ball down. His location is generally good. When it is off, he will get hurt.

One of Power's greatest assets is his attitude toward the game. Though his experience as a short reliever is limited, he has a knack for dismissing both good and bad outings. Frequently, he will come into a game, allow a hit and then settle down to retire the side in order. It is almost as if Power knows he is best under extreme circumstances.

TED POWER
RHP, No. 48
RR, 6'4", 220 lbs.
ML Svc: 3 years
Born: 1-31-55 in
   Guthrie, OK

1984 STATISTICS

W	L	ERA	G	GS	CG	IP	H	R	ER	BB	SO	SV
9	7	2.83	78	0	0	108	93	37	34	4	46	81

CAREER STATISTICS

W	L	ERA	G	GS	CG	IP	H	R	ER	BB	SO	SV
16	17	4.06	144	12	1	266	267	132	120	83	125	83

FIELDING, HITTING, BASERUNNING:

Power has an average move to first. He is a capable fielder, nothing flashy. He is slow but won't hurt his team on the bases by being thoughtless. His hitting is limited to being somewhat dependable in a bunt situation.

OVERALL:

Power is viewed as a "comer" with endorsements ranging from Schmidt to Garvey. Pete Rose has said he believes Power has "all the tools to be a stopper." But time will tell. There are still some reservations.

Campbell: "He can be a good right-handed short reliever. I don't think he's going to be of the caliber of Bruce Sutter because of Sutter's trick pitch (split-fingered fastball) or a guy like Goose Gossage, who is going to come in and intimidate hitters. But Power has been in pressure situations and proven himself. With John Franco down there--and given a couple of other arms--he could solidify the Reds' bullpen."

PITCHING:

Joe Price remains a precision pitcher whose location is the key to his success or lack of it. Generally, the control of his pitches is determined only by his control of his emotions. Last season, the lack in one area placed an extreme tax on the other. Price suffered uncharacteristic difficulties in 1984 and was unable to command any of his pitches. Illness and injury played an obvious role. Price will be shooting for a return to form in 1985.

When Price is right, he is both a pleasure and an enigma. His motion is deliberate to the extreme. He is not overpowering. His fastball is in the 85-88 MPH range. On a good day, it may even reach 90 MPH. Your Uncle Wilbur thinks he should be able to hit Price. But, like many big leaguers, Uncle Wilbur doesn't have a chance.

At his best, Price spots his slider, curve, change and fastball with the expertise of a surgeon. There is no single solution to Price. He will go to any of these pitches in a tight situation and will use any of them for an out. For Price, a start represents an investigation into what is working best for him and against him. Each hitter becomes a geometry problem for him, a pawn-and-queen situation to be solved. He is a thinking man's pitcher. He needs both his head and his stuff to win.

There is a dead giveaway as to whether or not Price is on his game. If it is his day, there will be a preponderance of pop-ups, routine grounders and opposite-field fly balls. If it is not his day, if his location isn't as true as it needs to be, someone will hit him hard right from the first inning--generally pulling the ball with authority. If Price is off his mark, he becomes more and more deliberate, taking his half-inning to a turtle's pace. Early

JOE PRICE
LHP, No. 49
RL, 6'4", 220 lbs.
ML Svc: 5 years
Born: 11-29-56 in
Inglewood, CA

1984 STATISTICS

W	L	ERA	G	GS	CG	IP	H	R	ER	BB	SO	SV
7	13	4.21	30	30	3	171	176	91	80	19	61	129

CAREER STATISTICS

W	L	ERA	G	GS	CG	IP	H	R	ER	BB	SO	SV
33	27	3.39	175	65	10	552	504	227	208	152	300	136

walks are also a sign of problems. On his best days, Price just does not walk anybody, such is his control.

FIELDING, HITTING, BASERUNNING:

Price's move to first is nearly as deliberate as his delivery to the plate: he won't pick off many people. He is an adequate fielder. As a hitter, well, Price just isn't one. He can't do it and he doesn't like it. Asking him to bunt is like trying to get your sister out of the shower.

On the bases, Price behaves like an uninvited guest. He is slow to move and a bit awkward once he gets going.

OVERALL:

Price can be nearly unhittable at times, while at others he is an easy touch.

Campbell: "He has had some shoulder problems in the past two years and that appears to be a factor. When his shoulder is sound and Joe is really on his feet, he is a very effective pitcher. But that shoulder has been suspect for a couple of years."

PITCHING:

Charlie Puleo has the desire to excel but not the stuff. With a fastball that tops out around 85 MPH and doesn't move all that much, with breaking pitches--a slider and a curve--that lack the nastiness it takes to succeed, Puleo seems destined to struggle in the big leagues.

His niche, if he has one, is in middle relief. Puleo will have a good day here and there. When he does, it is because of pinpoint location. But he does not display this type of control on a consistent basis. When Puleo succeeds, it is because his pitches are down in the strike zone, forcing hitters into routine pop flies and ground balls.

Puleo has a tendency to fall behind hitters on a regular basis. He will then challenge them, which is not the wisest course to take. Reluctant to issue any walks, Puleo gives in to hitters with a pitch down the middle of the plate. This scenario generally leads to big innings when Puleo is on the mound.

He is therefore at a crossroads in his career and looks to be one who will shuttle back and forth between the minors and the majors, picked up now and again when a club is desperate for an arm.

FIELDING, HITTING, BASERUNNING:

Puleo is an adequate fielder with an average move to first. Opposing pitchers needn't worry when he has a bat in

CHARLIE PULEO
RHP, No. 25
RR, 6'3", 190 lbs.
ML Svc: 3 years
Born: 2-7-55 in
  Glen Ridge, NJ

1984 STATISTICS

W	L	ERA	G	GS	CG	IP	H	R	ER	BB	SO	SV
1	2	5.73	5	4	0	22	27	15	14	2	15	6

CAREER STATISTICS

W	L	ERA	G	GS	CG	IP	H	R	ER	BB	SO	SV
16	23	4.55	72	53	1	350	359	201	177	191	192	7

his hands. Rarely on the bases, Puleo is a step-by-step man when he is on. He isn't fast and takes only the sure base.

OVERALL:

This is a case where the necessary skills just don't seem to be present.

Campbell: "Puleo has a lot of heart but not very much on the baseball. You can never say guys like this are completely finished because there are people like Bruce Sutter, who came up with a trick pitch, or Donnie Moore, who after treading water for 10 years and floundering around came up with a good year. In my heart, though, I don't see Puleo doing this."

HITTING:

Often used as a leadoff man because of his great speed, Gary Redus is probably best suited to be a No. 3 hitter.

A line drive hitter with power, Redus likes the fastball up and out over the plate. He's a pull hitter who wants to put the meat of the bat on the ball. In 1983, his rookie season, Redus was often fooled on breaking pitches. In 1984, he improved as a contact hitter, but there are still some holes.

Pitchers will work him down and in and down and away. He will still chase a bad pitch and strikes out with too much frequency for a leadoff hitter. Redus needs to refine his strike zone and exercise a bit more discipline at the plate. Like many relatively inexperienced hitters, Redus tends to look for "his" pitch too much.

He can bunt and has the speed to bunt for base hits. As a situation hitter, he needs work. He seldom goes to right field.

BASERUNNING:

Given adequate playing time and a strong enough on-base percentage, Redus will be near the top of the league in stolen bases. He has exceptional speed and a dramatic ability to accelerate. He has "flash" speed from first to third and displays good judgment. He can, and will, score from first on a base hit.

FIELDING:

This could be the biggest fly in Redus' pudding. His great speed is not complemented by good judgment, and his arm is neither strong nor accurate. He

GARY REDUS
OF, No. 2
RR, 6'1", 180 lbs.
ML Svc: 2 years
Born: 11-1-56 in
Limestone Co., AL

1984 STATISTICS

AVG	G	AB	R	H	2B	3B	HR	RBI	BB	SO	SB
.254	123	394	69	100	21	3	7	22	52	71	48

CAREER STATISTICS

AVG	G	AB	R	H	2B	3B	HR	RBI	BB	SO	SB
.247	268	930	171	230	44	14	25	80	128	103	98

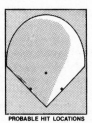

VS. RHP   VS. LHP   PROBABLE HIT LOCATIONS

is far from a disaster in the field, but he doesn't get a good jump all the time and occasionally he'll overrun a ball. There is definite room for improvement here.

OVERALL:

Redus plays well in spots. He is injury-prone: hamstrings are a continual problem and he had a troublesome shoulder in 1984. He appears to be one who needs to play on a regular basis for the best results.

Campbell: "I still think he has some holes in his game. He's improving, but he still has a way to go."

HITTING:

Mother Nature has been defied and Pete Rose is laughing in the face of Father Time. When he returned to the Reds as player/manager in August 1984, he proclaimed, "I can still hit." Then he went out and proved it.

Rose still hits in the clutch, still drives in the big run and still starts the key rally. His judgment of the strike zone may be the best around and his knowledge of opposing pitchers is demonstrated successfully day in and day out.

He is still a good two-strike hitter and still a great situation hitter, and he has taught himself to be a reliable pinch-hitter. He makes contact, finds holes and is very tough to strike out.

Generally, Rose's hits are right up the middle, ranging from left to right-center.

The apparent difference in this man today is that he is a far better hitter lefthanded than he is righthanded. When he faces lefthanded pitchers, he has a problem. If there is a successful way for a pitcher to work Rose, no one has found it yet. He taps on the low pitch, the high pitch, the pitch in, the pitch away--it doesn't matter. He thrives on hitting.

When he hits righthanded, the bat seems just a bit slower. His hits from this side will fade to right-center and right. Of course, this is Pete Rose and as soon as he is criticized he will re-bound to make his critics eat crow.

BASERUNNING:

The speed is gone but not the spirit. He'll still turn a single into a double and use his patented head first slide. He knows the opposition in every respect and knows when to take a chance. He may even try to steal a base. Anything can happen with this guy.

PETE ROSE
1B, No. 14
SR, 5'11", 203 lbs.
ML Svc: 22 years
Born: 4-14-41 in
Cincinnati, OH

1984 STATISTICS											
AVG	G	AB	R	H	2B	3B	HR	RBI	BB	SO	SB
.286	121	374	43	107	15	2	0	34	40	27	1

CAREER STATISTICS											
AVG	G	AB	R	H	2B	3B	HR	RBI	BB	SO	SB
.305	3371	13411	2090	4097	726	131	158	1243	1450	1077	187

  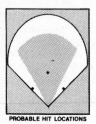

VS. RHP   VS. LHP   PROBABLE HIT LOCATIONS

FIELDING:

He's sound at first base, but that is probably the limit of his defensive ability. He never had a great arm and a recurrent elbow problem has restricted him even more. At first, he makes up for limited range with good positioning and knowledge of hitters.

OVERALL:

He's Pete Rose. He is older but still unique, still productive.

Campbell: "How do you review Pete Rose? He is still a pretty potent force. The greatest competitor I've ever played against or will ever see in this game, he never gives anything but his best. He knows baseball as well as any man alive. He has to be smart in playing himself; ninety-nine percent of the time he will probably play against righthanded pitchers."

PITCHING:

A power pitcher with good command of his pitches, Jeff Russell appears to require just one quality to become a reliable major league starting pitcher. He has to learn how to pitch.

A fierce competitor, this righthander has a fastball which peaks at the 92 MPH mark, a good slider, curve and change. His game is power. He relies on the fastball and slider, mixing in the off-speed pitches. Late in the 1984 season, he began to use the curveball to set up the fastball and slider. It was on those occasions that Russell seemed to have his greatest success.

He was tabbed as one of the most promising pitchers in the NL a year ago, and scouts still believe in Russell despite his off-year in 1984.

Russell has to learn how to pitch instead of just going out there and throwing the ball; he has to realize there is more to being a good pitcher than just throwing the ball and having good stuff.

"Refinement" may be the key word as far as Russell is concerned; "education" could be another. Certainly, Russell has every other tool. He can get out of trouble when he has to and there doesn't seem to be a hitter made who sends Russell running for cover. Right now, he is a winner who doesn't yet win.

There is one characteristic that is noteworthy regarding this young right-hander. He seems to get better as the game progresses. If Russell makes it through four innings, he has a shot at a complete game.

FIELDING, HITTING, BASERUNNING:

Russell is a good natural athlete. He fields his position exceedingly well,

JEFF RUSSELL
RHP, No. 46
RR, 6'4", 200 lbs.
ML Svc: 2 years
Born: 9-2-61 in
      Cincinnati, OH

1984 STATISTICS

W	L	ERA	G	GS	CG	IP	H	R	ER	BB	SO	SV
6	18	4.28	33	30	4	181	186	97	86	15	65	101

CAREER STATISTICS

W	L	ERA	G	GS	CG	IP	H	R	ER	BB	SO	SV
10	23	3.94	43	40	6	249	244	127	109	37	105	101

though his move to first leaves something to be desired. As a hitter, Jeff is dangerous. When he was a high school ballplayer, he won a home run hitting contest at Riverfront Stadium. As a big leaguer, he has home run capability. He held a season-long contest with Mario Soto for best batting average, runs batted in and homers among pitchers (Soto won it all). On the bases, Russell shows good instincts and good judgment.

OVERALL:

The jury is still out. Can Russell hone his natural skills and become a winner?

Campbell: "I thought he was going to become one of the great young pitchers of 1984. I look at Russell and say, Here is a pitcher with a good arm, good stuff and a good competitive spirit. But he has to learn that there are times during the season and during a game when you must get people out to win. I don't think he has learned that yet."

PITCHING:

Generally regarded as the best right-handed starter in the National League, if not in baseball, Mario Soto's forte remains the same: a fastball which ranges from 90-95 MPH and a change-up that is described in terms like "devastating," "awesome" and "unbelievable."

Both his fastball and change-up are thrown with an identical three-quarters motion. As National League hitters are all too aware, there is no tip-off as to what pitch is coming. They are faced with either a good moving fastball or the change, which drops dramatically.

Though Soto has a slider, he seldom uses it: He will toss it in once in a while to confuse hitters. Soto says that frequent use of the pitch hurts his arm and thus far he hasn't needed a third pitch. That time may be coming, however.

Although the fiery righthander had another banner season, he gave up 26 home runs, an excessive number. In most instances, they came on change-ups. The Reds' catchers said hitters had become aware of Soto's reliance on the change and simply waited on it.

Soto also continues to affected by his temper. In 1984, he was suspended twice for brawling. The total penalization of 10 days cost him a chance at winning 20 games for the first time in his career.

Similarly, Soto often allows umpires' calls and errors by his teammates to affect his performance rather than brushing aside such incidentals and continuing with the task at hand. But all this said, he is still one of the best: durable, masterful and dependable.

FIELDING, HITTING, BASERUNNING:

Soto is a good, quick fielder. His move to first is proficient enough to

MARIO SOTO
RHP, No. 36
RR, 6'0", 185 lbs.
ML Svc: 8 years
Born: 7-12-56 in
  Bani, DR

1984 STATISTICS

W	L	ERA	G	GS	CG	IP	H	R	ER	BB	SO	SV
18	7	3.53	33	33	13	237	181	102	93	26	87	185

CAREER STATISTICS

W	L	ERA	G	GS	CG	IP	H	R	ER	BB	SO	SV
77	58	3.22	222	149	59	1249	964	495	447	406	1025	189

keep baserunners from taking too many liberties. He takes special enjoyment in defensive play, as he does in hitting. He is aggressive in batting practice and showed himself to be a capable hitter in 1984. He can produce the key hit and is capable of hitting with occasional power. On the bases, he is quick and usually smart.

OVERALL:

He is one of the best, but he may need that third pitch and he may need to tame his emotions.

Campbell: "He wins even with a losing club, just a quality righthanded pitcher . . . even the best have flaws, though. He gives up too many home runs for a pitcher of his ability, particularly when he gets the change-up over the plate. The temper continues to hound him."

PITCHING:

When Reds' fans speak of their team's eventual return to prominence, this young man's name is frequently mentioned. Jay Tibbs joined the team from the minor leagues last July and quickly earned a reputation for effectiveness on the mound.

He is an overhand/three-quarters pitcher who survives on the basics. He throws a fastball, slider, screwball, curve and change and keeps all of them down and away from hitters.

"There is nothing overpowering about me," says Tibbs, whose intelligence on the mound far exceeds what would be expected of one with his limited experience.

His fastball is of average big league velocity (85 MPH). His breaking pitches are strong and consistently within his command. His strong suit is location. He spots the ball and mixes his pitches well. When his location slips, Tibbs relies on changing speeds. He is a worker on the mound who wastes no time.

"I've always felt you can think too much in this game," says Tibbs, "and no matter how much you think about it, sooner or later you have to throw the ball."

Tibbs's control is as good as his composure on the mound. Nothing ruffles him. He shakes off a bad outing and a bad pitch easily and gets on with business. He doesn't panic under pressure and is not afraid to throw any of his pitches for strikes.

Reds' catcher Brad Gulden assessed Tibbs's skills last season saying, "Jay has got it all. He stays ahead of the hitters and within himself. He throws

JAY TIBBS
RHP, No. 44
RR, 6'1", 180 lbs.
Born: 1-4-62 in
    Birmingham, AL

1984 STATISTICS

W	L	ERA	G	GS	CG	IP	H	R	ER	BB	SO	SV
6	2	2.88	14	14	3	100	87	34	32	4	33	40

CAREER STATISTICS

W	L	ERA	G	GS	CG	IP	H	R	ER	BB	SO	SV
6	2	2.88	14	14	3	100	87	34	32	4	33	40

strikes and gets outs. That's what this game is all about. He makes it look easy."

FIELDING, HITTING, BASERUNNING:

Tibbs is a fair fielder with an average move to first. He won't hurt his team in the field. He can lay down a bunt, but he is not dangerous at the plate. As a baserunner, Tibbs has average speed and gets the job done.

OVERALL:

Tibbs looks like a winner. What is impressive is that, unlike many young pitchers with good stuff who learn their craft later in their career, Tibbs appears to have cleared that hurdle already. Scouts say Tibbs looks like a winner. Pitching coach Jim Kaat loves to talk about this young starter who matches a good fastball with a strong screwball and good control.

HITTING:

Opposing pitchers didn't mask their relief or curiosity when they asked, "How can they keep this guy out of the lineup? In many cases, Walker was out of the lineup because of a lingering hamstring injury. When he was in, it was clear that he earned a lot of respect.

Walker hits with power, for average and in the clutch. A solid pull hitter, Walker will go deep to right and right-center. He's strong. He'll work on the inside pitch. A pitch out over the plate can be big trouble for opponents. He's selective at the plate and demonstrates good knowledge of the strike zone.

Walker has a quick bat. His vulnerability seems to be breaking pitches down. He can be fooled on occasion, but Walker seems to learn with each at-bat.

He is not one to be taken lightly. He can jump up and burn a careless pitcher with frequency. He will improve at the plate with experience.

BASERUNNING:

Walker has good major league speed. He will steal an occasional base and is not prone to error on the bases. He's alert and exercises good baseball sense here.

FIELDING:

Walker is generally consistent in the field. His best position is left field. He doesn't have a great arm, though he is usually accurate with his throws. At times, he is hesitant and doesn't get a good jump on a ball. If he tracks one down, he will make the catch. At other times, he'll come up with the sensational catch.

DUANE WALKER
OF, No. 26
LL, 6'0", 185 lbs.
ML Svc: 3 years
Born: 3-13-57 in
  Pasadena, TX

1984 STATISTICS

AVG	G	AB	R	H	2B	3B	HR	RBI	BB	SO	SB
.292	83	195	35	57	10	3	10	28	33	35	7

CAREER STATISTICS

AVG	G	AB	R	H	2B	3B	HR	RBI	BB	SO	SB
.246	278	659	75	162	32	4	17	79	80	136	22

  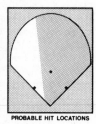

VS. RHP   VS. LHP   PROBABLE HIT LOCATIONS

OVERALL:

A solid offensive force, Walker will come through at the plate.

Campbell: "You have to like Walker, particularly as a hitter. He's like Denny Walling of Houston and Greg Gross of the Phillies. He's one who will go out and give you a solid effort and not over-impress you in any single facet of the game. Maybe he isn't quite good enough to play on an everyday basis yet, but he is certainly a valuable addition to any major league club."

RON ROBINSON
RHP, No. 58
RR, 6'4", 200 lbs.
ML Svc: 1 year
Born: 3-24-62 in
Exeter, CA

PITCHING, FIELDING, HITTING, BASERUNNING:

This young righthander lives by the creed "No walks!"

"I don't care anything about strike-outs," Ron Robinson says, "I just don't want to walk anybody. When I'm on my game, I don't walk people."

Robinson's analysis of his game is on the money. A control pitcher who blends a good fastball with a curve, change and slider, Robinson's strength is location. He spotted the ball well during 1984.

Using a three-quarters delivery, he lures hitters with pitches just off the plate and low in the strike zone. Many end up chasing pitches out of the zone.

When Robinson is on his game, the outs stack up quickly. A determined and relatively quick worker, Robinson is dependent upon his location. When it slips he can get in trouble quickly.

Robinson displays good composure on the mound and can pitch his way out of most trouble.

Robinson has quick hands and good reflexes. He fields his position well. He has an average move to first and does not become overly concerned with runners. As a hitter, he's fair as pitchers go. He can put down the bunt when called upon. Robinson can do the job on the bases.

OVERALL:

Robinson is promising, but it's early yet. He appears to be one who will make the most of his opportunities. He's a scrapper and will probably figure in the Reds' pitching staff sooner or later.

DAVE VAN GORDER
C, No. 23
RR, 6'2", 205 lbs.
ML Svc: 1 year plus
Born: 3-27-57 in
Los Angeles, CA

HITTING, BASERUNNING, FIELDING:

Dave VanGorder is another catcher who scouts cast as a backup player, not strong enough in any area to earn a starting position.

As a hitter, VanGorder is a singles man who has improved his contact. Generally, he'll go to shallow left and left-center. Occasionally, he'll take the outside pitch to right.

He doesn't strike out often. Even given his improvements from a year ago, VanGorder still cannot be categorized as a clutch hitter or strong RBI man. He has little power.

He can bunt and is pretty reliable in those situations. His bat is not quick. Power pitchers can handle him easily, others will work him down.

VanGorder is slow. He is not a threat to steal and will advance on the bases with care and good judgment.

VanGorder's game is behind the plate. He calls a relatively good game. His arm is a bit short but accurate. His release is a bit slow as well. He blocks the plate well. Few pitches get away from him (as in passed balls).

OVERALL:

VanGorder is another stop-gap, journeyman player. A player of his skills would not be in the majors at any other position.

Campbell: "Another in the mold of a plugger who will catch the baseball and doesn't offer much from the offensive side."

JOHN STUPER
RHP, No. 48
RR, 6'2", 200 lbs.
ML Svc: 3 years
Born: 5-9-57 in
    Butler, PA

PITCHING, FIELDING,
    HITTING, BASERUNNING:

Location and savvy are Stuper's main assets. A three-quarters to overhand pitcher, Stuper seems to survive on determination.

His fastball tops out at 86 MPH and has average movement. His breaking pitches, a curve and a slider, leave something to be desired, though he will throw them for strikes. Stuper tends to be behind in the count often and lacks the stuff to get out of trouble once he is there.

Stuper has to be on top of his control to be effective. When he is, he will spot the ball well, moving it in and out on hitters and mixing in his breaking pitches along with a straight change.

His determination and durability, however, are remarkable. Stuper is most known for his five hour and one minute outing in Game Six of the 1982 World Series, when he beat the Milwaukee Brewers by a score of 13-1. He struggles at times and often gets down on himself, allowing one problem to lead to another. Many feel that once Stuper defeats this aspect of his game he will be en route to a respectable career.

Stuper is a horrible hitter, a sure out. He can bunt effectively and is reliable on the bases. He will take some chances, but only when the odds are in his favor.

OVERALL:

Confidence is a question with this righthander who can be brilliant one moment and very mediocre the next. He must improve on his location. He has also been bothered by a tender shoulder which may impede his progress.

A starter by trade, Stuper may be best suited for middle relief at this stage of his career.

HOUSTON ASTROS

HITTING:

After being the Astros' starting catcher for the five previous seasons, Alan Ashby suffered a broken toe last April, yielded his starting job to rookie Mark Bailey and never won it back. This despite a .262 batting average, a 33-point improvement over 1983 and 26 points above his career average entering the season.

A switch-hitter, Ashby batted .304 lefthanded and .203 righthanded. Remarkably, though, he drove in 12 runs with only 16 hits from the right side and 15 runs with 34 hits lefthanded. Because of limited play, he didn't reach 200 at-bats.

Ashby is a high ball hitter, particularly righthanded. He's got more power lefthanded but homered only four times in 1984, twice from each side. He is primarily an alley hitter but will pull slow-pitching lefthanders down the left field line. He is a patient hitter and is willing to take a walk. He can be tough in pressure situations but has not adapted yet to pinch-hitting duties. Most pitchers have success changing speeds on him and keeping the ball down.

BASERUNNING:

He is a cautious runner who isn't a basestealing threat. Station-to-station baserunning is the rule with Ashby. But as catchers go, he is in excellent physical condition and he gives maximum effort. Injuries have affected Ashby throughout his career, and his toes are among his sore spots and sometimes slow him down.

FIELDING:

A funny thing happened to Ashby in 1984. Throughout his Astros career, he had started regularly except when Joe Niekro threw his fast moving knuckleball, giving way to others on those occasions. But from mid-season in 1984, Ashby's main responsibility was catching

ALAN ASHBY
C, No. 14
SR, 6'2", 190 lbs.
ML Svc: 10 years
Born: 7-8-51 in
    Long Beach, CA

1984 STATISTICS

AVG	G	AB	R	H	2B	3B	HR	RBI	BB	SO	SB
.262	662	191	16	50	7	0	4	27	20	22	0

CAREER STATISTICS

AVG	G	AB	R	H	2B	3B	HR	RBI	BB	SO	SB
.238	1561	2945	277	701	133	12	54	351	322	442	6

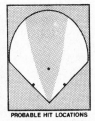

VS. RHP   VS. LHP   PROBABLE HIT LOCATIONS

Niekro. He responded well, probably handling the knuckler better than Mark Bailey.

Ashby is an intelligent man who calls a good game. He handles the pitching staff well but is quiet and not the type to take charge. One knock against him, perhaps attributable to so many injuries, is that he tends to move away from the plate to catch throws from the outfield, giving an approaching runner too much room.

OVERALL:

Ashby's future in Houston may depend on how he reacts to losing his starting job, assuming Bailey remains a regular in Houston. He wasn't especially happy with the circumstances of 1984.

Campbell: "I think he is a valuable guy to have on the club. He seems to be a quiet leader. All teams need a good backup catcher. Unless his salary demands are so overwhelming, I think he's settling into a role where he is going to give some team exactly that."

HITTING:

Mark Bailey made the jump from Class AA to the majors under emergency circumstances when Alan Ashby suffered a broken toe in late April 1984. He quickly showed he intended to stay, and a big reason was Bailey's offense.

A switch-hitter, he has good power, especially from the left side. Rather incredibly, he was the only Houston player to homer more than twice in the spacious Astrodome--Bailey hit seven out there. He accomplished two rarities: he had a home run in three consecutive games at the Dome and he homered both left and righthanded in the same game.

Based on early impressions, he seems to have a groove swing. As such, there is one area--about belt-high--that he prefers, and if a pitcher gets the ball in that spot, Bailey hits it well. His power comes when he gets his arms extended out over the plate. He appears to have more power lefthanded, but may prove to be a better "average" hitter righthanded.

He does have flaws in his swing: He can be pitched tight. High inside fastballs and low inside breaking balls are the best bets. Like any young hitter, he must learn to lay off the pitches he can't handle.

Bailey showed patience, though, as the season progressed, as indicated by 53 walks in only 344 at-bats.

BASERUNNING:

Like fellow Houston catcher Ashby, Bailey is no threat to steal, but he is a thin man and runs better than some backstops. He isn't aggressive, but once he commits, he isn't hesitant to slide hard.

FIELDING:

In the early season, he showed a strong, accurate arm. But later in the year, he seemed to tire, perhaps

MARK BAILEY
C, No. 6
SL, 6'5", 195 lbs.
ML Svc: 1 year
Born: 11-4-61 in
    Springfield, MO

1984 STATISTICS
AVG	G	AB	R	H	2B	3B	HR	RBI	BB	SO	SB
.212	108	344	38	73	16	1	9	34	53	71	0

CAREER STATISTICS
AVG	G	AB	R	H	2B	3B	HR	RBI	BB	SO	SB
.212	108	344	38	73	16	1	9	34	53	71	0

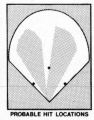

VS. RHP   VS. LHP   PROBABLE HIT LOCATIONS

because his prior professional career consisted of about 70 games catching in the minors.

Bailey is a converted infielder who has made quick progress. His footwork behind the plate is excellent, particularly for a big man, and this may be attributable to his infield experience. His set up and release were impressive in his rookie season. He blocks the plate much more aggressively than Ashby.

OVERALL:

As he learns his pitchers' nuances, he should get better. Already, however, Bailey seems to be an excellent young catcher. The new, shorter outfield dimensions at the Astrodome may make him even more valuable on offense.

Campbell: "When I first saw him, I assumed he had been a catcher all his life because he was doing a lot right. It was a revelation to find out he'd only been catching for a year or two."

HITTING:

After the All Star break, Kevin Bass hit almost .500 as a pinch-hitter. Given a starting opportunity in September, he hit safely in almost every game. But there are three problems facing Bass and their names are Jose Cruz, Terry Puhl and Jerry Mumphrey. Cruz hit .312, Mumphrey hit .290 and made the All Star team and Puhl hit .301. They left no room for Bass.

A switch-hitter, Bass hit 69 points better from the left side. If he were more consistent righthanded, he likely could earn at least a platoon role with Mumphrey, another switch-hitter whose weakness is batting righthanded. Bass can deliver the long ball righthanded on occasion.

Bass seems to hit the ball to all fields, though he is mostly a straight-away hitter. The best defense against him is to give him the lines and bunch the alleys in the outfield and jam the infield toward the middle.

The one statistic that jumps out at you is that he walked only six times in 331 at-bats. This puts limits on his pinch-hitting value because you sure wouldn't want him leading off an inning. Patience may be a problem. Despite the low walk total, he struck out 57 times: he isn't exactly a contact specialist.

He has a straightaway stance and a quick bat. But he needs more bat control, and experience may give him that.

BASERUNNING:

Bass has above average speed but stole only five bases. He only attempted 10 thefts, indicating a cautious approach, perhaps too cautious for a man with good speed. He needs to make better use of that quickness, and again experience probably is the answer.

FIELDING:

Bass has been an enigma on defense. He has excellent range, a strong arm and

KEVIN BASS
RF, No. 8
SR, 6'0", 180 lbs.
ML Svc: 2 years
Born: 5-12-59 in
Redwood City, CA

1984 STATISTICS

AVG	G	AB	R	H	2B	3B	HR	RBI	BB	SO	SB
.260	121	331	33	86	17	5	2	29	6	57	5

CAREER STATISTICS

AVG	G	AB	R	H	2B	3B	HR	RBI	BB	SO	SB
.238	239	559	64	133	24	8	4	48	13	93	7

  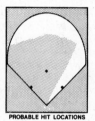

VS. RHP   VS. LHP   PROBABLE HIT LOCATIONS

a keen desire to do well. Occasionally, though, he will turn the simplest of fly balls into an adventure.

One likely problem is that he hasn't found a home. He platooned with Puhl early in right field, then took over for Mumphrey late in the season in center field. Bass didn't hurt the Astros in either position.

OVERALL:

Bass is a solid fourth outfielder who would get more opportunities elsewhere. He is a hard worker who hasn't complained--yet--but who is at that point when he needs to play more.

Campbell: "As long as Cruz, Mumphrey and Puhl are wearing Astro uniforms, it may take a trade to get Bass the playing time he needs."

HITTING:

The Astros' stated intention during spring training was to use Enos Cabell as their chief righthanded pinch-hitter, as a swing man at first and third and perhaps in the outfield. But right from the outset, starting first baseman Ray Knight didn't hit, Cabell did hit and Cabell took away Knight's job.

At the plate, Cabell is the type who will drive a pitcher crazy. One moment he looks as if he is falling down chasing a certain pitch; the next moment he is smacking that same pitch solidly for a double. He is often prone to the low outside curve. But just when you think he'll look goofy chasing it, he'll lay off it--or worse--drive it to right for a hit.

He is a spray hitter and excellent on the hit-and-run. He is primarily a high ball hitter. He didn't exhibit much power this year, but away from the Astrodome, he could hit 12-15 homers. He has improved as a contact hitter but he still doesn't walk often.

ENOS CABELL
1B, No. 23
RR, 6'5", 185 lbs.
ML Svc: 12 years
Born: 10-8-49 in
Fort Riley, KS

1984 STATISTICS

AVG	G	AB	R	H	2B	3B	HR	RBI	BB	SO	SB
.310	127	436	52	135	17	3	8	44	21	47	8

CAREER STATISTICS

AVG	G	AB	R	H	2B	3B	HR	RBI	BB	SO	SB
.278	1464	5340	686	1485	233	55	56	531	222	639	219

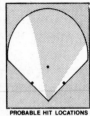

STRONG   STRONG

VS. RHP   VS. LHP   PROBABLE HIT LOCATIONS

BASERUNNING:

One of the league's real threats to steal during his first tour of duty with Houston in the late 1970s and in their 1980 Western Division championship season, Cabell has shown a marked decline in speed. He attempted only 19 steals in 1984 and was caught 11 times.

He will go from first to third on a single, though, and he'll score from second. He'll dive into first base or any other spot. He doesn't know what it is not to hustle.

FIELDING:

Shuffled from right field to third base to first base throughout his career, Cabell seems to have settled at the latter position. It's always been his best spot, probably his happiest spot, and he played steadily there in 1984.

OVERALL:

Enos returned to the league after two seasons with Detroit and had a heck of a good year, especially for a guy some folks thought had seen his better days. Offensively and defensively, he more than justified the Astros' investment in him as a free agent.

Campbell: "When Bob Lillis named him team captain (about mid-season), it seemed to give Cabell added enthusiasm. I think he wanted to lead by example. He always has been a pretty good baseball player."

HITTING:

In almost every offensive category, Jose Cruz was among the league leaders again in 1984. He was fifth in average and in the top 10 in runs scored and runs driven in, barely missing the 100 mark in both categories.

He remains a smart hitter who will go to left field if he's pitched outside and will pull with power if he gets inside heat. He is quick enough to get numerous leg hits and strong enough to rank among the league leaders in triples.

Cruz admits to adjusting his thinking completely. Thus, a remarkable accomplishment in the Astrodome, where he does not try to hit the long ball: he led the Astros with 12 homers and didn't hit even one at home.

He is tough to defense and tough to pitch. Righthanders sometimes can give him trouble with breaking balls down and in. He has been retired on change-ups. But he doesn't hit .300 every year missing those pitches over and over. If anything, he has become more selective and annually ranks among league leaders in walks.

The one negative is that he tends to start slowly, then hit about .370 or more from June until the finish.

BASERUNNING:

Cruz's offensive contributions don't stop at the plate. He stole 22 bases in 30 attempts in 1984, not bad for a man who's 37 years old. He doesn't run as often as in the past, but he picks his spots well. He also isn't as prone to pickoffs at first base as he was in the past.

FIELDING:

Excellent range atones for Cruz's occasional lapses in the field. He will

JOSE CRUZ
LF, No. 25
LL, 6'0", 185 lbs.
ML Svc: 14 years
Born: 8-8-47 in
   Arroyo, PR

1984 STATISTICS

AVG	G	AB	R	H	2B	3B	HR	RBI	BB	SO	SB
.312	160	600	96	187	28	13	12	95	73	68	22

CAREER STATISTICS

AVG	G	AB	R	H	2B	3B	HR	RBI	BB	SO	SB
.287	1907	6449	863	1851	316	82	134	881	772	798	294

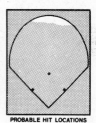

VS. RHP   VS. LHP   PROBABLE HIT LOCATIONS

make some errors, but they almost always are born of aggressiveness. His reactions are good. He handles shallow balls particularly well and he is difficult to score against from second base on a single. His arm is average in strength and accuracy.

OVERALL:

He has been Houston's Most Valuable Player for the past two seasons and in four of the last eight years. He may be the best player ever to wear the Astros' uniform, all things considered.

Campbell: "He's just an excellent baseball player, especially on offense. Watch out if he ever gets a fast start in April and May."

PITCHING:

At 240 lbs., Bill Dawley throws a good, hard fastball in the 90-92 MPH range and also uses a hard slider or, if you prefer, a slurve. His breaking ball is wicked to righthanded hitters.

If Dawley has a problem, it's against lefthanded hitters who are not intimidated by his three-quarters delivery and the combination of his fastball and effective breaking pitch.

Dawley was so effective during the first half of his rookie season (1983) that he made the National League All Star team. Then, he slumped in the second half, struggled during the Astros' 1984 spring training camp and started slowly in the regular season. Concern developed over whether he was a one-season fluke.

Dawley proved otherwise. He was untouchable in most late appearances, and overall he allowed only 82 hits in 98 innings in 1984. His ERA was 1.93. He saved only five games but, for some strange reason, seldom was placed in save opportunitites.

He is an imposing figure on the mound, a man who almost seems to sprint toward the plate to take the return throw from his catcher. He relishes competition and doesn't scare.

His strikeouts were down somewhat compared to his rookie season, and that's a figure to watch this season.

FIELDING, HITTING, BASERUNNING:

Despite his size, Dawley handles his position adequately. He gets few oppor-

BILL DAWLEY
RHP, No. 46
RR, 6'4", 240 lbs.
ML Svc: 2 years
Born: 2-6-58 in
  Norwich, CT

1984 STATISTICS

W	L	ERA	G	GS	CG	IP	H	R	ER	BB	SO	SV
11	4	1.93	60	0	0	98	82	24	21	35	47	5

CAREER STATISTICS

W	L	ERA	G	GS	CG	IP	H	R	ER	BB	SO	SV
17	10	2.34	108	0	0	177	133	50	46	57	107	19

tunities to hit, but works hard at it in practice. He is an average bunter. He won't win many foot races on the bases, but he won't hurt his team.

OVERALL:

Acquired four days before the start of the 1983 season from Cincinnati for catcher/first baseman Alan Knicely in a trade which was dismissed in both cities as a "nothing deal," Dawley turned into the Astros' find of the year. He came back strong in his sophomore season, too.

Campbell: "Astros manager Bob Lillis has a policy of not designating whether his relievers are 'short' or 'long,' and because of that philosophy Dawley's routine was altered repeatedly. Sometimes he was the stopper, sometimes not. He may benefit from a more certain role."

PITCHING:

In 1983, Frank DiPino and Bill Dawley were the Astros' one-two bullpen combination. Both had excellent rookie seasons. Neither fared badly in 1984, but their seasons took opposite directions. While Dawley struggled early and was highly impressive late, DiPino began strongly, then faded. Why? The Astros aren't certain.

He led the club with 14 saves, but he also had more save opportunities than any teammate. His 4-9 record and 3.35 ERA were below the team average.

He is especially tough against lefthanders in that he'll show the snapping curve, then zip the fastball past them. He is extremely self-assured. There is nothing fancy about DiPino. He goes after hitters in the belief he can beat their best with his best.

The major difference between the 1984 DiPino and the 1983 DiPino involved consistency. During his rookie season, he almost always controlled batters. Last year, at times he was dominating with his fastball, blowing away even the best hitters. But at other times he was hit hard or, more frequently, troubled by wildness.

His delivery is three-quarters to overhand. His fastball runs in to left-handed batters and away from righthanders. He'll get the big strikeout at the critical time.

The jury remains out as to whether he is best suited to starting or relief. He was converted to the latter role in 1983 because his history indicated his best performances came during the first four or five innings of games.

FIELDING, HITTING, BASERUNNING:

Considering the fact that he has not worked a large number of innings, he is

FRANK DiPINO
LHP, No. 46
LL, 6'0", 180 lbs.
ML Svc: 2 years
Born: 10-22-56 in
Syracuse, NY

1984 STATISTICS													
W	L	ERA	G	GS	CG	IP	H	R	ER	BB	SO	SV
4	9	3.35	57	0	0	75	74	32	28	36	65	14

CAREER STATISTICS													
W	L	ERA	G	GS	CG	IP	H	R	ER	BB	SO	SV
9	15	3.48	118	6	0	176	158	73	68	70	160	34

still an adept fielder. DiPino is quick enough to field his position well. He likes to hit and, if nothing else, takes his cuts. And he's no clog on the bases.

One negative: for a lefthander, he doesn't hold runners on especially well. Teams can run on DiPino.

OVERALL:

An intense competitor, DiPino may merely have experienced a one-time slump late in 1984. He's got good tools for a reliever--he throws hard and he doesn't scare. He's got an excellent attitude. And he has youth on his side.

Campbell: "I think DiPino has a bright future. With DiPino and Dawley, and with veteran Dave Smith healthy again, if the Astros get Joe Sambito back they could have as good a bullpen as there is in the league."

HITTING:

How often do you find two hitters in one body? Based on his two major league seasons, that's what Bill Doran seems to have. In April and May, he has been, in a word, terrible--no average, no power, no patience. In June, July, August and September, he has been among the most consistent offensive performers in the league--a .300 hitter, an on-base percentage of almost .400, numerous doubles and triples and lots of walks.

Unfortunately for Houston, Doran has typified the Astros' offensive plight the past two years. In 1984, for example, the Astros hit .237 through June 5, the worst in the league. But they finished at .263, a club record and four points off the league lead.

A switch-hitter, Doran was much more effective from the left side in his rookie season but hit almost 50 points higher righthanded in his sophomore year. He's got more pop lefthanded but also strikes out more. He tends to pull the ball more righthanded--thus, the change-up is a good pitch to throw. Most pitchers try to keep the ball down, but Doran will make a pitcher throw strikes. Because of his willingness to take a walk (66 in 1984), he is an ideal lead-off man.

BASERUNNING:

Doran became a bit more aggressive in his second season, stealing 21 bases, but he was caught 12 times. Experience at reading pitchers should be a big help. An intelligent young man, he can't help but become a better runner. Good speed enables him to move from first to third. His instincts are good. Given his high on base percentage, Doran could in time, steal 30 or 40 bases.

FIELDING:

The most impressive aspect of Doran's defense in 1984 was his adjustment to shortstop Craig Reynolds. All spring, Doran and Dickie Thon were touted as potentially the best middle infield combination in the league. Then, Thon was

BILL DORAN
2B, No. 19
SR, 6'0", 175 lbs.
ML Svc: 2 years
Born: 5-28-58 in
Cincinnati, OH

1984 STATISTICS

AVG	G	AB	R	H	2B	3B	HR	RBI	BB	SO	SB
.261	147	548	92	143	18	11	4	41	66	69	21

CAREER STATISTICS

AVG	G	AB	R	H	2B	3B	HR	RBI	BB	SO	SB
.267	327	1180	173	315	33	18	12	86	156	147	38

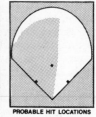

VS. RHP VS. LHP PROBABLE HIT LOCATIONS

hurt in the Astros' fifth game and did not return. Doran and Reynolds combined to rank high in double plays. That's the sign of a good infielder.

Doran's motions are smooth and he's a good playmaker around the bag. His arm is strong enough that under emergency conditions he played some shortstop. He is willing to dive for every line drive, and he made several spectacular plays during the season.

OVERALL:

Doran had a superb rookie season. But if you looked at his 1984 numbers on June 1, you had to wonder if he were a one-season fluke. He proved otherwise.

Campbell: "I compare him a lot to Alan Wiggins of the Padres. I think Doran is a better offensive player in that he can sting the ball a bit harder and with a little more authority. He's going to hit for a little higher average than Wiggins.

"I already consider Doran to be one of the premier second basemen in a league that has a lot of very good second basemen."

HITTING:

A veteran who was a world champion when he was with Oakland and Pittsburgh, Phil Garner only gets better as the pressure mounts. Indeed, after a slow start cost him his third base job, Phil won it back by stringing together several late-inning clutch hits. He had only 374 at-bats, but his nine game-winning RBIs ranked him second best on the club.

Garner is traditionally a slow starter. At Houston, that problem is endemic. In the early season, he showed little consistency, little power and little patience at bat. By June, as usual, he was demonstrating lots of each. Still, manager Bob Lillis experimented, and Garner platooned at third base mostly with lefthanded hitter Denny Walling.

He had always been a battler at the plate, as in all other areas. He is a high ball hitter, uses a closed stance and likes to dive into the ball. He's got good power to left-center field.

Garner will do whatever it takes to get runs. He will bunt, hit-and-run or drive the ball. When he is in a good groove, he'll draw walks, too. Once labeled the best No. 8 hitter in baseball, Garner is needed more in the heart of the Astros' order.

BASERUNNING:

Garner is, in a word, smart. He has lost some of his speed (witness his two steals in 1984), but he'll take the extra base on hits. He'll slide hard. He will break up double plays. His effort always is top-notch.

FIELDING:

Garner is the first to admit that he is a better second baseman than third baseman. With Bill Doran at the second, however, third is the only available job for Garner. Defensive shortcomings may keep him from being in the lineup every

PHIL GARNER
3B, No. 3
RR, 5'10", 177 lbs.
ML Svc: 10 years
Born: 4-30-49 in
Jefferson City, TN

1984 STATISTICS

AVG	G	AB	R	H	2B	3B	HR	RBI	BB	SO	SB
.278	128	374	60	104	17	6	4	45	43	63	3

CAREER STATISTICS

AVG	G	AB	R	H	2B	3B	HR	RBI	BB	SO	SB
.261	1490	5109	643	1336	253	69	89	622	471	678	203

  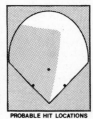

VS. RHP   VS. LHP   PROBABLE HIT LOCATIONS

day. But his reflexes, a problem in 1983 after so many years at second base, seemed to quicken in 1984. He'll make the occasional great play. His arm is no liability.

OVERALL:

Garner wasn't pleased at losing his starting job early in 1984 and requested a trade. But he played so well off the bench, management could ill afford to deal him. His unhappiness never showed on the field, which is a credit to him. He may split time with Denny Walling this year.

Campbell: "Garner was in the option year situation of his contract in 1984, and the best move the Astros could make was to re-sign him. He gives them some veteran savvy and can do well coming off the bench."

PITCHING:

After losing 28 of 39 games the previous two seasons, Bob Knepper made a superb comeback in terms of won-lost record. From the outset of spring training, he stressed the importance of being more aggressive on the mound. At the finish, he credited improvement in that area for his 15-10 record. With this new aggressiveness, however, came a tendecy to allow home runs, the first time that has happened during his up-and-down career. Opponents homered 26 times off Knepper, ten more than any other Astro.

As usual, Knepper was a durable worker, ranking among the league leaders in complete games, innings pitched and shutouts. His arm is strong. He never seems to get hurt. For all the past criticism about his lack of aggressiveness, Knepper has always wanted the ball.

A moderately fast worker, Knepper has a riding and tailing fastball and a slow curve and throws an occasional change-up. He'll throw a slider now and then to a lefthanded batter.

His problem last season, and often in the past, was one bad inning. He'll be sailing along, then something will go wrong and all of a sudden the other team has jumped on him for three or four runs.

Knepper has been characterized in the past as lacking mental toughness. He disputes that label. Regardless, he seemed to improve in that area in 1984. When he was at his best, he almost always won. And that wasn't usually the case in 1982 and 1983, even if Knepper were not to blame.

FIELDING, HITTING, BASERUNNING:

Knepper made a major improvement in one aspect and it shows in his record. Previously, he utilized a high leg kick,

BOB KNEPPER
LHP, No. 39
LL, 6'2", 210 lbs.
ML Svc: 8 years
Born: 5-25-54 in
 Akron, OH

1984 STATISTICS
W	L	ERA	G	GS	CG	IP	H	R	ER	BB	SO	SV
15	10	3.20	35	34	11	233	223	93	83	55	140	0

CAREER STATISTICS
W	L	ERA	G	GS	CG	IP	H	R	ER	BB	SO	SV
82	93	3.47	261	247	61	1646	1624	725	634	526	932	1

combined with a below average move to first base. This meant that a base-on-balls issued to a fast runner usually was, for practical purposes, a double. But Knepper worked hard in spring training to shorten his kick and he made excellent progess. Even without the good move to first, now the catcher has a chance of throwing the runner out.

Knepper has improved as a hitter, perhaps partly due to individual competition with teammate and close friend Nolan Ryan. He'll line pitchers' mistakes to right field. And every so often, he'll flash a bit of power.

OVERALL:

When he is good, he can be very good. When he is bad, he can be very bad. But most times in 1984, Knepper was good. His concentration level improved. He was not bothered by errors, as he had been in the past.

Campbell: "The big improvement was in his motion to the plate. But you have to wonder how many homers he would have permitted if half his games hadn't been at the Astrodome. Even so, a lot of good pitchers have given up home runs by the bunches. Robin Roberts was one, Denny McLain another."

PITCHING:

For the first half of 1984, Mike LaCoss didn't fit into a starting role or into the spot of late-inning relief specialist. His job primarily was as a mop-up man. But in his few opportunities, he made a positive impression. And when doubleheaders arrived and injuries affected other pitchers, suddenly LaCoss entered the starting rotation. He stayed there, too, despite an up-and-down performance.

LaCoss's chief weapon is a forkball that he has learned within the past two years. At least HE calls it a forkball. Several other clubs accused LaCoss of utilizing a foreign substance, and on one occasion he endured an inspection on the mound. "All that is just to my advantage," he said, and indeed it was. On those days, he pitched his best.

During July and early August, LaCoss pitched well enough to indicate he may have a future with the Astros. Then, in several key games, he was shelled. It seemed doubtful Houston would re-sign the potential free agent.

Previously a hard thrower, LaCoss has changed his pattern and uses as many as five or six different pitches, all at several speeds. His sinking forkball gives him the ability to secure the double play. He isn't likely to throw the ball past anybody, but he gets strikeouts because of his variety.

FIELDING, HITTING, BASERUNNING:

LaCoss was hurt by his fielding, a situation affected more by his height than his effort or desire. His move to

MIKE LaCOSS
RHP, No. 51
RR, 6'4", 190 lbs.
ML Svc: 7 years
Born: 5-30-56 in
Glendale, CA

1984 STATISTICS
W	L	ERA	G	GS	CG	IP	H	R	ER	BB	SO	SV
7	5	4.02	39	18	2	132	132	64	59	55	86	3

CAREER STATISTICS
W	L	ERA	G	GS	CG	IP	H	R	ER	BB	SO	SV
50	53	4.16	223	132	17	934	996	490	432	388	375	4

first base is below average, and his long leg kick is an invitation to steal. Offensively, he had only four hits in 31 at-bats. He is an awkward baserunner.

OVERALL:

La Coss has never helped himself with his attitude. He is an intense competitor, which is something that is in his favor. But he is constantly at odds with the press, despite receiving little negative coverage, and seems to relish putting down all around him, including his teammates. Basically, he lives in a world of his own.

Campbell: "His best shot at making any kind of a decent pitching staff would be as a fifth starter or long reliever. One positive note is that in 132 innings, he gave up only three home runs. But I don't think any team should count on him being a .500 pitcher as a regular starter."

HITTING:

Jerry Mumphrey always has had good tools and usually good statistics, but the knock against him was that he didn't drive in runs. There was one point in his career when Mumphrey actually feared going to the plate with runners in scoring position. Whatever the cause, he got rid of that problem in 1984, when he had 83 RBIs despite limited late-season playing time while the Astros were experimenting with youngsters.

A switch-hitter, Mumphrey, like most Astros, is far more effective lefthanded (.311, compared to .247 righthanded). After making the All Star team, he was platooned frequently in the second half. All nine of his home runs came lefthanded, as well as most of the RBIs.

He stands off the plate with a closed stance, has a fairly quick bat and will spray the ball around lefthanded. He prefers the ball up high but can handle low pitches, too. He is more of a slap hitter righthanded and tends to go to the opposite field. Throw him hard stuff when he's batting from the right side.

He showed good patience in 1984, walking 56 times, but he also led the Astros with 79 strikeouts.

BASERUNNING:

His running ability isn't what it was four or five years ago, but he is still a decent baserunner. He attempted only 22 steals in 1984 but was safe 15 times. He is a student of the game and takes advantage of pitchers' weaknesses. He doesn't make mistakes. He'll break up the double play.

FIELDING:

Jerry plays a deep center field. Not much gets over his head, but it seems that a lot of balls drop in front of him. He patrols the alleys well, and with Jose Cruz and Terry Puhl flanking

JERRY MUMPHREY
CR, No. 28
SR, 6'2", 200 lbs.
ML Svc: 11 years
Born: 9-9-52 in
  Tyler, TX

1984 STATISTICS

AVG	G	AB	R	H	2B	3B	HR	RBI	BB	SO	SB
.290	151	524	66	152	20	3	9	83	56	79	15

CAREER STATISTICS

AVG	G	AB	R	H	2B	3B	HR	RBI	BB	SO	SB
.212	1163	5259	527	1113	160	49	44	429	373	523	164

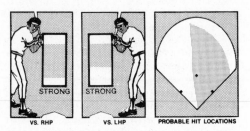

VS. RHP   VS. LHP   PROBABLE HIT LOCATIONS

him, not much gets past any of the Houston outfield.

Mumphrey's arm is his main liability. It's below average for a center fielder, and opponents took advantage last year.

OVERALL:

Mumphrey developed into one of the Astros' most dependable players in 1984. His attitude and approach were excellent. Previously known for his timidity, he became a team spokesman--always in a positive sense. When he was voted the Astros' All Star representative, there were no complaints from the media, fans or teammates. He deserved the recognition.

Campbell: "Personally, I was happy to see Jerry have such a good season. He is a heckuva nice guy. Acquiring him for Omar Moreno (August 1983) certainly is one of the best trades the Astros have made in recent years."

PITCHING:

At times in 1984, Joe Niekro's knuckleball seemed better than ever, if that is possible. He has been the Astros' most consistent pitcher over the past decade, and in the last eight years among National League pitchers only Steve Carlton has won more games.

As always, the knuckleball is the key, even though Joe, unlike his brother Phil, relies on other choices, too. He likes to mix in a fastball and a slider, and sometimes a curve, but when he needs to get a batter out, you can count on seeing the knuckler.

Control is important to Niekro in more ways than one. If he's not walking batters, he usually will have a very good outing. But when he is issuing free passes, the merry-go-round begins because with the knuckler, even though he has a quick move to first, he's open to the steal.

The quality of Niekro's knuckleball has little to do with his control. If it is too good--i.e., if it breaks too sharply--the catcher can't handle it. Many years ago, in an exhibition game at New Orleans, Niekro struck out five batters in one inning . . . and his catcher had five passed balls.

A hitter's only hope is to try to get ahead on the count and look for the fastball or slider. As Niekro's record indicates, however, that philosophy does not work often.

Under pressure, Niekro is only more determined than ever. And . . . at his best.

FIELDING, HITTING, BASERUNNING:

Joe ranks among the top four or five best-fielding pitchers in the league. Even approaching age 40, his reflexes are excellent, his judgment sound. He

JOE NIEKRO
RHP, No. 36
RR, 6'1", 190 lbs.
ML Svc: 17 years
Born: 11-7-44 in
   Martins Ferry, OH

1984 STATISTICS

W	L	ERA	G	GS	CG	IP	H	R	ER	BB	SO	SV
16	12	3.04	38	38	6	248	223	104	84	89	127	0

CAREER STATISTICS

W	L	ERA	G	GS	CG	IP	H	R	ER	BB	SO	SV
193	167	3.42	610	412	102	3074	2945	1314	1167	1019	1476	14

holds runners well, but the knuckleball is an automatic weapon for basestealers. Passed balls and wild pitches are problems, too.

A good hitter throughout most of his career, Niekro has been bothered considerably the past two years by a sore left shoulder which in no way affected his pitching but in every way affected his offense. Off-season surgery may correct the problem. He once went almost two seasons without failing to convert on a sacrifice bunt. He isn't quick, but he runs the bases well.

OVERALL:

If his knuckleball is on, you can be certain he'll give you a solid performance. He is, in every sense, a solid professional. Typical of most Astros, he hasn't received much national acclaim. But the record shows he has been among the game's best pitchers over the past decade.

Campbell: "If I were a manager and I had one game I had to win for a pennant, I would be more than happy to send Joe Niekro out to the mound."

HITTING:

Terry Puhl claims that the Astros' hitting instructor Denis Menke has completely changed his approach and attitude about swinging the bat--for the better. Certainly, Puhl has become more consistent. A notorious streak hitter, in 1984, Puhl avoided the one long slump that has characterized past seasons.

A line drive hitter, Terry seemed to forget about the home run in 1984. Still, he finished with nine, and by Houston standards, that's good. Club officials believe he will benefit more than any other player from shorter outfield dimensions in the Astrodome, because Puhl has made the warning track there a frequent target. His average may go down but expect his run production to improve.

If you're going to get him out, you have to throw him hard stuff inside. The Padres had good success in 1984 with that strategy. He likes the ball belt-high, maybe even a little above the belt. He sprays the ball to all fields. When he is hot, he is almost impossible to pitch to.

In the past, one criticism of Puhl was his failure to drive in runs. But he led the Astros with 10 game-winning RBIs in 1984 despite missing 30 games.

BASERUNNING:

Puhl is an excellent runner, but his stolen bases were down in 1984. So were his team's as a whole, and it may be because manager Bob Lillis doesn't emphasize the running game as much as Bill Virdon did. Normally a threat to steal 30 bases every season, Puhl was only 13 for 21 last year.

He is smart on the bases, moves from first to third well and enjoys heads-up baserunning.

FIELDING:

When Puhl dropped a line drive in 1984, it marked only the second time that had happened in seven years. He

TERRY PUHL
RF, No. 21
LR, 6'2", 197 lbs.
ML Svc: 7 years
Born: 7-8-56 in
   Saskatchewan, CAN

1984 STATISTICS

AVG	G	AB	R	H	2B	3B	HR	RBI	BB	SO	SB
.301	132	449	66	135	19	7	9	55	59	45	13

CAREER STATISTICS

AVG	G	AB	R	H	2B	3B	HR	RBI	BB	SO	SB
.283	1017	3720	528	1053	164	47	52	326	381	366	175

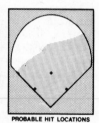

VS. RHP   VS. LHP   PROBABLE HIT LOCATIONS

holds several Astros fielding records. Nobody is more consistent. His range is good.

Like fellow outfielders Mumphrey and Cruz, Puhl doesn't have a strong throwing arm. Opponents will move from first to third base on him. But he sets up well, and his arm is accurate. He never throws to the wrong spot.

OVERALL:

Puhl's best season yet came in 1984, after he was injured in April and lost his starting job temporarily to Kevin Bass. Platooned at the outset, Puhl proved that he could hit lefthanders, too. Most officials in the Astros' organization only expect him to get better.

Campbell: "He is the type of guy you'd love to have on your club. What will be ideal is to see what guys like Puhl, Cruz and Mumphrey can do with the fences moved in at the Astrodome. I do not think King Kong could have hit more than 15 or 20 home runs the way that park was laid out."

HITTING:

Reynolds was the Astros' major surprise of 1984, as indicated by his second place standing to Jose Cruz in voting for club MVP honors.

Counted upon as the chief infield reserve, Reynolds was required to start all season at shortstop because of an eye injury to Dickie Thon. He responded by batting a strong .269 with 60 RBIs, third on the club behind Cruz and Jerry Mumphrey.

Reynolds's approach to hitting continues to defy logic. His stance is all wrong and he takes a slapping uppercut swing. He's tried to change to a more orthodox approach but with negative results. So all he does is what he has always done: beat pitchers his way.

Reynolds seems to have one simple objective at bat. If he sees the ball, he'll swing at it. He had 528 at-bats in 1984 and walked only 22 times. But he makes contact. He doesn't have good power, but he'll surprise you at times, especially if a pitcher hangs a breaking pitch.

Bunting is among Reynold's best weapons. He'll sacrifice almost every time he's asked, but he'll also drag bunt for hits. He is a tough man to pitch or defense mainly because of his free swinging, unorthodox approach.

BASERUNNING:

Considering his above average speed and intelligence, it's surprising that Reynolds doesn't steal more often. He isn't especially aggressive. Ignore him, though, and he'll beat you on the bases. He's among the quickest players out of the box, expecially on bunts. He doesn't make mistakes and will take the extra base on singles.

FIELDING:

He doesn't have great speed, great range or a great arm. But he gets the job done better than many shortstops. He seems to play hitters extremely well. His hands are good. He sets up well to

CRAIG REYNOLDS
INF, No. 12
LR, 6'1", 175 lbs.
ML Svc: 8 years
Born: 12-27-52 in
       Houston, TX

1984 STATISTICS

AVG	G	AB	R	H	2B	3B	HR	RBI	BB	SO	SB
.260	146	527	61	137	15	11	6	60	22	53	7

CAREER STATISTICS

AVG	G	AB	R	H	2B	3B	HR	RBI	BB	SO	SB
.258	956	3050	334	787	90	51	25	248	146	260	42

  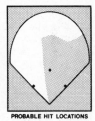

VS. RHP   VS. LHP   PROBABLE HIT LOCATIONS

throw. In short, he is highly consistent. He will dive after balls. He and Bill Doran developed into an excellent double play combination.

OVERALL:

Thrust into an unexpected and difficult situation, Reynolds, a potential free agent, produced an exceptional if unsung season and was rewarded with a new three-year contract. A quiet but dedicated performer, a former two-time All Star, he never complained when Thon took away his job in 1983 but instead continued to work hard in case he was needed. And he responded in truly professional fashion.

If Thon returns in 1985, Reynolds would become a reserve again in Houston. He likely could start for more than half the other major league teams.

Campbell: "I thought he did a superb job of replacing Dickie Thon. He proved in 1984 he can still play regularly in the major leagues for somebody. But the Astros can't afford to give up Reynolds at this time."

PITCHING:

Nolan Ryan's arm never appears to falter. Every problem he ever seems to have is with his legs, either a hamstring muscle or a calf muscle. It may be that these problems will end Ryan's career before his arm goes bad.

He still throws 95+ MPH on his good days, and in one game last season at Chicago, Ryan was clocked at 99 MPH seven times. If he is getting the curve over, too, school is out. Forget it. Offer congratulations.

He has worked on a change-up during the past two years and now uses it more and more often. It is effective at times, but some hitters consider it a favor when Ryan throws that pitch.

Critics used to say that Ryan was too precise, that he always wanted to make the perfect pitch, always aimed for corners and, as a result, walked far too many batters. But in the past few years, Ryan's control has improved (about one walk per three innings), and he believes he is a better pitcher (not necessarily thrower) than ever.

When he is right, he is almost untouchable. During the entire month of May, he allowed three earned runs. But his strength, by Ryan's own admission, comes from the legs. And when he is hurting, he has trouble.

FIELDING, HITTING, BASERUNNING:

He is a superbly conditioned athlete and, as such, he fields his position well enough. His move to first base is not particularly good. His motion is deliberate, but at 95+ MPH, at least his pitches get to the plate quickly.

NOLAN RYAN
RHP, No. 34
RR, 6'2", 210 lbs.
ML Svc: 18 years
Born: 1-31-47 in
Refugio, TX

1984 STATISTICS
W	L	ERA	G	GS	CG	IP	H	R	ER	BB	SO	SV
12	11	3.05	30	30	5	183	143	78	62	69	197	0

CAREER STATISTICS
W	L	ERA	G	GS	CG	IP	H	R	ER	BB	SO	SV
231	206	3.10	546	512	198	3704	2666	1463	1276	2091	3874	2

Ryan takes pride in his hitting, but for two years running he has established Astro records for consecutive outs in a season. He is a good bunter and an average runner.

OVERALL:

A resident of nearby Alvin, Texas, he has found happiness in Houston and is among the most popular of Astros with fans, teammates and management. If he could avoid injuries, it seems obvious that even at age 38 he could produce a big, big season. When he is at his best, nobody is better. And at all times, nobody works harder and nobody cares more about his team or community.

Campbell: "Nolan appears to have great off-the-field habits which have added to his longevity. His arm is still great. Only the legs are a concern."

PITCHING:

Joe Sambito, a former All Star reliever, returned to the majors in 1984 after missing more than two years because of a serious elbow injury that required three operations. Almost every scout who watched him agreed that he didn't throw hard enough to get batters out consistently.

But one rather significant footnote: Sambito DID get batters out. Repeatedly. He allowed only 39 hits in 47 2/3 innings. His control was good, too. Joe Sambito himself suggested that he was a better pitcher than ever, because during the preceding two years he studied the game carefully and gained more mentally than he lost physically.

Astros management handled Sambito with kid gloves. He pitched in 32 games and never once appeared with his team ahead or with a game on the line. Joe didn't like management's approach, preferring to be treated as an equal of other pitchers. But the aim was to avoid subjecting him to any undue pressure (on his elbow), and maybe that was good.

Sambito, who lost full feeling in his hand after surgery and was still gradually regaining it last season, hopes to increase the velocity on his fastball. Otherwise, he must use his smarts--and variety--to get batters out.

His confidence level seemed to build with every outing.

FIELDING, HITTING, BASERUNNING:

Sambito is an excellent fielder. His move to first base is average or above, and he doesn't fall asleep with runners on base.

He doesn't get as many hitting or running opportunities, but one characteristic of his earlier years was an

JOE SAMBITO
LHP, No. 35
LL, 6'1", 190 lbs.
ML Svc: 8 years
Born: 6-28-52 in
Brooklyn, NY

1984 STATISTICS

W	L	ERA	G	GS	CG	IP	H	R	ER	BB	SO	SV
0	0	3.02	32	0	0	47	39	16	16	16	26	0

CAREER STATISTICS

W	L	ERA	G	GS	CG	IP	H	R	ER	BB	SO	SV
33	32	2.43	353	5	1	534	441	168	144	155	421	72

unusually good eye for a pitcher at the plate. As an intelligent, dedicated athlete, he isn't apt to hurt his club in any area.

OVERALL:

The Sambito Comeback Story is one of sports' genuine success tales. His career seemed over after the third operation, but Sambito never gave up. He proved he can pitch again in the major leagues. Now, the question is whether he can regain his former role as a premier reliever. It's likely he'll get the chance this year under pressure.

Campbell: "I thought the Astros handled Joe well in 1984. They tried not to bring him into any situations where he would overexert himself. His numbers were good enough that he should regain a lot of confidence. He still got people out throwing 84 MPH last year, but in his heydey he was throwing 90+, and he could make mistakes and still overpower people. Last year, if he made a mistake, he got hit."

PITCHING:

A year ago, Mike Scott appeared to have turned his career around for the better, having won 10 of 16 decisions following a trade from the Mets to Houston. Then, he went backward again. He made 29 starts last season and won only five times, absorbing 11 losses and an incredible 13 no-decisions. His 4.68 ERA was terrible for a team which plays half its games at the Astrodome. His innings-pitched-to-hits ratio was very bad.

A significant factor to consider about Scott is that Astros management thought enough of him, despite the bad season, to keep him in the rotation. That's because he seems to have good stuff--his fastball travels in the mid-90s and was even was clocked at 97 MPH one game.

But in 1984, Scott's location with the fastball was seldom good. He was consistently behind in the count, had to throw the fastball over the plate and got hurt. He is supposed to have a good curve, but his breaking pitches definitely were not sharp last year.

Scott's season was so perplexing, even to himself, that by the midway point he had abandoned his slider, which had been his key pitch in critical situations in the past. "I just kept getting beat by it," he explained, "so I stopped throwing it." Expect him to re-tool the slider for 1985, though.

FIELDING, HITTING, BASERUNNING:

The best defensive quality Scott has going for him is one of the quicker moves to first base. Of course, he had lots of practice in 1984. He is annually among the league leaders in picking off runners.

MIKE SCOTT
RHP, No. 33
RR, 6'3", 215 lbs.
ML Svc: 5 years
Born: 4-26-55 in
 Santa Monica, CA

```
1984 STATISTICS
W   L  ERA  G   GS  CG IP   H    R    ER  BB  SO SV
5   11 4.68 31  29  0  154  179  96   80  43  83 0
CAREER STATISTICS
W   L  ERA  G   GS  CG IP   H    R    ER  BB  SO SV
29  44 4.45 139 113 5  663  736  377  328 211 307 0
```

As a hitter, bunter and runner, he is average, though he will occasionally help his team with the bat.

OVERALL:

Scott is a quiet man who seems to be a strong competitor but one who didn't put anything together last year. He may need new guidance or perhaps just better fortune. But he didn't throw well enough to win for any team in 1984.

He has experienced an up-and-down career and probably is at a crossroads entering the 1985 season.

Campbell: "If Scott gets behind in the count, he's in real trouble. I think if he's going to pitch in the major leagues, his only role is as a long reliever. You can't count on him to be any kind of consistent starter. He doesn't have the kind of stuff to be a short reliever. Scott is going to have to have a great spring to make the 1985 Houston team. Either that or Houston's pitching will not be very good."

PITCHING:

In 1980 and 1981, Smith teamed with Joe Sambito to form one of the best one-two relief combinations in baseball. Then, Joe Sambito was sidelined for more than two seasons because of an elbow injury. Smith was hurting, too, throughout that period. And though he was often able to pitch through the pain, soreness in his back, elbow and shoulder eventually took its toll.

Smith had an extremely bad 1983 season, and his Astros career was on the line. He rebounded strongly in 1984, though, even if he didn't quite return to his earlier form.

The forkball is Smith's best pitch. When it's working, he gets batters out. When it isn't, he gets hurt. His velocity improved last year, and that provided enough contrast to make his forkball more effective.

Smith also regained consistency. At times during the previous two seasons, he seemed to be using a different motion and delivery almost every appearance. Not in 1984; as a result, his control was much better and his innings-pitched-to-hits ratio was excellent.

Smith got few chances to save games, but when he did he usually responded. He is a battler who loves to win. He doesn't scare under pressure.

FIELDING, HITTING, BASERUNNING:

A back injury had adversely affected Smith's fielding the previous two years, but he was quicker off the mound last

DAVE SMITH
RHP, No. 45
RR, 6'1", 190 lbs.
ML Svc: 5 years
Born: 1-21-55 in
San Francisco, CA

1984 STATISTICS

W	L	ERA	G	GS	CG	IP	H	R	ER	BB	SO	SV
5	4	2.21	53	0	0	77	60	22	19	20	45	5

CAREER STATISTICS

W	L	ERA	G	GS	CG	IP	H	R	ER	BB	SO	SV
25	17	2.67	243	1	0	391	345	134	116	142	251	40

season. His move to first base is only average, but he pays close attention to runners. When his forkball is dipping 10 to 12 inches, it's tough to catch--thus, easy to steal against.

He has never been an adept hitter. But he bunts well. His running is average for a pitcher.

OVERALL:

Smith received some criticism here last year for being too heavy. He lost weight prior to the 1984 season and had fewer physical problems. Maybe the two were related. At times last year, Smith showed signs of regaining his old job as the Astros' stopper. Bill Dawley, Frank DiPino and Joe Sambito may have something to say about that, though.

Campbell: "He made a noticeable improvement in 1984."

HITTING:

Primarily a lefthanded pinch-hitter throughout his career, Harry Spilman has never had the chance to play regularly in the big leagues. But in July 1984, he was threatening to break the Astros' lineup when a serious leg injury ended his season.

Spilman is a good fastball hitter who likes the ball out over the plate. He is a line drive hitter but flashes occasional power. The best defense against him is to bunch the alleys and to give him the lines.

Perhaps due to his lack of playing time, Spilman is not a patient hitter. The key is to get ahead of him in the count, then throw him something far off the plate--he is apt to chase a curve in the dirt.

BASERUNNING:

He is not a threat to steal a base, but neither is he a threat to hurt his team by trying. Spilman is a slow runner and he knows it--so does everybody else. But he is also a smart runner and will break up double plays. He gives 100%.

FIELDING:

Unable to ensure his future in the big leagues as an outfielder or first baseman, Spilman volunteered to learn to catch two seasons ago. By mid-1984, he had become an adept backstop, and it was while making a superb catch of a pop foul that Spilman suffered the disabling leg injury.

Pitchers liked his determination behind the plate. Spilman has a sound arm,

HARRY SPILMAN
C/1B, No. 16
LR, 6'1", 190 lbs.
ML Svc: 5 years
Born: 7-18-54 in
   Albany, GA

1984 STATISTICS

AVG	G	AB	R	H	2B	3B	HR	RBI	BB	SO	SB
.264	32	72	14	19	2	0	2	15	12	10	0

CAREER STATISTICS

AVG	G	AB	R	H	2B	3B	HR	RBI	BB	SO	SB
.240	275	430	59	103	15	0	10	63	43	67	0

VS. RHP   VS. LHP   PROBABLE HIT LOCATIONS

but his mechanics need fine tuning. It is doubtful he will ever become a starting catcher.

He is most effective at first base, but with rookie power slugger Glenn Davis joining veteran Enos Cabell, not much playing time is available at first in Houston.

OVERALL:

Just when he got going, the leg injury spoiled Spilman's best season. Time will tell if he gets another chance. He is a hard worker who just wants the one chance to show whether he can--or can't --make it as a regular.

HITTING:

Since Dickie Thon batted only 17 times in 1984, not much has changed from last year's scouting report, other than the usual concern as to how any hitter will react to being beaned in the head by a fastball.

Thon's 1984 season ended April 8, in Houston's fifth game, when a Mike Torrez fastball hit him near the left eye, requiring surgery and causing impaired vision which continued even after the season ended.

One positive note was that he requested the opportunity to participate in the Arizona Instructional League last October, and in his first competition since April he was 3-5.

He promises that he will not be affected by the injury, that he will stand firm in the batter's box but that presumes his vision improves.

When healthy, Thon is a superb hitter, both for power and average. In 1983, his last full season, he homered 20 times, 17 on the road. With a smaller Astrodome, Thon's power potential increases. He is most likely to drive pitches into the alleys but will pull down the line on occasion.

Nothing retires him consistently, but the best bet is to keep the ball down, probably with breaking pitches. Beware the high breaking pitch, though. He'll rip it hard with regularity.

Under pressure, Thon only got better prior to the injury. In 1983, he led the league in game-winning RBIs, and that was for a third-place team.

BASERUNNING:

In his only full season as a starter (1983), Thon stole 34 bases, and that merely began to tap his potential. He is quick, aggressive and willing to take a chance. His instincts are excellent. He gets a good jump. Because his grandfather and father were so involved in baseball in Puerto Rico, they taught Dickie well--Thon knows exactly what it takes to win.

DICKIE THON
SS, No. 10
RR, 5'11", 175 lbs.
ML Svc: 6 years
Born: 6-20-58 in
South Bend, IN

1984 STATISTICS

AVG	G	AB	R	H	2B	3B	HR	RBI	BB	SO	SB
.353	5	17	3	6	0	1	0	1	0	4	0

CAREER STATISTICS

AVG	G	AB	R	H	2B	3B	HR	RBI	BB	SO	SB
.279	459	1550	208	433	80	22	23	142	115	176	84

  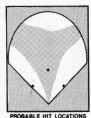

VS. RHP   VS. LHP   PROBABLE HIT LOCATIONS

FIELDING:

Only Ozzie Smith was more consistent --and more spectacular--than Thon prior to the eye injury. Range: excellent. Arm: excellent. Hands: excellent. Instincts: excellent. Last year's report ranked him among the top three shortstops in the league. There is no reason to change that viewpoint.

OVERALL:

Sadly, Thon's career hangs in the balance because of that one pitch which accidentally went awry. If he is the Dickie Thon of earlier years, he is among the best players in the game. But without good vision, his return is questionable.

Campbell: "As far as his excellent ability, nothing is changed. But all is subject to his recovering physically from the injury. He must also overcome the psychological barrier created by his circumstances."

HITTING:

Throughout his Astros career, Denny Walling has ranked among the league's best pinch-hitters. When he declared free agency following the 1983 season, the Astros thought enough of him to sign him to a long-term contract specifically as a late-inning specialist.

The irony is that during the negotiations Walling was in high demand but only as a pinch-hitter. Nobody wanted him as a regular. Disappointed, he signed with Houston only because he was convinced he wouldn't get the opportunity to play elsewhere and may as well stay where he was familiar and happy.

And what happened? Walling performed so well in the early season that he earned an opportunity to platoon both at third and at first and batted 249 times.

Not surprisingly, he hit. He's always hit. Walling batted .281 in 1984. He is primarily a fastball hitter and a first ball hitter. But he can tag the breaking ball, even from lefthanders.

He's got good power down the line and into right-center and should be aided by shorter Astrodome dimensions. He will take the outside pitch to left field, too. Walling studies pitchers, remembers every at-bat and doesn't get fooled often.

BASERUNNING:

Walling isn't particularly aggressive but he's got average to above average speed and, as indicated by seven steals in eight attempts, he picks his opportunities wisely. He'll take the extra base on singles. Throughout his career as an Astros reserve, he's fit the mold of an ideal pinch-runner--except that it has been necessary to save him for his bat.

FIELDING:

A first baseman/outfielder by trade and one who won't hurt his team at either position, Walling began to learn about third base in 1983. Even into the first part of last season, he was a liability there. But by August, Enos

DENNY WALLING
3B/PH, No. 29
LR, 6'1", 185 lbs.
ML Svc: 7 years
Born: 4-17-54 in
Neptune, NJ

1984 STATISTICS

AVG	G	AB	R	H	2B	3B	HR	RBI	BB	SO	SB
.281	87	249	37	70	11	5	3	31	16	28	7

CAREER STATISTICS

AVG	G	AB	R	H	2B	3B	HR	RBI	BB	SO	SB
.272	654	1406	189	382	52	22	21	191	168	162	33

VS. RHP

VS. LHP

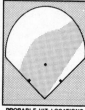

PROBABLE HIT LOCATIONS

Cabell and Ray Knight, two men who previously played third base for Houston and had no reason to exaggerate, were calling Walling the best in the league at the position.

Early on, his arm wasn't accurate. By late season, it was. And strength-wise, he says only the Padres's Luis Salazar is better than Walling. His reflexes improved with time. And when teams tried to bunt against him, Walling stopped them.

Indeed, in the early season manager Bob Lillis shied away from using Walling at third base because of questions about defense. After the All Star break, Walling was playing most days in large part due to his fielding.

OVERALL:

Until the second half of last season, his best position seemed to be first base, but his incredible improvements at third should cement him there.

Campbell: "Walling should benefit from the shorter dimensions in the Astrodome. I've seen him hit a lot of balls that would have been home runs elsewhere."

JIM PANKOVITS
PH/INF, No. 20
RR, 5'10", 174 lbs.
ML Svc: 1 year
Born: 8-6-55 in
    Pennington Gap, VA

He is an average runner, perhaps slightly above, who won't hurt a team on the bases. He is a good hustler.

Reports on Pankovits in the minor leagues lauded his defense. He didn't play enough for Houston to allow a thorough judgment. His range is good, his arm adequate.

He can play the outfield in emergency situations.

HITTING, BASERUNNING, FIELDING:

Jim Pankovits didn't figure in the Astros' plans when 1984 began, but injuries gave him two separate opportunities and he made the most of them.

In a brief starting role at second base, when Bill Doran was slumping, he got some key hits. But it was as a pinch-hitter late in the season that he made his mark. He likes to pull the ball, doesn't scare in pressure situations and if the ball is out over the plate, he'll drive it with power.

OVERALL:

Pankovits shares a problem with many other middle infielders in the Houston organization: he isn't going to take Doran's job away. Assuming Dickie Thon regains his health, he won't be starting at shortstop, either.

His future seems to be as a utility player with the Astros. If he can produce off the bench as he did late in 1984, Pankovits may stick this year because the Astros' weakness is righthanded hitting.

MIKE RICHARDT
2B, No. 2
RR, 6'0", 170 lbs.
ML Svc: 4 years
Born: 5-24-58 in
    Los Angeles, CA

Richardt had no real opportunity to play defense with Houston, but he is known as a steady second baseman who rarely makes a mistake. His range is above average, his arm average. He goes to his right especially well. And he's an aggressive fielder.

His speed is average, but given more playing time he could develop into a threat to steal on occasion. Pitchers must be aware of his presence on the bases.

HITTING, BASERUNNING, FIELDING:

Mike Richardt batted only 15 times for the Astros last season but did get four hits, including one game-winner. During a previous tenure with Texas, he had a reputation as a good clutch-hitter.

The book on Richardt in the American League was that he handled fastballs best but had trouble with curves, particularly low and outside. He has to battle over-aggressiveness in that he tends to swing at bad pitches with two strikes.

Primarily a contact hitter, Richardt lacks pure power but can drive the ball into the alleys. He has enjoyed more success against lefthanded pitchers.

OVERALL:

Richardt was among the Rangers' most highly regarded prospects for several seasons. Injuries cost him an opportunity to win a full-time job, and he was traded to Houston during the 1984 season. He spent most of last year in the minors and figures to have a tough time making the Astros in 1985, if only because of Houston's middle infield strength. His best chance is if he hits well enough in the spring to merit a pinch-hitter's role. The Astros are not loaded with righthanders off the bench.

VERN RUHLE
RHP, No. 48
RR, 6'1", 195 lbs.
ML Svc: 9 years
Born: 1-5-51 in
    Coleman, MI

PITCHING:

1984 is one season Vern Ruhle wants to forget. Nothing went right from the outset. His innings-pitched-to-hits ratio was terrible, usually indicative either of bad stuff or bad location. And with Ruhle, when we speak of control, we don't refer to wildness outside the plate, but within the plate. He is a pitcher who, without much speed, must rely on hitting spots. The record shows he didn't hit them often. When he throws down the middle, he's in trouble.

He throws five pitches--fastball, slider, curve, sinker, change-up--and has been effective in the past at changing speeds. He is an intelligent pitcher and a strong competitor. He didn't seem to have as much zip on his fastball last season as he had in the past.

FIELDING, HITTING, BASERUNNING:

A problem for Vern has been too much concern about baserunners. And in 1984, he had a lot of runners to be concerned about. His move to first base is good. But he throws so often one wonders if he devotes enough attention to batters. He is among the game's quickest workers with the bases empty, among the slowest with runners aboard.

He fields his position well. To his credit, he has worked hard to improve his hitting. He is a good bunter. Unlike some pitchers, he will draw a walk. He is an average runner for a pitcher.

OVERALL:

Campbell: "If anyone gives him a chance in 1985, it will be a make or break year for Ruhle. He can't expect to have another year like 1984 and stay in the major leagues."

JULIO SOLANO
RHP, No. 52
RR, 6'1", 160 lbs.
ML Svc: 1 year plus
Born: 1-8-60 in
    Aqua Blanca, DR

PITCHING:

Julio Solano has been a favorite of manager Bob Lillis since Lillis first noticed him during the 1983 spring camp. For a long time, one wondered what Lillis saw in Solano. During the second half of last year, Solano explained why with his talented arm.

In 50 2/3 innings, Solano allowed only 31 hits, one of the best ratios for any reliever. Control, a problem in the past, also disappeared except for rare instances. His 1.95 ERA was no fluke.

He mixes a better than average fastball with a forkball which dips radically, making it difficult for hitters to know what's coming. His poise and confidence seemed to improve with every game.

HITTING, FIELDING, BASERUNNING:

The jury remains out on Solano in these areas because he's had so few opportunities. He was 1-for-3 offensively. He is a quick fielder and an adequate runner.

OVERALL:

The Astros have debated whether his best role is as a short reliever or starter. His immediate future probably depends on what the Astros' need are entering the 1985 season. He's almost certain to be utilized often in one of the two areas because of his excellent performance last year. Lillis and his staff see great potential in this young man. If he progresses as much this year as he did last season--watch out!

MIKE MADDEN
LHP, No. 53
LL, 6'1", 190 lbs.
ML Svc: 2 years
Born: 1-13-58 in
Denver, CO

PITCHING, FIELDING,
    HITTING, BASERUNNING:

Mike Madden has a good fastball, a good curve and a good change-up. But, in 1984, he could not get any of them over the plate with any consistency. Touted last season in these pages as a future star, Madden literally walked himself back into the minor leagues. He gave up a whopping 35 walks in 40.2 innings.

If he can somehow regain his control, he will fit into the Astros' plans. He uses a classic delivery, almost straight overhand, and he bubbles with enthusiasm and confidence. He is an intelligent young man, and is effective when he does throw strikes.

It may be that Madden's arm hurt him more in 1984 than he was willing to admit. He has a history of arm trouble, but has downplayed any problems, perhaps out of his intense desire to remain active.

He has good reflexes in the field and fields his position well. He was a terrible hitter when he joined the Astros two seasons ago, but he has worked to improve, and has learned to make contact with the ball. He is an average runner.

OVERALL:

This is the pivotal season in his career. If he is healthy and can throw strikes, he has the stuff to help his team and to win. Until 1984, the only question was his health; now many are wondering about his ability as well.

LOS ANGELES DODGERS

HITTING:

In taking over the full-time duty as the No. 1 shortstop from longtime veteran Bill Russell, Dave Anderson turned in his first full year in the major leagues in 1984. Dave had excellent minor league seasons, but like most young players, he is quickly discovering that the step from the minors to the majors is a big one.

Anderson, who is 24 years old and a product of Memphis State University, does not hit for power. He is strictly a singles hitter who will stroke an occasional double. He has a straightaway stance and can hit to all fields.

This young player likes the ball up in the strike zone. Pitchers who come in on him in the upper part of the zone, or who can go down and away, will have the best success with him.

Anderson, a righthanded batter, handles lefthanded pitchers better than he does righthanders.

He likes to bunt and can handle the bat well. Dave runs very well and was utilized for a time in the leadoff spot.

At the plate, he is a disciplined hitter and seldom goes after bad pitches--two characteristics that teams like to see in a young player.

BASERUNNING:

Anderson has better than average speed, and he is a smart runner on the basepaths. He takes an average lead off first, and while he can steal bases, he is not considered a major basestealing threat, like Montreal's Tim Raines, for example.

Anderson will take the extra base and is always looking to the coach for his signs to help him out on the bases.

FIELDING:

Anderson has good range at shortstop and throws well from deep in the hole. He is a smooth fielder, though sometimes he tries to be a little too smooth. If there is a criticism of him as a field-

DAVE ANDERSON
SS, No. 10
RR, 6'2", 185 lbs.
ML Svc: 2 years
Born: 8-1-60 in
Richmond, TX

1984 STATISTICS

AVG	G	AB	R	H	2B	3B	HR	RBI	BB	SO	SB
.251	121	374	51	94	16	2	3	34	45	55	15

CAREER STATISTICS

AVG	G	AB	R	H	2B	3B	HR	RBI	BB	SO	SB
.231	182	489	63	113	20	4	4	36	57	70	21

STRONG

VS. RHP

STRONG

VS. LHP

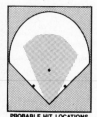

PROBABLE HIT LOCATIONS

er, it is his lack of aggressiveness on some routine plays. Like so many of the young players in the league, his fear of making a mistake in the big leagues stands in the way of executing the simple plays.

He has very quick feet, is able to get to a ball extremely well, sets up well and has a good release.

OVERALL:

In 1982, Anderson was selected by the managers in the Pacific Coast League as their "top major league prospect," and it appears that, in time, he is going to live up to that branding.

Campbell: "This is a player who will get better as time goes on. Dave has worked under Billy Russell and he reminds me a lot of Russell as far as the mannerisms he has. Dave Anderson will be the Dodgers' shortstop in the future. The only thing that may hold him back will be a physical one, a back problem he has had since birth."

HITTING:

The Dodgers obtained Bob Bailor from the New York Mets during the winter of 1983-84 with the notion he would be able to replace Derrel Thomas as their "man for all positions." Unfortunately from the start of his time with the Dodgers, the versatile Bailor needed replacing himself, when he dislocated his shoulder diving after a ground ball in a spring training exhibition game. Later in the season, he required arthroscopic surgery to repair an injured knee.

Nonetheless, Bailor is still thought of as one of the league's top utility players. At the plate he does so many things well: he can advance a runner, he can bunt and he can handle the bat very well in any given situation. He makes good contact with the ball, striking out only once his first 117 at-bats in 1984.

The veteran Bailor is a singles-type of hitter who will hit to all fields. He seldom hits down the lines, but he hits well up the middle. He does not go to the plate thinking long ball; rather, making contact is his bread and butter. Bailor has an excellent eye, waits well and is a patient hitter.

BASERUNNING:

Bailor is a good baserunner who stole 20 bases for the Mets in 1982. In 1983, he stole 18 bases in 21 attempts. He knows when to go and when to stay. He breaks up the double play as well as anyone on the club. It remains to be seen how much the knee he injured in 1984 will hold him back this season.

FIELDING:

Bailor can play well at second base, third base, shortstop or the outfield. He could catch, too, and in 1980, while he was with the Toronto Blue Jays, he even pitched when his team was in a jam. He made three appearances on the mound in August of that year, pitched two and one third innings, gave up four hits,

BOB BAILOR
INF/OF, No. 21
RR, 5'10", 160 lbs.
ML Svc: 9 years
Born: 7-10-51 in
Connellsville, PA

1984 STATISTICS

AVG	G	AB	R	H	2B	3B	HR	RBI	BB	SO	SB
.275	65	131	11	36	4	0	0	8	8	1	1

CAREER STATISTICS

AVG	G	AB	R	H	2B	3B	HR	RBI	BB	SO	SB
.265	881	2819	331	746	104	22	9	215	184	160	87

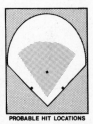

VS. RHP   VS. LHP   PROBABLE HIT LOCATIONS

two earned runs and walked one batter.

The outfield, however is probably his best position, though Bob won't give the Dodgers the kind of thunderous bat it takes to play there for any length of time.

In the infield, Bailor has good range and a good arm. He is a very aggressive fielder, as evidenced by the circumstances of his shoulder injury during the spring of 1984: the Dodgers were losing, 12-0, pretty much a lost cause, when Bailor dived after a ground ball.

OVERALL:

Bailor is a consistent hitter who also plays well defensively, wherever and whenever he is asked to play.

Campbell: "I think the Dodgers made a good acquisition in Bailor. He can play anywhere and will not embarrass you wherever you put him. A club needs a guy like him on the team, and, to me, he is a very valuable utility man."

HITTING:

The 1984 season was another disappointing one for Greg Brock, so much so that he was shipped back to the minors in the middle of the season.

There is no doubt that Brock has a discerning eye on pitches that are too high or low in the strike zone. There are also few who will disagree that he continues to have wonderful potential on the pitches that he can handle, but the problem is that he simply cannot hit pitches that are thrown inside on him. Brock will chase inside pitches, and until he learns to back off pitchers who throw him this way, his future in the majors will be in question.

He likes the ball out over the plate. Brock is a pull hitter and can also go straightaway, but he has the innate power to drive the ball to left as well. If a pitcher gets the ball high out over the plate, Brock is going to do some damage. A high pitch is the one he loves to see coming.

Until the time Brock learns to read the inside pitches better, the big thing for a pitcher to do is keep him tight-- jam, jam, jam should be the only thing a pitcher thinks when facing this young hitter. Many scouts feel that Brock's bat is just too slow to ever handle the inside pitch.

BASERUNNING:

Brock does not have blazing speed at all, but he is a good baserunner, taking eight bases in his first eight attempts.

FIELDING:

He is not a smooth first baseman. He is merely an average fielder, but while he still has difficulty coming up with throws in the dirt, Brock does have a good throwing arm and does not hesitate to go after the lead runner on a bunt play.

GREG BROCK
INF, No. 9
LR, 6'3", 200 lbs.
ML Svc: 2 years
Born: 6-14-57 in
McMinnville, OR

1984 STATISTICS

AVG	G	AB	R	H	2B	3B	HR	RBI	BB	SO	SB
.225	88	271	33	61	6	0	14	34	39	37	8

CAREER STATISTICS

AVG	G	AB	R	H	2B	3B	HR	RBI	BB	SO	SB
.222	252	743	98	165	21	2	34	101	123	123	13

  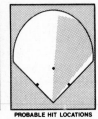

VS. RHP VS. LHP PROBABLE HIT LOCATIONS

OVERALL:

The Dodgers are still patiently waiting for Brock to unleash the power he displayed in the minors in 1982, when he hit 44 home runs at Albuquerque.

Brock was something of a brooder through the first part of the season. It was almost as if he did not want to go to the ballpark at all. When he returned to the Dodgers after a month-long exile to the minors, Greg came back with a refreshed attitude. His batting average, however, did not pick up to any great degree.

Campbell: "Pitchers can just keep coming in, in, in on him. I think the only way he is going to hit is to stay far off the plate, close up his stance and take anything that comes inside. He has got to learn to discipline himself to lay off that pitch."

PITCHING:

Carlos Diaz is a lefthanded control pitcher whose value to the club is in short relief. He was acquired by the Dodgers from the New York Mets as a replacement for Steve Howe, who was on the suspended list for a year. But Diaz proved to be a disappointment, and was returned to the minor leagues at mid-season. Diaz had a good year with the Mets, so it is obvious that the Dodgers were looking for more than what they got.

Diaz allowed, roughly, two men on base per inning, and when a relief pitcher does that, he's asking for trouble. Diaz's strikeout rate was not bad.

He throws a fastball, a slow curve and a screwball, the latter his most effective pitch. He comes to the plate with a three-quarters delivery. His fastball isn't much more than 80-85 MPH; his out pitch is the screwball. Diaz's strategy is to try to get ahead and use the screwball as a strikeout pitch.

FIELDING, HITTING, BASERUNNING:

Diaz isn't much of a hitter and, being in the role of short reliever, he gets few opportunities to go to the plate or run the bases. He is adequate at fielding his position.

OVERALL:

Diaz, still only 27 years old, had a

CARLOS DIAZ
LHP, No. 27
RL, 6'0", 170 lbs.
ML Svc: 2 years
Born: 1-7-58 in
Honolulu, HI

1984 STATISTICS

W	L	ERA	G	GS	CG	IP	H	R	ER	BB	SO	SV
1	0	5.49	37	0	0	41	47	26	25	24	36	1

CAREER STATISTICS

W	L	ERA	G	GS	CG	IP	H	R	ER	BB	SO	SV
7	3	3.35	114	0	0	153	146	65	57	72	116	4

minimum of big league experience until 1983. In 1982, he had a total of 23 games with the Braves and the Mets. In New York, he pitched in the shadow of Mets' ace Jesse Orosco in 1983. Last year was the first season he was "the man" in the bullpen, and he improved noticeably once he returned from Triple A ball.

Campbell: "Carlos has certainly been a disappointment, as illustrated by the fact he was sent out to the minors. The The Dodgers gave up an awful lot (rookie lefthander Sid Fernandez) to get him. I wonder if they got all that they bargained for."

HITTING:

Pedro Guerrero, a 30-homer/100 RBI slugger, fell far off his usual figures in 1984. He had a terribly slow start last season; he reported last spring three weeks late and 12 lbs. overweight. And while he greatly improved his average in the second half of the season, he did not pick up his home run or RBI production.

Guerrero signed a five-year, $7 million contract before the 1984 season, based mostly on his outstanding clutch hitting in 1982 and 1983. He did not have the same success at the plate in 1984. The loss of Dusty Baker in the Dodger lineup last season might account for some drop in his numbers—pitchers began to work around him quite often.

Guerrero likes the ball up in the strike zone. He likes high fastballs and especially high breaking pitches, but the 1984 season saw him having more trouble with them than he ever had before. His bat seems to have slowed down some, possibly a result of the extra weight he is carrying.

Pitchers must work him down in the strike zone with breaking pitches, although he can also go down to get a ball.

BASERUNNING:

Guerrero is an excellent baserunner. He has surprising speed for a big man. He continues to use a headfirst slide and it is the source of the shoulder problems that have plagued him for three years. He breaks up the double play very well.

FIELDING:

Guerrero has been tried in right field, at third base and even at first base, all with varying degrees of success. He was moved to center field late last season and the Dodgers think that center may be his best position.

PEDRO GUERRERO
3B, No. 28
RR, 6'0", 195 lbs.
ML Svc: 5 years
Born: 6-29-56 in
    San Pedro de Macoris, DR

1984 STATISTICS

AVG	G	AB	R	H	2B	3B	HR	RBI	BB	SO	SB
.303	144	535	85	162	29	4	16	72	49	105	9

CAREER STATISTICS

AVG	G	AB	R	H	2B	3B	HR	RBI	BB	SO	SB
.303	657	2294	342	694	112	19	101	364	233	406	63

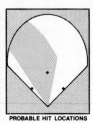

STRONG VS. RHP   STRONG VS. LHP   PROBABLE HIT LOCATIONS

Because of his shoulder injuries, he does not throw well. When Guerrero is playing in right field, the opposition will take a lot of liberties and run on him.

OVERALL:

It's Guerrero's bat, not his glove, that will keep him in the big leagues. He is a threat anytime he comes to the plate. Although he had a disappointing start to the 1984 season, he did begin to hit very well, including the long ball, in the final six weeks.

Campbell: "One of the problems the Dodgers have is finding a place for Guerrero to play. He obviously can't play third base. Opposing teams hate to see him come up with men on base because he really can change the game with one swing of the bat."

PITCHING:

Orel Hershiser was certainly one of the more pleasant surprises the Dodgers had in 1984. A righthander, Hershiser throws three-quarters to overhand. He has a good, hard, tailing fastball and a great breaking pitch, whether he calls it a slider, curve or a "slurve." When his breaking pitch is on, he gets batters out left and right.

In spite of the fact that he throws his breaking pitches better than half the time, Hershiser is considered more of a power type of pitcher. The breaking pitch seems to just explode at the plate, and the hitters have a very tough time laying off it.

Like most pitchers, when Hershiser starts to lose his effectiveness, his pitches get up in the strike zone and his breaking stuff is not quite as sharp as it should be.

One thing that many do not like about him is the fact he is one of the slowest working pitchers in the National League. He takes his time--an unusual amount of it--between pitches. Yet, while he can be extremely tiresome for his fielders to work behind and for opposing batters to face, Hershiser pitches games that don't seem to take very long. Not too many hitters reach base when he is on.

His fastball is in the 88-90 MPH range, but it is the breaking ball that is his big out pitch.

FIELDING, HITTING, BASERUNNING:

He is a better than average hitter

OREL HERSHISER
RHP, No. 55
RR, 6'3", 190 lbs.
ML Svc: 1 year plus
Born: 9-16-58 in
  Buffalo, NY

1984 STATISTICS
W	L	ERA	G	GS	CG	IP	H	R	ER	BB	SO	SV
11	8	2.66	45	20	8	189	160	65	56	50	15	2

CAREER STATISTICS
W	L	ERA	G	GS	CG	IP	H	R	ER	BB	SO	SV
11	8	2.70	53	20	8	197	167	71	59	56	20	3

and fields his position well. His move to first is very average, and he tends to throw very often, perhaps too often. He is a decent baserunner.

OVERALL:

Despite his innocent, boyish appearance, Hershiser shows good mental toughness on the mound. As catcher Steve Yeager noted, "Nice guys can be mean, too, once they get on that mound."

Campbell: "He was the National League pitcher of the month in July 1984 when he ran off a string of six or seven starts during which there couldn't possibly have been a better pitcher in baseball."

PITCHING:

Rick Honeycutt is a lefthanded, control type of pitcher who relies on his sinker and slider. He has a history of being a very good pitcher at the beginning of the season and then tailing off, and it was true again in 1984.

As he did in 1983, Honeycutt experienced arm problems in the last month of the season and, eventually, had to have surgery on his shoulder to correct an arthritis condition.

Honeycutt is a quality pitcher, the kind who usually keeps his club in the game. He does not throw his sinker much better than 85 MPH, but the velocity is not the important thing with him: location and movement are Rick's strengths. When Honeycutt is keeping his sinker down and tailing it away from righthanded hitters, he gets batters out all day with ground balls. He uses his slider against lefthanded hitters.

FIELDING, HITTING, BASERUNNING:

Honeycutt has a decent move to first base, and he fields his position well. He handles himself well at the plate--he was a college All American at the University of Tennessee as a first baseman, but until coming to the National League

RICK HONEYCUTT
LHP, No. 40
LL, 5'11", 190 lbs.
ML Svc: 7 years
Born: 6-29-54 in
    Chattanooga, TN

1984 STATISTICS
W	L	ERA	G	GS	CG	IP	H	R	ER	BB	SO	SV
10	9	2.84	29	28	6	183	180	72	58	51	75	0

CAREER STATISTICS
W	L	ERA	G	GS	CG	IP	H	R	ER	BB	SO	SV
68	84	3.87	212	191	45	1248	1313	608	536	359	482	0

in 1983, he had never gotten a hit in the big leagues.

OVERALL:

Honeycutt is a quality starter, but he has yet to prove it over an entire season. The Dodgers are hoping that his shoulder will be stronger following his surgery.

Campbell: "He does not appear to be durable enough to hold up over a long season."

PITCHING:

A starting pitcher throughout his career, Burt Hooton was relegated to bullpen duty for most of 1984. He began the season as the Dodgers' long reliever, then, because of injuries to the club's other relievers, he was utilized in a short relief role. By the end of the year, again because of injuries, he was once again starting.

Hooton has lost some of the zip off his fastball, and his knuckle-curve is not as devastating as it once was. Most hitters, especially the veterans, have grown accustomed to seeing Hooton's knuckle-curve because he has been throwing it in the big leagues for thirteen seasons.

Hooton also employs a slider and a straight change. His high leg kick, even with runners on base, makes him susceptible to the stolen base.

FIELDING, HITTING, BASERUNNING:

Hooton is not a good hitter (his career average is only slightly better than .100), but he is an effective bunter. In his ten years with the Dodgers, he has led the club in sacrifices five times.

OVERALL:

His days with the Dodgers may be num-

BURT HOOTON
RHP, No. 46
RR, 6'1", 210 lbs.
ML Svc: 13 years
Born: 2-7-50 in
Greenville, TX

1984 STATISTICS

W	L	ERA	G	GS	CG	IP	H	R	ER	BB	SO	SV
3	6	3.44	54	6	0	110	109	43	42	43	62	0

CAREER STATISTICS

W	L	ERA	G	GS	CG	IP	H	R	ER	BB	SO	SV
146	128	3.29	451	357	84	2527	2348	1034	924	759	1429	3

bered. The team is undergoing some recontruction, and the ax may fall to Hooton. A cross-over to the American League might not be a bad idea for him; those hitters have never seen his knuckle-curve. It would give a lift to his career.

Campbell: "Hooton's numbers weren't bad last season, especially since he was used in so many roles. He is not the pitcher he was two or three years ago. His best years are behind him, but it wouldn't hurt him to be traded to another club where he would get the opportunity to pitch more often."

PITCHING:

Ken Howell was one of the Dodgers' few bright spots in 1984. He came to the big leagues because the Dodgers suffered so many injuries to the pitching staff. He has pitched professionally for a short time but, immediately, he reminds scouts of a young Al Holland. Howell comes in and plays "challenge baseball." He displays tremendous confidence in himself.

Howell's strikeouts-per-innings-pitched ratio is excellent, and he has excellent control. He is not afraid of any hitter. He comes right after the hitter, no matter who it is.

His best pitch is the fastball, and he will only toy with the breaking pitch. By his own admission, it is his control that got him into the majors. While he was in the minor leagues, he was told to throw strikes; he could, he did, he came and he's a winner.

FIELDING, HITTING, BASERUNNING:

Ken is a good fielding pitcher and is involved in any play on the in field. His move to first base is average.

OVERALL:

For someone who has pitched only a

KEN HOWELL
RHP, No. 71
RR, 6'3", 200 lbs.
ML Svc: 1 year
Born: 11-28-60 in
Detroit, MI

1984 STATISTICS

W	L	ERA	G	GS	CG	IP	H	R	ER	BB	SO	SV
5	5	3.33	32	1	0	51	51	51	21	19	9	54

CAREER STATISTICS

W	L	ERA	G	GS	CG	IP	H	R	ER	BB	SO	SV
5	5	3.33	32	1	0	51	51	51	21	19	9	54

short time as a professional, Howell displays excellent poise on the mound. He was repeatedly brought into tough spots. Twice in one week he fanned the Braves' most dangerous slugger, Dale Murphy, in criticial, late-inning situations.

Campbell: "It seems that his pattern is this: when he comes out of the bullpen and there are another pitcher's runners on base, he goes right to the fastball and stays with it; when he goes out the next inning he begins to tinker with the breaking ball."

HITTING:

Ken Landreaux was a disappointment to the Dodgers in 1984 after signing a multi-year contract and coming off two strong seasons.

For someone with as quick a bat as his (Lasorda says that he has one of the best swings in baseball), his run production figures were far off expectations.

In the past, Landreaux has had most of his difficulties against lefthanded pitchers, but he had much better success against them in 1984. Landreaux likes the fastball down. Sinkerball pitchers give him fits.

BASERUNNING:

Landreaux is quick enough on the bases to be effective, but he does not make baserunning mistakes occasionally; he's run through signs and not picked up his coaches. He reads pitchers well, and he gets a good, quick jump off the base.

FIELDING:

Landreaux is not a good outfielder. He does not charge balls at all, although he does go back very well on long drives. He still plays far too tentatively, especially for a center fielder, which is one reason the Dodgers finally shifted him to right. He does not get a good jump on any ball, whether it is in front of him or over his head.

His throwing arm rates from below average to average.

KEN LANDREAUX
CF, No. 44
LR, 5'11", 185 lbs.
ML Svc: 7 years
Born: 12-22-54 in
   Los Angeles, CA

1984 STATISTICS

AVG	G	AB	R	H	2B	3B	HR	RBI	BB	SO	SB
.251	134	438	39	110	11	5	11	47	29	35	10

CAREER STATISTICS

AVG	G	AB	R	H	2B	3B	HR	RBI	BB	SO	SB
.272	899	3154	401	859	137	41	69	377	228	317	115

  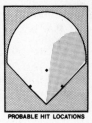

VS. RHP　　　VS. LHP　　　PROBABLE HIT LOCATIONS

OVERALL:

People look at Ken Landreaux and just marvel at his potential. That has been the case ever since he signed in the big leagues. He had two of the best overall years with the Dodgers in 1982 and 1983, but slacked off in 1984.

Campbell: "The Dodgers have got to do a lot of soul searching. They've got to make decisions on where some of their people should play, and Landreaux may be the odd man out."

HITTING:

Candy Maldonado, a righthanded-hitting outfielder, got off to a tremendous start in 1984, confirming, for a time at least, the tremendous faith shown in him by Dodger Vice President Al Campanis. He started the season in a platoon role in right field, but eventually played every outfield position as well as two games at third base.

His strength is batting against the pitch high in the strike zone. He hits lefthanded pitchers far better than he does righthanders.

He likes to shoot for the alleys and has some power, though he did not display it as much as the Dodgers had hoped he would.

Maldonado is only 24 years old and has had good numbers in the minors. 1984 was his first full season in the majors.

BASERUNNING:

Maldonado does not run well and is no threat to steal.

FIELDING:

Maldonado rates no better than average as a defensive outfielder. His forte is his throwing arm, which is very strong. Unfortunately, he often exhibits it at the wrong time and will attempt to throw out a runner at the plate in a lost cause. He also takes too much time getting rid of the ball, a source of concern to the Dodger coaching staff and a skill they have been working on with him to improve.

CANDY MALDONADO
OF, No. 20
RR, 5'11", 195 lbs.
ML Svc: 2 years
Born: 9-5-60 in
    Humacao, PR

1984 STATISTICS

AVG	G	AB	R	H	2B	3B	HR	RBI	BB	SO	SB
.268	116	254	25	68	14	0	5	28	19	29	0

CAREER STATISTICS

AVG	G	AB	R	H	2B	3B	HR	RBI	BB	SO	SB
.244	175	332	30	81	15	1	6	34	25	50	0

VS. RHP   VS. LHP   PROBABLE HIT LOCATIONS

OVERALL:

Maldonado played well enough in his in-and-out role in 1984. He was called upon to pinch-hit and did well in that role, responding with three home runs.

Candy is not yet the polished player the team believes he will be, but the Dodgers understand young players better than almost any team in baseball, and have confidence in his ability to improve.

Campbell: "I don't project Maldonado as an everyday player; perhaps his future is as a platoon player. He is a good guy to have on a club to fill that fifth outfield spot and come off the bench to pinch-hit."

HITTING:

Mike Marshall is still trying to put together his first injury-free season in the big leagues. Last season, he had an operation on his foot, then he had knee problems and, in the last two weeks of the season, he suffered a stiff neck that cut into his playing time.

When he is healthy and all is going well, Marshall has tremendous power to all fields. He is not yet a disciplined hitter; he swings at far too many bad pitches.

Marshall likes the ball out over the plate and is a high ball hitter. Pitchers should work him down and away. Those pitchers who pitch him high must also keep the ball inside because if Marshall gets a pitch out over the plate, he will jump on it.

Marshall is a streak hitter, and when he gets hot, he has the patience and maturity to suddenly stop chasing bad pitches and make contact.

Last year was only his second full season in big leagues, yet this young player has come a long way and made considerable strides from the time when he first appeared in the big leagues.

One of his problems last year was the fact that he stood alone in the lineup—the others around him were not hitting, and so, he became a more impatient hitter than he might have been.

BASERUNNING:

Though he is no basestealing threat, Marshall is aggressive on the bases and has good speed for someone who is so large (6'5", 220 lbs.).

FIELDING:

Marshall is not a good defensive player. But in his short time in the majors, he has played both left field and right field as well as at first base

MIKE MARSHALL
RF, No. 5
RR, 6'5", 220 lbs.
ML Svc: 3 years
Born: 1-12-60 in
Libertyville, IL

1984 STATISTICS

AVG	G	AB	R	H	2B	3B	HR	RBI	BB	SO	SB
.257	134	495	69	127	27	0	21	65	40	93	4

CAREER STATISTICS

AVG	G	AB	R	H	2B	3B	HR	RBI	BB	SO	SB
.266	337	1080	128	287	50	1	43	140	97	247	13

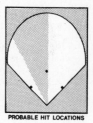

VS. RHP   VS. LHP   PROBABLE HIT LOCATIONS

(his position in the minors). His best overall position is probably first base, and in the outfield, he is a better left fielder. He does not have great range in the outfield and his throwing arm rates below average to average.

OVERALL:

Marshall is an extremely aggressive hitter who should improve as time goes along. He still stands in close to the plate, even after he was hit in the head by a pitch in 1983.

Campbell: "Even though he is a righthanded hitter, he can hit a ball to right-center field as far as any of the great lefthanded sluggers I have ever seen. When he starts to chase bad pitches, I have to believe it is because he thinks that he has to do a whole team's worth of hitting by himself."

PITCHING:

1984 was a disastrous year for Tom Niedenfuer, who is certainly one of the better pitchers in the National League when he's right. In 1983, when he had no ailments, he had the fewest-men-on-base-per-innings-pitched ratio of any pitcher in the league. Last season, however, shoulder and elbow miseries sidelined Niedenfuer several times during the year. On top of that, he suffered a painful kidney stone attack.

It is the problem with his shoulder, though, that is of the greatest concern to the Dodgers. The thought is that maybe Niedenfuer simply cannot take the wear and tear of the bullpen over the long haul of a season.

On the mound, Niedenfuer does not mess with trick pitches. His bread and butter pitch is his 93-94 MPH fastball. He also throws a hard breaking pitch, which possibly explains the arm and shoulder problems he has encountered.

He is extremely tough on righthanded batters. Niedenfuer throws a sinking fastball to lefthanded hitters.

Niedenfuer is a pitcher who has come along quickly in the majors; he actually pitched in the World Series the year he became a professional, 1981. Even now, he is only 25 years old.

FIELDING, HITTING, BASERUNNING:

For his large size (6'5", 225 lbs.), Niedenfuer handles himself well defen-

TOM NIEDENFUER
RHP, No. 49
RR, 6'5", 225 lbs.
ML Svc: 3 years
Born: 8-13-59 in
  St. Louis Park, MN

1984 STATISTICS												
W	L	ERA	G	GS	CG	IP	H	R	ER	BB	SO	SV
2	5	2.47	33	0	0	47	39	14	13	23	45	

CAREER STATISTICS												
W	L	ERA	G	GS	CG	IP	H	R	ER	BB	SO	SV
16	13	2.47	171	0	0	237	190	69	65	83	183	22

sively. His move to first rates as average; he can be run on. Like most short relievers, he rarely gets the opportunity to hit or run the bases.

OVERALL:

Niedenfuer has displayed excellent competitiveness in his short time in the majors. He has adapted well mentally to the rigors of short relief work. The only question is a physical one.

Campbell: "He knows how to pitch in tough situations. He became the Dodgers' bullpen ace very quickly, but there must be concern about the shoulder and elbow problems. The key to 1985 is going to be his health. The Dodgers are going to have to inject more depth into the bullpen to take some of the heat off Tom."

PITCHING:

Alejandro Pena, only 25 years old and already with two full seasons and parts of two others behind him in the major leagues, has blossomed into one of the National League's leading pitchers.

He has an extremely easy three-quarters to overhand motion. He pops the fastball at 95 MPH and has good location. Pena throws a slider as well, but his No. 1 pitch is his fastball.

Arm problems caused him to miss a couple of turns in the rotation in the second half of the 1984 season. Earlier in his career, he had to overcome an ulcer, and later, a migraine condition.

Each year he becomes more accustomed to pitching in the majors. When the Dodgers originally signed him out of his home in the Dominican Republic, he was only 19.

FIELDING, HITTING, BASERUNNING:

Pena is not afraid to throw to first base, and throws there often. His move is not especially good, but he is quick and not easy to run on. He is a decent fielder.

Pena is not impressive as a hitter, although he never gets cheated with the bat. He likes to go to the plate swinging.

ALEJANDRO PENA
RHP, No. 26
RR, 6'1", 190 lbs.
ML Svc: 3 years
Born: 6-25-59 in
  Cambiaso, DR

1984 STATISTICS

W	L	ERA	G	GS	CG	IP	H	R	ER	BB	SO	SV
12	6	2.48	28	28	8	199	186	67	55	46		13

CAREER STATISTICS

W	L	ERA	G	GS	CG	IP	H	R	ER	BB	SO	SV
25	18	2.81	105	54	12	436	393	166	136	129	167	3

OVERALL:

Pena is an intelligent young man who has come up quickly into the ranks of the top pitchers in baseball. He has both the stuff and the composure to be a big success in the majors for a long time.

Campbell: "I consider Alejandro to be one of the premier pitchers in the National League. His fastball is definitely his out pitch. As opposed to so many pitchers whose demeanor is often macho, show-offish and feisty, Pena is the complete opposite. He is very stoic on the mound, very professional, very poised. He just takes things as they come along."

PITCHING:

Lefthander Jerry Reuss had arthroscopic surgery on his left elbow in January of 1984, and it affected him throughout the year. He had pitched only 35 innings by June, and he didn't hurl his first complete game until September 8. He pitched another complete game two weeks later against the Astros, after which he pronounced himself "100%."

While Reuss was working his arm back into shape, he was throwing a fastball that had lost much of its pop. When his fastball is right, it is a very heavy sinker, and is clocked at 92-93 MPH. At no time during the 1984 season was that in evidence.

In the past, Reuss has been criticized for throwing too many breaking pitches and not relying enough on his fastball, but last year he did not have much of a fastball.

Reuss's curveball was also less effective in 1984, in part because the hitters knew that they did not have to sit on his fastball as they did in previous seasons.

FIELDING, HITTING, BASERUNNING:

Reuss has been around long enough to know how to field his position. He has

JERRY REUSS
LHP, No. 41
LL, 6'5", 225 lbs.
ML Svc: 14 years
Born: 6-19-49 in
St. Louis, MO

1984 STATISTICS

W	L	ERA	G	GS	CG	IP	H	R	ER	BB	SO	SV
5	7	3.82	30	15	2	99	102	51	42	31	44	1

CAREER STATISTICS

W	L	ERA	G	GS	CG	IP	H	R	ER	BB	SO	SV
178	147	3.48	484	422	118	2932	2900	1303	1134	943	1631	10

a good move to first. He is not a great hitter by any means, but he generally makes contact. In 1983 he hit .282.

OVERALL:

Off the field, Reuss is one of baseball's better practical jokers; he keeps the clubhouse good and loose. He needed to have a sense of humor in 1984, when he was not able to contribute as he had in the past because of his elbow problems. He was not at all happy working out of the bullpen.

Campbell: "The 1985 season will be the make-or-break year for Jerry Reuss."

HITTING:

Robert James "R.J." Reynolds displayed considerable dash and excitement last season, his first taste of the big leagues. After a late-season promotion from Double A ball, the Dodgers felt that without a doubt he was ready to stay. But R.J. was soon returned to the minors after some disappointments both at the plate and in the field.

Reynolds is a switch-hitter. He has decent power when he can get around on the ball, but not getting around on the ball was one of his problems. Pitchers consistently whipped the ball past him. He appeared to have better bat speed when he first came to the Dodgers in 1983 than at any time in 1984.

BASERUNNING:

Reynolds has excellent speed--he stole 43 bases in Double A in 1983--and he gets a decent enough jump off first base. He slides hard into second base on double plays, and he will take the extra base.

FIELDING:

Reynolds has the speed to go get a ball. He has a decent throwing arm, one that is slightly better than the major league average. He is, however, not a good outfielder as yet. One reason is that he played all three outfield positions in 1984, and he did not have enough playing time at any one of them to either perfect his skills or to win a permanent job.

R.J. REYNOLDS
OF, No. 23
SR, 6'0", 190 lbs.
ML Svc: 1 year plus
Born: 4-19-60 in
　　Sacramento, CA

1984 STATISTICS

AVG	G	AB	R	H	2B	3B	HR	RBI	BB	SO	SB
.258	73	240	23	62	12	2	2	24	14	38	7

CAREER STATISTICS

AVG	G	AB	R	H	2B	3B	HR	RBI	BB	SO	SB
.254	97	295	28	75	12	2	4	35	17	49	12

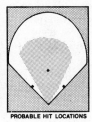

VS. RHP　　　VS. LHP　　　PROBABLE HIT LOCATIONS

OVERALL:

Reynolds made an impact when he came to the big leagues at the tail end of the 1983 season, but he was not as impressive in any area when he was called up early in the 1984 season.

Campbell: "The longer he played, the more deficiencies he showed. He needs another year in Triple A . . . another SOLID year in Triple A."

HITTING:

German Rivera, a rookie in 1984, is a high ball hitter: it did not take long for rival pitchers to learn to throw him something other than a high fastball.

He likes the ball out over the plate. Rivera has some power to the alleys but is more of a singles and doubles type of hitter. He is definitely not a home run hitter.

A pitcher who keeps the ball down and in will be effective against Rivera. He is not a good breaking ball hitter, and is especially vulnerable to the off-speed pitch. Rivera has a quick bat and he will jump on a pitcher's mistake, and can hammer a hanging breaking pitch.

BASERUNNING:

Rivera is not much of a threat to steal bases even though he does run fairly well.

FIELDING:

Rivera has an extremely strong throwing arm and he has better than average range at third base. He turned in some splendid plays, diving to his left or his right, but he also made a number of errors on routine plays.

OVERALL:

Rivera got into some hot water during

GERMAN RIVERA
3B, No. 25
RR, 6'2", 190 lbs.
ML Svc: 1 year plus
Born: 7-6-60 in
  Carolina, PR

1984 STATISTICS

AVG	G	AB	R	H	2B	3B	HR	RBI	BB	SO	SB
.260	94	227	20	59	12	2	2	17	21	30	1

CAREER STATISTICS

AVG	G	AB	R	H	2B	3B	HR	RBI	BB	SO	SB
.266	107	244	21	65	13	2	2	17	23	32	1

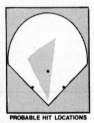

VS. RHP   VS. LHP   PROBABLE HIT LOCATIONS

the season because of what management described as "hot dogging," possibly a result of his rash of errors on routine plays. He was the Dodgers' opening day third baseman but failed in numerous clutch opportunities to drive in runs.

Campbell: "He has to learn the strike zone better before he can become a consistently strong hitter."

HITTING:

Billy Russell, a 36-year-old veteran, still makes good contact with the ball, he still handles the bat extremely well, he hits behind runners, he can bunt and he can hit-and-run.

Russell likes the ball up in the strike zone and will spray the ball to all fields.

He is not a power hitter, and he is not a big RBI man, but he is extremely valuable as a clutch hitter--and every team needs at least one. He may not drive in a lot of runs, but the ones Russell gets are the big ones.

BASERUNNING:

Although he was once considered an outstanding runner, wear and tear and increasing age, have no doubt taken their toll. Nonetheless, Russell does not make mistakes on the bases. In situations where a stolen base is necessary, Russell can still move down the line.

FIELDING:

Russell has probably played his best shortstop in the latter years of his career. He has gradually turned over his position to youngster Dave Anderson. In fact, Russell was used some in center field, his original big league position, and at second base, the spot he played earlier in his career.

He made a remarkable adjustment after the index finger on his throwing hand was shattered by a pitch in 1980. His future would appear to be as an all-purpose player.

BILL RUSSELL
SS, No. 18
RR, 6'0", 180 lbs.
ML Svc: 15 years
Born: 10-21-48 in
   Pittsburgh, KS

1984 STATISTICS

AVG	G	AB	R	H	2B	3B	HR	RBI	BB	SO	SB
.267	89	262	25	70	12	1	0	19	25	24	4

CAREER STATISTICS

AVG	G	AB	R	H	2B	3B	HR	RBI	BB	SO	SB
.264	2000	6933	756	1828	276	56	46	596	450	635	154

  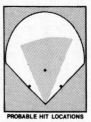

VS. RHP   VS. LHP   PROBABLE HIT LOCATIONS

OVERALL:

Russell is still a valuable asset for any club, because he is intelligent at the plate and in the field, as well as being an unassuming leader in the clubhouse.

Campbell: "Because of the unsettling nature of the Dodgers, with all of their young players, it would behoove them to keep Billy Russell around for quite a while. He is a pro's pro, and provides much-needed stabilization in the clubhouse."

HITTING:

Steve Sax's numbers fell off drastically in 1984. A .280-plus hitter in his first two years in Los Angeles, he was struggling late last season to reach the .240's. He was disappointing as a lead-off hitter, too, since he had difficulty getting on base.

His problem was one of impatience. So often, Sax would have a tendency to swing at the first pitch. When Steve is hitting well, he drives the ball through the middle and can hit line drives to right-center, but last season he tried to pull the ball.

He seldom bunts, which is too bad, because he has the ability to bunt and he runs well. Sax is a high ball hitter; he stands close to the plate and chokes up slightly.

A pitcher should work Sax down and in. He is aggressive at the plate, but sometimes his own aggressiveness works against him; he will forget to be patient at the plate. Instead of trying to work a pitcher for a base on balls, he will go to the plate swinging. That is not the best thing for a leadoff man to do.

BASERUNNING:

Sax is by far the Dodgers' best base-stealing threat, but he is also the club leader in getting caught, and by a quite a good margin. Last season, he was thrown out roughly once in every three attempts.

He gets his stolen bases when he gets a good jump, so it is a matter of learning the pitchers' moves.

FIELDING:

As long as he plays the game, Sax will be hounded by the horrors of the 1983 season, when he simply could not make the relatively easy throw to first base.

The problem was well-publicized. It was surely a mental problem (throws to

STEVE SAX
2B, No. 3
RR, 5'11", 175 lbs.
ML Svc: 3 years
Born: 1-29-60 in
Sacramento, CA

```
1984 STATISTICS
AVG   G   AB    R   H   2B  3B  HR  RBI  BB   SO   SB
.243 145  569   70  138  24   4   1   35   47   53   34
CAREER STATISTICS
AVG   G   AB    R   H   2B  3B  HR  RBI  BB   SO   SB
.270 481 1949  267 526  67  16  12  132  161  193  144
```

STRONG — VS. RHP | STRONG — VS. LHP | PROBABLE HIT LOCATIONS

first for a major leaguer are not physically difficult). As mysteriously as his throwing problem appeared, it went away: Sax started the 1984 season with 38 consecutive errorless games. Then, the bugaboo struck again, although this time Sax quickly harnessed it.

Sax has decent range, and while he has problems turning the double play at times, he is improving.

OVERALL:

Sax was a good offensive player his first two-plus years with Los Angeles but was among those who fell off sharply in 1984. Even though he was the National League Rookie of the Year in 1982, he rates only so-so, overall, on defense.

Campbell: "He had a very disappointing season, although late in the year it appeared Sax had solved that nagging throwing problem. He is still very unpredictable at second base. He will make the spectacular play but has trouble with the little ones."

HITTING:

Mike Scioscia has made tremendous strides to improve as a hitter. After hitting .276 in his first full season in the major leagues (1981), he dropped off dramatically in 1982, to .219, and questions were raised about his future in Los Angeles. He was injured for all but a few weeks in 1983, but he came back very strong in 1984.

Scioscia is a lefthanded batter and likes the fastball out over the plate. His stance is closed and he appears to be very relaxed at the plate. Mike does not have too much power; one of the reasons for his sharp dropoff in 1982 was the team's decision to make him a power hitter, a plan that was later abandoned.

Scioscia will drive the ball to the alleys, and he will also hit an occasional home run. He sprays the ball fairly well, and is aggressive at the plate.

He must be pitched inside with a breaking ball.

BASERUNNING:

No threat to steal, period. Scioscia is, however, very aggressive on the bases. He slides hard and is the best on the Dodger club at breaking up a double play.

FIELDING:

Scioscia was lost almost the entire 1983 season because of a shoulder injury he suffered while throwing out a runner. After a year of therapy, he came back strong, showing no hint of the malady.

MIKE SCIOSCIA
C, No. 14
LR, 6'2", 220 lbs.
ML Svc: 4 years
Born: 11-27-58 in
Upper Darby, PA

1984 STATISTICS

AVG	G	AB	R	H	2B	3B	HR	RBI	BB	SO	SB
.273	114	341	29	93	18	0	5	38	52	26	2

CAREER STATISTICS

AVG	G	AB	R	H	2B	3B	HR	RBI	BB	SO	SB
.256	402	1165	98	298	47	2	14	120	149	86	5

VS. RHP   VS. LHP   PROBABLE HIT LOCATIONS

He had particularly good success early in the year throwing out runners. He is improving with his ability to call a game behind the plate. Mike has no peer when it comes to blocking off the plate. He is fearless.

OVERALL:

Scioscia's return was most welcome, both for the Dodgers and Mike himself. His career was in jeopardy. He makes good contact as a hitter. Behind the plate, he displayed no sign of his 1983 problems.

Campbell: "Mike Scioscia is the best plate blocker I have ever seen."

PITCHING:

Fernando Valenzuela once again displayed his durability and his effectiveness by ranking among the National League leaders in innings pitched, complete games, strikeouts and ERA.

Valenzuela's won-loss record in 1984 is misleading because of the lack of offensive support he received. In a few games, he had to supply his own game-winning RBI, including one of his three home runs.

Lefthander Valenzuela is considered both a power and a control type pitcher. He can beat a club so many ways, and he just turned 24 years old last season. He conducts himself on the mound more like a 35-year-old veteran.

He throws a fastball, slider, curveball, and, his money pitch, the screwball. In fact, he throws two types of screwballs, a hard one and a change-up.

Fernando gets the majority of his strikeouts on the fastball, but it is the screwball that sets it up so beautifully.

FIELDING, HITTING, BASERUNNING:

Valenzuela has an excellent move to first base. He picked off Montreal speedster Tim Raines three times last season.

He is also an excellent fielder and notoriously dangerous at the plate. He

FERNANDO VALENZUELA
LHP, No. 34
LL, 5'11", 200 lbs.
ML Svc: 4 years
Born: 11-1-60 in
    Navajoa, Sonora, MEX

1984 STATISTICS

W	L	ERA	G	GS	CG	IP	H	R	ER	BB	SO	SV
12	17	3.03	34	34	12	261	218	109	88	106	24	0

CAREER STATISTICS

W	L	ERA	G	GS	CG	IP	H	R	ER	BB	SO	SV
61	47	3.01	141	131	50	1013	858	393	339	354	608	1

will not hit for a high average, but he is strong and makes contact. He will come through each season with more than a pitcher's share of home runs.

OVERALL:

Valenzuela is a total professional. When he keeps the ball down, he is virtually unhittable. When he has his pitches in good spots, it is very difficult to beat him.

Campbell: "He may have had a losing record last season, but I think that if the Dodgers ever wanted to trade him, every team in the majors would beat a path to their door."

PITCHING:

Righthander Bob Welch did not have a vintage year in 1984. He gave up more hits than innings pitched. He was also plagued on and off by arm injuries, forcing him to miss some turns in the starting rotation in the second half of the season.

Welch is still a challenge type of pitcher. He comes at the batter from over the top with a riding fastball. He has improved his breaking pitch considerably and he has also added a change.

When his fastball is humming, he will be in the 88-92 MPH range. Occasionally, he will intimidate hitters. He likes to get ahead in the count and make a hitter chase after a bad pitch.

Welch does not feel that his shoulder problem is anything serious, but it did cause him considerable pain at times.

FIELDING, HITTING, BASERUNNING:

He has a very quick move to first base. He has several "trick moves," and will use several different set positions. He is adept at keeping runners close to the bag at first.

Welch fields his position well, and is very average as a hitting pitcher.

BOB WELCH
RHP, No. 35
RR, 6'3", 190 lbs.
ML Svc: 6 years
Born: 11-3-56 in Detroit, MI

1984 STATISTICS

W	L	ERA	G	GS	CG	IP	H	R	ER	BB	SO	SV
13	13	3.78	31	29	3	178	191	86	75	58	12	0

CAREER STATISTICS

W	L	ERA	G	GS	CG	IP	H	R	ER	BB	SO	SV
79	60	3.22	201	176	26	1164	1059	464	416	389	703	8

OVERALL:

The last two seasons might label Bob as a "tough luck" pitcher. He has been hampered by a lack of offense and he has had occasional injury problems. In 1984, he was sent for a brief time to the bullpen and then came back strong before being sidelined with a shoulder problem.

Campbell: "Bob Welch is another LA pitcher who, I think, will have a big year in 1985. Two years ago, he was the Dodgers' most effective pitcher and one of the best pitchers in the National League."

HITTING:

Steve Yeager was used strictly as a platoon catcher in 1984, starting only against lefthanded pitchers. He is the kind of batter who, if a pitcher makes a mistake, will hit the ball a long way.

He is very strong and has the power to drive the ball. The catch is, however, actually hitting it. If a pitcher keeps the ball down, and keeps tossing breaking pitches, Yeager is going to have his troubles. But get the ball up-- look out!

BASERUNNING:

Like most catchers, especially those who are 36 years old, Yeager does not run well. He is aggressive on the bases and slides hard into second base on double plays, but he is no threat to steal.

FIELDING:

Yeager still rates as one of the finest defensive catchers around. He works well with the pitchers, urging them on, and he calls an intelligent game.

He has a strong, accurate throwing arm and he is active with it, whipping the ball to any base at any time. He still holds his own blocking the plate, but it cost him in 1984; he required knee surgery after breaking a leg in a home plate collision late in the season.

STEVE YEAGER
C, No. 7
RR, 6'0", 205 lbs.
ML Svc: 12 years
Born: 11-24-48 in
Huntington, WV

1984 STATISTICS

AVG	G	AB	R	H	2B	3B	HR	RBI	BB	SO	SB
.228	74	197	16	45	4	0	4	29	20	38	1

CAREER STATISTICS

AVG	G	AB	R	H	2B	3B	HR	RBI	BB	SO	SB
.229	1166	3333	343	764	112	15	100	389	323	679	14

VS. RHP

VS. LHP

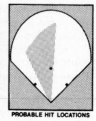

PROBABLE HIT LOCATIONS

OVERALL:

Yeager is one of the few remaining members of the so-called "Old Blue" among the Dodgers. He is one of the team's leaders. Steve has a year remaining on his contract, but at 36 and coming off knee surgery, how much he will contribute in 1985 is questionable.

Campbell: "He is still an asset behind the plate. Once one of the best in the game, he has come down some but only because of age. He is not quite the bulldog at the plate he used to be."

PITCHING:

Righthanded reliever Pat Zachry was one of the Los Angeles Dodgers' most versatile pitchers in 1984. He started the season as the club's middle reliever, then, because of numerous injuries, was moved into the short relief role.

Zachry, a nine-year veteran, has enough pitching savvy and know-how to pitch in almost any situation. He does not scare. He has an elastic arm and is able to come back frequently.

He was a starting pitcher for his first seven years in the majors, first with Cincinnati and then with the New York Mets. In 1982 at New York, he split his time between starting and the bullpen. In 1983, his first year in Los Angeles, he was used exclusively in relief, except for one emergency start.

One of Zachry's most effective weapons is his herky-jerky motion, making it difficult for hitters to pick up the ball. He throws a hard sinker, a slider and a good off-speed breaking pitch. He moves the ball around in the strike zone, but he's most effective when he keeps the ball down.

FIELDING, HITTING, BASERUNNING:

His move to first base is nothing special, although he does field his position well for someone as tall and

PAT ZACHRY
RHP, No. 38
RR, 6'5", 175 lbs.
ML Svc: 9 years
Born: 4-24-52 in
Richmond, TX

1984 STATISTICS

W	L	ERA	G	GS	CG	IP	H	R	ER	BB	SO	SV
5	6	3.81	58	0	0	82	84	38	35	51	55	2

CAREER STATISTICS

W	L	ERA	G	GS	CG	IP	H	R	ER	BB	SO	SV
69	67	3.52	283	154	29	1165	1133	522	455	484	661	3

lanky as he is.

As a hitter, he strikes little fear into the opposing pitcher.

OVERALL:

Zachry has the experience and the know-how to keep him afloat in the big leagues. He has been an extremely welcome additon to the Dodgers because of all their injury problems.

Campbell: "Zachry is a valuable man to have as a middle reliever. I don't think he can be terribly effective as a starter or a short reliever."

SID BREAM
1B, No. 33
LL, 6'4", 215 lbs.
ML Svc: 1 year plus
Born: 8-3-60 in
Carlisle, PA

HITTING, BASERUNNING, FIELDING:

Like so many of the young Dodgers, Sid Bream had excellent minor league seasons and now is looking to make it in the majors. One problem he faces is that he is a first baseman and, in terms of manpower at least, the Dodgers have no shortage of first basemen. They simply haven't decided which one will win the spot.

Bream, 24, is a tall lefthanded hitter. He showed some power in the minors but not in his two brief appearances in the majors. He is a line drive hitter who likes the ball up in the strike zone.

Of the Dodgers' three young first basemen (Stubbs and Brock are the other two), Sid Bream is the best defensively. He is aggressive at first base, always thinking to get the lead runner. He was selected as the Pacific Coast League's All Star first baseman.

OVERALL:

Bream appears to be ready to challenge for a big league job. The question now is, "where?"

RAFAEL LANDESTOY
INF, No. 17
SR, 5'9", 168 lbs.
ML Svc: 8 years
Born: 5-28-53 in
Bani, DR

HITTING, BASERUNNING, FIELDING:

Rafael Landestoy is an extremely valuable player for any team. He's highly versatile as a backup infielder, able to play second base, third base or shortstop.

If he could hit at all, he would be a prize for any major league club. But since hitting .266 and .270 in back-to-back seasons with Houston in the 1970s, Landestoy has struggled. He is a switch-hitter, and when he's playing somewhat regularly, he will make contact. With Los Angeles, he was used as an early-inning pinch-hitter.

OVERALL:

Because of his versatility (he can play the outfield, too), Landestoy is a valuable player. He works as hard as anyone but needs to hit better to become something else besides a defensive replacement.

FRANKLIN STUBBS
INF, No. 80
LL, 6'2", 215 lbs.
ML Svc: 1 year
Born: 10-21-60 in
    Laurinburg, NC

HITTING, BASERUNNING, FIELDING:

When Franklin Stubbs was rushed to the majors at mid-season as an emergency fill-in for the Dodgers' injured players, he exhibited some outstanding tools. His bat was quick and he played aggressively at first base.

But pitchers quickly learned his deficiencies--he is particularly vulnerable to the off-speed pitch--and he had his troubles, striking out almost once in every three at-bats.

It was the crush of injuries to the regular players that caused the Dodgers to advance Stubbs so rapidly; he should have remained in the minors. He was the Dodgers' No. 1 selection in the June 1982 draft, giving him only two full years of professional experience, and he spent most of the second one (1984) on the bench.

OVERALL:

Stubbs remains an excellent prospect. He is a natural first baseman but played the outfield in the minors before coming to Los Angeles.

Campbell: "He was force-fed because of all the Dodgers' injuries. He is not yet ready to play at the major league level, but I suspect that someday he is going to be an excellent major league hitter."

TERRY WHITFIELD
OF, No. 45
LR, 6'1", 200 lbs.
ML Svc: 5 years
Born: 1-12-53 in
    Blythe, CA

HITTING, BASERUNNING, FIELDING:

Terry Whitfield, who played the previous three seasons in Japan, looked to be quite a find for Los Angeles when the 1984 season started. Whitfield, a left-handed batter, started the season well, platooning in right field. But as the pitchers got sharper, Whitfield fell off sharply.

Whitfield likes fastballs belt high and out over the plate, but his bat has slowed down noticeably since his earlier days in the National League.

OVERALL:

Whitfield had a thumb injury that put him on the disabled list for a time. After a decent start, he simply did not provide what the Dodgers had hoped he would when they signed him to a three-year contract.

Campbell: "Terry Whitfield is probably one of the best hustlers in the game of baseball, but his skills have slowed down somewhat since the last time we saw him in the National League."

MONTREAL EXPOS

HITTING:

The fans in Montreal were down on Gary Carter when the 1984 season opened. By the time it ended, however, Carter surely had gotten them back on his side. He enjoyed one of the finer offensive seasons of his already illustrious career, rebounding from what was, for him, amildly disappointing 1983 season.

Carter changed his batting stance slightly in 1984. He began to stand more open at the plate, with his back foot fairly close to the plate and his front side open. Importantly, Carter continued to turn his front shoulder in toward the pitcher when the ball was released, so he still had a squared swing by the time the ball and bat would come through the strike zone.

Carter is a classic middle-of-the-order hitter, a clutch hitter and a run producer with home run power. He is a high ball hitter who, given his choice, likes the ball out over the plate. He loves to pull the ball to the left-center alley, but more and more he will rattle a double to right-center. Carter also has mastered the art of hitting the opposite way to advance a runner. All in all, he is a complete hitter.

The best chance of getting him out is by throwing him fastballs up and in, then getting him to chase a breaking ball down. And by all means, stay ahead in the count. Carter is an even more aggressive hitter when he's ahead.

BASERUNNING:

Carter did not have blazing natural speed to begin with, and he has been slowed more by years behind the plate. But he is aggressive and intelligent on the bases. He slides hard and loves to break up double plays.

FIELDING:

If he is not the best defensive catcher in baseball, he's close enough

GARY CARTER
C, No. 8
RR, 6'2", 215 lbs.
ML Svc: 10 years
Born: 4-8-54 in
  Culver City, CA

1984 STATISTICS

AVG	G	AB	R	H	2B	3B	HR	RBI	BB	SO	SB
.294	159	596	75	175	32	1	27	106	64	57	2

CAREER STATISTICS

AVG	G	AB	R	H	2B	3B	HR	RBI	BB	SO	SB
.272	1408	5018	683	1365	256	23	215	794	549	656	34

STRONG
VS. RHP

STRONG
VS. LHP

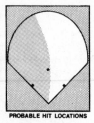
PROBABLE HIT LOCATIONS

that there's no point in quibbling. Carter has three attributes that make him a great defensive catcher--quickness, a strong throwing arm and brains. He has an excellent rapport with the Montreal pitching staff.

He has an extremely rapid release and a powerful, accurate throwing arm. He blocks the plate with determination and abandon. He plays balls in front of the plate well. He blocks all but the wildest of wild pitches. He runs down as many pop flies as any catcher. And he is a superb and intelligent caller.

OVERALL:

Campbell: "Sometimes you can see just traces of mustard; he can be a little bit of a hot dog at times. But he is a guy who enjoys playing baseball and happens to be very good at it . . . among the best in the National League. There really are no negatives about him."

HITTING:

Just when Andre Dawson's 1984 season appeared to be a complete wipeout, just when the Expos were pondering whether he should call it a year because of his arthritic knees, Dawson turned everything around. He was woefully ineffective at the plate during the first half of the season, hitting in the low .200s, but he resembled the Dawson of old in the second half, moving his overall numbers in the general direction of respectability.

He is a very aggressive hitter who is murder on pitches that are out over the plate and around the belt or higher. His only weakness as a hitter is his tendency to chase pitches out of the strike zone. He rarely walks, goes after a lot of high, inside pitches and will chase almost anything when he has two strikes on him. But on the other hand, it should be noted that Dawson often hits those stray pitches.

He has one of the quickest bats in the game. He really hacks at the ball, waiting a long time and then taking a vicious swing. This makes him a very good hitter against the breaking ball. He is a pull hitter for the most part and is never cheated at the plate, to say the least.

He hits for both power and average and is a solid run producer. Unless he's in a slump or injured, Dawson is one of the most dangerous hitters in the game.

BASERUNNING:

The bad knees have reduced Dawson's speed on the bases, but they have not had a discernible effect on his aggressiveness. He remains capable of stealing a base when his club urgently needs it. He is an intelligent baserunner who knows what to do and when to do it.

FIELDING:

As a concession to his knees, the Expos moved Dawson from center field to right field last season. The move isn't

ANDRE DAWSON
CF, No. 10
RR, 6'3", 192 lbs.
ML Svc: 8 years
Born: 7-10-54 in
Miami, FL

1984 STATISTICS

AVG	G	AB	R	H	2B	3B	HR	RBI	BB	SO	SB
.248	138	533	73	132	23	6	17	86	41	80	13

CAREER STATISTICS

AVG	G	AB	R	H	2B	3B	HR	RBI	BB	SO	SB
.282	1174	4603	698	1299	236	63	182	669	288	725	222

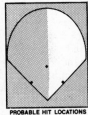

STRONG   STRONG   PROBABLE HIT LOCATIONS
VS. RHP   VS. LHP

necessarily permanent, but Dawson has all the attributes of an outstanding right fielder: a rifle for an arm, a quick release, adequate speed and excellent judgment on fly balls.

The move from center to right took some pressure off his knees, but having to play 120 games a year on artificial turf remains a very real problem. In center field, he had established himself as the leader of Montreal's outfield and as one of the best in the game at his position.

OVERALL:

All the questions about Dawson are related to his health. On his side are an enormous amount of natural ability and a truly outstanding attitude.

Campbell: "You would have to say that Dawson is in a decline in his career now from the standpoint of injuries. Whether or not they can be corrected, I don't know. But the second half of last season, he really seemed to get a second wind from somewhere."

HITTING:

Miguel Dilone's greatest asset as a hitter is his speed. Utilized last season as a reserve outfielder, pinch-hitter and pinch-runner, Dilone is a streak hitter who can go on tears when his confidence level is high.

He is a switch-hitter, more of a chopper than a hitter. He likes to take his cracks at the ball, thinking more in terms of putting it into play somewhere than in terms of driving it. His fundamental approach to hitting is to get the bat on the ball, put the ball on the ground and run, run, run.

He does not have much power; he rarely pulls the ball, generally hitting to the right side when batting righthanded and to the left side when batting lefthanded. The best way to pitch him, particularly when he is batting lefthanded, is to throw him a lot of slow stuff and try to force him to pull the ball. The worst way to pitch him is with fastballs out over the plate. He will chop down on them and many times beat them out or get them through a hole in the infield.

BASERUNNING:

More than hitting or defense, baserunning makes Dilone a major league player. He could be an asset to a team purely as a pinch-runner, although the Expos also utilize him as a pinch-hitter and reserve outfielder. His basestealing percentage (93%) was the best in the league last year. In 29 attempts, he was caught twice.

His greatest asset on the bases is his raw speed. But he also has great acceleration, both from home to first as a hitter and from first to second as a basestealer. Dilone is almost certain to go from first to third on a single to right. In addition to good speed and acceleration, he rounds out his value as a baserunner with good judgment and sound instincts.

MIGUEL DILONE
OF, No. 18
SR, 5'11", 160 lbs.
ML Svc: 8 years
Born: 11-1-54 in
Santiago, DR

1984 STATISTICS

AVG	G	AB	R	H	2B	3B	HR	RBI	BB	SO	SB
.278	88	169	28	47	8	2	1	10	17	18	27

CAREER STATISTICS

AVG	G	AB	R	H	2B	3B	HR	RBI	BB	SO	SB
.269	722	1871	296	504	67	22	6	122	133	177	250

VS. RHP   VS. LHP   PROBABLE HIT LOCATIONS

FIELDING:

He can be erratic in the field; this, along with some holes in his swing, represents his shortcomings. But his speed helps him immeasurably in the field, allowing him to compensate for some errors in judgment and/or lapses in concentration. He has only an average arm; all in all, he could be a creditable performer in left field.

OVERALL:

He has had his bright moments and his dark ones as a player, but he seemed to find a niche for himself in Montreal last season. He is not an everyday player, a fact he has had difficulty grasping, but he has the tools to help a team. Once he loses a couple of steps, though, he's finished.

Campbell: "To sum him up, he just chops at the ball and runs like the dickens."

HITTING:

Dan Driessen is the man who replaced Tony Perez in Cincinnati and years later, Pete Rose in Montreal. As a hitter, he has never quite exploded into the stardom once forecast for him, but he is a solid, dependable hitter.

He has, however, lost a little something at the plate in the last couple of years. He still is not the first guy you'd want to face in the clutch, but he does not drive in as many runs as he once did.

Driessen likes the ball up and out over the plate and has a very quick bat. If he is in a good groove, he is very tough for a pitcher to get inside on. The most effective means of pitching to him is keeping the ball down. Lefties can throw him the slider down and away; righties can throw him the fastball down and away. But he is a thinker as a hitter, and pitchers cannot be too predictable in facing him. If he knows that a pitcher is throwing him exclusively away, he will spray the ball to the opposite field.

BASERUNNING:

When Driessen first came into the league, he had exceptional speed and was capable of stealing 25-30 bases. But he has lost a couple of steps and now has only average speed on the bases.

Against a sleeping pitcher or weak-armed catcher, Dan will still swipe an occasional base. He is not overly aggressive on the bases.

FIELDING:

A lefthanded hitter, Driessen plays first base righthanded. A righthanded first base never looks as graceful as a lefthander but Dan gets the job done.

Driessen plays his position without flash. He still has better than average

DAN DRIESSEN
1B, No. 22
LR, 5'11", 190 lbs.
ML Svc: 12 years
Born: 7-29-51 in
  Hilton Head, SC

1984 STATISTICS

AVG	G	AB	R	H	2B	3B	HR	RBI	BB	SO	SB
.269	132	387	47	104	24	0	16	60	54	40	2

CAREER STATISTICS

AVG	G	AB	R	H	2B	3B	HR	RBI	BB	SO	SB
.270	1531	4886	681	1320	251	23	142	702	695	654	152

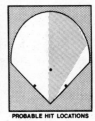

VS. RHP VS. LHP PROBABLE HIT LOCATIONS

range, a good arm, good hands and a good ability to handle high and low throws.

OVERALL:

The Expos have made a commitment to Driessen as their first baseman, and it will be interesting to watch in 1985 whether he responds to their show of confidence. He had some unhappy times in Cincinnati as the team declined and was frequently mentioned in trade rumors before finally going to Montreal.

For the first time in several years, he has a sense of stability; that could help him.

Campbell: "He is not the offensive force he was in the past. His average may be the same, but he's not quite as dangerous from a power or RBI standpoint, but he will still produce."

HITTING:

Doug Flynn has not made his mark as a big league player on the strength of his bat--his bat is not a strength at all. In fact, if you keep the ball down on him, you should get him out all day or all night long. He hits mistakes, not good pitches.

If Flynn gets a fastball up in the strike zone, he likes to spray it to the right side. Occasionally, very occasionally, he goes on a streak where he will pull the ball with surprising authority, but then he will revert to his more recognizable state.

Defenses generally play him to right, so he often gets extra bases when he pulls the ball.

He has the most trouble with low inside fastballs and with most good breaking pitches. He'll hit bad breaking pitches to left field. Flynn is a better than average bunter, but he does not have good bat control when it comes to the hit-and-run. He is not a good clutch hitter, and he does not have a good eye at the plate. Defenses should play him toward the lines and shallow.

BASERUNNING:

He is intelligent on the bases, but not much more than that. He has only average speed and moderate aggressiveness on the bases. He is not a threat to steal.

FIELDING:

His glove has given him a substantial big league career. Doug can play second base and shortstop, although second base is his natural position.

He is a very steady defensive player, not flashy, but steady. He does not have extraordinary range, but he plays hitters extremely well and has very good hands. He has a way of being in the right place at the right time, and he

DOUG FLYNN
2B, No. 23
RR, 5'11", 165 lbs
ML Svc: 10 years
Born: 4-18-51 in
Lexington, KY

1984 STATISTICS

AVG	G	AB	R	H	2B	3B	HR	RBI	BB	SO	SB
.243	124	366	23	89	12	1	0	17	12	41	0

CAREER STATISTICS

AVG	G	AB	R	H	2B	3B	HR	RBI	BB	SO	SB
.238	1267	3796	286	904	113	38	7	282	151	318	20

  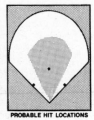

STRONG   STRONG

VS. RHP   VS. LHP   PROBABLE HIT LOCATIONS

knows what to do with the ball once he has it.

He has an accurate throwing arm and a quick release. As a second baseman, he turns the double play as well as anyone in the league.

OVERALL:

Had Doug Flynn been able to hit and run the bases a notch or two better than he has shown, he might have had a 15-year career as a starting middle infielder in the major leagues instead of a utility player. But as long as he can field, throw the ball and turn the double play, a team will find a spot for him, if only as a utility infielder. He also is a good influence on a club.

Campbell: "I've always felt his best position is second base because he turns the double play so well--in my opinion, as well as anybody in the NL. Doug's best asset now is his versatilility."

HITTING:

Terry Francona is a hitter, pure and simple. In that respect, he is reminiscent of his father, former big leaguer Tito Francona.

A lefthanded hitter, Terry got off to a strong start last season, battling San Diego's Tony Gwynn for the NL batting lead for much of the first half of the season. But Francona then went down with a knee injury (he has a history of this) and the rest of the season was wasted.

Francona is actually much like Gwynn as a hitter. Their swings are not similar, but they are both spray hitters who utilize the entire field, like the ball up, don't strike out very often and don't hit many long balls.

The best way to defense Francona is to give him both lines and bunch him in the middle, both in the infield and in the outfield. Francona has proven he can hit any pitch if it is up; the best way to pitch him is to crowd him with fastballs. He stands in the middle of the box and has a good knowledge of the strike zone. He is a good bunter.

He simply makes contact and has a way of finding holes. He is the kind of hitter a team looks at in spring training and figures will produce a .300 average but not many long balls.

BASERUNNING:

Knee and leg problems have hurt his speed. In 1983, he wore a three-quarter brace on his leg and in 1984, he wore an elastic support before reinjurying himself. With or without braces, he has severely limited speed and is no base-stealing threat. He is, though, an intelligent player, and this extends to his baserunning.

FIELDING:

He can play both the outfield and first base. First base is his better position, but the presence of Driessen figures to force Francona to the outfield. At both positions, his agility

TERRY FRANCONA
OF, No. 16
LL, 6'1", 175 lbs.
ML Svc: 3 years
Born: 4-22-59 in
    Aberdeen, SD

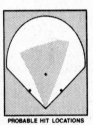

1984 STATISTICS											
AVG	G	AB	R	H	2B	3B	HR	RBI	BB	SO	SB
.346	58	214	18	74	19	2	1	18	5	12	0
CAREER STATISTICS											
AVG	G	AB	R	H	2B	3B	HR	RBI	BB	SO	SB
.300	258	670	64	201	33	4	5	57	24	49	3

VS. RHP   VS. LHP   PROBABLE HIT LOCATIONS

and range are compromised by the leg problems. He has good hands, particularly when playing first base. He will smoothly field any ball he reaches, in either the infield or the outfield. His throwing arm is average for a first baseman, slightly below average for an outfielder.

OVERALL:

The dominant questions about Francona concern his physical condition. He's had the last two seasons ended prematurely by injuries, and it is growing difficult for the Expos to count on him. He needs a solid healthy year--soon. But if injuries reduce him to this role he should be a fine contact hitter.

Campbell: "Sometimes, it looks like his bat has radar in it, the way his hits find holes. Ideally, a manager likes to have a first baseman who will hit 30 home runs and drive in 100 runs, but you look around and there's no one like that. Terry Francona is going to hit a solid .300 or more every year."

PITCHING:

Bill Gullickson is a good pitcher, but a lot of people keep waiting for him to become a great pitcher and a dominant figure in the National League. He has the tools.

He is a power pitcher who, when he's right, throws a 90+ MPH fastball and devastating breaking pitches. He calls his best breaking pitch the "slurve," a combination of a curve and slider. On his best nights, Gullickson likes to get two strikes on a hitter with fastballs and then strike him out with the slurve.

While he is a power pitcher, Bill also has extraordinary control. He throws mostly from over the top.

With the combination of the 90+ MPH fastball and the slurve, one wonders what keeps Gullickson from perennial Cy Young candidacy. One reason is that he has not developed a straight change, which would help. But the bigger factor is that Gullickson consistently is not sharp until two months or so into the season.

He rarely has any zip on his fastball until June or July, at which point he becomes very difficult to beat. But earlier, he throws his fastball in the mid 80s instead of the low 90s, a vast difference. Somehow, he needs to find a way to be ready to pitch in April.

He is a key member of the Expos' starting rotation and figures to remain there for years to come.

FIELDING, HITTING, BASERUNNING:

Gullickson still needs to refine his move to first base; baserunners tend to get too good a jump on him, which gives

BILL GULLICKSON
RHP, No. 34
RR, 6'3", 210 lbs.
ML Svc: 5 years
Born: 2-20-59 in
Marshall, MN

1984 STATISTICS

W	L	ERA	G	GS	CG	IP	H	R	ER	BB	SO	SV
12	9	3.61	32	32	3	226	230	100	91	37	100	0

CAREER STATISTICS

W	L	ERA	G	GS	CG	IP	H	R	ER	BB	SO	SV
58	49	3.42	147	141	27	1004	962	416	382	241	610	0

them a good shot to beat out catcher Carter's throws. Gullickson is adequate as a fielder.

He has never hit above .150 in the big leagues and probably never will. He is an unfamiliar sight on the bases.

OVERALL:

He is at the age and point in his career at which he should take off, vaulting from a good pitcher to stardom, if he is ever to make that jump. He needs to find consistency from April on. If he ever achieves that, it would surely help the Expos' chances of playing baseball in October.

Campbell: "What they need to do, even if it means intensifying his off-season training program, is find a way for him to be ready to pitch when April rolls around. Gullickson has got to lick that problem."

PITCHING:

For a long time, people in baseball have known that James had the tools to pitch in the big leagues. And he seems to be moving closer and closer to refining those tools.

He is best suited for use as a middle and short reliever, the roles in which the Expos utilize him. At times, he can be purely overpowering coming out of the bullpen.

James is a power pitcher who throws a fastball in the 91-92 MPH range. He can come into a game with runners on base and simply blow the hitters away with his velocity. However, he has a disturbing tendency to abandon the fastball when men are not on base, thus putting himself in trouble. In those situations, he tries to pick the hitters apart with his breaking ball rather than throwing his primary pitch.

James's breaking ball, a curve/slidder, is acceptable when he uses it off the fastball--but not when he tries to use it as a primary pitch.

But as long as he does throw the fastball, he can be an effective pitcher. With experience, he should get better and better.

FIELDING, HITTING, BASERUNNING:

He does not have a particularly good pickoff move to first base and is vulnerable to the stolen base. James needs to improve his move if he is to entrench himself as a short reliever. He's also no better than average in fielding.

BOB JAMES
RHP, No. 42
RR, 6'4", 230 lbs.
ML Svc: 2 years
Born: 8-15-58 in
Glendale, CA

1984 STATISTICS

W	L	ERA	G	GS	CG	IP	H	R	ER	BB	SO	SV
6	6	3.66	62	0	0	96	92	47	39	45	91	10

CAREER STATISTICS

W	L	ERA	G	GS	CG	IP	H	R	ER	BB	SO	SV
7	9	4.09	118	2	0	185	172	95	84	94	186	17

He is nothing special as a hitter. Because of the role in which he is used, James rarely gets to the plate and even more rarely gets to first base.

OVERALL:

He has had a mild problem with putting on extra weight, a problem that could become more serious with age. Other than keeping off the weight, James needs only remember to throw the fastball, throw the fastball, throw the fastball . . .

Campbell: "What I've noticed is that he is often more effective in his first inning in a game than in his second. He comes right at people in his first inning, especially if he inherits baserunners, but then seems to let up."

PITCHING:

In the first half of the 1984 season, Lea was as good as any pitcher in the National League. But in the second half, he fell back into the pack.

Still, he remains the ace of the Expos' starting rotation, a pitcher with a secure future. Unlike much of the Montreal staff, Lea is not a power pitcher. Rather, he is a control pitcher who spots his fastball (87-88 MPH tops), throws the breaking ball for strikes, changes speeds and plays mental games with the hitter.

He has good control of all of his pitches, but when he does fall behind 2-0 or 3-1 in the count, he remains willing to throw the breaking ball. This makes him a very effective pitcher. He changes speed well on his breaking balls, and he has good sinking movement on his fastball.

His basic pitching pattern is to throw the fastball in on lefty batters and away from righties. He likes to set up lefties with the breaking ball down and away and then put them away with a fastball in on the fists. But he also can use the breaking ball for an out pitch.

He is equally effective against left-handed hitters as against righthanders.

FIELDING, HITTING, BASERUNNING:

One much criticized aspect of Lea's game is the yawn-provoking frequency with which he throws to first base. He does not have a good move, it is not even an average move, but he persists in throwing to first base, even against runners who are not threats to steal.

Lea's constant throws to first base distract his fielders. Like waiting on line in the supermarket, the annoyance

CHARLIE LEA
RHP, No. 53
RR, 6'4", 190 lbs.
ML Svc: 4 years
Born: 12-25-56 in
 Orleans, FR

1984 STATISTICS

W	L	ERA	G	GS	CG	IP	H	R	ER	BB	SO	SV
15	10	2.89	30	30	8	224	198	82	72	68	123	0

CAREER STATISTICS

W	L	ERA	G	GS	CG	IP	H	R	ER	BB	SO	SV
55	40	3.29	127	120	22	791	704	324	289	289	462	0

of the moment can lead to lapses of concentration. Otherwise, Lea is sufficient as a fielder.

Lea is "just your typical pitcher" as a hitter and baserunner, but he has mastered one important aspect of hitting, especially for a pitcher: bunting. He is a very good bunter and can help himself with sacrifices; in fact, few pitchers in the league bunt better than Lea.

OVERALL:

He figures to keep getting better. When he puts together a full season like his first half of last year, Charlie Lea will be a Cy Young Award winner. The Expos must feel good knowing that he is only 28 years old and has his name carved in their rotation.

Campbell: "He is sort of the reverse of Bill Gullickson: Lea starts slowly and finishes strong. One maddening thing about Lea is his habit of throwing to first base all the time. It puts his ballclub to sleep. I assure you, it puts the broadcasters to sleep. Zzzzzzzz."

PITCHING:

Lucas is the type of pitcher who must be at his best to be effective; he does not have enough stuff to get hitters out with less than his best.

He is the antithesis of a power pitcher. Lucas is a control pitcher who is not going to overpower anyone, anytime. He throws sinkers and sliders and is actually most effective when he is getting the ball slightly OUT of the strike zone.

The key to Lucas's success is deception, making his pitches look as if they are strikes until the batter commits and then having them dip or dart off the plate. He can be brutalized when he's getting his pitches up in the strike zone. He must keep them down.

Lucas is a gangly lefthander who comes to the plate with a sometimes three-quarters, sometimes sidearm motion. The batter sees an unorthodox mass of arms and legs. It helps Lucas, who strikes out more batters than one would expect from a non-power pitcher.

Because of his sinker, the lefthanded Lucas often is more effective against righties than lefties; his sinker comes in on lefties, who sometimes can turn on it effectively.

He is purely a relief pitcher, but it is felt he is better suited for middle relief than short relief. He's capable of 16-20 saves a season, but he also has a history of losing a lot of games.

FIELDING, HITTING, BASERUNNING:

He is not the most natural of athletes and is not the smoothest of fielders. He has only an ordinary move to first and sometimes forgets about baserunners.

GARY LUCAS
LHP, No. 25
LL, 6'5", 200 lbs.
ML Svc: 5 years
Born: 11-8-54 in
Riverside, CA

1984 STATISTICS

W	L	ERA	G	GS	CG	IP	H	R	ER	BB	SO	SV
0	3	2.72	55	0	0	53	54	20	16	20	42	8

CAREER STATISTICS

W	L	ERA	G	GS	CG	IP	H	R	ER	BB	SO	SV
18	36	2.88	285	18	0	481	444	185	154	162	304	57

He fields bunts and other batted balls with no great distinction.

He is neither a hitter nor a baserunner. As a relief pitcher, particularly a middle reliever, he rarely gets to the plate, and when he does he's normally not there for long. He is a poor bunter.

OVERALL:

Lucas's biggest asset is that he is a seasoned lefthander, a precious commodity in a big league bullpen. He has a track record, and the Expos know what to expect. He won't exceed their expectations, but at least he is a known commodity.

Campbell: "Gary is a professional, but he's probably not the type of guy you'd want pitching the final innings with the game on the line. I don't say that for lack of heart; I say it for he is short on the ability side."

PITCHING:

Last season, David Palmer made a moderately successful comeback from his second elbow operation, and the Expos hope he will continue to progress. If so, he can help solidify their starting rotation.

When Palmer first arrived in the big leagues in 1979, he was blessed with a blazing fastball. His arm problems have taken some velocity off the fastball and forced him to put more emphasis on his breaking pitches. He has gone two full seasons, 1981 and 1983, without throwing a pitch because of elbow surgery.

Palmer still has youth and natural tools in his favor, but he has missed a lot of pitching time that would have made him a far more advanced, more refined pitcher by now. That is unfortunate. But if Palmer can stay healthy, and can complement a fastball that still pops in the 80s, he can win in the big leagues.

FIELDING, HITTING, BASERUNNING:

Missing all of two of the last four seasons has not helped any aspect of Palmer's game, including his fielding. Imagine going two years without fielding under game conditions. But he is a natural athlete and, except for his arm, has kept the rest of his body in good condition. He has only an average pick-off move.

Hitting and baserunning are the least of Palmer's worries this season. In the

DAVID PALMER
RHP, No. 46
RR, 6'1", 205 lbs.
ML Svc: 6 years
Born: 10-19-57 in
Glens Falls, NY

1984 STATISTICS

W	L	ERA	G	GS	CG	IP	H	R	ER	BB	SO	SV
7	3	3.84	20	19	1	105	101	45	45	44	66	0

CAREER STATISTICS

W	L	ERA	G	GS	CG	IP	H	R	ER	BB	SO	SV
31	16	3.12	98	63	7	441	404	177	153	142	264	0

past, he has shown that he has an idea or two about what to do at the plate, and he has average speed for a 6'1", 205 lb. pitcher.

OVERALL:

The only question really is his health. If his arm stays sound, he will win in the big leagues. If not, a career of such high promise will have been wasted.

Campbell: "I don't know why so many of the Montreal pitchers seem to have arm problems. I don't know whether the staff is more breaking ball oriented than some or what, but David Palmer deserves a good comeback."

HITTING:

Tim Raines is clearly one of the top four or five offensive players in the National League, not to mention one of the top four or five all-around players.

He has a rare, almost phenomenal, combination of abilities that make him ideal as either a leadoff batter or a No. 3 hitter.

He hits for a high average. He has a discerning eye and a small strike zone and thus walks a lot. He also is a good RBI man (71 RBI in 1983, for example) and will occasionally hit a long ball. To put it simply, Raines is a force.

To categorize him, you would have to say he is a contact hitter. A switch-hitter, he appears equally good from the left and right sides--amazing since he only began switch-hitting a few years ago. He is extremely difficult to strike out. At only 5'7", not only does he have a small strike zone but he is extremely selective at the plate. Because of his speed, pitchers do not want to walk him, and he makes certain they come in with a pitch in his hitting zone.

He likes the ball up and likes to shoot for the holes. The best way to defense him is to give him the lines and bunch the fielders toward the middle. He is generally a straightaway hitter.

BASERUNNING:

Raines has a natural gift of blinding speed, but that is not his only attribute as a baserunner. He also has very good instincts, and he also is very aggressive.

He studies and reads pitchers very well, gets good jumps and is one of the most alert baserunners in the game. He has the best speed in the league from first to second, and frankly, he can steal almost at will.

FIELDING:

He came up as a left fielder and even took a crack at second base, but Raines

TIM RAINES
CF, No. 30
SR, 5'7", 178 lbs.
ML Svc: 4 years
Born: 9-16-59 in
Sanford, FL

1984 STATISTICS

AVG	G	AB	R	H	2B	3B	HR	RBI	BB	SO	SB
.309	160	622	106	192	38	9	8	60	87	69	75

CAREER STATISTICS

AVG	G	AB	R	H	2B	3B	HR	RBI	BB	SO	SB
.293	581	2217	398	650	115	32	28	211	310	256	321

VS. RHP   VS. LHP   PROBABLE HIT LOCATIONS

played center field for the Expos much of 1984. There are few players in the game more effective at running down fly balls. In addition to the good speed, Raines judges fly balls very well and gets good jumps.

One flaw in his game is that he does not have a good throwing arm, but he usually does throw to the right base and hits the cutoff man.

OVERALL:

Tim has had back-to-back outstanding seasons after having an admitted drug problem in 1982. As a hitter, a baserunner, a defensive player and an all-around force, Raines is a franchise player.

Campbell: "He appears to have conquered his personal problems. He shows up every day, plays hard every day, and there is no hint of any of those interferences from the past. He certainly was one of the four or five best players in the National League in 1984."

PITCHING:

Jeff Reardon is a good, solid short reliever, but he has not been able to nudge into the elitist class with the Bruce Sutters, Rich Gossages and Lee Smiths of the league. At times, he is almost as overpowering as anyone, but at other times, his fastball seems to level out some and he is vulnerable.

The key with Reardon seems to be his handling. With two or three days' rest, he can be virtually unhittable. But if he is used, say, three days in a row, as many relievers are asked, he seems to lose a little velocity and a lot of movement off his fastball.

Although he is the Expos' primary short reliever, he probaby would be more consistent if not used in more than 45 games per season. Teammates Bob James and Gary Lucas can help by shouldering some of the workload, but a lot of managers like to have one dependable stopper who can go out to the mound 60-70 times a year.

Reardon, an over the top pitcher, has an adequate breaking ball, and he can get a surprise strikeout with it from time to time. But when the situation is delicate, he will throw his 92+ MPH fastball.

Reardon also has a history of back injuries dating to his childhood. It might explain his tendency to weaken if overused.

FIELDING, HITTING, BASERUNNING:

Reardon has a real problem with his move to first base; it is almost no deterrent at all to opposing baserunners. His move never catches runners by surprise, and he doesn't get the ball to the base very quickly, either. Reardon is a slightly above average fielder. His

JEFF REARDON
RHP, No. 41
RR, 6'1", 190 lbs.
ML Svc: 5 years
Born: 10-1-55 in
Dalton, MA

1984 STATISTICS

W	L	ERA	G	GS	CG	IP	H	R	ER	BB	SO	SV
7	7	2.90	68	0	0	87	70	31	28	37	79	23

CAREER STATISTICS

W	L	ERA	G	GS	CG	IP	H	R	ER	BB	SO	SV
33	29	2.52	331	0	0	489	400	153	137	194	403	86

back problem does not appear to handicap him in fielding bunts or other batted balls.

Reardon rarely bats and, on those even rarer occasions when he reaches base, doesn't extend himself, again perhaps because of the back problems and also the unfamiliarity of the situation.

OVERALL:

Reardon is 29 years old and probably has just about reached his level as a big league pitcher. He has a very impressive career ERA, and a lot of teams would like to have him, although not all see him as a No. 1 short reliever. With a front line lefthanded complement, Jeff could be extremely effective.

Campbell: "I don't know if Reardon can take the wear and tear of pitching 45 games or so--just as Steve Bedrosian of Atlanta can't. I have a feeling that, for a couple of years at least, Reardon could be a very, very good relief pitcher if Montreal could get a couple of guys to complement him."

PITCHING:

Because of a spring training arm injury, Steve Rogers fell off dramatically in 1984. Remember that in 1983 he won 17 games, completed 13 and led the league in shutouts with five. Last year, he was only a shell of his former self.

He said he was pitching without pain late in the season, but judging from his stuff, that was arguable. He clearly had lost four or five miles off his sinking fastball, and his breaking stuff did not have the same zip. He tried, sometimes successfully, to get hitters out by nibbling here and there.

Rogers, who delivers from a three-quarters motion, was one of the classiest righthanders in the league before last year. While it is true that he always did nibble around the plate, he did it with very good stuff until last season.

The Expos hope Rogers will be able to return to his old form and re-establish himself in the starting rotation. There are two hopes: first, that a winter of rest and rehabilitation will revive his arm and make him the pitcher of old; second, if not, that Rogers will be able to make adjustments to his pitching style and begin a sort of "second career" just as successful as his first. He is one of the more intelligent players in the game.

FIELDING, HITTING, BASERUNNING:

He always has been, and still is, a better than average fielder. Rogers achieves this distinction despite often being out of position at the end of his delivery. He has a snap throw to first which can be very effective as a pick-off move.

STEVE ROGERS
RHP, No. 45
RR, 6'1", 175 lbs.
ML Svc: 11 years
Born: 10-26-49 in
    Jefferson City, MO

1984 STATISTICS

W	L	ERA	G	GS	CG	IP	H	R	ER	BB	SO	SV
6	15	4.31	31	28	1	169	171	93	81	78	64	0

CAREER STATISTICS

W	L	ERA	G	GS	CG	IP	H	R	ER	BB	SO	SV
156	148	3.14	391	386	128	2801	2568	1097	977	856	1603	2

Rogers is an excellent bunter and in non-bunting situations is fairly adept at putting the bat on the ball. That is really all that one can ask of a pitcher as a hitter.

He is only an average baserunner, intelligent enough to know he shouldn't be hurting himself on the bases.

OVERALL:

Rogers's decline was one of the sad stories of the 1984 baseball season. He will be interesting to watch in 1985. No doctor or trainer can tell you with any certainty that you will ever again see the Steve Rogers who won 150 games between 1972 and 1983. Just wait and see.

Campbell: "You don't look at a Steve Rogers having a losing record and think it's the same guy. If anybody can come back, it's him. He has a lot of courage. The key will be rehabilitating the arm, getting the strength back."

PITCHING:

Three years ago, Dan Schatzeder was on the fringe as a big league pitcher, very close to oblivion. While he was with both Detroit and San Francisco, he simply did not seem to have the stuff to get big league hitters out.

Then he was dealt to Montreal, and he has looked better and better for the last two years. Suddenly and inexplicably, he picked up three to five miles on his fastball, a significant boost. Just as suddenly, just as inexplicably, his breaking pitches became sharper.

The result is that Schatzeder is now a valuable member of the Montreal staff, especially so since he is a lefthander. He can be used as a starter or a reliever, though he prefers starting.

Schatezeder has good control; his basic approach to pitching is to try to jump ahead in the count, then force the hitter to hit his pitch.

He pitches from a three-quarters delivery. His greatest weakness is that, more often than the Expos would like, he will give in to a hitter and be burned by the long ball.

FIELDING:

Dan is a better than average fielder and, because he is a lefthander, has a natural advantage in holding runners on first base.

He is an excellent hitter, unquestionably one of the best hitting pitch-

DAN SCHATZEDER
LHP, No. 43
LL, 6'0", 195 lbs.
ML Svc: 7 years
Born: 12-1-54 in
Elmhurst, IL

1984 STATISTICS

W	L	ERA	G	GS	CG	IP	H	R	ER	BB	SO	SV
7	7	2.71	36	14	1	136	112	44	41	36	89	1

CAREER STATISTICS

W	L	ERA	G	GS	CG	IP	H	R	ER	BB	SO	SV
49	49	3.59	249	102	17	884	796	378	353	312	473	4

ers in the big leagues. During his college baseball days (University of Denver where he was 21-11), Schatzeder played center field when he wasn't pitching, so his big league hits are not flukes. He also is a good baserunner.

OVERALL:

He got one or two extra chances to make good because of the premium placed on lefthanders with good arms. He took advantage of perhaps his last chance, securing a job with the Expos.

Campbell: "He was the plus of the Montreal staff in 1984 as he came back into the fold as big league pitcher."

HITTING:

It is his hitting that has kept Tony Scott from stardom in the big leagues. He is a star-caliber player in the other areas, defense and baserunning, but he falls short as a hitter.

A switch-hitter, Scott is a better hitter from the right side than the left side. He can do some damage as a right-handed pinch-hitter. The raps against him as a hitter are his lack of power and lack of run production; these deficiencies work strongly against an outfielder, in particular. He is also a streak/slump hitter, sometimes playing himself out of the lineup with brutally cold spells.

To pitch to him, keep the ball in on his fists, and you'll get him out. The opposing infielders must be alert, too, because he is a good bunter, particularly a good drag bunter.

BASERUNNING:

He has outstanding speed, the type of speed that could allow him to be among the top three or four basestealers in the league if he got on first base more often. You have heard the cliché, "You can't steal first base," and therein lies Scott's limitation.

When he does get on base, Scott has a tendency of occasionally doing something reckless, but he is generally a heads-up baserunner.

FIELDING:

He has perhaps been underrated as a defensive player. The fact is that he is one of the best defensive outfielders in the National League. He has few superiors when it comes to judging a fly ball, reacting to it, chasing it down and catching it.

Scott gets a great jump on the ball and is an acrobat in the outfield, often making diving, sprawling catches, often

TONY SCOTT
OF, No. 30
SR, 6'0", 195 lbs.
ML Svc: 11 years
Born: 9-18-51 in
  Cincinnati, OH

1984 STATISTICS

AVG	G	AB	R	H	2B	3B	HR	RBI	BB	SO	SB
.239	70	92	10	22	5	0	0	5	11	24	1

CAREER STATISTICS

AVG	G	AB	R	H	2B	3B	HR	RBI	BB	SO	SB
.249	991	2803	359	699	111	28	17	253	186	464	125

  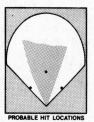

VS. RHP   VS. LHP   PROBABLE HIT LOCATIONS

reaching or leaping over fences, etc. He has only an average arm, but he does hit the cutoff man.

OVERALL:

With the Expos, his lot appears confined to being a reserve outfielder and righthanded pinch-hitter. But he is an able fourth outfielder and could command a large amount of playing time if the right circumstances develop. He can do enough things to stay around the big leagues for a long time.

Campbell: "The raps against him are connected to his hitting. He can't seem to give a team the kind of power and production that you need from an outfielder. It's hard to play baseball without a bat."

PITCHING:

Used as a starter by the Expos last season, Bryn Smith has a versatile arm and can be used in almost any capacity: starter, long reliever, middle reliever, short reliever. Smith was a starter throughout the minors and much prefers that role.

He is a control pitcher rather than a power pitcher. His fastball is normally clocked in the 86-87 MPH range, but his distinguishing pitches are the slider and palmball. The palmball is his speciality. It is a pitch which acts like a change-up/curve, as the ball dips and darts around the plate.

Smith pitches from a three-quarters motion and is good at isolating and exploiting a batter's weaknesses. He has to be fine with his control to win. If he is getting the ball up, he won't last very long. But if he is keeping the ball down, he often gets in a groove that is difficult for the opposition to break.

FIELDING, HITTING, BASERUNNING:

He does not hurt himself on the mound. Smith follows through in good fielding position, reacts quickly to bunts and other batted balls. He throws cleanly to first base.

He has an above average pickoff move to first base; he improved his move while working in high pressure relief situations.

BRYN SMITH
RHP, No. 28
RR, 6'2", 200 lbs.
ML Svc: 3 years
Born: 8-11-55 in
    Marietta, GA

1984 STATISTICS

W	L	ERA	G	GS	CG	IP	H	R	ER	BB	SO	SV
12	13	3.32	28	28	4	179	178	72	66	51	101	0

CAREER STATISTICS

W	L	ERA	G	GS	CG	IP	H	R	ER	BB	SO	SV
21	28	3.17	131	41	9	426	415	170	150	120	261	6

Bryn is nothing special as a hitter or as a baserunner. But say this for him, he thoroughly enjoys himself at the plate and does not get cheated out of his swings.

OVERALL:

Smith had a chance at a professional golf career before opting for baseball. His baseball career now seems firmly on track, and the Expos see him as a member of their starting rotation for 1985 and beyond.

Campbell: "I think he can be used in any role, but he seems to have more confidence as a starter. He can be very tough when he's in a groove."

HITTING:

Fortunately, Tim Wallach can hit. It makes him a big league player. He is the type of hitter whom a manager can look to each year for 17 home runs and more than 60 RBIs. At least!

He is extremely dangerous on balls out over the plate and down. He crowds the plate, but likes to get his arms fully extended to hit.

There is only one way to get him out consistently--pitch him inside, inside, inside. He has the ability to take the inside pitch that could be called either way, and he seems to get the ball called about 85% of the time. This keeps him alive.

The best strategy for a pitcher is to pound away at him inside, because Tim does a lot of damage if a pitcher moves the ball out toward the middle or outside of the plate. He has extremely strong wrists and can even flick a pitch that is an inch or two off the outside corner for an extra-base hit.

He looks as if he is hitting with an open stance, but Wallach actually closes his front shoulder off. He invites the pitcher to throw the ball away from him, and then he'll pop it into left field. He goes through periodic slumps where he looks helpless against the curveball.

BASERUNNING:

It's a good thing that Wallach is a power hitter because he has nothing that could be called speed. He also lacks aggressiveness on the basepaths.

He will go in hard and try to break up a double play, but he's reluctant to ever attempt to take the extra base.

FIELDING:

He is not a great third baseman. He does not have good hands, does not have

TIM WALLACH
3B, No. 29
RR, 6'3", 200 lbs.
ML Svc: 4 years
Born: 9-14-58 in
   Huntington Park, CA

1984 STATISTICS											
AVG	G	AB	R	H	2B	3B	HR	RBI	BB	SO	SB
.246	160	582	55	143	25	4	18	72	50	101	3
CAREER STATISTICS											
AVG	G	AB	R	H	2B	3B	HR	RBI	BB	SO	SB
.258	550	1982	218	511	98	11	70	254	157	319	9

  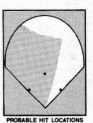

VS. RHP VS. LHP PROBABLE HIT LOCATIONS

a strong throwing arm and does not always know how to play batted balls.

Wallach does have an accurate throwing arm in his favor, however. Third base may not be his permanent position, he may wind up playing first base or left field.

OVERALL:

He hit 28 home runs in his first full major league season (1982), and has the potential to explode some day into one of the game's topflight power hitters.

Campbell: "He has a great attitude. He'll be a bit of a liability on defense and the basepaths, but he's going to hit and he's going to have a job for many years to come."

FRED BREINING
RHP, No. 48
RR, 6'4", 185 lbs.
ML Svc: 5 years
Born: 11-15-56 in
Pacifica, CA

PITCHING, FIELDING:

Fred Breining had been a steadily improving pitcher with the Giants, an impressive enough pitcher that the Expos dealt Al Oliver for him in spring training. Breining reported to the Expos with an injured arm, and his 1984 season was a waste.

At this point, it is pure conjecture as to how completely or how effectively he will be able to come back in 1985. However, he has the tools, if healthy, to be a member of the Expos' starting rotation or a pivotal member of the bullpen. When healthy, he is a versatile pitcher who can help a team.

His best pitch is the forkball; he also throws a fastball that moves and sinks, a curve, a slider and a change-up. He likes to move the ball around, in and out, up and down, and likes to out-think the hitter. He does not have overpowering velocity, but he sets the hitters up well, maximizing his resources. He has good control and, by keeping the ball down, gets a lot of ground balls.

He is an adequate fielder, quick and athletic off the mound. He reacts well to bunts and makes good throws. He has an average pickoff move to first base, giving the catcher at least a fighting chance.

OVERALL:

The question with Breining is his health. If is arm rebounds, he can help the Expos. He is not a superstar pitcher and probably will never be one, but he is a solid, workmanlike pitcher who can contribute as, say, a fourth starter or middle reliever.

Campbell: "The Expos claimed he was damaged merchandise when they made the trade for Al Oliver. He might have been but he just didn't get enough work to make the kind of evaluation that would have cleared up the question."

DAVE HOSTETLER
1B, No. 12
RR, 6'4", 215 lbs.
ML Svc: 3 years
Born: 3-27-56 in
Pasadena, CA

HITTING, BASERUNNING, FIELDING:

Hostetler is the ultimate streak hitter. When he's swinging well, he can hit the ball out of any park, mostly from left to right-center, when he gets a pitch up and out over the plate. He has shown the ability to go the other way with a pitch.

He gets down on himself when he goes into a slump and then seems even more likely to strike out. He has shown himself to be vulnerable to change-ups and has all kinds of trouble with breaking pitches.

Hostetler has below average speed. The best thing he does on the bases is the home run trot.

In the field, Hostetler has worked hard to improve himself defensively, but is still barely adequate. He does have a strong arm, but he lacks range and has trouble with sharp grounders hit directly at him. He prefers to play in the field and does seem to hit better when he has time as a fielder.

OVERALL:

The Expos fans are an enthusiastic and appreciative crowd. If they decide to take Hostetler into their hearts, it could be just the spark that this young but unsettled power hitter needs to open up and bang the ball.

BOBBY RAMOS
C, No. 44
RR, 5'10", 208 lbs.
ML Svc: 4 years
Born: 11-5-55 in
Havana, Cuba

HITTING, BASERUNNING, FIELDING:

He is not much of a hitter and not much of a baserunner, but Bobby Ramos is an outstanding defensive player.

He is the backup to Gary Carter, the Expos' starting catcher and one of the best anywhere at his position. As a result, Ramos is not going to get a lot of playing time.

When he does play, Ramos is no baby-sitter. Opposing baserunners best stand still. Ramos has a cannon for an arm. If the pitcher is doing his job in holding the runner, Ramos will throw him out. Ramos also blocks the plate well and appears to call a sound game.

As a hitter, he likes the ball up; if the pitcher keeps it down, he should be successful against Ramos. He doesn't run well.

OVERALL:

The Expos might like Ramos to contribute a little more offensively, especially as a righthanded pinch-hitter, but he serves well as backup to Carter.

Campbell: "His forte is defense. He has a tremendous, tremendous throwing arm. The fact is, however, no one is going to play much behind Gary Carter.

MIKE STENHOUSE
OF, No. 32
LR, 6'1", 195 lbs.
ML Svc: 1 year plus
Born: 5-29-58 in
Pueblo, CO

HITTING, BASERUNNING, FIELDING:

Mike Stenhouse is a lefthanded hitting outfielder whom the Expos visualize as their power hitter of the future. They seem him as the type of hitter who will make his mark with long balls and run production, not a high average.

Stenhouse appeared overmatched at times last season and does need to learn to hit for a better average. He may need more Triple A seasoning. He has particularly good power to right field, likes the ball around the belt or a little above and, like most power hitters, likes the ball out over the plate so he can get his arms fully extended.

To get him out, throw him hard stuff in and then breaking balls down. He will chase pitches out of the strike zone.

He is adequate on defense. He doesn't have much speed, but he is not mistake-prone, either on the bases or in the outfield.

OVERALL:

Mike has baseball in his blood; he is the son of Dave Stenhouse, a former pitcher for the Washington Senators. The jury is still out, however, on the young man as a big league player.

Campbell: "The key will be for him to raise his average some more. If he hits for a higher average, the home runs and RBIs will come."

MIKE RAMSEY
INF, No. 5
SR, 6'1", 175 lbs.
ML Svc: 5 years
Born: 3-29-54 in
Roanoke, VA

HITTING, BASERUNNING, FIELDING:

Mike Ramsey is a switch-hitting utility infielder whom the Expos obtained in a mid-season trade for veteran shortstop Chris Speier. He has never been much of a hitter, and he has slipped considerably as a defensive player. He still runs well, though.

As a hitter, Ramsey can be overpowered. Pitchers shouldn't do him any favors by throwing him breaking balls. Just throw fastballs to get him out. He is a slightly better hitter from the left side than the right, but he has no power from either side. Play him shallow and toward the middle of the field. Above all, don't walk him.

As a fielder, Ramsey once was among the best utilitymen in the league. With the Cardinals, he could play second, short and third with efficiency, and he had a strong, accurate throwing arm. Last season, however, he appeared very, very unsure of himself in the field.

OVERALL:

At one time with St. Louis, Ramsey appeared to be carving out a niche for himself as one of the game's outstanding utility players, along with Derrel Thomas and Jerry Royster. But he had a difficult time accepting the role and wanted to play regularly somewhere. He appears to have regressed. He will have to prove himself anew in 1985.

Campbell: "Two years ago, it was my opinion he might be the best utilityman in the National League, particularly defensively. But he has slipped considerably. It is a mystery to me how he slipped so far so fast."

JIM WOHLFORD
OF, No. 5
RR, 5'11", 175 lbs.
ML Svc: 12 years
Born: 2-28-51 in
Visilia, CA

HITTING, BASERUNNING, FIELDING:

Jim Wohlford is one of those rare hitters who somehow seems more effective coming off the bench than playing regularly. A righthanded hitter, he does not have a lot of power, but he knows the pitchers and knows how to make contact. He is difficult to strike out.

Wohlford is a high ball hitter who will drive the ball to the alleys. He is a straightaway hitter, so the best defense is to sacrifice the lines and to bunch the fielders toward the middle.

The best pitching strategy against Wohlford is to keep everything down and away. He is particularly vulnerable against down-and-away breaking balls. You can throw him fastballs--provided they are down and away--but do not get them over the middle of the plate or in.

He does not have great speed by any stretch of the imagination, but he is a good baserunner. He's aggressive and alert, and there is much to be said for that. He is not a basestealing threat of any magnitude.

OVERALL:

Wohlford has built a long career by getting the most out of his skills. He can only be categorized as a solid righthanded pinch-hitter.

Campbell: The biggest compliment I can give him is to say that he knows how to play the game. In this day and age, a grasp of the fundamentals is somewhat hard to find in young players, but Jim has been around and fills a need."

NEW YORK METS

HITTING:

After spending most of the 1983 season in the minor leagues, Wally Backman made a solid contribution to the Mets in 1984 and showed marked improvement as a hitter, from both the left and the right sides of the plate. With more experience and continued improvement, he could become a first-rate leadoff hitter.

Like most hitters, Backman is dangerous on pitches that are down the middle of the plate. He generally hits line drives or ground balls back through the middle of the field. He is not a pull hitter from either side of the plate. Backman is a more dangerous hitter from the left side (his natural side) than from the right side.

He is still only 25 years old and is adjusting to big league pitching. But after three years in the majors and a lot of time at Tidewater, he is showing signs of impending arrival.

BASERUNNING:

Backman is not a basestealing demon, but he is better than average. Last season, he really hustled and swiped 32 bases. He once stole 46 bases in a Triple A season, but that was against pitchers with minor league pickoff moves and catchers with minor league arms. Still, Backman has good enough speed to steal a valuable base when his team needs it. He also breaks from the batter's box very well. He is about as aggresive on the bases as you would expect from someone who is 5'9" and 160 lbs.

FIELDING:

He has made some strides as a defensive player, but Backman is still lacking in many areas. He can play shortstop or second base, but is primarily a second baseman. His range is average at best, and his aggressiveness in the field is questionable. His arm is accu-

WALLY BACKMAN
2B, No. 6
SR, 5'9", 160 lbs.
ML Svc: 3 years
Born: 9-22-59 in Hillsboro, OR

1984 STATISTICS

AVG	G	AB	R	H	2B	3B	HR	RBI	BB	SO	SB
.280	128	436	68	122	19	2	1	26	56	63	32

CAREER STATISTICS

AVG	G	AB	R	H	2B	3B	HR	RBI	BB	SO	SB
.276	303	868	128	240	35	6	4	60	122	139	43

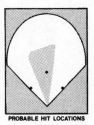

VS. RHP VS. LHP PROBABLE HIT LOCATIONS

rate, but it is not strong, and he takes too long before releasing the ball. Last season, he began to show some improvement in turning the double play.

OVERALL:

The Mets are still searching for the right combination in the middle infield; Backman is still one of the possible pieces in the puzzle. He'll have to continue to make consistent and substantial improvement if he is to establish himself as a full-time major league regular.

Snider: "He had a pretty good year last season, both as a hitter and as a fielder. He's an aggressive little player who bunts pretty well, will steal an occasional base and is beginning to look better when turning the double play."

PITCHING:

After being traded from the Reds to the Mets last season, Bruce Berenyi showed indications that he might be on his way to becoming a solid major league pitcher. When he was with the Reds, Berenyi was erratic, sometimes good and sometimes bad . . . but bad more than good. With the Mets in 1984, he showed some consistency late in the season; in 1985, he has a chance to establish himself as a member of their starting rotation. In this respect, 1985 will be a crucial season for him.

Berenyi benefited from working with pitching coach Mel Stottlemyre last season. One of Berenyi's problems while with the Reds was his wildness, but he was throwing quality strikes late in the year after several sessions with Stottlemyre. He has a strong arm and a good fastball, and he was also throwing a good breaking ball at the end of the year.

Berenyi has had--and may still have-- a tendency to sometimes aim the ball rather than put everything he has behind the pitch. He needs to challenge the hitters and pitch more aggressively. Perhaps it is a lack of confidence that causes Berenyi to feel for the plate rather than attack it. But if he continues to show the kind of improvement he did last season, his confidence should take care of itself.

FIELDING, HITTING, BASERUNNING:

Berenyi is an adequate fielder; his motion is smooth enough to leave him

BRUCE BERENYI
RHP, No. 31
RR, 6'3", 215 lbs.
ML Svc: 5 years
Born: 8-21-54 in
  Bryan, OH

1984 STATISTICS

W	L	ERA	G	GS	CG	IP	H	R	ER	BB	SO	SV
12	13	4.45	32	30	0	166	163	93	82	95	134	0

CAREER STATISTICS

W	L	ERA	G	GS	CG	IP	H	R	ER	BB	SO	SV
41	53	3.93	125	121	13	728	675	356	318	393	567	0

prepared for the batted ball. His move to first is average but could stand improvement, especially on a team without rifle-armed catchers. Berenyi seems to have a good time at the plate, but he doesn't do much damage. His baserunning isn't worth much.

OVERALL:

He has the velocity to do well in the big leagues. If he can overcome his control problems--and last season he appeared to be moving in that direction-- his acquisition could turn out to be a stroke of genius (or luck) for the Mets.

Snider: "He came a long way last season. I wasn't too impressed with him in Cincinnati, but he seemed to get away from aiming the ball and looked like a good pitcher. Sometimes a change of scenery is all a player needs."

HITTING:

Hubie Brooks's career has been peculiar. He hit .309 in 1980 and .307 in 1981, but then began to taper off. Last season, he showed some encouraging, although inconclusive, signs of reverting to his earlier offensive form. The Mets continue to harbor hopes that he will show up one season as a bona fide offensive force.

For now, however, Brooks can be handled with inside pitches and high fastballs; high, inside fastballs are particularly effective against him. Brooks likes pitches from the middle of the plate to the outside corner--ideally, around the waist.

Brooks hits most often to the opposite field, although he is trying hard to pull the ball more often. He is a good clutch hitter.

BASERUNNING:

He has good natural speed, but he has not learned how to transform this natural asset into an asset on the bases. He does not know which pitchers he can try to steal against, and he does not appear to have the instincts which tell him when to run. This applies not only to basestealing opportunities but to a variety of other situations that arise on the bases as well.

FIELDING:

Brooks was on his way to becoming at least an adequate third baseman when the Mets tried him at shortstop last season. He will never be a dazzling defensive shortstop, but he could play the position until the Mets find someone more naturally suited to it. Brooks contributes more with the bat than the prototypical shortstop, which theoretically should allow him to contribute a little less with the glove.

HUBIE BROOKS
3B, No. 7
RR, 6'0", 178 lbs.
ML Svc: 4 years
Born: 9-24-56 in
    Los Angeles, CA

1984 STATISTICS

AVG	G	AB	R	H	2B	3B	HR	RBI	BB	SO	SB
.283	153	561	61	159	23	2	16	73	48	79	6

CAREER STATISTICS

AVG	G	AB	R	H	2B	3B	HR	RBI	BB	SO	SB
.272	551	2043	196	555	85	11	28	219	128	325	28

  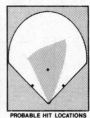

He has a very strong arm, for either a third baseman or a shortstop, but his arm is not as accurate as it should be. He gives first baseman Keith Hernandez a serious workout with his errant throws.

Brooks is an aggressive fielder. At third base, he pounces all over bunts; at short, he will take a shot at anything in the hole.

OVERALL:

Whether he plays short or third, Hubie benefits from Hernandez's presence at first base. It is hard to visualize Brooks as a long-term shortstop, but he has the offensive capability to play third base for a long time.

Snider: "He's a sincere guy, a hard worker who looks you straight in the eye when he talks to you. He has some sock in his bat and hit with more authority last season. I would like to see him continue to work to improve."

PITCHING:

Some people are very high on Ron Darling, and others are lukewarm. He is not the kind of pitcher who convinces you, on just one glance, that he will be a big winner. But the more you see him, the more you begin to think that this young pitcher has a chance.

Darling was in the Mets' starting rotation last season, and he figures to be there again this year.

Darling's biggest asset is his intelligence; he knows what he is doing on the mound and everywhere else. He also has a curveball that, at times, is as good as any in baseball. But at other times, the curve deserts him, and he gets into big trouble.

Darling's other pitches are a fastball and a change-up. His fastball has average velocity; if he could add an additional two or three miles an hour, he would do better with it. Last season, his fastball did not appear to have exceptional movement, although scouts say it moved better when he was in the minor leagues. Darling needs to continue working hard on his change-up as well. If he improved his straight change, his curveball would be much more effective.

Like many young pitchers, Darling struggles through stretches of wildness. It is possible, however, that now that he has had a full season of experience, Darling will be a looser pitcher next year. If he is, it may lead to increased velocity and better movement on his pitches.

RON DARLING
RHP, No. 44
RR, 6'3", 195 lbs.
ML Svc: 1 year plus
Born: 8-19-60 in
Honolulu, HI

1984 STATISTICS
W	L	ERA	G	GS	CG	IP	H	R	ER	BB	SO	SV
12	9	3.81	33	33	2	205	179	97	87	104	136	0

CAREER STATISTICS
W	L	ERA	G	GS	CG	IP	H	R	ER	BB	SO	SV
13	12	3.68	38	38	3	240	210	108	98	121	159	0

FIELDING, HITTING, BASERUNNING:

Darling worked hard last season on his move to first base, and the attention paid off. He has begun to show real improvement, and he'll keep working on it. As a fielder, Darling is alert and knows what to do with the ball when he has it. Don't look for much from him as a hitter or baserunner, however.

OVERALL:

Darling is only 24 years old, and the next couple of years should tell us what kind of future he will have. As he gains more confidence and better control, he could become a top-flight starter.

Snider: "I like his makeup. He needs more movement and more velocity right now if he is going to continue his progress. But he's a good competitor, and a good athlete all the way around."

PITCHING:

A few years ago, the Los Angeles Dodgers were hyping Sid Fernandez as the next Fernando Valenzuela. But the Mets were able to pry Fernandez away from the Dodgers for a marginal relief pitcher and a utility man. That alone should make you wonder if Fernandez might have been over-hyped. Major league teams, especially the Dodgers, are not in the habit of trading pitching phenoms for second-line talent.

In his first season with the Mets' organization, Fernandez did not look like another Valenzuela. At times, he did look like a pitcher who could contribute, and, with some improvement, perhaps he could contribute significantly. The Mets have a collection of pitchers who have a chance for strong careers --Fernandez, Ron Darling, Walt Terrell, maybe Brent Gaff--and the team just has to hope that a couple of them develop well enough to join Dwight Gooden as the nucleus of their rotation for the rest of the decade.

Fernandez did not show overpowering stuff last season, but he appeared to have good control. It is debatable at this point whether his stuff is good enough to enable him to win consistently in the major leagues--it appears to be borderline. His fastball is average, despite the earlier rumors that it was far above that, and his other pitches (curveball, change-up) are still in the refining stage. If he has a future, though, it is probably as a starting pitcher. The Mets will give him another good shot in 1985.

FIELDING, HITTING, BASERUNNING:

Fernandez is big and overweight--he doesn't look like much of an athlete--

SID FERNANDEZ
LHP, No. 50
LL, 6'1", 220 lbs.
ML Svc: 1 year plus
Born: 10-12-62 in
    Honolulu, HI

1984 STATISTICS

W	L	ERA	G	GS	CG	IP	H	R	ER	BB	SO	SV
6	6	3.50	15	15	0	90	74	40	35	34	62	0

CAREER STATISTICS

W	L	ERA	G	GS	CG	IP	H	R	ER	BB	SO	SV
6	7	3.66	17	16	0	96	81	44	39	41	71	0

shades of Fernando here, right? Wrong--sort of. Fernandez is actually a very good fielder. Considering the fact that he could stand to lose 15 pounds or so, he fields his position very well. He has a decent move to first base. His running style is not classic, but he gets around the bases adequately. In short, he does the little things well enough; it is his pitching that is the question mark.

OVERALL:

Fernandez needs to watch his weight. Sure, overweight pitchers can win in the big leagues, but he needs to be careful not to let his waistline get too far out of control. It is also possible that Fernandez would pick up a little velocity if he lost a little weight; it could make a big difference in his pitching.

Snider: "Normally, when a guy is big and heavy, it takes a little away from his fastball. Will he be a great one? You never know. But I think he needs to develop another pitch. What he has right now is not sufficient to get by these hitters a second season."

HITTING:

George Foster's entire existence as a major league player is tied to what he does with a bat in his hand. In his first season as a Met (1982), he was a colossal bust. In his second season, he matched the lowest batting average of his career, but did hit 28 home runs and drive in 90 runs. And last season, although still not the fearsome Foster of his prime years in Cincinnati, he put up the kind of numbers which few could complain about.

As always, Foster is a cautious, patient hitter, taking a lot of pitches and taking a lot of time between pitches. By playing mental gymnastics with the pitchers, Foster seems to sacrifice the aggressiveness a hitter of his power should display at the plate.

The same old raps against him apply: he chases too many bad pitches, takes too many good ones and goes into too many slumps.

He bats with a closed, upright stance and stands deep in the box. He is most dangerous when the pitcher gets the ball down and out over the plate. He waits well on the ball and is about as good a change-up hitter as any power hitter in the league. He strikes out a lot, as always.

In short, Foster remains the kind of hitter who can decide a lot of games with one swing of his big, booming bat.

BASERUNNING:

Foster does not have good speed--he does not, for that matter, have average speed--and he seems largely indifferent on the bases. He gives the impression that he does not like to slide and generally runs the bases one at a time. Last year, though, he seemed to be a little bit more into the games on the bases than usual.

FIELDING:

For most of his career, Foster has been a much-criticized defensive player;

GEORGE FOSTER
LF, No. 15
RR, 6'1", 195 lbs.
ML Svc: 13 years
Born: 12-1-48 in
 Tuscaloosa, AL

1984 STATISTICS

AVG	G	AB	R	H	2B	3B	HR	RBI	BB	SO	SB
.269	146	553	67	149	22	1	24	86	30	122	2

CAREER STATISTICS

AVG	G	AB	R	H	2B	3B	HR	RBI	BB	SO	SB
.277	1761	6287	899	1742	277	43	313	1120	596	1271	50

  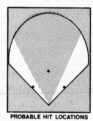

VS. RHP — STRONG   VS. LHP — STRONG   PROBABLE HIT LOCATIONS

the biggest rap against him is that he appears to view defense as a secondary role with which he would rather not be bothered. But last year, perhaps because the Mets were in contention, Foster seemed to extend himself more in the outfield. He made some catches not customary of him, and he even took on a wall here and there. Still, Foster does not charge balls well, has a weak arm and doesn't always get rid of the ball quickly enough or throw it to the correct spot. He's the stereotypical power hitter who plays left field.

OVERALL:

Foster is now 36 years old, but you look around the big leagues and see an increasing number of hitters producing in their mid-to-late 30s. There is no reason Foster cannot exceed his 1984 numbers in 1985.

Snider: "With his team in contention, George played the game a little differently in 1984. He is a clutch player who probably was very happy with the year he had."

HITTING:

Ron Gardenhire's career has been an elevator ride between New York and Tidewater--up and down, up and down. Three years ago, the Mets saw him as their starting shortstop. More recently, the prevalent view of Gardenhire has been as a utility infielder and role player.

Gardenhire struggles against quality major league pitching--and sometimes against not-so-quality pitching. He can hit the change-up, but pitchers learn this quickly and stop throwing it to him. He is vulnerable to low, inside curveballs, and he can be overpowered. He sees the high fastball well and can sometimes do damage on this pitch. He hits straightaway more than anywhere else, and hits it on the ground more than in the air. Occasionally, he will enter a hot spell during which he drives the ball with authority, and if he hits the ball into the gap, Gardenhire may get himself another triple.

BASERUNNING:

Gardenhire does not have blinding speed, but he runs very hard. He gets out of the batter's box quickly, accelerates well and never slows down. He seems to sense just how many bases he can get out of a batted ball--and he takes them. He is aggressive on the bases and seems to enjoy sliding. He is good at breaking up the double play and at forcing defensive players to make mistakes.

FIELDING:

He has worked hard at the game, but the fact remains that Gardenhire is somewhat below average as a defensive player. Given his offensive limitations, he must make himself into a sterling defensive player if he is to become an everyday player.

He has some raw tools that can help

RON GARDENHIRE
SS, No. 19
RR, 6'0", 175 lbs.
ML Svc: 3 years
Born: 10-24-57 in
Butzbach, GER

1984 STATISTICS

AVG	G	AB	R	H	2B	3B	HR	RBI	BB	SO	SB
.246	74	207	20	51	7	1	1	10	9	43	6

CAREER STATISTICS

AVG	G	AB	R	H	2B	3B	HR	RBI	BB	SO	SB
.235	259	671	52	158	25	2	4	47	38	111	13

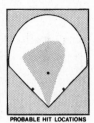

VS. RHP   VS. LHP   PROBABLE HIT LOCATIONS

him in the field: his arm is accurate, and he has good range at shortstop. He moves gracefully to his left, and he can throw on the run--important characteristics for a shortstop. He also benefits from having a manager who feels that defensive ability can be taught and cultivated.

OVERALL:

Gardenhire got a good shot at a roster position in 1982 but had lesser opportunities the last two seasons. While the final verdict on his future certainly has not yet been rendered, it appears unlikely that he has the multiple skills needed to be in the starting lineup.

Snider: "He's a good guy to have on the bench. He can be a team player--a role player. He gets the most out of what he's got; he tries hard and isn't afraid to get his uniform dirty."

PITCHING:

Oh . . . what do you say?

Start with this: Dwight Gooden has a chance to become the dominant pitcher of his era, the pitcher by whom all others of the 1980s and 1990s will be measured. He has a chance to be one of the truly great pitchers in baseball history. He has the makings.

Gooden, the National League Rookie of the Year and a high finisher in the Cy Young Award voting, exploded upon the league and left his mark. He is extremely poised and confident, and, with his stuff, why not?

He throws a 90+ MPH fastball and he hits spots with it. He throws an exceptional overhand curveball, which, during his delivery, is indistinguishable from his fastball. He is learning a change-up. Gooden has the ability to pitch through nine innings without losing too much velocity from his fastball. And, although Dwight is only 20 years old and has one year of major league experience and almost NO experience at the Triple A level, he knows how to pitch.

He has clearly established himself as the ace of the Mets' starting pitching staff, and, unless he slips badly, he will be the ace of the staff for a long time to come.

FIELDING, HITTING, BASERUNNING:

If you are looking for a flaw in Gooden as a player, you won't find it here. He is an excellent fielding pitcher, runs well enough to even steal an occasional base and swings the bat impressively. His pickoff move is better than you would expect from a 20-year-old

DWIGHT GOODEN
RHP, No. 16
RR, 6'2", 190 lbs.
ML Svc: 1 year
Born: 11-16-64 in
Tampa, FL

1984 STATISTICS
W	L	ERA	G	GS	CG	IP	H	R	ER	BB	SO	SV
17	9	2.60	31	31	7	218	161	72	63	73	276	0

CAREER STATISTICS
W	L	ERA	G	GS	CG	IP	H	R	ER	BB	SO	SV
17	9	2.60	31	31	7	218	161	72	63	73	276	0

but, still, he went to the Florida Instructional League last fall to work on it.

OVERALL:

Even if his stuff never improves a bit, Gooden should be a big winner for a long time. The only question may be how well he handles the enormous pressure of playing in New York City. He appears right now to be a humble, level-headed young man; the challenge lies in remaining that way.

Snider: "If he can handle all the New York notoriety, we might be looking at the next Bob Gibson, the next Juan Marichal, the next Sandy Koufax--name whoever you want. It's as Dwight told me last summer: 'I know nobody is unhittable, but I've got a chance to be quite a pitcher.' You bet he does!"

PITCHING:

When he was in the Montreal organization, the Expos had Tom Gorman ticketed as a potentially outstanding short relief pitcher. He never developed into that role for the Expos and was peddled to the Mets.

Gorman still is not an outstanding short reliever, but last season he was outstanding at times as a middle reliever. His key pitch is the forkball; without it, he is nothing as a major league pitcher.

To be effective, he must throw a lot of forkballs, to both lefthanded and righthanded batters, and he must keep the pitch down. He knows very well what he must to do be successful. He can complement the forkball with a fastball that moves well on good days, a curveball and a straight change. He knows how to move the ball around, and he has good control. He is tougher against righthanded batters than lefties.

Gorman's value to the Mets is as a pitcher who can keep games close until it is time for Jesse Orosco or Doug Sisk to enter. In this role, he also will pick up a few wins if he does his job and the Mets rally while he is the pitcher of record.

FIELDING, HITTING, BASERUNNING:

Gorman likes the game of baseball (unfortunately, that cannot be said of all players), and he works hard to play

TOM GORMAN
LHP, No. 29
LL, 6'4", 200 lbs.
ML Svc: 2 years
Born: 12-16-57 in
   Portland, OR

1984 STATISTICS
W	L	ERA	G	GS	CG	IP	H	R	ER	BB	SO	SV
6	0	2.97	36	0	0	57	51	20	19	13	40	0

CAREER STATISTICS
W	L	ERA	G	GS	CG	IP	H	R	ER	BB	SO	SV
8	5	3.81	78	5	0	137	124	61	58	38	96	0

the game better. Consequently, he is a capable fielder, hitter and baserunner. His move to first base is good enough to keep the average baserunner a half step closer to the bag--an often significant margin.

OVERALL:

Gorman should have a secure job on the staff in 1985. The way the New York staff is structured, he'll work in the fifth, sixth and seventh innings. If Sisk or Orosco is injured, then Gorman would move into shorter situations.

Snider: "He can be outstanding in middle relief. He was 6-0 last season and knows what he has to do to be effective."

HITTING:

Danny Heep is a classic example of a minor league slugger who has had to settle for a secondary role in the major leagues. He can devastate minor league pitching, but against big league pitchers, who tend to make far fewer mistakes, he is a much more ordinary hitter.

In 1983, when New York brought up Darryl Strawberry, Heep was platooning with Gary Rajsich in right field for the Mets. But since "The Straw That Stirs the Drink" arrived, Heep's primary role has been that of a lefthanded pinch-hitter. That figures to remain his role.

Heep has power and can be especially dangerous when pitchers make a mistake; he has the ability to decide games with one swing of the bat. He is a high ball hitter who can be deadly on pitches that are up and out over the plate. Heep can be neutralized by keeping the ball in on him, especially in on his fists or lower. He does not hit breaking balls as well as he hits fastballs.

An aggressive hitter, Heep does not have the patience or the inclination to accept a walk. He swings at too many pitches out of the strike zone; savvy pitchers use this against him. Still, when he gets his pitch, he can drive it for extra bases. When a sacrifice fly is needed, he is also a good man to have at the plate, assuming he doesn't strike out.

BASERUNNING:

He has deceptively good speed, but he is a very cautious baserunner. Occasionally, he will settle for a single when he really should turn it into a double. Heep goes in hard on double plays when the situation demands it.

FIELDING:

Danny has played first base and all

DANNY HEEP
PH/OF/1B, No. 25
LL, 5'11", 185 lbs.
ML Svc: 4 years
Born: 7-3-57 in
San Antonio, TX

1984 STATISTICS

AVG	G	AB	R	H	2B	3B	HR	RBI	BB	SO	SB
.231	99	199	36	46	9	2	1	12	27	22	3

CAREER STATISTICS

AVG	G	AB	R	H	2B	3B	HR	RBI	BB	SO	SB
.244	379	847	94	207	46	3	13	74	96	117	6

  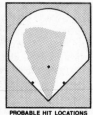

VS. RHP   VS. LHP   PROBABLE HIT LOCATIONS

three outfield positions, and he won't hurt his team at any of the four spots-- but he won't win you many games in the field, either. No matter: all four jobs are taken on the Mets, leaving Heep's primary value as a pinch-hitter.

OVERALL:

One day--soon--Heep should step forward as the Mets' No. 1 lefthanded pinch-hitter.

Snider: "He didn't hit for a very high average last year, but just when you think you've got him, Heep can hurt you with the bat. He can spell Keith Hernandez at first base, and he knows his role. He would like to play more often, but he is a team player and not a complainer."

HITTING:

Keith Hernandez's 1983 trade to the Mets from St. Louis raised an interesting set of possibilities: would he be completely out of place in New York, unable to handle the attendant hype and notoriety, or would Hernandez rise to the occasion? Rise to the occasion? Hernandez can leap tall buildings in a single bound!

At the age of 31, Hernandez is a better baseball player now than he has ever been. (Last season, he was second in NL MVP voting.)

He is one of the best lefthanded clutch hitters--one of the best hitters, period--in the league. Hernandez has a smooth, relaxed swing, and he strides forcefully into every pitch. He hits the ball to all fields against righthanders and goes the opposite way with lefthanders. He has an extraordinary eye at the plate, does not mind taking a walk and forces good pitches.

He has proved himself to be both a good clutch hitter and a good on-base percentage hitter. He will hit some home runs, but he hits more doubles and triples. He knows how to place the ball. There really is no pitch he cannot handle, no part of the field he cannot reach.

Devastating against lefthanded pitchers on a pitch between the waist and the knees, Hernandez is equally dangerous against righthanders on any pitch up and away.

BASERUNNING:

Baserunning is the only facet of his game which can be categorized as average. Despite a lack of speed, he will challenge the pitcher, taking a lead and playing the distracting role if he can. But he isn't a basestealing threat.

FIELDING:

Put it this way: Keith Hernandez is the best defensive first baseman in the National League and probably will be for

KEITH HERNANDEZ
1B, No. 17
LL, 6'0", 185 lbs.
ML Svc: 10 years
Born: 10-20-53 in
San Francisco, CA

1984 STATISTICS

AVG	G	AB	R	H	2B	3B	HR	RBI	BB	SO	SB
.311	154	550	83	171	31	0	15	94	97	89	2

CAREER STATISTICS

AVG	G	AB	R	H	2B	3B	HR	RBI	BB	SO	SB
.300	1414	4946	788	1486	304	53	105	726	746	667	91

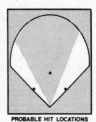

VS. RHP   VS. LHP   PROBABLE HIT LOCATIONS

at least a few more years. He is a precious commodity as far as other infielders are concerned, saving them countless throwing errors with his ability to pull balls out of the dirt and pull others out of the air by stretching. He also is accomplished at leaving the base for a wide throw and making a tag on the baserunner.

Hernandez has good range on batted balls and plays the bunt extremely well. Year in and year out, he will rank with the NL's top first basemen in chances and putouts. He has a strong, accurate throwing arm.

OVERALL:

If anyone in St. Louis thought that Keith might be slipping a bit, he has proved them clearly wrong. He is one of the best all-around players in the game and a valuable leader on a young, maturing Mets team.

Snider: "If it's possible, I think that Keith has become even better. He's a Gold Glove first baseman, a leader; it's just a pleasure to watch him play."

HITTING:

The injuries to John Stearns and the Mets' failure to settle on a front-line replacement have forced Ron Hodges to have more starts behind the plate than ideally would be the case. His abilities are more suited for use as a backup catcher or lefthanded pinch-hitter.

He is a low ball hitter who likes to drive these pitches to the opposite field. He is not a power hitter, but he does hit the ball hard whether it's on the line or on the ground.

Hodges is a good bunter and has good bat control, which makes him useful in hit-and-run situations. He responds well to clutch situations, making him a reliable pinch-hitter.

The best way to pitch to Hodges is to throw him hard stuff up and in or breaking stuff away. He does not go the opposite way with the ball very often.

BASERUNNING:

He is a one-base-at-a-time type of runner, and he can pretty much be discounted as a potential basestealer. He gets out of the batter's box slowly. Although he is a good bunter, his lack of speed and his slow start mean that he can rarely beat out a bunt. But he can sacrifice runners along, at least.

FIELDING:

When Stearns's injury forced Ron to put on the catcher's gear, Hodges proved to be adequate as a fill-in. His greatest asset is that he appears to have a working knowledge of the opposing hitters' strengths and weaknesses, and he uses this to call a solid game. His arm is strong, but his footwork sometimes falls into disarray. Hodges gets rid of the ball slowly. He also sprays throws around second base. Knowing this, oppo-

RON HODGES
C, No. 42
LR, 6'1", 187 lbs.
ML Svc: 11 years
Born: 6-22-49 in
    Franklin County, VA

1984 STATISTICS

AVG	G	AB	R	H	2B	3B	HR	RBI	BB	SO	SB
.208	64	106	5	22	3	0	1	11	23	18	1

CAREER STATISTICS

AVG	G	AB	R	H	2B	3B	HR	RBI	BB	SO	SB
.240	666	1426	119	342	56	2	19	147	224	217	10

  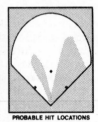

VS. RHP   VS. LHP   PROBABLE HIT LOCATIONS

sing baserunners will challenge him. As a receiver, he is good at blocking low pitches.

OVERALL:

It is not Ron Hodges's fault, but he simply does not have the tools to be a starting major league catcher. He can be an integral part of a team, though. Ideally, he should catch 30 or 35 games a year and spend the rest of his time as a pinch-hitter.

Snider: "He's been around a long time (in fact, he was on the Mets' 1973 National League championship team), and he knows just exactly where he stands on the ballclub. He is not the No. 1 catcher, but he can do an adequate job for a little while."

HITTING:

One of the Houston Astros' best hitters in 1982 and 1983, Ray Knight went into such a bad slump in 1984 that he not only lost his starting job but did not even fit into Houston's pinch-hitting plans. Thus, he was sent to New York in a late-season trade.

Knight stands away from the plate, is a high ball hittter and has a good ability to foul off tough pitches, making it difficult to get your best stuff past him. He likes to battle the pitcher until he sees what he wants. In 1984, though, he kept missing even those deliveries.

Except for last year, he has been an excellent clutch hitter and a good RBI man. Even so, it's difficult to bat him higher than sixth or seventh because he is so slow that he clogs the bases.

He can hit-and-run and adjust to any other situation. He may show more power away from the Astrodome. Until last year, he's always got the maximum from his ability.

BASERUNNING:

The heart is willing, but legs are not. Several injuries and Father Time have combined to slow Knight to a crawl. He doesn't make silly mistakes, though, and gives you the best he's got.

FIELDING:

If Hubie Brooks makes the transition from third base to shortstop, Knight may start regularly at third. The question then involves his arm. At Houston, he had trouble getting throws across the infield, precipitating a move to first base where initially he was terrible but where he developed into a more than adequate fielder. The Mets have Keith

RAY KNIGHT
1B, No. 22
RR, 6'2", 190 lbs.
ML Svc: 8 years
Born: 12-28-52 in
Albany, GA

1984 STATISTICS

AVG	G	AB	R	H	2B	3B	HR	RBI	BB	SO	SB
.237	115	371	28	88	14	0	3	35	21	43	0

CAREER STATISTICS

AVG	G	AB	R	H	2B	3B	HR	RBI	BB	SO	SB
.280	1013	3210	337	898	194	23	50	385	231	364	10

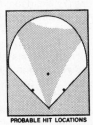

VS. RHP   VS. LHP   PROBABLE HIT LOCATIONS

Hernandez at first, a position off limits to anyone else. Lack of speed does not help him afield either.

OVERALL:

Whether Knight regressed in 1984 because of a slower bat or because of physical problems--kidney stones, vertigo--remains to be seen. A fresh start with a new team may help. Knight isn't a complainer, but he and Houston manager Bob Lillis didn't see eye-to-eye on everything in 1984.

Campbell: "After the physical ailments slowed him for a month and a half, Knight never got a chance to unwind last year. So 1985 becomes a make-or-break season for him in terms of our finding out if time has caught up with him."

PITCHING:

Ed Lynch looks like a power pitcher--he is 6'5", 207 pounds--but looks are deceptive in this case. He is a finesse pitcher in the purest sense.

A starter and spot starter for the Mets over the past three seasons, Lynch is not blessed with overpowering velocity. Instead, he battles, nibbling at the corners, changing speeds, trying to out-think and outguess the hitters.

Occasionally, he can pop a fastball in the 90-91 MPH range, but he likes to throw just as many curves and change-ups as he does fastballs. Lynch has also developed a slurve, which at times has a big break and is very effective. Generally speaking, none of his pitches are outstanding major league pitches. Lynch has good control and he cannot win without it. He also keeps the ball down consistently.

He is normally a five- or six-inning pitcher, not the complete-game type. He has a somewhat unorthodox delivery, holding onto the pitch a little longer than most pitchers and releasing it from far out in front of him. This cuts into the time the hitter has to watch the pitch. Lynch is the kind of pitcher who looks for every possible advantage.

FIELDING, HITTING, BASERUNNING:

Lynch is active and alert on the mound. He moves quickly and decisively to field bunts and other batted balls. He has worked hard on his move to first base, and it has improved. A few years ago, he had a tendency to forget about

ED LYNCH
RHP, No. 36
RR, 6'5", 207 lbs.
ML Svc: 4 years
Born: 2-25-56 in
Brooklyn, NY

1984 STATISTICS
W	L	ERA	G	GS	CG	IP	H	R	ER	BB	SO	SV
9	8	4.50	40	13	0	124	169	77	62	24	62	2

CAREER STATISTICS
W	L	ERA	G	GS	CG	IP	H	R	ER	BB	SO	SV
28	32	3.97	135	69	1	537	625	272	237	131	193	4

the baserunner, but he no longer does that. A good all-around athlete, Lynch likes running the bases--but he is rarely on them.

OVERALL:

Lynch is the type of pitcher who could be shoved off the Mets' rotation and/or staff by the emergence of younger pitchers with more natural ability. But that has not happened yet, and Lynch keeps outthinking and outguessing just enough hitters to hang on.

Snider: "If he gets the ball down low, he can make you hit it on the ground. He is a battler, and he did a good job off and on last season. The pressure is really on him because of the way the Mets' pitching staff is heading. The younger stars may make it difficult for Lynch to stay around."

PITCHING:

It is hard to remember, let alone believe, that just two years ago Jesse Orosco had a 4-10 record. For the last two seasons, he has been one of the best relief pitchers in the game.

He was always blessed with a great arm and a 92 MPH fastball, but he did not know how to pitch until 1983. He learned a lot from ex-Mets manager George Bamberger, who taught him the slider and how to take command of both himself and the game. Still, the fastball remains his best pitch; in addition to velocity, he has outstanding movement on the pitch. Being a lefthander helps in this regard.

Now, armed with his fastball, slider, good control and absolute confidence, Orosco is a feared figure for the opposition in any close game. Orosco can be virtually impossible for lefties to hit. But the slider has made it extremely difficult for righthanders to get anything off him as well.

A lot of relievers are inconsistent--good one year, bad the next--but Orosco has indicated by his performances in the last two seasons that he will be a consistent stopper year after year.

FIELDING, HITTING, BASERUNNING:

Orosco does himself favors on the field. He has an exceptional move to first base; he'll occasionally pick a runner off and, more significantly, will keep everyone close. This is particularly important since he often is working with one-run leads.

He fields his position well, getting

JESSE OROSCO
LHP, No. 47
RL, 6'2", 185 lbs.
ML Svc: 4 years
Born: 4-21-57 in
   Santa Barbara, CA

1984 STATISTICS

W	L	ERA	G	GS	CG	IP	H	R	ER	BB	SO	SV
10	6	2.59	60	0	0	87	58	29	25	34	85	31

CAREER STATISTICS

W	L	ERA	G	GS	CG	IP	H	R	ER	BB	SO	SV
28	26	2.46	202	4	0	358	272	117	98	140	298	53

off the mound quickly and never failing to cover first base. He has a better than average bat for a pitcher, but short relievers rarely get to the plate.

OVERALL:

The Mets are very fortunate to have Orosco in their bullpen, even more so because he is a lefthander. His arm is amazingly resilient, and he is a workhorse. The presence of Jesse Orosco in the bullpen has enabled the Mets to shape the rest of their pitching staff with confidence.

Snider: "Nobody had heard of him when Neil Allen was in the Mets' bullpen, but all of a sudden, Orosco got the opportunity and made the most of it. He just goes out there and gets outs; he has got tremendous stuff. He is the kind of guy that anybody would love to have on his staff."

PITCHING:

Like Jesse Orosco, Sisk received his opportunity when Neil Allen was traded to the Cardinals. And like Orosco, albeit to a lesser degree, Sisk has capitalized on the opportunity.

Sisk had been a workhorse for two seasons, going to the mound even more often than Orosco, until he was injured late last season. But he should be fine in 1985 and ready to resume his role as a middle/late reliever. That means he doesn't pitch the ultra-crucial ninth inning situations that go to Orosco, but he is trusted to pitch the eighth innings of tight games or finish games with, say, two-run leads.

His arm is durable; in 1983, Sisk pitched in 67 games, more than any other pitcher in Mets history. He has a good fastball (89-90 MPH, with good movement on it) and excellent control. He is tougher against righties than lefties. Sisk is a smart pitcher, and thinks before he throws. He places the ball well. He doesn't mind jamming a power hitter or flirting with the outside corner on a pull hitter. He does not give up many home runs, an important asset in his role.

Being a righthander, he is an ideal complement to the lefthanded Orosco; they provide the nucleus of a first-rate bullpen.

FIELDING, HITTING, BASERUNNING:

Sisk is an above average fielder who has a particularly good move to first base for a righthander. When he inherits

DOUG SISK
RHP, No. 39
RR, 6'2", 210 lbs.
ML Svc: 2 years
Born: 9-26-57 in
Renton, WA

1984 STATISTICS

W	L	ERA	G	GS	CG	IP	H	R	ER	BB	SO	SV
1	3	2.09	50	0	0	77	57	24	18	54	32	15

CAREER STATISTICS

W	L	ERA	G	GS	CG	IP	H	R	ER	BB	SO	SV
6	8	2.13	125	0	0	190	150	63	45	117	69	27

baserunners, as he often does, he holds them close. He fields bunts well because he is alert, quick, has sure hands and doesn't panic with his throws. He looks as if he could be mildly dangerous with the bat, but rarely gets an opportunity.

OVERALL:

All teams would love to go into a season knowing they had a bullpen tandem like Orosco and Sisk. But few teams have such a luxury. They are a perfect pitching complement--they are even roommates, sharing expenses and chores at home as well.

Snider: "The difference between Orosco and Sisk is that Sisk will give you a few more pitches to hit. Not many, but a few. Because of Orosco, he doesn't get the amount of saves he would if he were the number one man in the pen."

HITTING:

One word says all that needs to be said about Rusty Staub as a baseball player: Hitter!

Pure and simple, the man is a hitter, even at the age of 40. He knows every pitcher in the league; he knows what to expect in every situation, and he knows what to do with it. It is safe to say that he is the most dangerous pinch-hitter in the game.

Staub prefers the pitch down in the strike zone and out over the plate. He knows the strike zone as well as any hitter in the league. Against right-handed pitchers, Staub often hits to the opposite field. Against lefthanders, he goes up the middle or pulls the ball. Consequently, lefthanders should pitch him down and in, and righthanders should pitch him away.

Staub can hit for both power and average, and he can appear downright unbeatable in clutch situations. He is a streak hitter who, when hot, will turn just about any pitch into a line drive.

BASERUNNING:

Staub does not get paid to run. He lumbers around the bases more than he runs around them, always taking one base at a time. Often, after being used as a pinch-hitter, he will be lifted for a pinch-runner. An ordinary triple for most players is a standup double (maybe) for Staub.

FIELDING:

Although primarily a pinch-hitter, he will occasionally fill in at first base or in the outfield. He does his best at both spots. But his arm is not as strong as it once was, and he has no range at all.

RUSTY STAUB
PH/1B, No. 10
LR, 6'2", 230 lbs.
ML Svc: 21 years
Born: 4-1-44 in
  New Orleans, LA

1984 STATISTICS

AVG	G	AB	R	H	2B	3B	HR	RBI	BB	SO	SB
.264	78	72	2	19	4	0	1	18	4	9	0

CAREER STATISTICS

AVG	G	AB	R	H	2B	3B	HR	RBI	BB	SO	SB
.279	2897	9675	1187	2704	496	47	291	1458	1245	884	47

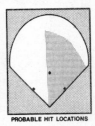

VS. RHP VS. LHP PROBABLE HIT LOCATIONS

OVERALL:

True, Staub has become a one-dimensional player, but his dimension is one that can win ball games in the late innings.

Snider: "If I had room for him, he would be on my team, even if I had to wheel him to the plate. He is a pure hitter. He's got the kind of swing that is very hard to get out of synch. I know that there are some hits left in his bat. He can win a game for you, or he can start a rally."

HITTING:

One year ago, no one hesitated to label Darryl Strawberry as "The Franchise." With the emergence of Dwight Gooden, Strawberry might have to share that distinction.

Strawberry had some struggles in his sophomore season, but he appeared to pull through well. Based on his rookie season and the general expectations of what was to follow, Strawberry's 1984 season was viewed as an off year. But he still looks like a player who will be one of the game's great offensive weapons--a player who should be able to hit for average, for power and for run production.

He has very quick wrists, and his hitting style has been compared by many enthused scouts to that of Ted Williams. He likes the ball down and out over the plate. Like most power hitters, he wants to get his arms fully extended in his swing. He is still learning to hit major league change-ups, but when he is in a groove, he's one of those hitters who can hit just about everything.

His problems last season more likely resulted from the mental adjustments to fame and celebrity status than from any deficiencies in his ability.

BASERUNNING:

Strawberry has all the natural tools, including the ability to run. He could eventually become a member of baseball's elitist 30-30 club (30 home runs and 30 steals in the same season). Being a lefthanded hitter helps him beat out a few more infield hits than he would otherwise get, and his 6'6" height allows him to cover a lot of ground in a single stride. But more importantly, he has agility, quickness and speed. He also has good baserunning instincts.

FIELDING:

Strawberry's defensive game appeared to suffer last season from lapses of concentration. But this, too, might have

DARRYL STRAWBERRY
RF, No. 18
LL, 6'6", 190 lbs.
ML Svc: 2 years
Born: 3-12-62 in
   Los Angeles, CA

1984 STATISTICS

AVG	G	AB	R	H	2B	3B	HR	RBI	BB	SO	SB
.251	147	522	75	131	27	4	26	97	75	131	27

CAREER STATISTICS

AVG	G	AB	R	H	2B	3B	HR	RBI	BB	SO	SB
.254	269	942	138	239	42	11	52	171	122	259	46

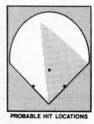

VS. RHP   VS. LHP   PROBABLE HIT LOCATIONS

been the result of struggling with the pressures of success in New York. The only physical limitation to his defensive game is that he has a below average throwing arm, particularly for a right fielder. He has good instincts in the outfield, but sometimes tends to trail the ball rather than go directly for it, and sometimes tends to stick his glove up rather than actively catch the ball.

OVERALL:

If he can handle all of the hype, if he can play despite what he reads about himself, then Darryl Strawberry should quickly become a full-fledged superstar.

Snider: "As a man who played in New York for 12 years, I know what the media hype is like. They make you feel as if you are the greatest thing since canned beer. I think Darryl will get it all together and let his natural talents catapult him to stardom. The best thing for him to do is not to buy a newspaper and just go out and play hard. But oh my, wouldn't you like to be his age and have his talent?"

PITCHING:

For now, Walt Terrell must be categorized in the middle echelon of pitchers. Solid but not spectacular, promising but not proven. Possibly a very good big league pitcher, not a sure thing.

Another member of the Mets' unusually large class of young pitching talents, Terrell has already distinguished himself with good control. His fastball is not overpowering, but it moves well and is thrown for strikes. Terrell continues to work on his breaking pitches, which clearly are the key to his future success. Right now, they are good enough to throw but not good enough to dazzle.

A righthander, Terrell moves the ball around well and doesn't mind coming inside on hitters. He keeps the ball down consistently. For the most part, he is not a nine-inning pitcher, and he could eventually be used in the bullpen (if there is ever room). On occasions, he will pitch a masterful game, but he hasn't really found a consistent major league groove yet. If he does, he'll be a solid member of the Mets' starting rotation.

FIELDING, HITTING, BASERUNNING:

Terrell is not an assertive fielder, sometimes bowing out of plays which he should make. His move to first is about average for a righthander, and that means it could stand a good deal of improvement. He is one of those pitchers who seems to thoroughly enjoy swinging the bat, and he does it much better than most pitchers. When he makes contact, he

WALT TERRELL
RHP, No. 49
LR, 6'2", 205 lbs.
ML Svc: 2 years
Born: 5-11-58 in
　　Jeffersonville, ID

1984 STATISTICS
W	L	ERA	G	GS	CG	IP	H	R	ER	BB	SO	SV
11	12	3.52	33	33	3	215	232	99	84	80	114	0

CAREER STATISTICS
W	L	ERA	G	GS	CG	IP	H	R	ER	BB	SO	SV
19	23	3.54	57	56	7	369	377	168	145	149	181	0

hits the ball with authority, and sometimes for distance.

OVERALL:

Terrell was a 33rd round draft choice of the Texas Rangers, so he already has done exceedingly well just to reach the big leagues. And he has the ability to achieve even more if he comes up with another pitch or improves one of his existing pitches.

Snider: "The son of a gun can hit; he comes out flailing. As a pitcher, he's not overpowering, but on any given day he can make a guy look bad. He doesn't have one pitch that stands out above the others at this point. The Mets are pulling out all the stops to make their pitching staff the best in the game, and Terrell is one fellow they may have to work on."

HITTING:

Mookie Wilson has two elements that make an ideal leadoff hitter: he is a switch-hitter, and he runs well. But he also strikes out too much and does not walk often enough. In short, he is a free-swinger, not a disciplined hitter.

Wilson had a pretty good season in 1984, but he continued to have trouble with good curveballs and with some fastballs. A natural righthanded batter, he continues to make strides from the left side of the plate. He is at an advantage when batting lefty because his speed allows him to beat out more hits.

From the left side, he likes the ball down and tries to keep it on the ground so as to maximize the speed advantage. Batting from the right side, he likes the ball up and tries to drive it. He has more power from his natural side, the right side of the plate. The best way to pitch to him is to keep the ball inside; he will chase far too many down-and-in breaking balls.

The Mets continue to ponder whether Wilson should bat first or lower in the order, say, sixth (as a "second leadoff").

BASERUNNING:

Wilson has extraordinary speed, but he needs to be more resourceful in reaching base to become a consistent thief of 70-80 bases per year. He bolts out of the batter's box, especially from the left side, and will beat out a lot of ground balls to the left side of the infield. He goes from first to third on singles quite often and almost always scores from second base on even a little hit.

FIELDING:

Wilson is perfectly equipped to play the spacious center field at Shea Stadium. The Mets need someone with his range and speed in center since Foster is in left; you will see Wilson play a

MOOKIE WILSON
CF, No. 1
SR, 5'10", 168 lbs.
ML Svc: 4 years
Born: 2-9-56 in
  Bamberg, SC

1984 STATISTICS

AVG	G	AB	R	H	2B	3B	HR	RBI	BB	SO	SB
.276	154	587	88	162	28	10	10	54	26	90	46

CAREER STATISTICS

AVG	G	AB	R	H	2B	3B	HR	RBI	BB	SO	SB
.275	584	2297	334	631	91	36	25	178	108	373	189

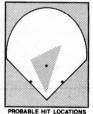

VS. RHP   VS. LHP   PROBABLE HIT LOCATIONS

lot of balls in left-center and occasionally catch a ball directly in front of Foster.

Wilson will occasionally misjudge a ball, but he usually can make up for that kind of error with his speed. He charges the ball well and has a strong, accurate arm. He always seems to have his mind on the game in the outfield, and does not carry his previous strikeout into the field with him.

OVERALL:

The Mets still would like Wilson to increase his on-base percentage, and he just might do it in 1985. He has, after all, consistently improved in all other aspects of his game.

Snider: "He is a free-swinger. It is possible that he hasn't learned to hit major league pitching yet. He does a very good job in center field and has amazing speed--he is like a bullet out of the box."

KELVIN CHAPMAN
2B, No. 11
RR, 5'11", 172 lbs.
ML Svc: 1 year
Born: 6-2-56 in
      Willits, CA

HITTING, BASERUNNING, FIELDING:

Kelvin Chapman played for the Mets in 1979, then dropped out of sight, falling into the anonymous reaches of their farm system and off the 40-man protected roster. Last season, he resurfaced.

A second baseman who has also played in the outfield, Chapman is a fringe player. He has a little pop in his bat, but good big league pitchers should be able to handle him. He will do the most damage on pitches out over the plate and around the waist.

He is a battler who holds his own in the field. He turns the double play adequately.

Chapman has good speed and, on occasion, will steal a base. He likes the game and has learned it well.

OVERALL:

He is the kind of player who can make miscellaneous contributions to a ballclub. Chapman will never be a superstar and may never be a big league regular for a prolonged period of time, but even when he's at the Triple A level, he is useful to have around in case of an emergency.

MIKE FITZGERALD
C, No. 20
RR, 6'0", 185 lbs.
ML Svc: 1 year
Born: 7-13-60 in
      Long Beach, CA

HITTING, BASERUNNING, FIELDING:

The biggest question regarding Mike Fitzgerald is whether he will hit enough to hold onto a big league job. Early last season, he appeared hopelessly overmatched at the plate. But later on, with some exposure to the pitchers, he started dropping in a few more hits. He did not tear up the minor leagues with his bat, so it is unlikely that he will ever do so in the majors.

Fitzgerald appears to be a good receiver. He doesn't let many pitches get past him, and he appears to have a good idea of what pitches to call from various pitchers in various situations. His arm was erratic last season.

He runs the bases like a catcher, which is to say he won't steal or perform any feats of fancy footwork on the basepaths.

OVERALL:

There are some people within the Mets' organization--and some people outside the organization--who think that Fitzgerald has a solid future. One factor in Mike's favor is the scarcity of promising young catchers. But he will need to improve several facets of his game to have a solid career.

Snider: "It's more difficult for a catcher than for a pitcher to jump to the big leagues. He just needs to keep progressing."

BRENT GAFF
RHP, No. 45
RR, 6'2", 200 lbs.
ML Svc: 1 year plus
Born: 10-5-58 in
   Fort Wayne, IN

PITCHING, FIELDING, HITTING, BASERUNNING:

The Mets see Brent Gaff primarily as a relief pitcher and, at this point, as a middle man. But in this era of fewer and fewer complete games and constantly increasing emphasis on the bullpen, middle relievers are becoming vital to a team. Gaff is the type of pitcher who can come into a game in the middle innings and keep the Mets in position to win until they go to one of their short relievers.

He has good stuff for this role: a good fastball, control of his breaking pitches and an adequate change-up. What he needs, of course, is experience; he got some when Sisk was injured late last season.

Gaff hasn't received a lot of major league exposure, but scouts say he is a good athlete who won't hurt himself in the field. He has an adequate pickoff move and does not make the mistake of forgetting about the baserunner.

At the plate, he is nothing special, but in his role as a middle reliever, he won't get many opportunities to swing a bat. He runs as well as most pitchers.

OVERALL:

He is the type of pitcher who might someday get an opportunity to take a larger role on a club, and he has the stuff to take advantage of that occasion. On a staff laden with promising young arms, Gaff fits in comfortably.

WES GARDNER
RHP, No. 57
RR, 6'4", 195 lbs.
ML Svc: 1 year
Born: 4-29-61 in
   Benton, AK

PITCHING, FIELDING, HITTING, BASERUNNING:

Wes Gardner has been overshadowed by the other young talents in the Mets' system, but he got a brief exposure to the big leagues last season. The Mets want to see more of him in spring training 1985.

If Gardner makes the team, it would most likely be as a long reliever or perhaps spot starter.

He has a good fastball, an adequate curveball and a change-up that needs work. He does not have a single pitch or an assortment of pitches that could put him in the class with his colleague Dwight Gooden, for example. But then, who does?

Gardner appears to have good control and a working knowledge of what to do with the ball. He doesn't mind challenging hitters, and that is not always the case with young pitchers. He is not-- and should not be--a nibbler.

Throughout his minor league career, Gardner has been a good fielding pitcher; he is quick and sure-handed. He does not get rattled by difficult plays. His move to first base is as good as one normally finds in a young pitcher. He has not appeared at the plate or on the bases often enough to offer an evaluation of his abilities there.

OVERALL:

Gardner is another of the Mets' pitchers looking to find his niche. He may or may not require more minor league seasoning, but the raw ability appears to be there.

RAFAEL SANTANA
2B, No. 3
RR, 6'1", 160 lbs.
ML Svc: 1 year plus
Born: 1-31-58 in
San Pedro de
Macoris, DR

HITTING, BASERUNNING, FIELDING:

As the Mets continued their search for a shortstop, Rafael Santana got an opportunity at the position last season. He did a decent job.

He covers a fair amount of ground and turns the double play adequately. He appears somewhat erratic in the field, although this could be attributed to his lack of experience. He looks stiff instead of fluid in the field.

As a hitter, Santana may develop into the type of hitter who will punch singles here and there, but he has trouble with good pitches.

On the bases, Santana has good speed.

OVERALL:

No one really knows who is the long-term answer at shortstop for the Mets. Hubie Brooks? Santana? Ron Gardenhire? Jose Oquendo? Or, most likely, someone else . . .

Snider: "He looked as if he did a halfway decent job at shortstop during the stretch he played there. The Mets must find someone to take over on a permanent basis at short if they are going to continue their quest for the title."

PHILADELPHIA PHILLIES

PITCHING:

Larry Andersen is a control pitcher who is used primarily in middle-inning relief. He is well suited to the role.

He doesn't possess that one overpowering pitch, such as a Goose Gossage fastball or a Bruce Sutter split-finger fastball usually associated with late-inning relievers. He gets a lot of ground balls with his sinker and is excellent at setting the table for a stopper.

Andersen uses a three-quarters side-arm motion to deliver a hard sinker, a cut fastball, a slider and a curve. His sinker is his out pitch, but his slider is excellent.

Andersen is most effective against righthanded batters since he is a low ball pitcher and lefties tend to be low ball hitters. He likes to jam right-handers with his slider. He can pitch under pressure and doesn't panic when he gets behind in the count.

For Andersen to be effective, his sinker must be working. When his pitches are up in the strike zone, he gets into trouble. His greatest strength is his ability to go into a game and get a ground ball when it's needed. He is not overpowering, which means he must get his pitches where he wants them if he is going to be effective.

FIELDING, HITTING, BASERUNNING:

Andersen has an average move to first but pays attention to baserunners. He takes his fielding seriously. He gets off the mound quickly, covers first well and backs up the right base.

Andersen isn't called upon to hit

LARRY ANDERSEN
RHP, No. 47
RR, 6'3", 205 lbs.
ML Svc: 5 years
Born: 5-6-53 in
  Portland, OR

1984 STATISTICS													
W	L	ERA	G	GS	CG	IP	H	R	ER	BB	SO	SV
3	7	2.38	64	0	0	90	85	32	24	25	54	4
CAREER STATISTICS													
W	L	ERA	G	GS	CG	IP	H	R	ER	BB	SO	SV
7	11	3.77	184	1	0	301	300	146	126	90	159	10

very often and is not dangerous at the plate. He does work on his hitting, however, and can bunt when called upon. Overall, he is an average hitter and baserunner.

OVERALL:

Andersen is a humorous man who loves to joke. His ability to laugh and make others laugh keeps him and the rest of the clubhouse loose. On the mound, he is highly competitive and competent, completely professional. His success has come through his ability to accept one of the least glamorous roles on a ball-club. He knows his limitations and works within them.

Snider: "Larry is a good man to have on a team. He's not overpowering, but he mixes up his pitches and he has good breaking stuff--he breaks an awful lot of bats. He doesn't have quite enough velocity to be a stopper, but he's been excellent as a middle-inning guy."

PITCHING:

Bill Campbell is the quintessential finesse pitcher. He was acquired by Philadelphia from the Chicago Cubs in the spring of 1984 to work in late relief along with Al Holland. But Campbell couldn't fill that role and finished the season in long and middle relief, jobs he's more suited to.

He has a jerky windup that makes it difficult for hitters to pick up the ball. He uses a three-quarters delivery.

Campbell is one of the few righthanders in the game who throws a screwball. He also possesses a fastball that has been clocked in the mid 80s, a slider and a curve. A third baseman who can pick it is important to Campbell, who throws his screwball to both left and righthanded hitters. Righthanders tend to pull the pitch down to third and lefties will hit it off the end of the bat toward third.

Campbell is a breaking ball pitcher who tries to finesse hitters. He will show hitters his fastball, but he does not get many outs with it. When he starts to lose it, his pitches are up in the strike zone. As long as he keeps his pitches down and throws strikes, he's fine. But when he's behind in the count, he gets too fine and ends up walking batters.

His greatest strength is his competitiveness. He'll battle hitters. But he has to throw his pitches exactly where he wants them. There is very little margin for error with Campbell.

FIELDING, HITTING, BASERUNNING:

Campbell is an above average fielder. He's good enough defensively to be used

BILL CAMPBELL
RHP, No. 39
RR, 6'3", 190 lbs.
ML Svc: 10 years
Born: 8-9-48 in
    Highland Park, MI

1984 STATISTICS

W	L	ERA	G	GS	CG	IP	H	R	ER	BB	SO	SV
6	5	3.44	57	0	0	81	68	43	31	35	52	1

CAREER STATISTICS

W	L	ERA	G	GS	CG	IP	H	R	ER	BB	SO	SV
75	59	3.49	609	9	2	1099	1020	480	426	449	782	119

in the outfield in a pinch. He has only an average move to first, but pays attention to runners and keeps them close.

Campbell is just a fair hitter, but as a reliever he doesn't get that many chances to bat. He is an average baserunner.

OVERALL:

Campbell has an excellent mental approach to the game. He is a well-conditioned athlete. His lack of success last season was due in part to his inability to use the whole plate and the inappropriate use of him as a late reliever.

Snider: "Campbell is a middle-inning guy at best. He wasn't able to fill the role that Philadelphia expected of him. If he falls behind in the count, he's in trouble. He can still pitch, but he's a marginal guy who's going to have his good games and his bad games."

PITCHING:

Steve Carlton is no longer the premier lefthanded power pitcher in the game. But he is still effective, still has his slider and is far from down for the count.

Carlton's money pitch is his slider, a nasty breaking ball that fools hitters into swinging at pitches in the dirt. It is not the dominant pitch it once was. Good hitters have taken some of the mystery out of the pitch by laying off it and taking it for a ball. When righthanded hitters don't flail away at the slider, they force Carlton to go to his fastball. His fastball doesn't have quite the velocity it had earlier in his career. Carlton tries to keep the fastball away from righthanders, and last season he turned it over quite often, giving it a sinking, tailing movement.

Carlton has a big sweeping curveball that he uses most often against lefties and a change-up that he uses once in a while. The change-up is, by far, his weakest pitch. If he is going to continue to use it this season, he will have to work to make it worthwhile.

Carlton has excellent command of his three best pitches, especially the slider, which he will throw at any time in the count. His ability to throw strikes with the slider prevents hitters from laying off the fastball when the count is 3-1 or 3-2.

You can tell when Carlton is tiring by watching his number of walks. He generally works deep counts, but rarely walks hitters when he's sharp. When he is missing with the slider, he must come in with his fastball, and the hitters have a chance against it.

He is an extremely fast worker and a pitcher who relies heavily on rhythm. Often, batters will step out of the box to disrupt his cadence. Carlton's greatest strengths are his concentration and his conditioning. His concentration level is extraordinary. He has the ability to shut out distractions such as fan noise and concentrate entirely on the hitter.

STEVE CARLTON
LHP, No. 32
LL, 6'5", 212 lbs.
ML Svc: 19 years
Born: 12-22-44 in
Miami, FL

1984 STATISTICS

W	L	ERA	G	GS	CG	IP	H	R	ER	BB	SO
13	7	3.58	33	33	1	229	214	104	91	79	163

CAREER STATISTICS

W	L	ERA	G	GS	CG	IP	H	R	ER	BB	SO
313	207	3.04	657	639	251	4785	4207	1837	1615	1603	3872

HITTING, FIELDING, BASERUNNING:

Carlton has an excellent move to first base and is extremely difficult to steal against. His move borders on a balk and umpires will sometimes call him for it, but Carlton gets the benefit of the doubt more often than not.

Fielding is the weakest part of his game. He is not quick off the mound or adept at deflecting ground balls up the middle to his shortstop or second baseman. He does not cover first well.

Carlton is an excellent hitter and must be taken seriously at the plate. With below average speed, he is not a good baserunner.

OVERALL:

Snider: "It looks like he's lost a little bit on his fastball. He's not throwing the ball with as much velocity consistently. He is turning the ball over an awful lot, making it run away from righthanded hitters. He knows the hitters exceptionally well. If hitters lay off that slider, it can be a long evening for him. He is still good enough to be a quality major league pitcher, but he is not the Steve Carlton we're used to seeing."

HITTING:

Tim Corcoran uses a straight-up, closed stance and stands well back in the box. He is a low ball, opposite field hitter with a little power to right and right-center.

Corcoran, who turns 32 years old in March, has spent much of his 12-year professional career bouncing around the minor leagues. Philadelphia signed him as a free agent in April 1982, and he spent the next two seasons in its farm system.

Though he was not an everyday player, he did spend all of last season with the big league club, batting .341 and driving in 36 runs while filling in at three different positions. Corcoran was particularly valuable as a pinch-hitter, batting .270 with 10 RBIs.

He likes pitches away that he can take to left. Pitchers generally pitch him away and teams defense him by over-shifting to left. Occasionally, pitchers will try to jam him. He has trouble with left and righthanders who work up in the strike zone.

He seldom hit against lefthanders, going 5 for 13. He was remarkably consistent, hitting .324 against righties, .348 on the road, .333 at home, .345 on turf and .333 on natural grass.

Corcoran is a patient, consistent hitter. He knows how to work a pitcher and will wait for his pitch. He is not called upon to bunt.

BASERUNNING:

Corcoran has below average speed on the bases and is not a threat to steal. He hustles on the bases and is aggressive at breaking up the double play.

FIELDING:

Corcoran plays both first base and the outfield. His best position is probably first, where he started 34 games, but he can play both left (four starts)

TIM CORCORAN
OF, No. 33
LL, 5'11", 175 lbs.
ML Svc: 5 years
Born: 3-19-53 in
    Glendale, CA

1984 STATISTICS

AVG	G	AB	R	H	2B	3B	HR	RBI	BB	SO	SB
.341	102	208	30	71	13	1	5	36	37	27	0

CAREER STATISTICS

AVG	G	AB	R	H	2B	3B	HR	RBI	BB	SO	SB
.283	400	861	108	244	40	3	12	106	99	82	4

  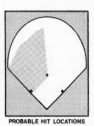

VS. RHP   VS. LHP   PROBABLE HIT LOCATIONS

and right (11 starts) without hurting a team. He committed only one error all season.

As a first baseman, Corcoran has good range and is excellent at digging balls out of the dirt. He has a strong, accurate arm. He is excellent at fielding bunts.

OVERALL:

Corcoran is a sound, fundamental player and a fine hitter. He was not blessed with any of the tools he has; he has had to work for everything. Defensively, Tim can play three positions well. He is best suited to coming off the bench, and in that role would be an asset to any ballclub.

Snider: "He knows what to do with the bat when he walks to the plate. He has got a little sock. He plays the outfield and first base, and gets the job done both places."

HITTING:

Sometimes, even the steadiest of players have off years. Ivan DeJesus had his in 1984.

DeJesus likes fastballs from the middle of the plate in. He has trouble with hard stuff and breaking balls away. Pitchers try to keep the ball away from him and teams defense him by overshifting to right field.

As the No. 8 hitter in the Phillies' lineup for three seasons, DeJesus proved himself to be a patient hitter. He is willing to give himself up to move runners along and is an excellent bunter.

DeJesus's biggest problem as a hitter is that he stands too far off the plate. If he stood closer to the plate, he would make better contact with outside pitches and be able to hit more balls up the middle.

He is a more effective hitter against lefthanded pitching since he has a tendency to pull breaking balls.

BASERUNNING:

DeJesus is average at getting out of the box, but he has good speed and is a threat to steal. But as the No. 8 hitter, DeJesus is rarely called upon to run.

FIELDING:

DeJesus dropped off significantly in 1984. He committed 29 errors in 144 games last year after making 23 in 158 games in 1983--the third fewest errors among National League shortstops.

DeJesus's defensive problems were more mental than physical. He has all the tools: a strong, accurate arm, quick feet, good hands, great range and aggressiveness. His greatest difficulty came on balls hit right at him, a sign that he may have lacked good concentration. The Philadelphia fans rode him hard for his errors, and the razzing seemed to have an effect.

The ballclub finally replaced him in September with Steve Jeltz. This spring,

IVAN DeJESUS
SS, No. 11
RR, 5'11", 182 lbs.
ML Svc: 9 years
Born: 1-9-53 in
Santurce, PR

1984 STATISTICS

AVG	G	AB	R	H	2B	3B	HR	RBI	BB	SO	SB
.257	144	435	40	112	15	3	0	35	43	76	12

CAREER STATISTICS

AVG	G	AB	R	H	2B	3B	HR	RBI	BB	SO	SB
.255	1289	4499	582	1146	170	48	21	316	460	641	192

STRONG

VS. RHP

STRONG

VS. LHP

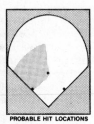

PROBABLE HIT LOCATIONS

Jeltz is being projected as the starting shortstop.

OVERALL:

DeJesus is a durable player. In nine years, he never missed a game because of injury. The steadiness that marked his game over eight major league seasons was gone last year. He became unpredictable in the field. One mistake seemed to breed another, and DeJesus put tremendous pressure on himself late in the season. He has the ability to bounce back, but at the end of last season his days with Philadelphia seemed numbered.

Snider: "Many fans don't realize that ballplayers can be affected by what they see and hear in the stands. Cheers of encouragement can help a slumping player while jeers can make him play worse. Ivan has been an excellent shortstop for a long time. Age may be catching up to him, but his play last season was probably just a bad slump he could not shake."

PITCHING:

John Denny is a control pitcher who blends a sinking fastball with one of the best curveballs in baseball. When healthy, Denny is as good a righthanded starter as there is. After suffering shoulder problems in 1982, he remained healthy in 1983 and won 19 games and the Cy Young Award. An elbow injury limited Denny to 22 starts last season. Still, he posted an excellent 2.45 ERA.

Denny uses an abbreviated windup and a three-quarters overhand delivery. He likes to run his fastball down and away to righthanded hitters. He has a good slider, but his out pitch is his curveball. He changes speeds with it and has one of the best slow curves in the game.

His control is well above average. He walked only 29 batters while striking out 94 in 154 innings pitched last season. But then, he is not a strikeout pitcher. Ground balls are his game.

Denny is so consistent that it is difficult to determine when he's tiring. He always keeps his team in a game.

There was a time in Denny's career when he was known as a pitcher who could be rattled. An error by one of his fielders or a bad call by an umpire could destroy his concentration. That changed last season. Under the tutelege of Gus Hoefling, the Phillies' strength and flexibility coach, Denny learned to block out distractions and take errors and bad calls as part of the game.

Denny's greatest strengths are his curveball and his control. His concentration has also risen to the point of being a strength. His weakness is his health; despite his hard work and dedication to fitness, arm problems have plagued him.

JOHN DENNY
RHP, No. 40
RR, 6'3", 190 lbs.
ML Svc: 10 years
Born: 11-8-52 in
    Prescott, AZ

1984 STATISTICS

W	L	ERA	G	GS	CG	IP	H	R	ER	BB	SO	SV
7	7	2.45	22	22	2	154	122	53	42	29	94	0

CAREER STATISTICS

W	L	ERA	G	GS	CG	IP	H	R	ER	BB	SO	SV
101	84	3.50	265	262	55	1745	1662	766	678	639	908	0

FIELDING, HITTING, BASERUNNING:

His move to first is excellent. He keeps runners close and varies the timing of his move, making it difficult for runners to anticipate his delivery. John is a good fielder, quick off the mound and excellent at covering bunts. He covers first well.

He will help himself with a bat. He is a conservative baserunner with below average speed, but seldom makes a baserunning mistake.

OVERALL:

Denny's mental approach to the game is impeccable. The key to his future is his durability. He will be a quality major league pitcher as long as his right arm holds up.

Snider: "All he has to do is come back healthy and he'll be the mainstay of the ballclub."

HITTING:

Bo Diaz crouches at the plate, keeping all of his weight on his right foot and cocking his bat over his wrists. He is a low ball, fastball hitter with excellent power to left and left-center.

Although he is a pull hitter, he can take outside pitches to right and is a surprisingly good hit-and-run man.

Diaz's weakness is the breaking ball away. He likes the ball from the middle of the plate in. He is an impatient, undisciplined hitter who likes to go after the first pitch. He will chase pitches out of the strike zone when he is behind in the count.

He sustained a knee injury early last season and underwent surgery which sidelined him for all but 27 games. In 75 at-bats, he hit a disappointing .213 and had almost as many strikeouts (13) as hits (16). He walked only five times and grounded into four double plays.

BASERUNNING:

Diaz is a catcher with bad knees, making him even slower than average. He is not a threat to steal. Managers will sometimes try to hit-and-run with him to avoid the double play. He consistently advances one base at a time and cannot score from first on a double.

FIELDING:

Diaz is a fine defensive catcher with a strong, accurate arm and a quick release. Potential basestealers must be wary of him. Diaz is an excellent receiver with good hands and blocks balls in the dirt well. On plays at home, however, he doesn't block the plate, nor does he attempt to bluff a runner into thinking there will be a play when the throw is actually going to another base.

The Phillies' pitching staff thinks highly of him as a signal caller. He

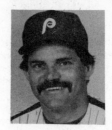

BO DIAZ
C, No. 6
RR, 5'11", 200 lbs.
ML Svc: 7 years
Born: 3-23-53 in
Cua, VEN

1984 STATISTICS

AVG	G	AB	R	H	2B	3B	HR	RBI	BB	SO	SB
.213	27	75	5	16	4	0	1	9	5	13	0

CAREER STATISTICS

AVG	G	AB	R	H	2B	3B	HR	RBI	BB	SO	SB
.257	507	1620	175	417	86	3	46	240	105	231	7

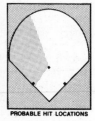

VS. RHP   VS. LHP   PROBABLE HIT LOCATIONS

has the ability to think along with his pitchers and knows how to set up the hitters.

OVERALL:

Because of the knee surgery, Diaz cannot be judged according to his performance in 1984. He is a major league caliber catcher and a hitter who can hurt pitchers with the long ball. The Phillies were trying to trade him during the off season, but they were not sure of his value because he was damaged goods.

Snider: "Bo was hurt last year, so this will be an important season for him. Nobody knows how well he will bounce back from the surgery. He is a fine receiver. He's got some strength in his bat, but he needs to learn some patience at the plate."

HITTING:

Greg Gross stands up in the box with an upright, closed stance. He is a singles hitter who likes pitches from the middle of the plate out.

He is an opposite field hitter with very little power who seldom pulls the ball to right. The vast majority of his hits are to left and left-center. Occasionally he will hit the ball up the middle. Fully 55 of his 65 hits last season were singles.

Greg has trouble with fastball pitchers who mix up their pitches and work in different spots in the strike zone. He rarely bats against lefthanders. He is patient at the plate, but will go after the first pitch if he's being used as a pinch-hitter. He has an excellent concept of the strike zone and is tough to strike out (11 Ks in 202 at-bats in 1984).

Gross is an excellent pinch-hitter. He hit .283 (.322 overall) in that role last season, making him a valuable commodity on the bench.

Gross is a consistent hitter who rarely goes into prolonged slumps. He is an excellent bunter who's not afraid to bunt for base hits down the third base line.

BASERUNNING:

Gross has below average speed, but is an intelligent runner who knows exactly what to do in any given situation. He's not a threat to steal.

FIELDING:

Gross has played all three outfield positions and first base in his tenure with the Phillies. He's not blessed with a lot of natural ability, but his fundamentals are supremely sound. He does not have a strong arm, but Gross charges balls extremely well in the outfield and gets them to the cutoff man

GREG GROSS
OF, No. 21
LL, 5'11", 175 lbs.
ML Svc: 11 years
Born: 8-1-52 in
York, PA

1984 STATISTICS

AVG	G	AB	R	H	2B	3B	HR	RBI	BB	SO	SB
.322	112	202	19	65	9	1	0	16	24	11	1

CAREER STATISTICS

AVG	G	AB	R	H	2B	3B	HR	RBI	BB	SO	SB
.295	1357	3134	391	924	115	43	6	265	418	209	37

  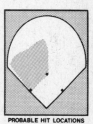

VS. RHP   VS. LHP   PROBABLE HIT LOCATIONS

quickly. He doesn't cover enough ground to play center on a full-time basis and doesn't have a strong enough arm to qualify as an everyday right fielder.

As a first baseman, Gross has good anticipation and digs balls out of the dirt well.

OVERALL:

Gross is the type of player who is more valuable coming off the bench than starting. Defensively, he can be used at any one of four positions and not hurt a team. But good pinch-hitters are hard to find, and Gross is a good one.

His versatility and his willingness to accept a bench role without complaining are two more reasons why Gross is most valuable as a reserve.

Snider: "He is a good guy coming off the bench. He is not in awe of anything. Situations don't bother him too much. It is nice to have people like him."

PITCHING:

A control pitcher, Kevin Gross has above average stuff including an excellent curveball. He was used primarily in long and middle relief last season after being used exclusively as a starter in 1983. The change left him without a clearly defined role on the pitching staff.

While he has shown that he is capable of handling both starting and long relief, Gross could probably be best used as a starter. However, the Phillies needed help in the bullpen last season and he was the pitcher most capable of making the transition from the starting rotation to the bullpen.

Gross has a compact delivery and throws with a three-quarters motion. He has a below average fastball that has been clocked in the mid 80s. His best pitch is his curveball. He can freeze righthanded hitters and get lefthanders out with it, but he uses it much too often. He also has an average slider.

He is inconsistent with his pitches. His control is only fair. He walked 44 batters in 129 innings last season. His strategy is to feed hitters his curve until they either hit it or he gets behind in the count. When he does get behind in the count, he tends to groove his fastball.

The best way to tell when Gross is losing it is when he runs deep counts. When he's throwing strikes, he can be effective. When he's not, he's very hittable. His greatest strength is his curve, which is of major league quality, and his willingness to learn. Claude Osteen, the Phillies pitching coach, has been teaching Gross to spot his fastball and to rely less on his breaking ball.

FIELDING, HITTING, BASERUNNING:

Gross has an average move to first

KEVIN GROSS
RHP, No. 46
RR, 6'5", 203 lbs.
ML Svc: 2 years
Born: 6-8-61 in
    Downey, CA

1984 STATISTICS

W	L	ERA	G	GS	CG	IP	H	R	ER	BB	SO	SV
8	5	4.12	44	14	1	129	140	66	59	44	84	1

CAREER STATISTICS

W	L	ERA	G	GS	CG	IP	H	R	ER	BB	SO	SV
12	11	3.88	61	31	2	225	240	112	97	79	150	1

and does not hold runners well. Overall, he is an average fielder. Gross is not taken seriously at the plate. He is a conservative baserunner with below average speed.

OVERALL:

Gross is highly competitive, but must learn to work hitters and alter his pitching patterns. He showed improvement in his control after walking 35 batters in 96 innings in 1983. He also reduced his gopher balls, permitting eight home runs after allowing 13 in 1983. This spring, the Phillies will give Gross a chance to win a job in the starting rotation.

Snider: "He's a breaking ball pitcher and has to keep the ball down. If he pitches up, he gets in deep trouble. Breaking ball pitchers have a tendency to make mistakes. If hitters are patient, they'll get a pitch to hit. If Gross gets the hitter looking for the breaking ball, his fastball picks up a foot or so. But he can't count on it unless he gets it in a perfect spot."

HITTING:

Von Hayes uses an upright, closed stance. He is a low ball, fastball hitter with good power all fields. The majority of his power, however, is to right field.

Last year, he was much more effective against righthanders, hitting over .300 against them as compared to .234 against lefthanders. Hayes prefers fastballs and has a tendency to top breaking ball pitchers, but he is a good "trick pitch" hitter. For instance, he has great success hitting Bruce Sutter's split-fingered fastball.

One phase of hitting in which Hayes has improved is the ability to react to pitches. He is still is a guess hitter, but unlike 1983, pitchers last season couldn't get him out consistently with the same pitch. They had to vary their patterns.

Hayes still has to work on his situational hitting. He does not drive in as many runs as he should. Last year, he had 49 extra-base hits, including a career-high 16 homers, but drove in only 67 runs.

Hayes gained a great deal of confidence while hitting .292 overall. After coming to Philadelphia from Cleveland for five players, Hayes put himself under a lot of pressure in 1983. His teammates didn't help him much by riding him constantly about the five-for-one deal. He survived and began showing signs last year that he has the potential to become a topflight major league player.

BASERUNNING:

Hayes has excellent speed, gets out of the box well and gets down the line very quickly. He is a definite threat to steal (he stole 48 bases last year). On the bases, he has a quite a few things to learn. He'll be better able to utilize his speed when he becomes a more intelligent baserunner.

FIELDING:

He can play all three outfield posi-

VON HAYES
OF, No. 9
LR, 6'5", 185 lbs.
ML Svc: 3 years
Born: 8-31-58 in
Stockton, CA

1984 STATISTICS

AVG	G	AB	R	H	2B	3B	HR	RBI	BB	SO	SB
.292	152	561	85	164	27	6	16	67	59	84	48

CAREER STATISTICS

AVG	G	AB	R	H	2B	3B	HR	RBI	BB	SO	SB
.269	469	1548	216	417	69	16	37	198	151	212	108

VS. RHP   VS. LHP   PROBABLE HIT LOCATIONS

tions as well as first and third base. The Phillies used him primarily in center field last year. He doesn't have a particularly strong arm and he doesn't get rid of the ball quickly.

He's better at going back on fly balls than at coming in for them, but he's not afraid to dive for sinking line drives or go into a wall for a long drive.

Hayes doesn't take charge on pop flies and doesn't communicate well with his fellow outfielders.

OVERALL:

Hayes can hit, run and field. He has work to do in all three phases, but with his renewed confidence he should continue to mature as a player.

Snider: "Von came around last season--He went out and had a fine year. He should be able to do even better in 1985. He has all the tools it takes. Von is a very good low fastball hitter, runs well and fields well."

PITCHING:

Al Holland is a one-pitch power pitcher who has been used exclusively in late inning relief by the Phillies. He doesn't use a windup; he rocks, pivots and throws with a direct overhand motion.

Although he was used as an occasional starter and in middle inning relief in San Francisco, he is best suited to late inning relief, the role he has played for the Phillies for the last two years.

Holland is a fastball pitcher and can make it rise or tail. He also has a below average breaking ball that he rarely uses. In 1983, Holland's fastball was clocked at about 94 MPH. Late last season, though, he was throwing an 86-90 MPH fastball. The loss of velocity hurt him. Holland's best pitch is his rising fastball when he throws it high in the strike zone. When he throws it at the knees, it tends to rise into a hitter's wheelhouse.

His pitching strategy is to overpower hitters with his fastball. Holland does not try to fool hitters. They know what to expect when he comes into a game. He works extremely well under pressure, the mark of a good late-inning reliever.

He works well when behind in the count. When Holland's velocity is down, he gets hit hard. Batters tend to tee off on him when he's not throwing at peak velocity.

Losing close games is part of a late-inning reliever's life. He can shake off the tough losses and come back and pitch effectively in his next appearance.

Holland's greatest strength is his fastball. When the fastball is humming, he can overpower any hitter in the league. His greatest weakness is his breaking ball, which he usually wastes.

FIELDING, HITTING, BASERUNNING:

Holland is a below average fielder.

AL HOLLAND
LHP, No. 19
RL, 5'11", 210 lbs.
ML Svc: 5 years
Born: 8-16-52 in
Roanoke, VA

1984 STATISTICS

W	L	ERA	G	GS	CG	IP	H	R	ER	BB	SO	SV
5	10	3.39	68	0	0	98	82	38	37	30	61	29

CAREER STATISTICS

W	L	ERA	G	GS	CG	IP	H	R	ER	BB	SO	SV
32	25	2.70	300	10	0	510	425	174	153	183	409	73

He is slow off the mound and does not cover first well. He has a below average move and rarely throws to first. He tends to forget about runners, making him vulnerable to the stolen base.

Holland is an average hitter who works at this phase of the game. He does not bat very often, nor is he called upon to run the bases.

OVERALL:

Holland fell into a horrendous slump last August and September. His problem was burn-out; he worked too many innings early in the season and was tired over the final two months. Better off-season conditioning would help Holland gain the stamina he needs to pitch effectively over the course of an entire season.

Snider: "He had a strange year. He lost the velocity on that high fastball of his. He reminds me somewhat of Al Hrabosky. When hitters learn to lay off the high fastball, they have a chance to beat Al Holland. It would be nice if he had another pitch to go with his fastball, something he could show the hitter. If he had a straight change-up, he'd be awesome."

PITCHING:

A power pitcher, Charlie Hudson again showed that, with maturity, he can become a quality major league starting pitcher.

Hudson uses a compact windup and a three-quarters or direct overhand delivery. He tends to work quickly with nobody on, but becomes deliberate with runners on base. He has a fastball that has been clocked in the low 90s, a hard slider, a curve and a straight change.

He has excellent movement on his fastball, which he likes to run in to both right and lefthanded hitters. His curve and change are his third and fourth best pitches, respectively. He shows them to hitters, but rarely tries to throw either for a strike. Hudson likes to work inside with his fastball and away with his slider against all hitters. He is at his best when he's throwing strikes. When he falls behind in the count, he has a tendency to groove pitches: he threw 12 gopher balls in 1984.

A strong competitor, Hudson has shown the ability to come back from a bad inning and throw well. Hudson's greatest strengths are his fastball and slider. His demeanor on the mound is also a strength. He's not afraid to establish the inside part of the plate . His weakness is his lack of knowledge of the hitters; with less than two full seasons of experience, Hudson is still learning the book on many hitters.

FIELDING, HITTING, BASERUNNING:

Hudson has a below average move and does not throw to first often enough. He doesn't hold runners well and is vulnerable to the stolen base. He is an average fielder. He gets off the mound quickly and covers first well.

CHARLIE HUDSON
RHP, No. 49
RR, 6'3", 185 lbs.
ML Svc: 2 years
Born: 3-16-59 in
Ennis, TX

1984 STATISTICS

W	L	ERA	G	GS	CG	IP	H	R	ER	BB	SO	SV
9	11	4.04	30	30	1	173	181	101	78	52	94	0

CAREER STATISTICS

W	L	ERA	G	GS	CG	IP	H	R	ER	BB	SO	SV
17	19	3.71	56	56	4	342	339	174	141	105	195	0

A switch-hitter, Hudson is weak from both sides of the plate. He is not taken seriously as a hitter, although he works on it. He has above average speed for a pitcher and is a good baserunner. He is capable of taking an extra base when the situation calls for it and is not afraid to slide. Overall, he is a below average hitter, but an above average baserunner.

OVERALL:

Last season, Hudson worked on moving his pitches around in the strike zone. When he learns to locate his pitches and gets a better knowledge of the hitters, he will be one of the better righthanded power pitchers in the league.

His continued improvement has once again earned him a spot in the Phillies' regular starting rotation.

Snider: "He has a chance to be a good pitcher in the National League. He has a pretty good idea on the mound and has good stuff. He's a good athlete, and I like his attitude. I look for big things from Charles Hudson."

PITCHING:

At the age of 41, Jerry Koosman is in the twilight of a magnificent career. He was once among the premier power pitchers in the game, but now he relies on control and guile.

Last year, Philadelphia used him as a starter, and he won 14 games as a member of the rotation. At the end of the year, however, the Phillies experimented with bringing him out of the bullpen. Koosman can fill the two roles; he was both a starter and a reliever with Chicago until the White Sox traded him to the Phillies in December 1983. At this point in his career, Koosman is best suited to the bullpen.

He has an economical windup and a three-quarters delivery. Koosman has a fastball that has been clocked in the high 80s (sometimes higher), a cut fastball, a change-up that he turns over and a slow curve.

His best pitch is the slow curveball, which he uses to fool hitters after setting them up with his fastball and cut fastball. He tries to mix up his pitching pattern throughout the game. He tends to work righthanders with his fastball, cut fastball and change-up, and likes to jam lefthanders with his fastball and get them off stride with his slow curve.

He has excellent command of all of his pitches and can throw each for a strike at any point in the count. A veteran of 17 major league seasons, Koosman knows how to pitch when he is behind in the count and does not panic after a bad inning.

When he is tiring, Koosman tends to nibble. He won't give in to a hitter, but he will try to finesse him with his breaking pitches. As good as they are, Koosman needs his fastball to set them up.

JERRY KOOSMAN
LHP, No. 24
RL, 6'2", 225 lbs.
ML Svc: 17 years
Born: 12-23-43 in Appleton, MN

1984 STATISTICS

W	L	ERA	G	GS	CG	IP	H	R	ER	BB	SO	SV
14	15	3.25	36	34	3	224	232	95	81	60	137	0

CAREER STATISTICS

W	L	ERA	G	GS	CG	IP	H	R	ER	BB	SO	SV
216	205	3.34	593	509	137	3729	3524	1552	1382	1165	2496	17

FIELDING, HITTING, BASERUNNING:

Koosman has an above average move to first. He holds runners well and throws there often. He pays attention to the baserunners and is difficult to steal against. He fields his position well and hustles to cover first and back up on infield plays.

He is a good hitter who must be taken seriously at the plate. He is an above average bunter and led the Phillies in sacrifice bunts last season with 14. He has below average speed on the bases and doesn't take any chances--but he is willing to slide if he must.

OVERALL:

He has been able to change his style from power to control and still be successful. Part of Koosman's success last season had to do with his fastball. In the early season, he was throwing the fastball in the low 90s, although it lost velocity as the year progressed.

Snider: "Jerry Koosman was a pro from day one. Now he is relying on finesse. He needs some runs to help him out a little; he is not going to get many low-scoring games."

HITTING:

Joe Lefebvre stands close to the plate, straight up in the box with a slight crouch and a closed stance.

He is a low ball, fastball hitter. His best stroke is an opposite field one. He has some power to right, left and left-center, but is not a home run hitter. He hits the ball hardest when he takes it from center to left.

Lefebvre likes the ball away, so pitchers try to jam him and make him pull the ball. He has trouble against righthanded breaking ball pitchers who work the inside of the plate--and all lefthanders.

A knee injury sidelined Lefebvre for all but 52 games last season. In that time, he hit a disappointing .250 and suffered through a prolonged slump. He was just beginning to come out of the slump when he caught a spike on the warning track in Wrigley Field and injured his knee.

Lefebvre changed quite a bit from the hitter he was before the Phillies acquired him from San Diego. The Padres needed power in the lineup and asked him to pull the ball. He was not very successful at that. With the Phillies, he developed into an opposite field hitter. He improved his knowledge of the strike zone, but was still susceptible to off-speed pitchers.

BASERUNNING:

Lefebvre has below average speed and is not a threat to steal. He's aggressive at breaking up the double play.

FIELDING:

Lefebvre is an average outfielder in terms of range and his hands. But he has one of the top five arms in the National League, which makes him well suited to right field.

JOE LEFEBVRE
OF, No. 23
LR, 5'10", 180 lbs.
ML Svc: 5 years
Born: 2-22-56 in
  Concord, NH

1984 STATISTICS

AVG	G	AB	R	H	2B	3B	HR	RBI	BB	SO	SB
.250	52	160	22	40	9	0	3	18	23	37	0

CAREER STATISTICS

AVG	G	AB	R	H	2B	3B	HR	RBI	BB	SO	SB
.260	433	1073	139	279	52	13	31	130	136	199	11

VS. RHP

VS. LHP

PROBABLE HIT LOCATIONS

OVERALL:

The question facing Lefebvre is how well he can come back from a debilitating injury. He is an above average right fielder with a way above average arm. In 1983 with Philadelphia, he showed himself to be a reliable RBI man and a good clutch hitter. His early season slump raised some questions about his ability to shake off a bad year. Lefebvre needs to come back and do well.

Snider: "Joe struggled early in the year and got down on himself. Then he got hurt, so it was a tough year for him. He should be able to bounce back. He hits the ball hard when he makes contact, but he has trouble with lefthanders. He has a great arm. It's strong and accurate."

HITTING:

Sixto Lezcano stands back in the box with a deep crouch and a closed stance. He cocks the bat over his left wrist and always swings from the heels.

Lezcano is a dead fastball hitter with great power to left, left-center and center. He is a pull hitter who likes fastballs out over the plate so he can extend his arms and drive the ball.

He is susceptible to the breaking ball from both righthanders and left-handers. Most pitchers feed him a steady diet of curves and sliders. He is an impatient hitter who likes to go after the first pitch. He is a below average bunter.

Lezcano had good power stats last season--22 of his 71 hits went for extra-bases; he also struck out 43 times and grounded into 11 double plays.

Lezcano improved his average against righthanders last season, hitting .283 against them after going hitless in 16 at-bats for Philadelphia in September, 1983. On the other hand, his .271 average against lefties was a disappointment.

BASERUNNING:

Lezcano has below average speed and is not a threat to steal. He is not aggressive at breaking up the double play.

FIELDING:

Lezcano is an above average right fielder with an excellent arm. His arm isn't the gun it used to be, but it's still respected by baserunners. He goes to his right better than he goes to his left. He charges balls well and will dive for line drives.

SIXTO LEZCANO
RF, No. 28
RR, 5'10", 190 lbs.
ML Svc: 10 years
Born: 11-28-53 in
Arecibo, PR

1984 STATISTICS

AVG	G	AB	R	H	2B	3B	HR	RBI	BB	SO	SB
.277	109	256	36	71	6	2	14	40	38	43	0

CAREER STATISTICS

AVG	G	AB	R	H	2B	3B	HR	RBI	BB	SO	SB
.273	1219	4018	544	1098	182	34	145	582	541	752	37

  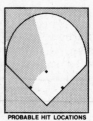

VS. RHP | VS. LHP | PROBABLE HIT LOCATIONS

OVERALL:

Philadelphia was Lezcano's fourth major league team in four years, and now he will be with his fifth in six years. That tells you he has a tendency to wear out his welcome wherever he goes. However, he did help the Phillies win the NL East after they acquired him from San Diego on August 31, 1983. In spring training, the Phillies were planning to platoon him in right. But he started only 57 games and spent much of the season riding the bench.

Snider: "He has the tools to be a good ballplayer. He has great power to left and will hit a few out for you. When he turns it on, he can play with anybody. The problem is, you never know when he's going to turn it on."

HITTING:

Garry Maddox uses a spread stance and a slight crouch. He doesn't step at all: his swing is all wrist.

Maddox is a first ball, low ball hitter with occasional power to left and left-center. He is an excellent breaking ball hitter but is susceptible to anything up in the strike zone. Righthanders and lefthanders both can get him out with anything high in the strike zone. They can also get him to chase outside breaking balls in the dirt.

He hits lefthanders well, but is a pedestrian hitter against righthanders. Maddox is a completely undisciplined hitter who rarely walks. That is because he hacks at the first pitch the vast majority of the time. Over the course of the last two seasons (565 at-bats), Maddox walked a total of 30 times, and has not drawn more than 20 walks in a season since 1978.

He is also a bad bunter.

BASERUNNING:

Garry has excellent speed out of the box and gets down the line quickly, but knee injuries have slowed him down and he is not the threat to steal that he once was. He does not know how to slide and is not aggressive about breaking up the double play.

FIELDING:

Once one of the premier defensive center fielders in the game, Maddox has won eight Gold Gloves. Among National League outfielders, only Willie Mays and Roberto Clemente won more.

In his prime, Maddox could cover huge amounts of territory. He has an excellent knowledge of how to play hitters. He gets a good jump on any ball hit in the air. He is slightly better at coming in for balls than at going back for

GARRY MADDOX
CF, No. 31
RR, 6'3", 190 lbs.
ML Svc: 13 years
Born: 9-1-49 in
   Cincinnati, OH

1984 STATISTICS

AVG	G	AB	R	H	2B	3B	HR	RBI	BB	SO	SB
.282	77	241	29	68	11	0	5	19	13	29	3

CAREER STATISTICS

AVG	G	AB	R	H	2B	3B	HR	RBI	BB	SO	SB
.286	1638	6106	754	1747	329	61	113	730	308	754	244

  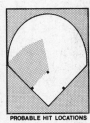

STRONG — VS. RHP   STRONG — VS. LHP   PROBABLE HIT LOCATIONS

them, but he does both well. He has only an average arm, while his accuracy is below average.

OVERALL:

Maddox is past his prime; he turns 36 years old in July and doesn't cover the ground he used to. He was injured for a good part of last season, appearing in only 77 games, and underwent disc surgery in September. The injuries, his age and his contract status make Maddox a candidate for retirement in the near future.

Snider: "Garry has been a great defensive player. He hit well last year when he was in there. I don't think too many hitters stand flat-footed in the box. He is not a disciplined hitter and he does not take the extra base. He makes a lot of offensive mistakes."

HITTING:

Len Matuszek uses an upright, closed stance. He swings from the heels and has a long sweeping stroke.

He is a low ball, fastball hitter with excellent power to right and right-center. He has some power to left-center, but the vast majority of his hits are to right.

Matuszek's most glaring weakness at the plate is up in the strike zone. Pitchers can get him out with hard stuff up either inside or outside.

His patience at the plate and his ability to wait on off-speed pitches depends on his frame of mind. When he is confident, Matuszek is a fine power hitter. When he is not, he is an easy out. Matuszek's level of confidence seems to rise and fall with his success of the moment.

If he is hitting, his entire game improves, but if he struggles for a few games, he gets down on himself and has a hard time snapping out of it.

He spent several injury-prone years in the Phillies' farm system when Pete Rose was their steady first baseman. When he was healthy, Matuszek had good years. In a couple of cameo major league appearances, Matuszek was unimpressive. Then, in September of 1983, he was recalled from the minors and helped the Phillies to win the National League East and effectively won the starting job at first base.

He opened the 1984 season as the team's platoon first baseman against righthanded pitching. But he was sidelined with a broken finger, and when he returned his confidence was gone. So was his job.

Matuszek has shown some ability as a pinch-hitter. He batted .417 with three homers and 10 RBIs as a pinch-hitter last season. But he believes himself to be an everyday player and does not like the role of pinch-hitter.

BASERUNNING:

Matuszek has average speed, does not

LEN MATUSZEK
1B, No. 12
LR, 6'2", 198 lbs.
ML Svc: 3 years
Born: 9-27-54 in
Toledo, OH

1984 STATISTICS

AVG	G	AB	R	H	2B	3B	HR	RBI	BB	SO	SB
.248	101	262	40	65	17	1	12	43	39	54	4

CAREER STATISTICS

AVG	G	AB	R	H	2B	3B	HR	RBI	BB	SO	SB
.237	167	392	54	93	25	2	16	63	47	79	4

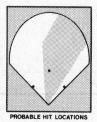

VS. RHP · VS. LHP · PROBABLE HIT LOCATIONS

get down the line well and is not a threat to steal. He isn't always aggressive at breaking up double plays.

FIELDING:

Matuszek is an average fielder. He has excellent range to his right, but overall does not cover a lot of ground. Matuszek is weak at digging out balls in the dirt. His arm is average.

OVERALL:

Like it or not, Matuszek may be destined for the bench. Philadelphia was thinking about dealing him in the off season. He has yet to get a chance to show what he can do over the course of an entire season. But he is 30 years old and that chance may never come.

Snider: "I am surprised about him. After 1983, I thought he was ready to take over a major league role. The injury did not help him toward that. He just isn't consistent enough."

HITTING:

Al Oliver stands back in the box and well off the plate with an upright, closed stance. He is a low ball hitter and an exceptionally good breaking ball and off-speed hitter. He is excellent at hitting off-speed stuff because he keeps his hands back and waits on pitches extremely well. He generally drives the ball to the alley in left and right-center.

Oliver has trouble with good fastball pitchers. Pitchers generally throw him hard stuff and try to keep the ball away from him. Even though he stands far from the plate, he can reach outside pitches because he steps into everything.

Oliver is an undisciplined hitter, but he rarely strikes out. His theory of hitting is as basic as they come: "See the ball, hit the ball." If it is a strike, that fine; if it's not, well, that's okay, too.

He has some power, but Oliver rarely swings for home runs. He went all of last season without a homer. He is not a good hitter with runners on base. He is a poor bunter. Oliver has estimated that he has attempted to bunt only ten times in the course of his 16-year major league career.

Oliver is a remarkably consistent hitter who has hit .300 or better in ten of the last eleven years, including the last nine straight.

He is not a team man. He is a one-dimensional hitter who rarely walks and does not bunt, lift fly balls to the outfield with a runner on third and less than two out or move runners along with ground balls to the right side.

BASERUNNING:

Oliver gets out of the box well and hustles down the base line. He runs out everything. But he has no speed, is not a threat to steal and is not agggressive at breaking up the double play.

AL OLIVER
1B, No. 0
LL, 6'1", 185 lbs.
ML Svc: 17 years
Born: 10-14-46 in Portsmouth, OH

1984 STATISTICS

AVG	G	AB	R	H	2B	3B	HR	RBI	BB	SO	SB
.301	119	432	36	130	26	2	0	48	27	36	3

CAREER STATISTICS

AVG	G	AB	R	H	2B	3B	HR	RBI	BB	SO	SB
.305	2272	8783	1168	2676	518	75	214	1295	523	732	83

VS. RHP   VS. LHP   PROBABLE HIT LOCATIONS

FIELDING:

Oliver is a deficit at first base. He has bad hands, limited range and no arm. Baserunners routinely challenge his arm. The quicker basestealers will run to second when they are picked off because they know they can beat Oliver's relay to the bag.

OVERALL:

Oliver is a proven .300 hitter, but he comes with his limitations. Because of his terrible defense, Oliver would be better suited to DH in the American League.

Snider: "There is no question that he is a fine hitter and that he is going to get 3,000 hits. He hits the ball to all fields. But Oliver is not the first baseman you need. You can't give a major league team more than three outs very often without it scoring on you. The arm is just not there."

PITCHING:

Shane Rawley is a lefthanded power pitcher with a compact motion and overhand delivery. After being acquired by the Phillies in a mid-season trade with the New York Yankees, Rawley was used exclusively as a starting pitcher. He went 10-5 in 18 starts and secured a spot in the Phillies' starting rotation this season.

Rawley has a fastball that has been clocked at close to 90 MPH. He also uses a slider, a change-up and a curveball. His fastball is his best pitch, and he uses it 80% of the time. Rawley moves his fastball around in the strike zone and throws his slider down and in to righthanded hitters. The slider is a good second pitch, but his change and curve are only fair.

Rawley is a pitcher who likes a challenge. Late last season, he outdueled Dwight Gooden, the Mets' rookie sensation, in a game in which Gooden struck ou. 16 batters.

He is a much better pitcher when he's ahead in the count. When Rawley falls behind, he tends to groove his pitches. His ability to come back after a bad inning improved after he began working with Gus Hoefling, the team's strength and flexibility coach. Gus uses a martial arts approach and teaches, among other things, concentration.

Rawley's greatest strength is his competitiveness. His greatest weakness is the gopher ball. He allowed 13 home runs in 120 innings for the Phillies. When Rawley begins to tire, the first thing he loses is the location of his fastball. He begins to pump it down the middle of the plate, where it is hit for long distances.

FIELDING, HITTING, BASERUNNING:

A good athlete, Rawley fields his po-

SHANE RAWLEY
LHP, No. 26
LL, 6'0", 155 lbs.
ML Svc: 7 years
Born: 7-27-55 in
   Racine, WI

1984 STATISTICS

W	L	ERA	G	GS	CG	IP	H	R	ER	BB	SO	SV
10	6	3.81	18	18	3	120	117	55	51	27	58	0

CAREER STATISTICS

W	L	ERA	G	GS	CG	IP	H	R	ER	BB	SO	SV
55	61	3.84	304	73	19	899	897	496	384	352	510	40

sition well. He is quick off the mound, covers bunts to the left side of the infield well for a lefthanded pitcher and covers first well. He has only an average move, but he will throw over when a good runner is on base.

After Rawley's stint in the American League, where he did not have to swing a bat, he surprised many people by doing well for himself at the plate. He had five hits in 43 at-bats. He takes his hitting seriously and works at it, making him something more than an automatic out. He is an average baserunner with average speed. He doesn't take many chances on the bases, but he's willing to slide.

OVERALL:

Snider: "It seems like he has learned how to pitch. He tries to pitch something like Carlton with that slider down and in. As long as the slider breaks down, he'll be okay."

HITTING:

Juan Samuel is a triple threat offensive player with superstar potential. He stands well back in the box, with a slight crouch and a closed stance. He can hit for average and for power, and has the speed of Mercury.

Samuel is a low ball, fastball hitter. He's basically an alley hitter who drives the ball, but he's fast enough to get a lot of infield hits. He is extremely quick getting out of the box and gets down the line quickly enough to force third basemen and shortstops to hurry their throws even on routine grounders.

Samuel has great hand strength and generates most of his power through bat speed. But he is also an undisciplined hitter who can be lured into swinging at fastballs around his eyes or breaking balls in the dirt. Righthanders with hard breaking stuff, such as Chicago's Rick Sutcliffe, own him. Samuel struck out 168 times last year--a rookie record --in a major league record 701 at-bats. He walked only 28 times, not nearly enough for a player who bats first or second.

BASERUNNING:

There is no one faster from the right side. He is always a threat to steal. Last season, Samuel broke a team record and a major league rookie record for stolen bases with 72, finishing second behind Montreal's Tim Raines for the league's stolen base title. Samuel stole on raw speed. He's just beginning to learn the pitchers.

FIELDING:

By far, fielding is the weakest part of Samuel's game. He committed 33 errors at second base last year and there was talk that the Phillies were considering converting him into an outfielder. But there are no guarantees that he can play the outfield. Samuel's problems in the field centered around his arm. He developed a bad habit of throwing sidearm, especially after making the pivot on double plays. The Philadelphia coaching

JUAN SAMUEL
2B, No. 16
RR, 5'11", 168 lbs.
ML Svc: 1 year plus
Born: 12-9-60 in
    San Pedro de Macoris, DR

1984 STATISTICS

AVG	G	AB	R	H	2B	3B	HR	RBI	BB	SO	SB
.272	160	701	105	191	36	19	15	69	28	168	72

CAREER STATISTICS

AVG	G	AB	R	H	2B	3B	HR	RBI	BB	SO	SB
.273	178	766	119	209	37	21	17	74	32	184	75

STRONG   STRONG   PROBABLE HIT LOCATIONS

VS. RHP   VS. LHP

staff worked with him to correct the problem, but it persisted throughout the year.

Samuel's footwork also left something to be desired. On plays behind second base, he consistently failed to plant his back foot, and consequently got nothing on his throws to first. There was also another factor: fatigue. Samuel clearly was a tired ballplayer at the end of the season and pressed both at the plate and in the field.

OVERALL:

How far Samuel's star rises will depend largely on how well he hones his raw talent.

Snider: "When you go to the ballpark and Samuel is playing, you sense an air of excitement. He is a great offensive ballplayer, but strikes out too much. He will learn the pitchers in a year or two. He needs to learn how to relax and glide a little bit in the field. Sometimes, it looks as if he has a pitchfork in his hand instead of a glove."

HITTING:

Another year, another home run title and another 100 RBIs. Mike Schmidt, one of the game's premier righthanded power hitters just kept rolling along. His 36 homers tied Dale Murphy for the National League title. He tied for the lead in driving in runs (106) with Gary Carter.

He used the same stance that he developed several years ago--upright, closed, back in the box and well off the plate. Schmidt is basically a pull hitter, but he has the ability to hit, and hit with power, to all fields. He is a low ball hitter who prefers fastballs, but can hit the breaking ball.

Schmidt stands so far off the plate, it would seem he should be susceptible to outside breaking pitches. Not so. Schmidt, a patient hitter with an excellent eye, usually lays off them. Occasionally, he will reach out and stroke an outside pitch to right.

Schmidt's position in the box makes it extremely difficult for pitchers to jam him. If they work him inside, they have to make sure their pitches are well inside. Otherwise, he'll hurt them.

But as Baltimore showed in the 1983 World Series, Schmidt can be pitched to. Breaking balls down and in and fastballs up and away give him trouble.

Schmidt is a streak hitter, given to prolonged slumps. He seems to go through cycles over the course of the season. Those who have observed him over the years feel that his slumps are more mental than mechanical.

Schmidt is a good bunter and will occasionally lay one down the third base line for a hit. He is never called upon to sacrifice.

BASERUNNING:

Schmidt has suffered chronic hamstring injuries over the last three or four years, but he still has above average speed and is an intelligent baserunner. He can steal a base, but doesn't run very often.

MIKE SCHMIDT
3B, No. 20
RR, 6'2", 203 lbs.
ML Svc: 12 years
Born: 9-27-49 in
Dayton, OH

1984 STATISTICS

AVG	G	AB	R	H	2B	3B	HR	RBI	BB	SO	SB
.277	151	528	93	146	23	3	36	106	92	116	5

CAREER STATISTICS

AVG	G	AB	R	H	2B	3B	HR	RBI	BB	SO	SB
.265	1789	6191	1161	1642	292	51	425	1180	1178	1543	167

VS. RHP — STRONG   VS. LHP — STRONG   PROBABLE HIT LOCATIONS

FIELDING:

His lateral movement has been hampered by his leg injuries. There are times when he has trouble bending over to field balls to either side of him. He has a strong, accurate arm and makes the charge-and-barehand play as well as any third baseman in the game. But he tends to have lapses of concentration in the field. Philadelphia experimented with Schmidt at first base late last season, but because of his leg problems, it would be tougher for him to play first than third.

OVERALL:

Schmidt's leg problems may eventually cause him to retire. He is 35 years old and has three years to run on his contract. At the plate, he remains a dangerous hitter, but one prone to abysmal slumps.

Snider: "I have all the respect in the world for Mike Schmidt. He's a super third baseman, but he's getting to an age at which the ballclub might need another one."

HITTING:

Jeff Stone is a low ball, opposite field singles hitter who sprays the ball between center and left.

Stone can hit fastballs and breaking balls, but he has a severe weakness up in the strike zone. Pitchers can pitch anything high and get him out.

He is a patient hitter, willing to take a walk. He is an excellent drag bunter, but he's not very good at laying down sacrifices to the left side of the infield.

Philadelphia recalled him from their Triple A Portland club in mid-June, but Stone went on the disabled list with a pulled groin muscle in early July. When he returned to the lineup in August, he slumped badly and was sent back to the minors.

The slump came from Stone trying to do too much at the plate. He stopped playing within his limitations and began to drive the ball. His fielding--the weakest part of his game--also affected his hitting. He tended to carry over his mistakes from one game to the next.

When Philadelphia brought him back in September, he came with a new attitude. He was resolved not to let his fielding affect his hitting and not to overreach his capabilities at the plate. He finished with a flourish and closed out the season hitting .362.

BASERUNNING:

Stone has blazing speed and has the potential to become one of baseball's premier basestealers. At Philadelphia, he stole 27 bases in 32 attempts.

At breaking up double plays, he is in the same category as Gary Matthews and Lonnie Smith--extremely aggressive. But Stone is not an intelligent baserunner. He makes a lot of mistakes.

FIELDING:

Stone is a defensive liability in

JEFF STONE
OF, No. 26
LR, 6'0", 175 lbs.
ML Svc: 1 year
Born: 12-26-60 in
Kennett, MO

1984 STATISTICS

AVG	G	AB	R	H	2B	3B	HR	RBI	BB	SO	SB
.362	51	185	27	67	4	6	1	15	9	26	27

CAREER STATISTICS

AVG	G	AB	R	H	2B	3B	HR	RBI	BB	SO	SB
.370	60	189	29	70	4	8	1	18	9	27	31

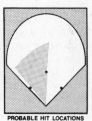

VS. RHP   VS. LHP   PROBABLE HIT LOCATIONS

left field. He has a below average arm. His speed gives him great range, but he has trouble simply judging anything hit in the air. He doesn't get a good jump on fly balls and ground balls often elude him. With work, he could become an average left fielder.

OVERALL:

Stone is a blue chip major league prospect. His offensive ability and his his basestealing potential far outweigh his defensive deficiencies. If he can learn to play left just a little bit, he'll be around for a long time.

Snider: "He's still learning how to hit. When he learns, he's liable to be something like a Tim Raines. He'll steal a bunch of bases, score a lot of runs, just tear you apart. You don't know how to defense him. His fielding can be worked on."

HITTING:

1984: the year Ozzie Virgil stopped being a slave to the breaking ball and proved himself to be a solid power hitter. A year ago, Virgil was a sucker for a breaking ball. He would chase it up, down, in or out, and rarely get any wood on it. He worked on his hitting after recovering from a gunshot wound in his right hand (Virgil was shot accidentally during a New Year's celebration).

Virgil is still a low ball, fastball hitter. But his improvement at hitting the breaking ball was easily noticeable. Virgil disciplined himself to lay off the breaking ball. When he does take a hack at a breaking pitch, he doesn't try to drive it, just stroke it for a single.

He is a pull hitter with excellent power to left and left-center. Occasionally, he'll take an outside pitch to right, but he goes to the plate looking to drive the ball. Virgil is only an average bunter and is seldom called on to do so.

BASERUNNING:

A catcher, Virgil has below average speed and is not a threat to steal. He is average at breaking up double plays.

FIELDING:

Fielding is another area where Virgil improved. He has become excellent at blocking balls in the dirt and his footwork has become a lot better on throws to second. He has a strong, accurate arm. His improved footwork and quicker release made it tougher to steal on him last year.

Virgil is not a good receiver. He does not work hitters well and as yet has not learned how to set up hitters. He doesn't think along with his pitchers. The veteran pitchers on the staff

OZZIE VIRGIL
C, No. 17
RR, 6'1", 205 lbs.
ML Svc: 3 years
Born: 12-7-56 in
Mayaguez, PR

1984 STATISTICS

AVG	G	AB	R	H	2B	3B	HR	RBI	BB	SO	SB
.261	141	456	61	119	21	2	18	68	45	91	1

CAREER STATISTICS

AVG	G	AB	R	H	2B	3B	HR	RBI	BB	SO	SB
.246	252	708	84	174	35	2	27	99	63	154	1

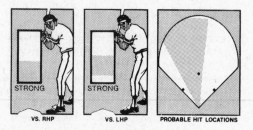

don't like to throw to Virgil.

OVERALL:

Virgil surprised everyone last year by playing adequately as a full-time catcher. Virgil's defense had been so suspect that Philadelphia had traded for John Wockenfuss to back up Bo Diaz. But then Diaz went down with a knee injury and Virgil filled in well. He hit .261 with 18 homers and 68 RBIs in 141 games, in- cluding 124 starts behind the plate. With time, he could improve his receiving and become more sophisticated at calling pitches.

Snider: "It looked like he recovered from all his wounds. Most people didn't think he could become a No. 1 catcher in the National League. He showed some that he's a better player than they thought he would be. He did a good job--not a great job--behind the plate."

HITTING:

Glenn Wilson has an upright, closed stance. He is a first pitch, fastball hitter who likes the ball up.

Wilson has trouble with sliders down and away. Pitchers rarely throw him inside. He is an alley hitter with good power to the opposite field. His ability to drive the ball was refelcted by his 30 extra-base hits last season.

Wilson had a disappointing season for Philadelphia after being acquired from Detroit last March. He hit .240 in limited appearances and struggled against righthanded power pitchers. His problem was that he tried to pull the ball too much.

Wilson is a very impatient hitter. If a pitcher throws him an inside fastball on the first pitch, he will go after it. If a pitcher opens Wilson with a slider away, there's an equally good chance he will chase the pitch and either pop it or hit it off the end of the bat.

His weakness for pitches away was reflected in his .219 average against lefthanders.

Wilson is not called upon to bunt.

BASERUNNING:

Wilson has below average speed and is not a threat to steal. He is aggressive in breaking up the double play.

FIELDING:

Many scouting reports claim that he has the ability to play all three outfield positions. Last year, however, he played much better in right field than in left field. Wilson does not have the range to play center field on a regular basis, but can fill-in in the late-innings if needed.

Wilson comes in for a ball much better than he goes back for it. He is good at charging a line drive or a ground

GLENN WILSON
OF, No. 12
RR, 6'1", 190 lbs.
ML Svc: 3 years
Born: 12-22-58 in
Baytown, TX

1984 STATISTICS

AVG	G	AB	R	H	2B	3B	HR	RBI	BB	SO	SB
.240	132	341	28	82	21	3	6	31	17	56	7

CAREER STATISTICS

AVG	G	AB	R	H	2B	3B	HR	RBI	BB	SO	SB
.267	360	1166	122	311	61	10	29	130	57	186	10

  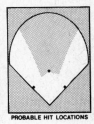

STRONG — VS. RHP   STRONG — VS. LHP   PROBABLE HIT LOCATIONS

ball and coming up throwing, but is weak at fading back for long fly balls. He should play deeper than he does.

Wilson has a very strong arm but is not accurate. While opposing baserunners must respect his arm, they will challenge him because of his inaccuracy.

OVERALL:

Wilson has two important tools: an arm and an ability to drive the ball. He is still highly thought of as a major league prospect, but he has yet to reach his potential. This season will be an important one for him.

Snider: "He has some pop, but he has a lot of work to do to make himself into a major league hitter. He can't keep chasing those breaking balls away. He's got to learn that pitchers make mistakes, too, and wait for them."

HITTING:

John Wockenfuss uses a unique stance. It is closed to the point of absurdity. A righthanded hitter, he also stands at the plate with his feet absolutely parallel.

The stance would seem to make him susceptible to inside pitches. But he looks inside and overcompensates and pivots his hips as he strides into the ball.

He is a fastball pull hitter who swings hard all the time. However, he does have the ability to take the outside pitch to right which makes him an excellent hit-and-run man. Wockenfuss likes pitches from the middle of the plate in. Pitchers can get him out with high fastballs and outside breaking balls.

BASERUNNING:

Wockenfuss has below average speed and is not a threat to steal. He is aggressive at breaking up the double play.

FIELDING:

A utility man, Wockenfuss can catch or play first base. Pitchers love to throw to him when he is behind the plate. He is excellent at calling pitches and has a good feel for setting up a hitter for the kill. But he doesn't shift well and doesn't block pitches in the dirt. He has bad hands and no arm. Runners steal on him routinely.

As a first baseman, Wockenfuss is adequate. He's decent on balls hit down the line, but he won't get many in the hole. He plays the position well enough to be a platooned first baseman, not an everyday one. He is clearly a better first baseman than a catcher.

JOHN WOCKENFUSS
C/INF, No. 14
RR, 6'0", 190 lbs.
ML Svc: 10 years
Born: 2-27-49 in
   Welch, WV

1984 STATISTICS

AVG	G	AB	R	H	2B	3B	HR	RBI	BB	SO	SB
.289	86	180	20	52	3	1	6	24	30	24	1

CAREER STATISTICS

AVG	G	AB	R	H	2B	3B	HR	RBI	BB	SO	SB
.264	763	2035	266	537	73	11	86	308	269	271	5

STRONG

VS. RHP

STRONG

VS. LHP

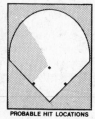

PROBABLE HIT LOCATIONS

OVERALL:

Wockenfuss is a sound utility man with power. He does not play defense well enough to be an everyday player, but he is valuable coming off the bench. He had some trouble hitting lefthanders last season, batting .238 against them. His bench value would increase if he were a better pinch-hitter. In that role, he hit .222 last year.

Snider: "He just eats sleeps and drinks baseball. He is dedicated to the game. He does have a strange stance, but there is no set rule in baseball that says how you should stand at the plate. He can set quickly into a fairly strong approach from that stance. He knows that he is a role player and accepts that. Those kind of guys are hard to find."

LUIS AGUAYO
INF, No. 16
RR, 5'9", 185 lbs.
ML Svc: 4 years
Born: 3-13-59 in
Vega Baja, PR

HITTING, BASERUNNING, FIELDING:

Luis Aguayo is a high ball, fastball hitter who uses a straight-up, closed stance. He is a pull hitter with surprising power for a man of his size (5'9", 185 lbs.).

Last season, Aguayo hit three home runs and drove in 11 runs in 72 at-bats. Projected over a full season, those numbers translate to 21 homers and 76 RBIs.

He has trouble with breaking balls down and away. Righthanded breaking ball pitchers and lefthanded sinkerballers usually have good success against him.

Aguayo is impatient at the plate and likes to hit early in the count. He is a good sacrifice bunter, but he doesn't bunt for base hits.

Aguayo has average speed and is not a threat to steal. He is a smart baserunner and is aggressive at breaking up the double play.

Entering his fourth season as a utility infielder, Luis is capable of playing third, short and second, but second is his best position.

He has a strong, accurate arm, good hands, and is an excellent pivot-man. His range at shortstop is questionable, however. Aguayo isn't quick enough to play that position on artificial turf.

OVERALL:

The jury is still out on whether Luis can play every day. But he has established himself as an excellent utility player.

KIKO GARCIA
INF, No. 18
RR, 5'11", 178 lbs.
ML Svc: 8 years
Born: 10-14-53 in
Martinez, CA

HITTING, BASERUNNING, FIELDING:

Kiko Garcia has an upright, closed stance. He is a singles hitter with very little power. He has a long, sweeping swing that really is inappropriate for the type of hitter he is. Pitchers get him out with fastballs and breaking balls away.

Garcia is a patient hitter and a good bunter, but generally has bad mechanics at the plate. He is somewhat effective against lefthanders, but righthanders own him.

As a baserunner, Garcia is below average. He does not have good speed and is not a threat to steal. He is aggressive at breaking up the double play.

Garcia is a utility infielder who can play shortstop, second or third. His natural position is shortstop, but he doesn't have the range to play the position on artificial turf. He can be an adequate third baseman, but his arm is below average, so he is best used there as an emergency fill-in.

OVERALL:

Garcia is a career utility man. He can help a clubs by doing the little things. Offensively, he is a liability. Defensively, he is nothing more than adequate, but he knows he's a role player and accepts it. He can be a handy guy to have around just in case, a luxury a lot of teams cannot afford.

STEVE JELTZ
INF, No. 15
RR, 5'11", 170 lbs.
ML Svc: 1 year
Born: 5-28-59 in
Paris, FR

HITTING, BASERUNNING, FIELDING:

Steve Jeltz uses an upright, closed stance. He is a singles hitter with very little power.

At Triple A Portland last year, Jeltz hit a meager .220. He came to the Phillies in September with a huge hitch in his swing. He worked on cutting down on his swing and punching the ball but hit only .197 against major league pitching.

Jeltz planned to go to the Florida Instructional League last winter to continue working on his mechanics. Jeltz is an excellent bunter.

He has above average speed and is a threat to steal. He will improve as a basestealer when he learns the pitchers. He's aggressive at breaking up the double play.

Jeltz excels in the field. He's an extremely aggressive shortstop. His quickness permits him to play very shallow on artificial turf. He has a strong, accurate arm, good hands and excellent footwork.

Last September, Jeltz was given a tryout at short and the Phillies liked what they saw. He has a chance to be their everyday shortstop this season.

OVERALL:

The Phillies say that if Jeltz can hit .240, they will be satisfied. The question is, can he hit .240? Steve's fielding will keep him in the majors but if he wants to play every day, he will have to learn to hit.

Snider: "If he hits, it looks like he's going to be a pretty good shortstop. It looks like he can handle himself out there."

RENIE MARTIN
RHP, No. 17
RR, 6'4", 190 lbs.
ML Svc: 6 years
Born: 8-30-55 in
Dover, DE

PITCHING, FIELDING,
HITTING, BASERUNNING:

Renie Martin is a control pitcher who relies on curves, sliders and finesse. He was used primarily in long relief after being acquired by the Phillies late last season. He has been a starter in his career, but was used primarily as a mop-up man and in long relief.

Martin has a below average fastball and average breaking pitches. He does not have very good control, to say the least. Martin tries to finesse hitters by moving his pitches around in the strike zone and changing speeds. His greatest strength is his willingness to accept whatever role a club has in mind for him.

He fields his position well. He is quick off the mound, plays bunts well and is adept at covering first. He does not make his infielders do all the work.

Martin is a good hitter and must be taken seriously at the plate on the rare occasions that he bats. He runs the bases well and is willing to slide if the situation demands it.

He is a good competitor and gives his best every time he takes the mound. But he is a marginal major league pitcher.

Snider: "Martin is a finesse pitcher with less than average stuff. He gives you a little of this, a little of that, and hopes to get you out."

JOHN RUSSELL
OF, No. 29
RR, 6'0", 190 lbs.
ML Svc: 1 year
Born: 1-5-61 in
Oklahoma City, OK

HITTING, BASERUNNING, FIELDING:

Last season, John Russell led his minor league team in home runs with 19 and was second in RBIs with 77 before the Phillies called him up to stay.

Russell stands upright in the box with a closed stance. He has a short, compact swing. He is a pull hitter with excellent power to left and left-center. With Philadelphia, 12 of his 29 hits went for extra bases. He is an intelligent hitter who knows what to do with the bat in any given situation. With two strikes, he goes for contact and doesn't try to drive the ball.

Pitchers can get him out with hard stuff away and can get him to swing at pitches out of the strike zone. More patience at the plate will help him cut down on his strikeouts: he had 33 in 99 at-bats last season with the Phillies.

As a baserunner, Russell has below average speed and is not a threat to steal. He is aggressive at breaking up the double play.

The Phillies are trying to find a position for him. He is a converted catcher who started mostly in left in the minors. In Philadelphia, however, he was used in right (16 starts) against left-handed pitching. He has a strong arm but a bad habit of overthrowing cutoff men. He has limited range in the outfield. He may wind up playing first base.

OVERALL:

Russell is the kind of player teams make room for. Philadelphia likes his power and his RBI ability. He has a chance to play regularly this season.

PITTSBURGH PIRATES

HITTING:

Dale Berra is a solid number eight hitter. He might hit even better if he is moved up in the lineup where he can't be pitched around.

Berra usually goes to the plate looking for fastballs, but pitchers don't have to throw them, knowing the pitcher follows him. That's why he can't be as aggressive as he would be batting early in the order. He hopes the early breaking balls miss and pitchers are forced to throw him a fastball. If the early breaking balls are over, Berra often finds himself behind in the count. He is a good low fastball hitter, although he has trouble with the fastball high and tight.

He is only a fair bunter, but can hit behind the runner when it's needed. Both are talents rarely utilized in a No. 8 hitter anyhow. He swings late which is the main reason he may set the lifetime record for reaching base on catcher's interference. Pete Rose holds the record with 28, Berra has 18.

BASERUNNING:

Berra prefers to make his baserunning errors on the side of caution. He can surprise you with a steal now and then, but you don't often ask a No. 8 hitter to steal. He's a below average runner out of the box, but can go from first to third well.

FIELDING:

Just when the manager is about to give up on Berra's fielding, he starts to play well. Annually, he makes a bundle of errors early in the season, then clears up as the season goes on. The team begins to think that he won't make it as a shortstop, then suddenly he starts to play better. Earlier in his career, you could excuse the slow start, saying he's liable to improve, but now he is a veteran shortstop. Also, earlier in his career, his errors came in the first few innings of the game where they didn't count much. Last year, he

DALE BERRA
SS, No. 4
RR, 6'0", 190 lbs.
ML Svc: 6 years
Born: 12-13-56 in
Ridgewood, NJ

1984 STATISTICS

AVG	G	AB	R	H	2B	3B	HR	RBI	BB	SO	SB
.222	136	450	31	100	18	0	9	52	34	78	1

CAREER STATISTICS

AVG	G	AB	R	H	2B	3B	HR	RBI	BB	SO	SB
.238	744	2291	215	545	96	8	46	255	186	376	31

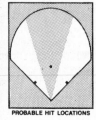

VS. RHP   STRONG   VS. LHP   STRONG   PROBABLE HIT LOCATIONS

made late-inning mistakes, the type good shortstops don't make.

He certainly isn't the acrobatic shortstop good teams need to win. He may be too musclebound and would be better off playing third. His arm is good, his range is good, but neither is excellent.

OVERALL:

This is a crucial year in Berra's career. If he doesn't get off to a good start at shortstop, he'll be benched or moved to third. While he has good power and RBI strength for a shortstop, the question lingers--can he hit well enough to be a third baseman? He's a good competitor, the type who plays hurt and never complains. He's a good team man who enjoys playing the game.

Snider: "There's something about Berra I don't like as a shortstop. He hasn't lived up to his minor league record as far as homers or RBIs, and he isn't the acrobatic shortstop most teams are looking for. I would imagine that the Pirates are shopping around at that position."

PITCHING:

The Pirates performed an interesting experiment with John Candelaria last year, using him in relief late in the season. Candelaria did well, getting 17 of the 18 batters he faced, with five strikeouts. He seemed to like relief pitching and had no physical problems with working often.

Candelaria does have some abilities that would make him a good relief pitcher. He has exceptional **control with a variety of pitches.** He can vary his style depending on what he needs. He can throw a sinker trying to induce a ground ball if he needs a double play, or resort to power if he needs a strikeout.

Candelaria is intense on the mound and a strong competitor. He is tough on the hitters in the middle of the lineup, but sometimes lets up on the seventh and eighth hitters.

He would be a good competitor in a late situation with men on base, but a manager would have to think long and hard about taking him out of the starting rotation.

He throws what hitters call a "heavy" ball, one that is difficult to drive. He is no longer a nine-inning pitcher and it doesn't seem to bother him. He will throw hard for six or seven innings, or until his back hurts. Then he is content to let the bullpen take over.

Candelaria likes to pitch outside, to the frustration of managers who would like him to change the pattern and bust a few guys inside occasionally.

FIELDING, HITTING, BASERUNNING:

Candelaria gets off the mound well to field balls in front of him, but his forward motion means he is often late in covering first. He is a big guy who has to suddenly change the direction of his body. He keeps runners close to the bag and has a good motion, but his de-

JOHN CANDELARIA
LHP, No. 45
SL, 6'7", 232 lbs.
ML Svc: 10 years
Born: 11-6-53 in
New York, NY

1984 STATISTICS												
W	L	ERA	G	GS	CG	IP	H	R	ER	BB	SO	SV
12	11	2.72	33	28	3	185	179	69	56	34	133	2

CAREER STATISTICS												
W	L	ERA	G	GS	CG	IP	H	R	ER	BB	SO	SV
122	80	3.10	284	271	45	1800	1681	689	620	113	1095	6

livery is slow and long. A good baserunner who studies him closely can steal against him.

Candelaria finally got his first major league home run last year, snapping his string of 566 major league at-bats without one. Only three active players have longer streaks: Don Sutton, Steve Rogers and Ron Reed. Candelaria was a good hitter early in his career but lost it and began experimenting with his swing. He can't decide if he is a lefthanded or righthanded batter.

OVERALL:

At age 31, Candelaria should just be moving into his prime. He has put on weight in the last few years, which can't help someone as prone to injuries as he has been. When physically and mentally sound, Candelaria is one of the best pitchers in baseball.

Snider: "If you have a happy John Candelaria, you have a heckuva pitcher. It's just a matter of what John wants to do. He's got good stuff and he's a good athlete. He's a little stubborn at times and sometimes he thinks too much. But overall, he's a plus."

PITCHING:

If Jose DeLeon can learn from last year, he can become one of the best pitchers in baseball. In his first full season, he made just about every rookie mistake imaginable. His other statistics aren't bad: 153 strikeouts and 92 walks in 192 innings with a 3.75 ERA, but his won-loss record was 7-13.

He would pitch well but then find a way to blow the game. Someone would make a bad play, or a hit would break up a no-hitter and DeLeon would get rattled. Suddenly, he would throw a ball away or walk someone he shouldn't and the other team would start a rally. No one doubts he has the pitches to become an outstanding pitcher. He is a power pitcher with a fastball, a slider, and a nearly unhittable forkball.

Hitters have started to lay off the forkball unless they are behind in the count. After all, if Pirate catcher Tony Pena can't catch it, how are they going to hit it? DeLeon is big and strong enough to pitch complete games, if only he can toughen himself mentally. He admits that he loves to strike hitters out, something he has to get over. Late in a game, he should just worry about getting them out. He needs to take advice better and pitch to a hitter's weakness rather than challenge everyone who comes to the plate.

FIELDING, HITTING, BASERUNNING:

DeLeon can make improvements in all three areas. He has no idea of how to keep runners close at first base. Even ordinary runners take advantage of him. DeLeon is slow off the mound and gets rattled when he fields a crucial bunt. He'll have to get smoother and turn those plays into routine ones. He also needs to react more quickly and get over

JOSE DeLEON
RHP, No. 25
RR, 6'3", 210 lbs.
ML Svc: 2 years
Born: 12-20-60 in
LaVega, DR

1984 STATISTICS

W	L	ERA	G	GS	CG	IP	H	R	ER	BB	SO	SV
7	13	3.75	30	28	5	192	147	86	80	92	153	0

CAREER STATISTICS

W	L	ERA	G	GS	CG	IP	H	R	ER	BB	SO	SV
14	16	3.42	45	43	8	300	222	122	114	139	271	0

to cover first better.

DeLeon is a poor hitter, a victim of the designated hitter rule since high school. He looks awkward at the plate and misses pitches by laughable margins. Perhaps he could improve with experience, but there are some pitching details DeLeon must work on first. He's on base so rarely, it's hard to tell what sort of runner he is. He is fast enough to be adequate, but it's hard to imagine he knows what to do.

OVERALL:

Will DeLeon be the next pitching superstar, or will he continue to make the mistakes that plagued him last year? He has the ability, but needs to correct a host of little things that added up to big trouble last year.

Snider: "DeLeon had his come-uppance last year. He's got good stuff, but he is still not a pitcher. He has to toe a fine line and he has to learn to pitch without losing his stuff. Jose has to throw to spots more but can't take the edge off his stuff."

HITTING:

Doug Frobel started slowly his rookie season, but he has enough hitting talent that it is too early to give up on him. He has a long looping swing that generates a lot of power, but it also means he strikes out a lot. Frobel started working on a crouched batting stance to cut down on strikeouts and get his power into the ball.

He must also study pitchers better. Too often he acted surprised at what pitchers would throw. If you are surprised by a pitch, you usually react too late and foul it off or swing when it's in the catcher's glove--even when it's a good pitch for you to hit. Frobel must also handle his strikeouts better. Too often he carries his previous at-bat to the plate with him. He must reconcile himself to striking out fairly often and concentrate on hitting for power. He'll never be a .300 hitter, but could develop into a .280/30 home run/80 RBI man with some time.

Frobel is a fastball hitter and will likely see a diet of breaking balls until he can prove he can hit them. He is an excellent low ball hitter, but has difficulty with high fastballs.

BASERUNNING:

Frobel has above average speed and good baserunning instincts, but is not yet an outstanding baserunner. He could improve with time, but first he must concentrate on hitting.

FIELDING:

Frobel spent most of his time in the minors at first base, but developed into an adequate outfielder. He is fast

DOUG FROBEL
OF, No. 51
LR, 6'4", 196 lbs.
ML Svc: 2 years
Born: 6-6-59 in
Ottowa, CAN

1984 STATISTICS

AVG	G	AB	R	H	2B	3B	HR	RBI	BB	SO	SB
.203	126	276	33	56	9	3	12	28	24	84	7

CAREER STATISTICS

AVG	G	AB	R	H	2B	3B	HR	RBI	BB	SO	SB
.216	174	370	48	80	15	4	17	42	29	112	9

  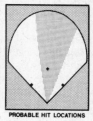

VS. RHP · VS. LHP · PROBABLE HIT LOCATIONS

enough and has a strong enough arm to be a better outfielder than he is. That, too, can come with time. He could be an outstanding left fielder and a more than adequate right fielder.

Snider: "Doug asked permission to work with me on hitting because a lot of people say he swings like I did when I was young. We worked on a hitting tee under the stands, and I tried to get Doug to crouch lower where he can get his natural strength into the ball and cut down on strikeouts. I think if he gets the proper stance and the proper approach, he will show some power. He has to get used to the fact that he will strike out 80-100 times a season if he is going to generate the power he can. I wouldn't give up on the guy."

HITTING:

Lee Lacy suddenly turned into an outstanding RBI man after several years in which he did everything but drive in runs. Lacy, 36 years old and on the last year of his contract, had his best season ever in 1984. He always said he could contend for a batting title if he played regularly, and he finished second in the National League with a .321 average.

Lacy is a line drive hitter who also legs out a lot of infield choppers. He hits many different kinds of pitching, usually where it is pitched. Nearly all of his home runs are to left against lefthanded pitching. He is less effective against righthanders who come in sidearm or with a three-quarters motion, and he has a tendency to bail out.

Lacy is an adequate leadoff hitter, but is even more valuable as a "second leadoff hitter," batting seventh in a good lineup, because of the power he can generate. His biggest asset remains his ability to come off the bench and get a base hit.

BASERUNNING:

Lacy is fast and a good baserunner, but is prone to spectacular baserunning mistakes. He once lost a grand slam when he passed the runner at first base. He loves to take the extra base and goes from first to third and from second to home with the best runners in the NL.

FIELDING:

Lee has found a home in the outfield. Once a poor outfielder, he has made himself into a good one. The Pirates had enough confidence in him last year to shift him from left field to right field all year, often in the middle of a game.

He has the speed to be a center fielder, but doesn't get a good enough jump on the ball. His arm is average for a left fielder and below average for a

LEE LACY
LF, No. 17
RR, 6'1", 175 lbs.
ML Svc: 12 years
Born: 4-10-48 in
Longview, TX

1984 STATISTICS

AVG	G	AB	R	H	2B	3B	HR	RBI	BB	SO	SB
.321	138	474	66	152	26	3	12	70	32	61	21

CAREER STATISTICS

AVG	G	AB	R	H	2B	3B	HR	RBI	BB	SO	SB
.289	1185	3308	469	955	154	35	64	335	264	442	168

  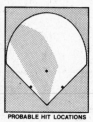

STRONG   STRONG

VS. RHP   VS. LHP   PROBABLE HIT LOCATIONS

right fielder. He is fairly accurate, but must get over his tendency to miss the cutoff man.

OVERALL:

Lacy has always been in excellent shape and is a "young" 37. He thinks he can play five more years and perhaps he can. He had the best year of his career last year, but don't expect that sort of production every year. Lacy is a good player on a bad team, a role player who can contribute to a pennant. He has power and speed and hits for a good average. And he is a rarity--a good pinch-hitter who can stay in the game on defense.

Snider: "I like Lee Lacy. He is an aggressive hitter who still runs well. He should be rested some, probably against the better righthanded pitchers, but he is the type of guy who can beat you."

HITTING:

Nagging injuries have bothered Bill Madlock for several years, but last year was completely shot by several major ones. He was never 100% after suffering an appendix attack at the beginning of spring training. Then he suffered shoulder, arm and leg injuries. At 34 years of age, he is young enough to make a strong comeback.

He is a nearly perfect hitter, as evidenced by his four National League batting titles. He hits for power with an amazingly compact swing that has virtually no backswing. His swing starts at his ear, comes straight down and hits the ball.

Madlock is the type of guy who breaks up no-hitters. He hits good pitchers even when they are pitching well. He loves fastballs, but has the compact swing to drive breaking balls into the gaps.

BASERUNNING:

Managers used to look for Madlock to steal 25 bases a season, but now they prefer him to conserve his body for hitting. He has lost some speed, but is still a good first-to-third runner. He is a smart runner who doesn't often run into outs. Madlock's rolling block slide can really break up double play.

FIELDING:

Madlock had trouble throwing early last year because of his injuries. If he doesn't recover, the Pirates may consider moving him to first base. He has limited side-to-side range, but charges bunts as well as anyone. He can catch anything he can reach, but with all the high bounces off the artificial turf, the Pirates often wish he were taller. He likes to block third base when a

BILL MADLOCK
3B, No. 5
RR, 5'11", 190 lbs.
ML Svc: 11 years
Born: 1-12-51 in Memphis, TN

1984 STATISTICS

AVG	G	AB	R	H	2B	3B	HR	RBI	BB	SO	SB
.253	103	403	38	102	16	0	4	44	26	29	3

CAREER STATISTICS

AVG	G	AB	R	H	2B	3B	HR	RBI	BB	SO	SB
.312	1443	5315	752	1659	286	33	124	687	492	364	157

  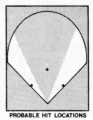

VS. RHP   VS. LHP   PROBABLE HIT LOCATIONS

runner is taking a lead.

OVERALL:

Madlock is one of baseball's better players and the Pirates' drop to last place last season can largely be attributed to losing him for most of the season.

He is the only righthanded hitter to win the National League batting title since 1971 and could contend again in 1985. He doesn't have the speed and range he once had, but he continues to strike fear in the heart of pitchers.

Snider: "He is still Bill Madlock, the type of player who makes things happen. He knows how to play the game. For instance, he makes up for the range he has lost by knowing how to play the hitters. I like his attitude. He is an aggressive player."

HITTING:

Lee Mazzilli is a good fastball hitter who has trouble with inside breaking balls. A switch-hitter, he has more power lefthanded. He stands erect, with his feet parallel to the plate. He is a straightaway hitter who rarely pulls the ball.

His biggest problem early in his career was a lack of concentration. In 1984, he hit well in streaks, but the last few years, he has had a dramatic dropoff in hitting both for average and for power.

BASERUNNING:

Once blessed with excellent speed, he is now just about average. He has good running habits, although he occasionally forgets that he just is not as fast as he used to be. He is a master of the hook slide, either to the left or to the right.

FIELDING:

Last year, manager Chuck Tanner took Mazzilli out of left field for defensive purposes, a move unthinkable when Lee was young and a good outfielder. He catches what he can reach, but his loss of speed in the outfield is dramatic and his throwing arm is poor. There is no way he can play center field anymore and with his poor throwing arm would be a liability in right field.

OVERALL:

Mazzilli's attitude seemed to improve

LEE MAZZILLI
OF, No. 16
SR, 6'1", 180 lbs.
ML Svc: 9 years
Born: 3-25-55 in
   Brooklyn, NY

1984 STATISTICS

AVG	G	AB	R	H	2B	3B	HR	RBI	BB	SO	SB
.237	111	266	37	63	11	1	4	21	40	42	8

CAREER STATISTICS

AVG	G	AB	R	H	2B	3B	HR	RBI	BB	SO	SB
.263	1051	3490	466	917	163	22	80	382	508	509	175

  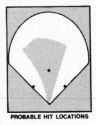

VS. RHP VS. LHP PROBABLE HIT LOCATIONS

last season, as he has apparently accepted the fact that he is no longer a superstar. He has good streaks and bad streaks. If he smoothed things out, he might be a good player again. He is concentrating too much on power and his batting average suffers.

Snider: "Lee's body is a slow body now instead of the quick body he used to have when he was young. In everything he does, he looks slower: throwing, running, and swinging the bat."

PITCHING:

Larry McWilliams became a good pitcher when he learned that it is not always what you throw but how you throw it.

He junked his long windup in 1981 for a no-windup delivery. Now, he suddenly charges off the mound and to a hitter; it seems as if he's running the ball at you. McWilliams throws a variety of pitches from this herky-jerky delivery. At times, he'll quick-pitch, and some hitters try to slow him down by stepping out of the batter's box.

He has a fastball, two different curveballs and occasionally throws a knuckleball, though he relies heavily on a forkball.

McWilliams is a rarity--a strikeout pitcher who is not a power pitcher. He has excellent control and is durable. He can close out a complete game, but his biggest asset is consistency--he rarely gets knocked out of a game early.

FIELDING, HITTING, BASERUNNING:

McWilliams is a good athlete who fields his position well. He is fast enough to be used as a pinch-runner. He is above average as a hitter and can help himself with a well-laid bunt.

LARRY McWILLIAMS
LHP, No. 49
LL, 6'5", 179 lbs.
ML Svc: 6 years
Born: 2-10-54 in
Wichita, KS

1984 STATISTICS

W	L	ERA	G	GS	CG	IP	H	R	ER	BB	SO	SV
12	11	2.93	34	32	7	227	226	86	74	78	149	1

CAREER STATISTICS

W	L	ERA	G	GS	CG	IP	H	R	ER	BB	SO	SV
58	47	3.66	179	150	27	991	961	453	403	313	640	2

OVERALL:

McWilliams is a consistent 15-game winner on an ordinary-to-worse team. He does all the little things that help a pitcher. He could even be a good relief pitcher if a team is starter-rich enough to switch him.

Snider: "Whatever he calls that pitch, a forkball or slider, it's a very good one. It comes to the plate, and it is as though the bottom drops out. What I like most of all is that he uses that funny delivery to go right at the hitters and get them out."

HITTING:

Jim Morrison likes fastballs, but he jumps all over bad breaking pitches. If you are going to throw him breaking balls, make sure they are good ones.

Morrison hits for good power and average and is excellent coming off the bench. He is a good contact hitter who excels at the hit-and-run. He can move runners up with a bunt, although he does not have the speed to bunt for a hit.

He is a disciplined enough hitter to take a walk in the right situation, but will swing from the heels if the team needs the long ball. His talents make him a tough out for junkball pitchers.

BASERUNNING:

Morrison is an average runner who must not let his enthusiasm get the best of him. He is fast enough to get all the doubles he deserves, but not fast enough to steal at will.

FIELDING:

While he is not good enough to be a regular at any infield position, Jim is good enough to fill in at three of them.

He does not have the range of a good second baseman or the throwing arm of a good third baseman, but he can play both adequately. Morrison is not really a shortstop, but could play there in a pinch. This versatility gives him a lot more playing time than if he could play only one position.

OVERALL:

Morrison is a better than average

JIM MORRISON
INF, No. 2
RR, 5'11", 178 lbs.
ML Svc: 7 years
Born: 9-23-52 in
 Pensacola, FL

1984 STATISTICS
AVG	G	AB	R	H	2B	3B	HR	RBI	BB	SO	SB
.286	100	304	38	87	14	2	11	45	20	52	0

CAREER STATISTICS
AVG	G	AB	R	H	2B	3B	HR	RBI	BB	SO	SB
.265	638	1963	227	521	95	10	70	241	118	278	27

  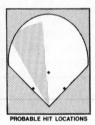

VS. RHP   VS. LHP   PROBABLE HIT LOCATIONS

utility player because of his versatility and late-inning hitting ability. He is not the type you build a team around, but without someone like him, your team has a hole in it.

Snider: "He is a great guy to have on a team because he has some pop in his bat and he can play several positions. He knows his role. He wants to play, but even when he is not playing, he still does all that he can to help a team. He is definitely an asset."

HITTING:

Tony Pena is a 15-home run hitter who someday may rise to 25. He is a streak hitter, partly because he needs to discipline himself and partly because backstops always are battling some little injury. If he played some other position, he might be a contender for a batting title.

Pena is best when he's hitting the ball to right field, although his home runs usually come to left field. He is a bad ball hitter, driving balls that are over his head to center field, or blooping balls that are at his ankles to right.

There is no pattern to pitching him because he hits all pitches at different times of the year. The pitchers have to hope he's in one of his slumps and not in one of his streaks.

He's a good hitter to bat fifth or sixth in the lineup because he likes to hit with men on base.

BASERUNNING:

Pena may be the fastest catcher in the league, although that isn't saying much. He should take a bigger lead off first base, but he is usually too busy chatting with the first baseman.

FIELDING:

Pena has a strong and accurate arm and often throws to first or third from his knees. He is an aggressive catcher, trying to pick runners off at any time. He catches everything one-handed and is probably the best at pop-ups in the National League.

Catching the Pirates staff last year was challenging, as the Pirates have several pitchers--John Candelaria, Rod Scurry and Don Robinson--who throw sharp breaking pitches into the dirt. Pena has missed a few, but is still very good at blocking pitches.

Pena has set a style among catchers by stretching his leg out and nearly

TONY PENA
C, NO. 6
RR, 6'0", 175 lbs.
ML Svc: 4 years
Born: 6-4-57 in
Montecristi, DR

1984 STATISTICS											
AVG	G	AB	R	H	2B	3B	HR	RBI	BB	SO	SB
.286	147	546	77	156	27	2	15	78	36	79	12
CAREER STATISTICS											
AVG	G	AB	R	H	2B	3B	HR	RBI	BB	SO	SB
.296	510	1816	198	538	87	11	43	229	92	236	21

  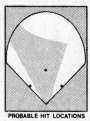

VS. RHP   VS. LHP   PROBABLE HIT LOCATIONS

sitting on the ground when there is no one on base. He thinks it keeps his legs loose and helps give the pitcher a lower target. The Pirates first tried to cure him of that habit because of the fear he might hurt himself when he tried to field a pop-up or a ball hit in front of the plate. But Pena has persisted and now other catchers think it has helped him prevent knee injuries and are beginning to copy it.

OVERALL:

Pena is one of the best players in the league and should remain so for the next half dozen years. He is an ironman who can play nearly every day.

Snider: "Whenever I walk up and talk with Tony Pena, he makes me feel good. He's always so happy, tickled to death to be playing in the major leagues. And when the game starts, he gives it all he's got. You really have to give him credit for the way he catches the Pirate staff."

HITTING:

Typical of Johnny Ray is the way he worked so hard at hitting righthanded that he actually hit for a higher average that way last year, .317 to .311. He still has much more power lefthanded, but his righthanded hitting is no longer a weakness. Ray is a contact hitter, one of the toughest batters to strike out in baseball.

He drives the ball into the gaps--one of the reasons he gets a lot of doubles. If he can continue to improve as a hitter, he might win a batting title one year soon.

Ray is a very good No. 2 hitter. He bunts well and is effective on the hit-and-run. He doesn't hit into too many double plays. Ray is a patient hitter who had surprisingly little trouble with breaking balls right from the moment he reached the major leagues.

BASERUNNING:

Ray is a good baserunner, putting his average speed to above average use. He gets the maximum lead off first base and could turn into a 30-base stealer. He goes from first to third and from second to home well, and rarely makes a base-running gaffe. Obviously, he knows his fundamentals.

FIELDING:

Ray has quickly developed into one of the better second basemen in baseball. He has dramatically improved his double play pivot and increased his range. His arm is about average for a second baseman, but you rarely see Ray make a bad throw.

JOHNNY RAY
2B, No. 3
SR, 5'11", 170 lbs.
ML Svc: 3 years
Born: 3-1-57 in
    Chouteau, OK

1984 STATISTICS

AVG	G	AB	R	H	2B	3B	HR	RBI	BB	SO	SB
.312	155	555	75	173	38	6	6	67	37	31	11

CAREER STATISTICS

AVG	G	AB	R	H	2B	3B	HR	RBI	BB	SO	SB
.289	499	1880	232	543	117	20	18	189	114	100	45

  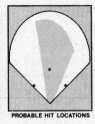

VS. RHP   VS. LHP   PROBABLE HIT LOCATIONS

In fact, you rarely see Ray make a mistake of any kind. He has soft hands that catch nearly every ball he reaches and can make a play out of a bad flip from the shortstop.

OVERALL:

Ray is a solid player, the type to build a team around. He's not a superstar, but still a very good player.

Snider: "Johnny Ray is an All Star as far as I'm concerned. He's shown us everything a second baseman could have. He runs the bases well, throws well, hits well. He's turned into a very good player."

PITCHING:

Rick Rhoden had the best season of his career last year, finishing 14-9 with a miserable team.

Rhoden is a control pitcher who won't blow anyone away with his fastball. He must keep the ball down and nip the corners to be effective. He walks very few hitters, less than three a game.

A hitter is in trouble if Rhoden gets ahead in the count because he'll start nipping corners. His fastball is accurate and stays inside on lefthanded hitters.

He throws a slider and an average change-up and often scuffs up the ball. He patterned himself after Don Sutton while both were in the Los Angeles organization. Rhoden calls himself "The Pupil" and Sutton "The Master." Rick is a battler, the type of pitcher who can win a game when he doesn't have his best stuff.

He reliably goes six or seven innings and knows how to close out a game. He has to be a starting pitcher because of the time it takes him to warm up. He needs a strong defense to catch all the ground balls and pop-ups he induces.

FIELDING, HITTING, BASERUNNING:

Rhoden would be a hitter instead of a pitcher if he didn't have a withered leg. Last year, he hit .333 with six doubles and four RBIs. His doubles have to be clean doubles since Rhoden runs at just over a trot. He had a 10-game hitting streak last year that would have

RICK RHODEN
RHP, No. 29
RR, 6'4", 200 lbs.
ML Svc: 10 years
Born: 5-16-53 in
  Boynton Beach, FL

1984 STATISTICS

W	L	ERA	G	GS	CG	IP	H	R	ER	BB	SO	SV
14	9	2.72	33	33	6	238	216	81	72	62	136	0

CAREER STATISTICS

W	L	ERA	G	GS	CG	IP	H	R	ER	BB	SO	SV
96	70	3.45	264	235	46	1650	1647	702	632	498	890	1

been longer except he made an out as a pinch-hitter. Rhoden fields his position extremely well, making few errors and a lot of plays.

He gets to first base before the runner almost every time, which makes you wonder why the faster pitchers can't. Rhoden has a good move to first base and works hard at keeping runners close.

OVERALL:

Maybe Rhoden is good at the little things because he had to be. Osteomyletis as a youth left him with a withered leg. He is the type of overachiever who is tough to root against.

Snider: "He's so businesslike, so professional, he's fun to watch. He makes the ball move and finds some way to get the hitters out. I'd like to have him on my team."

PITCHING:

After four in-and-out seasons with shoulder problems, the Pirates tried to ease the problem by making Don Robinson a relief pitcher. Robinson pitched more often, but in fewer innings, and had no problems last year.

Robinson has a hard fastball and a devastating curve. He recently developed a good palmball. His curveball is as much of a problem for the catchers as the hitters, as it often bounces into the dirt. Perhaps Robinson should shy away from it with runners on base, but if he does, it will make him more predictable.

When he first came up, he walked very few hitters, challenging everyone. But he has since learned that he must be more of a pitcher without issuing all of the walks, especially since shoulder problems have taken a little off his fastball.

Robinson is the aggressive type, one who likes the challenge of pitching in relief.

The Pirates eased him into the relief role last year and he responded well, with 10 saves and a 3.02 ERA, despite some inconsistency. The next step would be the role of the team's prime save man.

FIELDING, HITTING, BASERUNNING:

Robinson drives the ball as few pitchers can and has twice considered dropping pitching for hitting. Pitchers must treat him as a power hitter and home run threat and set him up with breaking balls before busting him with a

DON ROBINSON
RHP, No. 43
RR, 6'4", 231 lbs.
ML Svc: 7 years
Born: 6-8-57 in
Ashland, KY

1984 STATISTICS

W	L	ERA	G	GS	CG	IP	H	R	ER	BB	SO	SV
5	6	3.02	51	1	0	122	99	45	41	49	110	10

CAREER STATISTICS

W	L	ERA	G	GS	CG	IP	H	R	ER	BB	SO	SV
51	48	3.89	207	120	22	972	933	462	420	350	654	14

good fastball.

Robinson is a good fielding pitcher with an excellent move to first base. He is a tricky devil who will show a runner two or three ordinary moves before unleashing his best ones. He is an ordinary runner who rarely makes mistakes on the bases.

OVERALL:

In the Gossage era, a pitcher like Robinson could become as valuable as a relief pitcher as he was as a starter. Robinson could develop into the type of pitcher you turn the game over to in the seventh inning.

Snider: "Robinson has good stuff, but tends to be more of a thrower at times than a pitcher. He has to learn not to challenge everybody. But with all his attributes and the way he can hit, you have to like him."

PITCHING:

Rod Scurry pitched well at the end of last season, showing signs of recovering from injuries and a stay in a drug rehabilitation center.

Scurry has a devastating curveball that is the closest thing in baseball to an unhittable pitch. He is, however, erratic with it, walking hitters or resorting to an ordinary fastball when he gets behind in the count. Batters know what they will see when they face him—curveballs.

Since there are so few lefthanders, period, and even fewer throwing curveballs, Scurry basically throws a trick pitch hitters don't see often. Scurry should learn to spot the fastball better or figure a way to give it a little motion. He also could use a change-up.

Scurry must work on consistency with his curveball, a pitch that must be practiced.

FIELDING, HITTING, BASERUNNING:

Scurry is an average fielder who covers first base well enough to get by. He is a little lazy coming off the mound and sometimes throws a curveball to first base. He should develop a better motion to first base. Runners like to steal on him simply because of his long, slow delivery, and the fact that his curveball is liable to wind up in the dirt. The catcher has enough to worry about just catching the ball, let alone being ready to throw out the runner. Catchers rarely get a pitch from Scurry

ROD SCURRY
LHP, No. 19
LL, 6'2", 180 lbs.
ML Svc: 5 years
Born: 3-17-56 in
     Sacramento, CA

1984 STATISTICS

W	L	ERA	G	GS	CG	IP	H	R	ER	BB	SO	SV
5	6	2.53	43	0	0	46	28	14	13	22	48	4

CAREER STATISTICS

W	L	ERA	G	GS	CG	IP	H	R	ER	BB	SO	SV
17	27	3.14	227	7	0	330	267	130	115	196	303	32

that is good enough for them to throw out the runner.

Scurry is another of those pitchers who hasn't learned to hit because of the designated hitter rule. Luckily for Scurry, there are not many times when relief pitchers need to hit. Scurry is reasonably fast, but a stranger on the basepaths.

OVERALL:

This is a key year for Scurry, who is coming off a stay in a drug rehab center and arm injuries. At one time, he was considered a potential star, but he has been inconsistent for two years.

Snider: "Scurry throws a great curveball, but he's got to quit bouncing them in the dirt. He has a good arm; maybe he'll wake up one of these days."

PITCHING:

Kent Tekulve has lost a little bit off his fastball--though he call it a sinker. Consequently, his mistakes are hit harder than before. Tekulve also throws a slider, but could use a third pitch to keep the hitters off guard.

Righthanders find Tekulve difficult to hit, but lefthanders have been able to pull his pitches. A lot of them go down the line for doubles.

There are two ways to try to hit Tekulve. The first is to wait, hoping he misses the strike zone and has to throw the ball higher, where you can hit it. The second is to swing down on the sinker, trying to bounce it through the infield.

Tekulve rarely gives up home runs, so teams must string together a few hits to beat him. Tekulve is better on grass. On artificial surfaces, too many balls bounce over his head or the infielders' heads for hits.

He knows how to pitch and will pitch around the right hitters in the lineup and challenge the hitters he plans on getting out. Tekulve can no longer pitch the long inning regularly, but still he can pitch often.

FIELDING, HITTING, BASERUNNING:

Tekulve keeps runners close more with persistence than with an excellent move. He knows it's nearly as important to a relief pitcher as what he throws. He's

KENT TEKULVE
RHP, No. 27
RR, 6'4", 175 lbs.
ML Svc: 10 years
Born: 3-5-47 in
   Cincinnati, OH

1984 STATISTICS

W	L	ERA	G	GS	CG	IP	H	R	ER	BB	SO	SV
3	9	2.66	72	0	0	88	86	30	26	33	36	13

CAREER STATISTICS

W	L	ERA	G	GS	CG	IP	H	R	ER	BB	SO	SV
70	61	2.64	719	0	0	1014	893	349	297	362	548	158

a good fielder who is quick off the mound and covers first base regularly.

He cannot hit but hitting is not a prerequisite for a relief pitcher. On the rare times he gets on base, he's careful not to make a mistake.

OVERALL:

Tekulve's career is winding down, but he could still be valuable in a pennant race. Managers can use him one of two ways--as a ninth-inning man to wrap up the game--especially if a team has used up its lefthanded pinch-hitters--or as the first reliever out of the bullpen.

Snider: "Tekulve may not be quite as quick as he was, but he's still tough on righthanded hitters. His rubber arm is an asset."

HITTING:

Jason Thompson has a big, complicated swing that generates a lot of power but can also look bad. He is prone to slumps and streaks and can be a very frustrating hitter to follow. He will take a walk at the point in a game when the team needs a big hit to drive in a few runs. Yet, in the same game, he'll come up against a good pitch and drive the ball out of the park. Thompson can hit the ball out of any place in the park and is difficult to defense. He has trouble with breaking balls from left-handers, but when he's streaking, he's hard to take out of the lineup.

Thompson stands straight up at the plate, with his arms back. His swing has a lot of parts to it, a backswing, a downward motion, a forward motion and a follow-through—which is why he is prone to slumps and streaks.

When all the parts are synchronized, Thompson's swing drives the ball. When they aren't, he misses it. He takes far too many pitches, looking for only perfect pitches to hit. With his power, he could drive some semi-perfect pitches. Pitchers know this and pitch around him, figuring that a walk hurts a lot less than a home run. He could be a 30-home run hitter again, but he has to get more aggressive.

BASERUNNING:

Thompson is slow and clogs up the basepaths, another reason why pitchers aren't reluctant to walk him. Very often he robs the hitter behind him of a double. He is smart enough to know his limitations, though, and rarely runs into an out.

FIELDING:

Thompson is adequate around the bag. He catches the low balls thrown and hit to him, but doesn't have much range. He is hesitant to throw the ball and has a

JASON THOMPSON
1B, No. 30
LL, 6'3", 210 lbs.
ML Svc: 9 years
Born: 7-6-54 in
Hollywood, CA

1984 STATISTICS

AVG	G	AB	R	H	2B	3B	HR	RBI	BB	SO	SB
.254	154	543	61	138	22	0	17	74	87	73	0

CAREER STATISTICS

AVG	G	AB	R	H	2B	3B	HR	RBI	BB	SO	SB
.264	1265	4349	592	1146	183	11	196	717	714	792	8

  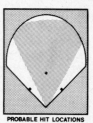

VS. RHP   VS. LHP   PROBABLE HIT LOCATIONS

below average arm. But overall, there is no reason to make him a designated hitter.

OVERALL:

The Pirates counted on Thompson to generate more power than he did last year when he hit only 17 home runs—four on the same day during a windy Wrigley Field doubleheader—and drove in 74 runs.

He could be a better power hitter if he were more aggressive at the plate. Part of his problem could be mental; he is a worrier, not the typical happy-go-lucky power hitter. Perhaps he needs a strong hitter batting behind him in the order to take some pressure off him.

Snider: "He's got some power, but sometimes you have to wait a long time for it. He's liable to snap back and have a fantastic year. If he changes his thought patterns, he might be better."

PITCHING:

Hitters watch John Tudor pitch and can't wait to get to bat--but feel much differently after he gets them out.

All of his pitches seem ordinary, but he mixes them extremely well. He throws a curve inside to lefthanded hitters, a strong fastball, and sometimes mixes in a knuckleball. But his best asset is his ability to change speeds and disrupt a hitter's timing.

He doesn't strike out a lot of hitters, but he doesn't walk many either. Last year, he walked two or fewer batters in 23 of his 32 starts, and he gave up just 25 hits in his last 17 starts.

Tudor will drop to three-quarters or sidearm to certain hitters, and lefthanded hitters find his sidearm delivery very difficult to hit. Righthanders look for his fastball late in a game, but he has learned to keep it outside.

When behind in the count, he comes inside to righthanded hitters with a fastball, but throws away from lefthanded hitters.

FIELDING, HITTING, BASERUNNING:

In his first National League season, Tudor was a surprisingly good hitter, finishing with a .211 average (11 for 76).

Tudor has an excellent move to first base--runners don't take advantage of

JOHN TUDOR
LHP, No. 24
LL, 6'0", 185 lbs.
ML Svc: 6 years
Born: 2-2-54 in
  Schenectady, NY

1984 STATISTICS

W	L	ERA	G	GS	CG	IP	H	R	ER	BB	SO	SV
12	11	3.27	32	32	6	212	200	81	77	56	117	0

CAREER STATISTICS

W	L	ERA	G	GS	CG	IP	H	R	ER	BB	SO	SV
51	43	3.79	138	126	27	848	845	395	357	264	499	1

him. He can field bunts and covers first base well. Tudor also has a move to second base that can fool a bad baserunner.

OVERALL:

Tudor has been a .500 pitcher under difficult circumstances. First, he was a lefthander pitching in Boston's Fenway Park, and last year he was on a Pirates team that didn't win very often. With a good team, he could turn into a big winner, perhaps an 17- or 18-game winner.

Snider: "Tudor is a heady pitcher with a good idea of how to pitch. The most important thing he does is stay within himself."

PITCHING:

The pitching-rich Pirates put Lee Tunnell in the bullpen early last season, which may have set back his career. Tunnell is often compared to Vernon Law, his minor league pitching coach.

Tunnell doesn't have a dominating pitch, but throws the curveball, fastball and slider well. To be effective, he has to use his head as well as his arm and pitch to a hitter's weakness. Good fastball hitters will get curveballs and vice versa.

Sometimes, Tunnell just can't seem to get the ball down in the strike zone. He uses a forkball for a change-up and has had good success with it. He doesn't strike out or walk many hitters.

He is a worrier who has done well when suddenly replacing an injured starter when he doesn't have time to think about it.

FIELDING, HITTING, BASERUNNING:

Tunnell is a good athlete, the type who could develop into a good fielder, hitter and runner. He needs to develop those things, since he'll need an edge. His move to first is good and he works hard at it.

OVERALL:

No one will know how good Tunnell is

LEE TUNNELL
RHP, No. 22
RR, 6'1", 180 lbs.
ML Svc: 2 years
Born: 10-30-60 in
Tyler, TX

1984 STATISTICS

W	L	ERA	G	GS	CG	IP	H	R	ER	BB	SO	SV
1	7	5.27	26	6	0	68	81	44	40	40	51	1

CAREER STATISTICS

W	L	ERA	G	GS	CG	IP	H	R	ER	BB	SO	SV
13	16	4.09	66	34	5	264	265	133	120	103	150	1

until he gets a chance to be a regular. He is the type of pitcher who needs to pitch a lot to be effective and is unsuited, at this point in his career, to being a long reliever.

It's likely he will struggle when first put in the rotation, but could improve when he gets more innings.

Snider: "Obviously, he didn't get enough work to be effective. I'd like to see him change his delivery--it's a little too easy to follow."

HITTING:

The Pirates hoped Marvell Wynne would progress as a hitter last year, but he stayed in a holding pattern. His batting average improved from .243 to .266, but his home runs dropped from seven to none. No longer does it seem as if he will develop into a power hitter.

Wynne has great difficulty with breaking balls, a weakness pitchers soon discovered. If he can't learn to hit them, he won't stay in the league.

His swing is a long one that looks pretty, but it is too long for a guy who doesn't hit for power. He could become a solid spray hitter, perhaps a .280-.290 hitter, if he gets a little better idea of what he's doing at the plate.

Sometimes he is hesitant, feeling for the pitch rather than taking a good solid swing. He hit 11 triples and 24 doubles last year and could turn into a St. Louis-type hitter, a contact hitter who puts the ball in play. A good fielder, 1985 is a crucial year for him at the plate.

BASERUNNING:

Wynne is just learning to use his speed. He stole 24 bases last year, but was caught 19 times. So far, he has had trouble timing his jump off first base. But otherwise, he is a capable baserunner who goes from first to third and from second to home very well.

FIELDING:

Catching the ball is Wynne's forte. He charges the ball very well and has excellent range from right to left.

The Pirates like their center fielder to play shallow and Wynne can do it. Wynne is not afraid of the walls, and seems to always know where they are. His throwing arm is average for a center fielder, but he rarely makes wild throws.

MARVELL WYNNE
CF, No. 36
LL, 5'11", 175 lbs.
ML Svc: 2 years
Born: 12-17-59 in
     Chicago, IL

1984 STATISTICS

AVG	G	AB	R	H	2B	3B	HR	RBI	BB	SO	SB
.266	154	653	77	174	24	11	0	39	42	81	24

CAREER STATISTICS

AVG	G	AB	R	H	2B	3B	HR	RBI	BB	SO	SB
.258	257	1019	143	263	40	13	7	65	80	133	36

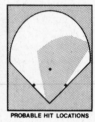

VS. RHP   VS. LHP   PROBABLE HIT LOCATIONS

OVERALL:

The promise Wynne showed his first season is still there, but he is beginning to have some doubters. No one questions his fielding, but he'll need to hit better and run better to be a solid major league center fielder.

Pirate manager Chuck Tanner played him every game until he was injured at the end of last season to give him experience, but Wynne's statistics suffered late in the season.

Snider: "Wynne is a good center fielder who wants to play. He's hustling every inning of every game. The artificial turf is tailor-made for him, and he should learn to take full advantage of it. He could get a lot of hits that way."

BRIAN HARPER
OF, No. 12
RR, 6'2", 195 lbs.
ML Svc: 3 years
Born: 10-16-59 in
Los Angeles, CA

HITTING, FIELDING, BASERUNNING:

Brian Harper played well last spring and was going to get a chance to play in the regular season when injuries wrecked his year. Annually, he has stong spring trainings partly because pitchers aren't throwing good breaking balls in Florida. He is a power hitter who likes to pull the ball, but he has had trouble with breaking balls.

He is an effective hitter against lefthanded pitching and will likely be platooned if his career ever gets off the ground. He has worked hard to increase his speed, improving from a slow runner to below average. But he is best advised to stay close at first and be conservative going from first to third.

Harper is a converted catcher who has worked hard at learning the outfield. If he gets a chance to play, he will probably struggle in the outfield at first; but he could turn into an adequate left fielder with more playing time.

OVERALL:

Harper is a hard worker with a drive to succeed. He works on staying in shape and improving his abilities. If and when he gets some playing time, Harper could develop into an effective role player on a good team.

Snider: "Harper's not as good defensively as I thought, but he looks like he could be a good hitter if he plays enough to get into a groove. The toughest thing in baseball is to be a young player who feels he has to hit in every game to play. It's tough going to the plate thinking an 0-for-4 will put you back on the bench."

MILT MAY
C, No. 14
LR, 6'0", 192 lbs.
ML Svc: 14 years
Born: 8-1-50 in
Gary, IN

HITTING, FIELDING, BASERUNNING:

Milt May is a strong hitter who can win a game with a home run. A good clutch hitter, he waits for a pitch he can handle even when he is under pressure.

He can hit to right-center, left-center and straightaway. He is an excellent pinch-hitter who is not afraid to take a walk if the situation calls for it, yet he drives the ball when he gets his pitch. He is effective against righthanders, but is susceptible to lefties.

Milt can no longer run, as his years of catching have caught up with him. He is smart enough to avoid mistakes on the basepaths, but must be lifted for a pinch-runner late in close games.

Pitchers like to throw to May behind the plate because he calls a good game. He blocks balls in the dirt well. He does not throw very well these days, and the good baserunners in the league can take advantage of him.

OVERALL:

Milt is a good backup catcher for a team with an ironman catcher like Tony Pena. He is no longer an everyday player, but can help complete a good team.

Snider: "Time is catching up with Milt May, but he is the type of player a manager likes. He knows his role, accepts it and does his job without complaining. He can get a pinch-hit for you when you need it."

BENNY DiSTEFANO
OF, No. 68
LL, 6'1", 195 lbs.
ML Svc: 1 year
Born: 1-23-62 in
Brooklyn, NY

HITTING, FIELDING, BASERUNNING:

Benny DiStefano looks like a Pirate hitter of the 1970s--a big, strong guy who attacks the ball. He is loose, attentive and seems to enjoy being at the plate.

He has a penchant for the spectacular, too. Although he hit only .167 in his short stay with the Pirates last year, he hit three home runs and two triples. He tripled in his first major league at-bat, hit his first home run as a pinch-hitter and hit a grand slam.

DiStefano hit .304 in Triple A last year, and the Pirates have only one question: Should he play next year and let him take some lumps, or should he have another solid year in the minors?

DiStefano is stiff-legged, certainly not a speedster. He'll never be a big basestealer, but he's not slow either. While he's young, he can probably play left field, but later in his career, he will most likely be a first baseman. He has good enough hands to field either position, but must work on his throwing.

OVERALL:

DiStefano is one of the bright lights in the Pirate organization, although there is a difference of opinion as to how close he might be to the majors. It might be wise to give him a shot, especially if the Pirates make a change in 1985 with Jason Thompson at first base.

Snider: "He's got some sock, and you have to like a kid like that. Every team likes a hitter who can break up a game with one hit, and DiStefano could become that type."

HEDI VARGAS
1B, No. 50
RR, 6'4", 205 lbs.
ML Svc: 2 years
Born: 2-23-59 in
Guanica, PR

HITTING, BASERUNNING, FIELDING:

Hedi Vargas is a power-hitting right-handed hitter who resembles Tony Perez in his appearance and in his style of swinging the bat. He could be a 20-home run hitter in the major leagues if he gets a chance to play regularly. So far though, he cannot handle major league breaking balls, but that is something hitters have to learn by playing.

If he were a capable outfielder, he would have already been a regular in the majors--he's passed through league waivers twice. But he doesn't hit for a high average and most teams already have a guy playing first base who projects the ability to hit 20 home runs.

Vargas isn't a spectacular fielder, either, and he has limited range. Perhaps he is too musclebound to get throws in the dirt. He is a bad baserunner and he is best advised to stay put at first base.

OVERALL:

Vargas may be one of those players with a promising minor league career who never does get his chance to play.

MIKE BIELECKI
RHP, No. 55
RR, 6'3", 200 lbs.
ML Svc: 1 year
Born: 7-31-59 in
      Baltimore, MD

PITCHING:

Mike Bielecki is a power pitcher who throws a fastball, slider and forkball. He's had over 100 strikeouts in each of the last four years in the minors. Last year, he was the righthanded pitcher of the year in the Pacific Coast League and led the league in wins with 19 and in strikeouts with 162. He had a 14-game winning streak snapped in the playoffs.

Bielecki did not give up a run in four relief appearances in the majors after he was recalled from Hawaii.

OVERALL:

For some reason, the Pirate farm system has begun spewing out pitchers the way it used to produce hitters.

Bielecki could be the best of them. There is little reason for him to return to Triple A, and the Pirates may make room for him in the rotation. It is likely that Bielecki will struggle until he gets used to the majors, but he could turn into a solid major league pitcher.

ALFONSO PULIDO
LHP, No. 58
LL, 5'11", 175 lbs.
ML Svc: 1 year
Born: 1-23-59 in
      Vera Cruz, MEX

PITCHING:

Alfonso Pulido is a control pitcher. He throws his screwball at three different speeds and spots his fastball and curve very well. He walked only 46 batters, and struck out 123, in 216 innings while with Hawaii of the Pacific Coast League last year.

Pulido was 18-6 in 28 games and named top lefthanded starter in the league. He led the league with 16 complete games and had four shutouts.

OVERALL:

Pulido and Mike Bielicki gave the Pirates a strong lefthanded/righthanded combination at Hawaii. Both deserve a chance to pitch in the major leagues this year. Pulido is likely to have more early success than Bielecki--his variety of pitches are liable to confuse the NL hitters for a while.

Much will depend on how well he handles the transition. Pulido must not be nervous or uncomfortable on the mound, otherwise, his control will suffer.

ST. LOUIS CARDINALS

PITCHING:

Neil Allen's best role might be as a short reliever, but with Bruce Sutter in the Cardinals' bullpen, he (or anyone else) has little chance to do that.

In 1984, Allen started one game but was mostly a middle reliever and won nine games out of the bullpen. His arm is durable and the Cardinals are able to use him in a variety of ways, although Allen would prefer to have one role established for him that he could stick with.

Allen would have to be classified as a thrower rather than a pitcher. He does not have the command of his pitches to be able to zero in on a certain part of the plate on one hitter and another on the next hitter.

When Allen's breaking ball is not on, he can be hit hard. Hitters have a tendency to look for the fastball at all times. When Allen throws a bad breaking ball, unless there are two strikes, a hitter can just look at it and not be bothered: he just sits there and waits for the fastball to come over.

FIELDING, HITTING, BASERUNNING:

He regards any hit he gets as a verifiable miracle. Although he had six hits last season, including one off Nolan Ryan, Neil feels that anyone who allows him to get a hit should be released immediately.

NEIL ALLEN
RHP, No. 13
RR, 6'2", 190 lbs.
ML Svc: 6 years
Born: 1-24-58 in
　　　Kansas City, KS

1984 STATISTICS

W	L	ERA	G	GS	CG	IP	H	R	ER	BB	SO	SV
9	6	3.55	57	1	0	119	105	54	47	49	66	3

CAREER STATISTICS

W	L	ERA	G	GS	CG	IP	H	R	ER	BB	SO	SV
44	52	3.57	305	28	5	622	600	275	247	276	425	72

As a fielder, Allen is quick off the mound and has a decent, if not special, move to first.

OVERALL:

Neil Allen was delivered to St. Louis in one of the most unpopular trades of the century, the one that sent Gold Glover Keith Hernandez to the Big Apple. Displaced Cardinal anger has haunted him since.

Snider: "Allen went to the Cardinals under most difficult circumstances. He has put undue pressure on himself in an attempt to make the deal look good and himself acceptable. He would help his own cause by developing some kind of trick pitch or a straight change."

PITCHING:

Joaquin Andujar finally put it all together for his first 20-game season. He is very proud of being the only pitcher in the National League to win 20 games in 1984. There is good cause for his pride, and the hitters had better recognize it.

He also led the league in shutouts and innings pitched and was second in complete games, as he erased the stigma of a 6-16 record the year before.

Andujar's forte is that he challenges each hitter. He does not use just one pitch. He has an uncanny knack of getting hitters out even though they have a pretty good idea of what is coming.

His success is partly attributable to the fact that he has developed from being a "thrower" to being a "pitcher." He throws a fastball with a little tail on it, and it is his most effective pitch against lefthanded hitters. His quick slider thrown inside can eat up left-handers, too.

He is, however, a more effective pitcher against righthanders. While he is an overhand pitcher, Andujar will occasionally drop to sidearm against them. Under these circumstances, no one can be sure where the pitch is going. It is not just the fastball that he will send from sidearm--the hitter might very well be getting a slider.

Andujar denies throwing inside. There are many who take issue with that. He claims that he CANNOT pitch inside. When he gets his butt kicked in bench-clearing brawls, he can't understand why.

He is one of the most exciting and excitable pitchers in baseball. Andujar wears his emotions on his sleeve.

FIELDING, HITTING, BASERUNNING:

Andujar forever fashions himself a power hitter. Last year, he put his

JOAQUIN ANDUJAR
RHP, No. 47
SR, 6'0", 180 lbs
ML Svc: 9 years
Born: 12-21-52 in
  San Pedro de Macoris, DR

1984 STATISTICS

W	L	ERA	G	GS	CG	IP	H	R	ER	BB	SO	SV
20	14	3.34	36	36	12	261	218	104	97	70	147	0

CAREER STATISTICS

W	L	ERA	G	GS	CG	IP	H	R	ER	BB	SO	SV
89	89	3.47	303	218	50	1588	1455	686	613	546	781	8

money where his mouth is. He ripped off two home runs, including a grand slam off Atlanta's Jeff Dedmon. If a pitcher just throws a pitch where Andujar is swinging, Joaquin can nail it. Other than these two heroic occasions, he struck out 47 times and generally hurt himself at the plate by failing to sacrifice or by swinging too hard when a normal swing might have meant a base hit.

He is one of the quickest fielding pitchers in baseball and his move to first may be the best.

OVERALL:

Andujar has developed a change-up. It helped him win more than one of his twenty games. He needs some more work on it, however.

Snider: "Andujar will probably always pitch worked up. For a while, it looked like he was going to settle down and not be quite so hotheaded, but it doesn't appear to be in his nature. Last year in this book, I suggested that he could become a 20-game winner if he controlled his emotions. Well, he is a fine pitcher, and did it in spite of himself."

PITCHING:

Danny Cox had an up-and-down year. He was 3-8 when he was sent to the minors, although the Cardinals had scored just more than a run a game for him in his losses. After nearly a month at Louisville, he re-discovered his off-speed pitch. Cox thereby returned to the big leagues to finish with a 9-11 record, and pitched both his first complete game and his first shutout.

When Cox gets behind in the count, he does not bear down and come in to the hitters. Rather, he is able to throw his change or breaking ball over for a strike. Normally on a 2-0 count, a hitter can look for and get a fastball--not so when Cox is on the mound. He has an excellent curveball, and the hitter may just get it.

He is a 6'4", 230 pound strapper who has been compared to former big leaguer Gene Cowley. Cowley also played professional basketball, and Duke Snider recalls that when Cowley was on the mound, he, like Danny Cox, came at the hitter with his size 15 feet and looked as if he was about to step right on your face.

Cox has made rapid progress in the majors, especially when you consider that he was in Class A ball in 1983. If Cox can remember that his 85 MPH fastball is not his best pitch, he may have a long future in the major leagues.

FIELDING, HITTING, BASERUNNING:

He turns his back on the plate after he releases the ball, making it tough for him to get balls up the middle. His move to first is better than average.

Cox takes a good swing at the plate, but does not get much accomplished. He

DANNY COX
RHP, No. 34
RR, 6'4", 230 lbs.
ML Svc: 1 year plus
Born: 9-21-59 in
   Northhampton, UK

1984 STATISTICS												
W	L	ERA	G	GS	CG	IP	H	R	ER	BB	SO	SV
9	11	4.03	29	27	1	156	171	81	70	54	70	0

CAREER STATISTICS												
W	L	ERA	G	GS	CG	IP	H	R	ER	BB	SO	SV
12	17	3.77	41	39	1	239	263	119	100	77	106	0

was a notably poor sacrifice hitter last season.

He is a good athlete, however, and runs the bases well.

OVERALL:

His pitching is coming along nicely, thank you, but oddly enough, he will have to start thinking about his own hitting. Many of the best pitchers in the National League have kept themselves in the game by being respectable hitters who a manager can watch at the plate without a bag over his head.

Snider: "Cox has a couple of good things going for him, not the least of which is his tremendous size. Tall, lanky pitchers are just a jumble of arms and legs and can be confusing to a hitter, though, after a while, you can time a skinny pitcher's motion. Cox, on the other hand, is such a big guy that there is an added dimension to be considered. Hitters will never get over the illusion that Cox is practically in your lap."

PITCHING:

Bob Forsch slipped to a 2-5 record last season after having missed most of the year because of surgery to correct a nerve problem in his back.

At age 35, Forsch's future is in some doubt, although the Cardinals have tremendous faith in his ability to recover completely. Throughout his career, he has never given less than 100% and has always been one of baseball's best competitors.

He pitched in the last month of the season even though it had been assumed by his doctors and trainers that he would have to wait until the spring of 1985 to begin his comeback.

Once a power pitcher, Forsch now has to have pinpoint control and needs to set up the hitters. He is one of those pitchers who needs to use his defense. Not coincidentally, the Cardinals have one of the best defenses in baseball.

What Forsch is going to have to do is come up with another pitch. For several years now, He has dabbled with a knuckleball on the sidelines but has rarely, if ever, tried to use it in a game.

This righthander has a good athletic body and is never out of shape.

FIELDING, HITTING, BASERUNNING:

He is one of baseball's best hitting pitchers and almost never fails to help himself by bunting. At one point, much

BOB FORSCH
RHP, No. 31
RR, 6'3", 215 lbs.
ML Svc: 10 years
Born: 1-13-50 in
    Sacramento, CA

1984 STATISTICS

W	L	ERA	G	GS	CG	IP	H	R	ER	BB	SO	SV
2	5	6.02	16	11	1	52	64	38	35	19	21	0

CAREER STATISTICS

W	L	ERA	G	GS	CG	IP	H	R	ER	BB	SO	SV
120	100	3.64	325	307	58	2005	1959	934	812	582	798	1

earlier in his career, he was a third baseman and still has the ability to hit home runs.

An excellent fielder, Forsch also has developed a quicker move to first by cocking his leg, somewhat like his former teammate Jim Kaat.

OVERALL:

An excellent student of the game, Forsch will have to call on all of his determination to fight his way back into the starting rotation.

Snider: "Bob has always been on top. I don't think that he will let his back up-end him. If anyone will fight to come back, it's him."

HITTING:

David Green is the power hope of the Cardinals, and he began to realize that last year when he hit 15 home runs, 11 of them after he returned in June from alcohol rehabilitation.

Green adjusted his swing to more of an uppercut, and his strikeout total mounted concurrently. He fanned 105 times and walked just 20, but when the ball jumps off his bat, it will go out of any ballpark.

It is said that Green could have a little more "bulldog" in him. That is to say that when Green steps into the box he should be a little meaner, a little more aggressive. This is not to say he should turn nasty, but first of all he has to work up a feeling of distinct competition with the pitcher and then transfer that to the baseball--a killer instinct, if you will. Green has not displayed that as much as he should have. A major league hitter has to really WANT to hit that ball.

At age 24, Green's potential is still enormous, even though he may never be the next Roberto Clemente, as some had fantasized.

If he could be more aggressive, he would hit 20 home runs, despite Busch Stadium's size. He could make up the difference on the road.

What Green does is basically up to him. He could be anything he lets himself be, but sometimes a player can let pressures affect him to the point where he never becomes the player he is expected to become.

Green is mostly a first ball, fastball hitter and he can be fooled with breaking stuff, especially on the outside corner.

BASERUNNING:

Green stole only 17 bases after swiping twice as many the year before, but

DAVID GREEN
1B, No. 22
RR, 6'3", 165 lbs.
ML Svc: 3 years
Born: 12-4-60 in
Managua, NIC

1984 STATISTICS

AVG	G	AB	R	H	2B	3B	HR	RBI	BB	SO	SB
.268	126	452	49	121	14	4	15	65	20	105	17

CAREER STATISTICS

AVG	G	AB	R	H	2B	3B	HR	RBI	BB	SO	SB
.273	369	1074	128	293	36	15	25	159	60	215	62

VS. RHP

VS. LHP

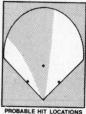

PROBABLE HIT LOCATIONS

he can still be classified as a legitimate threat to steal 30 bases a year. He is tremendously exciting going from home plate to third on triples.

FIELDING:

Green had his ups and downs in his first full season at first base. Many times, he wasn't even noticed, meaning that he was doing the job. There weren't many obvious mistakes.

OVERALL:

Snider: "He looks like he's a little more sure of himself in his approach to the game this season. Hopefully, his personal problems are behind him, and Dave can begin to crack the bat."

HITTING:

George Hendrick is still considered among the game's clutch hitters although he fell off to 69 RBIs before a thyroid operation short-circuited his season by three weeks.

Though he hit just nine home runs, Hendrick still has the reputation of coming up with key hits, almost unobtrusively.

He'll be 35 years old this season, but Hendrick is far from being considered washed up. If he is healthy, he should still have several good years left.

Hendrick is one of baseball's great wrist hitters although he isn't classified as a home run hitter. He would be classified more correctly as a singles and doubles hitter. He had 28 doubles among his 122 hits in 1984.

As they would with most players the size of the lanky Hendrick, pitchers try to tie him up inside with hard stuff so that he cannot extend himself and crack those wrists over the plate. He is especially deadly on a low ball over the middle of the plate.

BASERUNNING:

From first to home, Hendrick is a better than average runner. From home to first, he is far less. He tends to watch the ball sail off his bat, and he does not throw it into overdrive if he thinks that he is going to be out at first anyway. Hendrick is not a base-stealing threat and takes one of the shortest leads in baseball. He had no steals in 1984.

FIELDING:

Hendrick still is among baseball's top right fielders, although he might

GEORGE HENDRICK
RF, No. 25
RR, 6'5", 195 lbs.
ML Svc: 13 years
Born: 10-10-49 in
Los Angeles, CA

1984 STATISTICS

AVG	G	AB	R	H	2B	3B	HR	RBI	BB	SO	SB
.277	120	441	57	122	28	1	9	69	32	75	0

CAREER STATISTICS

AVG	G	AB	R	H	2B	3B	HR	RBI	BB	SO	SB
.267	1727	6260	842	1669	303	26	241	989	498	884	57

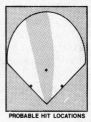

VS. RHP   VS. LHP   PROBABLE HIT LOCATIONS

prefer a less taxing position, such as first base, where he played in 1983.

He almost never throws to the wrong base and his arm still is strong and accurate.

OVERALL:

Hendrick has been a quiet leader for the Cardinals over the last six years, but he likely has seen his best and most productive years.

Snider: "I like the way he punches the ball. His strong wrists and quick flip of the bat are what you need to deliver. George is a quiet but important force for the Cardinals. They need him around, although most fans don't realize it."

HITTING:

Tom Herr returned to play in 1984 after being saddled with two bad years, but he has most likely seen his best and most productive years. He had arthroscopic knee surgery on his left knee in 1983, and there was question as to how far, or even if, he would come back.

But the Cardinals' second baseman had his most productive RBI season (49) last year, and hit .276, including a career-high .287 righthanded. He had never hit above .230 righthanded before, and last year, he had his first two home runs from the right side of the plate.

Herr's knees gave him little trouble and he played in 145 games before having to step out the last two weeks because of torn muscles in his left side.

Herr is one of the league's top second-place hitters, with the patience to take a pitch so as to help basestealers Willie McGee and Lonnie Smith, the intelligence to move a runner along and the punch to send the ball into the gap.

He may be the "guts" of the Cardinals and is not afraid to say anything critical if something is amiss.

FIELDING:

Herr's range came back gradually during the season, and he was running better at the end than he had been at the beginning. There are those, Herr included, who feel that he will be moving even better this year because it often takes a year or so to rebound from surgery.

Early on, Herr appeared to have trouble making plays behind second base, but in the second half of the season he was smooth. Herr made just six errors and, coupled with Ozzie Smith, helped the Cardinals to lead the league in double

TOM HERR
2B, No. 28
SR, 6'0", 185 lbs.
ML Svc: 5 years
Born: 4-4-56 in
Lancaster, PA

1984 STATISTICS

AVG	G	AB	R	H	2B	3B	HR	RBI	BB	SO	SB
.276	145	558	67	154	23	2	4	49	49	56	13

CAREER STATISTICS

AVG	G	AB	R	H	2B	3B	HR	RBI	BB	SO	SB
.276	562	2007	276	553	82	24	6	178	206	192	77

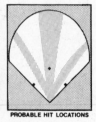

VS. RHP   VS. LHP   PROBABLE HIT LOCATIONS

plays. It might have been his best year defensively.

BASERUNNING:

A heady baserunner, Herr was able to steal just 13 times last year. With more mobility this year, he could return to the 20-steal category.

OVERALL:

Snider: "He turns the double play as well as anybody in the league. You can see that Ozzie Smith likes to work with him. That 'click' is especially important in the field. Tom is a take-charge guy--he won't let things go unsaid."

PITCHING:

Not blessed with a blazing fastball, Ricky Horton survives on his own intelligence. He has the ability to move the ball around and also has a great pickoff move. Both help.

He was the tenth man on the Cardinals staff when the team broke spring training, but had a 1.08 ERA in 15 relief appearances before he was clocked by Philadelphia in his first start of the year.

He earned eight of his nine wins as a starter. The Cardinals are going to use him only as a spot starter in 1985 and groom him further in the bullpen.

Horton's debut as a major leaguer was one for the books. His first two pitches were to Jeff Leonard and Chili Davis of the San Francisco Giants. One was a home run, the other a double.

After the first time around the league last season, Horton began to get hit a little more, not uncommon for a new pitcher. He still finished well, compiling a 9-4 record with a 3.44 ERA.

Horton has only an average fastball and sometimes likes it too much. It is not going to be an out pitch for him, and he must not think that it is. If he does, he will try to overthrow with something that is not there.

What he does do well, however, is establish the corners of the plate with his breaking stuff. While a great fastball is nice, the ability to pick the hitter's pocket with breaking balls is a delight to see.

FIELDING, HITTING, BASERUNNING:

Horton is not a good hitter, though

RICKY HORTON
LHP, No. 49
LR, 6'2", 195 lbs.
ML Svc: 1 year
Born: 7-30-59 in
Poughkeepsie, NY

1984 STATISTICS

W	L	ERA	G	GS	CG	IP	H	R	ER	BB	SO	SV
9	4	3.44	37	18	1	125	140	53	48	39	76	1

CAREER STATISTICS

W	L	ERA	G	GS	CG	IP	H	R	ER	BB	SO	SV
9	4	3.44	37	18	1	125	140	53	48	39	76	1

he is a good runner who has been used for pinch-running chores.

His move to first should stand as testimony to other pitchers who choose not to work on theirs. Horton does not throw any better than 90 MPH, and developed his tricky maneuver in high school. You must balance the scales: when you have not been given one thing, you must develop another. Last season, he picked 14 runners off first, akin to turning 14 double plays.

OVERALL:

Snider: "We may not see Ricky do any better than he did last season, but I have a feeling that the Cardinals would be happy with something along the same lines."

PITCHING:

After performing mostly as a reliever in his minor league days with the Cincinnati organization, Kurt Kepshire blossomed last year as a starter with the Cardinals. In 16 starts, he had only four poor ones and he finished the season with a bang by shutting out the NL East champion Chicago Cubs and the Montreal Expos.

Kepshire is a strong righthander with a better than average fastball and a good breaking ball. The best part about him is that he is not afraid of the hitters. He stands on the mound and goes right after them, giving everything he's got. This youngster has guts.

Kepshire was only 6-5 last season, but had two no-decisions against Philadelphia when his pitching was excellent.

As the Cardinals approach this season, Kepshire will likely be the No. 3 starter. With his added knowledge of the hitters in the league, he could be a 12- to 15-game winner.

FIELDING, HITTING, BASERUNNING:

Kepshire is strictly a lefthanded hitter, something quite unusual for a righthanded pitcher. Despite lusty swings, he is not a good hitter. He also needs to improve his bunting.

One of the things Kepshire worked on late last season and will have to address this spring is his move to first. It is slow.

KURT KEPSHIRE
RHP, No. 50
LR, 6'1", 180 lbs.
ML Svc: 1 year
Born: 7-3-59 in
   Bridgeport, CT

1984 STATISTICS
W	L	ERA	G	GS	CG	IP	H	R	ER	BB	SO	SV
6	5	3.30	17	16	2	109	100	47	40	44	71	0

CAREER STATISTICS
W	L	ERA	G	GS	CG	IP	H	R	ER	BB	SO	SV
6	5	3.30	17	16	2	109	100	47	40	44	71	0

His baserunning seems average, but it is really difficult to judge because he was rarely on base.

OVERALL:

The addition of an off-speed pitch will help Kepshire, although his current repertoire is more than adequate.

Snider: "For a young pitcher to attack the hitters with his best stuff the way Kepshire does is impressive. This season, we should see him complement his all-out approach with added knowledge of the hitters' weaknesses. How well he can hold up in Year Number Two will be interesting to follow."

PITCHING:

Jeff Lahti is Whitey Herzog's "jam" pitcher, meaning that he is the one most likely to enter a game with the bases loaded and one out in the sixth inning.

Despite a late season slump, Lahti allowed just 24 of 71 baserunners to score, and he retired the first hitter to face him 42 of 63 times, or 66.7%.

Lahti had his first career save last year, but his biggest value was in keeping his team close. On 28 occasions-- other than his save or his four wins --Lahti held the other team right where it was when he entered the game. He became an almost perfect setup man for relief ace Bruce Sutter.

On another team, Lahti could be the No. 1 reliever because of his 90 MPH fastball and hard breaking slider. Lahti also has considerable fire in him and his eyes almost seem to glaze over when he comes into the right situation.

Like many other pitchers, he can be hurt if he falls behind in the count. Hitters can then sit on the fastball. It makes all the difference in the world to a hitter when he knows that the pitcher is not going to come in with a breaking ball.

FIELDING, HITTING, BASERUNNING:

Middle relievers rarely bat, so Lahti has had little chance to apply himself. He generally is good for one Baltimore-chop hit a season.

JEFF LAHTI
RHP, No. 32
RR, 6'0", 180 lbs.
ML Svc: 3 years
Born: 10-8-56 in
   Oregon City, OR

1984 STATISTICS

W	L	ERA	G	GS	CG	IP	H	R	ER	BB	SO	SV
4	2	3.72	63	0	0	84	69	36	35	34	45	1

CAREER STATISTICS

W	L	ERA	G	GS	CG	IP	H	R	ER	BB	SO	SV
12	9	3.57	149	1	0	214	186	94	85	84	93	1

Lahti is alert in covering first base and he has at least an average move to first.

OVERALL:

Sutter would be the first to credit the work of Lahti and the team's other middle relievers. When Lahti is on his game, the Cardinals starters have only to give their team five good innings.

Snider: "Jeff has waited a few years for his chance in the big leagues. He really got it last year and the waiting seems to have made him want it badly. He practically breathes fire out there. The hitters cannot afford to be complacent when Lahti is hot or they will be cooling their heels in dugout before they know it."

HITTING:

Last season, Tito Landrum got more exposure than he ever had previously in his major league career, and became one of baseball's best fourth outfielders. In 173 at-bats, Landrum had 47 hits and drove in 26 runs.

His pinch-hitting average was in the .300s most of the year and that mark was exceptional considering that he hadn't been trusted to perform that role much before. For most of his career, Landrum has been a defensive replacement in the outfield, a platoon outfielder or a pinch-runner.

Landrum would have to be classified as a dead fastball hitter, although last season he began to show some progress in handling the curve. He can be pitched to if pitchers keep the ball away.

Last season, he seemed to swing with much more authority than ever before, and he probably hits the ball as hard as any Cardinal. Despite his above average speed, he does not get a lot of infield hits.

Landrum perfectly understands and accepts his reserve role and is one of baseball's real gentlemen.

FIELDING:

Landrum can play any of the three outfield positions and has a strong, accurate arm. Sometimes, it takes him a while to unload the ball, however.

BASERUNNING:

For all of his natural speed, Landrum is not a good basestealer. He had just three last year and sometimes seems hesitant on the bases.

TITO LANDRUM
OF, No. 39
RR, 5'11", 175 lbs.
ML Svc: 4 years
Born: 10-25-54 in
  Joplin, MO

1984 STATISTICS

AVG	G	AB	R	H	2B	3B	HR	RBI	BB	SO	SB
.272	105	173	21	47	9	1	3	26	10	27	3

CAREER STATISTICS

AVG	G	AB	R	H	2B	3B	HR	RBI	BB	SO	SB
.272	105	173	21	47	9	1	3	26	10	27	3

VS. RHP   VS. LHP   PROBABLE HIT LOCATIONS

OVERALL:

Landrum still would hope to play regularly, but at age 30 his future seems to be as a bench player. But after struggling to find himself in the major leagues, he has carved a niche for himself with the Cardinals.

Snider: "Landrum has bounced between both leagues in the past few years and finally returned to the Cardinals. Perhaps he decided that he did not want to be shuffled around anymore and decided to carve a niche for himself in St. Louis. He performed better last year than he had done in the past and now seems set to stay right where he is."

PITCHING:

Dave LaPoint has changed his style over the past two years. He is no longer trying to throw heat down the pike, but rather is "thinking" more now, finessing the hitters more than he has in the past.

He keeps the ball away from right-handed hitters. Then, when he catches them leaning inside, he can bust a fastball by them. His fastball actually isn't that fast, in the 85 MPH range, but his excellent off-speed pitch makes it look much faster.

LaPoint considers his off-speed pitch to be pretty much a change-up, but it has actions like a palmball or more likely a screwball.

If he could learn to throw a hard slider to righthanded batters, down and in around the knees, LaPoint would be more effective in complementing his other pitches.

With a weight clause in his contract, LaPoint is obligated to keep his weight down. Though he still appears a little heavy, it was a far cry from the spare tire noted on many other pitchers last year.

LaPoint was the Cardinals' opening day starter on the basis of a strong showing in spring training. He was never able, however, to get more than a game over .500 until he won his last three decisions to finish 12-10. LaPoint never has had a losing season in his eight years in professional baseball.

FIELDING, HITTING, BASERUNNING:

Prone to turn his back on balls hit up the middle, LaPoint does not help

DAVE LaPOINT
LHP, No. 39
LL, 6'3", 215 lbs.
ML Svc: 3 years
Born: 7-29-59 in
   Glens Falls, NY

1984 STATISTICS

W	L	ERA	G	GS	CG	IP	H	R	ER	BB	SO	SV
12	10	3.96	33	33	2	193	205	94	85	77	130	0

CAREER STATISTICS

W	L	ERA	G	GS	CG	IP	H	R	ER	BB	SO	SV
35	22	3.88	120	88	3	562	595	268	242	228	333	1

himself here as much as he could. His move to first base is getting better and he has improved his release in throwing to the plate.

A weak hitter, LaPoint stunned observers by knocking in three runs in a game at Cincinnati, including the game winner in a game he didn't last long enough in to win. His bunting is average, his baserunning considerably less.

OVERALL:

The Cardinals would like LaPoint to develop a curveball this spring, feeling that an extra pitch could make him a 15-game winner.

Snider: "Major league ballplayers, especially pitchers, have to keep themselves in good physical condition. While LaPoint is not as heavy as some other pitchers in the league, he should continue to keep his weight down to a respectable level. A trimmer pitcher is generally a better pitcher."

HITTING:

Whitey Herzog has always said that Willie McGee is never ahead in the count when it's 2-0 and never behind when it's 0-2--meaning that, McGee doesn't know, or care, what the count is. He'll hit the same regardless.

On one pitch, the fleet center fielder can look so bad that one would think that McGee could never hit that pitch. Then, seconds later, he'll drill the same delivery into the gap for a triple.

Nonetheless, McGee really should be a bit more selective at the plate. He gives the pitcher too much credit by swinging at everything he's thrown. Then again, you don't want to take the bat out of his hands.

Some days, McGee will have a stroke that enables him to chop down on the ball and take advantage of an artificial surface. The next day, he might be hitting lazy fly balls. Perhaps McGee does not remember his stroke from one day to the next, but he will somehow end up at about .290. He batted .291 last season.

McGee has pop from each side of the plate, belying his slim build, and he likes to extend his arms. His eleven triples tied him for fourth in the NL.

In the second half of the season, McGee became the Cardinals' leadoff man and he raised his average 16 points.

FIELDING:

McGee won a Gold Glove in only his second year in the league and probably is the best center fielder in the NL. His range is practically from wall to wall. His arm is above average and accurate and his judgment on throwing to the right base has improved considerably since he came into the league.

BASERUNNING:

McGee will steal some 50 bases a year

WILLIE McGEE
CF, No. 51
SR, 6'1", 175 lbs.
ML Svc: 3 years
Born: 11-2-58 in
San Francisco, CA

1984 STATISTICS

AVG	G	AB	R	H	2B	3B	HR	RBI	BB	SO	SB
.291	145	571	82	166	19	11	6	50	29	80	43

CAREER STATISTICS

AVG	G	AB	R	H	2B	3B	HR	RBI	BB	SO	SB
.290	415	1594	200	463	53	27	15	181	67	236	106

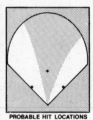

VS. RHP   VS. LHP   PROBABLE HIT LOCATIONS

for many years to come. He swiped 43 in 52 attempts last year, even though he takes a lead about a half-step shorter than the league's top basestealer, Tim Raines of Montreal.

OVERALL:

McGee has established himself as one of the best young players in the game. Given more control at bat, he should be a .300 hitter.

Snider: "It is hard to get a handle on him as a hitter, he switches his ways so much, but he will probably settle down and at least look more consistent. He is exciting to watch in center field, he has great range and covers a lot of ground. He is learning quickly."

HITTING:

An impressive rookie after he was re-called from Louisville in July, Terry Pendleton batted .324 in 262 at-bats. His average was considerably higher when he was batting lefthanded, but reports from Louisville were that Pendleton was a better hitter righthanded, so manager Whitey Herzog did not worry.

When Pendleton learns the pitchers better (he has been in pro baseball only three years), he has a chance to be one of the best young hitters in the league. He has a quick, compact stroke from either side of the plate. Though he had only one home run, he had 16 doubles and three triples, indicating that he does have some power.

In build and style, he reminds one of Pittsburgh's Bill Madlock, who has won four batting titles.

Pendleton hit third for St. Louis, which might not be his ideal spot, but the Cardinals' attack seemed so much better with him in the lineup that manager Whitey Herzog left him there.

Pendleton is the type of player who is always hustling. His enthusiasm for the game made many of the veterans on the team play better in the second half of the season after their lackluster first half.

How quickly he absorbs the learning process will dictate how quickly he will be a quality hitter. He must get to the point where he can see every pitcher's delivery in his mind's eye, and then he won't be surprised by too much. The pitchers of the league, far from a stupid fraternity, will know his weaknesses and he has to know theirs. He seems to be able to learn quickly, however.

BASERUNNING:

Pendleton stole only seven bases in the minors—three of them were steals of home—but he swiped 20 in his two and a half major league months.

He gets a reasonably quick jump and then dives into the bag headfirst.

TERRY PENDLETON
3B, No. 9
SR, 5'9", 180 lbs.
ML Svc: 1 year plus
Born: 7-16-60 in
   Los Angeles, CA

1984 STATISTICS

AVG	G	AB	R	H	2B	3B	HR	RBI	BB	SO	SB
.324	67	262	37	85	16	3	1	33	16	32	20

CAREER STATISTICS

AVG	G	AB	R	H	2B	3B	HR	RBI	BB	SO	SB
.324	67	262	37	85	16	3	1	33	16	32	20

  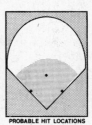

VS. RHP — STRONG | VS. LHP — STRONG | PROBABLE HIT LOCATIONS

Once he learns pitchers' moves, he should be a 30-plus basestealer. If that turns out to be true, the present St. Louis team would have six players capable of taking at least 30 apiece.

FIELDING:

Pendleton is a converted second baseman. He showed quick hands and an adequate arm at third, but must conquer his tendency to be indecisive on the rapid-fire turf-hit balls. Occasionally, he was caught backpedaling on balls and he caught in-between hops.

OVERALL:

Snider: "He seems to have a good attitude and is a very, very impressive young hitter. He will have to work out the kinks in his play at third base, but he is certainly interested in learning."

HITTING:

Darrell Porter is a strict uppercut hitter. He hit 11 home runs last year, but only two after a game-winning grand slam on July 18.

It may be that, at age 33, Porter is on a downward slide. His approach has not changed, but the Cardinals need more than the .232 average he gave them.

Last year, he seemed to adjust his hitting style in an attempt to hit more straightaway rather than pull the ball so much. In the past, Porter's success centered on his ability to drive the ball to the right side with a runner on first base or hit the sacrifice fly to right field with a runner at third.

He likes the fastball away and can be jammed with hard stuff inside. If a pitcher makes a mistake over the middle of the plate, he can take it deep. As an uppercut hitter, however, it's very difficult for him to hit for a good average. Home runs hitters have a little lift to their swing, not the big upper-cut Porter favors.

Porter is a hard-nosed player, a bear-down type of player. He still has the desire to bounce back for a big season. He is on the last year of his contract, which is fuel enough for some players, but Porter doesn't need any extra incentive.

FIELDING:

Porter appeared to have more trouble holding onto pitches and experienced difficulty in his shifting last year. His reactions seemed slow, especially late in the year, athough it probably wasn't laziness, but rather because he was tired from the rigors of the long season with little to excite him.

DARRELL PORTER
C, No. 15
LR, 6'1", 202 lbs.
ML Svc: 12 years
Born: 1-17-52 in
Joplin, MO

1984 STATISTICS

AVG	G	AB	R	H	2B	3B	HR	RBI	BB	SO	SB
.232	127	422	56	98	16	3	11	68	60	79	5

CAREER STATISTICS

AVG	G	AB	R	H	2B	3B	HR	RBI	BB	SO	SB
.248	1545	5014	695	1244	216	46	159	740	812	883	32

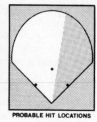

VS. RHP   VS. LHP   PROBABLE HIT LOCATIONS

BASERUNNING:

A good, aggressive runner from first to third, Porter is also a sneaky base-stealer. He swiped five last year, including the one that gave the Cardinals a single-season club record. He is also one of the toughest players at breaking up the double play.

OVERALL:

Snider: "I think that Porter should try some practice with a hitting tee. He could get away from his severe upper-cut swing and create a little lift in his swing. It would take a lot of practice to change his approach."

HITTING:

While Lonnie Smith enjoyed his best percentage year in stolen bases with a 79.4% success rate, he had his worst year at the plate. From a .316 lifetime average, Smith slipped to a mere .250, to the total mystification of one and all.

Perhaps the answer lies in the fact he was not as selective at the plate. He seemed to be swinging (and fouling off) a lot of pitches.

It is difficult to assess what the mental demands were on him in his first full year of playing after treatment for drug abuse. The fact was, he just did not seem to have the same pop in his bat.

At one time, he was the Cardinals' catalyst. Last year, he was dropped from the first to the third spot in the order for the last half of the season, and while there were brief surges of the Old Smith, his season was really a lost one.

Barring injuries, there is no reason why Lonnie cannot come back this season. He takes care of himself and he has a good attitude. The pressure to pick up where he left off may have made him "think" at the plate too much.

BASERUNNING:

Not only did he not hit very much last season, but "Skates" didn't fall down that much, either (in the past, Smith had been known to just fall down while running the bases, hence his nickname). Had he been able to hit anything at all, he probably would have swiped 70 bases.

Unfortunately, Lonnie did not get on base, and everybody knows that you can't steal first.

FIELDING:

He is exciting to watch in the field, though most times it is for all the wrong reasons. Smith is not a good de-

LONNIE SMITH
LF, No. 27
RR, 5'9", 170 lbs.
ML Svc: 5 years
Born: 12-22-55 in
  Chicago, IL

1984 STATISTICS

AVG	G	AB	R	H	2B	3B	HR	RBI	BB	SO	SB
.250	145	504	77	126	20	4	6	49	70	90	50

CAREER STATISTICS

AVG	G	AB	R	H	2B	3B	HR	RBI	BB	SO	SB
.300	447	2096	399	629	116	24	27	197	224	291	221

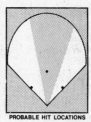

VS. RHP   VS. LHP   PROBABLE HIT LOCATIONS

fensive player, and often, very often, far too often, he throws to the wrong base.

Some players have good baseball instincts for some phases of the game, and other just don't. Smith doesn't appear to have been given the knack of defense.

OVERALL:

Clearly, this is a crucial year for Lonnie Smith. He will not improve his defense and the Cardinals are not looking for that. What he must do is regain his plate proficiences in order to do what he does best--rattle the defense and stir his team's offense.

Snider: "With Lonnie at age 29, you certainly hope that it's not over for him. I don't think that it is. He still has the capabilities of igniting his of-offense into high-octane efficiency. St. Louis has to have him back at full speed to play the kind of game they have built a team around."

HITTING:

Considering Ozzie Smith's .235 career average, his .257 mark last year should be considered as a bonus. It has been long said that if Smith hit .230, he would still be an asset.

He is a pecking type of hitter when he is batting from the left side, but is more effective righthanded. His basic problem from both sides of the plate is that he tries to hit everything too far and too hard.

Smith, however, can pull the ball into the corner, especially righthanded. His 44 RBIs represent a rather high total inasmuch as he missed five weeks after having a bone in his right hand broken by a pitch thrown by San Diego's Ed Whitson.

FIELDING:

Most baseball observers would say that Smith is the best defensive shortstop in the last 10 to 20 years. His arm is only slightly above average, but Smith never misses a play at first base even though the verdict may be by only half a step.

Smith has won five Gold Gloves in succession and unless he suffers a debilitating injury, he should go on to win ten of them.

His fielding best can be described as acrobatic, although Smith also is remarkably efficient on the routine plays.

BASERUNNING:

Smith stole 35 bases in three-quarters of a season and should be good for 50 in a full season. He probably is the best among the Cardinals at reading a pitcher and getting a lead.

OZZIE SMITH
SS, No. 1
SR, 5'10", 150 lbs.
ML Svc: 7 years
Born: 12-26-54 in
Mobile, AL

1984 STATISTICS

AVG	G	AB	R	H	2B	3B	HR	RBI	BB	SO	SB
.257	124	412	53	106	20	5	1	44	56	17	35

CAREER STATISTICS

AVG	G	AB	R	H	2B	3B	HR	RBI	BB	SO	SB
.238	1006	3688	446	877	138	31	7	266	384	219	241

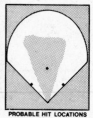

VS. RHP   VS. LHP   PROBABLE HIT LOCATIONS

OVERALL:

Smith may be the most valuable player on the Cardinals. Manager Whitey Herzog estimates that his shortstop saves 100 runs a year defensively.

Snider: "At shortstop, Ozzie is not just good, he is a performance. There are times when you are watching the Cardinals in the field, and, well, you just secretly hope that a hitter will send something Smith has to do a loop-de-loop for. Fantastic to watch, he is approaching the status of a legend in his own time."

PITCHING:

After the worst year of his major league career, Bruce Sutter rebounded to have his best in 1984. He had a National League record 45 saves (in 53 opportunities) and had a microscopic 1.54 ERA.

With Sutter as their stopper, the Cardinals lost only two games when they entered the ninth inning with a lead.

Sutter recaptured the consistency of his dreaded split-fingered fastball, retired the first hitter he faced 55 times in 71 games and allowed only nine of 45 runners on base when he entered the game to score.

The theory around the National League is to move up on Sutter in the batter's box. Some hitters, especially those on the Montreal Expos, try to move up four or five inches or even more. Hitters hope that by doing this, they can get to the split-fingered pitch before the bottom drops out of it. But, given the statistics, it seems that very few hitters have figured out the best approach to him.

In 1983, Sutter had difficulty putting together four or five good games in succession, but he was a different pitcher after Mike Roarke became the Cardinals' pitching coach. Roarke had been Sutter's coach in Chicago with the Cubs and had counseled him every year since. Roarke helps Sutter when he begins to have trouble with rhythm or location.

The hitters' dilemma is whether or not to swing at what seems to be a very hittable pitch at the knees. Often, it will not be a strike, as the split-fingered pitch starts its descent.

Sutter also has great ability to deliver a pitch and still have good quality stuff when he gets it up in the strike zone. When it's 2-0, he can come up and the pitch is still in a pretty good spot. Last year, however, his location was poor.

BRUCE SUTTER
RHP, No. 42
RR, 6'2", 190 lbs.
ML Svc: 9 years
Born: 1-8-53 in
    Lancaster, PA

1984 STATISTICS

W	L	ERA	G	GS	CG	IP	H	R	ER	BB	SO	SV
5	7	1.54	71	0	0	122	109	26	21	23	77	45

CAREER STATISTICS

W	L	ERA	G	GS	CG	IP	H	R	ER	BB	SO	SV
58	60	2.55	549	0	0	887	722	289	251	260	771	260

For lack of something else to compare it to, the split-fingered pitch is like a spitter, because of the drop that it takes, although no hitter ever has accused Sutter of throwing that slippery pitch.

There's no guarantee a Bruce Sutter or Rich Gossage is going to be able to do it every year, but seven out of eight years isn't bad.

FIELDING, HITTING, BASERUNNING:

Sutter went hitless for the second year in succession and does not enjoy being on base. He has other things to worry about in the ninth inning of a game. Now that his knee has healed from surgery of two years ago, he covers his position better and his release to the plate is excellent, giving Cardinals catchers time to throw out basestealers.

OVERALL:

When Sutter talked of off-season changes, manager Whitey Herzog said, "We can't even tie our shoes until we sign Bruce."

Snider: "Bruce Sutter is the franchise."

HITTING:

It is only a matter of time for Andy Van Slyke, despite the fact that nobody has figured out what his position is. He has played five positions, but given the development of first baseman David Green and third baseman Terry Pendleton, Van Slyke's primary position might turn out to be the outfield.

Offensively, Van Slyke has to deal with seeing pitchers more often and reacting to them. He has a tendency to take pitches he can hit and not to swing at those that make him feel uncomfortable. He must come to know himself and his own capabilities better. Having a good eye is fine, but not at the detriment of falling behind 0-2 or 1-2.

Basically, Van Slyke has to be more aggressive. He has to grit his teeth and go up to the plate watching each pitch and make a quick, precise decision. Standing in the batter's box with a major league stick in your hand is no time to be wishy-washy. If he doesn't adopt that attitude, he's giving the pitcher too much credit, and he will always get beat.

BASERUNNING:

Van Slyke stole 28 bases in 33 attempts and could be a 40-50 stolen base man with regular work.

FIELDING:

His further development will show Van Slyke to be one of the best outfielders in basball. He has a a strong, accurate arm and usually throws to the right base, although his mind has a tendency to wander when he's in the field.

Members of the Cardinals management,

ANDY VAN SLYKE
OF, No. 18
LR, 6'1", 190 lbs.
ML Svc: 2 years
Born: 12-21-60 in
Utica, NY

1984 STATISTICS

AVG	G	AB	R	H	2B	3B	HR	RBI	BB	SO	SB
.244	137	361	45	88	16	4	7	50	63	71	28

CAREER STATISTICS

AVG	G	AB	R	H	2B	3B	HR	RBI	BB	SO	SB
.252	238	670	96	169	31	9	15	88	109	135	49

  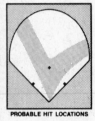

VS. RHP   VS. LHP   PROBABLE HIT LOCATIONS

coaches and scouts believe that his best defensive posture is in the outfield. Although teammates Willie McGee has a Gold Glove as a center fielder and George Hendrick should have had one in right, Van Slyke is considered the equal of both.

OVERALL:

Snider: "I'd like to see the hair on the back of his neck stick up when he is at the plate. I would like to see him really get mean. Andy has to start to take his chances against the pitchers; he has to believe that he really can hit the daylights out of a pitch, and if it doesn't do it that time, that he can do it the next."

STEVE BRAUN
INF/OF, No. 26
LR, 5'10", 180 lbs.
ML Svc: 14 years
Born: 5-8-48 in
Trenton, NJ

HITTING, FIELDING, BASERUNNING:

At age 36, Steve Braun became only the ninth man in baseball history to accumulate 100 pinch-hits. He finished the season with 102 pinch-swings and batted .283 (17-for-60) in his emergency role.

Generally, anyone who hits .200 to .250 as a pinch-hitter is considered good. Pinch-hitting is the toughest role in the game because of the concentration required during the game and the fact that there is only one chance for a player to hit.

Braun, who has served for four years as a pinch-hitter for the Cardinals, comes to the park early almost every day for extra batting practice. He also engages a hypnotist to keep his thoughts along positive lines.

Braun is tough to strike out because he doesn't have a long, looping swing. He also draws an inordinate share of walks. His on-base percentage is generally around .400.

Braun studies the game and knows what pitchers will throw in certain situations.

He is a straightaway hitter, although he will pull the ball when the occasion demands it. He is not a fast runner, and is often replaced for a pinch-runner when he gets on. Manager Whitey Herzog will occasionally play Braun in left field to keep him sharp, but he is not a good outfielder.

OVERALL:

Braun was disappointed in his hitting until late last season. He had two stretches of nearly a month during which he did not have a hit, but he is one of the best in the National League at what he does.

GLENN BRUMMER
C, No. 11
RR, 6'0", 200 lbs.
ML Svc: 3 years
Born: 11-23-54 in
Olney, IL

HITTING, BASERUNNING, FIELDING:

Glenn Brummer is a good third-string catcher, but the Cardinals may soon choose to keep only two of them, Darrell Porter and the youngster, Tom Nieto.

Brummer hit his first major league home run, off Chicago's Scott Sanderson, last year, but batted only .207 in 58 at-bats.

He missed part of the season with a bad ankle and was sent to Louisville for three weeks.

Brummer is a scrapper. He does everything he can to beat you and he knows his role.

Pitcher Dave LaPoint particularly enjoys having Brummer catch him--LaPoint's record is better with Brummer catching than with anyone else. Brummer also had good rapport with Joaquin Andujar, the Cardinals' 20-game winner.

Brummer is aggressive at taking out second basemen and shortstops on double plays and he occasionally is used as a pinch-runner, something highly irregular for a catcher. His steal of home in 1982 was one of the highlights of that championship season.

OVERALL:

Brummer is an ideal backup catcher who can play somewhere in the major leagues, even if it is not in St. Louis.

ART HOWE
INF, No. 18
RR, 6'1", 185 lbs.
ML Svc: 9 years
Born: 12-15-46 in
Pittsburgh, PA

HITTING, FIELDING, BASERUNNING:

After sitting out a year because of injuries, Art Howe batted just .216 as a part-time player. He was used at first, second and third and he took a couple of errorless turns at shortstop, a position that he had never played before in the major leagues.

There is a question how much the 38-year-old Howe has left in him, but whatever it is, the Cardinals will get it.

Last year was really the first year Howe had been a full-time pinch-hitter. He did very poorly in that role until the end of the season when he had four hits in four at-bats.

Pinch-hitting is probably the toughest job in baseball, and Howe should be better this year.

Howe is the type of player a team ·wants if it thinks it can win. He provides experience and considerable intelligence, as well as a winning attitude.

He is not fast on the bases, although he showed better range than expected at third base when he played there on a platoon basis.

OVERALL:

Howe will be the Cardinals' top back-up in the infield and their No. 2 right-handed pinch-hitter behind Tito Landrum.

MIKE JORGENSON
OF, No. 11
LL, 6'0", 192 lbs.
ML Svc: 15 years
Born: 8-16-48 in
Passaic, NJ

HITTING, BASERUNNING, FIELDING:

Mike Jorgensen falls into the category of "good guy to have around." He can play first base, take an occasional turn in the outfield and pinch-hit.

Although he is not a true pull hitter, he can hit behind the runner if he has to, or pull a grounder to the right side if he has to. He prefers to see the ball out over the plate.

Jorgensen was hitting in the .270s until a 1-for-18 slump left him with a .250 average for the season. He had three game-winning RBIs for the Cards and gave David Green a break at first base against especially tough righthanded pitchers.

Tight situations don't bother this 36-year-old and he is very reliable defensively. He is one of the top three or four first baseman in the league when only defense is considered. Jorgensen is not afraid to take the ball to second base on the 3-6-3 double play.

Jorgensen is not fast and is not a basestealing threat. He is, however, aware of this and doesn't try to exceed his limitations.

OVERALL:

Jorgensen is the perfect role player for a team which thinks it can win a championship. Pinch-hitting will be his role in the future and Jorgensen is gradually adapting himself to that.

Snider: "He has been around a while. Jorgensen is a good pinch-hitter on a team that has a lot of them."

RICK OWNBEY
RHP, No. 40
RR, 6'3", 185 lbs.
ML Svc: 3 years
Born: 10-20-57 in
    Corona, CA

PITCHING, FIELDING,
    HITTING, BASERUNNING:

A hamstring injury suffered by Rick Ownbey while he was working out before spring training set his progress back. Then, while trying to make the club, Ownbey re-injured the leg and wound up in Louisville, where he hurt it again. Finally, he came around physically and was called up the Cardinals in early July. Two starts later--two ineffective starts--he was sent back to Louisville. He emerged again in September and pitched seven innings of shutout ball against the Chicago Cubs in the last game of the season.

Ownbey's poor showings in July and another in September clouded the team's judgment of him for the spring. Once ranked as one of St. Louis' starting pitchers, this year he is fighting to make the club.

Ownbey is blessed with a 90 MPH fastball, but did more picking than pitching last year.

OVERALL:

Ownbey was being counted on to defray the cost of losing Keith Hernandez in that controversial June 1983 deal; he may be having his last chance with the Cardinals.

Snider: "Maybe he should be a thrower instead of trying to be pitcher. There are a few guys who are successful at being throwers because their ball does enough. If some guy starts to try to thread the needle all the time, then he's in deep trouble."

DAVE RUCKER
LHP, No. 36
LL, 6'1", 190 lbs.
ML Svc: 3 years
Born: 9-1-57 in
    San Bernardino, CA

PITCHING, FIELDING,
    HITTING, BASERUNNING:

Dave Rucker allowed 10 of 29 runners on base to score after coming into games in 1984. However, he did have an impressive statistic last year: he held the opposition at bay 31 times. In addition, he got credit for two wins.

Most of his good work was done when the Cardinals were behind in the game. When he was used in "game" situations, Rucker wasn't quite as effective. When he was not under pressure, he tensed.

Bruce Sutter gave Rucker considerable credit for helping him to attain his 45 saves.

Rucker, who has a 90 MPH fastball, also favors a hard slider as one of his out pitches. He struck out only four more batters than he walked, however (38-34)--but his ERA of 2.10 was the second best on the staff.

Rucker is an excellent athlete and takes an impressive swing although he has had a hard time getting hits. His move to first is more than adequate.

He does not get on base very often; when he does, he is adequate and takes no extra chances.

OVERALL:

Whitey Herzog is looking for more consistency in late-inning situations from Rucker, who, at 27 years old, is still capable of improvement.

Snider: "When a pitcher starts to squeeze the ball, he's going to make mistakes. That's especially true when you've been hurt the last time out. That probably happened a few times to him last year, but added experience will help him to overcome that error."

DAVE VON OHLEN
LHP, No. 38
LL, 6'2", 200 lbs.
ML Svc: 2 years
Born: 10-25-58 in
Flushing, NY

PITCHING, FIELDING,
HITTING, BASERUNNING:

Dave Von Ohlen has a good arm and his big breaking curveball can be effective against lefthanded hitters. Righthanded hitters give him trouble.

Von Ohlen was used mostly in middle and situational relief for the Cards. He had just three save opportunities in 1984 and he saved only one. Von Ohlen's most important contribution was his 14 "holds," meaning that the opposition did not extend its run count on those occasions.

Von Ohlen is the Cardinals' second or third lefthander in the bullpen and thus is about the 10th man on the staff. He started the season in Louisville for the second year in a row, but was recalled in June when Bob Forsch had back trouble.

He is an average fielder, but Von Ohlen last year was a 1.000 hitter (one for one).

OVERALL:

Given Whitey Herzog's general dissatisfaction with his lefthanded relief, Von Ohlen will have a difficult time reclaiming a job.

SAN DIEGO PADRES

HITTING:

Kurt Bevacqua has been around the big leagues a long time but will best be remembered for his 1984 post-season performance. As a hitter, Bevacqua has always thrived on clutch situations, so it should be no surprise that he produced as well as he did.

He has two values to the Padres: as a pinch-hitter and as a marvelous influence on the rest of the team. An upright hitter, he stands in the middle of the box, off the plate, and hits the ball where it is pitched. He really is not a home run hitter, but he has good power to the alleys and will hit some doubles. Pitchers should not throw him high fastballs; rather, they should keep the ball down on him and try to get him to chase breaking balls.

For years, Bevacqua has demonstrated that he is a better hitter off the bench than he is as a starter. But for a few days at a time, as he proved last October, he can produce regularly.

BASERUNNING:

Bevacqua was never a scintillating baserunner, and at age 38 he has lost much of whatever speed he once had. But he is a student of the game and knows HOW to run the bases.

FIELDING:

Although used primarily as a pinch-hitter, he can fill in at first base or third base or in the outfield. His arm is fine for first base, but it is below average for a third baseman or outfielder. His throws are generally accurate, but weak. He won't kill a team in the field, but he helps with a bat, not a glove.

KURT BEVACQUA
INF, No. 7
RR, 6'2", 195 lbs.
ML Svc: 13 years
Born: 1-23-47 in
    Miami Beach, FL

1984 STATISTICS

AVG	G	AB	R	H	2B	3B	HR	RBI	BB	SO	SB
.200	59	80	7	16	3	0	1	9	19	0	0

CAREER STATISTICS

AVG	G	AB	R	H	2B	3B	HR	RBI	BB	SO	SB
.235	899	1980	197	466	84	11	24	250	201	293	12

VS. RHP

VS. LHP

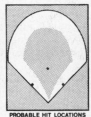

PROBABLE HIT LOCATIONS

OVERALL:

In five seasons with the Padres, Bevacqua has a pinch-hitting average above .300; and although he most often is used against lefthanded pitchers, he really seems to hit righthanders just as well. A contending team must be able to call on its bench for base hits, and Bevacqua provides that element for the Padres.

Snider: "Every team needs a guy like him. He keeps you loose, and when the umpire says, 'Play ball,' he's ready. He's not exceptionally strong at any defensive position, but he certainly can hit. He's getting to the age at which he's not going to be playing the game an awful lot longer, so it's good to see him have the kind of post-season he had."

BOBBY BROWN
OF, No. 20
SR, 6'1", 207
ML Svc: 6 years
Born: 5-24-54 in
Norfolk, VA

HITTING:

Earlier in Bobby Brown's vagabond career, there were people who felt he might one day establish himself as a big league regular capable of many great things. They saw him as the type of player who might hit for average, for some power and for good run production while also stealing a lot of bases and playing good defense.

Brown never quite developed into that type of multi-dimensional, front-line player. But in the last two seasons with San Diego, he has shown unequivocally that he can use his myriad skills to help a team as a role player. And he does this primarily as an offensive player.

He is a switch-hitter who has some power. He always has been a better hitter from the left side of the plate than the right, in terms of both average and power, but hard work has allowed him to make great strides from the right side. He is a streak hitter who can really help a team if he gets in the lineup for a week or two while he is hot. As with most streak hitters, Brown also goes through stretches during which almost anything gets him out; when he's hot, the best way to pitch to him is with breaking balls. Because of his impatience, he will chase bad pitches.

From both sides of the plate, Brown crouches in the middle of the batter's box, with his feet spread. He always has struck out more often than someone with his speed should allow, and he has problems with breaking pitches. He is not a patient hitter, and that always worked against him when teams were trying to make him a leadoff hitter.

Brown is a good bunter who could use that skill for more base hits if he were so inclined.

BASERUNNING:

Brown is a very good baserunner, largely because of his far above average natural speed. He is among the league's elite in going from home to first, especially when batting lefthanded, and he gets a good jump off first on basesteal-

1984 STATISTICS											
AVG	G	AB	R	H	2B	3B	HR	RBI	BB	SO	SB
.251	85	171	28	43	7	2	3	29	33	16	4
CAREER STATISTICS											
AVG	G	AB	R	H	2B	3B	HR	RBI	BB	SO	SB
.251	423	1193	175	300	35	12	26	124	111	201	67

VS. RHP — STRONG

VS. LHP — STRONG

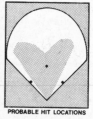

PROBABLE HIT LOCATIONS

ing attempts. But sometimes he gets too good a jump off first, breaking before the pitcher has started his motion to the plate. On those occasions, he's dead.

FIELDING:

Brown's biggest asset as a defensive player is his speed. But he also judges the ball well and can do a good job in left field or center. He is more experienced and seems more comfortable and content in center. His arm is marginal at best, a liability at worst.

OVERALL:

This much-traveled player seems to have found his spot with the Padres. As a fourth outfielder, a switch-hitting pinch-hitter and a pinch-runner, he clearly has value.

Snider: "Bobby is another of those role players. He'll hit a few key home runs and make a few key plays in the outfield, but he is not an everyday type of player. You have 25 players on a ball club, and he is an integral part of San Diego's 25."

PITCHING:

Back in 1982, Luis DeLeon was one of the more effective relief pitchers in the league. But he was slightly less effective in 1983, leading the Padres on their wild Goose chase for Rich Gossage, and he was an injured non-entity for much of 1984.

But it will be interesting to watch where his pitching career goes from here. The skinny righthander with the three-quarters delivery has the stuff to be a stopper in the bullpen: an 88 MPH fastball, an exceptional slider that is murderous to righthanded batters, a hard sinker that induces ground balls and outstanding control. He also has the arm resiliency to pitch frequently, and he has the confidence needed in a short relief pitcher.

He is, it should be noted, substantially more effective against righthanded hitters than lefthanded hitters, who sometimes can hit hanging sliders a long way. This is the one flaw that might keep DeLeon from becoming a prime finisher, the type of pitcher who will be on the mound no matter who is batting for the opposition in the closing moments of a tight game.

The other raps against him are that he sometimes becomes flustered and sometimes seems to suffer concentration lapses.

FIELDING, HITTING, BASERUNNING:

He is a natural athlete, strong and agile, and that shows when he is running the bases or fielding his position. He has a good move to first base, but he would be better served by hastening his delivery to the plate.

LUIS DeLEON
RHP, No. 35
RR, 6'1", 153 lbs.
ML Svc: 3 years
Born: 8-19-58 in
     Ponce, PR

CAREER STATISTICS

W	L	ERA	G	GS	CG	IP	H	R	ER	BB	SO	SV
15	12	2.37	134	0	0	228	177	63	60	46	158	28

As a hitter, DeLeon's athletic skills do not manifest themselves. He seems to enjoy himself at the plate, but he usually ends up by striking out. He is also a poor bunter.

OVERALL:

His pitching tools notwithstanding, DeLeon fell out of favor in San Diego last season, and there is every reason to believe the Padres will attempt to find him a new home to 1985. He could be a worthwhile addition to some team.

Snider: "He was not used much last season, and may not have much opportunity if he remains with the Padres. Occasionally, when he is pitching, his mind seems to wander--and a relief pitcher cannot afford even a momentary lapse in concentration. Luis might do better in new surroundings, where he can start fresh and fix his mind on the game. He has the potential to become a member of baseball's elite stoppers."

PITCHING:

Unless a lot of people--i.e., almost everyone--are wrong about Dave Dravecky, he has a golden future on the mound. The question now is only how his future will unfold--as a relief pitcher or as a starter. Dravecky has shown the arm and the skill to be extremely successful in either role. He has enough pitches, enough stamina and enough intelligence to be a starter, and he has enough arm resiliency to be a reliever.

On top of everything else, he has the great advantage of being a lefthander. Everybody is looking for a lefthanded pitcher with this kind of ability.

He has gained notable velocity on his fastball in the last two years and now throws it in the 86-88 MPH range. He also has outstanding control and breaking pitches. His fastball, which sinks, and his slider make an effective combination against righthanded hitters. And his hard stuff, off-speed stuff and intelligence make him virtually impossible for a lot of lefties to hit. Like all of the cherished lefthanders in the game, he has a lot movement on his pitches.

Dravecky could still improve his change-up and be a bit less predictable when behind in the count. But he usually is ahead in the count, often putting batters in fast 0-2 holes. For a still-young pitcher, he has good poise on the mound.

FIELDING, HITTING, BASERUNNING:

Dravecky is a natural athlete, but he is more than that; he is also a good student of the game. He has a decent move to first base and is substantially above average at fielding his position. He is a good and improving bunter, and

DAVE DRAVECKY
LHP, No. 43
RL, 6'1", 195 lbs.
ML Svc: 3 years
Born: 2-14-56 in
    Youngstown, OH

1984 STATISTICS

W	L	ERA	G	GS	CG	IP	H	R	ER	BB	SO	SV
9	8	2.93	50	14	3	156	123	53	51	51	71	8

CAREER STATISTICS

W	L	ERA	G	GS	CG	IP	H	R	ER	BB	SO	SV
28	21	3.12	109	52	12	444	390	168	154	128	204	10

he likes to take his swings at the plate. He is not exactly dangerous there, however--no Tim Lollar, for example.

OVERALL:

There isn't a team in either league which wouldn't like to have Dravecky on its pitching staff. Some teams would like to have him as a much-needed lefthanded starter, some as a lefthanded short reliever. And some would use him as the Padres have used him, a combination of middle-to-short reliever and spot starter. Given the scarcity of top-quality southpaw starters in the game, don't be surprised if he eventually steps forward as a starting pitcher.

Snider: "I really like him and would like to have him on my team. He has a good attitude, good stuff, keeps the ball down. I like the way he goes about his business. He has a durable arm, and if I needed a lefthanded starter, I wouldn't hesitate to use him. He has the team in mind first, and that's good."

HITTING:

He was able to command more playing time when the Padres were a lesser team, but, ironically, Tim Flannery now may be a better player--especially a better hitter--than when he played regularly. He now makes better, more consistent contact, appears to have refined his eye for pitches and knows how to pull the inside pitch.

He is a very good high fastball hitter, but continues to have problems with the harder throwers because of his relatively slow bat speed. It used to be that Flannery hit all fastballs to left field, thereby allowing left fielders to play him exceedingly shallow and take away most of his would-be hits, but he now has learned to pull the less than overpowering fastballs.

From the bench, he has become a student of hitting. And while he'll never be a great hitter, maybe not even an above average hitter, he has a good concept of outs. Because he makes contact, he rarely strands a runner at third base with less than two out.

He is a better hitter against right-handers than lefthanders and, because of his slow bat speed, hits breaking balls much better than he hits fastballs. The best way to pitch him is with power; righthanders can jam him with fastballs.

BASERUNNING:

Flannery is not blessed with exceptional natural speed, but he is aggressive and attentive on the bases. He is serious about breaking up double plays. He is an intelligent baserunner, and this intelligence entails recognizing the limits of his speed.

FIELDING:

He has played both second base and third base, without positive or negative distinction. His arm is not as strong as a team would like in a third baseman, and he doesn't turn the double play as

TIM FLANNERY
INF, NO. 11
LR, 5'11, 170 lbs.
ML Svc: 5 years
Born: 9-29-57 in
Tulsa, OK

1984 STATISTICS

AVG	G	AB	R	H	2B	3B	HR	RBI	BB	SO	SB
.273	86	128	24	35	3	3	2	10	17	4	1

CAREER STATISTICS

AVG	G	AB	R	H	2B	3B	HR	RBI	BB	SO	SB
.246	454	1145	109	282	37	15	5	94	91	98	7

  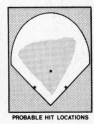

VS. RHP   VS. LHP   PROBABLE HIT LOCATIONS

well as a team would like in a second baseman. But he does have an accurate arm, plays hard in the field and doesn't mind having a ball hit to him in the clutch.

OVERALL:

He has improved himself as a player, perhaps as much as his limited natural abilities would permit. Earlier in his career, he was able to play regularly because the Padres were a bad team. Now, he is playing a more realistic role, and he has improved enough to do a good job at it.

Snider: "It is a somewhat odd situation, a bit like the case of which came first, the chicken or the egg. Tim has improved so much, that I find myself thinking that he should be playing more. Should he play more often because he is good, or is he good because he doesn't play often? I'm not sure, but there is a whole school of thought which doesn't argue with success."

HITTING:

Any discussion of Steve Garvey, the hitter, is almost superfluous at this point. His style of hitting and his accomplishments as a hitter are well known and well documented. And oh, how consistent.

Garvey crouches in the back of the batter's box, fairly close to the plate in a slightly closed stance. As he hits, he exudes confidence, waiting eagerly for a pitch he feels he can drive.

He is an aggressive hitter with a history of power and production, although his home runs have fallen off in recent years. The drop in home runs represents the only change in Garvey in the past few seasons; his average and run production have remained tantalizingly consistent.

He can hit any pitcher, especially in a clutch situation, but he is particularly productive against lefthanders. And because he can both pull the ball and go the opposite way, he can hit any pitch. One less recognized aspect of Garvey's offensive game is his bunting ability; he gets on base with surprise bunts more often than you might realize.

Garvey does occasionally go into a slump, usually because he is playing with some nagging injury or because of a rare mental lapse. During these slumps, Garvey will fall into the habit of chasing bad pitches, especially low, two-strike breaking balls off the outside of the plate.

BASERUNNING:

At his peak, Garvey had slightly above average speed, but he has lost a step or two. He seldom attempts to steal a base. However, he is an experienced, knowledgeable baserunner who will occasionally take the extra base by recognizing and exploiting a fielder's weak arm. He is aggressive when there's an opportunity to disrupt a double play.

FIELDING:

There are two aged criticisms of Garvey as a first baseman: his height

STEVE GARVEY
1B, No. 6
RR, 5'10", 190 lbs.
ML Svc: 14 years
Born: 12-22-48 in
 Tampa, FL

1984 STATISTICS

AVG	G	AB	R	H	2B	3B	HR	RBI	BB	SO	SB
.284	161	617	72	175	27	2	8	86	64	1	2

CAREER STATISTICS

AVG	G	AB	R	H	2B	3B	HR	RBI	BB	SO	SB
.299	1988	7548	1000	2257	382	37	233	1137	460	791	83

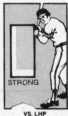

(5'10") prevents him from bringing down a few of the wildly high throws that other first basemen might retrieve, and his woefully weak throwing arm hurts him on those occasions when he has to throw to second for the start of a double play or make a play at the plate or third base. It is undeniable that Garvey's arm is a liability, although much less so at first base than at third base, his original position. However, his inability to come down with a few high throws is more than offset by his adeptness at digging low throws out of the dirt.

OVERALL:

He is 36 years old, but just as dedicated and motivated as ever. Garvey is a model citizen, a model baseball player, one of a kind.

Snider: "Garvey just walks up there like a mechanical man. He always has the same expression. You can see the determination and the intensity on his face. There is no uncertainty in his eyes, and that is what has made him a great player."

PITCHING:

Everybody likes to ponder the question of whether Goose Gossage has lost a little bit of velocity off his fastball. And the answer, most likely, is yes, he has. But so what?

He is still overpowering and he still can put 96-98 MPH behind a pitch when he needs it. And he remains among the most feared relief pitchers in the game.

If he has lost anything, it is in the frequency with which he can throw his maximum fastball. While he still will pop a few like old times, others seem to have dropped a little velocity. Again, so what?

He is making better use of his curveball against righthanded batters, and he has the enormous advantage of knowing that batters can never wait on the breaking pitch from him. Despite the curve, it would be a foolish mistake to categorize Gossage as anything other than a power pitcher.

He does not throw to spots with his fastball and presumably never will; he simply rears back and throws. His attitude: "Here it comes, hit it if you can." And obviously, more failed than succeeded last season. He is at the age at which batters increasingly feel they may be able to sit on his fastball, but he scoffs at that.

He throws three-quarters, loves and thrives on pressure and is equally effective against lefties and righties.

FIELDING, HITTING, BASERUNNING:

All those years in the American League eroded whatever offensive skills Gossage might have possessed, but as a short reliever he never gets much chance to flaunt them, anyway. As a fielder, he is below average.

This primarily is because he is off balance after releasing the ball to the plate. Occasionally, batters will try to exploit this by bunting for base hits against him. His pickoff move, like his fielding in general, is below average.

RICH GOSSAGE
RHP, No. 54
RR, 6'3", 217 lbs.
ML Svc: 13 years
Born: 7-5-51 in
  Colorado Springs, CO

1984 STATISTICS
W	L	ERA	G	GS	CG	IP	H	R	ER	BB	SO	SV
10	6	2.90	62	0	0	102	75	34	33	36	84	25

CAREER STATISTICS
W	L	ERA	G	GS	CG	IP	H	R	ER	BB	SO	SV
89	79	2.86	630	37	16	1338	1063	474	425	555	1160	231

But he tries to compensate for the poor quality of his move by throwing to first base often. Even so, his throws seem somewhat half-hearted, and it is clear his focus is on the batter, not the baserunner. He has a speedy delivery to the plate, making it more difficult for runners to steal against him.

OVERALL:

The addition of Gossage, more than anything else, put the Padres over the top last year. He gave them the quality short reliever that, in this era, every championship team must have. A lot of opposing managers feel that if their team had signed Gossage last year, they could have made a 10-15 game improvement in the standings. In addition to the velocity he carries to the mound, he also exudes confidence, and that was a valuable contribution to a young team striving for a pennant.

Snider: "He has the ability on any given day to blow everybody away. He is a thrower, not a pitcher, but not everyone can go out there and be successful like Gossage. In recent seasons, he has lost a little bit off his fastball."

HITTING:

Last year, in THE SCOUTING REPORT: 1984, the report on Tony Gwynn read, "Some scouts believe that Tony Gwynn has the talent to lead the NL in hitting once he has had a few seasons under his belt." Well, it didn't take a few seasons; it happened in 1984.

He had a marvelously consistent season and was never challenged for the batting title after Montreal's Terry Francona was injured. This is how he did it . . .

He is a straightaway hitter who crouches slightly and stands in the middle of the batter's box with a moderately closed stance. He hits fastballs, up or down, in or out, as well as anyone in the game. He also hits hanging breaking balls as well as anyone in the game. And last year, he began to hold his own against low breaking stuff, which had given him trouble in the past. He is an extremely disciplined hitter--he will not chase bad pitches--and he has a studious knowledge of the strike zone. He forces the pitcher to throw him a good pitch, and then he hits it.

The big improvement in Gwynn last year was in the way he hit lefthanders. Also, he toughened up noticeably with two strikes on him by pecking away until he could find a hole somewhere. He is principally a line drive hitter, but there is reason to believe he will become more and more of a home run threat. In short, there is every reason to believe Tony Gwynn's first NL batting championship will not be his last.

BASERUNNING:

He has good speed from home to first, and this speed put a few extra points on his league-leading average. He has enough speed so that the opposing pitcher and catcher cannot rule out the possibility of a stolen base. It wouldn't hurt for him to become a bit more aggressive on the bases, however.

FIELDING:

He showed improvement as a right

TONY GWYNN
OF, No. 19
LL, 5'11", 185 lbs.
ML Svc: 3 years
Born: 5-9-60 in
    Los Angeles, CA

1984 STATISTICS

AVG	G	AB	R	H	2B	3B	HR	RBI	BB	SO	SB
.351	158	606	88	213	21	10	5	71	23	33	18

CAREER STATISTICS

AVG	G	AB	R	H	2B	3B	HR	RBI	BB	SO	SB
.329	298	1100	155	362	45	14	7	125	60	70	33

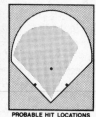

VS. RHP — STRONG   VS. LHP — STRONG   PROBABLE HIT LOCATIONS

fielder last season. His throwing arm remains weaker than is ideal for a right fielder, and it probably always will be. It is an accurate arm, however, and Gwynn was much better last year at hitting the cutoff man. He has good range in the field, judges the ball well and plays the wall well.

OVERALL:

For such limited big league experience before last season (he had played in just 140 games) Gwynn's accomplishments are remarkable. He is still only 24 years old, so look for him to be a National League All Star for a long, long time to come.

Snider: "He got there, didn't he? He is one of the best hitters in baseball right now. He really came into his own in 1984. We had heard for a couple of years that Tony Gwynn could be an outstanding hitter, and last season we found out. He's got a chance to lead the league for years with the way he swings the bat."

PITCHING:

Not so long ago, Greg Harris was a highly regarded prospect, the type of pitcher who is seen as a potential staff ace. In 1984, however, he was a role pitcher for the Padres--more useful than invaluable. His greatest contribution was as a middle reliever.

Harris is not and never has been overpowering, but he has an extraordinary curveball. He spots his fastball well, but his out pitch is the breaking ball. His problem, as with most other pitchers through the years who have tried to exist mostly on the curveball, is that the pitch inevitably lends itself to costly mistakes. Throw as many curveballs as Greg Harris throws, and inevitably some will hang. And inevitably, some will land out of the park.

Harris probably needs to come up with a new wrinkle or two in his repertoire; otherwise, with hitters increasingly familiar with him, he may go downhill. But he has a good arm and appears to be the type of pitcher who can come in when the starting pitcher has been ineffective, stabilize the game and give his team a chance to catch up.

FIELDING, HITTING, BASERUNNING:

He is acceptable in all these areas. He can swing the bat a little bit, which is to say he swings it a little better than the average pitcher. He runs like a pitcher, and he fields his position well. And not that it's terribly significant, but he likes to shag fly balls with his throwing hand.

GREG HARRIS
RHP, No. 42
SR, 6'0", 168
ML Svc: 1 year
Born: 11-2-55 in
    Lynwood, CA

1984 STATISTICS

W	L	ERA	G	GS	CG	IP	H	R	ER	BB	SO	SV
2	2	2.48	34	1	0	54	38	18	15	25	45	3

CAREER STATISTICS

W	L	ERA	G	GS	CG	IP	H	R	ER	BB	SO	SV
7	13	4.23	85	25	1	215	201	113	101	93	167	5

OVERALL:

He has just enough stuff, just enough natural ability, that there'll be a team willing to give him a shot until he flops conclusively. Right now, he has that shot with the Padres.

Snider: "I do not see Harris becoming a major league caliber pitcher until he learns to control his curveball. A good curveball is a cherished possesion to a pitcher, but few of them come naturally. He must stop hanging so many of them; these big league hitters know a hanging curveball when they see one--and they know how to hit it into the seats."

PITCHING:

There are people who think that, one season soon, Andy Hawkins simply will explode into one of the greatest pitchers in the game. In the opinion of some scouts and opposing players, he has the best stuff among San Diego's starting pitchers. He is a big, quiet righthander with a smooth three-quarters delivery. His motion is fluid and easy, and his fastball, which sinks, carries 87-89 MPH velocity. He also has an above average (although erratic) slider. Because of his sinking fastball, he gets a lot of ground balls. That, of course, is good, but it does make Hawkins a lesser pitcher on artificial turf than on natural grass.

Hawkins's biggest problem--one that there is reason to think he is overcoming--has been an unnecessary tendency to nibble at the corners rather than to challenge the hitters. He has the stuff to challenge, and needs only the confidence and assertiveness to match. He's working on that, and you can almost see him becoming more aggressive, more determined.

FIELDING, HITTING, BASERUNNING:

At 6'3", 200 pounds, Hawkins lumbers more than he runs; in other words, he won't steal a base or beat out an infield hit. He won't hit much but has worked hard to become a good sacrifice bunter. His fluid pitching motion leaves him in good fielding position, and he's alert on the mound. He is, however, sometimes tentative about playing difficult chances. Like most young right-

ANDY HAWKINS
RHP, No. 40
RR, 6'3", 200 lbs.
ML Svc: 2 years
Born: 1-21-60 in
Waco, TX

1984 STATISTICS

W	L	ERA	G	GS	CG	IP	H	R	ER	BB	SO	SV
8	9	4.68	36	22	2	146	143	90	76	72	77	0

CAREER STATISTICS

W	L	ERA	G	GS	CG	IP	H	R	ER	BB	SO	SV
15	21	3.94	72	51	7	329	315	173	144	147	161	0

handers, he could use some work on his pickoff move.

OVERALL:

He is reaching a decisive stage in his career--that transition stage between bright, young prospect and established, proven pitcher. There is reason to believe he'll make it to the third stage, which is from proven pitcher to exceptional pitcher. He needs to continue concentrating on aggressiveness, on challenging the hitters, on resisting that inherent urge to nibble at the corners. When he nibbles, he sacrifices some of his natural velocity and movement--plus he walks too many hitters.

Snider: "Most of the Expos players feel he has the best stuff on the San Diego staff, at least among their starters. It is just a question of control and not making quite so many mistakes."

HITTING:

Kennedy entered last season as one of the National League's most productive, most feared hitters. But he was a colossal underachiever in 1984.

There's really no way to isolate why that happened. He looked the same at the plate, but the results were drastically different from those in 1983, when he hit 17 home runs and drove in 98.

A lefthanded batter, Kennedy crouches in a slightly closed stance. In good seasons, he pulls fastballs while also waiting well enough to jerk off-speed pitches, and he jumps all over pitches which are out over the plate and up in the strike zone. But last season, he had all kinds of problems with all kinds of pitches, especially fastballs that crowded him. After hitting the ball authoritatively in 1983, he hit it softly in 1984.

He tried to maintain his aggressiveness at the plate, but nothing seemed to work. And his run production, so prolific the year before, fell off dramatically.

BASERUNNING:

Kennedy is a big man (6'4", 220 lbs.) and is not going to beat out many infield hits or steal many bases. He has had knee surgery in the past, which has further reduced his speed.

FIELDING:

He does not have a good reputation for throwing out opposing baserunners, making it all the more vital that he make substantial offensive contributions. He has slow footwork for a catcher and slow release time on throws. He can get a lot on the ball, but it often is too late by the time he releases it.

TERRY KENNEDY
C, No. 16
LR, 6'4", 220 lbs.
ML Svc: 6 years
Born: 6-4-56 in
Euclid, OH

1984 STATISTICS

AVG	G	AB	R	H	2B	3B	HR	RBI	BB	SO	SB
.240	148	530	54	127	16	1	14	57	99	1	2

CAREER STATISTICS

AVG	G	AB	R	H	2B	3B	HR	RBI	BB	SO	SB
.275	678	2409	247	663	128	8	60	346	236	291	4

  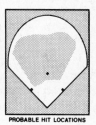

VS. RHP   VS. LHP   PROBABLE HIT LOCATIONS

It doesn't help him, either, that the Padres' pitching staff collectively is below average at holding runners on base.

OVERALL:

There is no reason, at this point, to believe Kennedy cannot return to his offensive form of 1983; and until he proves otherwise, 1984 probably should be viewed as one of those inexplicable slumps that lasted a full season. It might help Kennedy's hitting if he could move to first base, but Steve Garvey's presence precludes that for at least a few years.

Snider: "He had an off year--and I don't know why--but there's no reason he can't bounce back. He's a leader, a good, tough player."

PITCHING:

Here you have a classic case of a pitcher adding just one pitch and transforming himself from the fringes to the forefront of major league pitchers. For Lefferts, that pitch was the screwball.

Craig Lefferts was an afterthought in the three-way deal in 1983 involving the Padres, Cubs and Expos, but his emergence as a fine big league pitcher probably tilted the scales of the trade in favor of San Diego. The screwball changed him from a journeyman to a most significant pitcher.

When he was with the Cubs, he had been a fastball/breaking ball pitcher who seemed destined to be no more than a so-so middle reliever. But then he came up with a screwball and for a beginner, Lefferts threw it with outstanding control.

Though he was just an afterthought only one year ago, Lefferts now appears to be a mainstay for the Padres.

FIELDING, HITTING, BASERUNNING:

He fits into the same category as most pitchers: doesn't hurt himself (or significantly help himself) as a fielder, doesn't do anything notable as a hitter, and rarely gets on base.

OVERALL:

Last season, he looked as if he were

CRAIG LEFFERTS
LHP, No. 37
LL, 6'1", 180 lbs.
ML Svc: 2 years
Born: 9-29-57 in
   Munich, W. Ger.

1984 STATISTICS												
W	L	ERA	G	GS	CG	IP	H	R	ER	BB	SO	SV
3	4	2.13	62	0	0	105	88	29	25	24	56	10

CAREER STATISTICS												
W	L	ERA	G	GS	CG	IP	H	R	ER	BB	SO	SV
6	8	2.97	118	5	0	194	168	64	64	53	116	11

a pitcher who had found the added element necessary to survive in the big leagues. But because such discoveries can be fleeting, 1985 will be an interesting year for him. Still, there is every reason to believe he will again be successful.

Snider: "It is amazing what another pitch can do for a pitcher. I am reminded of Charlie Hough with his knuckleball and of Warren Spahn, who added ten years to his career by coming up with a slider. I'd say that Leffert's going to be around a long time."

PITCHING:

When Tim Lollar won 16 games at the age of 26 in 1982, many people thought he would immediately develop into a 20-game winner. He didn't, however, instead regressing to a seven-game winner during an injury-plagued 1983 season. But he did approximate his 1982 form last season, and the summer of 1985 just might be the one in which Lollar finally fulfills the promise he showed in 1982.

He is an overhand pitcher with a much better than average fastball, which he consistently throws in the low 90s. He also has a good change-up and a very good slider that is particularly effective against righthanded hitters. He mixes the fastball and slider wisely, throwing the fastball about two of every three pitches, and occasionally mixes in a change-up. He has to be careful with his slider, because a hanging slider often lands out of the park.

For Lollar to have particularly good outings, he needs his slider and his control. Even without the slider, he is excruciatingly tough on lefthanded hitters, but the slider makes him equally tough on righthanders.

With experience, he continues to develop more poise and more intelligence on the mound, and he seems to have fewer concentration lapses than in the past.

FIELDING, HITTING, BASERUNNING:

No matter how effectively Lollar pitches, he always will be known, too, for his hitting. He is such a good hitter that Padres manager Dick Williams even considered using him as a designated hitter in the 1984 World Series.

He has outstanding power, and there is probably no better-hitting pitcher in the big leagues. If he comes to the

TIM LOLLAR
LHP, No. 48
LL, 6'3", 195 lbs.
ML Svc: 4 years
Born: 3-17-56 in
　Poplar Bluff, MO

1984 STATISTICS

W	L	ERA	G	GS	CG	IP	H	R	ER	BB	SO	SV
11	13	3.91	31	31	3	195	168	89	85	105	131	0

CAREER STATISTICS

W	L	ERA	G	GS	CG	IP	H	R	ER	BB	SO	SV
37	42	4.04	133	107	8	712	650	339	320	348	467	3

plate with a runner in scoring position, there is a good chance he'll get the runner home. Pitchers often make the mistake of trying to challenge him with fastballs; he is a good fastball hitter, though he will not do as much damage against a breaking ball. Curiously, while Lollar obviously has skill with the bat, he is a below average bunter.

As a baserunner, he also is below average. As a fielder, he is adequate, and being lefthanded helps him hold runners on base.

OVERALL:

You hear this about every lefthanded pitcher of above average ability, but it bears repeating in Lollar's case: the great lefty pitchers normally do not peak until they reach their mid-to-late 20s. Lollar still has time to take his place among them. And he has the stuff.

Snider: "He really hasn't changed any; he is still one of the league's best young lefthanders. And he is a tremendous hitter."

HITTING:

The jury remains out on Carmelo Martinez, a young power hitter. The preliminary reports were that the Cubs may have dealt him away mistakenly, but Martinez's first season with San Diego was uneven and ended with continuing debate about whether he'll be a first-rate big league hitter over the long term.

He has a big, looping swing, the type that is going to result in a lot of strikeouts. But it is the type that also will result in some home runs. For now, anyway, there are holes in his swing, and he is troubled by breaking balls and by a lack of discipline (or knowledge) at the plate.

He had a good first half with the Padres last season, but then tapered off. Pitchers seemed to frustrate him with breaking balls down and away. It may be another year or two before we really know if Carmelo Martinez is going to be an Orlando Cepeda-type hitter or a journeyman player.

BASERUNNING:

He is not a good baserunner, in terms of either speed or instincts. He lumbers more than he runs.

FIELDING:

Remember that Martinez is a natural first baseman who has to play left field in San Diego because Steve Garvey occupies first base. Martinez has a long, long way to go as a left fielder. More than anything else, he appears to simply stick his glove out and hope the glove catches the ball. He doesn't throw

CARMELO MARTINEZ
INF, No. 12
RR, 6'1", 190 lbs.
ML Svc: 2 years
Born: 7-28-60 in
Dorado, PR

1984 STATISTICS

AVG	G	AB	R	H	2B	3B	HR	RBI	BB	SO	SB
.250	149	488	64	122	28	2	13	66	82	1	3

CAREER STATISTICS

AVG	G	AB	R	H	2B	3B	HR	RBI	BB	SO	SB
.251	178	577	72	145	31	2	19	82	86	20	3

STRONG   STRONG

VS. RHP   VS. LHP   PROBABLE HIT LOCATIONS

well, either, and his lack of speed hurts him in the field.

OVERALL:

Martinez is an interesting player to watch, but he needs to sharply refine his offensive and defensive abilities to hold down a starting job.

Snider: "Potentially, he will hit some home runs and will become a more selective hitter. He is still a baby in the art of hitting. I wouldn't say that he plays an outstanding left field . . . he just plays left field."

HITTING:

There never was any educated doubt as to whether Kevin McReynolds would develop into a top-flight major league hitter, not even while he struggled with a .221 batting average in 1983. And last season, the general confidence in him was rewarded with a banner season.

A righthanded hitter with power, he crouches in a sharply closed stance with his left foot near the front corner of the plate. In 1983, he appeared over-anxious and started guessing at the plate. But in 1984, he was a confident, determined hitter, thoroughly in control of the situation.

He can hit any kind of fastball, although he occasionally will be troubled by one thrown inside, and he can hit the breaking ball remarkably well for someone his age. He is extremely aggressive at the plate and, in fact, would probably benefit from more selectivity. He loves to pull the ball, but he is knowledgeable enough to go to right field with outside pitches.

Most scouts look at McReynolds and see an offensive talent capable of hitting near .300 with 30-plus home runs and 100-plus RBIs. Judging from last season, he is well on his way to a long, illustrious career.

BASERUNNING:

McReynolds did not get to the big leagues with his baserunning, and he knows that. However, he has slightly above average speed and slightly above average quickness. With experience, he could accumulate some mildly surprising stolen base numbers. He showed signs last season of becoming more aggressive on the bases.

FIELDING:

McReynolds is not one of those sluggers who simply has to play somewhere-- he is a good center fielder. He has good

KEVIN McREYNOLDS
OF, No. 18
RR, 6'1", 205 lbs.
ML Svc: 2 years
Born: 10-16-59 in
        Little Rock, AK

1984 STATISTICS
AVG	G	AB	R	H	2B	3B	HR	RBI	BB	SO	SB
.278	147	525	68	146	26	6	20	75	69	3	6

CAREER STATISTICS
AVG	G	AB	R	H	2B	3B	HR	RBI	BB	SO	SB
.266	186	665	83	177	29	7	24	89	81	32	8

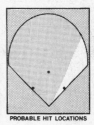

VS. RHP   VS. LHP   PROBABLE HIT LOCATIONS

range, partly because he runs in long strides and partly because he reacts well to the batted ball. His weakest tool is his arm, but that weakness has been exaggerated by some. While opposing baserunners know that he does not have a Roberto Clemente-type arm, they also have learned that he is not an open invitation to run.

OVERALL:

He has successfully made the monumental adjustment from the minor leagues to big leagues, and his career appears to have taken off. The statistical stratosphere is the limit for him.

Snider: "He carried that ballclub at times, and with a year under his belt, I think he should have an even better season. He's quiet, and lets his bat and body do the talking. He'll be heard from for quite a few years; he's just going to get better and better."

HITTING:

There was a time last season when Graig Nettles appeared finished as an offensive player, a futile sight at the plate. But then he went on a mid-season tear and looked like a close approximation of his former self.

Nettles is a lefthanded hitter with power, and it seems safe to say that he will still make a pitcher pay for a mistake. Beyond that, it will be interesting to see what kind of offensive damage he can do in 1985.

He is a pull hitter who likes the ball down, and still has that characteristic Yankee Stadium swing. He may not hit for a high average, but the Padres hope he can hit for production (some doubles, a few homers, some RBIs) for at least one more year.

BASERUNNING:

He runs hard, has great instincts and is alert on the bases. What he lacks is speed--he is not a basestealing threat, but he doesn't clog up the bases during rallies.

FIELDING:

Sadly, this must be stated: Graig Nettles is not the defensive player he used to be. But this, too, must be said: A lesser Graig Nettles is still better than a lot of players who play third base in the big leagues.

At his peak, nothing got past him. He could stop everything, it seemed, between shortstop and the line. Now, he has lost a small amount of quickness, and hitters can squeeze a few hits past him. But while Nettles may make fewer "impossible plays" these days, he still makes all of the routine ones and most of the difficult ones. He still has

GRAIG NETTLES
3B, No. 9
LR, 6'0", 185 lbs.
ML Svc: 18 years
Born: 8-20-44 in
San Diego, CA

1984 STATISTICS

AVG	G	AB	R	H	2B	3B	HR	RBI	BB	SO	SB
.228	124	395	56	90	11	1	20	65	55	0	0

CAREER STATISTICS

AVG	G	AB	R	H	2B	3B	HR	RBI	BB	SO	SB
.250	2245	7922	1070	1980	284	26	353	1151	941	989	31

VS. RHP   VS. LHP   PROBABLE HIT LOCATIONS

those indescribably good hands and that strong, accurate throwing arm.

OVERALL:

Nettles clearly is playing toward the end of his career but he is doing it happily and in a winning environment. And, most importantly, he is contributing.

Snider: "He was so happy to be in San Diego last year and away from the situation he had been in while in New York. He had that little twinkle in his eye. He is loose, a great guy on a ballclub, a guy who'll help the other players. How much longer he'll play, that's the question."

HITTING:

His playing time and plate appearances were curtailed by the presence of Graig Nettles, which reduced Salazar to playing mostly against lefthanders. The Padres, though, would not have been tempted by Nettles's availability had it not been for Salazar's declining batting average over the previous two seasons.

He has been unable to resist swinging at high fastballs and distantly outside breaking balls. Pitchers need not throw him strikes; he'll swing at pitches many inches out of the strike zone. He is almost impossible to walk and much too easy to strike out.

But it also must be noted that his undisciplined aggressiveness sometimes can make him a dangerous hitter. He has the natural tools to hit mistakes. He tends to uppercut the ball, collapsing his left arm in the swing. He hits to all fields, slapping some pitches to right field and pulling others with power to left.

With more discipline and restraint at the plate and with some knowledge of the strike zone, Salazar possibly could be a very, very good hitter.

BASERUNNING:

Salazar has far above average speed and gets a good lead off first base. He is a definite basestealing threat; in the two seasons before Nettles arrived, Luis averaged 28 steals. He also is good at going from first to third on singles, at scoring from second and at beating out infield hits.

FIELDING:

This may not be common knowledge, but as a third baseman, Salazar has dazzling range and a powerful throwing arm. But he doesn't necessarily use these attributes to his advantage. Because of his range, he is able to reach some balls on

LUIS SALAZAR
INF, No. 4
RR, 5'9", 180 lbs.
ML Svc: 4 years
Born: 5-19-56 in
Barcelona, VEN

1984 STATISTICS

AVG	G	AB	R	H	2B	3B	HR	RBI	BB	SO	SB
.241	93	228	20	55	7	2	3	17	38	11	7

CAREER STATISTICS

AVG	G	AB	R	H	2B	3B	HR	RBI	BB	SO	SB
.269	625	1802	192	484	61	22	29	187	103	268	85

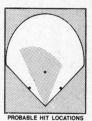

VS. RHP   VS. LHP   PROBABLE HIT LOCATIONS

which he has no play. But he often throws the ball away instead of holding on to it. And he likes to flaunt his powerful throwing arm by delaying his throws to first base, challenging baserunners rather than releasing the ball quickly and throwing them out routinely.

OVERALL:

He has some valuable tools: speed, a strong arm and natural hitting ability. He's only 28, so there's time for him to become more disciplined and selective at the plate and have a fine career as a regular player.

Snider: "He is a pretty good guy to have on a ballclub. He has the enthusiasm you like on a team. But for now, he will play mostly against lefties."

PITCHING:

Only a poor post-season performance detracted from Eric Show's 1984 season, in which he solidified himself as a top-quality starting pitcher. He's 28 years old, is entrenched in the Padres' starting rotation and should be entering the prime of his career.

He has the pitches to be a 20-game winner. He has an above average fastball that moves well (drops, rises or rides in) and a hard sinker. Movement is more important than velocity for Show, but he nevertheless can pop the fastball close to 90 MPH.

The key is that he must keep the ball down and avoid sporadic spurts of wildness. He must be careful with his third pitch, a slider, which he tends to hang too often. And he must be careful not to give in with fastballs down the middle when he falls behind in the count.

When he gets the ball up, he is vulnerable to long balls; when he walks too many hitters, he is vulnerable to short outings. Generally, he is more effective against righthanders than lefthanders.

But in addition to very good pitches, Show has intelligence going for him on the mound, and this should enable him to keep improving with experience. He is a student of philosophy, religion and physics, and some people try to explain his bad outings by saying he "thinks too much on the mound." That, of course, is a shallow argument.

FIELDING, HITTING, BASERUNNING:

Show showed some improvement last season as a fielder, and it is imperative that he develop his fielding skills as much as possible, because his sinker generates a lot of ground balls back through the middle. In many cases,

ERIC SHOW
RHP, No. 30
RR, 6'1", 185 lbs.
ML Svc: 3 years
Born: 5-19-56 in
Riverside, CA

1984 STATISTICS

W	L	ERA	G	GS	CG	IP	H	R	ER	BB	SO	SV
15	9	3.40	32	32	3	206	175	88	78	88	104	0

CAREER STATISTICS

W	L	ERA	G	GS	CG	IP	H	R	ER	BB	SO	SV
41	30	3.47	129	79	9	579	510	243	223	219	334	6

Show's glove is the difference between these balls being 1-3 outs and base hits into center field.

He has a good move to first base and a quick delivery to home plate, so he gives his catcher a good chance against opposing baserunners. He's probably a bit better than the typical pitcher as a hitter, and he's working diligently on his bunting.

OVERALL:

Although somewhat anonymously, Show has been a winner throughout his professional career. And he is in a perfect position--a good pitcher on a good team with a good bullpen--to continue posting winning records.

Snider: "He has a tendency to pitch up a little too much. He is not overpowering, and he has to get the ball down where it belongs. He has a really good attitude. He will be even more effective when he changes speed better and stays ahead in the count more."

HITTING:

While not living up to his promise as an offensive player, Garry Templeton is one of those rare switch-hitters who is just about as dangerous from one side of the plate as the other. From the left side he hits for slightly higher average. But from the right side, he hits with slightly better power. From the left side, Templeton hits line drives and grounders up the middle and to the opposite field. From the right side, he is more inclined to pull and drive the ball.

As a lefthanded hitter, he likes the ball down and out over the plate. Pitchers often find success against him by jamming him with sliders and fastballs. As a righthanded hitter, he likes fastballs up and out over the plate.

He has never become a disciplined hitter, and that--along with two arthritic knees--might explain why he has never blossomed into a superstar offensive player. He loves to swing at the first pitch. He could add a few points to his average if he were a better bunter.

BASERUNNING:

Templeton's knee problems have reduced his basestealing capabilities. He has good speed, when not slowed by the knees, and gets good jumps. The Padres have tended to take Templeton's baserunning out of their offense, a concession to his health.

FIELDING:

He is a more dependable shortstop than he was a few years ago, and he still has extraordinary range going to both his left and right. One area of improvement is that he now gets rid of the ball much more quickly, and his throwing is much more accurate than in the past. Occasionally, he will still drop a routine play, probably because of concentration lapses, but he also will

GARRY TEMPLETON
SS, No. 1
SR, 5'11", 170
ML Svc: 8 years
Born: 3-24-56 in
  Lockey, TX

1984 STATISTICS

AVG	G	AB	R	H	2B	3B	HR	RBI	BB	SO	SB
.258	148	493	40	127	19	3	2	35	81	8	3

CAREER STATISTICS

AVG	G	AB	R	H	2B	3B	HR	RBI	BB	SO	SB
.288	1130	4506	641	1298	189	82	36	420	222	526	184

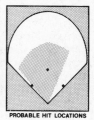

VS. RHP   VS. LHP   PROBABLE HIT LOCATIONS

make more than his share of difficult plays. He loves to chase pop flies into the outfield.

OVERALL:

There are few players in the game with more natural ability. But Garry has had to play with injuries, and he hasn't always had the best attitude. He certainly appeared to have it all together in the playoffs and World Series last fall, however.

Snider: "If he'd take out onto the field the attitude he had in the playoffs and Series, he'd get back to being one of the best all-around shortstops in the National League. I hadn't seen that enthusiasm in Templeton in a long time. He played with that kind of enthusiasm when he first came up with St. Louis, but after a while, he crawled into a shell. He came out in the playoffs and World Series. He has all there is in physical tools."

PITCHING:

Mark Thurmond has bounced around the San Diego organization since 1979, not always taken completely seriously as a potential big league pitcher. But he improved each year in the minors, working his way up to Triple A after three years in the Texas League and then getting a shot in the big leagues in 1983. Last season, he took a significant step toward establishing himself there.

A lefthander, he is the type of pitcher who impresses more with result than style. His stuff can be categorized in no terms more glowing than "pretty good," but last season he demonstrated that he knows what to do with what he has. What he has is an average fastball, average curveball, average slider and an average change-up.

His success hinges on pinpoint control. He had good control most of last season, and because he was able to put his pitches where he wanted them, he was largely successful. He must keep the ball down to have a chance against good hitters. He is more effective against lefthanders than righthanders and is particularly valuable against teams that have predominately lefthanded power.

Throughout his career, he has principally been a starting pitcher, but he has the type of arm that hints that he perhaps could be an effective relief pitcher as well.

FIELDING, HITTING, BASERUNNING:

He batted only five times in his minor league career, and that shows every time he steps to the plate in a

MARK THURMOND
LHP, No. 58
LL, 6'0", 180 lbs.
ML Svc: 2 years
Born: 9-12-56 in
    Houston, TX

1984 STATISTICS

W	L	ERA	G	GS	CG	IP	H	R	ER	BB	SO	SV
14	8	2.97	32	29	1	178	174	70	59	55	57	0

CAREER STATISTICS

W	L	ERA	G	GS	CG	IP	H	R	ER	BB	SO	SV
21	11	2.86	53	47	3	293	278	110	93	88	106	0

big league game. His baserunning prowess, if existent, is a moot point. He does not hurt himself as a fielder, making all the plays which he should make and a few which are marginally improbable. He holds runners on base well, and he gets the ball to the plate quickly enough.

OVERALL:

Remember that he is a lefthander, and remember that lefthanded pitchers are precious commodities in baseball. As long as he throws the ball where he wants it, he has a good future.

Snider: "He has pretty good stuff, but I wouldn't say that it is outstanding. He has to keep the ball down, and I mean down, down, down. If he starts to get it up in the strike zone, he will get tattooed."

PITCHING:

He had a strong and timely season and is ready to cash in on his success. His career, though, has been erratic enough that one must wonder if last year marks a flash of success or a lasting change.

Throughout his career, which has taken him from Pittsburgh to San Francisco to Cleveland to San Diego, scouts have felt that Whitson had the tools for greatness. But his 1984 season was the closest Whitson has come to realizing his potential.

Still, he's only 29 years old, so maybe he's right on schedule.

He is a hard thrower, with a fastball that exceeds 90 MPH and a nasty slider. He is a hard competitor. He complements his fastball and slider with a palmball; he's always struggled with his off-speed and breaking pitches, but last season he appeared to bring them under some mastery.

He throws from a three-quarters motion and occasionally is plagued by control problems that lead to his aiming the ball. And aiming the ball tends to lead either to more walks or home runs. But last year, Whitson seemed to worry less about walks, and consequently he pitched more assertively.

FIELDING, HITTING, BASERUNNING:

He is an aggressive, competitive person, and this is reflected in the manner in which he attempts to hit, the way in which he runs the bases and how he fields his position. He plays batted balls aggressively and is conscientious about covering first base. But he is so

ED WHITSON
RHP, No. 31
RR, 6'3", 200 lbs
ML Svc: 7 years
Born: 5-19-55 in
   Jefferson City, TN

1984 STATISTICS												
W	L	ERA	G	GS	CG	IP	H	R	ER	BB	SO	SV
14	8	3.24	31	31	1	189	181	72	68	42	103	0

CAREER STATISTICS												
W	L	ERA	G	GS	CG	IP	H	R	ER	BB	SO	SV
53	56	3.60	243	143	14	1023	995	457	409	374	567	8

focused on the batter that he sometimes overlooks the baserunner, not throwing to first base frequently enough.

OVERALL:

With his stuff, Ed could (should) have had four or five 15-win seasons by now. But his problem, at least until last season, was a tendency to lose close games because of mistakes in decisive situations. Last year, though, he appeared more relaxed and more confident than he had in previous seasons. It will be very interesting in 1985 to see if Whitson can sustain his success of 1984.

Snider: "He became a pitcher in 1984 instead of a thrower, and a lot of times he got the job done. He has quality stuff, especially when he is letting it go."

HITTING:

A switch-hitter, he is one of the "igniters" at the top of the Padres' batting order. Along with Tony Gwynn, Alan Wiggins makes things happen.

From the right side of the plate, he can drive the ball into the left-center and right-center alleys. From the left side, he punches the ball more than he drives it and also is more likely to bunt. But he looked more confident from the left side last year than ever before.

From either side of the plate, he is most vulnerable to hard stuff inside, although he handled that pitch better last season than ever before. He can hit breaking balls very well, and he can hit anything that is out over the plate.

Wiggins will never be a home run hitter, but he can bounce doubles against the walls and--increasing his offensive value--he has a good eye and doesn't mind taking a walk.

ALAN WIGGINS
OF, No. 2
SR, 6'2", 160 lbs.
ML Svc: 3 years
Born: 2-17-58 in
 Los Angeles, CA

1984 STATISTICS

AVG	G	AB	R	H	2B	3B	HR	RBI	BB	SO	SB
.258	158	596	106	154	19	7	3	34	57	70	21

CAREER STATISTICS

AVG	G	AB	R	H	2B	3B	HR	RBI	BB	SO	SB
.266	389	1367	233	363	42	12	4	71	136	132	122

VS. RHP   VS. LHP   PROBABLE HIT LOCATIONS

BASERUNNING:

His speed--plus, of course, his ability to get on base--makes him an ideal leadoff batter. He studies pitchers, gets good jumps and goes in hard at second base. He is going to steal a lot of bases every season; there is no defense against his speed.

FIELDING:

Wiggins made a very unusual transition last year, moving from left field to second base so that the Padres could get Carmelo Martinez into the lineup in the outfield. Wiggins made the move successfully--and, impressively, without apparent backlash on his offensive performance.

He did a fine job at second base, turning the double play adequately, demonstrating sufficient range and making strong, accurate throws. It is tough for a tall, lean person to play second base, but Wiggins did it.

Still, he probably is better in left field, where he is one of the best in the majors at going to the line to cut off extra-base hits. And he might well be back in the outfield in a few years, if not sooner.

OVERALL:

An outfield of Wiggins-Tony Gwynn-Kevin McReynolds would be outstanding. But for now, the Padres like the makeup of their team with Wiggins at second base. His speed and overall offensive ability make him a volatile force as a leadoff hitter.

Snider: "He is a catalyst, one of their guns at the top of the order. And their gamble of moving him to second base didn't hurt them at all."

BRUCE BOCHY
C, No.15
RR, 6'4", 229 lbs.
ML Svc: 4 years
Born: 4-16-55 in
   Landes de Boussac, FR

HITTING, FIELDING, BASERUNNING:

Bochy is the backup catcher on a team which has a workhorse starting catcher, Terry Kennedy. So, his role is limited.

But he fills it well. He calls a good game and has an adequate throwing arm, so his presence in the game is not disruptive. He can chip in with a timely hit here and there, and the Padres are not concerned that he doesn't run very well.

Although Kennedy had an off-season last year, the Padres know he will be their front-string catcher for a long time, so Bochy is seen purely as a backup. He'll catch an occasional day game after a night game and the second games of double headers, and he'll catch when Kennedy is hurt. But that's about it.

OVERALL:

Bochy undoubtedly would like a more prominent role. But the role he has with the Padres, or one like it, will keep him in the big leagues for a while.

Snider: "You've got to have guys like him on a club. Kennedy will do most of the catching, but Bochy is an adequate backup guy. He is a role player who never complains."

GREG BOOKER
RHP, No. 45
RR, 6'6", 230 lbs.
ML Svc: 1 year
Born: 6-22-60 in
   Lynchburg, VA

PITCHING, FIELDING,
   HITTING, BASERUNNING:

Greg Booker looks like the type of pitcher who can fill a limited but significant role on a staff. He looks like the type of pitcher who can be used in the early-to-middle innings--the third, fourth, fifth, possibly sixth--to keep a game under control. He does not appear to have the stuff to be used as a primary short reliever or as a starter. But there are a lot of games in which the starter is knocked out early that ultimately can be won if the long/middle reliever keeps the score from getting further out of hand.

Booker has two qualities going for him on the mound: control and intelligence. He must have pinpoint control to be effective, and he must keep the ball down, down, down. He is not overpowering, relying on location and breaking pitches. He is strong physically, with a sound, resilient arm.

As a hitter and baserunner, Booker has average skills. In his role, he will rarely get an opportunity to hit and even more rarely an opportunity to run the bases. He is conscious of baserunners and holds them on reasonably well. He won't hurt himself as a fielder.

OVERALL:

Incidentally, he is the son-in-law of Padres general manager Jack McKeon. But more significant to his future with the team, he is the type of role pitcher that a staff needs. Not a standout, but a contributor.

Snider: "He looks like he'll have to be a middle-man or maybe a spot starter. He looks like a good competitor."

MARIO RAMIREZ
SS, No. 12
RR, 5'9", 173 lbs.
ML Svc: 3 years
Born: 9-12-57 in
 Yauco, PR

HITTING, BASERUNNING, FIELDING:

Ramirez is the prototypical utility infielder, a good fielding middle infielder without a threatening bat. It is doubtful he'll ever be a regular player, but he could survive a while as a utility man.

He has made great strides as a defensive player since the early years of his career; consider that he committed 46 errors at shortstop in the Midwestern League in 1976 and 46 errors at short in the International League in 1978. But incredibly, one year after making those 46 errors, he committed only nine (in just as many chances) and led International League shortstops in fielding percentage. Since then, he has been an accomplished defensive player with good hands, good range and a good throwing arm.

In addition to shortstop, Ramirez can play second base and third base. His best minor league batting average was .251, at Hawaii in 1981. He runs well.

OVERALL:

The Padres like Ramirez. Proof is that they drafted him from the Mets' organization in 1980 and, five years later, are holding on to him. And although this will be his tenth year in pro baseball, he's only 26 years old.

CHAMP SUMMERS
1B, No. 24
LR, 6'2", 205 lbs.
ML Svc: 9 years
Born: 6-15-48 in
 Bremerton, WA

HITTING, BASERUNNING, FIELDING:

It appears that Champ Summers is nearing the end. He has always had a good, powerful bat and probably can still win some games with hits off the bench. But he may have lost a little bat speed in the last year or so, and he undoubtedly has gotten rusty by a lack of playing time and plate appearances.

It is unlikely he would be used much in any role other than as a lefthanded pinch-hitter. Summers is a liability defensively, and he has below average speed on the bases.

He can hit, however, especially when he is facing righthanded pitchers and especially in certain parks.

OVERALL:

Snider: "He's getting down near the end of the line. After sitting around so much through the years, a player begins to regress. You sit on the bench and sit on the bench, you lose a little something. Champ probably has needed to play a little bit. But he's a role type of player, a lefty pinch-hitter."

SAN FRANCISCO GIANTS

HITTING:

Considering all that he went through, Dusty Baker did not have a bad year at the plate. He missed spring training and had leg injuries, but contributed as a part-time player and reached his life-time batting average.

He is primarily a pull hitter and pitchers can get him out on good stuff inside and breaking balls away. Then again, you could say that about most hitters. His timing was off last year and so his power was not as evident as it had been in the past.

What Baker does have is savvy. He knows the pitchers and he knows his limitations, so he doesn't strike out much and is a good man to have at the plate in clutch situations.

Baker really did not have a fair chance to show what he could do last year, although he played in 100 games. It remains to be seen whether he will ever have the chance to be a regular again. That certainly doesn't seem likely in San Francisco, which has a set outfield.

With the Giants, he is a part-timer at best, but could recapture the hitting magic with another club that needs some sock. He has played enough to show that he can still hit, but it isn't known if he will ever approach the home run and RBI totals of his more productive Los Angeles years.

BASERUNNING:

Merely a shadow of his former self on the basepaths, Baker is still a heady runner, stealing second, third and home in one inning last year. He once stole 24 bases in a major league season, but 12 years and many bumps and bruises later, that's impossible now.

FIELDING:

Baker, who was never a great out-fielder, finds himself on a team blessed with three good ones. It has cut down his playing time.

DUSTY BAKER
OF, No. 12
RR, 6'2", 200 lbs.
ML Svc: 13 years
Born: 6-15-49 in
      Riverside, CA

1984 STATISTICS

AVG	G	AB	R	H	2B	3B	HR	RBI	BB	SO	SB
.292	100	243	31	71	7	2	3	32	40	27	4

CAREER STATISTICS

AVG	G	AB	R	H	2B	3B	HR	RBI	BB	SO	SB
.280	1845	6532	891	1831	297	22	224	942	685	842	135

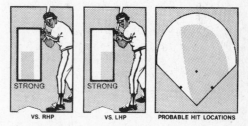

His arm is merely average, but he rarely misses the cutoff man and is not a detriment in left field, though he doesn't get to balls as quickly as he used to.

OVERALL:

An extremely proud veteran, Dusty insists he can be a productive regular, but he may not get that chance, especially in the San Francisco organization. He came through a tough 1984 with respectable statistics despite an upsetting separation from the Dodgers, a contract hassle and varied injuries.

There's no question he can be even better this year in the proper frame of mind.

Campbell: "It was more or less a lost year for Dusty. All of his injuries have really slowed him down. The key will be to find an everyday job, because Baker makes too much money to remain a part-time player."

BOB BRENLY
C, No. 15
RR, 6'2", 210 lbs.
ML Svc: 3 years
Born: 2-25-54 in
  Coshocton, OH

HITTING:

Bob Brenly enjoyed tremendous success for a guy who wasn't even a regular in spring training last year. He finally responded to former Giant manager Frank Robinson's prodding and had the type of year he was capable of putting together.

Brenly's power-hitting reputation probably hurt him in the past. Both he and Mike Schmidt share several college records, so Bob came to the majors looking for homers. Last year, he finally got smart.

He gained confidence with a .373 May and made the All Star squad. He took off from there with a .319 July and batted .312 with eight home runs and 29 RBIs in August to stay above .300 for most of the season.

Brenly reached career highs in virtually every offensive category by learning to use the entire field and shedding his image as a pull hitter. He also became more patient at the plate.

At one time, Bob thrived on high heat and had a weakness for low pitches. Better discipline has enabled him to cover most of the strike zone, eliminating that glaring flaw, a sharp contrast to his slump-filled 1983.

BASERUNNING:

Hardly a slug on the basepaths, Bob runs better than most catchers and is not a liability in that area. But he is not surprising opponents anymore, so don't expect a lot of steals. He is also aggressive on the bases and will score from second on a single.

FIELDING:

One of the top priorities last spring was to make Bob a take-charge guy behind the plate. And while Brenly's attitude definitely improved, there was not much to take charge of on the San Francisco pitching staff.

He has a merely average arm and an average release, but he improved greatly last season in throwing out runners. More improvement is needed, however.

1984 STATISTICS											
AVG	G	AB	R	H	2B	3B	HR	RBI	BB	SO	SB
.291	145	506	74	147	28	0	20	80	48	52	6
CAREER STATISTICS											
AVG	G	AB	R	H	2B	3B	HR	RBI	BB	SO	SB
.255	333	1012	141	276	46	4	32	133	109	130	22

VS. RHP

VS. LHP

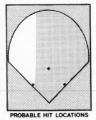

PROBABLE HIT LOCATIONS

OVERALL:

Brenly finally put it all together last year to give the Giants a solid all-around season behind the plate. He might have done it sooner had it not been for a broken collarbone in the spring of 1982. The big thing last year was the confidence factor. Once he knew he was pretty good, he maintained a level of consistency heretofore not evident.

This catcher is also a very aggressive athlete with a good attitude about the game. A popular and well-respected player, he was voted Giants' MVP last year by his teammates.

Campbell: "He was outstanding offensively last year, but it's tough to get a reading on him as a signal-caller. When the pitching staff lacks quality, it really doesn't matter what finger you put down. He will go into 1985 knowing the job is his, which could mean an even better year."

HITTING:

Just when he seemed to place all his problems behind him last year, a knee injury prevented Jack Clark from having an outstanding season. He played only about one third of the season, but it was an important 57 games for him.

He got over the threshold of his slow starts by hitting .284 in April and .382 in May. That should serve him well as he prepares mentally for 1985. So should a lineup packed with successful hitters. Clark has superstar potential if he ever stays healthy and can fuse his skills into an awesome season.

He likes the ball outside and belt high and he never gets cheated at the plate, though pitchers will often work around him. Jack is a good cripple hitter, and becomes more aggressive when he's ahead in the count. He will chase fastballs up and breaking balls down when pitchers have the edge.

A streak hitter, Clark can hit anything when he is in a groove. His high career game-winning RBI total is testimony to his ability in the clutch. The Giants are afraid to trade him because of the big numbers they know he is capable of putting together.

BASERUNNING:

Baserunning blunders throughout his early years have given him a reputation he's not likely to shake. This is the weakest part of his game because his mind seems to wander on the basepaths and he has been made to look foolish at times.

FIELDING:

He was a third baseman in the minors, so the probable switch to first base shouldn't be a problem. Besides having a glut of outfielders, the Giants look at the move as a means of placing less of a burden on his knee following his 1984 surgery. Clark has become a decent outfielder, especially in a tough right

JACK CLARK
OF, No. 22
RR, 6'3", 205 lbs.
ML Svc: 8 years
Born: 11-10-55 in
New Brighton, PA

1984 STATISTICS

AVG	G	AB	R	H	2B	3B	HR	RBI	BB	SO	SB
.320	57	203	33	65	9	1	11	44	43	29	1

CAREER STATISTICS

AVG	G	AB	R	H	2B	3B	HR	RBI	BB	SO	SB
.275	1044	3731	597	1034	197	30	163	595	497	566	60

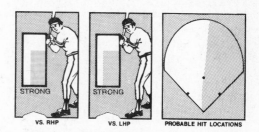

STRONG   STRONG

VS. RHP   VS. LHP   PROBABLE HIT LOCATIONS

field such as Candlestick's, but has had problems with his erratic arm.

OVERALL:

Clark made tremendous strides off the field last year and now appears to have the mental stability to go with his physical ability. He quit his griping, which had earned him a "bad boy" label, impressing former manager Frank Robinson enough to name him team captain.

There was some skepticism over his reluctance to return to action after the knee mended last season, but he did not want to risk further injury on a team that was going nowhere. He didn't offer to return any pay, however.

Campbell: "We were told that he would be out for three or four weeks, and it turned out that he didn't play for the last four months. His attitude has been suspect in the past and he seemed to spend more time sniping at the front office than playing baseball. It's hard to shake that kind of reputation."

HITTING:

The mystery man of the 1983 season fooled everyone in 1984, posting his most solid season at the plate and easing fears he might be a failure following a banner rookie season in 1982.

Chili Davis contemplated abandoning switch-hitting at one point, but he declined to do so because he didn't want to give up the advantage--smart move. If he had stopped going both ways, he would have most likely concentrated on hitting righthanded, where he had previously had more success.

Presto! Chili changed his stance, stopped going for homers and thought about making contact while switching to a lighter bat (he started using teammate Duane Kuiper's). The results were staggering.

He became a better hitter from the left side, belting all but two of his 21 career-high homers as a southpaw swinger. He also notched a career RBI high (81) while popping the longball without consciously trying.

The best way to bother him is to throw good, hard stuff inside regardless of which way he's batting. He's a much more disciplined hitter now, cutting down his strikeout total by more than 25% over his 1983 total.

BASERUNNING:

This is the area of his game which has suffered the most. Chili set a club stolen base mark for a rookie in 1982, but he has a different role now that he no longer is leading off. Moreover, he has not become a smart baserunner and gets caught often enough to discourage himself.

FIELDING:

The strength of Davis's game in center field was his arm; that becomes an asset as he shifts to right field, where he can do a better job defensively than Jack Clark. In fact, Davis, Leonard and

CHILI DAVIS
OF, No. 30
SR, 6'3", 195 lbs.
ML Svc: 3 years
Born: 1-17-60 in
Kingston, JAM

1984 STATISTICS

AVG	G	AB	R	H	2B	3B	HR	RBI	BB	SO	SB
.315	137	499	87	157	21	6	21	81	42	74	12

CAREER STATISTICS

AVG	G	AB	R	H	2B	3B	HR	RBI	BB	SO	SB
.247	436	1641	228	439	69	14	51	216	143	299	48

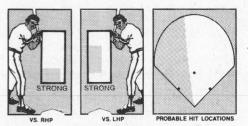

Gladden form a solid fielding trio, one that might become the best in the NL.

OVERALL:

One of the smartest moves owner Bob Lurie made last year was saying no to a spring deal that would have sent Davis to the Cubs. While it may have kept Chili from a winner, it also protected the Giants' investment in a rather rare commodity: a productive switch-hitter.

One year after he was briefly demoted to the minors because of a season-long funk, Davis reached the All Star game and finished with a flurry to post the highest average among the full-season regulars. He also had an 18-game hitting streak down the stretch, the best since Clark's 26 in 1978.

Campbell: "He started to fulfill the promise he showed as a rookie. Chili had a lot of problems at the plate in 1983, but he straightened himself out and is a valuable guy to have around, especially with the Giants having so many right-handed hitters."

PITCHING:

Mark Davis was undeniably the biggest disappointment of the staff last season after going 5-1 down the stretch in 1983 and being the most reliable starter in spring training. Davis was spiked on his left thumb last April and never regained his form.

He had the best stuff among the starters in the spring of 1984 and was counted on to emerge as a standout after being the so-called sleeper in the deal that sent Joe Morgan and Al Holland to the Phillies following the 1982 season.

Instead, he fell asleep last year, squandering his obvious talent by being too true; he gave the hitters too many pitches to hit. He appeared to straighten out with a bullpen stint, but reverted to his old habits shortly thereafter.

Consequently, Mark became one of the major league's biggest losers last year. He has a better than average fastball (88-89 MPH), a sharp breaking ball and change-up, but he hasn't put it all together either physically or mentally.

FIELDING, HITTING, BASERUNNING:

A decent hitter, his two triples represented one more extra-base hit than the rest of the pitching staff combined. Davis is also the best bunter among the pitchers, totaling 15 sacrifices in the last two years. He has a good move to first and runs well, but topped the staff with three errors.

OVERALL:

Davis must revert to his 1983 form if he is to remain in the starting rota-

MARK DAVIS
LHP, No. 13
LL, 6'4", 195 lbs.
ML Svc: 2 years
Born: 10-19-60 in
Livermore, CA

1984 STATISTICS

W	L	ERA	G	GS	CG	IP	H	R	ER	BB	SO	SV
5	17	5.38	46	27	1	174	201	113	104	54	124	0

CAREER STATISTICS

W	L	ERA	G	GS	CG	IP	H	R	ER	BB	SO	SV
12	25	5.00	77	57	3	335	347	203	186	133	241	0

tion, though being lefthanded and young gives him an advantage. The Giants took a gamble on him because of the arm problems he had while in the Phillies system, and they apparently still like his stuff or he would never have had been given the chance to lose so many games.

His problems seem mental as much as physical. He frets when things go badly, as was the case often last year, and he admittedly didn't relax until he had gotten past the point of no return down the stretch.

Campbell: "I'm sure he's a bit of an enigma to the Giants. He has a good, live arm and enough zip, though it seems to me that his problem is location. He has enough off-speed stuff, so hitters can't gear in, but it appears he puts too many pitches in the middle of the plate. Maybe he just pitched on the wrong days."

HITTING:

Along with Bob Brenly and Chili Davis, Dan Gladden was the most pleasant surprise among the non-pitchers on the club last year, stamping himself as a potential superstar with his glove, bat and feet.

Gladden wisely decided that at 5'11" and 180 lbs. he wasn't going to make the grade as a power hitter, so he altered both his stance and his thinking to take best advantage of his speed and keen batting eye.

By choking up more and opening his stance, he began spraying the ball all over the field and came up with some astonishing results. After tearing up the Pacific Coast League to the tune of .397 for half a season, he continued his batting binge when he joined the Giants to stay.

This compact athlete maintained a .350 pace, one exceeded only by Tony Gwynn, and he did it with more than 300 at-bats, suggesting it wasn't a fluke.

At the same time, Gladden solved the club's quest for a leadoff hitter and appears ready, at age 27, to finally make a major contribution with the Giants, winning a starting job on a club well stocked with outfielders.

BASERUNNING:

The man can fly and makes things happen on the basepaths. He set a Giants rookie record for stolen bases while playing only half the season. He is also the best bunter on the club and has the potential to score a lot of runs before his promising career concludes.

FIELDING:

Danny possesses merely an average arm, but he compensates with great speed and has demonstrated good judgment in

DAN GLADDEN
CF, No. 25
RR, 5'11", 180 lbs.
ML Svc: 1 year plus
Born: 7-7-57 in
  San Jose, CA

1984 STATISTICS											
AVG	G	AB	R	H	2B	3B	HR	RBI	BB	SO	SB
.351	86	342	71	120	17	2	4	31	33	37	31

CAREER STATISTICS											
AVG	G	AB	R	H	2B	3B	HR	RBI	BB	SO	SB
.222	104	405	77	134	19	2	5	40	38	48	35

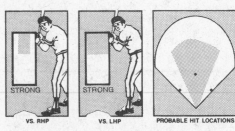

STRONG   STRONG
VS. RHP   VS. LHP   PROBABLE HIT LOCATIONS

tracking down balls. Gladden is so good in center field that he forced the shift of Chili Davis to right and helped to make room for Jack Clark at first base.

OVERALL:

If his three-month spree of 1984 is indicative, there's really nothing this man can't do. Only the presence of Dwight Gooden and Juan Samuel obscured Gladden's rookie feats, including more than 200 hits combined at Phoenix and San Franciso. The guy can play, adding an exciting dimension to the Giants despite the team's horrid performance.

Campbell: "A very pesky player; he has a great eye and will take the walks. Dan is an exciting baserunner and he obviously can hit. He revamped his game plan and it really paid off for him. He has the potential to be a big star."

PITCHING:

Atlee Hammaker is the best pitcher on the San Francisco staff when he is healthy, which unfortunately wasn't very often last year. He had only six starts, to be exact, but he was 2-0 with a 2.18 ERA after leading the National League with a 2.25 ERA in 1983.

He didn't win again in 1984 after July 10 as a result of what was suspected to be a tendinitis problem in his shoulder. It turned out that Hammaker had a tear which required rotator cuff surgery. The rehabilitation was slow, so he managed only six starts before elbow trouble cropped up. Arthroscopic surgery in September removed two bone spurs and a bone chip.

As a result, he missed 90% of the 1984 season, and it cost the Giants dearly. When he's on top of his game, Hammaker is as effective as anyone in the league because of his impeccable control, an assortment of off-speed pitches and a 90 MPH fastball.

FIELDING, HITTING, BASERUNNING:

He did not have enough work to make a determination last year, but there's no question that pitching is his strength. He does not have a good move to first base, especially for a lefty, and is not a good hitter or baserunner. He is, however, a good athlete. He attended college on a basketball scholarship, so these areas can improve once he gets his arm squared away.

OVERALL:

It would be a shame if this promising southpaw doesn't regain his touch. It

ATLEE HAMMAKER
LHP, No. 14
LL, 6'2", 195 lbs.
ML Svc: 3 years
Born: 1-24-58 in
  Carmel, CA

1984 STATISTICS

W	L	ERA	G	GS	CG	IP	H	R	ER	BB	SO	SV
2	0	2.18	6	6	0	33	32	10	8	9	24	0

CAREER STATISTICS

W	L	ERA	G	GS	CG	IP	H	R	ER	BB	SO	SV
25	20	3.33	68	62	12	419	412	177	155	81	264	0

will be a big adjustment mentally as well, because he knows how good he can be following his 1983 success and it would be a big step backward if he is not able to recapture the magic.

He is an exceptional talent when he's right. A unique pitcher because he has such great control, contrary to most young lefthanders. He changes speeds well and throws a tailing fastball, but it may be too much to expect a total comeback in 1985.

Campbell: "I don't know whether he will be able to come back following a pair of operations, but if the Giants are going to make a move in 1985, he's going to have to be in top form. He was the club's stopper in 1983, and when he was unavailable, the Giants really fell apart. When healthy, Atlee is one of the best young pitchers in the game."

PITCHING:

Mike Krukow was strictly hot and cold in 1984, with an emphasis on the cool side. He enjoyed a 5-1 record in July, but was mediocre for the rest of the season, getting into ruts he just could not escape. Krukow was extremely disappointing to the Giants because he was supposed to be a steadying influence for a young staff, not the bad example he turned out to be.

He throws three-quarters and has all the pitches for success, but the key factor is getting the curve over the plate. His is a slow curve and the hitters have to sit on it. They either have to do that or sit on his fastball.

He pressed hard in 1983 because of the success Al Holland was having with the Phillies following a trade, but that excuse was gone last year. Nonetheless, Krukow is a good competitor who's not afraid to keep the hitters loose or to retaliate to protect his own hitters--just ask Joaquin Andujar.

FIELDING, HITTING, BASERUNNING:

Krukow is a good hitter as pitchers go (he batted as high as .254 two years ago), but he slipped at the plate in 1984. He also knows what he's doing on the basepaths.

His move to first base is a quick one for a righthander, but he is not a great fielder.

OVERALL:

It was hoped that he would blossom as a stopper last year with Hammaker out

MIKE KRUKOW
RHP, No. 39
RR, 6'4", 205 lbs.
ML Svc: 7 years
Born: 1-21-52 in
Long Beach, CA

1984 STATISTICS
W	L	ERA	G	GS	CG	IP	H	R	ER	BB	SO	SV
11	12	4.56	35	33	3	199	234	117	101	78	141	1

CAREER STATISTICS
W	L	ERA	G	GS	CG	IP	H	R	ER	BB	SO	SV
80	84	4.05	249	237	21	1419	1488	730	638	568	953	1

and with one year under his belt in San Francisco. Instead, Krukow remained mediocre, perhaps suggesting that he's nothing more than a .500 pitcher.

He is a veteran who seems to have all the ingredients for success, but great performances are few and far between. He also isn't very lucky. Last summer, he blanked the Mets for nine innings with a career-high of 10 strikeouts, but was matched against Dwight Gooden and lost, 2-0, in the 10th.

Campbell: "He's either very, very good, or very bad--and you usually know after an inning or two. He has a problem with one bad inning per game, and it usually costs five or six runs. Mike has always struck me as a good competitor, a guy who is capable of having a great year."

PITCHING:

Like team ate Mike Krukow, Bill Laskey's season was marred by inconsistency. He also had trouble getting past the middle innings and became labelled as a "five-inning pitcher," a categorization which rankled this tough competitor.

Laskey is a low ball pitcher, throwing sinkers and sliders in and out. A muscle tear in his side reduced his effectiveness in 1983, but he held up for an entire season last year and logged his most innings ever.

After topping the staff in victories in his first two seasons in the majors, Laskey went into stretches when he just couldn't buy a win. He had too many dry spells on a club that begged for a stopper, and his work proved disappointing despite his own tough luck and non-support.

He has the four basic pitches, and uses them with excellent control and good poise.

FIELDING, HITTING, BASERUNNING:

Rangy and awkward, Laskey has a clumsy move to first base and is not a good fielder by any means. His greatest weakness is his inability to hold runners on base—a common malady among 1984 Giants pitchers.

On the basepaths, he is not a good runner, and his hitting has gone downhill over the last three years.

OVERALL:

A good attitude and tenacity are two

BILL LASKEY
RHP, No. 19
RR, 6'5", 190 lbs.
ML Svc: 3 years
Born: 12-20-57 in
    Toledo, OH

```
1984 STATISTICS
W  L  ERA  G   GS  CG IP   H   R   ER  BB SO SV
9  14 4.33 35  34  2  207  222 112 100 50 71 0
CAREER STATISTICS
W  L  ERA  G   GS  CG IP   H   R   ER  BB SO SV
35 36 3.89 92  90  10 544  559 261 235 138 240 0
```

of his greatest assets. There is some concern because his unusual pitching motion places a strain on his arm, causing skepticism surrounding his long-term prospects for success.

He thrived under pressure as a rookie and his work in tough situations drew former Giants manager Frank Robinson's admiration. In last two years, however, he has become better known for amazing control even when he's losing. If Bill could find a way to miss some bats, his problems would be solved.

Campbell: "Like so many Giants pitchers, his problem is lack of stuff. They need pinpoint control to win. Bill is the type of guy who's learned he has to do everything to win. I like his poise and his competitiveness."

PITCHING:

"Pudge" became the Giants' record-holder for pitching appearances last season, surpassing Christy Mathewson, but it has become obvious that the many outings have taken their toll on the knees and arm of this fairly consistent relief specialist.

He has a good, tailing fastball, making lefthanded hitters dread facing him when he's on his game. He has a high leg kick and his fastball bores in on the hitters. He can make them look bad on breaking balls and occasional short change-ups.

For the most part, Gary Lavelle was a solid pitcher in 1984, but a handful of poor outings kept him from having a truly outstanding year. His problems are usually caused by control difficulties, but a 90 MPH tailing fastball makes him a pain to hitters.

FIELDING, HITTING, BASERUNNING:

A pathetic hitter and a poor baserunner who doesn't get the chance to prove it often, Gary nevertheless fields his position well. He also has an odd move to first base, which keeps runners guessing. Once Lavelle commits to the plate, however, a runner can steal second standing up if he guesses right. If he doesn't, he's dead. Gary's high kick adds to the deception.

OVERALL:

How long can Lavelle be an effective reliever with his brittle knees and per-

GARY LAVELLE
LHP, No. 46
RL, 6'1", 200 lbs.
ML Svc: 10 years
Born: 1-3-49 in
Sacramento, CA

1984 STATISTICS

W	L	ERA	G	GS	CG	IP	H	R	ER	BB	SO	SV
5	4	2.76	77	0.	0	101	92	34	31	42	71	12

CAREER STATISTICS

W	L	ERA	G	GS	CG	IP	H	R	ER	BB	SO	SV
73	67	2.82	647	3	0	981	910	359	307	382	696	127

iodic arm problems? Somehow, he keeps getting the job done and basically has been quite effective ever since his major league debut in 1974.

The Giants may have made the mistake of holding onto him too long. They tried to move him to a contender last year, but the asking price was apparently too high. He's the type of pitcher who could lose it all of a sudden, leaving the club holding the bag.

Campbell: "He has broken more bats than any lefthanded reliever in the National League. He has a good fastball and a hard slider. His fastball seems to rise and he's murder on lefthanders. He blew more hot and cold than usual last year and the Giants offered him around, but the deals fell through."

HITTING:

Suspicions were confirmed last year when Johnnie LeMaster returned to mediocrity at the plate, continuing a pattern which has had him playing well and poorly in alternate years.

"Bones" found moderate success as the leadoff batter early in 1983, blossoming as a formidable basestealer, but the move also gave him delusions of grandeur. He could not hit well enough to stay in the top spot, so he was dropped to No. 8 in the lineup and brooded sufficiently to have it affect his overall play.

To get LeMaster out, which isn't a great accomplishment, keep the ball down and stay ahead of him on the count. Do not get into a position where you have to groove a pitch to him.

He seems to have worn out his welcome with the club because of a less than positive attitude, but there is no better shortstop on the squad, so the team may have to endure another year with him as a regular if they don't come up with somebody in a trade.

LeMaster also seems to wear down if he's not given an occasional breather. He's had difficulty putting two good halves together, and some years he does not do it offensively for even one half a season.

BASERUNNING:

LeMaster proved in 1983 that he can be an above average basestealer, but batting eighth and not getting on base enough greatly curtailed his running last season. With Dan Gladden on the club now, batting leadoff for LeMaster is out of the question, making his 39 thefts of 1983 an unapproachable total.

FIELDING:

The strongest part of LeMaster's game is his glovework, but even that slipped during a dismal 1984. He can go to the

JOHNNIE LeMASTER
SS, No. 10
RR, 6'2", 180 lbs.
ML Svc: 8 years
Born: 6-19-54 in
   Portsmouth, OH

1984 STATISTICS

AVG	G	AB	R	H	2B	3B	HR	RBI	BB	SO	SB
.217	132	451	46	98	13	2	4	32	31	97	17

CAREER STATISTICS

AVG	G	AB	R	H	2B	3B	HR	RBI	BB	SO	SB
.228	974	3073	312	695	109	19	21	220	234	537	93

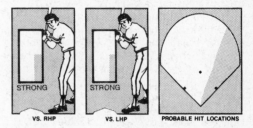

VS. RHP   VS. LHP   PROBABLE HIT LOCATIONS

hole with the best of them and has a rocket arm, but he'll bobble the routine play. The club will have to determine whether his glove can compensate for his liabilities in other areas.

OVERALL:

The Giants seemingly would be better off without him if they could come up with someone better. Trade rumors say that Brad Wellman may get a shot, but Johnnie's glove can keep him in the lineup if he comes to the realization that all he has to do is field well to help a club that does not need more hitting.

Campbell: "He improved considerably as an all-around player in 1983, but was back to his old ways last year. The guy has too many holes in his bat, so he can't make use of his excellent speed. He's highly regarded as a shortstop, but is prone to mistakes. The total package isn't very impressive."

HITTING:

Jeff Leonard enjoyed his second straight solid season last year. With Jack Clark out of the lineup for most of the season, Leonard turned into one of the club's most dangerous hitters.

He's a dead fastball hitter, so you can get him out with curves. "Hack" was more disciplined during the first half of last season, but his strikeout totals increased as the season progressed and he reverted to his former free-swinging ways. Except for a late-season dry spell, however, Leonard had more success in the final half, batting .340 in July and .339 in August before cooling off.

Leonard deserved to be named to the All Star squad and there were some hurt feelings when Chili Davis was selected instead of Jeff; these two players have a friendly rivalry, finishing with almost identical statistics last year.

If you keep the ball low and away on him, you won't have much trouble, but if a pitcher gives him a fastball up--look out. The guy has tons of power and he's tough with men on base.

Somewhat of an underrated hitter, this gifted athlete is not fully appreciated by those who aren't frequently around him. He reached the finals of the National League home run hitting contest, which attests to his raw power.

BASERUNNING:

An aggressive baserunner and a smart basestealer, Leonard could have much higher stolen base totals if he took some time to concentrate on that aspect of his game. But he hits in the heart of the order and has emerged as a solid RBI man, so there's less of a need to steal where he bats. He is definitely a man with 30-homer, 30-steals potential.

FIELDING:

His good fielding is another part of Leonard's game which is overlooked. He piles up assists in left field and is

JEFF LEONARD
LF, No. 26
RR, 6'4", 200 lbs.
ML Svc: 6 years
Born: 9-22-55 in
  Philadelphia, PA

1984 STATISTICS

AVG	G	AB	R	H	2B	3B	HR	RBI	BB	SO	SB
.302	136	514	76	155	27	2	21	86	47	123	17

CAREER STATISTICS

AVG	G	AB	R	H	2B	3B	HR	RBI	BB	SO	SB
.272	640	2116	282	591	96	25	58	324	187	459	93

VS. RHP

VS. LHP

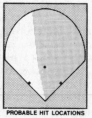

PROBABLE HIT LOCATIONS

proficient at gunning runners down at the plate, yet he doesn't get much recognition for his fielding, a snub which annoys him.

He charges the ball well, but has occasional difficulty going back on rising drives--but who doesn't at Candlestick?

OVERALL:

An outstanding talent who got his personal life together in 1983 and became an all-around star, Leonard has difficulty shaking off his moody past. He realizes his worth, however, and is eligible for free agency following the 1985 season if he doesn't sign with the Giants. He can hit, run, throw and pop the ball, so superstardom may be on the horizon, like it or not.

Campbell: "He's the kind of a guy who saunters to the beat of his own drummer. I really don't know if his attitude has changed or not, but you've got to respect his ability. He can do a lot of things."

PITCHING:

Greg Minton has saved 40 games over the last two years without being a truly effective reliever. His success usually boils down to whether his sinker sinks or not.

He appeared overweight last year, lending credence to claims that a huge contract made him fat in more ways than one. When his sinker isn't working, the hitters can't wait to take their cuts at it because he hasn't much else to give them.

Minton's slider can be wicked at times to righthanded hitters, and his sinker ranks with the best of them when he has got it together. However, he is simply not the pitcher he was in the late 1970's.

Minton holds the major league record of 269 1/3 innings without yielding a home run (1978-82), but he has been hit for 16 homers in the last two seasons. He signed a million-dollar contract following a career-best performance in '82.

FIELDING, HITTING, BASERUNNING:

After batting .545 in 1983, it seems now that he has even lost his hitting touch. His batting average dropped below .100 last year. Minton is a decent fielder, but he's not good at holding runners on and is merely average as a baserunner.

OVERALL:

It seemed the Giants placed him in a lot of save situations last year to try to justify his huge contract. As inef-

GREG MINTON
RHP, No. 38
SR, 6'2", 190 lbs.
ML Svc: 7 years
Born: 7-29-51 in
   Lubbock, TX

1984 STATISTICS

W	L	ERA	G	GS	CG	IP	H	R	ER	BB	SO	SV
4	9	3.77	74	1	0	124	130	60	52	57	48	19

CAREER STATISTICS

W	L	ERA	G	GS	CG	IP	H	R	ER	BB	SO	SV
35	44	3.11	421	7	0	681	666	275	235	280	272	115

fective as he has been in relief, it is amazing that he's had so many chances in the late innings.

With his penchant for getting into trouble, Minton always seems to be working with runners on base, making already tense situations tougher. When he can squirm out of it, he's sensational, but judging by his record and his ERA, he didn't squirm often enough.

Campbell: "If he pitched against the Padres all his life, Minton would be outstanding. They can't seem to get the ball out of the infield against him. But when his sinker flattens out and stays in the strike zone, he's in trouble. He does not scare, and almost likes it better when the situation is hopeless. When his sinker is working, he's as good as any reliever in the league. Obviously, however, there have been a lot of days when it doesn't work."

HITTING:

Hitting is definitely the strength of Steve Nicosia's game, making him a solid backup catcher. He has been a .300 hitter ever since he joined the Giants late in 1983, forming a solid offensive tandem with teammate Bob Brenly.

Nicosia proved to be much more productive with the Giants than he was with the Pirates. He did some eye-catching things last season, like collecting a club record eight hits in a row, two shy of the league record. And while he is by no means a fast runner, he also tripled twice in one game.

Aggressive at the plate in typical Pirates fashion, he doesn't get cheated. Steve won't walk and can hit to all fields, so the best strategy is for a pitcher to move the ball around and for the fielders to play him straightaway.

BASERUNNING:

Definitely a reckless baserunner, he doesn't have much speed and is not a threat to steal a base. Unlike Brenly, Nicosia runs like a catcher, plodding along more than running.

FIELDING:

Nicosia was obtained in an effort to improve the Giants defensively behind the plate. He's better than Milt May, for whom he was swapped, but that isn't saying much. Steve definitely does not have much of an arm, but he is a take-charge guy and blocks the plate well.

OVERALL:

Nicosia is a good man to have around because he can give Brenly a breather

STEVE NICOSIA
C, No. 7
RR, 5'10", 185 lbs.
ML Svc: 6 years
Born: 8-6-55 in
　Paterson, NJ

1984 STATISTICS

AVG	G	AB	R	H	2B	3B	HR	RBI	BB	SO	SB
.303	48	132	9	40	11	2	2	19	8	14	1

CAREER STATISTICS

AVG	G	AB	R	H	2B	3B	HR	RBI	BB	SO	SB
.246	310	852	82	217	50	3	11	86	79	79	4

VS. RHP

VS. LHP

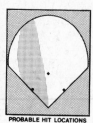

PROBABLE HIT LOCATIONS

without much punch being lost. He came out of Tony Pena's shadow when he left Pittsburgh and saw the Giants as an opportunity to play more. But Brenly's development last year cast Nicosia in a familiar backup role. He has handled it well and is a clubhouse cut-up who helps keep the players loose. Last year, they definitely needed it.

Campbell: "He's a tough, hard-nosed kid adequately suited for a reserve role. He doesn't hurt you with the bat, can be used as a pinch-hitter and is a team leader. He makes the most of his limited ability."

PITCHING:

Jeff Robinson came virtually out of nowhere, jumping from Class A minor league ball to enter the Giants' rotation at the start of last season. Just the mere fact that such emergency measures were required shows the sorry state of the Giants pitching staff in 1984. Nonetheless, he responded well to the pressure of the situation, poise being one of his strengths during a most rude awakening.

He is another pinpoint control specialist who has to compensate for a lack of speed. He throws three-quarters and drops lower. When he hits the corners, he can be quite effective, but that did not happen often in 1984.

Robinson would pitch well in spurts and then succumb to mistakes in one or two fateful innings.

FIELDING, HITTING, BASERUNNING:

He fields respectably and doesn't run badly, but his hitting is below average. Jeff collected a game-winning RBI in his first major league plate appearance, but added only one more RBI the rest of the season. It's just too early to make any determinations based on his first major league season.

OVERALL:

Anyone with such poise and control deserves a longer look, but Robinson has

JEFF ROBINSON
RHP, No. 49
RR, 6'2", 220 lbs.
ML Svc: 1 year
Born: 12-13-60 in
    Santa Ana, CA

1984 STATISTICS

W	L	ERA	G	GS	CG	IP	H	R	ER	BB	SO	SV
7	15	4.56	34	33	1	171	195	99	87	52	102	0

CAREER STATISTICS

W	L	ERA	G	GS	CG	IP	H	R	ER	BB	SO	SV
7	15	4.56	34	33	1	171	195	99	87	52	102	0

to be virtually perfect to be successful because his fastball is in the 85-86 MPH range. If his control isn't sharp, he is going to get blasted.

This youngster has courage, jumping from the college campus to the majors in one year and performing decently under trying circumstances. It was not his fault he had to do his on-the-job training in the majors.

Campbell: "He makes one or two good pitches to a batter, but seldom three. When he makes a mistake, hitters jump on it because he doesn't have enough power to push the ball past them. But I like his poise--nothing seems to bother him."

HITTING:

Invited to spring training as a non-roster player, desperate for a job, this former Cubs prospect was a pleasant surprise, making the club by hitting .319 in exhibitions and clearing the way for the trading of utility man Dave Bergman to Detroit last season.

Thompson was especially effective as a starter, but was mediocre as a pinch-hitter, batting under .200 in that role. Overall, however, he was above .300 most of the season, proving to be a bargain for the club.

Despite his size, Thompson is virtually devoid of power, but occasionally can drive the ball deep into the alley in right-center. When Al Oliver was on the club, it was curious that neither first baseman had a home run.

Thompson is a spray hitter who hits mostly to center and right-center. He is particularly valuable to the Giants because they are short of lefthanded hitters. Consequently, he will be used to give Jack Clark a breather at first base this year and, the Giants hope, will boost his pinch-hitting productivity.

BASERUNNING:

Scot stole a base or two last season, but is merely an average runner, despite the fact that in his youth he once stole 35 bases in the minors. He isn't used as a pinch-runner, which tells you all you need to know.

FIELDING:

At first base, Thompson is extremely adequate, looking even better when he replaced Oliver. He is agile around the bag and doesn't err often. He has played other infield positions, so his defense isn't a weakness.

SCOT THOMPSON
INF/OF, No. 41
LL, 6'3", 195 lbs.
ML Svc: 5 years
Born: 12-7-55 in
Grove City, PA

1984 STATISTICS

AVG	G	AB	R	H	2B	3B	HR	RBI	BB	SO	SB
.306	120	245	30	75	7	1	1	31	30	26	5

CAREER STATISTICS

AVG	G	AB	R	H	2B	3B	HR	RBI	BB	SO	SB
.273	475	1042	118	284	43	8	5	90	89	110	17

  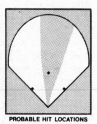

VS. RHP   VS. LHP   PROBABLE HIT LOCATIONS

Scot can also can play the outfield, and is a valuable utility man right out of the Dave Bergman mold.

OVERALL:

A good guy to have on the team because he can help you in more ways than one. Moreover, he's a rare breed, a player who will accept his utility status and remain a good team man. He has been inconsistent in the majors, enjoying three good seasons and three turkeys when he was a perennial prospect with the Cubs.

Campbell: "His best role is as a pinch-hitter and part-time player. His numbers are not conducive to playing everyday."

HITTING:

A broken bone in his right hand, suffered when he was struck by a Steve Rogers pitch, cost Manny Trillo dearly on offense in his first year with the Giants. He had been off to a good start and was batting .295 with three homers in April, but his average took a dive and he added only one homer after missing almost two months because of the injury.

This is a man capable of hitting in the .270-.290 range, so he has to be respected as a hitter. Trillo is a good hit-and-run man, ideally suited to batting second, and he knows what to do in the clutch.

Cool under pressure, he likes the tough situations and has good bat control. Manny waits on the ball well and can handle breaking pitches, often going to the opposite field.

The best way to handle him is with hard stuff low. He is a high ball hitter and pitchers must keep the ball down. Also, don't give him too much slow stuff because his bat control will enable him to "hit 'em where they ain't."

BASERUNNING:

Manny has never been a good basestealer because he lacks speed. He bats second, so he doesn't have to be much of a threat. It is more important that he stay close to the bag and give the No. 3 hitter a bigger hole.

He runs the bases with intelligence and is not prone to baserunning errors.

FIELDING:

Fielding is absolutely the strength of his game. He has lost some range with age, but there's nobody smoother around the bag and it's doubtful that another second baseman has a better arm.

A perennial Gold Glove winner, Manny can pick it, making only six errors last season and virtually guaranteeing an out

MANNY TRILLO
2B, No. 9
RR, 6'1", 164 lbs.
ML Svc: 10 years
Born: 12-25-50 in
Caritito, VEN

1984 STATISTICS											
AVG	G	AB	R	H	2B	3B	HR	RBI	BB	SO	SB
.254	98	401	45	102	21	1	4	36	25	55	0
CAREER STATISTICS											
AVG	G	AB	R	H	2B	3B	HR	RBI	BB	SO	SB
.265	1374	4930	495	1304	200	31	48	487	361	599	52

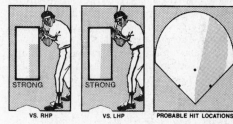

STRONG VS. RHP · STRONG VS. LHP · PROBABLE HIT LOCATIONS

if he gets to the ball. He has an unusual snap and throwing motion, but it obviously isn't a detriment.

OVERALL:

They say he's slowed down appreciably, but the Giants didn't notice the difference, welcoming ANYONE who could play defense on a club annually near the bottom in fielding. Until he was injured, Trillo was enjoying an All Star season. The club feels he has a couple of good years left if he can remain healthy.

A true professional, he makes fielding look easy and is a smooth, graceful performer.

Campbell: "Manny's better days are behind him. He's not the force he once was, losing a lot of range, but he still has sure hands and one of the best arms in the league. Hitting behind the runner and executing the hit-and-run are his main weapons on offense."

PITCHING:

The most pleasant surprise on the disappointing pitching staff last year, Frank Williams gave the bullpen a new look with his sidearm delivery and had an outstanding hits-to-innings-pitched ratio.

He throws almost submarine style, and his fastball runs in on righthanders and away from lefthanders. Williams also sports a sweeping breaking pitch and the ability to throw strikes.

Like Jeff Robinson, Williams came from nowhere and showed unusual poise for a rookie. He is unflappable under pressure and appears headed to become Greg Minton's replacement as the right-handed ace of the bullpen.

Because of Minton's presence, Frank wasn't used in many save situations, but he was far more effective than Minton. Going 9-2 is a good trick on a team with more than 90 losses.

FIELDING, HITTING, BASERUNNING:

Fielding is not his strength, evidenced by three errors in not so many opportunities. He doesn't run very well either, but he can swing the bat, hitting above .200 last year.

His very deliberate delivery makes it fairly easy for runners to steal on him. He is fully aware of this and spends a lot of time throwing to first.

OVERALL:

The Giants expect a promising future for the man nicknamed "Chief" because of his Indian heritage. He will most like-

FRANK WILLIAMS
RHP, No. 47
RR, 6'1", 180 lbs.
ML Svc: 1 year
Born: 2-13-58 in
Seattle, WA

1984 STATISTICS

W	L	ERA	G	GS	CG	IP	H	R	ER	BB	SO	SV
9	4	3.55	61	1	1	106	88	49	42	51	91	3

CAREER STATISTICS

W	L	ERA	G	GS	CG	IP	H	R	ER	BB	SO	SV
9	4	3.57	61	1	1	106	88	49	42	51	91	3

ly be a reliever, even though Williams certainly has proven that he can start. He only had one start and it was a rain-shortened, five-inning shutout at St. Louis.

Williams was a starter in the minors until 1983 and pitched well enough to earn a lot more saves, but the Giants insisted on making Minton earn his pay. The rookie, however, enjoyed victories in each game of a doubleheader sweep at New York last August, setting a Giant record.

Campbell: "One of the few positives on the Giants staff last year. Like Robinson, he showed me a lot of poise as a rookie. He also has an advantage with his unorthodox delivery and is not afraid to throw strikes. With a little help from his friends, he could have a bright future."

HITTING:

After belting a career-high of seventeen home runs as a reserve in 1983, big things were expected of Joel Youngblood when he became the regular third baseman last year. It didn't work out. The new position placed a lot of pressure on his defense, and it ultimately affected his hitting.

Despite his low average last season, Youngblood is regarded as a tough out. He possesses a quick bat, is very aggressive at the plate and is reliable in the clutch.

Last year's results should be thrown out because they are uncharacteristic of his career to date. The fact that he developed a home run swing in 1983 also created some unrealistic demands. It became a "mind game" for him in 1984, and he lost.

He likes the ball high, and his bat quickness enables him to wait on the slower pitches. Youngblood is a strong pull hitter but streaky as a power hitter, belting most of his homers in a three-week span last season.

Keeping the ball low and changing speeds is the best way to handle him.

BASERUNNING:

"Blood" was a decent baserunner in his youth, but he hasn't been the same since a knee injury in 1981. He's not a threat to steal, but runs the bases well and is a heady baserunner. He once stole 18 bases for the Mets, but he isn't the same runner today, though he does the job with intelligence.

FIELDING:

Fielding ratings for Youngblood differ in accordance with the position he is playing. His play at third base was an abomination last year. He led the majors with 37 errors, and he didn't even play the final month. No more third base.

He will return to the outfield, where

JOEL YOUNGBLOOD
INF/OF, No. 8
RR, 5'11", 175 lbs.
ML Svc: 9 years
Born: 8-28-51 in
  Houston, TX

1984 STATISTICS

AVG	G	AB	R	H	2B	3B	HR	RBI	BB	SO	SB
.254	134	469	50	119	17	1	10	51	48	86	5

CAREER STATISTICS

AVG	G	AB	R	H	2B	3B	HR	RBI	BB	SO	SB
.271	988	2913	374	781	150	23	65	330	256	467	54

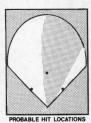

VS. RHP VS. LHP PROBABLE HIT LOCATIONS

his strong arm makes him a better than average fielder. He also filled in well at second base in 1983, but third base is out of the question--everyone has seen enough.

OVERALL:

Youngblood has been starving for regular duty. He got it last year, but his fielding dragged him down with the help of a tough Candlestick turf. He is back in a reserve role now and his success could hinge on how well he accepts the return to utility man status.

If his head is on right about the deal, he could be a big plus because of his versatility and hitting ability. He is a much better player than he showed in a troubled 1984.

Campbell: "He had just enough offense to be an infielder, but he's not a good one. His best position is right field and he's a tough out who can be quite effective offensively."

CHRIS BROWN
3B, No. 52
RR, 6'0", 185 lbs.
ML Svc: 1 year
Born: 8-15-61 in
   Jackson, MS

HITTING, BASERUNNING, FIELDING:

Chris Brown had a taste of big league pitching in the final month of 1984 and showed some ability following a .283 campaign with nine home runs in the minors.

A strong, well-built youngster, Brown has some power, as evidenced by a monstrous home run at San Diego, but the Giants were looking a lot less at his bat than at his glove. He utilizes the opposite field and is a line drive hitter who likes the ball up and over the plate.

Teammate Joel Youngblood's fielding problems at third base sent out an SOS, and Brown was the leading candidate to step in. He played the position better than his predecessor, but it wouldn't have taken much.

Brown displayed a strong arm, but his range wasn't adequately tested in the times that he played. He backed up on some balls and got into trouble doing so. He's merely an average runner on the basepaths.

OVERALL:

It is difficult to truly tell with Brown because his trial was so brief. It remains to be seen whether he is the answer at third base, but he definitely played the position better than anyone else on the 1984 roster. He has a reputation for requiring motivation after periods of languid play in the minors, but he didn't show it in his first major league chance.

Campbell: "He looks like an aggressive hitter and a decent fielder with an above average arm. Play him straightaway and hope he hits the ball at somebody."

BOB LACEY
RHP, No. 19
LR, 6'4", 190 lbs.
ML Svc: 5 years
Born: 8-25-53 in
   Fredericksburg, VA

PITCHING, FIELDING,
   HITTING, BASERUNNING:

Bob Lacey seemed to be a smarter (but also heavier) pitcher when he returned to the majors last year following a tryout with the Giants farm team. He does not have much on the ball, but he gets his pitches over the plate. The biggest asset in his comeback was his ability to throw strikes. He throws three-quarters and is a control/breaking ball pitcher who changes speeds on his slider and curve.

Once a promising youngster with the Oakland A's, Lacey was known for his wild ways which earned him the nickname of "Spacey," and had him in his former manager's (Billy Martin) doghouse. He has had to reform in an effort to find his way back to majors.

Lacey has been around long enough to be a respectable fielder. He has a decent move to first base, and surprised everyone as a hitter last year. He had never batted in the majors before, yet he managed to lead the Giants pitchers in batting with a .333 average.

OVERALL:

Lacey might be squeezed out in the numbers game, but he did a respectable job last year considering he didn't have spring training and was even contemplating another form of work. He looked a lot easier to hit than he was, but he is a long shot to make the staff this year.

Campbell: "He's a journeyman who's been around, so he knows what he's doing. He throws strikes and doesn't give hitters much to hit, so he can be effective when all his pitches are on."

FRAN MULLINS
INF, No. 55
RR, 6'0", 182 lbs.
ML Svc: 1 year
Born: 5-14-57 in
Oakland, CA

HITTING, BASERUNNING, FIELDING:

The Giants drafted Fran Mullins from the Reds organization and they must have liked him because they didn't give him back. Apparently he fills the bill as a utility infielder. He does not hit for a high average, but he shows some pop at the plate.

Mullins likes high pitches and he sprays the ball to all fields. He is nothing special as a baserunner but did a decent job as a backup infielder. His injuries prevented him from having a stronger rookie year.

If the Giants don't acquire a third baseman over the winter, Fran has the best chance of battling Chris Brown for the job. If Mullins's minor league statistics are indicative, he has more power than Chris, and that could work in his favor.

OVERALL:

Probably best suited to a utility role, Mullins hasn't shown enough to merit strong consideration for a regular job. He's a good team man, accepts his role and will likely serve the Giants as the No. 1 utility infielder.

Campbell: "Mullins is probably not the infielder of the future, but he seems to go to the hole well defensively. He's the utility infielder type who won't hurt you in that capacity."

JOHN RABB
1B/OF, No. 5
RR, 6'1", 180 lbs.
ML Svc: 2 years
Born: 6-23-60 in
Los Angeles, CA

HITTING, BASERUNNING, FIELDING:

A solid power hitter throughout his minor league career, John Rabb seemed lost with the Giants last year. He did not play enough to stay sharp and was ineffective as a pinch-hitter. But at age 24, he's too young to be discarded, especially with his hitting potential, including three homers in very few at-bats last year. Former Giant manager Frank Robinson, in particular, liked his power potential, but not enough to play him often.

The question remains where to play him. Rabb had a throwing problem when he reached the majors as a catcher; as a result, he is now regarded as a part-time outfielder and first baseman. He's merely adequate defensively, but he has not played long enough anywhere to grow into a position. He runs well for an ex-catcher.

OVERALL:

It doesn't look as if his big league future, if there is one, will be with this organization. The Giants are loaded with outfielders and have more on the way up. They are also solid with Clark and Thompson at first base. Rabb would probably be better off starting anew.

One gets the feeling, however, that Rabb would do some hitting if he played with more regularity.

Campbell: "Tremendous strength, but his problem is consistency. He can be pitched to, but if you make a mistake up, he can drive it 450 feet. He doesn't show much defensively, but he could develop into a pretty good pinch-hitter."

BRAD WELLMAN
INF, No. 36
RR, 6'0", 170 lbs.
ML Svc: 2 years
Born: 8-17-59 in
    Lodi, CA

HITTING, BASERUNNING, FIELDING:

Groomed as the club's second baseman of the future, Brad Wellman's progress was delayed when the Giants acquired Manny Trillo one year ago. Wellman shows enough pop in his bat and enough fielding skills to loom as a threat to teammate Johnnie LeMaster at shortstop.

Wellman played a lot of short last September and was respectable there, though he is not the fielder LeMaster is. After having spent many years at second, Brad's arm has to be strengthened to handle the longer throws from short. If successful, he could be a candidate for the regular spot.

Wellman has had good Triple A hitting figures and is capable of contributing more offensively than LeMaster. Right now, Brad is a better fielder at second, making the double play particularly well. He is also a decent baserunner who easily would reach double figures in steals if he played regularly.

OVERALL:

The Giants definitely like him and are trying to make room for him. He has a winning attitude and shows an aggressiveness unfound in LeMaster. If he can't move in at short, he might have to wait until Trillo steps aside at second.

Campbell: "He seems to be on a treadmill between San Francisco and Phoenix. Wellman will hit in the .230 area and he reminds me a lot of Doug Flynn. He looks like he could improve offensively, but he has to do more with his stance, perhaps square away a bit and do something about strengthening his forearms and upper body."

PLAYER INDEX